T0365149

Metaphysics AND Mystery

The Why Question
East and West

Volume 1: West

THOMAS DEAN

METAPHYSICS AND MYSTERY
THE WHY QUESTION EAST AND WEST

iUniverse books may be ordered through booksellers or by contacting:

iUniverse
1663 Liberty Drive
Bloomington, IN 47403
www.iuniverse.com
1-800-Authors (1-800-288-4677)

ISBN: 978-1-5320-7613-8 (sc)
ISBN: 978-1-5320-7614-5 (e)

Library of Congress Control Number: 2019942722

Print information available on the last page.

iUniverse rev. date: 06/21/2019

For Susan

Contents

PART TWO
Answering the Why Question: (I) West

CHAPTER FOUR
John Post: The Metaphysics of Theism 163

CHAPTER FIVE
Quentin Smith: The Metaphysics of Feeling 200

CHAPTER SIX
Milton Munitz: The Mystery of Existence 325

Preface

Philosophers are not born philosophers. One becomes a philosopher. The road to philosophy begins in experience. It goes further when that experience becomes reflective. The long journey ends only if and when one no longer needs to do philosophy. A strange journey indeed.

The arguments of this book owe their origin to the inarticulate but unforgettable experiences of the author long before such experiences could have been expressed in the language of philosophy or religion.

A Midwestern boy, lying on his back staring up at the night-time sky, awe-struck by the infinite distances of the starry heavens above, an unknowable reality that overwhelms his understanding but stirs his imagination.

A teen on a canoe trip in the Canadian wilderness, standing at the edge of an island in the deepening dusk, facing the dark pines looming up on the opposite shore, rendered speechless by the mystery of their silent presence.

A young man sitting amid the dunes on the edge of Lake Michigan, watching the sun slowly sinking below the distant horizon, sharing wordlessly in a drama repeated from time immemorial.

Perhaps the reader of this book has had similar experiences. That would not be surprising, for such experiences are universal, common to all cultures, knowing no boundaries, East or West.

The reality and truth of such experiences are 'origin-al.' They precede, give rise to, are not confined by, and endure long after philosophers and religious thinkers have had their say.

They have implications for spirituality too. They collapse the distinction between sacred and secular, holy and ordinary. They point to the 'origin-al' miracle, the wonder of being, from which stems all religion and philosophy. They are an 'eschatology of the everyday.'

Many other experiences went into the making of this book. Not only experiences of adult life, marriage, children, but also study of philosophy and religion in universities, American and German, and subsequent teaching of philosophy.

Yet those experiences remained grounded in the formative spiritual experiences of childhood and youth. Without those experiences, the philosophical and religious thinking recorded in the following pages would have been, as Thomas Aquinas once said of his own much more impressive achievements, "so much straw."

I would like to thank, first, those who have enabled this book to see the light of day – Donna Ansetey, Gustavo Benavides, Denise Benefiel, Emily Carter, Will Cerbone, Sharla Clute, Frederick Courtright, Donna Crilly, Ola Czajkowski, Orla Davies, Annette Day, Yi Deng, David Dilworth, Arnold Fisher, Naoko Fujieda, Robert Gall, Jill Gaynor, Paulette Goldweber, Diane Grossé, James Heisig, Hee-Jin Kim, Alison Kleczewski, Gereon Kopf, Agnieszka Kozyra, Gerald Lalonde, John LoBreglio, Alexandra Makkonen, John Maraldo, Kayla McLaughlin, Laura Milunic, Stephanie Munson, Uri Nodelman, Wynona Owens, Shelagh Phillips, Patricia and John Post, Sheik Safdar, Reed Samuel, Diana Taylor, Karin Tucker, Michiko Wargo, Jan Westerhoff, Stephen Williams, Pamela Wilson, and Edward Zalta.

Next I would like to thank the persons who have made possible the intellectual and spiritual journey recorded in these pages – teachers and writers of philosophy and religion, Western and Asian, past and present, some whose names appear in the bibliography, a cloud of witnesses too many to single out. They introduced me to the life of philosophy and religious thought and I shall be forever grateful. This offering is a sincere but poor repayment. May they forgive me.

There are two people to whom I owe special thanks – my brother Jeff Dean and sister-in-law Jill Weber Dean, who have been our friends over the years, welcoming us into their home, providing their love and hospitality. This two-volume work would not have been possible without their continuing encouragement and support.

Finally, there are two individuals to whom I owe a debt beyond calculation.

The first is my former wife, Susan Dean, former professor of American literature and women's studies at Bryn Mawr College, mother of our two children, Maggie and Frank. The first volume of this study, on the Western part of the journey, is dedicated to her.

The second volume, on the Asian part of the journey, is dedicated to my wife, Seiko Yoshinaga, past professor of Japanese literature and women's studies at Grinnell College. We divide our time between my hometown of Madison WI and her native city of Tokyo.

Whatever value the reflections in this study have, they would not have come to fruition without the love, companionship, and friendship of these two remarkable persons. My gratitude to them cannot be measured.

Credits

I would like to thank the following publishers, journals, online sites, and individuals for permission to cite excerpts from the works listed below.

Absolute Nothingness: Foundations for a Buddhist-Christian Dialogue, Hans Waldenfels, trans. J. W. Heisig, Copyright@1980, Paulist Press, reproduced by permission of Paulist Press.

Being and Time, Martin Heidegger, translated by John Macquarrie and Edward Robinson, Copyright@1962 by Harper & Row, Publishers, Incorporated, reprinted by permisişon of HarperCollins Publishers.

"Between Immanence and Transcendence: Religion and Non-Dualism in the Thought of the Kyoto School," Gereon Kopf, American Academy of Religion, Nashville: November 2000 (unpublished paper), reproduced by permission of Gereon Kopf.

The Collected Dialogues of Plato including the Letters, ed. Edith Hamilton & Huntington Cairns, Copyright@1961 by Bollingen Foundation, Pantheon Books, reprinted with permission of Princeton University Press

Dogen and the Koan Tradition, Steven Heine, Copyright@1994 by State University of New York Press, reproduced by permission of State University of New York Press

Dogen on Meditation and Thinking, Hee-Jin Kim, Copyright@2007, State University of New York Press, reproduced by permission of State University of New York Press.

Dogen Studies, ed. William R. LaFleur, Copyrigh@1985 by University of Hawaii Press, reprinted with permission of by University of Hawaii Press.

"Nishida Kitarō," John C. Maraldo, *The Stanford Encyclopedia of Philosophy* (Winter 2015 Edition), Edward N. Zalta (ed.), URL = <https://plato.stanford.edu/archives/win2015/entries/nishida-kitaro/>.

Nishida Kitaro, Nishitani Keiji, trans. Yamamoto Seisaku and James W. Heisig. Copyright@2016 by Chisokudō Publications, reprinted with permission of Chisokudō Publications.

Nishida Kitaro (1870-1945): The Development of His Thought, David A. Dilworth, Ph.D. dissertaton, Department of Philosophy, Columbia University, New York, Copyright@1970, reproduced by permission of David A. Dilworth.

"Nishida Kitaro and Some Aspects of His Philosophical Thought," Toratoro Shimomura, in Kitaro Nishida, *A Study of Good*, Copyright@1988, Greenwood Press, reprinted by permission of Greenwood Press.

"Nishida Kitaro's Logic of Absolutely Contradictory Self-Identity and the Problem of Orthodoxy in the Zen Tradition," Agnieszka Kozyra, Copyright@2007, *Japan Review*, 20, 60-110, reproduced by permission of the author.

Notebooks 1914-1916, Ludwig Wittgenstein, ed. G. H. Von Wright and G.E M.Anscombe, Copyright@1961, Blackwell publishing, reproduced by permission of Wiley-Blackwell Publishers.

"Nothing Gives: Marion and Nishida on Gift-Giving and God," John C. Maraldo, in *Japanese and Continental Philosophy: Conversations with the Kyoto School*, eds. Bret W. Davis, Brian Schroeder, and Jason M. Wirth, Copyright@2011, Indiana University Press, reproduced by permission of John C. Maraldo.

Nothingness in Asian Philosophy, Douglas L. Berger & JeeLoo Liu, Copyright@2014 by Routledge Publishing, reproduced by permission of Taylor and Francis Group, LLC, a divison of Informa plc.

On Buddhism, Nishitani Keiji, trans. Seisaku Yamamoto and Robert E. Carter, Copyright@2006, State University of New York Press, reproduced by permission of State University of New York Press.

Introduction

Why is there something rather than nothing? Philosophy's central, most perplexing question. – Bede Rundle.

How comes the world to be here at all instead of the nonentity which might be imagined in its place? The question of being [is] the darkest in all philosophy. All of us are beggars here, and no school can speak disdainfully of another or give itself superior airs. – William James

Mystery is a thing with paradoxes.– Janet Maslin

Not every religion or philosophy involves belief in God. But most religions and many philosophies believe there is something that gives ultimate meaning and direction to human life.

What is that 'something'? Why is there something rather than nothing? Why does the universe exist rather than nothing at all? What are we marveling at, wondering about? Not this or that – though this or that can give rise to the question – but the fact of the universe itself – not this universe but any universe, anything, rather than nothing at all. It is the ultimate Why question – what one philosopher called 'the super-ultimate Why.' Many attempts have been made to answer this question: religious stories of creation, theological doctrines of God, philosophical theories of a first cause, scientific cosmologies of the origin of the universe.

Some thinkers have argued, however, that it is not possible to answer this question. They say that we will never be in a position to know the answer, either because there are empirical limits-- limits to our factual knowledge, or because there are logical limits – limits of language built into the question itself. Still others have contended that it is not even possible to ask this question. They claim that it is a pseudo-question resting on conceptual or logical confusion. At best it is the expression of a deep emotion masquerading as a genuine question. Despite its

1

grammatical appearance and despite the long history of attempts to answer it, it is not really a question at all. Thus any attempts to answer it lack sense as well. Finally, some have suggested that perhaps it is not even a universal question, one found in all cultures or present in every human consciousness. Perhaps it is peculiar to a limited intellectual tradition – the monotheistic religions of the West and the philosophies influenced by them.

Whatever the case, the Why question – pseudo- or genuine, deep or confused, universal or parochial-- would appear to point to a long-standing human concern with the origin of the universe and the implications of that origin for our lives, for what it means to be a human being in a world whose origin is imagined or conceived in a particular way.

A discussion of this question requires that we consider the several viewpoints indicated above. First, in view of the doubts raised about the possibility of even asking, let alone answering this question, we will have to assess the empirical and the logical status of the question. What reasons would be relevant to that analysis? Of course, if we should determine that it is not possible to ask the question, presumably that would relieve us of the necessity to consider possible answers to it. The inquiry would seem to have come to an end.

On the other hand, what if it is possible to ask the question but not possible to answer it? What would make it impossible to answer a question as fundamental and important as this one? Further, if the question can be asked but not answered, what are we to make of the answers – religious, theological, philosophical, scientific – that have been put forward over the centuries in response to it? Can they possibly make sense? If they do, are they compatible with one another? Do they contradict one another? Are they incommensurable with one another? While appearing to answer the same question, are they in fact answering quite different ones?

The fact is we cannot seem to let go of this question, or perhaps the question does not let go of us. We keep on wanting to ask and answer a question that either cannot be asked or cannot be answered. This suggests that the situation is more complex, more nuanced than at first appears. Perhaps it is not possible to ask let alone answer this question in any straightforward empirical or logical way. But what if it is possible to ask, that is, to analyze the question and the answers to it, in some other way consistent with those logical or empirical limitations? What sort of question – what kind of asking – and what kind of answers would that entail?

If it is possible to provide an alternative analysis of the question, perhaps some if not all of the answers given in the past – religious and philosophical, if not scientific – could be seen to make sense after all once they are understood in terms of that alternate framework. The question would then be seen as the expression of a deep human concern – an expression of the question how, when confronted by the ultimate limits of our knowledge and existence, we should conduct our lives. Even if we find that the question cannot be asked without violating the logical and conceptual framework of empirical or scientific inquiry, we might still be able to understand it as the place-holder for a situation or reality that confronts us with the question of how to live and act in a world without an ultimate Why. That would make it one of the, if not *the* most important question we can ask. Our answers to this question would be among the most important we can give as human beings.

For a full analysis of this question, therefore, we must consider three possibilities: Can this question be asked? If it can be asked, can it be answered? If it cannot be asked or answered, can it be understood -- asked and answered – in some other way? Philosophy began with wonder. Those with answers are metaphysicians. Is metaphysics faithful to that wonder? Such are the questions we must consider in this inquiry into metaphysics and mystery, East and West.

PART ONE

Asking the Why Question

Something. World/ Universe

Something

Our first task in this section is to ask what the term "something" refers to. If that cannot be determined, we must consider whether the notion can be given any meaning at all

With regard to the term "something" the first thing we should note at the outset is that here we are not (yet) asking why there is a world or a universe at all rather than nothing, nor are we asking the seemingly similar but rather different question why the universe or the world exists. Rather, we are asking whether it makes sense to talk about the fact that there is "something" rather than nothing at all, whether, therefore, it makes sense to ask why this "something" exists rather than nothing at all.

What is this "something"? What does it refer to? What does it mean? The first problem with the notion of the "something" is that it would seem to be too indeterminate in its reference to be about anything at all, let alone anything in particular. As one philosopher, Munitz, has argued, the question itself, "why is there anything at all, or something, rather than nothing" itself is "not properly framed, since the words 'something' or 'anything' are wholly indeterminate in their reference." (Munitz, 1965, 45)

An early version of this critique is seen in a passing comment by Plato in his dialogue, *Sophist*: "Surely we can see that this expression 'something' is always used of a thing that exists. We cannot use it just by itself in naked isolation from everything that exists, can we?" (Plato,1963c, 237d). Implicit in this criticism, seconded by Quine, is a view of the referential function of language that does not operate unless it points to something determinate, that is, to particular things or objects that exist -- unless, that is, its use reflects a particular metaphysical or ontological presupposition that the function of language is to serve primarily an "ontic" orientation to "entities." (Quine, 1969, 12-13) The concept of language, on this view, involves "objectification," the positing, or talking about, or referring to particular existing things or objects. In other words, language, at least in its ordinary use, but also in the scientific and metaphysical uses built upon that ordinary use, involves an implicit form of, and commitment to, "entification." (Quine, *op. cit.,* 1) Thus, those who, like the philosopher Heidegger, take this question seriously thinking that it makes sense to talk about "something" or "anything" (or, as we shall see, "nothing"), have been, in Quine's view, "beguiled" by the "confusion" of the indefinite singular term "something" with a definite singular term. (Quine, 1960, 133)

Heidegger, for his part, would reject the criticism by Munitz and Quine of the alleged "indeterminacy" of the terms 'something' or 'anything.' For Heidegger, what the alleged "indeterminacy" of these terms points to, or if it may be put that way, *refer* to, is "no mere lack of determination, but rather the essential impossibility of determining it" (Heidegger, 1977a, 103). For Quine, the function of language is to determine what, for Heidegger, is *in principle* indeterminate. Heidegger's claim of a positive concept of *indeterminacy-in-principle* will prove crucial to a defense of the meaning, rather than incoherence, of the Why question.

There is a second feature of the "indeterminacy" of reference that gives added meaning to its use in the Why-question. As Munitz points out, the Why-question, either because of or in spite of its indeterminacy, "does not suggest any order of priorities among existences with respect to their capacity to arouse our sense of the mystery of existence." (Munitz, 1965, 45-46) Thus "the spectacle of [Kant's] the starry heavens" does not have any "pre-eminence" in provoking one to ask the Why-question. Anything can and in fact often does suffice – from the humblest, most insignificant to the grandest, most awe-inspiring – the mere fact that this or that thing exists, in fact, that any thing exists at all. Anything can, though it need not and most often does not, lead us to ask the question why it, why anything, exists, rather than nothing at all.

THOMAS DEAN

Nevertheless, Munitz, though perhaps neither Carnap or Quine, thinks the Why-question may have a better chance of making sense if the indeterminate term, "something," is replaced by the determinate term, "world" or "universe" – that to ask "why does the world, or universe, exist rather than nothing at all," since it has a concrete reference, may make sense, whereas with the terms 'something' or 'anything' it appears not to. Put another way, perhaps the term 'something' in the Why question, despite its grammatical or surface indeterminacy, in fact refers, in a linguistically misleading but more concrete way, to the world or universe, that is, to "anything" in the sense of any and all "things," the "world" as "the totality of things that exist," "the world as a whole" or "the world as such." (Heidegger refers to this with the phrase, *das Ganze des Seienden*, "the totality of *beings/entities*" "*beings* as a whole," which he distinguishes from *Das Sein des Ganzen*, "the *be-ing/exist-ence* of the totality." This distinction will prove to be important in our discussion of the notion of the "world" in the following section.)

So let us turn to Munitz' claim that the Why-question may have a better chance of making sense if the indeterminate term, "something," is replaced by the determinate term, "world" or "universe." Since it makes concrete reference to the "world" or "universe" as the totality of what exists, it would appear that, in this alternate formulation, the question "why does the world, or universe, exist rather than nothing at all?" does indeed make sense.

World/Universe

Presumably, according to Munitz, we could avoid the problems associated with the difficulty of assigning determinate meanings to the seemingly absolute notion of "something" *tout court* and what we shall later discover to be the equally absolute and even more paradoxical notion of "nothing (at all)," if it could be shown that the Why question could be asked without appealing to them. This, says Munitz, might be possible if we use an alternate formulation that replaces 'something' with 'world'. Rather than asking, "Why is there something at all rather than nothing?" we might reformulate the question as "Why does the world exist?"

In other words, if the idea of 'something (rather than nothing at all)' does not refer to anything in particular, if it lacks any concrete meaning, then, according to Munitz, perhaps we can rescue the question of the mystery of existence by replacing the notion of an indeterminate 'something' and a paradoxical 'nothing at all' with a more concrete term like 'world' or 'universe.'

According to Munitz, "the formulation of the question 'Why does the world exist?' does not, in itself, tacitly imply reference to the idea of absolute nothing. What the mystery of the existence of the world is, can be expressed without making use of the term 'nothing.' Instead of referring in some wholly indeterminate way to 'anything' or 'something,' we shall be dealing, in the substituted question, with a more determinate subject matter, that is to say, with the 'world'." (Munitz, 1965, 46-47)

The question we must now ask, therefore, is whether Munitz's substitute formulation of the question can do what it is advertised as being able to do, or does it simply create new difficulties that lead us further away from a solution to the original question?

Munitz' reformulation replacing the "indeterminate" notion of 'something' with the more "concrete" notion of 'world' in fact turns out to be highly problematic. Not only does the introduction of the notion of 'world' bring with it a host of problems in its own right having to do with the possible reference and/or meaning of the term (to which we will return), it also introduces a deep if not fatal ambiguity into the question itself.

For now the question can be seen as running together and confusing two very different issues. On one interpretation the question has little if anything (dare one say 'nothing'?) to do with nature and intent of the original conundrum. It becomes a question which is not philosophical, i.e. metaphysical, at all, but rather one which belongs to the quite different provenance of scientific cosmology. For on this interpretation the question, 'Why does the world exist" can be taken as referring to this already-existing-as-ordered world and as asking how or why this organized ordered cosmos came to exist and to exist in the particular way it does, why it has assumed the particular order or taken the particular form it has.

On the other hand, the question of the mystery of existence, reformulated as 'Why does the world exist?' can be taken, as it does in its original formulation, as a purely philosophical one referring simply to

THOMAS DEAN

the fact that this or, for that matter, any 'world' exists. But this is, after all, simply another way of asking why anything at all (rather than nothing) exists. In other words, Munitz' substitute formulation can itself be seen as still relying implicitly upon the problematic notion of 'nothing.' For on this reading it can seen as asking: "Why does a world or universe exist rather than nothing at all?"

In other words, when Munitz attempts to reformulate the question by replacing the term 'something' with the term 'world' and dropping the term 'nothing,' the 'nothing' (as Heidegger might have put it) simply conceals itself in the unwelcome guise of ambiguity.

It is important to note and insist upon this ambiguity and the hidden presence of the 'nothing' in the question, "Why does the world exist?" because it will affect the rest of our discussion.

But let us assume, for the moment, that Munitz' formulation is not troubled by any ambiguity and that it can successfully function as an alternative, and superior, way of phrasing the question of the mystery of existence without implicitly involving the problematic notion of an (absolute) 'nothing.'. For this we turn first to the problem of the reference and/or meaning of the term 'world' (or 'universe'; I shall use these terms interchangeably, unless otherwise indicated). As we have noted, Munitz introduces this term as a substitute for 'something' (or 'anything') and as a way of overcoming the problem of referring to 'nothing' in addressing the question of the mystery of existence.

Our first task here is to ask: What is it that the more concrete-looking notion of the "world" refers to? Is it possible, its appearance of 'concreteness' notwithstanding, that it fails to refer to anything at all, or that at least here too another ambiguity surfaces? If so, we would have to consider the possibility that the notion lacks any clear, univocal meaning. Unless we can unravel this tangled matter, the question of the mystery of existence, at least in Munitz's formulation, would seem to have ended in a blind alley. In that case either the inquiry with which we began this essay will have come to an abrupt, all-too-sudden end, or the Why question will have to be rethought all over again from the start.

In may prove that the task of making sense of the vague notion of "something" and questionable notion of "nothing at all," difficult as it may have initially appeared, was in fact relatively straightforward compared to the task of analyzing the much more complex, indeed daunting set of issues swirling around the seemingly more concrete notion of "world" or "universe." We may end up wishing we could go back to the seemingly simpler notions of "something" and "nothing" after all!

The Concept of 'World.'

We can break down the general question of the reference and meaning of the term 'world" into a subset of two more specific questions: First, what are we referring to with the term 'world' or 'universe'? What are we talking about? What sort of "thing" or "entity" is the world or the universe? Can we in fact refer to something called 'the world' or 'the universe' at all? Second, what properties or attributes can we ascribe to, or use to describe, this alleged "object," reality, or phenomenon? What do such terms mean when applied to 'the world as such,' or 'the universe as a whole'? Can they in fact be applied to such an alleged, and allegedly concrete, "entity"? Can we say anything at all about 'the world' or 'the universe'? Let us examine each of these issues in turn.

Reference of 'World/Universe.'

What are we referring to, what do we mean, with the term "world" or "universe"? The problem is that there is already an ambiguity in the reference and meaning of the term 'world' or 'universe.' In what follows we shall try to spell out what that ambiguity is and what bearing an attempt to disambiguate the term might have on a formulation of the Why question that relies upon the term.

In more recent discussions other philosophers, such as John Post and Bede Rundle have, like Munitz, resorted to using the terms 'world' or 'universe' rather than 'something' and 'nothing' to address the Why question. But in all three cases there is already an unclarity about the reference of the term. Both Munitz and Post, for example, introduce a further distinction between two senses of 'universe.' They distinguish between what they label the "manifest" or "observable" universe, and what they refer to as the "true" or "real" universe, the universe "beyond" the manifest universe, the universe "to which" the observed universe "belongs," the Universe "itself" or "as such." What do they have in mind with this distinction between two different senses of 'world' or 'universe,' and how do they think it can be used to answer the Why question? Do different rules apply, is there a different logic involved, in talking about the two senses of 'universe'? How does this distinction relate to the distinction we have introduced above between questions about the how, why and what of the existing universe, and the question about the fact that there is any universe at all? Despite attempts to clearly differentiate between two senses of 'universe,' do they not introduce an ambiguity into attempts to formulate the Why question as a question about the mystery of the existence of the 'world' or 'universe'?

Problems with the notion of the 'world' do not end there., there is another troubling issue that arises in determining its reference. Even if restrict the question about the existence of the world to the world or universe in some more univocal sense, there is another troubling issue that arises in determining its reference. What are we referring to when we talk about the world or universe? Do we have in mind the universe as an 'entity' that, like other entities 'within' it, has in principle a measurable spatio-temporal extent, starting with the Big Bang? Or is it a spatio-temporal 'totality' of entities? Or is it a spatio-temporal 'whole' that itself lacks specific spatio-temporal dimensions – a 'whole' that makes a 'world' out of the 'totality of entities' thought to be its 'parts'? Further, is it even a unified 'whole,' or is it more what William James referred to as a "multiverse" or "pluriverse'? Can we use a definite, or even an indefinite (indeterminate) article to talk about 'the' universe or 'a' universe at all? Again, do different rules, a different logic, obtain when we try to talk about these two (or more) senses of the manifest universe?

Finally, is the world or universe even something we can "experience" at all? Or is it rather, as the philosopher Immanuel Kant argued, simply a "regulative" idea that we use for heuristic purposes to give unity to the body of our experiences of spatio-temporally ordered entities 'within' the world, but not itself a concrete 'something,' a spatio-temporal entity, totality of entities, or 'whole' 'within' which such entities are located and which could be the 'object' of a separate experience itself. Once again, do different rules, a different logic apply to attempts to talk about, let along formulate a question about, the "existence" of, the world?

'Manifest'/'Observable' Universe or 'True' /'Real' Universe? The first difficulty we must confront lies in the distinction between two senses of 'universe,' the 'manifest' or 'observable' universe and the 'true' or 'real' universe. By 'manifest' or 'observable' universe is meant "the known universe, the universe as conceived through our present scientific

categories" (Post, 116), "that which is implicitly defined by the traits assigned to it by some cosmological model" (Munitz, 1965, 58). By the "true" universe they mean "the true physical universe, or the Universe" that lies "beyond" the manifest universe (Post, 116), or again, the universe "to which the observed universe belongs" (Munitz, 1965, 58). If we adopt this distinction, we must conclude that these two senses of 'universe' do not mean or refer to the same thing. As Munitz puts it, "short of begging the question, it is by no means the case that we are required to say of the universe1 – 'that to which the observed universe belongs' – everything that we can properly say of the universe2 – 'that which is implicitly characterized by the use of some cosmological model.'" (Munitz, 1965, 58). In fact Post explicitly says, "the two are not the same" (Post, 129). Munitz adds that there is a further distinction between two dimensions of reality – the observable universe and what he calls 'boundless existence,' a wholly unintelligible, transcendent aspect of reality that nevertheless should not be confused with a theistic conception of God. This observation will prove important when we come to the question of what properties or attributes can properly be ascribed to the 'universe,' that is, what statements can be made about the 'universe,' and correspondingly what sorts of explanations can be asked for and what kind of answers given regarding the question of the existence of the 'universe.'

The problem that confronts us, then, is to which universe does the question, "Why does the universe exist at all?" refer? Since Munitz and Post understand the "manifest" universe to refer only to that universe as currently known or conceived, that is, the universe whose nature, not whose existence, is contingent upon the best available cosmological science, it would seem that this universe cannot be a candidate for a question whose thrust is, "Why does any universe exist at all?", i.e., a question that asks not why this particular universe as currently known or conceived exists, but why any universe exists.

For the purpose of addressing that question, it would seem that the concept of the "true" or "real" universe, "the Universe" itself or as such, whatever the state of our current knowledge or concepts of it, is the better candidate as the universe referred to in the Why question. For as Post states, we must assume that, whatever the state of our current knowledge, "the Universe is there to be characterized." In other words, "the Universe exists in addition to (or perhaps instead of) what we may call the 'manifest' universe" (Post, 117).

THOMAS DEAN

This clarification might appear to permit us to go on to the problems mentioned above, save for the fact that, as both Munitz and Post admit, it is not entirely clear, after all, just what the notion of 'the Universe' really means beyond saying that it does not mean or refer to the physical universe as presently known or conceived. In other words, we can say what it is not, but not what it is. "Intuitively," Post says, "the Universe is the unknown (or incompletely known) whole about whose part physics attempts (or ought to attempt) to give us descriptions that are true and complete." However, he goes on to admit, "There is not much one can do to make this intuitive idea more specific; we do not know specifically what we mean when we speak of the whole that is the Universe, or of its parts" (Post, 156). Post qualifies this qualification, when he adds that, despite the fact we have only an "intuitive" idea of the "true physical Universe," since our current physical descriptions do refer, if only incompletely, to something that really exists, "the Universe is not to be thought of as some completely uninterpreted reality, a thing-in-itself outside all conceptual schemes." (Post 157-8)

Nevertheless, it would seem we are left back where we started. The "manifest" or "observed" universe cannot, for the reason we have suggested, be the 'universe' referred to in the question, "Why does any universe exist at all?" But when we insert instead the idea of the "true Universe," it turns out we cannot give more specific content to that term either. It seems no more "concrete," in fact just as "indeterminate," as the "something" whose indeterminacy was objected to in the initial formulation of the Why-question and that led to the proposal to substitute the more "concrete" term of "world" or "universe" instead!

"The World"/"The Universe." Let us assume that the preceding distinctions can somehow be reduced to a single and "concrete," univocal meaning for the phrase 'the world' or 'the universe.' The problem remains. Is the universe even a unified 'whole'? Is it a universe, or is it even *one*? Or is it only one of many universes beyond what we can conceive, let alone know? Can we use the definite, or even an indefinite (indeterminate) article to talk about *the* or *a* universe at all?

Post, for example, speaks variously of the universe as "the whole of existence, the sum total of what there is," the "unique spatiotemporal whole," and the "whole of spacetime" (Post, 116, 120, 126). It is not clear whether he would distinguish between the two notions of 'whole' and 'sum total,' or whether he takes them as simply two different ways of saying the same thing. Nor whether he would distinguish between the universe as a 'whole' that is the 'sum total' or 'totality' of what there is, the 'whole' that is the 'whole of spacetime,' and the 'whole' that is the 'unique spatio-temporal whole.' Nor is it clear whether he means any or all of these to apply to either or both the 'manifest' and 'true' universe.

For his part, when Munitz proposes to introduce the term 'world' into the Why-question in place of the "indeterminate" term 'something,' he admits that the term is "far from being clear, precise, non-controversial, and univocal, indeed the very opposite is the case." Thus he asks: "Is a statement about the world about an individual? Or is it about a class of objects? Or is the world an absolute whole?" The best we can do, he suggests, is to "reduce" but not "eliminate" this unclarity, because "there is a residual and uneliminable vagueness, or indeterminateness in the reference of the term 'the world' that [is] essential to it." (Munitz, 1965, 52-3)

The question, however, is whether the substitution of the "indeterminate" term 'world' for the "indeterminate" term 'something' indeed advances us toward a solution to the Why question, or whether it simply results in a further confusion of the issue. A closer look at the problems associated with the term 'world' may reveal whether, contrary to Munitz's claim, the ambiguities of the term can in fact be "eliminated." If they can, we will then be in a position to decide whether the term can help us toward a solution of the Why question, or whether, despite clarification, it still confuses the issue. If we find it still confuses the issue, or if we find that in fact the term resists being further clarified, we must then decide whether we want to go ahead with it anyway, or whether it might be better to go back to 'something' after all.

Entity. Munitz suggests that we might perhaps think of "the world" (in line with his distinction between the 'observed' and the 'true' universe) as referring to "the 'entity' that includes, first of all, the vast, though raggedly defined, observed universe" (Munitz, 1965, 69). "But what," he asks, "of the wider world to which the observed world belongs?" He answers that the claim that the wider, 'real' world may itself be viewed as an 'entity,' "if taken as having an ontological warrant, must be challenged an unsubstantiated." The notion that the real world itself may be taken as an 'entity' is "at best, an ideal of reflective inquiry," in other words, what Kant refers to as a 'regulative idea' (Munitz, *op. cit.*,70-1). In other words, Munitz concludes, "there is no way in which we can establish that the world is at all like *that.*" Still, he claims, if the idea of 'world' is used "critically," "this term serves as a perfectly adequate name for that 'entity'–such as it is–whether it is whole determinate or partly indeterminate, whether it is wholly comprehensible or only partly so–to which the observed world, and such contents and such order in it as we have already succeeded in identifying, belong." (Munitz, *op. cit.*, 71) But should we rest easy, take comfort, in this qualified endorsement, this claim that, if we do so "critically," we can nevertheless think of the observed world and/or the real world to which it belongs as like, as analogous to, the entities within it? The notion that the universe, observed or real, either is like or is an entity and that, like the entities 'within' it, it has in principle a measurable spatiotemporal extent, is not an idea that finds many other takers. It is, in fact, a philosophical or, to use Munitz' own word, an "ontologic" rather than empirically verifiable claim. As Rundle puts it, "the universe is not to be aligned with the things within it, things which, like planets and stars, pose answerable why-questions" (Rundle, 124). Rundle here alludes to one of the reasons why the attempt to view the universe, no matter how "critically," as like an entity confuses rather than clarifies the Why question itself.

Totality. We turn next to a more widely entertained possibility that the universe is like a totality of entities rather than a sort of mega-entity vis-a-vis the entities within it. Post, for example, in one place describes the universe as "the whole of existence, the sum total of what there is" (Post, 116), presumably meaning by "the whole" the totality of the things that exist. As the formula runs: "the world is the totality of whatever exists." (Munitz, 1965, 67). Munitz notes that this concept of the 'whole' in modern scientific cosmology, when taken to mean "the totality of what exists," is "derived from analogy with the use of totality-concepts" in mathematics and the physical sciences. "Thus, the universe is said to be a whole, in the sense that it is a *class* of bodies, events, and processes thought to belong to a field, whose structures can be specified by geometries [and] presumed to form a *physical system*; the laws or principles bind the various units and segments in a single interrelated framework." (Munitz, *op. cit.*, 59-60)

Here too, however, as with the concept of the world as (like) an 'entity,' this concept of the world as a 'whole' in the sense of a 'totality' runs in to a similar problem. As Munitz argues, "Even our using the phrase 'the world' is misleading, if it presupposes a single unity or order, an all-inclusive totality" (Munitz, *op. cit.*, 71). Why does he think so? He is not saying the concept should be rejected, but that a note of caution is in order. The notion of a 'totality,' like that of an 'entity,' again if used "critically," can serve as a "perfectly adequate" name for the world, observed or real. But here too it is important to remember that the notion functions at best only as an analogy, or in scientific terms, as a model for the observed universe. It should not mislead us into thinking that the world actually is a unified whole in the sense of an all-inclusive totality. As a Kantian regulative idea, or in scientific terms as a methodological postulate, while it may be useful, and indeed even necessary for a scientific cosmology to so regard the world, ontology need not be bound by this to draw any conclusions about the real nature of the world (Munitz, *op. cit.*, 60-1).

Once again, despite these notes of caution, the same critical reservation presents itself. It presumes that the questions we can ask of empirical wholes or totalities of entities that are, as Munitz himself points out, "discriminated against a background of other objects and events," can be asked of the world or universe itself. But, as he himself asks, "what is the background against which to discriminate the world?" (Munitz,1965, 65). It is precisely at this point that, as in viewing the world as an 'entity,' viewing it as a 'whole' in the sense of a 'totality of entities' breaks down, not despite the analogy but because at this point analogies are all we have, beyond which we cannot go.

Whole. To resolve these seeming conundra scientific cosmologists, and metaphysicians drawing on their work, have turned to what is perhaps the most basic and widely advanced notion about the nature of the universe -- that it is (like a) spatiotemporal whole, however one that is absolute and unique. Since Post provides an extended discussion of this notion, perhaps it is there that we can find the clear sense of reference and meaning for 'the world' required for advancing us toward a solution to the question of the Why of the world's existence. As we begin, we should keep in mind two questions: What analogy does Post draw on to present a metaphysical interpretation of the scientific-cosmological notion of the world as a 'whole'? What questions can philosophy put to a metaphysical definition of the world as a 'whole' based on an analogy taken from scientific cosmology?

Post begins with the claim, "If the whole of existence is to be identified with the physical universe, then the physical universe plus everything in it forms a whole." (Post, 118) The problem then becomes how to understand the nature of the relation between the things "within" this whole and the

THOMAS DEAN

whole itself which, on this definition, appears to be more than just the sum total of the things that are said to exist "within" it. Here Post turns to a mathematical set-theoretic analysis of the part-whole relation to give meaning to a more-than-sum-total sense of a 'whole.' He notes: the part-whole uses a "spatiotemporal whole-part relation to define a notion of 'the universe as a whole'" no matter what particular "spacetime" we happen to be in. (Post, 119) This seems to be a standard move in scientific cosmology, for as Munitz also observes, the use of the notion of a 'whole' in scientific cosmology is derived by analogy from totality concepts in mathematics and physical science.

The philosophical questions that must be raised at this point are, of course, what are the limits of the part-whole analogy, and what are the implications of having to resort to analogy to talk of the universe as a whole? Does this mean the concept of the world as such lacks any specifiable literal meaning? Post himself goes on to ask: "What of spacetime itself? Is it merely a convenient abstraction, just our way of representing the system of spatiotemporal relations among the concretely existing things and events? Or is it a physical thing, somewhat like an electromagnetic field?" His claim is that casting the part-whole nature of the world as a spatiotemporal whole in the (abstract) mathematical language of sets enables him to "to bypass such controversies, since it is neutral among the competing positions" (Post, 120). But does it? He asks, "How shall we capture this intuition rigorously in a definition?" He replies: by defining what is meant by a physically existing entity, and then explaining how, in what sense, "physical existents form a whole or a 'series' with an 'upper limit' or upper bound." (ibid.) In other words, by this analogy, further specified in set-theoretic terms, the universe "need not be an object or an individual or even a whole in any ordinary sense. But it *is* an array. In this minimal sense the universe is a thing, an entity, an existent." (Post, 126)

It is beginning to sound as if the spatiotemporal whole that Post has in mind is, after all, another way of talking about the universe as the sum total of what exists, in itself being in some sense a, or the, mega- or meta-entity, the upper limit of the series of all those other things that exist "within" it. If so we are back with the notion of the world as a totality, in fact, with the notion of world as an entity, with all the problems we saw with those two variations in the previous two sections. For as Post goes on to say: "The manifest physical universe is the ST-sum [i.e., totality] of all the entities that are either physical entities of a listed kind or ST-sums of physical entities of listed kinds. Thus our very concept of the physical universe, like our concept of a physical entity, is a function of the kinds or categories used in physics at any given time." Post, *ibid*.)

But now he comes to the, for the philosopher, critical question: Is the physical universe identical with the whole of spacetime? His answer: "That depends on what one means by 'the whole of spacetime.' A spacetime from the point of view of mathematics is just a specially defined abstract set, even if it is the spacetime 'of' the universe. Viewed this way, no spacetime could be identical with the physical universe, which is a whole or sum, not a set. If the spacetime were defined not as the set but as the ST-sum of the locations or regions of all the physical existents (events, fields, objects), still the spacetime would not be identical with the whole physical universe" (Post, *ibid*.) This returns us to Post's initial distinction between two senses of 'universe'–the physically manifest universe and the Universe "beyond." So far it would appear that his discussion of the world as a spatiotemporal whole has been limited to the empirically accessible universe. But this lands us right back in the earlier conundrum: When we ask the Why question about the world, the universe, which world, what universe are we asking about?

As Post admits: "'Beyond' expresses a spatial metaphor, or perhaps spatiotemporal. There is nothing literally beyond the universe, since by definition it is the ST-sum or supremum of everything. This is the physical universe. We can define no other. Any such definition must be based on a list of predicates from contemporary physics, and on a contemporary theory of spacetime. Otherwise, the definition is either obsolete or too vague." (Post, 154)

But of course this is just the problem. As he says, "Even though the whole it speaks of is a spatiotemporal whole, no one yet knows which spacetime is involved, or even whether it is any of the spacetimes that so far have occurred to us. Hence we do not know specifically what we mean when we speak of the whole that is the Universe, or of its parts, which physics attempts to describe and explain, since the definition of the whole requires that a spacetime be specified." Even if we use the current list of predicates of physics, he says, one must ask: "The true and complete account of *what*? The Universe? The physical existents or phenomena? Either answer lands us in circularity, if we are looking for a definition of the Universe, or for some characterization more specific than the intuitive one above" (Post, 156).

Post draws on the familiar image. The universe "stands to us roughly as the elephant stands to the blind men of the story. Like the blind men, we believe that our predicates and hypotheses, though revisable, are somehow prompted in part by a reality that our instruments touch here and there. We believe that the Universe is a causal factor in our adopting certain predicates and hypotheses, and in our rejecting them eventually in favor of still others. The Universe has a say in the ongoing trial by prerequisites. It is not completely uninterpreted, or 'ineffable'" (Post, 157-8).

As Munitz observes: the necessity of having to resort to analogy to depict the world or universe – whether as a unique mega- or meta-entity, or as an absolute whole or totality -- is an expression rather of a metaphysical vision, a quasi-theological faith. It is "the projection of what is a human need" – a need for "total intelligibility, and of belief in a unifying structure" – onto "an allegedly antecedent ontological fact," the meta-physical reality of the world or universe, of which scientific cosmologies are only the most recent examples of a quest reflected in the myths of creation and the theological doctrines and metaphysical systems that have succeeded them. It is the dream captured in the very word the Greeks have given us, *kosmos*: "an ordered totality that binds all phenomena in a universal scheme, and whose details are accessible to patient rational inquiry" (Munitz, 1965, 68). As Rundle observes, "philosophers and physicists nowadays are disposed to think of a universe as a determinate species of thing of which there may be many, ... but talk of *a* universe will require that the system of things conjectured be unified in some way" (Rundle, 32). And yet, using the term 'the world' *as if* it referred to a unique entity or ordered whole, an all-inclusive totality, turns out to be misleading (Munitz, 1965, 71). For it was Kant who showed, against such views of the universe, that "all these notions of a unified system of thought express, at best, a *regulative ideal* of inquiry" (Munitz, *op.cit.,* 68). The fact is, as Munitz reminds us, even the manifest universe of cosmology may, for all we know, have "elements of disorder, or refractory indeterminateness," may be more like a *chaos* than a *kosmos*, frustrating the desire for an "all-encompassing intelligibility" (Munitz, 1965, 69). One thinks in this connection of William James' critique of the notion of what he called the metaphysician's "block universe," his suggestion that the "universe" is instead still a work in progress, a "pluriverse" that is and may forever be "unfinished."

It would seem, therefore, that the expression, 'the world' or 'the universe,' lacks a "clear, precise, univocal, non-controversial" – i.e., "concrete" or "determinate" -- meaning. We cannot think of it as an individual, a member of a class or series of actual or possible worlds, a totality, or a whole. There is no clear use in this unique case for the definite article ("the" world), let alone the indefinite article ("a" world). While some of the philosophers we have been discussing may believe it possible to reduce these unclarities, it would not seem possible to entirely eliminate the vagueness or indeterminateness of the term. (Munitz, 1965, 51-2) This suggests, contrary to Munitz's own proposal, that substituting the allegedly more determinate term 'world' for the indeterminate term 'something' in the Why question, does not after all advance us toward solving our conundrum. We seem to be back where we started before Munitz criticized the "indeterminacy" of 'something' in the original formulation of the Why question

Whether we choose to refer to 'the world' or 'the universe' as an 'entity,' a 'totality,' or a spatiotemporal 'whole,' if we think we are doing anything more than speaking in meta-physical tongues, if we think we are referring to something "concrete" rather than deploying an abstract mathematical construct or scientific model taken from the realm of things "within" the universe and extended beyond to refer a "whole" of which such things are said to be "parts," we would appear to be indulging in the same sort of wish-fulfillment, or committing the same sort of intellectual error, as those metaphysicians or theologians who think that, by use of myths, metaphors or analogies, they can convey positive information about the existence and nature of God.

The Experienced World/Universe. Let us assume that the 'world' or 'universe' of scientific cosmology, an abstract 'world' or 'universe' fashioned out of the building blocks of mathematical set theory and reprised in the abstract concepts of a materialist or theological metaphysics, may indeed be just that, an intellectual construction with no purchase in concrete reality. That is not the world, the universe, of our concrete lived human experience – the universe which struck awe in even such an abstruse thinker as Kant when he spoke of his direct experience of the 'starry heavens above.' Here once again, however, the hydra-headed monster rears its ugly visage. Harking back to Post and

Munitz' distinction between the observed universe and the universe beyond, *which* universe was it that stirred Kant's lofty emotion? The universe of "phenomena" he experienced or the world of "noumena" he posited as existing beyond?

Given our problems in trying to determine just which 'world' or 'universe' and what kind of 'world' or 'universe' these terms refer to, it appears, however counter-intuitive it might seem, that nevertheless we can experience 'it', whatever that 'it' might be. There may be no way to directly experience the 'true' or 'real' universe beyond the 'manifest' or 'observed' universe to which the latter is said to belong (cf. Munitz, 1965, 62). Given the difficulty if not impossibility of determining the nature of the 'manifest' or 'observed' universe – a mega-entity? a totality? a unique spatiotemporal whole? in any case, an abstract mathematical or physical construct – it is not clear that our concrete and undeniable experience of entities "within" the universe – Kant's starry skies, for example – entitles us to claim that we can experience the universe "itself." (The use of 'within' in this setting itself gives rise to further confusion if taken as a literal rather than figurative expression.) True, Post says that the physical universe "presents itself to us as an array or spread of things" (Post, 128). But in light of the foregoing discussion, would it not be more accurate to say, following Kant, that we re-present it to ourselves as a 'whole' based on the sophisticated use of what turn out to be metaphor or analogy?

But perhaps these difficulties in reference are themselves more apparent than real. For what is a reference other than a congealed set of properties, a place-holder for the descriptions we use to pick out and orient ourselves to things, a shorthand way of referring not to "things" existing independent of language but to the predicates by which we "construct" those "things" and then in turn "attach" to them an "independent" reality. If we can give a clear sense to the terms we use to characterize or describe the 'world' or 'universe,' perhaps in this way we can, as Munitz suggests, "reduce" the confusion surrounding them, even if we cannot eliminate it altogether. The world or universe does seem, after to all, to be a unique case calling for a use of language that is correspondingly unique.

Properties of 'World/Universe.'

In light of our discussion of problems regarding the reference of the terms 'world' or 'universe' we are compelled to ask whether there are in fact any properties or attributes, any descriptive features, we can ascribe to or use to characterize the world or universe that might apply to that unique 'entity' regardless of whether we conceive it to be an entity-encompassing 'entity,' a 'totality' of entities, or a spatiotemporal 'whole.' If there are, can they be applied in a straightforward way, or do the circumstances of their ascription inevitably render them hopelessly ambiguous if not impossible? Munitz claims that "reflection about the way in which we understand the terms 'the world' and 'exists,' and the assertion 'The world exists,' reveals that, far from these expression being clear, precise, non-controversial, and univocal, indeed the very opposite is the case." (Munitz, 1965, 51) If so, there would appear to be a difficulty, in fact several difficulties when it comes to talking about the world itself or as such. What problems arise when we try to apply properties to such an 'entity'? Can they be applied to such an 'entity' at all? If not, what else can we say about the world or universe? If we cannot say anything about it, how can we ask any questions about it, let alone expect any answers to our questions? As Wittgenstein maintained, "a question only where there is an answer, and this only where something can be said" (Wittgenstein, *Tract.*, 6.51) To address these matters, let us first inquire into the status of propositions about the world or universe. Then let us turn to the major attempts to say something about that unique 'entity' via the part/whole analogy, the distinction between necessary and contingent propositions, and finally, the difference between negative and positive attributes.

The Status of Propositions About the World/Universe. The first difficulty we face concerns the nature or status of propositions about the world or universe itself or as such, not about entities existing within the world or universe. Are they empirical propositions, for example, propositions of a scientific cosmology, as in theories about the Big Bang or the Steady State universe? Or, given the unique status of the world or universe vis-a-vis the entities within the world, are propositions about that 'entity' themselves unique in nature – that is, not ordinary propositions of an empirical or scientific sort, but rather extra-ordinary propositions, perhaps of a transcendental or metaphysical kind? According to Aristotle, the originator of the discipline, metaphysics was literally *meta*-physics, a

THOMAS DEAN

'science' that comes 'after' or goes 'beyond' [*meta*] 'physics.' As a meta-'science' it was alleged to deal with unchanging principles or realities that transcend and systematize, give order to, render coherent and explicable a *kosmos* – a 'world' that might otherwise seem a "blooming, buzzing confusion" (William James), a chaos of ever-changing things, *ta phusika* that make up the subject matter of 'physics.' Or, more counter-intuitively still, are propositions allegedly 'about' the world or universe, i.e. expressions allegedly referring to something in reality, whether empirical or metaphysical, in fact not expressions about the world at all, but rather disguised expressions about our grammar? Perhaps they are "mixed" assertions, statements misleadingly cast in the form of descriptive statements about reality, but in their actual content reflections or expressions of the grammatical rules or regulative principles governing the ways we go about talking about the world or universe. For example, Wittgenstein did not view metaphysical propositions, in this case, propositions about the world, as statements referring to some empirical or meta-empirical reality, but rather as grammatical propositions masquerading as truths about the world. (Rundle, 5; Wittgenstein, *Tract.* 6.53)

To get further purchase on these knotty issues, including that last rather astounding claim that when we thought we were talking about the world or universe we were in fact not talking about the world or universe at all but engaging in a kind of mystified and mystifying meta-speak -- talking about our talking about the world, not about the world itself -- let us turn to some of the main ways philosophers have tried to unpack and resolve these puzzlements that seem to arise when all we wanted to do was simply talk straightforwardly and directly about the world itself, the universe as such, without having to take some sort of linguistic detour through the grammar of such talk.

The Analogy of Part/Whole. The first possibility for understanding the nature of propositions about the world or universe is to see them as relying on the use of analogy, somewhat the way theological propositions rely on analogy to talk about the unique being of God. Perhaps world-talk or universe-talk too, like God-talk, requires the use of analogy to say what it wants to say. If so, in the case of the world the analogy of choice, perhaps for obvious reasons, is that of part and whole, the world being the 'whole' to which the entities within the world, as its 'parts,' are said to 'belong.' A further possibility, as Munitz and Post have suggested, is to regard the visible universe itself as being 'part' of a 'whole' universe to which it in turn 'belongs.' In any case, we need to look more closely at how, or whether, the part/whole analogy can be used to understand the nature of statements about the world or universe.

One way of using this analogy, one that at first glance seems the most plausible, is to regard the descriptive features or properties of things within the (visible) universe as applying to the universe itself. The working assumption is that in many cases a whole will share the attributes of its parts. For example, if all the parts of a chair are, say, brown, the chair as the whole made up of those parts will itself be brown. Of course in other cases this assumption may not hold. If all the parts of a machine are light, it does not follow that the machine itself will be light; it could prove very heavy. To assert otherwise, in the absence of any compelling evidence to the contrary, would be to commit the so-called "fallacy of composition," the fallacy of reasoning that a whole possesses a certain property because each of its parts has that property (Edwards, R. B., 264-7).

Our first question, then, must be whether the analogy of part/whole can be validly used to make descriptive assertions about the nature of the (visible) universe as a whole by applying to it the properties of the entities said to be its parts. Specifically, if each of the 'parts' of the universe is an entity extended in space and time, can we then say, invoking the part/whole model, that by analogy the (visible) universe, the 'whole' made of these parts, can itself be described as an entity extended in space and time? This seems, at least at first, reasonable to conclude. After all the evidence of scientific cosmology would appear to support just such a conjecture. It indicates a temporal beginning (and thus finite age) of the (visible) universe with the Big Bang some 13.7 billion years ago, and estimates the spatial extent, the edge or limit, of the (visible) universe to be somewhere in the region of 73 to 93 billion light years. On the face of it, therefore, invoking the part/whole analogy in this case would not seem to be committing the fallacy of composition. Given the scientific evidence, it seems safe to conclude that the (visible) universe, like the entities within it, is itself a spatio-temporal entity, the only difference being simply that it exists on a breathtakingly larger, all-encompassing scale.

There is one difficulty in this argument, however. It rests on the assumption that, even restricting ourselves to the visible universe, we can talk intelligibly, let alone scientifically, about the universe *as a whole*. As we have seen in our previous discussion of the referent of the

THOMAS DEAN

terms 'world' or 'universe,' this is already a problematic assumption. What further complicates the situation here is that our understanding of the spatio-temporal nature of the entities within the universe rests on a scientific method that involves appeal to a variety of instances of such entities, whereas in the case of the universe it would appear, at least at the outset, that we are dealing with only one such 'instance,' a 'unique' entity, making it difficult to characterize in the same terms as the entities within it. Despite its apparent spatio-temporal extension does the universe itself really exist *in* space and time? With no other actually existing 'universes' to juxtapose it to spatially or temporally, can we be so confident in our assumption? Though in one sense 'extended in' space and time the universe may itself not *exist in* space and time; as the 'whole' of space-time, it may itself be a 'time-less' existent with no spatial 'location' of its own. As one philosopher argues, "If scientific method investigates only natural occurrences [i.e., entities existing within time and space], then it cannot investigate nature as a whole, since the whole of space-time is not an occurrence [i.e., an entity existing] within space-time." (Edwards, R. B., 149)

A second way of invoking the part/whole analogy is to regard the visible universe as 'part' of another 'whole' to which it 'belongs.' The difference from the first use of the analogy is that here we are speaking not of 'parts' but of a (unique) 'part.' This involves the distinction, which we have met before, between the "manifest" or "observable" universe and the "true" or "real" universe, the universe "beyond" the visible universe "to which" the latter "belongs"– the Universe "itself" or "as such." Let us assume for the moment that we have overcome the difficulty of applying the features of entities within the visible universe to the visible universe as a whole. The question here is whether the descriptions that apply to the visible universe can be applied, by analogy, to the universe beyond the visible one.

The problem is that not only do these two uses of 'universe' not refer to the same thing, in the absence of any knowledge about what the universe beyond the visible universe might be like, we have no basis, empirical or logical, for saying anything further about it whether by analogy or by any other kind of reasoning. Everything at this point reduces to imaginative speculation of which, needless to say, there has been a good deal. Perhaps ultimately the *uni*-verse is rather, as the philosopher William James opined, a *pluri*-verse "ridden with chance and mishap and always denying any intellectual or conceptual closure"; or perhaps, as some cosmologists have ventured, it is a *multi*-verse of other universes of which ours is only one. It would seem, then, that despite our attempt to apply the part/whole analogy to the instance of the present universe in relation to something "beyond," the fact remains, as earlier observed, that "it is by no means the case that we are required to say of that to which the observed universe belongs [i.e., the universe--or universes--'beyond'] everything that we can properly say of that which is implicitly characterized by the use of some cosmological model [i.e., the visible universe]." (Munitz, 1965, 58)

To clarify this point further, it is already problematic enough, as we have earlier seen, to regard the visible universe itself as a 'whole.' As Munitz reminds us, "even if the [visible] universe were in some sense finite and wholly explorable by actually or theoretically available instruments, the statement that what is thus observationally explored is in fact the universe as a whole would not be warranted by observational evidence alone. What comes within the observational reaches of the astronomer is definitely not the universe as an absolute whole, if there is fact such a whole." (Munitz, 1967, 238-9). But if we cannot be sure that the visible universe is in some sense a whole, how can we say with any confidence that the universe beyond our observational reach is nevertheless a 'whole'?

As Munitz points out, "Cosmology aims at articulating the character of the universe *as* a whole. To that extent, then, it rests on the methodological postulate that the universe *is* a whole. Therefore the statement 'The universe is a whole' is in this context an analytic statement, a matter of definition. Not only does cosmology require that, as a matter of definition, the universe be thought *as* a whole, it also postulates that the universe as a whole is unique or absolute. But what if 'the universe' means 'that to which the observed universe belongs'? Is the statement 'the universe is an absolute, unique whole' still analytic? To this the answer must be no. In contrast to the case of the universe as defined by a cosmological model, we are no longer committed by the basic methodological postulate of cosmology to saying that the universe *is* a whole" (Munitz, 1967, 243). Munitz says, "when we use 'the universe' in this sense, we move from methodology to ontology." Post on the other hand seems to have no reservations about making this metaphysical leap: "Roughly speaking, the Universe [i.e., the universe beyond the visible universe] is the unknown (or incompletely known) whole about whose parts physics attempts (or ought to attempt) to give us descriptions and explanations that are true and complete" (Post, 129; cf. 116-117, 156-158).

As Munitz explains, "Indeed, even if we grant that the observed universe is structured in some manner, this does not entail that the wider universe of which it is a part is also pervasively structured. Nor does the fact that we describe the observed universe as 'part of' or 'that which belongs to' something else require us to say that the universe to which it belongs is a unique or absolute whole. For our reliance on such terms as 'part,' whole,' and 'belong' reveals merely that the mind, in reaching into the unfamiliar, must use *analogies* in order to relate the unfamiliar to what it already knows." (Munitz, 1967, 243)

Munitz concludes, "The universe as the 'something more' than the observed universe may well be a complete, unique and intelligibly structured whole. But the claim that we are able to say so is something to which we need not commit ourselves. It is better left as an open question, since, strictly speaking, it is one on which we neither have nor can have any knowledge." (Munitz, 1967, *ibid.*) Of course, we might want to go further than Munitz at this point and ask, following Wittgenstein, what kind of question it could be, let alone an open one, if we cannot say anything about it, let alone have any knowledge about it? (cf. Wittgenstein, *Tract.*, 6.51)

The situation is even more dire than Munitz suggests. The attempt to predicate anything of the universe as a 'whole' leaves us not with an 'open question' but with a set of what Kant called 'antinomies,' a series of unresolvable paradoxes. In the case of the universe of time and space, taken as the absolute completeness of a given whole of appearances, that is, as what Munitz refers to as a given cosmological model of the observable universe as a structured, systematic whole, we are confronted by a pair of opposing and logically contradictory propositions, each of which seems to be plausible, but neither of which can be demonstrated as true, namely, on the one hand, "the world has a beginning in time, and is also limited as regards space," and on the other, "The world has no beginning, and no limits in space; it is infinite in both" (Kant, 396).

The underlying problem with all of these attempt to use of the part/whole analogy is that they require extending our concepts for things that exist within the spatiotemporal universe to something that lies beyond their normal range of application, whether that be the visible universe as a unique 'whole' or an alleged 'whole' that is even more inaccessible 'beyond.' The most difficult philosophical question, as one philosopher notes, is whether such efforts to use words to describe something that transcends the conditions of their ordinary application make any sense at all (Nagel, 2004). "Whether in speaking of God or of the universe, we are at risk of making misconceived projections of our language: what makes sense with respect to things within universe may cease to do so when God, or universe as whole, is at issue" (Rundle, 191).

To take just one example, though perhaps the most prominent and consequent for trying to answer the Why question, namely, the notion of causality. When scientists, philosophers or theologians think to look for an ultimate explanation, i.e., cause, for the existence of the universe, what they are trying to do is find a quasi-scientific or meta-physical explanation that uses a concept of causation that applies to relations of things within the world to something that is not an entity within the world. The concept of causation, like concepts of beginnings and endings, though having innumerable instances within the world, resist extrapolation to the universe itself (Rundle, 44). As Rundle goes on to observe, while we are wary of extending to God descriptions applying to human beings, we tend not to be equally wary of applying descriptions of something *within* universe to the universe itself. It is as if we are treating the universe as something existing *in* space and time. So "it is whether we may intelligibly speak of a cause at all in this instance that is problematic" (Rundle, 75).

And yet, on the other hand, as Nagel points out, while it is risky to use ordinary or even scientific language to reach beyond its existing limits, or even to its edges, we feel impelled by the Why question to do so over and over again, however inadequately, despite or perhaps even because of our recognition that our understanding of the world is incorrigibly limited, that all we have at our disposal are what Kant refers to as "categories of understanding" designed to make sense of phenomena within the universe, categories that at the same time tempt yet frustrate our every attempt to extend them beyond the boundaries of their legitimate use. (Nagel, 2004)

Necessary and Contingent Existence. There may, however, be another way to get at talking about the universe as a whole, or the universe as such, one that does not involve using the analogy of part and whole drawn from talk about entities within the world. We can ask instead whether it is possible to talk about the universe as existing in a completely different way than the things that exist within the universe, that is, as having a totally different mode of existence altogether– namely, one of necessary rather than contingent existence. If so we may be able to say something about the universe after all, namely, we may be able to make unique descriptive assertions that match the uniqueness of the phenomenon itself. The advantage of turning from attempts to describe the world/ universe using the parts/whole analogy to a discussion of whether the existence of the universe is itself contingent or necessary is that it does not involve us in trying to extend notions describing the contingent existence of things within the world beyond the context of their ordinary use and applying them to apply to the universe as a whole. Instead it raises the more general, and perhaps logically prior question, whether the universe can be said to exist in a contingent (i.e., empirical or quasi-empirical) sense at all, whether instead its unique status entitles us to say it has necessary existence (necessarily exists, exists necessarily).

In other words, if unlike empirical entities within the world which exist contingently, that is, which can be conceived without contradiction as not existing, the universe itself it cannot be conceived not to exist, then statements about it will share in that necessity in a manner analogous to the necessary truths of logic or mathematics. If so, this would be a descriptive feature, perhaps one we could call meta-physical or ontological, applying uniquely to the universe and to the universe alone. This would make it possible to talk about the universe in itself or as such after all, and would in fact take us a long way toward answering the underlying question with which we are concerned, namely, why there is a universe at all, why the world exists rather than nothing at all. So let us examine more closely the question whether the existence of the universe is uniquely necessary or whether, like the entities within it, in fact it too after all exists only contingently. In the latter case we would have landed back in the dilemma with which we began.

Necessary Existence and Necessary Truth. In metaphysics a distinction is frequently made between two kinds of existing entities: "those that exist but could have failed to exist, and those that could not have failed to exist. Entities of the first sort are contingent beings; entities of the second sort are necessary beings." These entities, if they exist, could include "God, propositions, properties, states of affairs, possible worlds, and numbers" (Davidson, 2013). Our question, of course, is whether the world or universe could be included in that list as well. Metaphysics also makes a parallel distinction between two classes of propositions: "those that might have been false and those that could not have been false (or those that have to be true)" (Van Inwagen, 2014). What Leibniz calls "truths of reason," that is, necessary truths, depend for their truth on the principle or law of contradiction, whereas what he terms "truths of fact," that is, contingent truths, depend on something less stringent, namely, the principle of sufficient reason–that for whatever entity that exists or event that happens, there must be a sufficient reason, causal or otherwise (Hamlyn, 199). Our question, again, is whether propositions about the world or universe could be included in the class of necessary truths, of propositions that could not have been false, that in fact, have to be true. There is a linkage between these two questions, for as van Inwagen notes, "The modality of propositions is called modality *de dicto*. But modality would seem to be an undeniably metaphysical topic if one admits the existence of modality *de re*—the modality of things."

The Necessary Existence of the Universe. When we turn to consider the mode of existence of the world or universe, what do we find? The grounds for asserting the necessity of its existence would seem to lie in the claim that, at least according to one philosopher, "The universe did not come into existence, nor will it cease to exist. And this is not just a matter of empirical fact: there is nothing we could intelligibly describe as the universe's coming into existence or its ceasing to exist. Beginnings and endings join causation in being concepts which, while having innumerable instances within our world, resist extrapolation to the universe itself." (Rundle, 122).

In view of the scientific cosmology of the Big Bang and estimates of the age and extent of the universe this would seem, on the face of it, a counter-intuitive claim. However, Rundle rejects the assertion that the scientific account of the Big Bang refutes his philosophical brief. "Big Bang or no Big Bang, there has never been a time when there was nothing, and our conception of the Big Bang has to be accommodated to that consideration." The notion of there ever having been an initial point of time before there was nothing, "a point of division between the start of an event and an eventless period which preceded," is logically incoherent (Rundle, 123). To cap off his argument and lay to rest this alleged conflict between philosophy and science, he brings in the preeminent cosmologist Stephen Hawking, who says in apparent agreement, "if the universe is really completely self-contained, having no boundary or edge, it would have neither beginning nor end: it would simply be" (Hawking, 149, cited in Rundle, 123). As Rundle concludes "There just is no alternative to being" (Rundle, 112).

In short, the universe cannot not exist; it not only "simply 'be's'," it has to be. Its existence is necessary, not contingent, and the statement that it does exist is a necessary, not a contingent truth. It would seem, therefore, that we are finally able to say at least one thing for sure about the universe – something not dependent upon extending to the universe descriptions that apply only to entities existing contingently within the universe, something that is true whatever the current state of empirical knowledge about the visible universe – that it is a necessary truth that the universe not only exists, but does so necessarily.

Are we entitled, then, to conclude, with Rundle, that in effect we have answered the question, why does the universe exist rather than nothing? If the universe cannot not exist, if its existence is necessary, there is nothing further that needs to be said or that can be said. It would seem our questioning has reached its end. The universe exists because ... it simply is. (One is reminded of Heidegger's famous tautological neologisms, *die Welt weltet* and *das Sein west* – "the world worlds" and "being be's"). We could pack up our philosophical and cosmological baggage and go home, perhaps none the wiser about the empirical universe but at least with our metaphysical itch scratched. Unfortunately, Rundle's argument, and even Hawking's pithy imprimatur, leave some questions still up in the air, and insofar as they do, we cannot return from our lofty speculations to terra firma quite yet.

To change the metaphor, there are at least two flies in this metaphysical ointment. First, there is an ambiguity in Rundle's notion of the 'universe.' Then there is the ambiguity in what he or Hawking mean by 'be' as applied to the alleged necessity of the universe's 'existence' or 'being.' Until or unless these can be disambiguated and the confusions they engender cleared away, it is premature to think our inquiry has reached its goal.

We have already encountered the distinction between the visible universe and the universe beyond, the universe itself or as such. This distinction, unless carefully observed, can wreak havoc on otherwise sensible arguments. Rundle does not make use of this distinction. He may think it a non-starter, that the two notions in fact refer to the same thing. As a metaphysical 'materialist' or 'realist' he regards his use of the term 'universe' as having a univocal meaning, basically the notion of the visible universe, the universe as observed by astronomy and modeled by mathematical physics. But in fact his use of the term conflates a rather different pair of notions which compromises, fatally, his argument that the 'universe' exists necessarily. For example, in the passages we have been citing he conflates the phenomenon of 'the universe' as the structured, systematized spatiotemporal whole of scientific cosmology, the ordered *kosmos*, with the unstructured, unsystematized 'singularity,' the 'no-thing' or primordial *chaos*, from which the manifest cosmos of space and time originated in the Big Bang. Thus, while he may want to argue that primeval chaos has to exist, that it is in some sense necessary, this does not entitle him to say that the particular universe which has happened to emerge from that singularity itself exists necessarily. We can imagine, and cosmologists and philosophers have indeed imagined, other possible universes, in fact a multi-verse of possible universes that could also have emerged from out of that fiery singularity. Therefore, there would seem to be no logical contradiction in saying of the visible universe that it could have failed to exist.

Perhaps related, if not prior to the preceding ambiguity, there is the question of just what Rundle, or for that matter, Hawking have in mind when they say of the universe that it might "simply be." The phrase would seem to be taken here as a synonym for 'necessary existence.' But this is extremely puzzling. For one thing, there seems to be no contrasting sense in this context for the notion of 'simply being,' no sense, that is, of 'simply not being'; whereas for the notion of 'necessary existence' we do have the contrasting concept of 'contingent existence.' Further, and apart from this, it is not at all clear why we should not take the notion of something's 'simply being' as a synonym instead for 'contingent existence,' for what Munitz, in speaking of the universe, refers to the "pure contingency" of its existence (Munitz, 1965, 158).

Negative and Positive Attributes of the Universe. Whatever the case, let us assume for the moment that the universe exists necessarily, or alternatively, that it has the property of necessary existence, that propositions ascribing to it existence are necessary truths. Even granting this, we face new questions. Does this statement really tell us something positive about the existence and nature of the universe, as on its face it appears to do? (Post entitles his book *The Faces of Existence*.) Or is it a statement with nothing more than negative import, one that tells us only what the univers is not? Or is it not even that? Is it yet another instance of "mixed" discourse, a statement of grammar masquerading as a profound truth of metaphysics or cosmology, a statement about the limits of our ability to talk about the universe pretending to be a meaningful proposition about the universe itself? Or is there yet another possibility? Might it be not a proposition of cosmology, metaphysics or grammar at all? Might it be rather a "speech-act" having another function altogether, the expression of a response not to "how" the world is but simply "that" it is? (cf. Wittgenstein, *Tract.*, 6.44; also, 6.432) Let us consider each of these possibilities in turn.

One way to test the positive import of the claim that the universe exists necessarily is to see if it lends support to other positive statements about the properties of the universe. That is what at least two of our philosophers argue. According to Rundle, given that the universe is the spatiotemporal whole of existence, that the Big Bang was not an expansion in time and into space but an expansion *of* time and space, in other words, then since space and time are properties internal to the universe, it follows that we cannot talk of a time "outside" or external to the universe when it began to exist or when it will have ceased to exist. "There is no such time with respect to the universe" (Rundle, 120-1). However paradoxical it may sound, the universe of space and time does not itself "exist" in space or time. The universe, as Hawking said, has "neither beginning nor end," it is not itself a spatio-temporal 'entity'; it simply "is" (Rundle, 123; Hawking, 149).

Now maybe, Rundle concedes, these assertions do not entitle us to make any positive assertions about the universe; perhaps they constitute at best a *via negativa*. Nevertheless he sees "the failure of certain descriptions to apply to the universe 'came into existence' and 'was caused to be' [as] part of the resolution of our problem rather than the source of a difficulty" (Rundle, 191). How so? Because, as the title of his book, *Why there is Something rather than Nothing*, indicates, as does his citation of Hawking, not only does the universe "simply" exist, it has to exist. In other words, the *via negativa* leads to at least one positive metaphysical proposition -- that the universe exists necessarily. But that is not all. The *via negativa* in fact has implications for additional positive assertions about the universe, as a second philosopher spells out in detail.

As Post argues in the subsection of his chapter, "Universe," entitled "Eternal Universe" (Post, 138-58), whatever the case with the three-dimensional world of our ordinary experience, the four-dimensional world of cosmology, that is, the whole of spacetime, not only exists necessarily but is eternal. Further, as metaphysically necessary it is the self-existent First Cause of all that is, the Unmoved Mover on which all else is dependent: "the universe is an explanatorily or metaphysically necessary being. Those of its properties that have no explanation by reference to properties of its parts also enjoy this sort of necessity. They are not contingent, nor are they brute, gratuitous, absurd, or irrational. They are metaphysically necessary. From physics to metaphysics is but a step" (Post, 135, 153; also, 115, 116-17, 129).

What are some of those metaphysically necessary properties? They are contained in the assertion that the universe is eternal in a five-fold sense, namely, that it is immutable, does not exist in time, is timeless, exists "all at once," and is without beginning or end.

- The universe is immutable. "It is not subject to change, to becoming, to process, or to corruption or decay" (Post, 153; cf. 141-144).
- The universe does not exist in time. "Its existence cannot be dated as past, present, or future or as before or after some event" (*ibid.*, 153; cf. 144-145).
- The universe is timeless. "It is not be described by means of tensed verbs" (*ibid.* 153; cf. 145-146).
- The universe exists "all at once." It has "no parts distinguished by being transiently past, present, future, or still to come, relative to one another" (*ibid.* 153; cf. 146-148).
- The universe is without beginning or end. "Its 'duration' is such that it neither ceases to exist nor comes into being" (*ibid.* 153; cf. 148-153)

At this point Post, like Rundle, points out something very interesting. These positive-sounding affirmations employ negative predicates. As he notes, "We *can* say of the universe beyond that it is eternal, but only because 'eternal' is characterized negatively, by denying certain temporal properties" (Post, 158, emphasis in original). He returns in the last pages of his study to make the point again: "the Universe beyond satisfies the key negative predications," viz. immutable, not in time, tenseless, without beginning or end, not created, not explanatorily dependent on any being. This means that "we must refrain from any positive physical predications about it – plus other positive descriptions as well – so that in this sense it 'transcends every form which our intellect attains'" (Post, 361). And yet these propositions are clearly regarded as having positive, metaphysical significance. In other words, both Rundle and Post regard the *via negativa*, which refuses the attribution of positive temporal ('physical') predicates to the universe as somehow, by "but a step," becoming a *via positiva* that ascribe positive, nontemporal ('meta-physical') properties to the universe. In effect by a metaphysical sleight-of-hand (that small "step") they transform negative assertions about the universe into positive assertions, propositions that say what the universe is not into propositions that describe what the universe is.

So what is going on here? Is this just another instance of "mixed" grammatical or 'transcendental' statements about the limits of our language masquerading as positive metaphysical claims? Or is it a misuse of empirical science to justify jumping to metaphysical conclusions? Is there another way of interpreting the negative predicates in Rundle and Post's accounts without taking a metaphysical leap?

The Contingency of the Universe. The alternative, drawing a different conclusion from the same observations about the limits of our language vis-a-vis the universe, is to argue that the universe exists not necessarily but contingently. The argument here is that scientific cosmology, whether observational astronomy or the theoretical models of physics, not only does not but cannot support metaphysical claims about the nature of the universe. Scientific method cannot yield metaphysical theories about the properties of the world as a spatiotemporal whole, for example, that it is eternal, self-sufficient, nonpersonal, exhaustive of reality, or necessary (etc.), because the subject matter of scientific method involves contingent possibilities (Edwards, R. B.,149). "If scientific method investigates only natural occurrences, then it cannot investigate nature as a whole, since the whole of space-time is not an occurrence within space-time" (Edwards, R. B., *ibid.*). For example, returning to the attempt to use the part/whole analogy to make assertions about the world as a whole, science does not discover in experience "any necessary whole (that cannot not be) composed entirely of contingent parts (that can not be). To say that the relation between the world of nature and its parts is the only exception to this generalization would be simply to beg the question" (Edwards, R. B., 167).

Nevertheless, having noted the limits of science or cosmology when it comes to talking about the universe as a whole, are we not still faced with having to choose between one of two positions? Does the universe as a whole, unlike its parts, exist necessarily, dependent on nothing else for its existence, or does it, like its parts, exist only contingently, dependent upon some other, 'higher' cause? As Rundle might argue, is matter 'eternal, self-sufficient, and indestructible'? Or if the concept of 'matter' has been rendered untenable by modern physics, is there a more elemental form of 'formless" energy that is 'eternal, self-sufficient, and indestructible'? As Edwards observes, "Here is where the real problem ultimately lies, and here is where we may have reached the limits of human knowledge." Can we say that we know matter or energy has those additional metaphysical properties? "Is it an empirical problem, one that experience could resolve? Is it a conceptual problem?" (Edwards, P., 268).

Proponents of physicalism like Post or materialism like Rundle, precisely because they hold self-consciously metaphysical standpoints, have no hesitance about going beyond ('meta-') the limits of empirical science ('-physics') in their advocacy of the 'necessary, eternal, self-sufficient (etc.)' side of this question. On the other hand, philosophers of religion or theologians defending a theistic version of a first-cause 'meta'-physics have an interest in coming down on the side of the universe as 'contingent.'

Metaphysical Agnosticism about the Universe. This suggests another possibility – metaphysical agnosticism. It is Munitz, remember, who pointed out, as does P. Edwards, that the notion of the universe as a spatiotemporal whole is a methodological concept, not a metaphysical one. Thus it does not warrant the leap (let alone a 'step') to bold metaphysical assertions of the kind advanced by Rundle or Post. At best it permits a modest agnosticism, if not skepticism, concerning propositions about the universe as a whole. The relapse into metaphysical certainty that one sees in Rundle or Post goes far beyond the probabilities of empirical science. So to the question whether the universe exists necessarily or only contingently, Munitz says, "we have no way of assuring ourselves either as to an affirmative or negative answer to this question. It follows that the only sound philosophic view to adopt in connection with this entire matter, is one of agnosticism" (Munitz, 1965, 178, also 220-54 passim). Edwards too concludes perhaps echoing Munitz, "Could we not simply be agnostics, abandoning the possibility of a definite answer?" (Edwards, P., 269).

Conclusion and Transition

For these several reasons it seems an unwarranted leap to conclude of the visible universe that its existence is necessary or, on the other hand, that its existence is purely contingent. Or either. At this point it seems that about all we can say is that (*pace* Heidegger) *die Welt 'weltet'*, the world 'worlds,' the universe 'universes.' We cannot say whether it "came into being," "will end," or even that it "just simply is." The meaning of the latter is as opaque as Heidegger's *das Sein west*, "being be's." We seem to have arrived at an impasse. It would seem premature, therefore, to end our inquiry into the Why question here.

Transition

We began this discussion of the world or universe by trying to follow out Munitz' suggestion that we could rescue the question "Why does something exist rather than nothing?" by replacing the indeterminate notion of 'something' with the more concrete term 'world' or 'universe.' It seems to safe to say, however, that this substitution has not done what it was advertised as being able to do. Instead, it has simply created new difficulties that lead us further away from a solution to the question. The notion of the world or universe has turned out to be highly problematic in its own right. The reference of the term proved burdened with a fatal ambiguity, while attempts to describe the world have also led to a logical impasse. It would seem, therefore, that we must return to our starting point and think the matter all over again

As we said at the start, while the question, Why is there something rather than nothing at all?, seems rather simple and straightforward, like many questions it contain several parts. In this section we have been discussing the first of the questions-within-the-question, "Why is there *something* rather than nothing at all?" The subject referred to by indeterminate term 'something,' at least if Munitz is to be believed, turned out to be something more determinate, 'world' or 'universe.' Having arrived at an impasse in our attempt to answer this first part of the Why question – at least temporarily, since we may wish to return to the more indeterminate term 'something' at a later point in our inquiry -- we turn to second part of the Why question, "Why *is there* something rather than nothing at all?" Here the focus shifts to a consideration of the feature of this "something" (or world or universe) that is being asked about, namely, the fact that this 'something' (world, universe) exists. We are not asking about its content, its makeup, its extent in space and time – what Wittgenstein referred to as the 'how' of its existence, but rather the 'that' of its existence, the fact that it exists.. We are asking simply about the existence or being of that 'something' (world, universe). We are interested in the fact that *there is* something. Perhaps if we can get clear about that, we will be able to get clear at the same time about the subject matter our first question-within-the question -- the *'something'* (world, universe) whose existence the question is asking about.

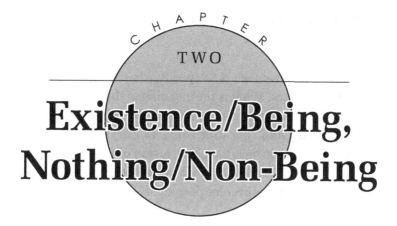

C H A P T E R

TWO

Existence/Being, Nothing/Non-Being

"This word 'is' hides the riddle of all riddles, the mystery that there is anything at all." – Tillich, *Biblical Religion and the Search for Ultimate Reality*

In this second part of our question, "Why *is there* something rather than nothing at all?," the focus shifts to the basic feature or property of this "something" (world, universe) that is being asked about – the fact that it *exists*. We are not asking about its content, its structure, its extent in space and time – the 'what' or, as Wittgenstein put it, the 'how' of its existence. Nor are we here asking, at least not yet, about its 'why,' the reason or explanation for its existence. Rather we are asking simply about the 'that' of its existence, the fact that it exists, what medieval philosophers referred to as its *haecceity*, its "this-ness" or "that-ness." We are asking simply about the existence or being of that 'something' (world, universe). We are interested in the fact that *there is* something. If we can gain clarity about that, we might be able to get clear at the same time about the subject matter of our first question-within-the-question -- the 'something' (world, universe) whose "is-ness" or "existence as such," the question is asking about.

Concepts of Existence.

The Problem/Question of the Meaning of Being/Existence/Exists

The first problem we face is to specify what is meant by saying of something that it 'exists.' What is the meaning of the term 'existence' (or 'being,' or 'exists')? As Heidegger observes in the opening citation of his magnum opus, *Being and Time* (Ger: *Sein und Zeit*) from Plato's *Sophist*, 244a: "For manifestly you have long been aware of what you mean when you use the expression '*being*' [Grk: '*on*']. We, however, who used to think we understood it, have now become perplexed" (Heidegger, *Sein und Zeit*, 1/*Being and Time*, 19)

Perhaps having Heidegger's quote from the *Sophist* in mind, the author of the article "Existence" similarly observes: "Like many philosophically interesting notions, existence is at once familiar and rather elusive. Although we have no more trouble with using the verb 'exists' than with the two-times table, there is more than a little difficulty in saying just what existence is. On the face of it, there would seem to be no way at all in which we can explain what existing is. If one thinks that 'exists' is readily dispensable in favor of some other (less troublesome) expression, then there will be no difficulty in dismissing the thought of there being some such property or attribute as existence. Alternatively, if one thinks that 'exists' is not to be dispensed with in this way, then one might be inclined to continue pursuing the puzzle of just what existence is" (Miller, 2002).

As the writer explains: "'real' is what has been called an 'excluder' predicate, meaning thereby that it attributes nothing positive to Tom, but operates in a purely negative fashion simply to exclude Tom from being imaginary, mythical, fictional, and the like. To say that 'exists' meant 'is real' would be to say *inter alia* that it attributed nothing positive to Tom; and that would do much to relieve our frustration at being so fluent in our use of 'exists' despite having no idea of its attributing anything positive to Tom. It would be a relief to discover that 'exists' attributes nothing positive to him at all. Unfortunately, this won't do; for among all the negatives that 'is real' might be applying to Tom would be not only 'not imaginary', 'not mythical', etc., but also 'not nonexistent'"(Miller, *ibid*.).

Just before th passage cited by Heidgger in the *Sophist*, Plato's Stranger had said: "Possibly, then, our minds are in the same state of

THOMAS DEAN

confusion about being. We profess to be quite at ease about being and to understand the word when it is spoken, though we may not understand the nonbeing, when perhaps we are equally in the dark about both" (Plato, *Sophist*, 243c). Thus puzzlement about the meaning of, and link between, 'being' [exists, is real] and 'nonbeing' [the nonexistent, unreal] was established already at the very beginning and foundation of the Western philosophical tradition.

Heidegger goes on to explain the difficulty in trying to understand or define the seemingly evident, all-too-familiar concept of being or existence. Nowadays, he says, the notion is dismissed by philosophers as the most universal and hence emptiest of concepts. It is therefore regarded as the most indefinable of concepts. And since everyone uses it all the time, its meaning is obviously already understood; in fact, its meaning is self-evident. "In this way," Heidegger notes ironically, "that which the ancient philosophers found continually disturbing as something obscure and hidden has taken on a clarity and self-evidence such that if anyone continues to ask about it he is charged with an error of method" (Heidegger, *BT* 21, *SZ* 2). Heidegger further explains why, given these three alleged features of the term, it is no longer felt necessary to trouble ourselves with Plato's perplexity about 'being' and 'nonbeing':

It is said that being/existence is the most *universal* of concepts. It is already included in our understanding of all beings/entities. Its universality, therefore, is not that of a higher class or genus. But this means that rather than being the clearest of concepts, in no need of further inquiry, it is rather, says Heidegger, "the darkest of all" (*SZ* 3, *BT* 22-23).

It is said that being/existence is, as a consequence, *indefinable*. It cannot be conceived of as a being or entity. Nor can it be defined by some logically 'higher' concepts or described through any 'lower' ones. In other words, it cannot be 'defined' like other terms. This does not mean, however, that the problem of its meaning is thereby finessed. Rather, says Heidegger, "it demands that we look that question in the face" (*SZ* 4, *BT* 23).

Finally, it is said that of all concepts it is the most *self-evident*. Whenever one says anything about anything some use of being/existence is implied. It has "an average kind of intelligibility," which means that in fact the term is unintelligible. Thus in every statement about entities as entities, in every relationship to beings as *beings*, says Heidegger, "there lies *a priori* an enigma." Though we implicitly refer to and presuppose an understanding of its meaning, the explicit meaning of being/existence remains "veiled in darkness" (*SZ* 4, *BT* 23).

Therefore, Heidegger concludes, "it is necessary in principle to raise this question again." It is."not only that the question of Being lacks an answer, but that the question itself is obscure and without direction" (*SZ* 4, *BT* 24). As Miller also concluded, "one might be inclined to continue pursuing the puzzle of just what existence is."

Heidegger's inquiry in *Being and Time* subsequently proceeds in the direction of an "existentialist" analysis of the meaning of being/existence. That is a direction this inquiry too may eventually take. For now, the discussion of the meaning of being/existence (and nonbeing) will be confined to the "cosmological" (scientific or metaphysical) context within which for the most part the ancient and modern philosophical tradition has discussed it. That means, for the purposes of this essay, Aristotle, Kant, and modern logical theory.

The Many Meanings of 'Being' according to Aristotle

As Rundle observes, the notion of being or existence is so broad that "the only limit that can be imposed on what can be is to be found in the demand for consistency or coherence. The notion itself is totally indifferent to *kinds* of thing. No form of existence seems privileged, all seem thinkable away" (Rundle, 166). We hear here an echo of Heidegger's critique, that modern philosophers dismiss the notion of being/existence as so "broad," i.e. universal, that paradoxically it lacks any specifiable purchase on "reality" at all, and that as a consequence any use of the term is not only indefinable, it is "thinkable away," readily dispensable (Miller, 2002). However, Rundle goes on to add, "this point notwithstanding, there are forms or modes of existence that are derivative or dependent" (Rundle, *op. cit.*). With this observation being/existence is brought back into the discussion.

When we go back to the beginning of the tradition of philosophical speculation, we find Plato's student Aristotle arguing that being has in fact not just one but many meanings. But this seems to deepen the original "perplexity." What is the relation among these many meanings? Is there an underlying meaning that unites them? Or is one of them more fundamental than the others in relation to which the others are "derivative or dependent"? Is there at least a partial overlap in meanings, or have they completely different meanings? It would seem rather that the field for discussion has been opened even more widely.

What, according to Aristotle, are the many meanings of being/existence, and what are their relations to one another? In his account of the things there are (*ta onta*, beings) in his *Categories* (1a25), Aristotle divides 'beings' into ten categories -- substance, quality, quantity, relation, etc. Of these Aristotle privileges the first, substance (*ousia*). Substances are independent entities. The items in the other categories all depend on substances. Qualities are qualities of substances, quantities are the amounts and sizes that substances come in, relations are the way substances exist in relation to one another. These other categories of 'being' all owe their 'being' to substances. They 'exist' only 'in' substances. A fundamental relation of inherence links these other 'beings' to the primary being of substance. (Cohen, 2008)

In his *Metaphysics* (Bk IV, 2, 1003a), Aristotle tell us, similarly, that 'being' is "said in many ways." "There are many senses in which a thing may be said to 'be'" That is, the verb 'to be' (*einai*) has different senses, as do its cognates 'being' (*on*) and 'entities' (*onta*). Cohen asks, does this mean a universal science of being qua being [ontology] founders on an equivocation? How can there be a single science of being when the very term 'being' is ambiguous? (Cohen, *op. cit.*) If the term 'being' were ambiguous, Aristotle's science of being *qua* being would indeed be impossible, says Cohen. But Aristotle argues that 'being' is not ambiguous in this way. 'Being' indeed is "said in many ways," but it is not simply "homonymous," i.e., sheerly ambiguous. Rather, the various senses of 'being' have a *"pros hen"* ambiguity -- they are all related to a single central sense. (The Greek phrase *"pros hen,"* Cohen explains, means "in relation to one.") As Aristotle continues, "but all that 'is' is related to one central point, one definite kind of thing, and is not said to 'be' by a mere ambiguity" (Aristotle, *op. cit.*). (It is interesting to note that in this same passage Aristotle adds, "It is for this reason that we say even of non-being that it *is* non-being" – a point to which we shall return.).

In a later book of the *Metaphysics* (Bk VII.1), speaking of substance, i.e., the primary sense of being, Aristotle repeats what he said earlier. 'Being' is said in many ways, but the primary sense of 'being' is the sense in which substances are beings. There again he assigns to the other categories a secondary or dependent, derivative sense of 'being'. Aristotle concludes that "the question which was raised of old and is raised now and always, and is always the subject of doubt, viz. What being is, is just the question, what is substance? And so we also must consider chiefly and primarily and almost exclusively what that is which *is* in *this* sense." (*Metap.*,1028 a-b).

The problem with Aristotle's discussion of the many senses of 'being' and his assigning of priority to 'substance' understood as 'independent beings' is that it does not, at least on its face, seem to address our opening question. For our problem, as stated above, is not the 'what' of being/s ("independent entities") or the 'how' of being/s (beings as not "dependent" upon others for their being), but the 'that' of being/s (that 'there *is*' being, that 'there *are*' beings, that being/s '*exist*'). Talk of 'be-ing' as 'beings' does not address the issue of what it means 'to exist.' Aristotle does talk elsewhere of the meaning of 'to exist,' but we will understand his comments better if we place them in the context of the analysis of the many meanings of 'is' in modern logical theory, in particular the question whether 'exists' is a descriptive predicate (Kant).

The Meanings of 'Is' or 'Exist' in Modern Logic

As Miller observes, it seems clear that the question of the meaning of being or existence is "inextricably intertwined" with the question of the meaning of 'exists' (Miller, *op. cit.*). And here "the predominant view on existence among contemporary philosophers of an analytic persuasion might be summarized in two theses, the first of which is the Frege-Russell distinction between four different meanings of 'is' — the 'is' of existence, of identity, of predication, and of generic implication (inclusion)" (Miller, 2002). Thus:
'Socrates is' – the 'is' of existence
'Cicero is Tully' – the 'is' of identity
'Socrates is wise' – the 'is' of predication
'Man is an animal' – the 'is' of generic inclusion

The problem for our inquiry is that, as Miller observes, "the different uses of 'is' entail correspondingly *different meanings,* so different in fact as to have *nothing whatever in common.* That is to say, they are casually ambiguous rather than being merely systematically ambiguous or analogical, which would have been the case had their meanings been inter-related though without being univocal in any way—not even partially" (Miller, *ibid.*). If Aristotle's many senses of being seem to have complicated the matter, at least the other categories of being referred back to the primary sense of 'substance.' They were, in Miller's term, at least "inter-related," even if they were not "univocal." Here, on the other hand, in modern logical theory, it would appear that the search for the meaning of 'being' or 'existence' has broken down completely

And yet is the situation as dire as all that? Reviewing these four senses of 'is,' can we not say, following Aristotle, that the 'is' of existence is primary, the others being dependent upon it? The 'is' of predication presupposes reference to the 'substance' (Socrates) named in the 'is' of existence. The 'is' of identity likewise presupposes the 'substance' to which the two names refer. And the 'is' of generic inclusion refers back to the 'substances' included in the genera.

In any case, and these are complicated matters in logic as well as metaphysics, it would seem from the above list of uses of 'is' that the use which is the focus of our inquiry is the first on the list, the 'is' of existence, the 'is' of 'exists.' If so, the next question is, what does it mean to say of an entity that it 'exists.' Are we in fact saying anything about it at all? Counter-intuitive though it may appear, perhaps in saying of something that it exists we are not predicating anything of it at all. If existence is not a predicate, if saying of something that it exists is not telling us anything about it, then are we saying anything meaningful when we assert of the world that it exists, or when we ask why it exists rather than nothing at all?

Is Existence a Predicate?

These questions turn on the underlying question whether the notion of existence is a predicate. As Miller notes, "the second thesis commonly, though not universally, held by analytic philosophers might be summed up in the familiar dictum, 'Existence is not a predicate'." (Miller, *op. cit.*).

Before this claim was recast in the symbolic notations of modern logic, it had already been addressed by Hume and Kant. Hume argued that "the idea of existence must either be derived from a distinct impression, conjoined with every perception or object of our thought, or must be the very same with the idea of the perception or object" (Hume, 1960, Bk. I, Part II, sect. vi). And since, Hume said, nothing pointed to the presence of any such impression from which the idea of existence could be derived, therefore the notion of existence adds nothing to "the idea of what we conceive to be existent." (Miller, 2002.) Hume's claim that to say of an entity that it exists "makes no addition" to the description of that entity was developed in further detail by Kant.

According to Kant, "By whatever and by however many predicates we may think a thing — even if we completely determine it — we do not make the least addition to the thing when we further declare that this thing is. If we think in a thing every feature of reality except one, the missing reality is not added by my saying that this defective thing exists." (Kant, 1958, B628) In other words, paradoxical as it may seem, the verb 'to exist' tells us nothing about the entity to which it is applied. As J. L. Austin humorously observed, "The word is a verb, but it does not describe something that things do all the time, like breathing, only quieter – ticking over, as it were, in a metaphysical sort of way." (Austin, n. 68, cited by Munitz, 1965, 92). If so, this adds one more problem to the Why question about the world's existence. For as Munitz pointedly asks, if Kant (and Austin) are right, then 'exists' as a verb does not really describe any activity of the world (Munitz, *ibid*.). Normally, to say of an entity that it exists is to say it "persists in carrying on some particular activity" as a "loose surrogate for other terms that can be substituted." 'Exists' can always be eliminated and replaced "by specifying the particular activity" (Munitz, 1965, 92-3). But in the case of the world, what 'activity' could that possibly be? We shall return to that question below.

In the meantime it should be noted that for Kant, while 'being' or 'existence' is not a real predicate, not a predicate that describes any additional feature of a subject, it can be thought of as a logical predicate. In that case its function is either to assert simply that an entity exists (along with its various properties) or to assert that its properties exist (in relation to that entity). Take, for example, the two statements "x is" (exists) and "x is y" (has the property y). As a logical predicate, the role of 'is' in both cases, says Kant, is simply to posit (the German verb is *setzen* – to put, place, set, posit) the existence of the entity. In the former instance, it posits the subject (x) "in itself with all its predicates" (whatever they are), while in the latter instance it posits the predicate (y) in relation to the subject (x). The 'is' in the former and the 'is' in the latter seem for Kant to be merely two uses of the one notion (Miller, 2002).

Kant's distinction between these two aspect of 'is' as a logical predicate, one positing the existence of the subject *tout court*, one positing the relation of the predicates to the subject, finds an interesting anticipation in Aristotle. While some think the Frege-Russell distinction of four different and unrelated uses of 'is' cannot be found in Aristotle, others think that the 'is' of existence, of predication and identity can be found in his works – in particular a sense for the first two as, contra Frege-Russell, related in their meaning. There is still a difference of view about the nature of that relation, however. On the one hand, as Miller explains, "In so far as this applies to the existential and predicative uses, some have explained the former as being merely elliptical for the latter. Thus, 'Socrates is' would be merely elliptical for 'Socrates is a something or other', where the permissible substitutions for 'something or other' are any of Socrates' essential predicates. On this view, therefore, 'is' would be unambiguous because its use was always predicative, either explicitly as in 'Socrates is a man' or merely implicitly as in 'Socrates is'. Not only was the one sense being used, it was being employed with the same force in each case, namely, predicative" (Miller, 2002).

On the other hand, however, there are passages in Aristotle that would seem to conflict with the ellipsis hypothesis. For example: "For it is not the same thing not to be something and not to be *simpliciter*, though owing to the similarity of language to be something appears to differ only a little from to be, and not to be something from not to be" (Aristotle, *De Soph. El.* 167a4–6) Here too, the two uses of 'is' ('to be' and 'to be something') are not, says Miller, as unrelated as might first appear. "So far as the existential use [i.e, Kant's 'is' as a logical predicate] is concerned, the earlier quotation is pertinent as showing that the existential and predicative occurrences of 'is' are indeed related to each other as absolute and relative uses of the same notion. Although being used with existential force in the former but predicative force in the latter, 'is' has the same *sense* in both" (Miller, 2002).

In the first case, the 'is' of 'to be' *simpliciter* is absolute because it involves positing the existence of a substance in itself, and as we recall, for Aristotle it is substance that has being or existence in the metaphysically primary or independent, 'absolute' sense. Whereas in the second case, the 'is' of 'to be something,' i.e., the 'is' of something in relation to which certain predicates stand, is an 'is' used in a relative use, because, as we recall such predicates, i.e., qualities, have 'being' only in a secondary sense, that is, only in their relation to the absolute sense of the primary being of substance. Here then we seem to have a precursor of Kant's distinction between two uses of 'is' having the same sense as a logical predicate, in one case with what is here designated existential force (the 'is' of 'to be') and in the other instance predicative force (the 'is' of 'to be something').

Modes of Existence, Necessary and Contingent

On the assumption that 'existence' is not a descriptive predicate (Kant: a 'real' predicate) that adds anything to our concept of a thing, but that it does have meaning ['sense'] as a term that posits the existence of a thing either *simpliciter* or together with its predicates (Kant: a logical predicate), our next question must concern the extent of its application as a term for positing the existence of something. Is its meaningful use in the positing sense restricted to positing the existence of things that exist only contingently, entities the denial of whose existence does not involve us in logical contradiction? Or can 'exists' be used to posit entities whose existence is necessary, entities the denials of whose existence would land us in logical contradiction?

More specifically, is its use to posit the existence of entities that exist contingently limited to entities that exist within the parameters of space and time? Or can its use in this sense be extended to the existence of the world itself? Can we view not only things existing within space and time but the whole of spacetime itself as existing contingently? If so, the possibility of the world's not existing could be affirmed without landing us in a logical contradiction. That would seem to put the Why question back in play – why then does the world exist, rather than nothing at all? On the other hand, can 'exists' also be posited of entities whose existence is necessary? If so, and if the world itself is deemed to be such an 'entity,' that would seem to render the Why question moot. Why does the world exist? Because it simply has to. Getting clear about the extent of the application of 'exists' as a term for positing existence is therefore important for any conclusions we may wish to draw about the Why question itself.

There is of course a third possibility. It could be that, paradoxical as it might seem, we cannot say of the world either that it exists contingently or that it exists necessarily. It may be that we cannot apply to the world the term 'exists' in either of its senses, 'real' or 'logical,' descriptive or positing. In other words, it may be impossible to say of the world that it 'exists' in any sense of the term, even to distinguish it from 'nothing.' Lest this seem an idea from out of 'nowhere' or 'nowhen,' we only need to remind ourselves of the first and fourth of Kant's 'antinomies' (unresolvable paradoxes or contradictory theses) in his *Critique of Pure Reason*:

First Antinomy: "Thesis: The world has a beginning in time, and is also limited as regards space." "Antithesis: The world has no beginning, and no limits in space; it is infinite as regards both time and space." (Kant, 396)

Fourth Antinomy: "Thesis: There belong to the world, either as its part or as its cause, a being that is absolutely necessary." "Antithesis: An absolutely necessary being nowhere exists in the world, nor does it exists outside the world as its cause." (Kant, 415)

If Kant is right, we may have to resign ourselves to a kind of metaphysical scepticism regarding assertions about the existence of the world, and hence about alleged answers to the Why question. The Why question may simply have to go unanswered. Whether or not that is a philosophically satisfactory answer may not matter, for it may well be that the question is in principle unanswerable. It would seem, therefore, that a lot hangs on the answer to the question of the meaning and scope of application of that harmless looking, ubiquitous little verb, 'to exist.' We need to look more closely, therefore, at the notion of 'to exist' in relation to that of 'the world.'

Existence and the World

How is it then with 'existence' and 'the world'? The most extensive treatment of this question is in Munitz, *The Mystery of Existence*. Echoing the conclusions of the preceding section, the first thing to be noted about 'the world' and 'exists' and 'the world exists,' says Munitz, is that none of them of these expressions are "clear, precise, non-controversial or univocal" (Munitz, 1965, 51). In particular, it would seem that "the ordinary analysis of existence-statements does not apply to the analysis of the statement 'the world exists'" (Munitz, *op. cit.*, 52). It may be, in other words, that while "the statement 'the world exists' does say something about the world, [it] does not commit one to the view that the world is contingent; nor, at the same time, does it follow, by this denial, that one has to say that the existence of the world is, in any way, necessary" (Munitz, *op.cit.*, 72-73). It may be rather than in this case the term 'exists' is "uniquely descriptive" (Munitz, *op.cit.*, 73). But this only deepens the mystery. How can else anything, the world included, be said 'to exist' if not contingently or necessarily? It would appear that Munitz, and we, still have a lot of explaining to do.

The Relation of 'Exist and 'the World' in 'the World Exists.'

We look first at the reasons Munitz gives for saying 'exists' in 'the world exists' is "uniquely descriptive." In making his case he wishes to argue, first, that "'the world' includes 'existence' as one of its defining characteristics"; and second, that "the fact that the world exists is discovered in experience, though not in a narrowly conceived sense-experience" (Munitz, 1965, 77; cf. 83). On the basis of these two premises he then concludes, drawing on Kant's classification of judgments, that "it would be best to classify the judgment 'The world exists' as analytic *a posteriori*" (Munitz, *ibid.*).

Kant classifies judgements as regards, first, the relation of the subject to the predicate, there being two kinds: analytic – the predicate is contained in the definition of the subject, and synthetic – the predicate adds something to the definition of the subject; and, second, in terms of how knowledge of the judgement is obtained, there being two ways: *a priori* – by simple inspection of the meaning of the terms alone, and *a posteriori* – by resort to experience beyond the meaning of the terms alone. At least two kinds of judgement follow from this classification. First those that are *analytic a priori* – those in which the predicated is known to be contained in the subject by virtue of the meaning of the terms; and secondly, those that are *synthetic a posteriori* – judgements whose predicates add something to the content of the subject, a fact which can only be known through appeal to experience.

Kant goes on to argue, more controversially, for a third kind of judgement, those that are *synthetic a priori* – judgements in which the predicate adds something to the subject, a truth which, however, can be known apart from any prior experience. Kant's example of this latter are 'transcendental' principles that organize our experience such as 'every event has a cause.' This principle has the necessity of an a priori judgement, it is not grounded a posteriori in an inductive survey of empirical evidence; however, it is synthetic insofar as the relation of the predicate to the subject cannot be shown by a proof based on concepts alone.

Munitz, though referring to Kant, in fact, goes beyond what even Kant would allow by introducing a fourth kind of judgement, one that is *analytic a posteriori* – a judgement whose predicate is contained by definition in the subject, yet the truth of which can only be known through experience. Such a judgement would have the necessity of a conceptual truth, and yet would be a judgement whose truth, paradoxically, could not be determined by analysis of the concepts, requiring instead an appeal to experience. The sole, unique instance of such a judgement, says Munitz, is the judgment, "the world exists." The proposition is necessarily true, but its truth can only be discovered through experience. Munitz acknowledges that for Kant that is one kind of judgement too far: "there is, for Kant, nothing that corresponds to an analytic aposteriori judgement" (Munitz, 1965, 83). How, then, or why does Munitz propose to rush in where even Kant feared to tread?

Another Meaning of 'Exists.' As we have noted, Kant rejects the possibility that 'exists' adds any further descriptive features to the concept of thing. But, asks Munitz, what if the concept of a thing "already contains, as part of its very meaning, that its object exists?" (Munitz, 1965, 81) "It makes no sense," says Munitz, "to say that the world, as identified in our experience, does not exist." Thus, "to actually deny (or even entertain the possibility that one might deny) the existence of world is, therefore, contradictory of the meaning of the term" (Munitz, *ibid.*). If, says Munitz, 'the world exists' is analytic, then we cannot deny the world's existence without contradiction. Yet it the truth of the proposition is not a priori, since the world's existence is only known through experience. (Munitz, *op. cit.*, 82-83) It would seem, therefore, that the function of 'exists' in the statement 'the world exists' is different from its alleged function as a predicate in statements of the sort with which Kant was concerned, namely, judgments about things that exist within the world.

In other words, if, says Munitz, 'exists' means 'having the status of belonging to the world,' then it cannot be used to describe the world. If 'exists' applies only to things within the world, it could not be predicated of the world. "The world could not, meaningfully, be said 'to belong to the world'" (Munitz, *op. cit.*, 91). Therefore, since it does make sense to say "the world exists," there must be another meaning of 'exists' in that unique instance, and that means, a different kind of the 'experience' that justifies us in affirming the world's existence (Munitz, *ibid.*)

What, according to Munitz, is distinctive about our experience of the world's existence, and how does it justify the claim that 'exists' can in that instance be *descriptive* of the world? On the one hand, though 'the world exists' is analytic, that fact is not known by conceptual analysis. On the other hand, the existence of the world is not, however counterintuitive it might seem, known by experience either, that is, by the kind of sense-experience that gives us knowledge of things that exist within the world (Munitz, *op. cit.*, 78). Yet, says Munitz, "the knowledge of the existence of the world is nevertheless part of ordinary experience. We have no common name for it; one might call it 'cosmic consciousness'" (Munitz, *op. cit.*). It is not, however, a mystical experience with portentous metaphysical implications. Rather, "the awareness of the existence of the world is the most primordial, commonplace, and universally shared experience. We are likely to overlook it only because it is so trivial and omnipresent" (Munitz, *op. cit.*, 78-79). This awareness is "primary and not reducible to any other type of experience." It is "uniquely directed" to one object, "the world as existing" (Munitz, *op. cit.*, 79)

'Exists' As Descriptive Of The World. It may well be the case that the experience of the world itself, as such, or as a whole is of a different sort than experience of things within the world. But how does Munitz think this enables him to evade the Kantian critique that nevertheless 'exists' has no descriptive (real) function, at best merely a positing (logical) one? Munitz grants that normally "a verb suggests some form of activity; it describes what things or persons *do*." But what sort of activity, if any, does he propose 'exists' ascribes to the world? (Munitz, 1965, 92) Munitz maintains that the world does not 'exist' in the same sense that things within the world can be said to exist. But is that any reason to think that in its 'cosmic' application 'exists' thereby suddenly acquires a descriptive function lacking in its humbler uses?

THOMAS DEAN

Well, yes, says Munitz. Agreed, normally to say of something that it 'exists' is an "elliptical or foreshortened way of saying that [it] persists in carrying on some *particular* activity as a loose and general surrogate for other terms that can be substituted for [it]" such that one can always eliminate it in favor of describing that particular activity (Munitz, 1965, 92-3). But what about 'exists' in the case of the world? Here, says Munitz, "[it] does have a distinctive and unique role to perform: it designates *what the world does*" (Munitz, *op. cit.*, 93). Now this is a 'bodacious' (bold and audacious) claim. What on earth can the world, the universe, be said to be *doing*? What sort of *particular activity* can it be said to be engaged in? Munitz' surprising answer is worth citing in full:

> What then does the world do? Well, the world does what the world does. It cannot be assimilated or literally compared to anything else. All other terms of description would be, at best, analogical, or only partially enlightening. But how can we describe what the world does, distinctively? The term used to describe its mode of 'activity' would be irreducible to any other; it should not be replaceable by some other term. It is to serve as such a distinctive and unique term to describe what the world does, and nothing else does, for which we may use the term 'exists.' The mode of functioning that is appropriate to the world is – to exist. Instead of saying 'The world worlds' or The world carries on as a world,' we say 'The world exists.' To exist is all the world can do; this is what it is 'fit' to do; or–to use traditional terminology–the essence of the world is its existence" (Munitz, *op. cit.*, 93-4).

Now what is at stake in Munitz' astonishing claim? Consider the alternatives, he says. If, on the one hand, we said that 'exists' is not descriptive of the world, if it is only used to posit the world as the subject for other terms that be predicated descriptively of it, then the Why question would come to a halt. How so? The question, 'Why does the world exist?' only makes sense if we can predicate existence of the world, for the question asks

why the world has the specific feature it has, namely,
'that it exists' (Munitz, *op. cit.*, 94-95).

On the other hand to insist that 'exists' is a descriptive predicate of the world would seem to land us in an opposite dilemma but with the same end result, namely, rendering the Why question moot. How so? If 'exists' in 'the world exists' "describes the world uniquely, is part of the meaning of the term 'the world,'" then once again the question why the world exists turns out to be "futile and beside the point." If 'exists' is just what the world does, where or what is the question? To say 'the world exists' would be "to affirm a tautology, and to deny it would be self-contradictory" (Munitz, *ibid.*). The Why question "purports to look for a reason, whereas at bottom, there is only a question of definition involved" (Munitz, *op. cit.*, 96).

Which horn of this dilemma, then, would Munitz have us adopt? On the one hand he rejects the view that the existence of the world is contingent in the sense that things within the world are contingent. He wants to say that the truth of its existence is an analytical truth, that its 'essence' is 'existence,' hence a necessary, tautological truth. On the other hand, he rejects the opposing view that the existence of the world is necessary in the way that the truths of logic are necessary, i.e. without need of resort to experience, insofar as the fact of the world's existence is discoverable only through experience, albeit via a unique, 'cosmological' experience.

Munitz has advanced a number of controversial claims in defense of this position. Questions abound here, and while we cannot at this point resolve them all, if any, it is important to put them on record before we go further. Munitz argues:

"The essence of the world is existence." But is this so? It reminds one, of course, of Anselm's famous *argumentum* ("proof") for the existence of God. God's essence is existence, so to assert the possibility that God, so defined, does not exist is to fall into self-contradiction. Whether the argument is valid or not – Kant's strictures against existence as a predicate were designed to refute Anselm's argument – can such a claim be sustained if the subject is the world? God's existence is certainly different from that of entities within the world. But if Kant's argument applied to Anselm, why would it not apply with equal if not greater force to Munitz?

"To deny the existence of world contradicts the meaning of the term." But again, is this so? As with the Anselmian argument, is it a contradiction to imagine the possibility of the world (God) not existing? Is that not the point of the Why question? Not to deny the world's existence, but to imagine the possibility of its not existing. Referring back to the previous point, if Kant's critique of 'existence' as a (descriptive, 'real') predicate applies validly not just to things within the world, but to the world itself, then there would be no contradiction in conceiving the possibility of the world's not existing.

"If 'the world exists' is analytic, then we cannot deny the world's existence without contradiction. Yet the truth of the proposition is not a priori, since the world's existence is only known through experience." To say 'the world exists' is analytic is not to say the world's existence is necessary. Further, and here we return to our earlier discussion of the ambiguities in reference of the term 'world,' what does Munitz think the term 'world' refers to when he speaks of it as the object of "cosmological awareness"? Is it Kant's empirically observed "starry heavens above"? Is it a mathematical model of the universe of cosmological science? Is it the unknown 'true' universe 'behind' or 'beyond' the 'manifest' universe? Or is it not an object of experience at all, but rather a Kantian regulative ideal, a categorial construct, whose function is simply to guide our empirical study of the universe? Until we can get clear about these matters, it is not clear just what we mean -- what we are referring to -- when we speak of experiencing the existence of the world.

"The knowledge of the existence of the world is nevertheless part of ordinary experience." Since Munitz distinguishes the 'cosmic consciousness' of the world from our non-cosmic experience of things within the world, in what sense is it 'part' of 'ordinary,' presumably non-cosmic experience? Is it not rather the foundation, presupposition, or ground of our ordinary experience of things either as an all-embracing whole or as the guiding principle of empirical research? Is it somehow both? It seems there is more to unpack in his concept of 'cosmic consciousness' or 'cosmological awareness' before we can be sure of the relation between 'exists' and 'the world.'

This awareness is "primary and not reducible to any other type of experience." It is "uniquely directed" to one object, "the world as existing." But wonder at the existence of things is not limited to the existence of the world as such. As the world's religions amply testify, and as many scientists would concur, wonder at the existence of things can be aroused by encounter with the humblest of entities. We need more precision, then, if we are to give to experience of the world's existence some sort of exceptional, privileged status setting it off from the existence of things within the world. Absent that, it would seem Kant's strictures still apply.

"'Exists' is an "elliptical or foreshortened way of saying that [it] persists in carrying on some *particular* activity. [We] can always eliminate it in favor of describing that particular activity." Here, of course, Munitz is simply reporting Kant and Austin's claim that existence is not a predicate. But is it so easy to "eliminate" that little verb, when, as Heidegger among others would argue, the reality of being or existence is implied, implicitly present, presupposed by, every activity? Yes, it may be eliminable as a descriptive ('real') predicate, but it is nevertheless still present as a positing ('logical') term in its 'there is...' sense. Modern logical symbolism expresses this fact clearly when it notates, for example, "the boy is running" as (Ex)[xB . xR] – read as: *there is, i.e., there exists* an x (entity, object) such that x is a boy and x is running. The nature of the verbal *activity* may have been relocated inside the brackets, but the fact of *existence* is still present in the "there is" (E) and the "x."

Munitz claims that, in the exceptional case of the world, however, 'exists' functions both descriptively and as a positing term. The question this raises is whether logical symbolism is able to accommodate the distinctive use of 'exists' in the case of 'the world.' If not, is it logic or is it Munitz' claim that needs to give way? In the notation of logic, does it make sense to say there is, i.e., exists, an entity such that the entity is the world and the entity exists (Ex)(xW . xX)? Have we not duplicated the 'exists' and thereby uttered nonsense, at least logically speaking? If not, what kind of descriptive content can we give to the term 'exists' in its application to the world? The passage from Munitz cited at length above does not really tell us. What we get are simply variations on an underlying tautology: 'existence exists': "the world does what the world does. The mode of functioning that is appropriate to the world is – to exist. Instead of saying 'The world worlds' or The world carries on as a world,' we say 'The world exists.' To exist is all the world can do." Not terribly informative.

The Why question "purports to look for a reason, whereas at bottom, there is only a question of definition involved." Here Munitz is reporting the critic who submits that the Why question is rendered moot by the tautological nature of 'the world exists.' This, by the way, is a position to which our other two interlocutors, Post and Rundle, would presumably subscribe. The question here is whether to say of a proposition that it is necessarily true is the same as to say that the subject of the proposition necessarily exists. Further, as noted above, the deep unclarity in what we mean by 'world' makes it difficult if not impossible for either the critic or Munitz himself to say that 'the world exists' is true by definition. At best, perhaps, one can say that it is analytic that 'something exists' is true, but whether that 'something' is to be taken to mean 'the world' is yet to be determined. That, of course, would be problematic for Munitz' position in particular, since it was he who touted the advantage of substituting 'the world' for 'something' in the original formulation of the Why question.

Munitz' position, as we noted above, rests on the contention that the existence of the world cannot be understood as either contingent, in the ordinary sense ascribed to entities existing within the world, nor necessary, if that is taken to eliminate the need for turning to experience to verify its reality. But if his 'third way,' viewing 'the world exists' as an analytic a posteriori judgement, is in fact problematic, as the previous reservations suggest, perhaps we should look more closely at his reasons for rejecting the two obvious alternatives, that the world does indeed exist contingently, or that like God is said to do, it exists necessarily.

Contingent Existence and the World

Munitz says that a sense of the world's contingency, apart from arguments grounded in theology of scientific cosmology, arises in a particular, more direct experience of the world. Specifically, it occurs when we are confronted, as the theologian Paul Tillich said, by the 'shock of non-being,' or as Heidegger said, by the dread-full or angst-ridden experience of 'the Nothing,' by a sense of astonishment, or despair, "that there might have not been a world at all, that there might have been nothing" (Munitz, 1965, 142). This sense of an 'existential' rather than metaphysical or cosmological 'nothing' in turn leads to a very different understanding of 'contingency' and 'world.' But, asks Munitz, are the highly subjective, emotion-laden words in which this "primordial" experience is expressed meaningful or true in any other sense? Do they have any cognitive meaning? Do they refer to a possible objective state of affairs? Philosophical opinion is divided. According to one thinker cited by Munitz:

> It is possible that there might have been nothing for such a state of affairs, though unimaginable, is not inconceivable – there are many statements (in physics for example) which describe situations which cannot be visualized. To show that the proposition 'Nothing might have existed' is inconceivable it would be necessary to show that it is self-contradictory or otherwise logically malformed, and there seems no good reason to assert this. (Smart, 51, cited in Munitz, 1965, 143)

As we might expect, Munitz, as would Rundle and Post, categorically rejects this line of argument. If 'the world exists' is analytic, and therefore a necessary truth, then the statement, 'nothing might have existed' is in fact, contra Smart, self-contradictory. One might add further, though here Munitz most likely would disagree, that if as we have previously argued the term 'the world' is totally lacking in clarity, then both the statements 'the world exists' and 'nothing [no world] might have existed' and indeed reference to the notion of the 'contingency' of the world would seem, pending clarification, to run the risk of being "logically malformed." Would the same stricture apply if in place of 'the world' we were to return to 'something'? That is a matter to which we will have to return.

As that may be, Munitz further argues (and here again he would be supported by Rundle and Post), "the statement 'There might have been nothing,' if taken to mean no more than 'Why does the world exist?', may be allowed to stand, though, redundantly, as part of our way of expressing the mystery of existence. However, if the term 'nothing' is intended to designate some independently conceivable possibility with which the existence of the world can be contrasted, then this manner of speaking must be rejected as being inherently unintelligible. It follows that if the concept of the contingency of the world is made to depend on some intelligible and metaphysically defensible idea of 'nothing', there is no warrant in speaking of 'the contingency of the world' (Munitz, 1965, 143-4).

There are several questions we might want to raise about Munitz' argument, however. Why should we grant that the Why question is simply a way of expressing "the mystery" of existence? It is not yet clear, of course, just what is being asked for, but it seems premature to dismiss it as an expression of existential astonishment or angst rather than a legitimate question in its own right.

Next, what exactly does Munitz mean by referring to the concept of 'nothing' (if indeed it is a concept) as intending an "independently" conceivable possibility? "Independently" of what? Does he mean an independently existing possibility? What "manner of speaking" is he speaking of that he finds so "unintelligible"? Perhaps the clue comes in his use of the world "metaphysically." Munitz seems to position his discussion of the world within the context of traditional metaphysics with its opposition of being and nonbeing.

But what if, in the Why question, the presence of the word 'nothing' refers not to an (im)possibility within the realm of metaphysics, but to an attempt to go beyond that framework, not necessarily to "eliminate" or "overcome" metaphysics, nor to effect its "deconstruction" or "closure," but to open thinking up to possibilities beyond the traditional binaries of metaphysics? We cannot explore that possibility further here, but we will return to it when we discuss the notion of "nothing (at all")" and the "Why" dimension of the Why question itself. In the meantime, what is involved in the claim that the world exists not contingently but necessarily, and what is Munitz' objection to this alternative possibility?

Necessary Existence and the World

There are, of course, some philosophers who would argue that the world exists necessarily. Among them we might include Rundle and Post. However, Munitz rejects this notion. To get clearer on what is at dispute, we will first look at the proposition that the world indeed exists necessarily. We will then turn to Munitz' reasons for rejecting this claim. We have already seen that he rejects as well the seemingly opposite claim that the world exists contingently. We shall consider his own view, his 'third way,' when we come to the 'Why' portion of the Why question.

The Proposition 'the World Exists Necessarily.' The claim that the world exists necessarily involves us in distinguishing and considering the relation between two kinds of 'necessity,' necessary propositions (judgements, truths) and necessary existence. Addressing the first kind of necessity, Van Inwagen says that "there is an important distinction to be made within the class of true propositions: the distinction between those that might have been false and those that could not have been false (or those that have to be true)" (Van Inwagen, 2014). Or as Leibniz formulated it, "there is a difference between truths of reason, or necessary truths, which depend on the principle or law of contradiction, and truths of fact, or contingent truths, that depend on something less stringent, the principle of sufficient reason." (Hamlyn, 199). Truths of logic and arithmetic are paradigm examples of necessary truths (Davidson, 2013). This distinction invokes the notion of modality, i.e., "pertaining to possibility and necessity," and refers to what philosophers call 'modality *de dicto*,' the modality of propositions.

There is a second kind of modality called 'modality *de re*,' the modality of things. Here we are speaking of two sorts of entities: those that exist but could have failed to exist, and those that could not have failed to exist. Entities of the first sort are contingent beings; entities of the second sort are necessary beings. There are various entities which have been said to have necessary existence: for example, God, propositions, relations, properties, states of affairs, possible worlds, and numbers. Note, says Davidson that the first entity in that list is a concrete entity; the rest are abstract entities. (Davidson, 2013). Note, too, however, that this list omits the actual existing world or universe. And yet that it is the very 'entity' (if such it is) the status of whose being is the object of our concern.

A problem arises, says Van Inwagen, when we ask about the relation between these two types of modality, and their corresponding senses of necessity. If the modality of possibility/necessity applies only to modality *de dicto*, the discussion could be safely confined to the realm of logic. But if the modality of possibility/necessity (contingent/necessary) can be extended to modality *de re*, it becomes "undeniably a metaphysical topic." In this latter case we become involved in a discussion not only about the contingent being or existence of things within the world, or the alleged necessary being or existence of God, but also about the metaphysical status of the world's being or existence..

Consider first the existence of things, says Van Inwagen. If there is such a thing as a contingent being, a being that might not have existed, and if there is the idea of a contingent being, then the complementary idea of a necessary being would seem to make sense – the idea of a being of which it is false that it might not have existed (Van Inwagen, 2014). Take next the properties of things. Like existence, properties too are subject to modality.

So, if there is an idea of "having a property contingently," one might think it also makes sense to speak of having a property not contingently but necessarily. A thing can be said to have a property necessarily "if it could not exist without having that property" (Van Inwagen, *op. cit.*). Finally, says Van Inwagen, if we can speak of possible worlds, we can say that "a necessarily true proposition is a proposition that would be true no matter what possible world was actual" (Van Inwagen, *op. cit.*)

How do these distinctions apply to the mode of the world's existence? Let us assume that the idea of a necessary being having a property necessarily makes sense. Let us further assume that we can distinguish between these notions as applying in any possible world and as applying to the actual existing world. Can we say of the actual existing world, as does Munitz, that its existence is a necessary property? If so, does that entitle us to the further claim that it exists necessarily? For reasons we shall come to, Munitz does not want to take that additional step.

But what if, contra Munitz, we do want to claim that the world exists necessarily? Then we are confronted by yet another question. As Davidson points out, "What grounds the being of necessary beings, then? What makes it the case that they exist in every possible world? Perhaps the best that can be said about this is that *nothing* accounts for their necessary existence. It is a 'brute' fact that they exist necessarily. But this is no explanation. Perhaps this "lack of grounding" is objectionable, however, perhaps ontological grounding applies only to contingently existing objects" (Davidson, 2013.) We seem to have returned to Munitz' position. On the one hand, appeal to the notion of necessary existence does not seem to be an "explanation" that could answer the Why question. On the other hand, if ontological explanations apply only to contingently existing objects within the world, where does that leave the mode of the world's existence? As Davidson concludes, "The issues here are deep, though, and there is much room for further philosophical inquiry" (Davidson, *op. cit.*).

Both Rundle and Munitz try to find a way out this metaphysical conundrum. Rundle asks whether it is not possible, contra Davidson, that some existential propositions, propositions stating that an entity exists, may be necessary truths. (Rundle, 109). Clearly Munitz thinks 'the world exists' is one such, if unique, case. Now a necessary proposition, according to Rundle, is one that is consistent with all states of affairs. Presumably the world is consistent with all possible states of affairs within the world. This would suggest that the existential proposition, 'the world exists,' is a necessary one. However, Rundle rejects this inference. The statement 'the world exists' is not in fact an "existential proposition." If it were, it would be possible to conceive or imagine the world not existing at all. But, he says, contra the supposition of Smart cited above, we cannot conceive or even imagine there being nothing at all. "Existing and not existing fit into the scheme – existing now, not existing then, and, more radically, there being a so and so and there being no so and so – but the contrast is still within how things are" (Rundle, 113).

At this point Rundle introduces a further, very interesting distinction: "it could be that no being can be held to exist of necessity, and yet it was a necessary truth that something existed" (Rundle, 109). This is an intriguing line of speculation. Is Rundle saying that by the very fact of its existence, it is necessary that something (namely, the world) exist? Or is he saying that it is not necessary that the world exist, only that something exist? What would that 'something' be? Clearly this latter is contrary to the direction that Munitz proposed when he replaced the indeterminate notion of 'something' with the more determinate notion of 'the world.'

Rundle's distinction forces us to confront the central point. Just what does 'exist' mean in the case of 'the world'? The attempt to clarify the meaning by applying the modal distinction of contingency/necessity has either been illuminated or further muddied by Rundle's apparent reintroduction of 'something' in place of 'the world.' Can Munitz help us find a way back out of this maze?

Critique of 'the World Exists Necessarily.' Those who would argue that the world exists necessarily must, says Munitz, adapt to the existence of the world some version of the ontological argument for the existence of God. The ontological argument says that because God is, by definition, understood as that being than which none greater can be conceived, we cannot deny the existence of such a being without falling into self-contradiction. To say that it is possible that such a being might not exist is to deny that it is in fact a being than which none greater can be conceived, since it is greater to exist in reality as well as in conception than to exist in conception alone. Ergo such a being not only exists, but exists necessarily. The question whether the world exists necessarily then turns on whether the ontological argument for the (necessary) existence of God can be applied to the existence of the world as well.

Munitz argues that it in one sense it can, but in an important sense it cannot. On the one hand, the ontological argument, as for example the theologian Karl Barth and the philosopher Norman Malcolm have argued, "is not essentially, or strictly, an argument, but at best only a way of making explicit (in the 'conclusion') the full meaning of what is already contained in the premiss" (Munitz, 1965, 163). We have already seen that Munitz regards 'existence' as part of the 'essence' or definition of 'the world.' His only proviso in accepting this argument is that in the case of the world at least, knowledge that the world exists is not a matter of intellectual intuition, as it would be for an a priori truth but requires direct experience (Munitz, 1965, *ibid.*). "At best, an 'ontological argument' for *the world's existence* only serves as a discussion that helps clarify what one means by saying that the world exists, and what kind of warrant this assertion does have." (Munitz, 1965, 163-4)

However, he immediately adds, to conclude from this, as do those who use this argument to prove the necessary existence of God, "that the existence of the world is a necessary existence is another matter altogether." (Munitz, 1965, 164) No appeal to any experience can establish that further claim in the case of the world, he says. It is precisely for that reason that while he accepts the ontological argument as clarifying the analytic or conceptual truth (by definition) of 'the world exists,' he rejects its further extension as an existential truth established *a priori* rather than *a posteriori*, by appeal to experience. Even in granting a limited truth to the argument, his bracketing of the expression 'ontological argument' makes this reservation clear.

To say that an entity, for example God, has necessary existence is to say that it is not dependent for existence on some other entity, that its existence is not in that sense contingent. Further, if its existence is to be intelligible, to make sense, it can only be dependent for its existence upon itself. In the term of the metaphysical tradition, it must be *causa sui*, its own cause. That means "it would not only explain everything that it derivatively contains or encompasses, but itself as well" (Munitz, 1965, 168). Implicit in this argument is an appeal to the Principle of Sufficient Reason. A potential problem rears its ugly head here, however, for as we recall from above, according to Leibniz the principle of sufficient reason applies only to contingent facts or truths. But the truth of the world's existence, says Munitz, is a necessary truth, a truth which, according to Leibniz, depends only on the Principle of Contradiction.

This suggests, says Munitz, contra the metaphysical tradition, that in fact we do not have a "clear and distinct idea" of what is meant by saying of an entity that its existence is *causa sui*, 'cause of itself,' exists necessarily simply by virtue of its own. So to clarify the possible confusion, Munitz introduces a new distinction, that between a negative and a positive way of interpreting 'necessary existence.' The term has a "double meaning." To say, for example, that God exists necessarily could mean, negatively, that God's existence is unlimited, not contingent upon, not explainable by, anything else. But taken positively it would mean that God's existence is intelligible, explainable in terms of his own nature or essence, namely, as *causa sui*. (Munitz, 1965, 169)

Drawing on this distinction Munitz says, "If by saying that the world's existence is necessary, one means only that the existence of the world is not causally dependent on some transcendent reality, there need be no objection (in this special, negative sense of 'necessary existence') to saying that the world has necessary existence' (Munitz, 1965, *ibid.*). However, in saying this, have we really said anything positive about the world's being? Those metaphysicians, and theists who draw upon them, who give a positive interpretation of the notion of 'necessary existence' are explicitly or implicitly presupposing, as noted above, the Principle of Sufficient Reason. As a Kantian regulative principle or methodological postulate guiding the quest for meaningful relations among entities within the world, there is no problem. But deployed as a metaphysical axiom about the ultimate intelligibility of the world, "there is nothing but faith to warrant [its] adoption" (Munitz, 1965, 170). Munitz concludes, "the world's existence *may* have a reason, but there is no way in which we can know this, or be assured that it must be so. To assert that the existence of the world, along with everything else, *must* have a reason, is something for which we have no philosophic warrant" (Munitz, *ibid.*).

"How, then," Munitz, asks, "is the statement that the world *necessarily exists*, any different from the statement that the world *exists*? The latter statement we already know to be true. Though true, however, we still ask the question – which the truth of this statement in a way makes irrelevant: '*Why* does the world exist?'" (Munitz, 1965, 173)

As A.N. Prior observes, "'It is necessary that there should be something' does not mean or entail 'There is something that "is" necessarily,' anymore than 'There is bound to be someone who wins' entails 'There is someone who is bound to win.'" (A.N. Prior, 145). In other words, it may be necessary that *something* exist, but not that the *world* exist. As proponents of 'possible worlds' or of a 'multiverse' or 'multiple worlds' are happy to remind us, the existing universe may only be one of many possible alternative worlds. Its existence is not obviously necessary, therefore, but neither for that reason is it necessarily contingent. The question remains, therefore, why does the world exist rather than nothing, nothing at all?

Nothing/Non-Being

"One should both say and think that being is; for to be is possible, and nothingness is not possible." – Parmenides
A philosopher proposed "the 'is' of existence to be understood as elliptical for 'is something that can be experienced.'" Frege replied: "Affirmation of existence is in fact nothing but the denial of the number nought." – Frege, Die Grundlagen der Arithmetik; cited in Barry Miller, 2002.
And, nothing himself, beholds
Nothing that is not there and the nothing that is. – "The Snow Man," Wallace Stevens

Absolute and Relative Nothing/Non-Being

At first glance it would seem that, it is in fact quite easy to specify a clear and legitimate use of the term "nothing." There is an entirely valid and logically respectable use in contexts in which it simply means "nothing" as "the absence of something." For example one might say "there is nothing here" in the context in which one is searching in a drawer or a room for a particular item and not finding it. We can call this contextually specified use of "nothing" its relative meaning. So far no problem.

The problem arises when we ask, what does this mean for the Why question which, on its face, would appear to require an 'absolute' notion of "nothing"? In the absence of such a notion, it would appear that the question is only a pseudo-question. If there is in fact no alternative to there being in fact something, or the world/universe, the alleged question is simply, in good Wittgenstinian fashion, "dissolved" and with it any purported "answers," including traditional theological ones, as well as any lingering "mystery" about the existence of something or the world. Perhaps the world simply exists, and that's the end of the matter. This, as we shall see, would appear to the position of Munitz and Rundle.

However, what if the concept of absolute nothing could be shown to have sense? This would appear to put the Why question back into play.

So, then, what about the notion of "nothing at all"? Is the idea of *absolutely* nothing at all, as opposed to the *relative* "nothing" (the absence of something) even conceivable? There are at least two issues here. Can the phrase "nothing at all" be a referring phrase at all? How can one refer to "nothing" without illicitly substantivizing it? How can we speak of "the nothing that is"? If we cannot, can the term 'nothing' at least be given – what might seem a paradox -- a positive meaning? Is it a counter-concept to being? Is it a unique "anti-concept"? Is it a concept at all? If not, it would seem the entire phrase, "something rather than nothing," and with it the Why question would dissolve into meaningless incoherence; the question would mean "nothing at all"! The concept of 'nothing' presupposed in the Why question would appear to be a concept of absolute 'nothing (at all),' not 'nothing' in its relative sense. In its absolute sense it is taken to mean not only that there is nothing in the desk, but nothing in the universe itself, in fact that there is no universe at all, just absolutely ... nothing. If 'nothing' in this absolute sense is meaningful, then the Why question is meaningful. If it is not meaningful, then the Why question itself must be called into question. A lot seems to hang on 'nothing'!

We will look first at a critique of the absolute sense of 'nothing,' then at its implications for the Why question, and finally at a possible defense of the notion in the context of the Why question.

Critique of the Concept of Absolute Nothing

A classic discussion of this question in the Western philosophical tradition occurs in Plato's *Sophist* where Plato, in consonance with his famous predecessor, Parmenides, critiques the attempt to give meaning to an *absolute* sense of 'nonbeing' or 'nothing' as 'the contrary or opposite of being.' The Greek term in question is *me on*. Regarding the attempt to talk about an 'absolute nothing,' Plato's "Stranger" says to young Theaetetus: "The audacity of the statement lies in its implication that 'what is not' [*to me on*] has being. But the great Parmenides from beginning to end testified against this, constantly telling us 'Never shall this be proved– that things that are not [*me eonta*] are'(Plato, *Sophist*, 237a). Well, this much is clear at any rate, that the term 'what is not' [*to me on*] must not be applied to anything that exists (Plato, *op.cit.*, 237c). So it seems to follow necessarily that to speak of what is not 'something' is to speak of no thing at all (Plato, *op.cit.*, 237d). Must we not even refuse to allow that in such a case a person is *saying* something, though he may be speaking of nothing? Must we not assert that he is not even saying anything [*pantapasi meden*] when he sets about uttering the sounds 'a thing that is not' [*me onti*]? (Plato, *op.cit.*, 237e). How then can anyone utter the words 'things which are not' [*me onta*] or 'that which is not' [*me on*]? You see the inference then. One cannot legitimately utter the words, or speak or think of that which just simply is not [*me on*]; it is unthinkable, not to be spoken of or uttered or expressed (Plato, *op.cit.*, 238c). The nonexistent [*to me on*] reduces even one who is refuting its claims to such straits that, as soon as he sets about doing so, he is forced to contradict himself. (Plato, *op.cit.*, 238d). I have not only just now but at this very moment spoken of it as one thing, for I am saying '*the* nonexistent' [*to me on*]. In applying that term 'being' to it, was I not contradicting what I said before? (Plato, *op.cit.*, 238e) And again in applying the term 'the,' was I not addressing it as a singular? And again in speaking of it as 'a thing not to be expressed or spoken or uttered,' I was using language as if referring to a single thing (Plato, *op.cit.*, 239a)."

Turning next to clarify a legitimate, relative use of 'nothing' in contrast to this notion of an absolute use of 'nothing,' Plato says: it is necessary to establish "that what is not [*to me on*], in some respect has being, and conversely, that what is, in a way is not." (Plato, *op.cit.*, 241d). In other words, "When we speak of 'that which is not' [*to me on*] it seems that we do not mean something contrary to what exists [*enantion ti tou ontos*], but only something that is different (Plato, *op.cit.*, 257b). It does not mean what is contrary to 'existent,' but only what is different from that existent. (Plato, *op.cit.*, 258b) Whereas we have not merely shown that things that are not, are, but we have brought to light the real character of 'not-being' [*me on*] (Plato, *op.cit.*, 258d). Then let no one say that it is the contrary of the existent [*touvantion tou ontos*] that we mean by 'what is not'[*to me on*], when we make bold to say that 'what is not' [*to me on*] exists. So far as any contrary of the existent [*touvantion tou ontos*] is concerned, we have long ago said goodbye to the question whether there is such a thing or no and whether any account can be given of it or none whatsoever (Plato, *op.cit.*, 258e). And if it were about nothing [*medenos de on*], it would not be a statement at all, for we pointed out that there could not be a statement that was a statement about nothing [*medenos de on*]" (Plato, *op.cit.*, 263c)

Plato further distinguishes the notion of *me on* from *ouk on*, another term used to signify a negative in relation to, not contrary to, existence. As Gerald Lalonde explains, "After reading all of the passages [in the *Sophist* cited above] where the negative is always *me*, it seems clear that the metaphysics is related to the grammar, in that the grammatical negative of unreality (*me*) is intrinsic to an ontological statement of not-being. Grammatically *ou(k/ch)* is the negative of the factual, etc., what you call the 'relative' sense of nonbeing, and *me* is the negative of the unreal, such as imperatives, wishes, unreal conditions, etc. I am guessing that the words *ouk on* would be found only in an attributive statement of being – e.g. in the expression *to ouk on kalon*, 'the thing that is not good.' As the Stranger would say, one could not translate that phrase as 'not-being is good,' because it would be nonsense to attribute anything to not-being. So, if a Greek wanted to say 'not-being is good,' he would have to say *to me on kalon*" (Lalonde, 2009).

Implications of the Critique of 'Nothing' for the Why Question

Munitz agrees with Plato in rejecting the idea of an absolute nothing. If, he says, by including the phrase 'nothing at all' in the Why question we mean "to refer to absolute nothing, and not merely to the relative absence, or nonexistence, of some particular object or entity, it is highly doubtful whether this idea can be given a sufficiently clear meaning" (Munitz, 1965, 46). It makes perfect sense if we ask in the relative sense of 'nothing' "Why does this chair exist?," since, says Munitz, "the alternative to 'this chair existing' is not absolute nothing" (Munitz, *ibid.*). However, "if the term 'nothing' is intended to designate some independently conceivable possibility with which the existence of the world can be contrasted, then this manner of speaking must be rejected as being inherently unintelligible." (Munitz, *op. cit.*, 144).

Munitz cites in support of this claim the views of several modern philosophers who, expanding upon Plato's critique of 'what is not' (*me on*), have formulated several other approaches showing that the concept of (absolute) 'nothing' is 'thoroughly muddled or inconsistent." The French philosopher, Henri Bergson, says the idea of absolute nothing is empty because it is self-contradictory. To talk about there *being nothing*, of *nothing existing* is like talking about square circles (Munitz, 1965, 145-7, citing Bergson, 1998, 283). The Austrian philosopher, Rudolf Carnap, in his famous critique of Heidegger's talk about 'the Nothing,' "called attention to the mistake involved in using the term as if it were a name for some special type of entity" (Munitz, 1965, 147; citing Carnap, 71, referring to Heidegger). In the terms of modern logic and theory of language, "any attempt to state, in a coherent language, that there is no world, is self-defeating. [T]he terms 'nothing' or 'the non-existence of the world do not describe any possible situation; they cannot be given any meaning in any logically definable language" (Munitz, *op.cit.*, 148).

But, contends Munitz, this many-sided critique of the concept of absolute nothing does not mean we cannot still ask the question, "Why does the world exist?" Even though the question seems to go beyond a relative sense of 'nothing' (to what other "particular object or entity" would we contrast the world's existing?), nevertheless it "does not, itself, tacitly involve reference to the idea of absolute nothing. What the mystery of the existence of the world is can be articulated without making use of this term." (Munitz, 1965, 47) In other words, it is still possible "to give a proper formulation to the mystery of existence without using the concept 'Nothing,'" one that would "constructively serve the interests of philosophy" (Munitz, *op.cit.*, 151). But this is rather surprising. How can the Why question be posed without reference to 'nothing at all,' without, that is, reference to 'nothing' in an absolute sense? Just saying so does not yet constitute an answer to the question.

Munitz then adds another surprise. "[T]he term 'Nothing' might still continue to be used – no longer, misleadingly, as a name for some special type of entity – but merely as a way of underscoring the mystery of existence" (Munitz, 1965, 151-2). In other words, though 'nothing' lacks cognitive meaning, it may still have expressive meaning. Munitz is not suggesting that somehow having a sense of the mystery of the world's existence will help us toward a positive answer to the 'why' of its existence. But absent an explanation of how the Why question can be answered without invoking the notion of 'nothing,' the mystery must reside for the moment in his position. We shall return to Munitz' views when we discuss the 'why' in the Why question. But in the meantime, perhaps Rundle's analysis of 'nothing' vis-a-vis the Why question can move us a step closer to a resolution of this conundrum.

Recall the discussion of the notion of 'existence,' in particular the claim that existential propositions are limited to entities that exist contingently. The question naturally arises: If there is "an essential contingency about affirmations of existence," is it not possible to speculate that "there might indeed have been nothing whatsoever"? Rundle answers that "our attempts at conceiving of total non-existence are irredeemably partial. We are always left with something, if only a setting from which we envisage everything having departed, a void which we confront and find empty" (Rundle, 110). In fact, attempts to conceive of 'nothing' are not simply partial, they are entirely without sense. Well, one might counter, perhaps we cannot conceive of 'nothing,' but we can at least imagine it. Rundle rejects this possibility as well. What we think of as imagining there was 'nothing' in fact always ends up tacitly assuming the existence of a 'setting.' For example, "we suppose we can imagine the stars ceasing to exist one by one, but we still look to where they were" (Rundle, 111). In other words, we are not left with nothing, "as if this could be the state of affairs." The concept of a totally empty space, "like that of an empty world, is surely itself empty" (Rundle, *ibid.*). In short, "to have literally nothing seems not to make sense" (Rundle, 112).

Let's follow this argument a bit further. There are, says Rundle, two strands to his argument. The first refers to the particular 'setting' of space (though it could also be extended to time, he says) within which contingent things exist. Talk about there possibly having been nothing seem to imply that first there was nothing, and then for some reason a cosmic event occurred, a universe "spontaneously sprang into being." But where was that "there," when was that "then"? The attempt to think away everything, to imagine a space emptied of every thing, "gives no more substance to the possibility of there being nothing than does imagining an empty cupboard" (Rundle, 116). 'There might have been nothing,' says Rundle, is not a truth about anywhere or any-when. It does not describe any possible state of affairs, it does not describe anything at all. (Rundle, 112).

The second strand argues "not that, specifically, a setting is a *sine qua non* of the states of affairs envisaged, but simply that *something* is always presupposed when existence affirmed or denied" (Rundle, 116-117). Here he appeals to the more general binary of 'existence/nothing,' "We cannot," he says, echoing Plato, "conceive of there being nothing, but only of nothing being this or that, and this use of 'nothing' presupposes there being something." An intelligible, that is, relative use of 'nothing' always contrasts with states of affairs within 'being,' within the already existing universe (Rundle, 113). To put it perhaps paradoxically, the contrast of 'existence' and 'nothing,' of 'being' and 'nonbeing' only makes sense and only takes place within 'being' itself. "There is," says Rundle, "just no alternative to being. This is as far as it goes" (Rundle, 113, 114).

Summing up his argument, Rundle concludes that the proposition that 'there might have been nothing' fails on both counts. First, it involves the "highly dubious" positing of a state of affairs where 'Nothing is anywhere' or 'Nowhere is (there) anything.' And second, it is simply incoherent as formulated, viz. Nothing is anything' (Rundle, 117). Talk of 'nothing' "requires that 'nothingness' be interpreted as something like 'the void,' retaining the existential implications which are so difficult to evade" (Rundle, 118). We may wonder, he says, how we could have ever had the idea that there might have been nothing if in fact, as Rundle has argued, it is neither a logical nor a real possibility (Rundle, 191). His answer: It is because of our proneness to argue by analogy from the empty cupboard or the removal of the stars from the universe to the emptiness of the world itself and beyond that to the existence of nothing at all. But is that so strange? As his phrase, 'the existential implications,' perhaps unintentionally suggests, given its double meaning (the existence of physical entities; the experience of human beings), perhaps the idea springs from a source "older than logic" (to cite a phrase from Heidegger), from a "cosmological awareness" that arises at the boundaries of human existence under the conditions of space and time. As Munitz himself observes, in his review of the arguments critiquing the notion of 'nothing':

> Although one may admire the acuity with which these criticisms have been carried out, one cannot help suppressing the belief, nevertheless, that somehow they do not go to the root of the matter.. It is not in the least likely that those who are given to using the concept 'Nothing' will, in any way, be deflected by these attacks, or moved to alter their ways of expressing their philosophic insights or claims. The use of the concept 'Nothing' cannot be easily dislodged by the above means because it is indissolubly linked with the need to voice the mystery of existence. They cannot, and would not, suppress their sense of wonder at the existence of the world, and as one device, among others, they use the expression 'Nothing' to reinforce and convey their sense of astonishment at the fact of the existence of the world" (Munitz, 1965, 150-1).

Is there anything further that can be said about 'nothing' at the existential edge of these reflections? Perhaps. But before we turn to that possibility, what can we say about Rundle's two-pronged case against using 'nothing' in support of the Why question?

First, as to his claim that it is not possible to conceive or imagine that 'there might have been nothing.' Even if it is true that for things existing within the universe imagining their disappearance would leave the spatiotemporal 'setting' in place, it does not follow that this argument holds when we try to apply it to the spatiotemporal whole itself. As Munitz asks, what does 'exist' mean in the case of the universe itself? This question gains added force if we make the further distinction between the observable universe and the universe beyond the observable universe. And if it is unclear what 'exist' might mean in those cases, can we be so clear in ruling out the notion of 'nothing'? In effect, the analogy upon which Rundle's argument relies tacitly presupposes that the universe is an item within the universe. To use an observation of his own against him, this would seem to be "harbouring a presupposition that is damaging to this supposed possibility" (Rundle, 116) -- in this case, the supposed impossibility of imagining 'there might have been nothing.'.

Second, as to his claim that the binary schema of 'being/nonbeing,' 'existence/nothing' does not function in the case of the proposition that 'there might have been nothing.' This argument rests on the claim the 'nothing' only makes sense relative to contexts where it contrasts with 'being' within "how things are" (Rundle, 113). It would seem that, *ceteribus paribus*, all other things being equal, 'being' too only makes sense relative to contexts where it contrasts with 'nothing.' But if this is so, is it not problematic for Rundle to conclude in rejecting the concept of 'nothing' that, in some absolute sense, "there is just no alternative to being" (Rundle, 112), that in the case of the universe, contrary to it use in all other contexts, there is no contrasting sense to 'being'? Here, as in the preceding point, he is presupposing that the sense of 'exist' that applies to entities within the universe can apply straightforwardly to the universe as a whole. But whether this is so or not is precisely the point in dispute. To assume otherwise is simply to beg the question

At this point therefore, it seems the only thing we can safely say about whether it makes sense to refer to 'nothing' in the Why question is that we can't say, one way or the other. Is there any way to extricate ourselves from this agnostic impasse?

Defense of the Concept of 'Nothing' in the Why Question

An at least prima facie case can be made for the meaning and necessity of including an absolute concept of 'nothing' in the Why question. In his review of Rundle's book, the philosopher Thomas Nagel says, "The most difficult philosophical question posed by Rundle's critique is whether efforts to use words to indicate something that transcends the conditions of their ordinary use make sense. The question is especially acute with regard to the why-question itself. Though it is likely to make you giddy, it is hard to cast off the thought that there might have been nothing at all – not even space and time – that nothing might have been the case, ever." Nagel notes, contra Rundle, that this thought "is not the thought of an empty universe." Rather, "it seems an alternative to all the possible positive ways the world could have been – an alternative both to the actual universe and to all the other possible universes that might have existed instead" (Nagel, 2004).

Nagel appears to agree with the philosopher of religion, Ninian Smart, who argued that "It *is* possible that there might have been nothing for such a state of affairs, though unimaginable, is not inconceivable – there are many true statements (in physics for example) which describe situations which cannot be visualized. To show that the proposition 'Nothing might have existed' is inconceivable it would be necessary to show that it is self-contradictory or otherwise logically malformed, and there seems no good reason to assert this" (Smart, 51). As the philosophical theologian Paul Tillich argues in accord with this, "Thought is based on being, and it cannot leave this basis; but thought can imagine the negation of everything that is" (Tillich, 1973, 163-4). We have suggested, with Nagel and Tillich and contra Rundle, that to argue otherwise rests on assumptions that beg the question.

Nagel now introduces an unexpected and intriguing analogy for imagining the possible non-existence of the universe. It is not Smart's appeal to physics, nor is it, significantly, the 'empty cupboard' of Rundle. Rather, he says, "each of us can imagine it on the analogy of our own non-existence. From the objective point of view this is a perfectly imaginable state of affairs, but it is not an alternative possible course of experience for you: subjectively it would be not something different, but nothing." (We recall Plato's distinction between what he regarded a legitimate sense of 'nonbeing,' i.e., "being different," and what he regarded as an illegitimate use of 'nonbeing' as simply 'nothing.') "The possibility that there should never have been anything at all" says Nagel," is the objective analogue to the subjective possibility that you should never have existed."

Nagel's interjection is unexpected because it takes its analogy not from the physical or metaphysical context of cosmology but from the existential dimension of what Heidegger calls our 'being-in-the-world.' It is intriguing because it suggests an entirely different way of understanding and hence dealing with the Why question itself. Munitz too in the previously cited quotation hints at this different direction. Added support for this line of speculation can also be found in the existential-ontological speculations of Tillich. "[T]he question 'Why does anything exist rather than nothing at all?' is not aroused by any particular puzzlement over the explanation of some phenomenon or other, but by the shock of contemplating the possibility that nothing might exist" (Smart, 51). This is what Tillich calls "the shock of non-being." The Why question is not simply a stumbling-block at the limits of our knowledge, it is also and inextricably an existential shock that goes to a core of our own existence.

In other words, this philosophical question and the double-barreled situation, scientific-cosmological and existential-ontological, out of which it arises suggests that even if Rundle is right, that one can give a logical demonstration of the metaphysical necessity of 'something exists' and the corollary logical impossibility of 'there might have been nothing,' we might still be left asking 'why is there something rather than nothing.' And so, finally, we must come to the third element in the question, the 'Why' itself.

Presumably we could be spared resort to an absolute sense of 'nothing (at all)' if it could be shown that the Why question can be asked without invoking it. This is what Munitz claims, at least as applied to his alternate formulation replacing 'something' with 'the world.' He argues that the question, 'Why does the world exist?' does not, in itself, tacitly imply reference to the idea of absolute nothing, "for what the mystery of the existence of the world is can be articulated without making use of this term." (Munitz, 1965, 46-47). What are his "reasons why"?

THREE

Reasons Why

Who can explain it?
Who can tell you why?
Fools give you reasons
Wise men never try.
– "South Pacific," 1958

"What's on the other side of our Unity? or Why Something, Why not nothing?—this is our unshakeable 'ontological wonder-sickness,' our craving to crack being. Absolute existence is absolute mystery, for its relations with the nothing remain unmediated to our understanding."
– William James

Preliminary Remarks

Let us review the questions we have dealt with so far and the remaining question to which we must now turn. We began by noting that the Why question, "Why is there something rather than nothing at all?," though seemingly simple and straightforward, contained, like many questions, several parts, and that each of them, though related, had to be addressed separately before we could decide whether, taken together, they made possible an answer to the initial question.

The first part of the question, "Why is there *something* rather than nothing at all?" addressed *what* was being asked about, namely, the 'something' or, as Munitz proposed, 'the world' or 'universe' as such. The second part of the question, "Why *is there* something rather than nothing at all?" asked what *feature* of this 'something' (or world/universe) was being asked about, namely, its *existence*. We now come to the third part of the question, indeed the core: "*Why* is there something rather than nothing at all?" Here we want to *know* about the existence of this 'something,' whether there is a *reason why* it, rather than nothing, exists, and if so, what that reason is We want to know, for example, whether there is a purpose, or a cause, or an explanation that could help us to understand why the world or the universe exists. We feel there must be a reason *why* there is something rather than nothing at all. Once we have answered this question, we should then be in a position to decide whether the original question, "Why is there something rather than nothing at all?" can or cannot be asked, and in either case, why.

Two Ways of Asking the Why Question

We should note at this point that there are at least two ways the 'Why' aspect of the Why question can be understood. This is owing to the apparently common reference to the existence of the world. There is, on the one hand, what we could call the 'objective' mode of posing the question, a scientific or metaphysical way of asking that looks for, say, the cause for the world's existence – perhaps a First Cause. This is the way of asking the question we have been following so far, the way presupposed in the discussions by Munitz, Post and Rundle. There is another way of asking the question, however, what we might call a 'subjective' or existential query that links the question of the existence of the world to the meaning of our own being-in-the-world, perhaps reflecting what William James called our 'ontological wonder-sickness.' This is a mode of questioning that is followed by existentialist philosophers like Heidegger or existentialist theologians like Tillich. Curiously, however, it also crops up fleetingly in the objectively-oriented treatments of Munitz, Post and Rundle. Depending on the outcome of our current reflections, we may want to return for a closer look at these subjective 'moments' in such scientifically or metaphysically oriented thinkers. For now, however, we shall continue in our objective mode, hoping to find a sufficient answer therein.

Four Meanings of 'Reason.'

Munitz has a very useful discussion of four different meanings of the notion of 'reason' alluded to above when we ask of something 'why' (Munitz, 1965, 178-89). By the 'reason' for something we may be asking for its purpose, its explanation, its cause or the evidence. As a preliminary we need to ask, which of these meanings is involved in the Why question?

The first sense of 'reason' asks, is there a purpose behind the existence of the world/universe? It would seem, however, that the first meaning does not apply, at least when the Why question is asked in the objective (scientific-cosmological) mode. Of course one could be asking the question in a theological mode. For example, was the universe designed by a creative Being? Or does it exist as a testing ground for 'soul-making'? Insofar as this mode involves metaphysical claims, it can be referred to in the following senses of 'reason.' On the other hand, insofar as it has a more metaphorical and spiritual import, it suggests a subjective (existential) mode of responding to the mystery of the world's existence.

The second sense of 'reason' asks, is there an explanation for the existence of the world/universe? It seems more likely that when we ask the Why question we have in mind the search for the explanation of the world's existence understood in a scientific (or metaphysical) mode, although again the reference to a creative Being cannot be ruled out. The difficulty here, of course, as Munitz points out, is that the world is not an individual event of the sort explained by appeal to empirical laws or regularities. The existence of the world, as he repeatedly reminds us, is unique. It cannot be brought within the scope of explanations of events or regularities within the world. Unless we can refute this claim by some metaphysical or theological argument, it could be concluded that in fact there is no explanation for the world's existence, that the world in this sense exists 'without reason,' 'without why.'

The third sense of 'reason' asks, is there a cause for the existence of the world/universe? The notion of cause, Munitz notes, is actually a hybrid. Depending on the context, it could mean the purpose for an action – "purposive action by a conscious agent," for example, a creative Being; or the explanation for an event – "explanation of events by means of empirical laws"; Munitz, 1965, 185). The problematics in using the term 'reason' in either of those senses are thus the ones pointed out above.

The fourth sense of 'reason' asks, is there evidence to support a 'reason why' for the existence of the world/universe? In this sense the term seems at first glance not to apply to the Why question. Evidence is usually sought in support of statements or beliefs. But, Munitz notes, the existence of the world is not a statement (Munitz, 1965, 194-7). Moreover, it would seem strange to ask someone for the evidence of their belief that the world exists as if this were something that could or needed to be proven. If the evidence being called for referred to statements or beliefs about the purpose, explanation, of cause of the universe, that would return us to considerations of 'reasons' in the first three senses of 'reason.'

In light of these four meanings of 'reason' and their application to or implications for the Why question, we shall at this juncture limit ourselves to the explanatory and causal senses of 'reason' in asking 'why' the world exists, reserving the right to return, should it prove necessary or desirable, to a consideration of the purposive sense. As we proceed it is important to remember the ambiguity of the term 'world' or 'universe' – is it meant to refer to the observable universe or to the universe 'beyond' it? We will have to consider what implications, if any, there are in asking whether there is a casual or explanatory 'reason' for the world's existence.

It is interesting to note the precedents, parallels and differences of Munitz's four uses of 'reason' with analogous discussions in the Western philosophical tradition. The most obvious comparison is, of course, with Aristotle's classical discussion of the four kinds of 'causes': final (purposive), formal (explanatory), efficient (causal) and material (evidential). The closest modern comparison, though at first it might not seem so, are Kant's four "Antinomies" (intellectual paradoxes or contradictions) that problematize what he calls "the System of Cosmological Ideas." These antinomies present conflicting metaphysical theses about the 'phenomenal' (observable) world and the 'noumenal' world (universe 'beyond'). (Kant, 390ff, 396ff, 402ff, 409ff, 415ff.)

Regarding *purposive* 'reason,' Kant's third antinomy deals with the conflict between the causality of nature obtaining within the phenomenal realm, and the 'causality of freedom,' purposive or teleological in nature and ascribed to the noumenal realm. A scientific-cosmological account of the observable universe does not appeal to the concept of purpose. That notion is reserved for the realm of what Kant calls 'practical' reason, reason dealing the motives for human actions. Whether it can be extended to the universe 'beyond' the observable universe is the question.

Regarding *explanatory* 'reason,' Kant's first antinomy presents the conflict between two theses regarding the existence of the world as the spatiotemporal whole – that the world has a beginning in time and is also limited in space and the claim that the world has no beginning and no limits in space but is infinite in both dimensions. Here a scientific-cosmological account of the observable universe would seem to run up against the limits of explanation, unable to decide, on purely empirical grounds, between one thesis or the other.

For *causal* 'reason,' both the third antinomy above, but also the fourth antinomy seem relevant. The latter deals with the conflict between contingent and necessary causality in explaining the existence of the world – between the claim that there is, either as part or as the cause of the world, a being that is absolutely necessary, and the claim that no absolutely necessary being exists either within the world or outside it as its cause. Here again a scientific-cosmological account of the observable world seems to reach a dead-end, unable to prove one thesis or the other.

Finally, as regards evidential (Aristotle's material cause) 'reason,' Kant's second antinomy deals with the conflict between the claim that there is an absolute completeness in the division of the whole of the material existence of the world into its simple parts and the claim that there are no final simple parts of composite things in the world. Here too the attempt of a scientific-cosmological approach is unable to find conclusive evidence in support of either of these material alternatives concerning the basic structure of the observable universe.

Reasons Why the Why Question Cannot be Answered or Asked

Munitz speaks of the 'mystery' of the world's existence. Munitz appears to take this to mean that in the final analysis there is no 'reason why' (in the explanatory sense) for the world's existence. In that case one might conclude not only that the Why question cannot be answered, it cannot even be properly asked. At most, perhaps it can be taken only as an expression of "a mystery in some *other* sense of the term, perhaps a feeling that *something* is strange, uncanny, eerie, weird, full of wonder" (Post, 78; Post cites Heidegger as holding this view; cf. Munitz, 1965, 13, 43). For a metaphysically inclined philosopher like Post, however, such 'mystery-mongering' will not do. As he observes, the Why question "expresses a mystery only if it seeks an explanation" (Post, *ibid.*).

Let us briefly sketch these opposing positions before entering into a more extensive discussion of the case for and against theological, scientific and metaphysical attempts to explain the 'reason why' the world exists.

First, Munitz. Munitz notes two possible reasons why the Why question cannot be answered, thus preserving what he calls the 'mystery' of the world's existence.

The question can be meaningfully asked and it may be that there is answer, it is just that can never know what it is. If so, minimally we would have to adopt a position of agnosticism if not scepticism as regards the matter. (Munitz, 1965, 104)

However, it may not be simply an inability to say what the reason is, it may be that we cannot even say whether there is a reason at all. This would indicate an even deeper intellectual paralysis. (Munitz, *ibid.*)

To this we might add several further reasons which could still preserve the 'mystery.'

It may be that there is a reason and that we can say and know what it is, but because it lies at the boundaries of our ordinary kind of knowledge, we cannot say anything further about it; or, in a weaker version, there is a reason and we can say what it is, but we cannot fully know it (e.g., it is a creative Being beyond our ken). In either case we are at the edge of the unknown and, in that sense, the mysterious.

It may be that there is no reason, no explanation. The world simply exists and that's all there is to it. It exists 'without Why.'

It may be that the question itself needs to be rejected as unaskable, whether for empirical or metaphysical or logical reasons. As an inference from the preceding, if no explanation is possible, what is the question? Wittgenstein famously observed: "For an answer which cannot be expressed the question too cannot be expressed" (Wittgenstein, *Tract.* 6.5: *Zu einer Antwort, die man nicht aussprechen kann, kann man auch die Frage nicht aussprechen*).

A Metaphysical Response

None of these positions would entirely satisfy the metaphysical urge of traditional philosophy. For Western philosophy down through the millenia the wonder reflected in the Why question is seen as simply the starting point of a quest for knowledge that must, if successful, end in a discovery of truth that transforms the initial sense of wonder into a settled sense of certitude. Aristotle says, "For it is owing to their wonder that men both now begin and at first began to philosophize" (Aristotle, *Metap.* 982b). But he quickly goes on to say, "Yet the acquisition of [knowledge] must in a sense end in something which is the opposite of our original inquiries. We must end in the contrary and the better state, as is the case in these instances too when men learn the cause." (Aristotle, *Metap.* 983a). Post, a true heir of Aristotle in this regard similarly observes, "philosophy beings in wonder," but then immediately adds, "and we hope that it ends not only in truth but in relevant truth – truth that answers some question, or helps to answer it, perhaps by showing that it is not a genuine or well-formed question in the first place" (Post, 71)

It seems there is a repressed fear motivating this sense of the relationship of philosophy to its origin in wonder – a concern that by surrendering to it the sense of critical inquiry that lies at the origin of philosophy may be polluted by relapse into ignorance or worse, by a falling back into fascination with the "wonders of myth" from which philosophy since its inception has struggled to free itself (Aristotle, *Metap.* 982b). As Post says, if we are told the Why question expresses "mysteries unfathomable" by us, "we may thereby feel relieved of any responsibility to inquire." Or if told that "while such questions are answerable, the answers are not to be found by science or reason," that they are "matters of faith, perhaps of mystical insight, completely beyond the reach of reason," again we may feel relieved of the responsibility to inquire any further. (Post, 74)

It is in line with this concern and the long philosophical tradition of the West that Post proposes a definition of 'mystery' that enables him to bypass this worry: "let us characterize a mystery as what is expressed by a question to which we do not know the answer, though *there is* a true answer to be known" (Post, 75). The Why question, then, should be understood as an "explanation-seeking why-question" (cf. Munitz's second kind of 'reason') that asks, "What is the explanation of the existence of the universe?" The question "presupposes that there is some explanation" – in particular, an explanation grounded in what philosophers call the Principle of Sufficient Reason [PSR], that for every existing event there is a (causal) explanation. For as Wittgenstein also observed: "If a question can be put at all, then it *can* also be answered" (Wittgenstein, *Tract.*, 6.5). It follows, says Post, that "The mystery, if there is one, is *what* the explanation is" (Post, 79).

On the other hand, if it should prove there is no explanation, then it must be that "the question is based on a false presupposition" (Post, *ibid.*), an assumption that PSR applies when in fact it does not. In that case the Why question "would be perfectly meaningful or well-formed, but out of order. It would be unfathomable only in the sense that there is nothing to fathom" (Post, *ibid*). There is of course the still further possibility that, as Post suggests above, it was not "a genuine or well-formed question in the first place."

Now having said all this, Post thinks in fact that the Why question *is* a meaningful one and that there *is* an answer to it, one that can be known and one that accordingly dissolves the alleged mystery alleged to surround the world's existence. We will return to his answer in the section on "Metaphysics" below.

Before we do, however, we should note two things about Post's definition of 'mystery.' First, his use of the indefinite phrase '*a* mystery' extends the notion of mystery beyond the context of its use in the Why question, whereas the use of 'mystery' presupposed in the Why question is, as Munitz argues, understood as referring to a unique case, not *a* mystery but *the* mystery, the *meta*-mystery of the world's existence *as such*. Second, by limiting his definition of mystery to questions for which there is a true answer to be known, he has in effect begged the question whether there is or could be at least one question, namely the Why question, for which either there is no answer or at least one that can never be known. But that is precisely the question in dispute.

The Core Issue

Post's disagreement with Munitz shows the core issue to be whether scientific or metaphysical truth permits philosophy to satisfy its originating sense of wonder by ending, as Aristotle says, in "something which is the opposite," or whether the sense of an ultimate and irreducible mystery, though it frustrates philosophy's desire for conclusive explanations is, paradoxically, necessary for protecting and preserving the very existence and truth of philosophy itself.

Can the Why Question be Answered Scientifically?

With this issue in mind, let us look first at whether the Why question can be answered scientifically. As Wittgenstein remarked, "For an answer that cannot be expressed the question too cannot be expressed. If a question can be put at all, then it *can* also be answered – a question only where there is an answer" (Wittgenstein, *Tract.*, 6.5, 6.51) The argument in this section will be that in fact science cannot answer the Why question and that the Why question therefore is not a scientific one. We shall first look briefly at what is required for questions about the world and answers to such questions to be scientific ones. We shall look next at why the Why question cannot be answered scientifically. We will conclude by arguing that the Why question is not a scientific question at all. If the Why question can neither be asked nor answered scientifically, we shall have to look in other directions, perhaps theological and/or metaphysical, to determine what sort of question it is, what sorts of answers to it are or are not possible, or whether, despite its grammatical appearance, it is even a question at all.

What makes a question and answer about the world scientific?

According to British cosmological scientist Stephen Hawking, "The usual approach of science of constructing a mathematical model cannot answer the questions of why there should be a universe for the model to describe. Why does the universe go to all the bother of existing? Up to now, most scientists have been too occupied with the development of new theories that describe *what* the universe is to ask the question *why*." As Hawking's observation suggests, for questions and answers about the world to be scientific, they must focus on models, theories and observations made about the already existing universe, scientific accounts that describe and make understandable what the observable world is like in its theoretical structures and empirical particulars. What they apparently do not do is answer the question why the universe is there in the first place presenting itself as the object of our scientific investigations. As Munitz observes, perhaps cosmological science can make the visible universe comprehensible in its details, but does it thereby answer the question of its existence, that is, how it is that it came into being in the first place? (Munitz, 1965, 263).

Why the Why question cannot be answered scientifically

It could be objected, *pace* Hawking and Munitz, that science does answer the Why question. What about the various scientific accounts of the origin of the universe, its beginning, for example, in the Big Bang? Doesn't that provide a scientific answer to the question why the world exists rather than nothing? There are several problems with such a claim. First, it assumes the reference of the Why question is to a universe, whereas as we have seen in its original formulation it referred only to the indeterminate 'something', not necessarily to a determinate 'world'. But even assuming the reference is to a universe, the claim refers only to the actually existing universe, whereas as we have seen before that the existing universe could be only the visible manifestation of another universe beyond, a universe beyond the reach of science; or it could be only one of a multiplicity of other worlds, also unknown to science. However, let us assume, for purposes of the examining the claim, that only the actual existing universe exists. Even in that case the claim assumes it is possible for science to explain how it came into being. But can it? As we shall see, two of our philosophers, Munitz and Rundle, argue that in fact science cannot establish that the universe had an origin in time. We must now see why.

Munitz argues that "it is a complete mistake to suppose that scientific cosmology, *qua* science, could, in principle, establish that the universe did have a beginning" (Munitz, 1965, 128). Of course, on the face of it, as we have just noted, this seems an absurd claim, for that appears exactly what the Big Bang theory of the origin of the universe does. So let us follow Munitz' argument. First, he says, cosmology provides us with three models of the existing universe: an origin from a unique physical singularity in the past with "an ever-increasing expansion"; an oscillating universe with "an endless series of cycles of expansion and contraction";

a steady-state model with an infinite time-scale (Munitz, 1965, 130-1). The current reigning model is that of the origin from a unique singularity popularly referred to as a Big Bang beginning at 'time-zero' (and presumably in 'space-empty'). It is this notion, Munitz contends, which, though imaginatively intuitive, is philosophically indefensible. There are two ways of defending this claim, he says. The first shows why the very concept of "the origin of the universe" is not a meaningful one. The second is to appeal to the "regulative criteria of the method of science" to show that the concept fails to satisfy those criteria, that, in short, it is not a scientific idea. Granting that opinion is divided on the first point, Munitz adopts the second line of attack, arguing that "any cosmological model seriously maintaining there was an absolute origin of the universe fails to satisfy the criteria of scientific method and so must be rejected as even a scientific hypothesis" (Munitz, 1965, 133-4).

As regards the first point, some have tried to argue that the concept of the origin of the universe is meaningful as indicating the "first instant in time." But, says Munitz, the idea of a first instant in time arising in a supposedly 'pre-' existing state where time is not yet predicable is in fact a self-contradictory one. Another attempt to defend the concept argues that 'beginning' as used in ordinary discourse need not presuppose a pre-existing state of affairs, e.g. "the beginning of the process of tooth decay." To the contrary, replies Munitz, the beginning of a process presupposes an *earlier* state of affairs over against which the 'beginning,' i.e. *later* stage, can be discriminated. (Munitz, 1965, 134-5)

Turning to the second point, the claim that the idea of 'the origin of the universe' is incompatible with the use of the scientific method, Munitz begins by recalling Kant's classic discussion of the 'antinomies,' in particular the first antinomy which presents the conflict between two theses regarding the existence of the world as the spatiotemporal whole – that the world has a beginning in time and is also limited in space, versus the claim that the world has no beginning and no limits in space, but is infinite in both dimensions. (Kant, 390, 396-402). A scientific-cosmological account of the observable universe here runs up against the limits of explanation. It is not possible to decide, on purely empirical grounds, between one thesis or the other. Since it is possible to give strong arguments in favor of each of these opposite views, according to Kant, Munitz says, "a rational solution to this question is doomed to failure" (Munitz, 1965, 136).

Here we again encounter the Principle of Sufficient Reason (PSR). For Kant the PSR is usefully and legitimately employed "as a *methodological postulate of science*." However, it oversteps the limits of reason if employed to draw metaphysical conclusions, for example, of the sort found in theistic arguments. (We shall return to this consideration in the next two sections.) The strength of Kant's point, says Munitz, is that the attempt to establish that the universe did or, alternatively, did not have an origin in time "runs counter to the very conception of science" (Munitz, 1965, 139). Empirical science, including the science of cosmology, rightfully employs PSR in its search for the causes or explanations of *any* event occurring *within* the visible universe. But "[t]o say that there is some unique event, marking the beginning of the universe [as a spatio-temporal whole] for which no explanation *can* be given, is to say something contrary to the method of science" (Munitz, *ibid.*) In other words, to say that there is some unique event called 'the origin of the universe,' an event that not only *has* no existing antecedents, that indeed there cannot *be* any such antecedents, is not only "to block the way" of scientific inquiry, it is "to deny the possibility" of an explanation at all (Munitz, 1965, 140).

On both counts, therefore, because the concept of 'the origin of the universe' is an empirically impossible notion and because it is a logically self-contradictory one to boot, to ask why the universe exists rather than nothing at all is to ask a question that cannot be answered scientifically.

Rundle takes up the argument against the possibility a scientific explanation of 'the origin of the universe' and develops it in a more metaphysical direction. Like Munitz, he locates the basic issue in the claim not only by some metaphysicians and theologians but even by scientific cosmologists who think it possible that from nothing something could come. Some cosmologists claim to have theories that explain how the universe emerged from nothing. In a book on the implications for cosmology and metaphysics of 20th C. particle physics, Columbia University science historian Robert Crease refers to some who speculate that "On the far side of the Big Bang is a mystery so profound that physicists lack the words even to think about it....Just as there is a tiny chance that virtual particles will pop into existence in the midst of sub-atomic space, so there may has been a tiny chance that nothingness would suddenly be convulsed by the presence of a something" (Crease & Mann, 405; cited in Rundle, 118).

Such a claim, of course, runs exactly counter to Parmenides' assertion, spelled out further by Plato in the *Sophist*, that *ex nihilo nihil fit*, "nothing comes from nothing," or as ancient Greek cosmology already have argued, that it makes no sense to talk about a time interval in which a world did not exist, since nothing could be created *ex nihilo* in the first place. Rundle agrees. If we inspect the theories of such cosmologists it turns out that "Talk of nothingness...requires that 'nothingness' be interpreted as something like 'the void,'" that is, as an existing 'something.' In other words, despite the negative connotations of 'nothing' or 'nothingness' in those scientific cosmologies, such talk turns out to have "existential implications ... difficult to evade." Therefore, he concludes, "We are spared from having to fathom a mystery on the far side of the Big Bang, since there is no far side." (Rundle, *ibid.*)

But let us explore the science and metaphysics of this a bit further, he says. The current theory of the 'origin" of the universe locates its 'beginning' with the Big Bang. But, says Rundle, with nothing 'outside' the universe, the only way to make sense of an event like the Big Bang is to understand it in an *internal*, not *external* way; that is, it is to understand the 'origin' or 'beginning' following the Big Bang "as an expansion *of* space rather than an expansion *into* space"; similarly as an extension *of* time, not an extension *in* time. These are features *intrinsic* to the universe, determinable, says Rundle, without going 'outside' of it. (Rundle, 120) It was a theologian, Augustine, who, Rundle reminds us, famously said in *The City of God*, "the world was not created *in* time but *with* time" (Augustine, 1972, cited in Rundle, 120).

This means we cannot draw a dividing line between a state of no universe and that of a universe; we cannot speak intelligibly about an origin of the universe from absolutely nothing. "If the notion of an event, a coming to be, is inapplicable here, to ask why the universe began to exist will be to compound the error" (Rundle, 121). By the same reasoning, he says, we cannot talk of a time when the universe will cease to exist: "there is no such time with respect to the universe" (Rundle, *ibid.*). It follows, he concludes, that there was and will *always* be a universe

On the basis of this argument, Rundle then advances the metaphysical claim that the universe *has* to exist, *must* exist, exists *necessarily*. That we cannot speak of the universe as either having come into existence or someday ceasing to exist "is not just a matter of empirical fact." The notion of beginnings and endings which we ascribe to things and events *within* the world "resist extrapolation to the universe itself." Here, of course, Rundle is in agreement with Kant, who had already argued that the concepts of beginning and endings that apply to our knowledge of empirical phenomena have no metaphysical purchase when applied to the world as a whole. But unlike Kant, Rundle goes on to grasp the other horn of Kant's first antinomy by asserting that we *can* speak of the world as extending indefinitely in time and space. This is a further step that Kant would not take. We will have to return to this disagreement in the section on the metaphysics of the Why question for it leads into the core of attempts to answer it. For the moment let us content ourselves with raising the question whether negative predicates ('no beginning in space and time') applied to the world as a whole license positive ascriptions ('extends indefinitely in space and time') to the world.

In the meantime, let us conclude that Munitz and Rundle pretty conclusively have "ruled out the possibility of any explanation in answer to the question, 'Why does the universe exist?' when, namely, this has force of 'What brought the universe into being?'" (Rundle, 124) This conclusion understandably frustrates our desire, if not our conviction, that the universe in which we live must be accessible to human intelligence. As Rundle notes, "The universe may initially be supposed in the category of those things for which we can expect an explanation to be forthcoming, so something for which its absence is troubling." However, as both he and Munitz have argued, "the universe is not to be aligned with the things within it, things which, like planets and stars, pose answerable why-questions." (Rundle, *ibid.*) Even scientists, when they reach the outer limits of their own observations and theories and cosmological models, are tempted to look beyond science for "ultimate explanations." But, says Rundle, as we have seen, "what they hanker after is a quasi-scientific explanation" drawing on concepts applicable to things and events within the universe as if, contra Kant's strictures, they could be extended to the universe as a whole.

There is a further implication to the preceding critique. If indeed the universe poses "unanswerable questions" to the scientific cosmologist, this means (remembering Wittgenstein's observation "a question only where there is an answer") that *the Why question is not a scientific question at all.* As Munitz maintains, to ask 'Why is there a world at all?' is not to ask a scientific question (Munitz, 1965, 4). If by a cognitively meaningful question we mean a question for which a scientific answer is possible, then by definition, says Munitz, "this would rule out the metaphysical question, 'Why does the world exist?' as not having cognitive meaning" (Munitz, 1965, 43).

How else to explain the otherwise unsettling (for science) fact that while science makes ongoing progress in its understanding of things and events within the world, including its spatio-temporal expansion from the Big Bang, when it comes to attempts to answer the Why-question, "[we] are confined to reiterating the question, and cannot either claim any progress in its past study, or ... believe that the prospects for answering it are likely to be better in the future, than they were when men first asked this question?" (Munitz, 1965, 4) The conclusion must be: a question that cannot be answered scientifically is a question that cannot be asked scientifically.

It seems we face a dilemma. "When existence is at issue, is there any alternative to a [*scientific*] interpretation of a why-question? ... It does not seem that an answer to our why-question is to be sought in this direction... How, then, can it be answered?" (Munitz, 1965, 124). How then indeed! In fact, as we have just argued, how can it even be asked? As might be expected, not all philosophers, and perhaps philosophers especially, are ready to thrown in the towel when science has reached its limits in understanding things cosmological. Nor, above all, are theologians. Could it be that philosophically-inclined theologians, especially the metaphysically-minded among them, can provide an answer to the Why question where scientific cosmology fears to tread? Let us explore that possibility next.

Can the Why Question be Answered Theologically?

If, as argued in the preceding section, the concept of 'the origin of the universe' is both an empirically impossible and a logically self-contradictory notion, then to ask why the universe exists rather than nothing at all is to ask a question that cannot be answered scientifically. But perhaps the question can be answered via a different approach. Traditionally the leading candidates for answering questions that transcend the limits of science have been theology and metaphysics. Let us consider theology first, in particular, the type most common in

Western discussions of cosmology and the one most relevant to this formulation of the Why question, namely, theism.

According to traditional theism, in particular the so-called "cosmological" arguments or "proofs" for the existence of God, the answer to the question why the universe exists rather than nothing at all is found in the concept of God as the "creator" or "first cause" who brought the world into existence *ex nihilo*, "out of nothing." The metaphysical version of this theistic claim makes several assumptions: the universe, like the entities within it, exists contingently; contrary to the arguments in the preceding section, it *does* make sense, if not empirically at least logically and metaphysically ("meta-empirically"), to speak of the 'origin' of the universe, of its 'coming into being'; the Principle of Sufficient Reason, which is used to explain the (contingent) existence of entities within the universe, can be extended to explain the (contingent) existence of the universe as well – the universe was 'caused' by God; the existence of the universe satisfies the demand of intelligibility; there is no mystery why the universe exists; and finally, ultimate mystery, if such there be, lies hidden in the being of God.

What can be said against these claims? For Munitz, who wishes to defend the notion of the mystery of the world's existence, the theistic answer must be rejected, precisely because, by offering an explanation, a 'reason why,' it eliminates the sense of mystery. The mark of a genuine sense of mystery, he says, is precisely that no explanation is forthcoming (M, 104; we remember Post's opposing definition of a 'genuine' mystery, following Aristotle, as precisely one which does result in an explanation, in scientific truth). Of course, Munitz is aware that the wish to defend the mystery of the world's existence does not, in and of itself, suffice to rule out a theistic explanation. Turning to a critique of the theistic answer he says that in fact it suffers from logical obstacles that are difficult to surmount.

First, it commits what is called the fallacy of composition – the assumption that attributes of the parts of a whole can automatically be extended to the whole itself. The assumption of the so-called "cosmological" argument is that because the world's 'parts,' the entities that exist within the world, exist contingently – that there is no logical impossibility in conceiving of their non-existence, no logical impossibility in conceiving of them as having come into being at some time in the past or passing out of being at some time in the future – therefore the world,

THOMAS DEAN

the spatiotemporal whole composed of those contingent parts must share the same feature of existential contingency. "[T]he crucial step is that in which the argument proceeds to make a judgment of the same type about the world, as it makes about any individual object or event within it, namely, that the world, too, is contingent. It is this step that is open to serious doubt." (Munitz, 1965, 108, 117)

Further, even if it were granted that the world exists contingently, that it can be conceived without logical contradiction as having come into being, that still does not license the inference that there must be a Necessary Being to explain that primordial cosmic event. To assume it does is to commit yet another logical error, the fallacy of begging the question: "To say the world is contingent, in the sense intended [i.e., for the theistic argument] is already to presuppose that it is created out of nothing, and thus begs the question." (Munitz, 1965, 108, 120) The central question is whether in fact it makes sense to speak of the world as contingent, to say that it might not have existence, and that therefore it owes its existence to some other being. For it we wish to say so, we need to offer reasons for thinking so. The problem is simply to characterize the world's existence as contingent does not by itself offer a ground or reason for believing in the existence of a creator or first cause. To think that it does is tacitly to employ the concept of God, that is, it is to presuppose in the definition the very thing the theist is trying to prove, namely, that the world was "created" or "caused." In other words, as we have already seen in the previous section, there seems to be no question-begging way to make sense of the notion of the contingency of the world if this requires that we speak of its 'origin' or 'coming into being.'

Then is there some other, non-question-begging way to conceive of the world as existing contingently that does not require positing the existence of a necessary being to account for its existence? And if not, must we conclude that perhaps the world itself exists necessarily, that it, paradoxically, is the Necessary Being theology seeks? Or is the concept of necessary existence, like that of contingent existence, likewise logically inapplicable to the world's being? If so, would we then have to agree with Munitz that perhaps the existence of the world is a permanent mystery?

We will address these questions in a moment. But first perhaps we should ask, with Munitz, about another of the assumptions that lies behind the theist's cosmological argument. "[W]hy need we presuppose that the existence of the world *must* be intelligible? What grounds have we for asserting *that* there is a reason for its existence?" That there may be no reason, that perhaps one *cannot* be given, "this is precisely where the mystery of existence its to be located." (Munitz, 1965, 125)

Admittedly, as rational beings, we should like to have reasons for everything; but there is no metaphysical reasoning that has yet been given, of a sufficiently compelling character, to show that the world must fulfill or satisfy such demands of *our* reason. To appeal to the metaphysical Principle of Sufficient Reason for this support, is already to commit oneself to the belief that the world's existence *can be explained.* The appeal to the metaphysical Principle of Sufficient Reason, as a backing for the belief in a Necessary Being, is thus only a disguised way of affirming the belief itself. (Munitz, *ibid.*)

Munitz' observation is a tantalizing one, but to the philosophically-minded it has to be disturbing. Is it correct? Might there be another metaphysical route into the Why-question, one that can answer it via the notion of Necessary Being without presupposing the PSR? For that we must turn to arguments put forward by Rundle and Post.

Rundle certainly agrees with Munitz that "the pressure to find an explanation should not lead us to accept uncritically just any hypothesis [in this instance, the theistic one] having a superficial claim to provide an answer. The status of explanation is one that has to be earned." (Rundle, 30) He also agrees with Munitz that the cosmological argument based on the claim of the causal dependence of the universe on God, that is, employing the PSR, has been centrally important to making the case for theism. (Rundle, 75-76).

Here he introduces a new line of attack focused on another of the assumptions of the theistic cosmological argument, namely, the attempt to extend what is involved in creating something to defend the notion of 'creation' out of 'nothing.' The notion of 'creation' with which we are familiar as the 'bringing into existence' of entities simply means and always involves "no more than the inducing of a change in some persisting substratum; old matter is simply endowed with a new form" (Rundle, 93). For the concept to make sense do we also need an additional explanation of the existence of the underlying substratum? No, at that point, the need for further explanation simply comes to an end. If we ask about the 'substratum' of the existing ordered cosmos, all we can say it, whatever it might be, is that it is already there, it already exists. To extend that concept to the 'creation' of the universe, therefore, he says, makes no

THOMAS DEAN

sense. Or rather, it cannot be used to support the classical case for theism. Theism requires that there be no pre-existing substratum from which God might have shaped the existing universe. To posit such an already existing reality alongside and independently of the divine being would be to compromise God's ontological status as the source and cause of all being other than Himself.

At this point Rundle makes a startling new claim. The God-hypothesis is metaphysically unnecessary, because the substratum of the ordered cosmos not only already exists, it *has* to exist, it exists *necessarily*. The universe itself is the Necessary Being for which the theologian rightly but wrong-headedly seeks. The universe itself is, as it were, the answer to the question of its own existence! To say that the universe, the spatiotemporal entity consisting of all that exists contingently, cannot itself exist necessarily, is once again simply to beg the question. It is not the notion of something existing necessarily that is the problem, the concept is not, says Rundle, obviously incoherent. It is that the theistic argument for that necessary existent being God was fallacious. (Rundle, 96)

Rundle's claim that it is the universe, not God, that is the Necessary Being theologians and metaphysicians have sought for would seem to entail that others of the ontological predicates traditionally ascribed to God may in fact be transferable and applicable to the universe instead. This, at least, is what Post claims. But first to set the scene: Post argues, as does Rundle, that if the physical universe is the whole of "what there is," if there is nothing else "outside" of it, then nothing could have "created" it, it could not have "come into being" from anything. From this it follows that the universe is "uncreated." "Indeed it is not the sort of thing that could have such a creator...since by hypothesis every existent is part of it." (Post, 130).

But from the fact the universe is not created, it does not follow that there is no explanation for its existence. The list of metaphysical possibilities – and predicates -- has not been exhausted. For example, perhaps the universe exists by reason of its very nature, that is, as the medievals said of God, perhaps its *essentia* is *existentia*, its "essence" is "existence." Perhaps, as Hawking put it, its nature is simply "to be." Or, if this seems too facile, if some sort of metaphysical cause is called for, perhaps, as theologians also say of God, the universe is *sui causa*, "self-caused."

Post will have none of this. First, he says, to explain the existence of something by appealing to its "essence," its conceptual "nature," is simply to "mask the absence, strictly, of any explanation properly so-called" (Post, 81). The notion that the universe exists necessarily by virtue of its nature misconstrues the notion of necessity: "the notion or notions of necessity presupposed apply not to extralinguistic things but to our statements about them" (Post, *ibid.*; also, 96-98). As for the notion of any kind of self-necessitation, that the universe as it were brought itself into existence, as Rundle put it, a kind of "bootstrap operation" (Rundle, 98), Post says "[t]he notion of something's being its own cause, literally, is as troubled as the notion of something's existing by the necessity of its own nature." (Post, 131)

If we cannot explain the existence of the universe by means of such ontological "transcendentals" as *causa sui, essentia and existentia*, if we must content ourselves, as Post suggests, with saying the universe is "uncreated," that is, that it has no explanation either scientific or metaphysical, that it exists, as it were, "without why," then, if we are to avoid falling back into what Post calls "mystery mongering," what *can* we say about its existence?

The first thing we must be clear about, Post says, is that the universe as that which exists ultimately, whatever metaphysical features, positive or negative, it might have of the sort traditionally ascribed to God, it "seems most unlikely to have the personal attributes of divinity" (Post, 117). Even if true, this might not give a theist pause, for there is an ancient and honorable tradition in Western theology that readily admits that the "God of the philosophers," the God to which a number of positive metaphysical predicates might be ascribed, is not the "God of faith," the personal God of scripture-based religions. But Post's position rules out that defensive maneuver, for the God of theistic faith is still conceived of as a being, even if the highest or supreme being. But in Post's science-based "physicalist" metaphysics, as in Rundle's similarly based "materialist" metaphysics, says Post, "God seems nowhere to be found in the inventory of what there is" (Post, 328). Nor, for scientific or metaphysical and logical reasons, as we have seen, can there be.

This brings Post, then, to a discussion of what can and cannot be predicated of a universe viewed as "uncreated." Surprisingly, having rejected the ontological notions of necessary existence, self-existence and the cosmological notion of "first cause" when applied to a being existing "outside" the universe, he now turns around and ascribes them to the universe itself as "the uncreated, explanatorily independent, metaphysically necessary, self-existent First Cause of all that is" (Post, 328). How, in view of what he labels his own "austere physicalism," can he now declare such extravagant features to have been rehabilitated and made once again metaphysically respectable?

It follows, he says, if we reflect upon what we mean when we say the universe is "uncreated." It means the universe, spacetime as a whole, is "eternal." In its everyday sense, he says, "'eternal' signifies everlastingless." But this is not how it is meant in the context of metaphysics or classical theism, where it refers to that which is "not conditioned by time." (Post, 138). Instead, the uncreated universe in this metaphysical (and theological) sense is "eternal" in a five-fold sense (Post, 138; 139-153; 328):

"it is not subject to becoming, to change, to process, or to corruption and decay"

"it is not in time thus not to be dated as past, present, or future"

"it is a 'tenseless' existent"

"its parts not distinguished by being transiently past, present, future, or still to come, relative to one another"

"it is of such 'duration' that neither ceases to be nor comes into existence"

But still we want to ask: what sorts of properties are these? Are they telling us anything positive about the nature of the universe? Or does the apparently unavoidable – why? – use of negatives in each of these predicates suggest that what Post offers us are at best the cosmological equivalent of "negative theology," a secular version of the uninformative Upanishadic *neti-neti*, "not this, not this"? *Not* subject to becoming, *not* in time, *not* having tenses, *not* distinguishable parts, *not* ceasing to be, *not* coming into existence. Fine, but does this tell us anything about *what* the universe *is*? As Post himself says of these negative predicates "we must refrain from any positive physical predications" about the true universe, "the Universe beyond the universe" (Post, 361).

Post had already said of the physical (manifest) universe that "we are reduced to a via negativa: we are not entitled to ascribe any positive predicates... Nothing positive is known about it, even if nothing negative is known about it either. To this extent it is wrapped in mystery." But we now see that of the Universe beyond the universe we are also forced to rest content with, at best, another via negativa, even though it seems that in this case something "negative is known about it," and to that extent the mystery is partially unwrapped. But is that really the case? One suspects that here too, as Post says of more positive-sounding notions like "essence is existence" or "necessary existence," that these predicates of the Universe beyond the universe – not subject to becoming, to change, to process, or to corruption and decay, not in time thus not to be dated as past, present, or future, a 'tenseless' existent, parts not distinguished by being transiently past, present, future, or still to come, relative to one another, of such 'duration' that neither ceases to be nor comes into existence, uncreated, explanatorily independent, metaphysically necessary, self-existent First Cause of all that is – "mask the absence, strictly, of any explanation properly so-called" (Post, 81).

If so, we must agree with Munitz, contra Rundle and Post, the existence of the universe remains "wrapped in mystery." As a firm believer in the metaphysical enterprise, Post believes in the "Aristotelian moral" that the transition from (the scientific truths of) physics (of the manifest universe) to (the positive assertions in "negative" formulation of) metaphysics (of the Universe beyond) is "but a step" (Post, 131). If Munitz is correct, however, this attempt to go from the "austere physicalism" of scientific cosmology to a full-blown metaphysics of the *kosmos* sporting the rehabilitation all the predicates of classic Greek metaphysics and medieval theology, both positive and negative, is more than just a *step*, not even just a step too far, it is a *leap* into the abyss of the mystery of being and nothingness that post-classical, post-medieval thinkers like Kant dared not venture, that Wittgenstein backed off from, that even Heidegger, despite appearances to the contrary, did not jump into in his reformulation of the Why-question with talk of 'the Nothing' underneath our being-in-the-world.

And yet we persist in asking the Why-question. What exactly is the nature of this question we are trying to ask? Do we fully understand what it is we are asking for, what sort of answer, what sort of explanation we are so earnestly seeking? Are there not other kinds of explanation than scientific explanations drawing on the causal principle of sufficient reason, than theistic appeals to the necessary existence of a creative divinity, or metaphysical ventures into a universe beyond the universe? As Rundle himself says, if we cannot find answer to the Why-question via the route of scientific or metaphysical causality, whether theistic or other, must we not therefore look in another direction? (Rundle, 124).

THOMAS DEAN

As Post too says, since theism is seen by science as a "bad explanatory hypothesis" (what I term "science minus") inasmuch as it means positing a superfluous entity for purposes of scientific or metaphysical explanation, must not the "reason" for the existence of the universe, if it has one, must lie elsewhere? (Post, 72) It would seem, therefore, that if we are to come to any kind of closure on the Why-question, we need to go back and take a closer look at the kinds of answers, the kinds of explanations available, and, by implication, the kinds of questions we can, or cannot, ask.

Can the Why Question be Answered Metaphysically?

· Two of our philosophers, Rundle and Post, argue that the reason why the world exists can be given a metaphysical answer in terms of the nature of the universe itself, making superfluous the positing of an entity outside or beyond the universe, though one of them (Post) is open to a revisionist (naturalist) form of theism. Our other thinker, Munitz, agrees that the existence of the universe cannot be explained theologically. But, he argues, neither is there a metaphysical reason for its existence. There is no "reason why" for the existence of the world. Its existence is a permanent mystery. The Why question is unanswerable.

Having arrived at this point, the choice seems clear: either the Why question has a metaphysical answer and the alleged mystery is dissolved, or there is no explanation for the world's existence and the mystery remains. So which side has the better of the argument – the metaphysicians of the *kosmos* or (as Post labels them) the 'mystery mongers'?

Rundle's Materialist Metaphysics of the World

Creation and Conservation

Rundle's claim that there is a metaphysical explanation for the world's existence is grounded upon his distinction between a traditional metaphysical explanation based on the notion of *causality*, one that appeals to the Principle of Sufficient Reason (PSR), which he rejects, and a metaphysical account based on the (a-causal) notion of necessary being, in particular, the necessary existence of *matter*, which is the approach he defends.

Given that we should be wary of applying causal explanations of entities or events *within* the universe to the universe itself, as if the universe were something in space and time rather than spacetime itself, he says, "whether we may intelligibly speak of a cause at all in this instance...is problematic" (Rundle, 75). The question, in fact, is whether the universe *needs* a causal explanation at all, divine or otherwise, or whether rather the *need*, the "necessity" in question, is of a different sort (Rundle, 76). Rundle is assuming, of course that there is, if not a causal, at least some other kind of ultimate explanation for the world's existence, one cast in terms of metaphysical "necessity."

The problem, however, is spelling out just why it should be assumed there is a need for an ultimate explanation, and if there is, just what the nature of the alleged metaphysical necessity is. From the point of view of the scientific cosmologist or the metaphysical theist, if the notion of an *external* cause cannot be evoked to explain why the universe exists, if the universe cannot in some sense even be regarded as *causa sui*, its own *internal* cause, "then we have seemingly blocked all avenues that might lead to an explanation, and are forced to conclude that the universe exists as no more than a brute, causally inexplicable, fact" (Rundle, 85). That, however, is also a position which Rundle, as a metaphysician, wishes to reject. The question, however, is whether he has painted himself into an explanatory cul de sac. How does he propose to get out of it?

We can begin to move a step forward from this "bleak conclusion," he says, it we reject the notion that the universe came into existence. "A universe whose existence had a beginning, but for which any cause of that beginning is to be excluded, is a universe that remains puzzling, but if that exclusion can be joined by an exclusion of what it is called upon to explain, the puzzlement will have been lifted significantly" (Rundle, *ibid.*). But if that means the universe has existed for an infinite time, then we face "another formidable problem," because we still do not know *why* it exists. "The universe may neither have, nor be susceptible of, a causal explanation, but the why question seemingly remains. Not 'Why does it exist?' where a cause of becoming is sought, but "Why does it exist?' where the query is motivated by considerations of modality: the universe need not have existed, surely, so the fact that it does is a fact that calls for explanation" (Rundle, *ibid.*).

The problem with saying the universe "need not" or might not have existed is that it appears to presuppose or rely on the applicability of the notion of contingent existence to the universe, and therefore tacitly on the notion of a cause. This, as we have seen, is a position Rundle rejects in favor of some sort of notion of metaphysical necessity. The problem he must address, however, is whether these modal categories of contingency and necessity also break down when one tries to extend them to the universe as a whole.

We may find a hint of how he intends to proceed from his discussion of what it means to "bring (something) into existence." In the case of material entities at least, "bringing into existence is no more than the inducing of a chance in some persisting substratum; old matter is simply endowed with a new form." However, that leaves us with the question: What explains the continuing existence of this "substratum"? If it is not to be explained causally as something that is itself "brought into existence," then what sense are we to make of this notion? (One is reminded of Aristotle's 'prime matter' or before that, Plato's *khora*, the 'receptacle' upon which the Forms are imprinted.) Does its existence in turn require an explanation but of some other sort? Or is this the point at which metaphysical explanations run out? If so, what is to distinguish this 'substratum' from "a brute, causally inexplicable, fact"? (Rundle, 93)

Essence and Existence

It is at this point that Rundle introduces his startling claim. The God-hypothesis is metaphysically unnecessary, because the substratum of the ordered cosmos not only already exists, it *has* to exist, it exists *necessarily*. The universe itself is the Necessary Being for which the theologian rightly but wrong-headedly seeks. The universe itself is, as it were, the answer to the question of its own existence! For the metaphysical theist to claim that the universe, the spatiotemporal entity consisting of all that exists contingently, cannot itself exist necessarily, is simply to beg the question. It is not the notion of something existing necessarily that is the problem. The concept of necessary existence is not, says Rundle, obviously incoherent. It is that the theistic argument for that necessary existent being God was fallacious. (Rundle, 96)

Whether There Might Have Been Nothing

How, then, does Rundle defend this audacious claim that the universe *has* to exist, that it exists *necessarily*? Here we come to the core of his argument. It revolves around the notion of necessity, in particular, the claim that some existential proposition – the assertion of the existence of something -- could be a necessary one. A necessary proposition is one that is consistent with all possible states of affairs, all possible worlds. It need not be a necessary truth about a particular individual existent. "It could be," says Rundle, "that no *being* can be held to exist of necessity, and yet it was a necessary truth that *something* existed" (Rundle, 109, emphasis added). Returning to the notion of the 'substratum,' which he takes to be 'matter,' a 'mass' term that is not the name of an individual, he says, we could argue not only that "there *has* to be *something*" but that "if *anything* exists, *matter* does" (Rundle, *ibid*.) If, as he claims, these two premises are necessarily true, the conclusion follows: it is necessarily true that, for all possible worlds, matter exists, that, metaphysically speaking, it *has* to exist (Rundle, *ibid*.).

Of course we might demur already at this stage of his argument. Granted the distinction between there having to be some *particular* thing and there having to be *something*, to claim the latter as a necessary truth might strike one as introducing in a premise that which has yet to be proved. Further, what does it mean to apply the concept of 'existence' to a 'something' called 'matter'? Might we not want to argue rather that the 'something' that allegedly *has* to exist is not a 'mass' something but rather a unique 'individual,' the universe itself? Let us simply note these as questions for now.

Rundle continues his argument by asking: should we not insist that it is simply not possible that there could be, or at some time could have been, nothing at all, that there simply had to be something? Is this not at least a supposition strong enough, even if seemingly "weaker" than a theistic one, to "enable us to answer the original query, why is there anything at all? If there just has to be something, the inescapability of this fact suffices to lay that query to rest." (Rundle, 110) Of course that is a mighty big IF. It would seem, at least at first glance, not an "answer" at all, but simply a giant petitio. What is there to recommend this claim apart from the apparent ease with which it resolves the Why question in a grand linguistic flourish?

Rundle imagines his opponent asking: but are not affirmations of existence, whether of particular entities or something general, essentially contingent in nature? If so, it is not logically impossible to conceive of there being or having been nothing at all (Rundle, *ibid*). Rundle is quick to reject this alternative supposition: attempts to conceive total non-existence, he says, are "irredeemably partial," by which he means, there is always something left, "if only a setting from which we envisage everything having departed, a void which we confront and find empty, but something which it makes sense to speak of as having once been home to bodies, radiation, or whatever" (ibid). In other words, imagining something said to be nothing is just that, it is "not imagining anything, which is simply failing to imagine, not imagining at all:" (Rundle, 111). The plain and simple fact of the matter is that "There is just no alternative to being" (Rundle, 112).

To clinch his argument, Rundle brings in Hawking. "The universe would be completely self-contained.... It would neither be created nor destroyed. It would just BE." (Hawking, 144; also, 149). "But if the universe is really self-contained...it would have neither beginning nor end: it would simply be. What place, then, for a creator?" (Hawking, cited by Rundle, 123). Is it nitpicking to observe, however, that there is a vast difference between claiming, as does Rundle, that an indeterminate 'something' (for example, matter) has to exist and Hawking's saying that a determinate something, namely, the universe, perhaps just IS?

There is a fundamental problem here. Rundle claims that "We cannot conceive of there being nothing, but only of nothing being this or that, and this is a use of 'nothing' that presupposes there being something." He says this contrast only makes sense "within *ways of being*" (author's emphasis). Again, 'existing, not existing' fit into a scheme: "existing now, not existing then, and, more radically, there being a so and so and there being no so and so–but the contrast is still *within* how things *are*... This is as far as it goes, there being something and there being nothing not being contrasting poles with respect to the way things *might* be" (Rundle, 113, emphasis added). The problem is that, as Rundle himself has pointed out, these contrasts apply to things that exist *within* the universe. How do we know, then, that we can apply them to the universe itself, let alone the mysterious 'something' that allegedly *has* to exist? It is not clear, for that matter, how Hawking's notion of "just BE" or "simply be" is meant to apply to the universe *as a whole* when, unlike in the case of things existing *within* the universe, there is no intelligible contrasting notion of 'not existing,' of 'not being this or that,' of 'there being no so and so' – i.e., of there 'not being a universe.' What does "exist" mean in the case either of an indeterminate 'something' or a determinate universe? If it lacks meaning, then can the distinctions between contingent existence and necessary existence, or between coming (or bringing) into existence and an allegedly *absolute* sense of existence, of 'just being,' make any sense in this context?

Beginning And Ceasing To Be

Rundle thinks that, nevertheless, these distinctions still do make sense even when applied to a context *'outside,'* as it were, that of the events and things *within* the universe–i.e., when applied in the context of the universe itself. To reinforce his claim that there is not alternative to the universe 'simply (and necessarily) being,' he expounds further upon his argument against the possibility of talking coherently about either the beginning or the ceasing to be of the universe.

If we reject on philosophical grounds the theistic doctrine of *creatio ex nihilo* and on scientific grounds misguided attempts of cosmologists to trespass the boundaries of their discipline, and thus assuming that there is in fact nothing 'outside' of on the 'far side' of the universe, then, says Rundle, we have to make sense of the 'origin' of the universe "in a purely *internal* way," not in an 'external' way. That is, "the expansion of the universe following Big Bang was an expansion *of* space rather than an expansion *into* space" and similarly with time. In other words, we are talking here about the *"intrinsic* features" of the universe determinable without going 'outside' of it (Rundle, 120). If so, then the real dividing line is, for example, "between a sunless period and the birth of a sun... but not between no universe and universe" (Rundle, 121). Even the great theologian, Augustine, held that "the world was not created *in* time but *with* time" (Augustine, 436, cited by Rundle, 120). Therefore, if the notion of an event, of something coming to be *in* time, is not applicable to the universe as the spatio-temporal whole, then to ask why the universe began to exist is, logically speaking, a non-starter (Rundle, *ibid.*). By parity of reasoning, neither can we talk of a time when the universe will have ceased to exist (Rundle, 121-122).

Now, if for reasons of logical coherence we can talk neither of a time when the universe began to exist nor conceive of a time when it will have ceased to exist, then the only apparent alternative, logically speaking, is that the universe exists necessarily. "Here we glimpse grounds for invoking a notion of necessity. The universe did not come into existence, nor will it cease to exist. And this is not just a matter of empirical fact: there is nothing we could intelligibly describe as the universe's coming into existence or its ceasing to exist. Beginnings and endings join causation as being concepts which, while having innumerable instances within our world, resist extrapolation to the universe itself" (Rundle, 122).

We should pause here for a moment to remind ourselves that, as noted earlier, Kant like Rundle had already argued that the attempt to apply the concepts of beginning and ending, as well as causation, to the existence to the universe led to logical antinomies, to insuperable contradiction. But we should also recall that, unlike Rundle, Kant also argued that applying the concept of metaphysically necessary existence to the universe fared no better. And so we must ask, how does Rundle think he can avoid a similar logical conundrum in claiming to prove that the existence of the universe is in fact metaphysically necessary? And why does he think he *has to* make such a claim? Is it because he thinks it is somehow necessary to meet and vanquish theologians on their own metaphysical ground lest they try to re-enter from 'outside?

The Necessity Of The Physical

Let us return to the nitpicking question raised a few paragraphs earlier about the difference between an indeterminate 'something' and that uniquely determinate 'something,' the visible universe. It will be recalled that Munitz opted for addressing the Why question via the latter, more concrete notion rather than the vague, perhaps empty notion of 'something' ('rather than nothing at all'). Remember too our earlier discussion of another distinction between the *fact that* there is something and the *what*, the particular features, of the visible universe. We need to keep these two distinctions in mind as we turn to the specifics of Rundle's argument for what he calls "the necessity of the physical" – a provocative juxtaposition of categories usually regarded as metaphysical distinct.

Rundle maintains, as we have just seen, that the question, why there is something rather than nothing, can be answered, at least to his satisfaction: "*that* there simply has to be something or other." But, as he now notes, this answer simply raises a new question: "why is there *what* there is? Why has reality taken the *form* it has? " (Rundle, 125; emphases added). It turns out that the 'what,' the 'reality' and the 'form' he has in mind is not the visible universe, but that indeterminate 'something' to which he now gives the label 'matter,' i.e., 'the physical.' What are we to say, he asks, about the 'particular character' of this something, this 'reality'? Since he rejects the claim that 'it' is the product of divine design, are we, he asks, to accept 'it' as simply "a brute, inexplicable fact"? Accept what? Accept the existence of the universe? Accept the existence of matter? Are these the same things? His referring terms go back and forth. We need to disambiguate a few things.

There seems to be a fundamental confusion in the argument at this crucial point. The question of the 'what' of this 'it' is not the question asked in the Why question. The Why question is not asking why the visible universe has the *form* it has, nor is it asking *what* its ultimate constituents are -- 'matter' or something else. Those are questions that can be and are dealt with by the cosmological sciences, primarily mathematical physics at the small-scale and large-scale ends of the spectrum. They are not questions requiring the help of philosophers, in particular the speculations of metaphysicians, theist or materialist. *That* there is something rather than nothing, *that* the, or a, universe exists, that is an entirely different question altogether. It is Rundle's answer to that question – *that* there simply *has* to be something -- that is the focus of our concern here, not his argument that the ultimate constituent of the universe is matter.

It would seem that Rundle wants to conflate two different things. On the one hand, he has argued the metaphysical necessity of the existence of an indeterminate something. No further specification of the nature (the 'what') of that something seemed necessary for that phase of his argument: "there simply has to be something or other." On the other hand, he now wants to cement his case against a theistic metaphysics of the necessary existence of God by introducing a rival metaphysics based on the necessary existence of a *particular form* of existence, 'matter' or 'the physical.' The question then becomes: how does one square the notion of *necessary* existence with that of *physical* existence? In the philosophical tradition of the West, at least, these two terms have been at the opposite ends of the metaphysical spectrum. Things having physical existence have usually been thought to exist only contingently, entities having necessary existence have usually been thought to be non-physical in their 'what-ness.'

However, since Rundle clearly wishes to argue that, on the contrary, it is indeed precisely the matter of the universe itself that exists with metaphysical necessity and not some divine being outside the material universe, how does he propose to make this astonishing and counter-intuitive case?

Given, he says, that we cannot think away everything – a point he feels he has proved, then "what has persisted so obdurately was the domain of the physical," that is, "the apparent inescapability of a spatio-temporal setting" (Rundle, 129). He does not mean by 'the physical' or 'a spatio-temporal setting,' however, a 'world' consisting of "just events, just energy, just forces" (ibid.). Why not? Because, he says, "the grammar" of those terms stands in the way of their having the 'key feature' of 'independence,' the metaphysical attribute that theists, for example, ascribe to God and that is required for any 'substance' claiming the 'status' of 'ultimate reality' (Rundle, 129-130). We can now proceed to take "the final further step to our conclusion if we can equate substance to material substance" (Rundle, 130).

True, he says, some might question whether 'matter' is the right term for this cosmic-metaphysical role, since it could be argued that "matter was a *product* of the Big Bang." But the point is that "there must have been *something* falling within a general category of the physical' that in time led to the creation of matter" (Rundle, 131, emphasis added). He notes: "The constraints here are grammatical rather than empirical." In other words, whatever that 'something' was, it cannot have been too different from what eventually emerged as the physical universe, lest we undermine the very intelligibility of this entire cosmological-metaphysical argument.

In pausing to evaluate Rundle's case before going on to his final conclusion, there are several points to note. First, the fundamentally *metaphysical* not empirical or scientific nature of his cosmological argument. This is made clear when he says that God is the chief rival to 'matter' for the status of the basic substance explaining the existence of the universe. Matter has a "decided existential advantage: we know that it exists, which is more than we can say for God." (Rundle, 146). But as his remark on the grammatical rather than empirical nature of the category makes further clear, his argument for the primacy of matter is not a scientific hypothesis based on empirical evidence or a theoretical model of the universe.

Further, it is not entirely clear what his notion of matter refers to. In the case of Plato's *khora*, or material "receptacle," or Aristotle's "prime matter," for example, 'matter' "exists" only in various spatio-temporal entities ('forms' or 'substances'), not abstractly, and certainly never independently, as it would seem to have to do to be considered a 'reality' or 'substance,' unlike, for example, the being of God in metaphysical theism. Rundle might reply, yes, but "prima facie, it is easier to argue for the inescapability of something all-pervasive, as is matter, than for the inescapability of some particular individual," for example an individual with "all the problematic characteristics of deity." Given that something exists, "the case for matter, or for the physical more generally, would appear overwhelming" (Rundle, 146-147).

Again that niggling word *'something'* together with an attempt to back off the term 'matter' by referring to 'the physical more generally.' The problem here, in addition to the indeterminate sense or reference of these terms, is that the argument assumes something does in fact exist. But that is not the Why question. The Why question asks why it is *that* something exists, not *what* it is that exists. Of course Rundle can reply, but the point is that *what* exists, matter or the physical more generally, does not just happen to exist, it exists *necessarily*, and because of that, it simultaneously answers the question why it is *that* something exists. With the necessary existence of matter you get *two* questions answered for the price of *one*! And in the bargain you get the dissolution of Munitz' alleged 'mystery of existence'! It is simple, elegant, entirely unproblematic. "It is just: there has to be matter; something has to be material. It is only necessity as indestructability that applies to a given volume of matter, as this persists throughout the transformations it undergoes" (Rundle, 147).

Nevertheless, we should remind ourselves that, despite the simplicity and elegance of this 'solution,' it is a metaphysical argument through and through, not an argument based on empirical evidence or scientific theory. As with Plato's *khora* and Aristotle's 'prime matter,' what is it that, in the final analysis, distinguishes Rundle's metaphysical concept of 'matter' of 'the physical more generally,' that is, or 'something' (we know not what) from 'nothing'? Rather, it would seem like those earlier notions more like an *anti-concept*, a straw grasped at when in fact our attempts to understand the universe have reached their conceptual limits, their breaking point.

An End To Explanations

In an sense Rundle might agree. He might say, yes, that's true; with what you call the 'anti-concept' of matter we have indeed reached "an end to explanations" (Rundle, 183). But where we disagree is that I interpret 'end' to mean that with the notion of the necessary existence of matter we have reached the 'final, ultimate explanation,' whereas apparently you want me to concede that my notion of matter represents a dead-'end' to the attempt to provide any explanation at all, that at this point there simply is 'no explanation' for why the universe exists. I find this deeply irrational, and I will tell you why.

Let's go back a step. With what you call the Why question we are asking "whether there can be any ultimate explanations, whether the regress of explanations can ever be brought to a satisfactory end" (Rundle, 167). Well, what is the situation we face when we are dealing with the universe itself, not something existing within the universe? What have we argued so far?

First, that we cannot *extend* the notion of causation, the Principle of Sufficient Reason, which explains the existence of things or events *within* the universe, to the existence of the universe itself. Causal explanations apply to members within a series, and at bottom to the successive transformations of the matter that persists throughout the changes in that series (Rundle, 182-183). So, if, as I have also argued, there is no question of a *transcendent* cause existing outside the universe, then "something other than a *causal* explanation will have to be sought" for the persistence of matter (Rundle, 183, emphasis added). "Or so it would seem."

Having eliminated the notion of a *purposive* explanation (i.e., a theistic one) and now a *causal* explanation (i.e., an empirical-scientific one), what other kind of explanation is possible? Clearly, only an explanation based on the notion of the *necessary* existence of 'the physical'—if you will, literally a *'meta*-physical*'* explanation.

Second, we have argued that, since it makes no sense to talk of the coming to be of the physical universe, "its being is always a matter of its continuing to be." And since, I would argue, "continuing in being is not something that requires explanation, the fact that the physical universe exists is not, it would appear, a fact in need of explanation"–at least not in the causal sense associated with the coming or bringing into being of an entity within the universe (ibid).

Of course "we may surely ask whether there *had* to be something of this nature, something that continues to be." But "since there is no time at which the universe might not have existed, it is not possible that the universe should not have existed, so it exists of necessity. If this is accepted, then, while a *causal* explanation is not wanted, it does not matter whether we say that the existence of the universe is in *no need* of explanation, or that an explanation is to be found in the *unthinkability* of its non-existence" (Rundle, *ibid.*, emphases added).

On the face of it this is a strange argument! Rundle appears to be saying that there is no difference between saying the universe *does not need* an explanation and saying that the non-existence of the universe is *unthinkable*. On the one hand, to say the universe "does not need an explanation" is ambiguous. Does it mean the existence of the universe *lack*s an explanation or does it mean the reason for its existence is *self-explanatory*? On the other hand, to say the non-existence of the universe is not thinkable, does appear in fact to offer an explanation, a reason, for the existence of the universe. Why then would he say the universe does not need an explanation?

He has in mind the argument of a fellow non-theistic philosopher, Anthony Flew. Flew argues that it is not a defect in a "naturalistic" (i.e., non-theistic) cosmology to arrive at a point where explanations run out. "For it is not a contingent fact about one sort of system, but a logical truth about all explanations of facts [that] we must necessarily find at the end of every explanatory road some ultimates which have simply to be accepted as the fundamental truths about the way things are" (Flew, 83; cited in Rundle, 184-185).

Commenting on Flew's argument, Rundle says if the claim is that ultimate facts are *not further explicable*, that is unproblematic, but if the claim is that explanations end in "unexplained and *inexplicable* truths," we need to make a further distinction. For there is another possibility, namely, of having arrived at a point where "the demand for explanation is seen to be misconceived." In that case, we would be left not with "something inexplicable," but with "something which simply does not need explaining" (Rundle,185). Lack of explanation, he says, is only a problem, not -- note -- a 'mystery,' in the face of something "for which there *could* be an explanation ... but the explanation eludes us" (Rundle, *ibid.*). But that is not the present case.

Rundle bases his case on the intelligibility of applying the notion of 'necessary existence,' a concept usually attributed by theists to the being of God, to the existence of 'matter, or the physical more generally.' It plays, he says, "a key role in answering, and answering in a logically satisfactory way, our initial query why is there something rather than nothing?... If there *has* to be a *physical* reality, then *that* there is *such* is, it could be said, self-explanatory–better: something that is not in need of explanation– however much an explanation is needed for why, more *specifically*, the universe is *as* we find it" (Rundle, 191-192; emphases added).

This summation of Rundle's answer to the Why question calls for comment on two points in particular.

First, as his last comment betrays, Rundle appears at times to conflate, at times to distinguish, two different meanings and referents of the term 'universe.' In the former instance, this serves to confuse, if not undermine his argument that the 'universe' exists necessarily. On the one hand, he sometimes uses the term, as just seen, to refer to "the universe as we find it," that is, the determinate, structured 'cosmos' which is the object of the empirically-based theoretical models of scientific cosmology. In this use, it cannot be said the universe exists necessarily. Propositions affirming the necessary existence of material entities do not lie in the province of empirical science however comprehensive or unified the theoretical model employed.

On the other hand, and as more frequently is the case, he seems to collapse this determinate notion of the universe into his indeterminate notion of 'matter or the physical more generally,' an indeterminate 'something.' In this latter sense the 'universe' could be apparently almost anything, any meta-physical esoterica such as the "ten-dimensional string theory whose breakdown gave rise to matter, perhaps" (Rundle, 131) – in other words, the 'universe' *before* it takes the 'form' of "the universe as we know it." His speculative claim regarding the nature of 'matter, or the physical more generally' – of *something*, whatever it might be -- is rendered even more uncertain and indeterminate by the little afterthought he tacks on to the end: "perhaps."

Thus, whatever else it is that Rundle may have demonstrated, it is not that the universe, in the generally accepted sense of the visible, physical cosmos, exists necessarily. To get from 'matter, or the physical more generally' to 'the universe as we know it' would involve something more than Post's "but a step" (Post, 135). It would take a leap over a chasm 70,000 fathoms deep – a leap from the alleged necessary existence of a 'something' indistinguishable from 'nothing' to the presently existing universe that originated, contingently, out of the mother of all leaps, the Big Bang at the beginning.

But second, as problematic if not more so, is his claim that something physical, matter, can exist necessarily. To believe this we would have to make a conceptual leap in the reverse direction, as it were, namely from the physical entities, including the visible universe, of empirical science and cosmology that exist contingently to the necessary existence of a *meta*-physical something *beyond*, "on the far side" of, the limits of empirical investigation, a line that scientific cosmologists, unless they mistake themselves for metaphysicians, do not and dare not cross.

Rundle, of course, makes no bones about the fact that his claim about the necessary existence of matter is not an empirical claim. Nor, he claims, does it involve a causal explanation. Then what sort of claim is it? He sometimes refers to it as a grammatical or logical claim: "What is important here is that there must have been *something falling within a general category of the physical* if we are to speak of it as *having given rise to matter*; whatever can be reckoned there without a predecessor, it has to be, logically if not literally, sufficiently *in the same space as the ensuing matter* for us to make sense of *its generation* of the latter. The constraints here are grammatical rather than empirical" (Rundle, 131, emphases added). What is interesting to note about this passage is its appeal to the Principle of Sufficient Reason. Whatever it is that allegedly *has* to be, the 'necessity' is governed by the logical need, based on the Principle of Sufficient Reason, to posit a *cause*, something "having given rise to" matter. However, since this alleged cause exists in the "same space" as its physical effect, the logical necessity that posits its existence does not, by that fact alone, establish that such a physical cause has the metaphysical status of necessary existence.

What is interesting about Rundle's overall approach is in fact its metaphysical character. It raises he question, why is he trying to meet and beat metaphysical theists on their own turf? For if one of the compelling features of whatever reality is nominated for the status of a metaphysically necessary being is simplicity, it would seem the advantage here would go to the theist's notion of the ontological purity, unicity and freedom from any taint of materiality of the being of God. Given not only the problematic nature of any proofs of the existence of such a necessary being, let alone of the very concept of necessary existence itself, would it not have been better on Rundle's part to have abjured an attempt at a metaphysical "explanation" altogether? Would it not have been better to simply stop the process of giving explanations at the point to which he himself alluded above, namely, to simply say, perhaps with Flew, that "at the end of every explanatory road some ultimates which have simply to be accepted as the fundamental truths about the way things are" – that at this point we have indeed come to an "end of explanation" – that here we have arrived at something that must forever remain an "unexplained and inexplicable" mystery – *that* there is, in fact and in truth, something rather than nothing?

Perhaps the temptation to think otherwise lies in the problematic nature of metaphysics itself. When we reach the limits of our language, as we do with the Why question, metaphysical arguments seem inevitably to land us in confusion due to their very nature as a 'mixed' form of discourse. Cast in the surface grammatical form of pseudo-scientific, meta-empirical or meta-factual assertions, on the one hand, their depth grammar reveals them instead to be, as Rundle himself on occasion seems to note, claims about the logical or 'transcendental' features of our language – claims about what we are logically constrained to say, but also as if not more importantly, claims about limits beyond which are not logically permitted to go. Particularly in this latter instance, if we adhere to such 'Kantian' or 'transcendental' strictures, this must place severe constraints on any alleged fact-stating claims about the necessary existence of some 'reality' or other put forward in propositions clothed (or masked) in metaphysical garb.

In view of these two points, the temporary verdict on Rundle's two-part answer to the Why question – that there *has* to be something, and that the 'something' *has* to be 'matter, or the physical more generally' – must be: not proven, at least not without further clarification.

Rundle ends his long study of the Why Question with this focus on the nature and need for a *metaphysical* explanation. This provides a convenient segue into Post's focus on what he calls 'ultimate explainers' in his own not dissimilar physicalistic metaphysics of the universe.

Post's Physicalist Metaphysics of the Universe

Post's basic claim, like that of Rundle, is that the universe, not God, is the metaphysically Necessary Being for which theologians and metaphysicians have traditionally sought, and that, consequently, there is no unresolved mystery as to why there is something rather than nothing. Post's claim rests on presuppositions concerning the nature of mystery vis-a-vis explanation and the explanatory value of the notion of necessary being.

Mystery and Explanation

We recall that for Post, as for Aristotle, wonder is not a fundamental perduring aspect of the human condition as such, but rather functions as a goad to scientific inquiry aimed at arriving at a truth that satisfies the initial condition of wonder, the "why" questions that prompted it in the first place. As he says, "Philosophy begins in wonder, and we hope that it ends not only in truth but in relevant truth – truth that answers some question, or helps to answer it, perhaps by showing that it is not a genuine or well-formed question in the first place" (Post, 71). We might reply, that may be well and good for things that exist within the world, but does not the existence of the world involve wonder of a different order? Does it not point to an ultimate mystery that transcends our every effort to find a scientific explanation? No, Post argues, any legitimate "why" question, even that posed by the existence of the universe itself, can lead to a final answer, what he terms an "ultimate explainer," that can in principle dissolve if not the emotional at least the cognitive dimension of that initial sense of wonder. There can be no such thing as an ultimate mystery unanswerable, unexplainable, in principle. He make his position clear already in his working definition of 'mystery': "let us characterize a mystery as what is expressed by a question to which we do not know the answer, though *there is* a true answer to be known" (Post, 75).

The problem with this definition is that it eliminates from the outset the possibility of there being, in the case of the existence of the universe at least, a situation in which there is not a (true) answer to be known, in which there is a more fundamental sense of mystery than the one captured by his definition. One could argue, in other words, that his definition begs the question under consideration, that it is, in the language of the trade, a *petitio principii*. Of course Post does not rest with simply putting forth his working definition. He proceeds to argue vigorously in its defense.

But why, we might want to ask, does he feel compelled to reject the possibility of a fundamental mystery where the existence of the universe is concerned? Part of the reason is a legitimate concern for the ethics of inquiry. If told the Why question expresses a mystery unfathomable to us, he says, we might feel *"relieved of any responsibility"* to pursue the matter further. Part of it is the history of the so-called warfare between science and religion involving attempts by some theologians to place such inquires off limits to philosophers. We might be told that while the question is indeed answerable, it involves *"matters of faith, perhaps of mystical insight, completely beyond the reach of reason"* (Post, 74). But, we might persist, is it not possible to argue that the existence of the universe involves a fundamental mystery with violating either the ethical or scientific guidelines that govern, or should govern, intellectual inquiry? Post, for one, with good reason, is deeply skeptical.

Let assume with Post that we can set aside the emotional power of the Why question and any off-putting theological answers, limit our focus to its cognitive dimension, and do so in an ethically and scientifically responsible way. Keeping in mind that, on his definition, a mystery involves a question for which, whether we know the answer or not, there is in fact a (true) answer, what is Post's understanding of the relation of mystery, in this sense, to the Why question? "If," he says, "the question is to express a mystery of the profound sort intended, it must be construed as an explanation-seeking why-question. In that case the question one is asking is '*What is the explanation* of the existence of the universe?' Hence the question 'Why does the universe exist at all?' presupposes that *there is* some explanation. The mystery, if there is one, is *what* the explanation is" (Post, 79, emphases his). If, on the other hand, there is no explanation, then "the question is based on a false presupposition" (Post, *ibid.*).

Here again, however, we return to the point made above. Post himself operates from could be labeled a "false presupposition," namely, his presupposition, going all the way back to Aristotle, that the only cognitive situation that shall be counted as a legitimate source of wonder or mystery is one which it is possible to convert via scientific explanation into (true) knowledge. ["Scientific" explanation in the Aristotelian context, as for Post, includes "metaphysical" explanation as well.] In other words, this presupposition empties the Why question of the possibility of pointing to a mystery that, while otherwise observing Post's strictures, is a permanent and positive feature of our cognitive situation vis-a-vis the existence of the universe as such.

Before we turn to Post's attempt to offer a cognitive ("scientific," i.e. metaphysical) explanation for the existence of the universe, we should be alert to another dimension of the problem. Post argues not only that there is no ultimate mystery to the existence of the universe, but also that there is no explanation based on anything *outside* the universe. In other words, if there is an explanation, as he believes there is, it must be based on something "included in the sum total of what there is," an "internal explanation" (as Rundle also argued), specifically an explanation in terms of "the nature or essence" of the (whole) universe itself (Post, 80-81). He admits that it "sounds odd," (we could add, "medieval") to say that the essence of something explains its existence. And so he inserts a cautionary note: "Do we really know what we mean when we speak of an explanation by reference solely to the nature of essence of the thing? Does such 'explanation' really explain, or does it *mask the absence, strictly, of any explanation properly so-called*?" (Post, 81, emphasis mine). One thinks of Anselm's so-called "ontological" argument at this point (and its critics), the attempt, and critique of the attempt, to "explain" or ground the existence of God in God's ontological essence, an argument that relies on the notion of necessary existence or what Post will call "explanatorily necessary being." We should keep Post's warning in mind as we look at his own "internal" explanation.

Post wants us to understand one other matter before proceeding further. His answer to the Why question, though it will be cast in terms of the notion of necessary existence, does not, appearances to the contrary, involve an appeal to the Principle of Sufficient Reason (PSR). He gives several reasons why the PSR is insufficient *tout court*, among them the fact of quantum theory. But the version of PSR most relevant for our (metaphysical, not physical or empirical) purposes is one he calls "Strong PSR," the claim that "every existing thing has an explanation of its existence either in the existence and power of something else or in the necessity of its own nature" (Post, 95-96). PSR assumes, in other words, the legitimacy of the explanatory use of the notion of necessary being. There is a question, however, "whether the very idea of a necessary being is legitimate, and with it whether the very idea of the explanation of a thing by reference to the necessity of its nature." The problem, says Post, is that "to assume Strong PSR is to beg the question...Strong PSR presupposes the existence of a necessary being, the very point at issue" (Post, 96).

And yet, while rejecting Strong PSR as question-begging, Post nevertheless appeals to the notion of an explanatorily necessary being to answer the Why question. At first this seems puzzling. If he can defend the notion of a necessary being independently of appeal to PSR, can he not then invoke PSR in a non-question-begging way to answer the Why question? How can an answer to the Why question that draws on the notion of explanatorily necessary being not be seen as also lending support to a rehabilitated notion of PSR? It would seem Post has work to do. As we shall see, he does not shy from the task.

Necessary Being and Ultimate Explanation

Post begins by drawing a distinction between what we might call ordinary explanations or "explainers," explanations that do not necessarily bring the chain of explanations to a final halt, and what he calls final explanations, or in his terminology, "ultimate explainers." By a "final or ultimate explainer" he means an explanation which "is explained neither by itself" nor by any other factors, one which "would not only be unexplained; it would be ineligible for explanation, not even a candidate, neither admitting of nor requiring any explanation." They are, as he provocatively puts it, "the unmoved movers" of explanation, "unexplained explainers, or ultimate explainers" (Post, 100).

As an "unexplained" explainer, he says, an ultimate explainer is "a terminus, a finality, a conversation stopper" beyond which (though not necessarily *about* which) nothing more can or need be said. "The most garrulous must stand mute and accept. The reason is that to ask an explanation-seeking 'Why?' about an ultimate explainer is necessarily to ask a question based on a false presupposition The question is equivalent to 'What is the explanation?'... But of course there is none, in the case of an ultimate explainer... Hence the question can express no mystery, unfathomable or otherwise" (Post, 101).

One might be tempted to say that while the ultimate explainer does not involve an appeal to anything beyond itself, nevertheless unless we are to risk falling into total incomprehension just at the point where we had to hoped to achieve clarity, surely a final explanation of things should at least make sense in terms of the nature of the *explanans* itself. By saying that an ultimate explainer is not explained by itself, however, Post appears to have ruled out seeing an ultimate explainer as being, or referring to, something that has the explanation of its existence "in the necessity of its own nature." As have seen, he specifically rejects the strong version of PSR that assumes "the legitimacy of the explanatory use of the notion of necessary being .... the very idea of the explanation of a thing by reference to the necessity of its nature" (Post, 95-96).

And yet we might still want to know *what*, in the case of the universe, the ultimate explainer is. Post lists a number of what the traditional "candidates" for filling this position have been, that is the realities "taken to be the most fundamental or basic existents, according to the various schools of metaphysics." As might be expected, the list is a mixed bunch, some of the candidates internal to the universe, competing perhaps with Post's own "physicalist" metaphysics, some of them external to the universe, as for example those of theists: "'the indefinite,' atoms-and-the-void, Platonic forms, Aristotle's unmoved mover, Spinoza's one substance (God-or-Nature), spirit, pure consciousness, a life force, quanta, mass-energy, Being-as-such, process, History, God, Shiva, Tao (in its aspect as *tzu-jan*, the 'self-so')" etc. If there is any mystery here, Post says, it concerns "just what the ultimate explainers are" (Post, 102).

At this point there seems a confusion. Post uses the notions of 'explanation' and 'explainer' interchangeably. But are they simply two different words for the same thing? In particular the term 'explainer' seems to travel back and forth between two different semantic regions, one theoretical, one metaphysical. An 'explainer,' as an *explanation*, is a *theoretical account* one gives of things, the *reasons* for it. It may or may not, depending on the context, involve a reference to an entity that 'causes' something else. The something referred to, in that case, could also be considered an 'explainer,' but it is an 'explainer' in the sense of the *reality* (e.g., one of the "candidates" on Post's metaphysical list) *referred* to in the explanation, not the *theoretical account* itself. There is a difference between words and things, reasons and realities.

To anticipate: Post will argue that the physical universe is the ultimate explainer in the sense of the ultimate *What*, the ultimate reality in the metaphysical scheme of things, a reality whose existence (somehow) explains the existence of all other things metaphysically subordinate to it. But whether reference to that ultimate *What* answers the ultimate *Why* question is a different claim and one that would still need to be argued.

As we have just seen, Post has ruled out an explanatory account in terms of the necessity of the ultimate What's nature. Therefore, he has rejected the explanatory use of the notion of the What (the universe) as a necessary being, that is, as an entity that exists necessarily. On the other hand, for Post the existence of the universe is not contingent either. Its existence is not to be explained by reference to something else. It would appear, therefore, that while the universe exists as the ultimate explanation for everything else, its own existence has no explanation, either contingent or necessary. It simply exists, for no reason, without Why. It would seem, however, that this has been Post's own argument all along. Surely a strange state of metaphysical affairs, dare one say, a mystery? So where is the problem?

Let us try to get at the question another way. In what sense can it be argued that the *existence* of the universe as such, not its *nature* as a structured whole, as a *kosmos*, but simply the sheer fact that it, that something, *exists* at all, is the 'ultimate *explanation*' for why the things that exist, including the physical universe as a structured whole, *do* exist? Explanations in the realm of the physical sciences at least – setting aside for the moment "metaphysical" explanations of the sort Post's 'ultimate explainers' appear to be – normally take one of two forms. Either an individual physical event is brought under some empirical law or regularity, or an empirical law or regularity is itself made intelligible by being brought under a broader scientific theory (cf. Munitz, 1965, 181-183).

The question is, in which, if either, of these senses can the mere fact that something exists at all be considered the explanation for why the things that do exist, exist? The existence of the universe cannot be considered an individual instance of an empirical regularity, let alone an empirical regularity or meta-level physical theory itself. Simply put, what does the *existence* of the universe explain at all? The mere fact that something exists not only seems to have no explanatory value in itself, it seems to have no explanatory value for the existence of anything else as well. Once again, we seem confronted by the fact that the existence of something, whether the universe or not, seems not only to have no explanation in itself, but seems unqualified to be a candidate for the position of "explainer" for everything else as well. Far from being an ultimate 'explainer,' the fact that something, the universe, exists at all seems to be an ultimate mystery.

And yet, says Post, insofar as the search for explanation of why things exist runs out at this point, can we not say, as the dimension of *ultimacy* in this case suggests, that the universe is in perhaps a *unique* sense of 'explanation,' a *meta*-physical sense, the (final) 'explainer' of everything else within the universe without falling back upon, without lapsing into, an appeal to mystery? Perhaps we need to clarify this notion of 'ultimate explanation-*sive*-ultimate explainer' a bit more.

One thing an ultimate explainer is not, says Post, is a *logically* necessary being, that is, a being such that its nature ('essence') would logically entail its existence. Again, think here of Anselm's attempt to make that case in his ontological argument for the logically necessary existence of God. Not only is the idea of such a being "highly problematic," says Post, it is not in any case needed for the case he wishes to make. Whatever it is that ends the chain of why questions, he says, though it is not a logically necessary being, "nevertheless enjoys an unproblematic kind of necessity just by virtue of being ultimate," not a *logical* necessity but an *explanatory* necessity (Post, 102).

It is interesting that in developing this distinction between logical and explanatory necessity, Post seems willing, indeed compelled to concede that, logically speaking, it is possible to conceive that the universe might not have existed (Post, 103). Here he would appear to diverge not only from Rundle, who says conceiving such is impossible, but also from the metaphysical tradition going back to Plato and Parmenides who, as we have seen, argue that the notion of there having been nothing at all is logically as well as metaphysically untenable.

Post makes a further interesting step in his argument. He says that, insofar as ultimate explainer is not "explanatorily dependent" on anything else, it can be said that, in that respect, it is not "explanatorily contingent." From this he then takes the "small step" to concluding that, if so, "the existence of the universe is explanatorily necessary" (Post,

103). (Munitz might refer to this notion of explanatory necessity of the universe's existence as a *negative* sense of "necessary existence"; it does not yet, without a supplemental argument, yield a positive sense what could be meant by speaking of the "necessary existence" of the universe; Munitz, 1965, 169, n. 12.)

To give the merely *negative* notion of *explanatory* necessity a philosophically more robust significance, it would have to be shown that it entails a *positive* notion of *metaphysical* necessity as well, yet without claiming, on the other hand, that such metaphysical necessity involves any *logical* necessity. That seems like a tall order indeed. How does Post propose to support such a claim? Explanatory necessity is distinct, he says, from "natural and physical necessity," from "causal and factual necessity" (Post, 103). But that is not the question here. The question is whether it entails a *different kind* of necessity called "metaphysical necessity" that is neither logical, on the one hand, nor natural, physical, causal or factual on the other. What is the positive, metaphysical import of the notion of "explanatory necessity" – if any?

It would seem that, despite Post's claim, the notion of explanatory necessity in fact has no further metaphysical or ontological import other than that imported by linguistic fiat. To wit: "In light of the finality and ultimacy of an explanatorily necessary being, and in light also of strong similarities between our argument for such a being and a certain strand of philosophical tradition, we *may call* the being metaphysically necessary. Thus metaphysical necessity may be *construed as* explanatory necessity.... [A]n ultimate explainer is metaphysically fundamental *in some sense*; it enjoys *some sort of* ontological priority" (Post, 103-4, emphases added).

Once again there is an interesting slippage from word to thing, from reasons to reality, from talking about an 'ultimate explainer' as an ultimate *explanation*, on the one hand, to referring to it as an explanatorily necessary *being*, on the other. There may indeed be "strong [*formal*] similarities" between the *role* an ultimate *explanation* plays in the *cognitive* realm, in the realm of *concepts, reasons or ideas*, and the *role* an alleged ultimate *reality* plays in the *metaphysical* or *ontological* realm, the realm of *being or reality*. But surely there is an even greater ["*material*"] difference, am immense gap, a yawning abyss, *between* the two realms that cannot be traversed by Post's "small step," even by a leap.

Why, given that his notion of explanatory necessity refers neither to the logically necessary being of an ultimate explainer, nor apparently to any kind of physical (natural, causal, factual) necessity, why does Post feel it important to "construe" *explanatory* necessity as "in some sense" *metaphysical* necessity? What is his underlying concern? What is the problem with saying that while the visible universe of scientific cosmology in some sense provides the ultimate explanation for all things existing within it, its *existence* as differentiated from its physical *structure*, that is the fact that there exists anything at all, has for all we know no metaphysical necessity? Perhaps the only thing we say about it is that, as Hawking put it, "it just is." That may not be any kind of explanation, and that may be the ultimate (and ultimately mysterious) truth of the matter.

Not surprisingly, Post anticipates this objection. In answer to the Why question, he says, it is tempting to say, "That's just the way the world is.'" There are two problems with such a suggestion, he says. It "is not exactly wrong, but it is not nearly strong enough, and it is potentially quite misleading." First, as he has said before in stipulating his definition of a legitimate versus illegitimate sense of 'mystery,' the Why question is "improper" insofar as it is based on "the false presupposition that there is an explanation, known or unknown." And second, the answer is misleading because it suggests, "as often it is meant to suggest–that [the world's existence] is merely contingent and in no sense metaphysically necessary" (Post, 104).

Regarding the first point we might say that whether or not the Why question rests on a false presupposition (i.e., an appeal to PRS) is relative to his stipulated definition of 'mystery.' But if that definition involves a begging of the question, then it is not clear that someone asking the Why question is necessarily invoking PRS. But it is the second point that brings us to the center of Post's concern. His concern, as the phrase "as often it is meant to suggest" betrays, is that someone making Hawking's point may be suggesting that the existence of the universe, in not being "metaphysically necessary," is therefore "contingent, brute, gratuitous, absurd, irrational, an accident or mere happening, *in crucial senses of these terms*" (ibid, my emphasis). That is quite a string of adjectives, shorthand for a variety of different and incompatible "metaphysical" philosophies. It would take time to unpack them individually or severally. But it is not necessary that we do so. Why? Because underlying that list is Post's own "false presupposition," that the Why question and/or the Hawking statement are necessarily committed to making that suggestion. Post's concern, understandable enough, is that to buy into that list of adjectives is "to imply that [the world's existence] fails to satisfy some norm," specifically – in this context of the giving of explanations -- "some norm of rationality" (Post, 105). And what is that norm? That there be an explanation, which in turn assumes PSR, "usually some version according to which every logically contingent thing has an explanation" (Post, *ibid.*). But since, as he has argued, "PSR could be a norm of rationality only if were valid," which it is not, it follows that the world's existence, as an ultimate explainer, "does not fail to satisfy a norm or expectation of rationality to the effect that [everything] must have an explanation .... A correct conception [of rationality], which rejects PSR [i.e., "an erroneous and obsolete conception of rationality and its norms"], does not permit us to call something irrational, absurd, brute, or gratuitous merely because it is ineligible for explanation" (Post, *ibid.*).

However, Post's argument relies on a version of PSR that involves reference to "logically contingent" things. But the Hawking point, in saying that the world may not exist *necessarily*, that instead it might "just be," does *not* entail that the world exists *contingently*. However cogent Post's argument may be as regards some versions of some of the views summarized in that list of metaphysical adjectives, he is here begging the very issue under discussion. For as the Hawking quote instead suggests, and as we remember from Kant, at the limits of metaphysical explanations perhaps neither the categories of necessity nor contingency apply.

Post makes an interesting concession at this point: "Of course if 'brute' and 'absurd' meant no more than 'has no explanation,' then [the world's existence] would be brute and absurd" (Post, *ibid.*). However, in the next breath, taking back his concession, as it were, he adds: "But the words do mean more. They have strong pejorative meanings and are intended to have them." But this is precisely where the nub of the argument lies. Do such words necessarily have such a negative meaning? Is it not possible to give an alternative reading, if not of the words, then of the underlying metaphysical situation to which they, "misleadingly," refer?

It turns out that the focus of Post's animus, or at least of his concern, is the one position he singles out from among the adjectival list for special opprobrium: the so-called "irrationalists." Post rejects their irrationalism because it rests on a presumed PSR view of rationality, a norm which, in their judgement, the existence of the universe fails to satisfy. But given a "correct" view of rationality, in which explanatory rationality reinstates a notion of metaphysical necessity without appealing to

PSR, we may conclude that the existence of the universe, which as an ultimate explainer exists, by definition, without ultimate explanation, is nonetheless rational and metaphysically necessary withal!

What it comes down to is this: Post rejects that list of "pejorative" metaphysical adjectives – "contingent, brute, gratuitous, absurd, irrational, an accident or mere happening" – because he subscribes – along with the mainstream of the Western metaphysical tradition going back to Aristotle's notion of philosophy beginning in 'wonder' but issuing in rational truth -- to the belief, subscribed to by metaphysicians of all stripes, that there is an ultimate necessity at the base of all things, a necessity that is rationally perspicuous, and that as a consequence there is no final mystery as to why something exists rather than nothing. He is, of course, right to reject the pejorative use of those terms, but not for the reason he does. It is not because such terms can be used to promote an underlying "irrationalism" or can be misused to license what he calls "mystery mongers" (Post, 114). It is because a pejorative use fails to convey the *positive* insight that can underlie them and to which Post himself proves sensitive when, in the last chapter of his study, he turns to the question whether human values have any ground in existence. We will return to that rather different question in Part Two of the present study.

In the meantime, Post feels he can now use "the proven existence of ultimate explanations to legitimize the idea of a metaphysically necessary being, which then proves not to be contingent, absurd, irrational, gratuitous, or brute, and about which there can be no mystery as to why it exists" (Post, 110).

In other words, he believes has thereby succeeded in putting "paid" to the Why question once and for all. The view of the Why question he has been concerned from the outset to rebut points to an allegedly ultimate mystery that posits "an absolute limit on the pretensions of science and of 'reason generally'" (Post, *ibid*.). But on his analysis, based on his definition of 'mystery,' his critique of an "erroneous and obsolete" view of rationality that presumes the universal validity of PSR, and his presuppositions about the nature of ultimate explanations-*sive*-ultimate explainers, the alleged mystery expressed by the Why question, namely, "Why does anything at all exist, why not rather nothing?" is equivalent to, i.e. reduces to "Why does the universe exist?," which in turn is equivalent to, i.e. reduces still further to "What is the explanation of the existence of the universe?" And the assumption on which *that* question is based is the (false) presupposition that there *is* some explanation (Post, *ibid.*).

So, says Post, while "it is true that science cannot fathom why there is something rather than nothing," that does not license the conclusion that the existence of things must remain forever a mystery. The problem rests not in the alleged limitations of "the pretensions of science and of reason generally." No, says Post, "What is pretentious is the question." The Why question "does not cease to have a false presupposition" just because of the "co-presence of a curiosity-feeling" when we raise it (Post, *ibid.*). (As an aside: it is interesting that here Post uses a put-down phrase borrowed from that notorious "tough-minded" positivist, Terence Penelhum, for whom Aristotle's and Post's own initial sense of "wonder" is reduced to mere "curiosity"!)

Post ends his discussion of "Mystery and Ultimate Explanation" (chapter 2 of his book) by returning from these meta-level (metaphysical as "meta-physical"?) reflections to the realm of scientific reason to "apply some of these lessons to physical cosmology," i.e., to a physicalist metaphysics of the existence of the universe. Referring to the cosmological theory of the "big bang," he says that to ask "Why?" about the big bang "would be idle" unless the question is meant to suggest there is an alternative physical cosmology in which what was unexplained in the big bang theory finds a better explanation. Absent such an alternative theory, however, in current cosmological theory the big bang serves as the ultimate explainer. In the context of this theory, therefore, the existence of the universe is not "brute, gratuitous, absurd, irrational, or a mere happening." Since "none of these term applies to an ultimate explainer," and since the big bang is an ultimate explainer, "we must say of the big bang that within our present best cosmological theory (or theories) it is metaphysically necessary" (Post, 115). Thus Post concludes: "From physics to metaphysics is but a step" (Post, 135).

But is it? Is it a step, or is it rather a leap from one domain of discourse to an entirely different one where different rules of conceptual logic apply? As Post himself observes, in an interesting aside about the difference between explanation and reality whose implications he himself then proceeds to cast aside, "most philosophers simply took for granted, until recently, that explanation is an objective relation among the things explained, and that a parade of explanations corresponds with an order in reality, a hierarchy or chain of being. They forget that explaining is something *we* do in order to satisfy *our* wonder about the whys of things, and that what we wonder about and what satisfies our wonder are very variable affairs. So explanation may well not correspond with any objective or invariant relation among existents. If not, this powerfully limits the metaphysical significance of an ultimate explanation" (Post, 106-107).

But that is precisely the question! Why should we think that a *cosmological theory* entitles us to conclude that the *physical existent* posited by that theory, the 'big bang' or (to accommodate future theories) the physical universe itself is *ontologically necessary,* and that, therefore, the *physical* universe also has all the traditional *metaphysical* attributes ascribed to an allegedly *necessary* being, as Post further claims (Post, 135)? If we are correct in rejecting Post's claim, then where did his argument go wrong?

In concluding our discussion of Post's problematic "step" from physics to metaphysics, we can make several observations.

First, it is clear that for Post, no matter what the cosmological theory, big bang or any other, the existence of the world will always be rationally intelligible. There will always be an ultimate (scientific) explanation, thus an ultimate (metaphysical) explainer, a 'world' of whatever sort that has the properties of a metaphysically necessary being. In other words, the existence of the world *cannot* be mysterious, cannot transcend the limits of "science or reason more generally." That possibility has been ruled out from the start, a priori, by his stipulated definition of mystery and by his metaphysical interpretation of the notion of 'ultimate explanation.' But why should we accept that initial stricture and its corresponding metaphysical interpretation?

Next, Post's smooth and apparently effortless slide from the original formulation of the Why question, "Why does anything at all exist, why not rather nothing?" to the alleged equivalent "Why does the universe exist?" and from there to "What is the explanation of the existence of the universe?" is highly problematic. He assumes that the only way the Why question can be understood is as a request for an ultimate scientific explanation, and in particular, one that presuppose the validity of PSR. Much of traditional Western metaphysics would suggest he is correct. But the Why question could be performing a different function, one belied by its surface grammar. If so, Post's critique, which is limited to the latter, may not be conclusive.

Finally, going back to a distinction he himself set out, there seems to be a continuing ambiguity of reference in Post's characterization of the 'universe' as a final explainer. Is he referring to the visible universe as described and explained by contemporary cosmology, or is he referring to what he calls the 'true' universe, the universe 'beyond' the universe of present-day cosmological theory? Does the visible universe in some sense exist 'within' the true universe? Are its properties the same? Which universe is the one said to be a metaphysically necessary being? Is it the universe that currently serves as the ultimate explainer for cosmological theory (originating in the Big Bang), or is it the universe posited as existing 'beyond' the known universe of scientific theory? Do we see here another instance of the slippery slope he refers to as "but a step," this time a slide in reverse from science to cosmology to metaphysics? At the very least, these things remain unclear.

The strength of Post's analysis is his argument showing that when in cosmological theory we arrive at an ultimate explanation, positing the existence of an ultimate explainer, we have gone as far as scientific reason can take us. What we find at the end of this chain or "parade" of explanations is something that, as Hawking put it, "just Be's." About that final explainer, as Post shows, it makes no sense to ask for a further explanation as to *why* it "just is." That's the point of saying the explanation and explainer are 'final,' are 'ultimate.' That's the point of that little word 'just.'

However, where his case breaks down is precisely when he ventures that little 'step' across the boundary separating the realm of physics, the realm of contingent beings, from the purported realm of metaphysics, the realm of allegedly necessary being. For to say with Hawking, for example, or as Post himself implies, that the universe "just Be's" is to take the verb "to be" out of the realm of its ordinary use, where the distinction between contingent and necessary being has its home, and apply it to a limit- or boundary-situation where that and related distinctions break down, where talk about opposites such as 'Being' and 'nothing at all' seem paradoxically to coincide. And that lands squarely back in the Why question itself: "Why *is there something* rather than *nothing at all*?" That suggests a mystery remains.

Munitz and the Mystery of Existence

If in fact the Why question does not have an answer that can be cast in metaphysical terms, if, further, it is not based on a false presupposition (i.e., does not depend on some version of PSR), and if, finally, it is not logically ill-formed – if, in other words, while there is no apparent explanation for the world's existence, metaphysical or any other, nevertheless the Why question is not obviously nonsensical, we would seem to have an additional puzzlement on our hands in addition to that of the Why question itself. How are we to understand a question that makes sense but cannot be answered, not just for scientific or metaphysical reasons, but in principle? What sort of logic must this involve?

Munitz believes he can straighten this out for us, and in so doing, clarify how it is that we can intelligibly say that the existence of the world is ultimately a mystery that has no explanation. This will involve a logical analysis of *questions and answers*, why we cannot apply categories of either *contingency* or *necessity* to the world's existence, and why there are no "*reasons why*" for the world's existence.

However, even if Munitz can establish his case that the existence of the world is ultimately a mystery, will that explain how it is that, nevertheless, we still want to ask the Why question, that it still makes sense to ask it, and if so, what kind of answers to it, if not scientific or metaphysical ones, make sense? An exploration of those questions will be the subject of Part Two of this essay.

Questions and Answers

Aristotle understood "wonder" about the world in a very specific way as the question: "How did the world get to be the way it is at the present time? Through what process of transformation and growth did it pass before it emerged as the ordered structures [*kosmos*] it is found to be now?" (Munitz, 1965, 3) This "wonder" could in principle be dissolved by scientific cosmology. It this understanding of "wonder" to which answers have been given from Aristotle's pre-Socratic predecessors up to the latest theories of 21st C. cosmological science. This understanding of "wonder" was also adopted by Post in his stipulative definition of "mystery." However, Munitz begins his own discussion of the "mystery" of the world's existence by claiming that "there is another side to human wonderment not considered by Aristotle that finds expression in a different kind of question from that which he listed under the heading 'the origin of the world'" (Munitz, 1965, 4).

Munitz has in mind the question we have been calling "the Why question." This is not the question how the world came to be in its present structured form as a *kosmos*, a question for which we look to science for an answer. It is rather the question why is there anything at all rather than nothing. This question science does not pretend to answer. If our criticisms of Rundle and Post are correct, it cannot be answered by a super-science called meta-physics either. However, there could be a very simple reason why neither science nor meta-science can answer this question. It could be, as Post maintained, that it is not a genuine question at all, rather it is a pseudo-question based on a false presupposition. Masquerading as a real question, it is simply a misleading expression of awe in the face of the wondrous universe we find ourselves inhabiting.

If so, is Munitz's talk of a different sense of "wonder," a different sense of "mystery," really saying anything different? What if Post were willing to grant, as perhaps he might, that his own notion of "ultimate explainers" is not in any ordinary sense of the term an "explanation" for the world's existence. And what if Rundle, similarly, might be willing to concede that his own claim that the world just "has" to be, or Hawking's notion that the world "just is," is not in any ordinary sense of the term an "explanation" for the world's existence. In rejecting such "explanations," Munitz wants to argue that the world's existence is ultimately a *mystery* for which there is *no* explanation, metaphysical or any other. But, we must ask, is there any real difference between saying with Munitz there is "no explanation at all" and saying with Post or Rundle that there is "a metaphysical explanation but not an explanation in any ordinary sense"? Are these not simply different ways of expressing the same thing, our awe at the existence of the world?

To unravel this we must first look at how Munitz understands the logic of questions and answers, in particular, questions which ask for the "reasons why" of things. We must then see how this bears on what he thinks we can ask and say about the world's existence. Perhaps then we can determine whether there is a difference between the answers ("reasons why") Post and Rundle give for the existence of the world and Munitz's "no answer" (no "reason why") view.

Munitz begins by noting that whereas scientific types of questions are agreed to be understandable and, at least in principle, answerable, not all would agree that the Why question is even an askable let alone answerable one. "Some reject, outright, both the question and any attempt to find an 'answer' to it, on the ground that the very asking of the question is itself a mistake and philosophically vacuous" (Munitz, 1965, 4,7). It could argued, for example as Post does, that the Why question results from a confusion of thought, a misuse of language. It reflects "an intellectual knot into which we get ourselves in asking a meaningless, because unanswerable question" (Munitz, 1965, 5). If so, it needs "disentangling" by linguistic analysis. "We should then find that the mental cramp will have disappeared--the question will have dissolved, and will no longer bother us." (Munitz, *ibid*) As Wittgenstein famously said at the end of his *Tractatus Logico-Philosophicus*, "For an answer that cannot be expressed the question too cannot be expressed. *The riddle* [mystery] does not exist. If a question can be put at all, then it can be answered. Whereof one cannot speak, thereof one must be silent" (Wittgenstein, *Tract.* 6.5, 7). The solution to the Why question is seen in its dis-solution. It may indeed persist as a grammatically misleading expression of an emotional response to the universe, but logically and cognitively speaking, it is *tohu wa bohu*, "without form and empty."

However, what if the Why question is askable but not answerable? What if it has the logically unique function of pointing to, serving as a place-holder for, a phenomenon that is not only emotionally resonant but cognitively significant without being an "answer" to a "question" in any ordinary sense of those terms? To show this Munitz must clarify his understanding of what it means to say a question is answerable or, alternately, unanswerable.

As noted, critics of the cognitive significance of the Why question invoke a "principle of answerability" modeled on the questions asked by science. In saying that the Why question is not answerable, says Munitz, critics charge that language is being used in a way that, "strictly speaking, has no literal cognitive meaning" (Munitz, 1965, 33). It does not do to reply that such a question simply reflects "a difficulty that cannot be resolved because of the inherent limitations of the human intellect" (Munitz, *ibid*.). To argue that way is to open the door to all sorts of illogical nonsense and unverifiable claims. It is a prescription for irrationality masquerading as metaphysical profundity. The principle of answerability, upon which any sound common sense must rest in philosophy too, not just in science, requires as Wittgenstein states that "every meaningful question must have a possible answer" (Munitz, 1965, 34).

But are things so simple, so open and shut as that? Perhaps there are more types of "unanswerability" than are dreamed of in the universe of logical positivists and doctrinaire empiricists. Munitz distinguishes three types of unanswerable questions (Munitz, *ibid.*):

The first involves "those violating accepted rules of linguistic use" – "linguistic use" here referring to the various linguistic conventions, the rules that dictate the meaningful use of terms, and "accepted" referring to some standardly deployed scheme of (empirical) knowledge and (logical) category distinctions that make explicit in the asking of the question the minimal relevant conditions for answering it. (Munitz, *op. cit.*, 34-35)

The second involves "those resting on false presuppositions". While the question may not violate the rules of use referred to above, nevertheless it relies upon presuppositions that are problematic if not false -- e.g. Post's rejection of the Why question on the grounds that it presupposes an illegitimate attempt to apply PSR to the universe as a whole. (Munitz, 1965, 35)

In both of these cases in which the question is prevented from having any possible answer, the solution is not to try to find answers to them, but to point out the logical mistakes that prevent them from being meaningfully asked in the first place. In short, it consists in dis-solving the question. (Munitz, 1965, 35-36)

But this leaves a third kind of "unanswerable" question, says Munitz, "those for which no answer is obtainable by a known rational method." The Why question is *the* unique instance of this kind of unanswerability. Critics like Rundle and Post reject the question as being logically malformed and/or cognitively meaningless because it violates the two rules above. It is not that they reject the idea that there are unanswerable questions. There are questions that are unanswerable, but if so, it is for technical or practical reasons, not for logical reasons (Munitz, 1965, 39). But questions that violate the two rules are not even meaningfully askable in the first place. In those cases the issue of their answerability simply does not and should not arise.

But for Munitz it is precisely the meaningfulness of the third kind of "unanswerable" question upon which his case for speaking of the mystery of the world's existence stands or falls. The key then is what exactly Munitz means by "rational method" (cf. Munitz, 1965, 189-193), and whether his formulation of this third kind of "unanswerability" rests on this notion. If it proves problematic, does that mean Rundle and Post will have the last word after all? Or can the case for the Why question still be made via a reformulated version of this alleged "third" kind of unanswerability?

To begin with, Munitz rejects as philosophically "irrelevant" to the Why question a *general* criterion of meaning limited to what he considers a *narrowly* empiricist ("positivist") view of language. The positivist use of the Principle of Answerability limited to the two rules above at best simply formulates a stipulated *definition* of scientific or more broadly empirical meaning, but nothing more than that. One cannot rule out *ab initio* the possibility of asking other types of meaningful questions without engaging in a *petitio principii*, without begging the very issue at stake! (Munitz, 1965, 41, 189-193)

But what about the positivist claim (including that of a metaphysics like Rundle's or Post's) that the Why question is not completely lacking in meaning. It may lack cognitive meaning, but it can still have deep emotive meaning. Munitz agrees: "if 'cognitive' means 'that which can be treated by the method of science,' or, as applied to questions, 'that which can receive a possible scientific answer,' then this definition would rule out the metaphysical question 'Why does the world exist?' as not having cognitive meaning" (Munitz, 1965, 43). However, he adds, this restriction of meaning "reflects a classification wholly inappropriate for identifying the principal use of language in raising a question of the type 'Why does the world exist?'... Such use of 'cognitive' is too narrow." (Munitz, *ibid.*) Clearly we need a broader sense of "cognitive" and along with it of "reason" and "logic."

Rather we must see in the Why question "a use of language that, even if non-scientific (*i.e.*, non-cognitive in the positivist sense) is not simply emotive. I am not denying, of course, that there is an emotive component (connected with the feelings of awe and cosmological astonishment) in the statement of the mystery of existence. But I deny that this is *all* there is to it, or even its principal feature. These are feelings derivative from the realization of the unanswerability of the question 'Why does the world exist?'" In a broader sense of "cognitive," therefore, I am arguing, he says, even the Why question can be classified as "cognitive." (Munitz, 1965, 43-44)

This is a highly provocative and perhaps even problematic passage. It raises several questions, and not just for positivist reasons. What, precisely, does Munitz think the relationship is between the emotive and cognitive elements in the Why question? Does he think the emotive component, though "derivative" and not even the "principal" feature of the question (i.e., therefore apparently not sufficient as the initial motivation of the question), is nevertheless necessary for understanding the question? If so, does this make it not only a philosophical question (he prefers 'philosophical' to 'metaphysical,' a term of which he is skeptical in so far as metaphysics proposes to "answer" the question), but also an inherently religious one? If religious, but not metaphysical, how are we to understand that? Specifically, are the feelings derivative from the realization that the question is unanswerable? Or is it not rather vice versa? Is it not the feeling of awe that gives rise to the sense the question is "unanswerable"? If the question derives from the feeling, then what does this say about the cognitive import of feelings? Does the bifurcation of emotive and cognitive meaning apply in the unique case of the Why question? Do we not have here what in Buddhist philosophy might be termed the co-arising inter-dependence of the spheres of cognitive and emotive meaning? Is this not part of what makes it cognitively unique? At the very least we, if not Munitz, need to clarify these questions in coming to our own understanding of the nature and significance of this allegedly "unanswerable" question.

Contingency and Necessity

What is at least clear so far is that Munitz rejects any attempt to use what he regards a narrowly empiricist criterion of meaning to deny the intelligibility of the question "Why does the world exist?" But in saying that although the question can be meaningfully asked it cannot be meaningfully answered, he seems also to be denying that we can answer the Why question by invoking either of the two traditional categories of metaphysics normally used to "answer" the question – *contingency* and *necessity*. We might want to reply: It is one thing to argue that the existence of the world as a whole or as such lies outside the purview of the empirical sciences, focused as they are on answering questions about events and objects that exist within the spatio-temporal framework of the world. But it would seem quite another to argue that the "meta-science" of metaphysics, which draws on categories transcending those of the empirical sciences, cannot use such categories to "answer" the Why question. Why should metaphysical answers like those proposed by Rundle or Post be ruled out as solutions to the alleged "mystery" of existence? How does Munitz propose to argue that?

Against the Contingency of the World's Existence

The chief roadblock to Munitz's claim that the existence of the world is ultimately a mystery is Rundle's and Post's claim that the world exists necessarily. But to prepare the ground for his rejection of that claim, Munitz begins by ruling out what might seem the alternative claim, that the world's existence is contingent. Normally the sense of contingency involved here entails the dependence of the existence of something on some other existent. In the case of the world's existence, this has traditionally involved dependence on something that exists necessarily, for example, in the tradition of theistic metaphysics a God whose existence is necessary. But, Munitz asks, what about the argument that there is another sense of contingency independent of theology or even scientific cosmology? What about the more "primordial" sense of the contingency of the world's existence experienced, for example, in Tillich's existential awareness of the "shock of non-being"? Or even more radically in the "ontological" awareness expressed by Why question itself – the sense of astonishment expressed by the fact "there might have been nothing, yet there is a world"? (Munitz, 1965, 142) This existential or "ontological" sense of contingency would seem to point to an alternative "logic" of "question and answer" than the one presupposed by the tradition of the empirical or metaphysical "sciences" and embodied in PSR.

However, says Munitz, there is still a problem. If the alleged alternative logic of the Why question depends on the intelligibility of the notion of 'nothing,' the question is a non-starter. Here he agrees with Rundle, Post, and Western metaphysics from Parmenides and Plato on. An absolute sense of 'Non-Being' or 'Nothing' lacks meaning. If, he says, the statement "there might have been nothing" means no more than "why does the world exist?" then it is, redundantly, simply another way of expressing awe at the world's existence. However, if the term 'nothing' is meant to

THOMAS DEAN

refer to "some independently possibility with which the existence of the world can be contrasted, then this manner of speaking must be rejected as being inherently unintelligible." (Munitz, 1965, 143-144) This means, however, that if some alternative sense of 'contingency' depends on "some intelligible and metaphysically defensible idea of 'nothing,' there is no warrant in speaking of 'the contingency of the world.'" (Munitz, 1965, 144)

But what if the Why question does not depend on an attempt to make metaphysical sense of 'nothing'? Munitz acknowledges that despite the force of critiques of the notion of an absolute 'nothing,' "one cannot help suppressing the belief, nevertheless, that somehow they do not go to the root of the matter." It would seem that somehow the word 'nothing' is needed to express the underlying primordial sense of wonder at the world's existence. And yet, he says, we cannot arrive at a solution to the Why question that will "constructively serve the interests of philosophy" unless we can give "a proper formulation of the mystery of existence without using the concept 'Nothing.'" (Munitz, 1965, 150-151). Until we see what Munitz substitutes as a "proper formulation" of the question, it is not clear why he thinks that, despite the fact some feel the "need" for using the term 'nothing,' a reformulation of the question without the term is what is needed. Would it still express the same feeling? Would it still ask the same question? And, could we still speak of the contingency of the world?

Munitz's skepticism about a formulation of the Why question that relies on the use of the term 'nothing' is that is implies a notion of the contingency of the world that stands or falls with a particular metaphysical tradition. The Greeks, he reminds us, did *not* ask *why* the world exists, but rather *how* it got to be the *way* it is (Munitz, 1965, 156). That question only arose in the interval between the Greeks and its metaphysical formulation by Leibniz with the intervention of what he terms "Hebraic-Christian creationalistic theism," in particular, the creation *ex nihilo* doctrine (Munitz, 1965, 157). Once the question was taken over by the metaphysical tradition there is a tendency to forget one very crucial underlying fact, says Munitz, and that is that the Why question, when formulated in dependence on an absolute sense of 'nothing,' relies upon theism for its sense. "It would be a mistake.. to assume that this question is meaningful apart from the context of theistic metaphysics" (Munitz, *ibid.*). Apart from that context, Munitz argues, the question has no independent meaning.

In fact, says Munitz, the statement, "there might not have been a world," which is derived from the question "why does the world exist rather than nothing?" is in fact a "depleted or degenerate," a "malformed" expression. It cannot stand on its own apart from that historical context of theism. Further, the assumption that the question itself *must* have an answer itself rests, as Post also pointed out, on the false presupposition of the PSR. In other words, by ignoring the theistic framework which alone gives it meaning and the discredited metaphysical principle it tacitly supposes, the Why question is "a gross example of begging the question ... In the absence of this background, the statement lacks meaning; with the use of this background, it begs the question" (Munitz, 1965, 157-159).

Nevertheless some might reject theism and still insist that the Why question makes non-question-begging sense. They might argue that the idea that the world might not have existed is "complete and intelligible" in its own right. They would reject Munitz's claim that adding the word 'nothing' "does not...in any way enlarge or add to this question." (Munitz, 1965, 159). They might wish to say that in fact invoking the notion of 'nothing' "is intended to express...the fact of the *pure* contingency of the world." (Munitz, 1965, 158, my emphasis). Munitz does not really reply to this suggestion, and yet it contains *in nuce* the possibility of an entirely different approach to the Why question, one that does not rely upon a theistic metaphysics, one that in fact abjures such a context as itself misleading for a proper understanding of the meaning and "answer" to the question. That, at least, is a line of inquiry that should not simply be dropped without further discussion. Otherwise one might suspect Munitz himself is guilty of begging the question.

What makes the idea of the *pure* contingency of the world so suggestive is its use in a *non-relative,* that is, *absolute* sense of the term. A "non-relative" or "absolute" sense of contingency would not be dependent for its meaning upon any contrastive notion of "necessary" existence such as ascribed to God in a theistic context. This is brought out in particular by its pairing with an equally "pure," i.e. non-relative or absolute sense of 'nothing.' This has further ramifications. If the relative distinction between contingency and its metaphysical opposite, necessity, collapses in a "pure" use of "contingency," what must this imply for its dialectical partner? At the conceptual limits of the use of these terms, does the distinction between them itself collapse into an "identity of opposites"? Or is it simply as Kant argued that the attempt to apply either of these terms to the existence of the world generates only "antinomies," irresolvable paradoxes, logical contradictions? A formulation of the Why question that includes an apparently "absolute" sense of 'nothing,' if it is to have meaning apart from a theistic metaphysics, must require a "logic" as unique, as "absolute," as the question itself.

Against the Necessity of the World's Existence

But let us, for the moment, defer that possibility, and instead acquiesce in Munitz's argument that the appearance of the word 'nothing' in the Why question makes no sense apart from a theistic context, and that accordingly it makes no sense to speak of the contingency of the world's existence save as a misleading way of expressing awe at its existence. If this is his position, it would seem he is committed to some version of Rundle's or Post's argument that the world *has* to exist, that the world's existence is *necessary*. And yet Munitz rejects this view too. But why and how?

Munitz acknowledges that there are those such as Rundle and Post who argue that "there is no genuine mystery of existence since the existence of the world is *necessary*...in the sense that its existence is entirely self-sufficient and self-explanatory." However, Munitz proposes to argue that, on the contrary, "we are not helped, in the slightest degree, by this line of thought, to dispense with the need for recognizing a mystery in the existence of the world, and that, moreover, there are no good reasons for saying that the existence of the world is necessary" (Munitz, 1965, 160-161). On the face of it this is an astonishing claim! If the existence of the world is not contingent upon some other, presumably necessary reality, then surely its existence must be necessary in and of itself! How then can we continue to speak of a "mystery" unless, to quote Munitz back at himself, this is simply a misleading way of expressing our awe in the face of that tremendous fact. It would seem Munitz still has some work to do.

The problem with the notion of "necessary existence," says Munitz, is that to be intelligible what it is that is said to exist necessarily would have also to be *causa sui*. Not only would it have to explain the existence of everything else, it would have to explain itself. (Munitz, 1965, 168). That means it would be invoking the Principle of Sufficient Reason to explain its own existence. However, says Munitz, "we do *not* have a 'clear and distinct idea' of a being whose existence is necessary by its own nature, or that is *'causa sui'*" (Munitz, 1965, 169). Munitz cites the case of Spinoza's for whom "necessary existence" (which he ascribes to the being of God) has a *double* meaning or what he might call "a negative and a positive aspect." Negatively, "to say God necessarily exists means that God's existence is unlimited, i.e., not contingent on something else." Positively, it means that "God's existence is intelligible, i.e., to be explained by reference to His own nature." (Munitz, 1965, 169)

Applying this distinction instead to the existence of the world itself, Munitz says, "If by saying the world's existence is necessary, one means only that the existence of the world is not causally dependent on some transcendent reality, there need be no objection (in this special, *negative* sense of 'necessary existence') to saying that the world has necessary existence." (Munitz, *ibid.*) But this is "necessary existence" in only a "limited, negative, special sense." It does not require invoking PSR. The problem is that this negative sense of "necessary existence" in no way licenses the further *positive* claim that the world's existence is necessary in the sense that its existence is intelligible by virtue of its own nature. (Munitz, 1965, 169-170). And yet that is what is required if we are to say that the world's existence is not ultimately a mystery.

Like Post, Munitz argues that the attempt to give positive meaning to the notion of necessary existence involves appeal to PSR, namely, the (false) presupposition that *some* "explanation" must be found for the world's existence. And while appeal to PSR is alright within the bounds of scientific explanation, its extension to a metaphysical principle is what Munitz, like Post, finds problematic. Further, says Munitz, the use of such expressions as 'necessarily exists,' 'necessary existence,' and *'causa sui'*, or for example the claim by "naturalistic" philosophers that the world is 'self-sufficient,' "far from serving to make the existence of the world intelligible, are, in fact, verbal disguises for the failure to contribute to such understanding." (Munitz, 1965, 171) Perhaps we can see them as hidden tautologies, those who employ them hoping that if they repeat them often enough, like philosophical mantras, we will be lulled into thinking we have actually said something positive and meaningful.

In concluding his critique of the notion, Munitz asks: "How...is the statement that the world *necessarily exists* any different from the statement that the world *exists*? ... We are not helped...by being told the world exists because it has necessary existence. All that is being done, in the absence of a genuine explanation, is to repeat the very fact to be explained, and to offer this fact as its own explanation... we don't know any more, in the sense of having an explanation of the existence of the world, in being told it is part of the essence of the world. To say it is part of the essence of the word, is merely to restate the fact which calls for an explanation; it is not to give the explanation." And so, we still find ourselves asking, "*Why* does the world exist?" (Munitz, 1965, 173). Unless and until we can answer that question, the mystery remains.

We have already heard this criticism of a "positive" notion of "necessary existence" somewhere else. It is Post's argument rejecting the intelligibility of a notion of necessary existence as logically self-explanatory. And yet Post does not conclude that therefore the world's existence ultimately remains a mystery. He argues that it can still be said that the world's existence is necessary in a positive sense insofar as it functions as a metaphysical "ultimate explainer." But if so, we must ask once again, is Munitz's conclusion really differ from such an account? Perhaps what Munitz means by saying the existence of the world is ultimately a mystery is nothing more than saying the existence of the world is not its own explanation though necessarily it is the final explainer of everything else. To this Post would certainly agree.

And yet. For Munitz the problem with metaphysical answers that use the categories of contingent existence or necessary existence, even if that latter is reinterpreted in terms of "ultimate explanations/ultimate explainers," is that they rest on a false presupposition. They assume that the *kind of mystery* pointed to by the Why question can be answered in the "scientific" (empirical or metaphysical) way that has characterized the philosophical tradition from Aristotle to the present. In other words, they assume that there is a *reason why* for the existence of the world, that a *rational account* can be given. But, as already suggested, what if the "logic" of this question is unique? What if it points to a phenomenon for which there is no "reason why"? What if the world exists "without why"? Is this what Munitz intends to argue in his reformulation of the question? Or does his own formulation itself finally fail to capture the odd "logic" that gives sense of the question? To decide this final matter, we must examine what he means when he says there is no "reason why" for the existence of the world, that the world's existence is at bottom a mystery.

Munitz on Reasons Why

To defend this claim, the question Munitz must answer is this: "Is there any way in which we can formulate what the mystery of existence is, without adopting either the Principle of Sufficient Reason, or one or another of the views that the existence of the world is contingent or that it is necessary?" (Munitz, 1965, 177)

Munitz's strategy is to reformulate the Why question by eliminating the word "why" because, he claims, it inevitably brings with it the misleading assumption that there is a reason to be found, specifically by way of PSR. He has also already eliminated the word "nothing" because of its history of association with theistic metaphysics. To avoid these two problems, he proposes to ask instead, "Is there a reason for the world's existence?" However, he will argue that even this question too is unanswerable, that it is simply another way of expressing "the proper mystery of existence." By "unanswerable" he means "there is no rational method already known...by which this question can be answered." If he can establish this claim, "that we have no way of assuring ourselves either as to an affirmative or negative answer to this question," we will then be in a position to conclude that "the only sound philosophic view to adopt ... is one of agnosticism." (Munitz, 1965, 178)

In evaluating Munitz' strategy and conclusion we will ask several questions of our own: Is the question about the world's existence, as reformulated, the same question, cognitively considered, as the original question, just phrased differently? Is the question as reformulated the same question, emotionally considered, as the original question? Does the answer, that is the "non-answer" of philosophical agnosticism, convey the cognitive import and emotive force of the statement that the existence of the world is ultimately a mystery?

Let us stay with Munitz' reformulated version and see where it takes us. It is not clear how his reformulated version avoids the assumption of PSR. If it does not, is it any better than the original formulation? Munitz himself says the question in this reformulated version is unanswerable. This suggests that he knows it does not represent any improvement over the original, at least in this regard. His solution of philosophical agnosticism confirms this suspicion, for it too tacitly makes sense only if one assumes PSR. If so, it is possible that his reformulated version together with his declared agnosticism, rather than concluding the matter, simply creates new problems.

But let us see. His argument rests on applying the notions of "reasons" and "rational method" to the mystery of the world's existence.

"Reasons."

As we have already seen, he breaks down the notion of a "reason" into four types: a reason as the purpose of, say, an action; a reason as the explanation of some phenomenon; a reason as the cause of some phenomenon; and a reason as the evidence of a statement or belief. (Munitz, 1965, 180) Given his rejection of theism, it is clear that asking for the reason of the world's existence is not asking for the purpose of its being. He has also ruled out providing a reason for the world's existence in terms of a transcendent cause or a notion of self-caused being (*causa sui*). Nor is it asking for the reason of the world's existence a matter of asking for evidence of its existence. It would seem, therefore, that asking for the reason of the world's existence must mean asking for an explanation for its being. So his reformulated question, "Is there a reason for the world's existence?" cannot be answered by citing a purpose or cause, but rather must be understood as asking "Is there an explanation for the world's existence?".

"Rational Method."

Munitz notes that when "rational" is used to characterize a method it has not only a descriptive but also an evaluative sense. (Munitz, 1965, 190). A method involves a distinctive "logic" that spells out the specific rules and criteria that belong to a particular discipline and define the epistemic force of evidence for that area (Munitz, 1965, 192). Different types of inquiry, different "sciences" such as mathematics, law, the empirical sciences, philosophy, theology, metaphysics, will all be characterized by the different "logics," different rules of discourse, that sketch the boundaries of that "science." The problem in the allegedly unique case of the world, however, is whether there is a "logic," a rational method, that limns an epistemological space within which one can ask and evaluate answers to the question about its existence. If there is not, that is tantamount to saying that the question, whether in its original form or its reformulated version, is meaningless – either logically ill-formed or resting on a false presupposition. Would even the stance of philosophical agnosticism be sustainable in that case? On the other hand, if there is a "logic" supporting the question of the world's existence, what must it look like?

Reason, Rational Method, and the World's Existence

With these preliminary considerations of "reasons" and "rational method," Munitz turns to the question, "Is there a reason for the world's existence?," more specifically, "Is there an explanation for the world's existence?" If there is, this means there a rational method which legitimates the search for an explanation of the world's existence, in other words, a logic which gives sense to the question and its possible answers. Munitz's answer in brief will be: There is no reason for the world's existence, no explanation can be given, because there is no rational method by which we could answer such a question, no logic that would give sense to the question or any answer to it. (Munitz, 1965, 194) But this sounds like Post's claim. How then is Munitz's "philosophical agnosticism" saying anything different? Let us look first why Munitz thinks there is no reason for the world's existence. We will then consider why he thinks there is no known rational method by which the question of the world's existence could be answered.

To begin with, he says, none of the four senses of the term 'reason' contribute to making sense of the notion of 'reason for the existence of the world.' (Munitz, 1965, 194) The world is not a "statement" for which evidence could be sought. (Munitz, 1965, 194-197). Since Munitz has already rejected a theistic amount, he rejects the view that the world is something that was "made" for which a purposive cause could be sought. (Munitz, 1965, 201-209). Finally, the world is neither an occurrence, an individual event that could be explained by an empirical law or regularity, nor is it a regularity for which an explanatory theory could be sought. (Munitz, 1965, 197-201). What is meant by 'the existence of the world' is, by definition, unique. (Munitz, 1965, 199) Though Munitz does not explicitly say so, the point is not that the existence of the world (i.e. in the sense of the known cosmological order) is empirically unique (there may be other 'worlds'), it is that it is logically unique. Munitz alludes to this point when he observes, "Though we are given the world *as existing,* we are not given the world *as designed.*" (Munitz, 1965, 209; my italics). What is unique is not the empirically known *kosmos,* it is the *fact* that there *exists* a world (or worlds) *at all.* In sum, there is no "plausible ground either of applying directly, or extending, the normal use of these terms, to serve the purpose of clarifying what might be meant by 'a reason for the existence of the world.'" (Munitz, 1965, 202)

With this apparently negative conclusion, have we then come to the end of our exploration? Munitz recognizes that some might think so. He thinks, however, that there is more to be said, more that is positive, at least to the extent of supporting a position of agnosticism. Let us follow his train of reasoning.

One way to sum up what has been said to far is to say that 'the mystery of existence' means, *in part,* "There is no reason for the existence of the world, *because* it makes no sense to look for it." Why does he add, "in part"? Does he think there is anything more to be said about the phrase, 'the mystery of the world's existence'? For if not, then we must agree with those critics who argue that the phrase hides a confusion of thought. If there is no point to speaking of a reason for the world's existence then there is no point to asking the question, nor is there any reason for "puzzlement at the lack of finding an answer." Therefore we should simply "dissolve our original problem altogether." We should say that the phrase "no longer identifies a genuine human experience of the world; it expresses a misguided and confused way of thinking about it." In saying there is no reason for the world's existence, "we should be saying all that can properly be said from a critical, philosophical point of view." (Munitz, 1965, 210)

If we adopt this critique, however, we are not saying, and here Munitz agrees with the point Post strongly made, that 'the world is irrational.' On this view the existence of the world would be neither rational nor irrational. Such terms, says Munitz, apply to statements or explanations, not to the existence of the world itself. (Munitz, 1965, 210-211) Rather, if we accept this line of critical reasoning, we would be saying simply that the discussion must end at this point. The only alternatives, says Munitz, are the two stated at the outset of his inquiry: The phrase, 'the mystery of existence,' or the question, 'is there a reason for the world's existence?,' expresses a "confused and misguided way of thinking." Or, if "clarified and reconstructed," it could have "positive, conceptual value, and should be incorporated into any sound philosophy." The critic is opting for the first alternative. Munitz, however, wishes to plump for the latter. To opt for the first, he says, "would be unsatisfactory ... this does not provide for a complete analysis; it does not give us any clue as to what, in addition, the phrase can be taken to connote" (Munitz, 1965, 211).

But having reached the conclusion that there is no reason for the world's existence, how can Munitz think there is still any "positive, conceptual value" to be found in that negative conclusion? In particular, why should we think his notion of agnosticism has any positive philosophical meaning beyond the critical position just described? But there is a positive meaning to the phrase, 'the mystery of existence,' he insists. The notion of 'mystery' is "a useful conceptual shorthand for a genuine philosophic idea," namely, 'agnosticism.' Thus, "the complete idea of the mystery of existence...can then be summed up by the following two statements: There is no *reason* for the existence of the world; we have no way of knowing, by any *rational method*, whether is, or is not, a reason-for-the-existence-of-the-world." (Munitz, 1965, 212, italics mine). In short, the very fact that the question, is there a reason for the existence of the world is unanswerable is "an essential part of what we mean by the mystery of existence." (Munitz, 1965, 214).

What if there were a reason-for-the-existence-of-the-world [REW], says Munitz. "It would have to be an explanation as unique as the unique fact of the world's existence itself." It could not be an explanation of any of the four types of reason already noted, i.e., explanations regarding beliefs or statements, purposive actions, or empirical events or regularities. "It would explain *that* existence, and nothing else." (Munitz, 1965, 213-214.) But since we do not know whether or not there is an REW, "all we can say is that, if there were such...and if it were known, it too, would explain in its own distinctive way, its distinctive object–the existence of the world." Therefore, if we wish despite that agnosticism to continue to speak of a REW, at best if would have to be viewed as "gap-schema," a place-holder holding open "a 'place' in the 'logical space' of explanations or reasons... All we are entitled to do...is to leave room for such a reason, if it exists." (Munitz, 1965, 214)

Munitz has more to say in defense of his understanding of philosophical agnosticism, but before we consider that, a few comments seem in order on the foregoing.

First, it seems strange to argue that, while (we *do know* that) there is *no reason* for the existence of the world, yet we *do not know* (have no rational method for knowing) whether there is *no reason* (or a reason) for the existence of the world. Does adding hyphens to the latter phrase somehow undo the apparent contradiction of trying to hold the two beliefs simultaneously?

Even if that dilemma can be resolved, it is hard to see how adding a second 'no' – not only *no reason* but also *no rational method* – can somehow convert those two negatives into a "positive" philosophical position.

Third, there seems to be another inconsistency. On the one hand, he says there is no reason, no explanation for the existence of the world that would satisfy any of the well-established notions of reason or explanation, unless it was as "unique" as the existence of the world itself. This seems a throw-away gesture since it implies that in fact there is no reason, no explanation. On the other hand, he then apparently back-tracks, at least to the extent of saying, well, perhaps we can leave that question open, leave a logical space for a possible reason or explanation. This reflects the ambiguity, if not contradiction, between the two parts of his "complete idea" of the mystery of existence. One would have to be nervous that such an logical space would leave an opening for reintroducing, say, the famous 'God of the gaps.' Again, how would such philosophical agnosticism differ, for example, from Kant's critique of metaphysics that "left room for faith"?

Philosophical Agnosticism

Perhaps Munitz can clarify these matters by spelling out what he means by "philosophical agnosticism." He identifies four possible types of human experience involving "intellectual activities" that could be classed as rational methods: common sense, science, religious experience, and philosophy. We can pass over the first two, common sense and its more formal expression in science. He has already argued that the forms of rational explanation in science do not apply to the unique case of the world's existence.

But what about this third type, religious experience? We have seen how Post has said that while the Why question may lack cognitive significance, it may express a powerful religious or mystical emotion vis-a-vis the awe-inspiring fact of the universe. By "religious experience" Munitz means "a non-inferential mode of awareness...regarded as having transcendently important cognitive worth...commonly recognized to be wholly different in character and subject matter from other modes of experience." (Munitz, 1965, 223) By this definition Munitz means to exclude any theological metaphysics since religious experience is held to be valid apart from appeals to rational argument. That does not mean it is therefore 'non-rational,' but insofar as religious experience is thus restricted, what *cognitive* value can it have as a 'method' for establishing a REW? (Munitz, 1965, 223-225). Are such experiences "merely expressions of deeply felt human yearnings, or the projections of human imagination and its myth-making propensities". Or are they, to the contrary, "revelations of some independently existing, objective reality?" (Munitz, 1965, 225)

The problem with religious experience, on this definition at least, is that "one cannot appeal to the experiences themselves to establish [the latter possibility]; they are not self-authenticating." How distinguish the genuine from the false claims of such experiences apart from "supporting, public tests, or independent criteria of corroboration"? (Munitz, 1965, 226). Such an appeal would mean going beyond "the domain of feeling and private experience." In other words, it would mean having resort to the fourth kind of "intellectual activity" for determining the truth of things, philosophical argument based on an independently warranted "scheme of metaphysics or theology."

Before we turn to that fourth kind of 'method,' a few comments on Munitz's understanding of religious experience. He explicitly relies on Rudolf Otto's famous account of religious experience as involving a "sense of the numinous", a complex of allegedly transcendent awareness and emotion, feelings and attitudes, "that baffles and defeats all attempts at rational, conceptual understanding" (Munitz, 1965, 224). The problem with this account of religious experience is that Otto's description, along with similar interpretations put forward by William James and others, as some kind of conceptually innocent, theoretically ineffable "subjective" or "private" experience, has been subjected to devastating critique by Wittgenstein and others. According to this alternative analysis, there is no such thing as "pure" religious experience that is not already theory-laden. Contrary to Munitz's claim, there are in fact "supporting, public tests and or independent criteria of corroboration" for attesting to the cognitive meaning and significance of such experience. For this reason, at least, we perhaps should not be so hasty as Munitz to dismiss the possibility that religious experience, for all its emotive and attitudinal content, may also have cognitive import. We should at least say at this point, case not (yet) proven.

That brings us to Munitz's fourth type of rational method for addressing the REW, philosophical argument grounded in schemes of metaphysics or theology. Munitz examines "the two types of philosophical activity ... 'conceptual analysis' and 'construction of a metaphysical world-view'." (Munitz, 1965, 227)

Munitz dismisses the first type of philosophy as offering a method for answering the REW question. Philosophy as *conceptual analysis* limits itself, as the name implies, to the analysis of concepts, it does not engage in making factual assertions about what exists. To be sure, if an analysis of the concepts involved in the REW question can show the question is logically malformed, then that can *dissolve* the question. But if it can be shown that the question is not logically malformed, as Munitz has previously argued, then the method of conceptual analysis cannot provide an answer one way or the other to the factual question, 'is there a reason for the existence of the world?' "The philosopher qua conceptual analyst is ideologically neutral." Munitz, 1965, 231, 227-234 passim)

Munitz next considers whether philosophy as *metaphysics*, in particular as the construction of world-views, can provide a method for answering the REW question. He canvasses several varieties of metaphysics so defined, dividing them roughly into two kinds, 'realist' and 'conceptualist.' According to the metaphysical realist (Post would be a good example), metaphysics is "a body of discourse whose statements and arguments can be judged in terms of their literal truth and falsity; it is the proper task of metaphysics to give us a uniquely correct picture of the world" (Munitz, 1965, 239). Munitz finds this traditional view of metaphysics inadequate. While he grants he cannot prove that claim, the very notion of "the world as it really is" already presupposes some particular metaphysical *interpretation* (Munitz,1965, 252). This means we need to consider a 'non-realist,' that is, 'conceptualist' or 'instrumentalist' views of the cognitive nature of metaphysics.

According to one version of this view, metaphysics develops conceptual models employing analogies or 'root metaphors' for integrating a wide range of facts into an overarching theory about the nature of the world. (Munitz, 1965, 241-244) On another version, the cognitive status of metaphysical statements and arguments rests on 'absolute presuppositions' that provide an ultimate conceptual framework for ways of understanding the world. (Munitz, 1965, 244-245) In a third version, metaphysics does not give explanations of a factual sort, but rather provides a 'point of view' for arguments of all kinds, like a lawyer might do in building a case. Metaphysics on this view calls not for proof or verification but for decision, advocacy, for a particular vision of the world. (Munitz, 1965, 246-248).

Munitz concludes that the metaphysical construction of "world-views," despite its intellectual power to integrate an unrestricted range of facts, is nevertheless unable to offer a rational method for answering the REW question. Metaphysics "constitutes a way of regarding the world, and nothing more." (Munitz, 1965, 251) It is a way of interpreting *how* the world is, not explaining *why* it is, let alone addressing the fact *that* it is. We cannot step outside of our metaphysical systems to look at the world "directly" in order to determine which particular world-view is truer than some other. The only course of wisdom, therefore, is to abstain from making such judgments altogether (Munitz, 1965, 253). Faced with the question 'is there a reason for the world's existence?' the only *positive* position we can adopt is philosophical *agnosticism*.

Munitz anticipates there will be objections to his view of philosophy, metaphysics, and agnosticism. For example, it could be argued that, despite his claim that his agnosticism is philosophically grounded, what his sense of mystery in the final analysis amounts to "simply a sense of astonishment, an emotional reaction, and nothing more." (Munitz, 1965, 256) Further, it could be argued that he locates the mystery in the wrong place. It is the existence of the world, not the human inability of answering the Why question, that is the primary fact in analyzing the mystery of existence. (Munitz, 1965, 258)

In reply to the first objection, Munitz contends that the very *asking* of the Why question together with the fact that we *know* that it is unanswerable by any rational method "is as essential to what the mystery is, as the feeling that accompanies it." Thus we are not "reducing" the awareness of the mystery to "nothing more than an emotion of astonishment." (Munitz, 1965, 257)

As for the second objection, Munitz agrees that it is the *fact* of "the existence of the world which arouses our sense of mystery." Further, "if mystery were nothing more than statement of human ignorance – a fact about us alone -- and not, also, about the world, the analysis would be faulty." However, "it is not the existence of the world, alone, that is the mystery; it is the fact that we, who are aware of the existence of the world, ask the kinds of questions we do.... The mystery, so to speak, is in the relation, or interaction, between the puzzled mind and the existence of the world, not in either one, taken separately." That the Why question is unanswerable "tells us something about ourselves *responding* to the existence of the world *in a special way*, in terms of an unanswerable question." (Munitz, 1965, 258, my italics)

Munitz's replies are helpful, but as always, raise further questions. Perhaps the basic question about his philosophical 'agnosticism' at this point, in addition to the two he addresses, is this: Why do we have "no way of knowing"? What do we mean when say that? Does it necessarily mean there could be a reason but we cannot know whether there is or not? This would imply that it makes sense to ask an unanswerable question, that in some sense the rules of reason still apply. But there is another possibility, not that do not know the answer one way or the other, but that here knowledge runs out, that in that respect the question does not make cognitive sense. It would not be an issue of suspended cognition, except to say that we know that the question cannot be asked, or answered, at all at this point. Perhaps in that sense Post is right. Here explanation, the quest for an explanation, runs out, makes no sense. The difference from Post is that we would not then try to make positive metaphysical statements about the necessity of the world's existence. The point is rather the necessity of the limits of knowledge, of asking and answering. In a sense it could be said we *do* know something, not that we do not know the answer to the mystery of existence, but that at this limit it makes no sense to speak either of knowing *or not knowing*.

At this point, then, we can sketch four positions. *Rundle*: the Why question makes sense and we can know the (metaphysical) answer, namely, that the world exists necessarily. *Post*: the Why question does not make sense, but paradoxically we can "answer" it: the existence of the universe is itself the final (metaphysical) explainer, the ultimate (metaphysical) explanation of all else, though not of itself. *Munitz*: the question makes cognitive sense, but there is no known way which we can answer the question one way or the other, thus (metaphysical) agnosticism. A fourth possibility: In one sense the question make no sense in that, as Post argues, the world simply exists but for no reason. We can also say, however, with Munitz, that it makes no sense to ascribe necessary existence to the universe either. As Hawking says (minus Post's metaphysical ascriptions), the universe just exists, just be's. That is not an answer to any question. And yet there is still the possibility to be considered, as alluded to by all three of these thinkers, that the Why question does make sense insofar as it points to the ultimate limits of reason *in a way* that calls for an existential response to the cognitive situation of not-knowing in the face of the just be-ing of the world.

To conclude: For Munitz, this analysis of the mystery of existence provides "some first (or last) words that need to be said in working out a more complete philosophical outlook on the world at large" (Munitz, 1965, 263). The positive contribution of Munitz's analysis lies in his preservation of our primordial sense of the mystery of existence, and in his insistence upon the cognitive significance of the Why question, his refusal to reduce it to the feelings to which it gives rise. What is lacking and only touched upon in his two replies to the anticipated objections, however, what we still need, is a more explicit analysis of the nature of the link between that cognitive awareness and the feelings of awe and astonishment and existential responses of joy and gratitude to which it can give rise. That is the subject we will address in the Part Two of this study.

In the meantime, perhaps we can conclude this first part of our discussion of the Why question by applying to it Winston Churchill's oft-quoted phrase: "It is a riddle, wrapped in a mystery, inside an enigma; but perhaps there is a key." That "key" is the subject of Part Two in which we move from considering the foregoing arguments that the question of the mystery of existence cannot be asked or answered to a different set of claims that the Why question *can* be answered. The "key" will be found in an epistemic register that draws on a "way of thinking" – a "logic" and "reason" – as unique as the existence of the world itself – of something, rather than nothing.

PART TWO

Answering the Why Question:

(I) West

Whatever our final theory of physics, we will be left facing an irreducible mystery. For perhaps there could have been nothing at all. Not even empty space, but just absolutely nothing! ... The religious person is left with a mystery which is no less than the mystery with which science leaves us. – Steven Weinberg

God is a question, not an answer. – Kamel Daoud, *The Meursault Investigation*

Introduction

The Why Question Revisited

As we previously noted in the first part of this study, there are at least two ways the 'Why' aspect of the Why question can be understood. This is owing to the apparently common reference to the existence of the world. There is, on the one hand, what we could call the 'objective' mode of posing the question, a *scientific* or *metaphysical* way of asking that looks for, say, the cause for the world's existence – perhaps a First Cause, whether 'natural' or 'super-natural.' This is the way of asking the question we have been following so far, the way presupposed in the discussions by Post, Rundle and even Munitz, even though Munitz could be listed under the 'ultimate mystery' view. There is another way of asking the question, however, what we might call a 'subjective' or *existential* mode of inquiry that *links* the question of the existence of the world to the meaning of our own being-in-the-world, perhaps reflecting what William James called our 'ontological wonder-sickness.' This is a mode of questioning followed by existentialist philosophers like Heidegger or existentialist theologians like Tillich. Curiously, however, a gesture in that direction also crops up fleetingly in/as subjective 'moments' in the objectively-oriented (scientifically or metaphysically oriented) treatments of Post, Rundle and especially Munitz.

And so in Part Two we propose to consider the possibility of another analysis of the Why question, an alternative logical and conceptual framework or "logic" for understanding the question. This will involve an analysis of the logical and cognitive significance of the "affective" or "existential" phenomena linked with the original question.

At the end of our previous discussion, we arrived at a point where the choice seemed clear: either the Why question has a metaphysical answer and the alleged mystery is dissolved (Post, Rundle), or there is no explanation for the world's existence and the mystery remains (Munitz).

One way of trying to reconcile the two apparently conflicting views was to see each as a version of the underlying claim that the existence of the world was a 'brute fact,' that the world was 'just there,' or as Hawking put it, that the universe 'just Be's' – whether necessarily so or for reasons beyond our fathom.

But on one matter all three thinkers seemed to agree: the Why question is almost always accompanied by a strong affect that is left unsatisfied, unaddressed, no matter the philosophical answer, whether scientific, metaphysical, or even theological. This suggests that there is an additional dimension to the question, that it conceals an additional level of meaning or some further kind of sense, some reason we have not yet uncovered as to why in pointing to the ultimate limits of reason it does so in a way that elicits an emotional response to the cognitive situation of the 'just be-ing' of the world. If so, the question is why. The original Why question, til now considered only in its cognitive meaning, seems to bring with it this further question about an apparent link between its cognitive dimension and the affective responses it provokes.

This suggests that we must rethink the Why question as serving a different or more complex interrogative function. If so, we may find that, thus reconsidered, perhaps it can be both meaningfully asked and meaningfully answered, and, moreover, in way that protects and preserves the ultimate mystery of existence. More specifically, I shall argue that the original Why question itself can and indeed must be, can only be finally be, understood by means of an alternative, existential-ontological approach to being and nothing, of world and thinking, of which the categories of 'cosmological metaphysics' presupposed by the three thinkers we have been considering thus far may be seen as 'derivative' forms.

I shall argue that only this alternative approach makes it possible to give a satisfactory answer to the co-primordial aspect of the Why question -- an aspect which we have touched on but not yet addressed, having left it to one side in our discussion so far. That is the question of the logical link between our cognitive awareness of the mystery of existence and our existential responses -- the deep emotions, negative and positive -- to which that awareness gives rise. It is a question which, though they have spoken to it, none of our three thinkers, insofar as they rely on traditional categories of metaphysics, have given a satisfactory answer.

One might ask, however, why the question of our emotional responses to the Why question is even a problem, or at least a problem insofar as trying to answer the Why question itself is concerned? What bearing do our emotional responses have on either the logical construal or a possible metaphysical answer to the question why there is something rather than nothing? That such emotions may be inevitable, even subjectively important accompaniments to the question may be granted, but whether they have any relevance to a cognitively meaningful answer to the question seems, on the face of it, at the very least questionable (in German, *fragwuerdig*) if not completely irrelevant.

And yet just as the Why question itself seems to nag at us, despite our best philosophical efforts either to answer or to dissolve it, so it is puzzling why we should continue to react to it so strongly in either case. Is it because of the apparent cognitive impasse we seem to have arrived at vis-a-vis the Why question, or is it in spite of the metaphysical dead-end? Do we need to justify our emotional responses to the awareness of the mystery of existence? Can we, even? Are such emotions simply 'non-cognitive,' that is, as the terminology has it, merely 'expressive'? Just as the world can be said to 'just Be,' can we not say that our emotional responses to that fact 'just Are' – and, as in the case of the world's existence, just let it go at that? But even in that case, does this not suggest that there is, after all, a link of some sort, causal, logical, whatever, between the two facts, the mystery of the world's existence and our existential response to that mystery? Surely, we want to say, there has to be more to the matter than a simple dismissal of such feelings as non-cognitive and hence philosophically extraneous to the question. And in fact, none of the philosophers we have so far considered would deny that these emotional responses are accompanying aspects of the Why question, and that, further, there is some sort of meaningful link between them.

And so, proceeding on that assumption, let us examine further the thesis that, for an answer to the Why question to be philosophically satisfactory it must answer both the cognitive and emotional aspects of the question. More specifically, an answer shall be judged inadequate unless it can explain why particular 'existential' (emotional and evaluative) responses to the Why question are appropriate, that is, justified by criteria reflecting cognitive aspects of the world's existence.

We shall demand of each approach that it explain *why* we respond emotionally to the Why question in the ways we do. It will not be sufficient simply to tell us *that* we do, it will be necessary that they explain *how* and *why* we do in the first place, how and why our emotional responses, both negative and positive, may be said to be justified on rational and cognitive grounds. We must be able to justify the philosophical, more specifically, the metaphysical and epistemological presuppositions that underlie these responses, showing how those presuppositions support the general phenomenon or truth of the fact that our emotions have more than merely 'subjective' force, that they have 'objective,' cognitive force as well.

In what follows we shall examine the answers to this question of the link between the Why question and our emotional responses to it provided not only by the thinkers we have so far considered, but also by other philosophers who have addressed this specific aspect of the question. To make the case that only an existential-ontological interpretation of the original Why question and its link to our existential responses to the Why question is fully satisfactory, we will first have to show how and why the answers to this question offered by Munitz, Post and Rundle are inadequate. This will involve introducing some new participants to the discussion as well.

Witherall on the Why Question

The first of these is the Australian philosopher, Arthur Witherall, who in his book *The Problem of Existence* has perhaps more clearly and explicitly posed the question of the link between the emotive and cognitive aspects of "the problem of existence." I shall turn to him for help in elaborating on and making more precise the rationale for, and issues at stake in, this part of our study. He address the question in the first chapter of his book, "The Fundamental Question of Metaphysics," a title he takes from Heidegger's launching of the question in *An Introduction to Metaphysics*. Witherall says of the question, 'Why is there something rather than nothing at all?' precisely because it is 'fundamental,' there is no ordinary context for addressing it. It arises "at the extreme end of philosophical inquiry... Transcending all of the normal conceptual structures and standards, asking for an explanation beyond any explanatory framework, it seems both inescapable and incalculable." In treating of it, he says, a satisfactory answer, if there is one to be had, must explicitly "draw upon both the intellectual and emotional aspects of human thought" (Witherall, 1). He devotes the remainder of his opening chapter defending his claim.

The context of philosophical questions–for example, questions dealing with reality as a whole, the existence of God, moral values, etc.--he argues, unlike those of science, is too "open-ended." They inevitably involve other considerations as well. Thus, "we cannot understand our answers to philosophical questions in their entirety without understanding the motives and feelings that have occasioned them." This does not mean "rationality" should be excluded, but that "our responses to philosophical questions are often without a background method" that can provide a determinate answer. In such cases "we must therefore draw upon the resources of human nature as a whole" (Witherall, 1).

Witherall then makes an observation that will be crucial for our subsequent discussion of the emotional responses to the Why question: "The range of feelings that may be appropriately occasioned by sincerely asking why anything exists is relatively narrow." If, he says, the question is "interpreted properly," if we understand that it is concerned with "the fact of existence," that "the feelings we have about this fact are prompted in part by the nature of 'our encounter with (possible) nothingness,' then the response-feelings evoked, whether negative or positive, will inevitably be "extreme reactions because they represent the extreme limits of thought." They will mostly lie in the region of such passions as "awe, astonishment, amazement, gratitude, joy, and exultation," what Witherall calls 'positive appreciations' reflecting "a positive encounter with the fact of existence," or their negative counterparts, 'negative appreciations' such as fear, anxiety, despair, nausea or hopelessness expressing a negative response in the face of existence (Witherall, 2).

Several points make this observation philosophically significant for our inquiry. First, as Witherall says, it puts "limits to the emotional basis" of an answer. It rules out certain kinds of emotions. For example, not only feelings such as "contempt, lust, revenge, pride, anger or pity, but even "moral emotions are largely irrelevant" as answers to what is "a strictly metaphysical question." On the other hand, "some religious feelings may be relevant," gratitude or joy, though others such as piety or holiness not (Witherall, 2).

Next, and even more intriguing, he maintains that both kinds of 'extreme' appreciations, positive and negative, lead to the formulation of corresponding particular answers to the Why question. Here we find a clue to the link between the emotional and intellectual aspects of the question. What is especially interesting about it, however, is the direction of the logical movement between them that his remark suggests. The answer proceeds from the emotional to the intellectual, not, as we have perhaps been assuming, vice versa. This will call for serious rethinking of some fundamental assumptions of the Western philosophical tradition. The question is where we can look to find resources for such fundamental rethinking (Witherall, 2).

Finally, given that the question evokes "distinctive" emotional responses, the question is "whether an answer, if there are any legitimate answers at all, helps to alleviate these feelings." Normally, as we saw in the case of Aristotle's discussion of 'wonder,' an answer eliminates the initial puzzlement that prompted the question. The problem in the case of the Why question is that "it seems possible to continue feeling overwhelmed with awe and wonder, even if one has finished with the problem on an intellectual level." It is, says Witherall, "a peculiar sort of question....it is *essentially* disturbing." (Witherall, 4; my emphasis)

What gives the Why question this "oddity," says Witherall, it is that it is in a sense "the oddity of our total situation." In this question we confront the universe "in its wholeness" like a "predicament in which we find ourselves placed.... When we call the existence of the world into question, we are asking...for some sort of total justification for our 'total situation." The Why question puts not only the world in question, it puts our own existence in question as well. The fact that nevertheless we somehow see ourselves as living a meaningful life in a universe whose existence seems void of any explanation – well, it all "seems very strange." (Witherall, 13)

As the title of his chapter indicates, Witherall acknowledges his debt to Heidegger. While Heidegger was "not the first to address the fundamental question," he did provide an account of "the [intellectual] contexts in which the question has significance, and the kind of [emotional] intuitions we have within those contexts." (Witherall, 14; bracketed insertions mine). Heidegger spoke of the "hidden power" of the question, arising in "moments of great despair, when things tend to lose all their weight and all meaning becomes obscured," but also "is present in moments of rejoicing, when all the things around us are transfigure and seem to be there for the first time," or again "in boredom, when we are equally removed from despair and joy." It is in such moments, says Heidegger, that the Why question "is evoked in a particular form." (Witherall, 14, quotations from Heidegger, 2000, 1-2).

Witherall comments: "What a strange thing this question is.... What kind of meaning must it have to enjoy all of these features?... But if such starkly different moods are all *appropriate* occasions for the question, a problem arises. Do the incompatibility of these moods illustrate that there is some sort of internal inconsistency in the meaning of the inquiry?" Can the Why question be a meaningful and internally consistent one, questions of explanatory framework aside, if it is compatible with all of these incompatible moods? But there is no problem here, he argues, "because joy, despair, and boredom, though mutually exclusive,, are intelligible emotional contexts for addressing the same fact." How so? Because "these different emotions are actually different appreciations of 'the world as a whole'." If so, "then these feelings are not so much occasions for asking a question as they are forms of understanding the world itself."

Does this then mean that the question itself is "superfluous"? Or if it continues to be "relevant," is it because each mood which gives rise to it presupposes the same fact, "namely that there is no reason for the world"? But if this so, "if there is absolutely no reason for world to exist, then there is a correct response to the fundamental question," not that it is an ill-formed query but that "it ends in a blank" (Witherall, 14-15). This of course does not constitute an "answer" in the sense of an "explanation," but Witherall's use of the word "blank" could be construed as saying that the question preserves an "open space" for an appropriate depth-response to our existence vis-a-vis the world-as-a-whole.

In any case, as Witherall says, this response "helps to clarify the oddity of our total situation." If for some thinkers this situation is "so unsettling that it is unacceptable," for others it opens up the possibility of seeking "a different kind of answer." But as Witherall observes, even such an alternative answer will not "dissolve the oddity" of the Why question. "If such a dissolution is what we seek when asking this question, then I do not believe that we shall have it" (Witherall, 15) A "strange question," a strange situation indeed!

In the face of this oddity, this strangeness at the extremities of language and reason, then what should the proper role of philosophy be? Witherall concludes the introductory chapter of his book by turning to this question. "If the fact of existence properly and reasonably produces feelings such as wonder and astonishment," and "if [philosophy] has the ability to explain existence, then does it also have the ability to reduce or eliminate these feelings?" Witherall observes that, as we have already seen with Aristotle and philosophers like Post, "most scientific explanations, when they are successful, immediately dissolve the mystery of the phenomenon which is explained." Providing solutions to theoretical problems may indeed be part of the traditional role of philosophy. That would certainly include assessing the answers philosophers and theologians have put forward in an attempt to answer the Why question as well using "the same general criteria of rationality" used in dealing with other intellectual problems (Witherall, 15)

There is, however, another dimension to the problem, and supremely so in the case of the Why question, and that is its emotional aspect. The question here is whether, as Witherall believes, "philosophy can also seek to elucidate *and encourage* certain feelings" in situations of "profound and intense concerns" like those which confront us vis-a-vis the existence of the world-as-a-whole. Witherall proposes that it be the task of the philosopher to express their analysis of the Why question in such a way as "*to elicit a certain kind of response*." For this purpose a philosophical "answer," whether considered as an "explanation" or not, cannot be cast in "straightfowardly literal terms," but must rather must retain "metaphoric dimensions" of the sort more suited to the expressive nature of the response (Witherall, 15, emphasis mine).

Even then, because of the oddity of trying to answer a question that in one sense cannot even be asked, a "question" arising where explanations have run out, where even the resources of metaphor falter, we must be prepared to acknowledge that "nothing, in the end, will entirely satisfy us." The philosophical must face the fact that "we do not necessarily find that reason if comforting. Sometimes, reason can lead us to its own limits. Questions may remain with us, and retain their enchanting power, forever." (Witherall, 15-16) That "blank" at the end of our investigations must retain its oddity, its strangeness, its "hidden power" to move, disturb, unsettle, frustrate, lure, beckon, invite us. Some questions, the Why question preeminently, Witherall says, resorting to metaphor himself, "even though they are answered and explained, linger on in our souls because the explanation, simple though it may appear, somehow leaves an echo of eternity." Philosophy is thus, or should be, a lesson in

Socratic humility, "a way of flourishing within the wisdom we can attain, whatever that may be (Witherall, 16)

At the conclusion of his book Witherall asks: "How it is possible to seek, let alone to find, a resolution to such an inquiry? Is it not too much for us– and at the same time, do we not demand it all the more passionately because we feel it cannot be obtained?" (Witherall, 154-155) This question, which cannot be answered, cannot even be asked, the Why question, 'the fundamental question of metaphysics,' is perhaps the philosophical question par excellence, the perfect and purest expression of the "love of wisdom," the desire, the passion for truth which, in the face of the mystery of existence, perpetually eludes our final grasp even as it lures us ever on. "Philosophy," says Witherall, "can fulfil itself in its questions." For his part, Witherall leaves us with the following questions:

– what is the nature of the link between certain emotions and the Why question?

– what is the direction of 'movement' between those emotions and the Why question?

– are there limits to the sorts of emotions appropriate vis-a-vis the Why question?

– what is the relation of such emotions to moral, ethical or religious experiences?

– do the explanations or "answers" alleviate, or even eliminate, such emotions?

– is the task of the philosopher not only to account for but to elicit or encourage such emotions or certain emotions in particular?

– does the fact that both negative and positive emotions appear to be compatible as responses to the Why question undermine the coherence of the question itself?

– does the Why question and emotional responses to it call for a different kind or sense of rationality?

– can metaphorical or symbolic language be used to answer the question if literal or scientific language cannot?

– what is the proper 'object' of the Why question – the existence of the world–as-a-whole or the fact that something exists rather than nothing?

– does the difference between these two 'objects' mean different kinds of emotional response are 'appropriate'?

We will do well to be guided by these points as we turn to the answers that other philosophers have given to the Why question. We will be looking in particular at how they illuminate the links between certain 'appreciations,' negative or positive, and our awareness of the existence of the world-as-a-whole or, alternatively, of the fact that there is something rather than nothing.

John Post:
The Metaphysics
of Theism

We turn first to thinkers who give what I term 'cosmological-metaphysical' answers to these questions – John Post and Quentin Smith. In the final three chapters of his book, *The Faces of Existence*, Post returns to explicate more fully an issue he touched on earlier in the book, the question whether human values have any ground in existence. As we noted in our earlier discussion of Post, he dismissed the Why question as a 'pretentious question': "It does not cease to have a false presupposition 'merely because of the co-presence of a curiosity-feeling' when we ask it" (Post, 110). On the other hand, he also referred to "*our* wonder about the whys of things" (Post, 106, emphasis his). Curiosity or wonder? Not quite the same thing. This suggests we must examine whether the explanation he gives of the relation of values to what there is also addresses the phenomenon with which we are concerned, the 'co-presence' of feelings such as awe vis-a-vis, not simply the curious fact that *this* universe exists but, the wondrous fact that there exists anything *at all* rather than nothing.

Metaphysics and Theism

We will begin by looking at his scattered remarks in earlier chapters of his book before turning to a closer look at his extended argument in the concluding chapters. In the opening chapters he lays out the parameters within which he will conduct his analysis of 'values' and 'existence.' Already at the outset he introduces a surprising twist. His grounding of values in existence will include and indeed culminate in his introducing into his rigorously physicalistic but 'nonreductive' metaphysics an unexpected guest – theism! But consistent with his entirely this-worldly metaphysics of the universe, this theistic dimension or 'face' of existence will not include reference to any sort of transcendent entity. "The only metaphysical or ontological theses theologians would need to assume are the physicalist's minimal ones." Beyond that, "theism thus construed would be not a matter of what there objectively is but an equally objective matter of how we ought to experience and talk about what there is... What theologians would need to add to the physicalist's metaphysics is a *normative* argument... even though theologians would still have work to do, it would be work in value theory, or axiology, rather than in metaphysics, or ontology. They would not need to multiply entities beyond what there objectively is in order to defend theism. Thus freed of worries on the score of what there is, they could concentrate instead on persuading us what objectively there ought to be." (Post, 18-19).

Theism as traditionally presented offered an account of the existence of the universe. But in the light of today's cosmology, Post says, this can be dismissed as "a bad explanatory hypothesis." It posits "a superfluous entity...superfluous that is for the purposes of scientific explanation." One is reminded of the legend that Napoleon is said to have asked the famous 18th C. French scientist Laplace where in his mathematico-mechanistic system of the celestial orbits he had included the hand of 'God.' Laplace is said to have replied, *"Je n'avais pas besoin de cette hypothèse-là"* ("I have no need for that hypothesis"). Post nevertheless maintains that theism may still be "crucial in other respects... such rational justification as theism may have...if any, and its point, must lie elsewhere"–namely, in the realm of values (Post, 72).

The word 'objectively' qualifying 'values' in the citation above indicates that Post is advocating a doctrine called 'moral realism.' This is the claim that values are grounded, that is, 'determined' objectively, by what there is. One might ask, however, why such a metaphysics of values should be labeled 'theistic.' It appears to be an attempt to transpose into a naturalistic context values originally grounded in traditional theism but without the transcendent backing required for them. But is such a translation possible? Post himself notes that "many a metaphysical dispute is really a value dispute in disguise." Is the dispute between traditional theism and Post's revisionist theism in fact such a dispute? We will return to these issues when we come to his later chapters. For now we simply note that for Post there is something he labels the objective values of theism, but they are determined by 'what there is,' the existing universe as explained by scientific cosmology, not by anything transcendent to it.

Mystery and Metaphysics

We have already criticized Post's reductive dismissal of the phenomenon of mystery in the context of the Why question. However, though he rejects the question itself as 'falsely posed' and 'pretentious,' in his comments on the emotions that often accompany the alleged question it turns out that he has a lot more to say. So let revisit his remarks.

As we have seen, for Post the only legitimate use of the term 'mystery,' at least in connection with a scientific or metaphysical inquiry, is if the puzzle it poses "seeks an explanation" (Post, 78). Otherwise, as he says, such a question, and preeminently the Why question itself, is simply engaged in 'mystery-mongering.' But in that same chapter on 'Mystery and Ultimate Explanation' Post nevertheless tries to account for the frequent juxtaposition of certain distinctive emotions and values with the Why question. People ask, he notes, "If there is no reason for the existence of the universe, how can there ultimately be any reason for mine?. ... Mustn't they be grounded somehow in the world and thereby in some explanation of why the world is here at all? What if it should prove to be some sort of reptilian indifference to us and our hopes?" (Post, 73-74). Clearly the Why question, whatever its logical status, humbles the mind and stirs the imagination.

True, Post says, and yet in asking the Why question, "are we seeking some sort of explanation? Or are we expressing an emotion?" Often, he suggests, citing Munitz, "it is the latter; we may be expressing anxiety, estrangement, helplessness, regret, astonishment, awe, affirmation, or even joy and exuberance at the fact of existence" (Post, 77; citing Munitz, 1965). But, he argues: "If I am expressing an emotion in asking the question of being...the question expresses no mystery unless I am at the same time also seeking an explanation." At this point Post seems to allude to another possibility. It is possible, he says, that the Why question "might express mystery in some *other* sense of the term, perhaps a feeling *something* is strange, uncanny, eerie, weird, full of wonder" (Post, 78, emphasis his). He adds: "we must never lose the gift of wonder. Indeed, the 'question of being' is used by some philosophers to symbolize the importance of wonder, a holy seeking prepared to transcend received categories of thought and feeling, if need be, to satisfy our hunger to understand" as, for example, Heidegger seems to do (Post, *ibid.*).

Unfortunately he does not explore further what that *'other'* sense might be other than what he has just noted, a 'feeling' unconnected in his mind to any inquiry having possible cognitive sense. Rather, as he immediately adds, "if I express the feeling that the existence of the universe is a wonder, it is hard to see how I would not also thereby be expressing the feeling that its existence is mysterious... that there is... some question about it to which we do not know the answer. And the only question in the neighborhood that might express mysteriousnesss in this deep sense is 'Why does the universe exist at all?' But it expresses a mystery only it seeks an explanation" (Post, *ibid.*) And so he returns to his basic Aristotelian definition of mystery that we have already seen. We may regard this as a lost opportunity to push the question of 'mystery in some *other* sense' further. What if there is another way to understand the Why question, not as seeking an explanation but with a cognitive sense as distinctive as the question itself? In that case might there indeed be another sense of 'mystery' that can account for the link between the Why question and the distinctive emotions cited by Post?

One of the distinctive emotions associated with 'the question of being,' reflected not only in philosophy but in literature and life, is the feeling of the absurdity of existence, including the absurdity of human existence. So-called 'existentialist' philosophical novels like Sartre's *Nausea* or Camus' *The Stranger* can stand as representative expressions. Before concluding his discussion of 'mystery' vis-a-vis (ultimate) explanations, Post addresses the philosophical problems posed for his position by this emotion in particular. "Sometimes when people say that existence is absurd they mean that human values have no ground in existence, that the universe provides no meaning or purpose for life, no reason for our existence." But, he argues, "even if existence were absurd in the sense of not conforming to a norm of rationality by virtue of having no explanation, still it would not follow that existence is absurd in the sense of failing to satisfy the human demand that it ground our values and give meaning to human life. Existence could do these things and yet have no explanation" (Post, 105-106).

But absent a transcendent ground, for example, something like 'the mystical' to which Wittgenstein referred as the ground of 'absolute' values, how would that be possible? How could the fact that the universe exists without explanation, namely, that it 'just be's', satisfy our ethical demand for values or our spiritual demand for meaning and purpose? As Post asked at the beginning of his chapter, "If there is no reason for the existence of the universe, how can there ultimately be any reason for mine?" The answer, he says, is simply and straightforward, though it will require the last three chapters of his book to establish: "Something *within* existence" could ground the values, provide the meaning or meanings (Post, 106).

With this reply, we come to the heart of Post's case for the grounding of values *within* existence, that is, within the universe described by scientific cosmology and interpreted by a physicalist metaphysics. To establish how and why it is that theism plays a foundational if paradoxical role in a naturalist metaphysics, he must first make the case that moral values are grounded in descriptive facts. This he does in a chapter on *facts and values*. Next he must discuss whether it is possible for some values to have ultimate priority over others. This he does in a chapter on *values and worlds*. He will then be in a position to argue that theistic values are grounded in the facts of this world (including the universe as a whole) without the need for appeal to an entity transcending the world. This he does in his concluding chapter on *values and God.*

Facts and Values

In his chapter on the relation of facts and values, Post presents a naturalist but non-reductive version of moral realism. This is a twofold claim. There is a *necessary* dependence of moral facts on natural facts. There can be no moral difference between two states of affairs without some factual differences. Moral facts are in some way *determined* (his term) by natural facts. Hence it is a *naturalist* account of moral values. However, this determination by natural facts is not *sufficient* for a full account of moral facts. Hence it is a *non-reductive* version of moral realism. In the technical language of analytic philosophers like Post, moral facts *supervene* on, in some sense are 'added on' to, natural facts.

Post's theory of a naturalist but non-reductive relationship between values and facts is particularly promising because it could provide a rational account of why certain emotions such as awe or wonder not only "accompany" but are cognitively grounded in the fact of (the world's) existence and thus are not merely subjective expressions of feelings. The alternative to Post's moral realism would be non-cognitive theories of moral value which reject the claim that ethical statements are objective fact-stating propositions describing some feature of the world and which could therefore be true of false. One version, the emotivist theory of logical positivists, claims that ethical statements are primarily emotional expressions of one's attitudes rather than statements of cognitively-grounded moral facts. Another version, prescriptivism, holds that rather than being fact-stating, ethical statements are universal imperatives which prescribe behavior. However, on Post's view both of these versions of noncognitivism ignore the reality that emotional and prescriptive reactions are in fact determined, at least in part, by descriptive features of the world. Hence they are unable to explain, in particular, the cognitive link between awe or wonder and the fact of (the world's) existence.

Though we cannot go into the details of Post's arguments for a naturalist but non-reductive theory of moral values, we can at least get a sense of its major points. The general question we are interested in is this: how can moral facts be said to be *determined* by natural facts, yet values be said to *supervene* on, not be *reducible* to, those facts? To put the issue in somewhat ideological terms: "The basic issue in moral philosophy is precisely how value and obligation fit into the scientific conception of the world." (Post, 274, n. 44: citation from Harmon, 29.)

Post makes it clear at the outset that "What a true moral judgment corresponds with, what makes it true, is a definite class of objective, natural facts, not some shadowy Platonic realm." In other words his version of moral realism does not refer to or posit "any sort of entity or reality" outside of space and time, whether Platonic forms, mathematical entities, or a transcendent deity (Post, 256). Crucial to Post's argument, then, is an answer to the question, "what in the world does a true moral judgment correspond with, and what precisely is this relation of correspondence?" (Post, 266). It is sufficient to defend the core of the moral realist thesis, says Post, if one can show that a moral judgment corresponds ("in a perfectly intelligible sense of 'corresponds'") with at least "a specific piece of the world" (Post, 279).

Post says what he is plumping for is "a new kind of position in meta-ethics–an alternative to the bleak trichotomy entrenched in the aging trivium of naturalism, intutionism, and emotivism." His position of 'determinationism,' he says, differs from a strict naturalism in arguing that "ought is not (or need not be) derivable from is, or definable by or reducible to is, so that moral properties are (or can be) nonnatural properties." On the other hand, it differs from intuitionism "in not making a mystery of the connection between natural and nonnatural properties but explaining it, via determination" (Post, 281). His position differs, in other words, from noncognitivist views such as emotivism and prescriptivism. Post says that he can therefore agree with an Existentialist such as Sartre when he says that ontology cannot formulate ethical values, that "we cannot possibly derive imperatives from ontology's indicatives" (Post, 282, n. 65, citing Sartre, 625), on the one hand, while also agreeing with an Idealist such as Plato that nonethless we can "ground the moral truths in what there is." This is possible, he says, because "moral imperatives are grounded in nonmoral fact, in the sense of determination, even if such grounding by itself enables no one to formulate or derive the imperatives from any indicatives" (Post, 282).

The surprising conclusion to this line of argument is that finally, Post observes, there is no such thing as a "purely scientific description" of the world that is "ethically neutral." Thus, he says, "we are free to regard nature and value as ontologically reunified" (Post, 283). For, as he pointed already in the Introduction to his chapter on Fact and Value, in one sense there is no such thing as "purely descriptive truth." Our decision to talk of objective, natural fact or descriptive truth, "however objective the discourse is, reflects or presupposes as well as reinforces values we may scarcely perceived.... The discourse comes trailing clouds not just of etymology but of value, purpose, emphasis, and mood." So while, in one sense, "there is such a thing as purely descriptive truth," yet in another, perhaps more fundamental sense "no discourse, including the purest description, is value-free. For our decision to use one discourse rather than another reflects and reinforces certain values, even if–strictly speaking–the discourse, via its distinctive vocabulary, expresses none" (Post, 252-253).

Post's ontological observations on the value-laden nature of the discourse of "objective, natural facts," of the sense in which moral fact and natural fact are, in the end, "ontologically unified," is an important contribution to our search for the link, not only cognitive but now possibly metaphysical or ontological as well, between our feelings of awe or wonder and the fact of (the world's) existence itself. Of course he leaves us with several questions at just this point:

What does Post mean when he states that even 'purely scientific description' is 'not ethically neutral'? Does this mean that all descriptions of natural facts are already value-laden? Would it not dissolve the *fact-value distinction* he needs to make the case for a naturalist (though non-reductive) theory of moral values? How can he reconcile that with the claim that while we can ground all moral facts in natural facts, the opposite does not hold true?

What is the notion of *'ontology'* at work in Post's argument? Is it the same use of the term as in the citation from Sartre, which suggests that the realms of fact and value, the indicative and the imperative, cannot in fact by ontologically 'unified'? What is the alternative notion of 'ontology,' what is the concept of 'being' that would support Post's claim that the two realms are or can in fact by ontologically 'unified'? Can it be a strictly physicalistic metaphysics such as Post's if the discourse of that metaphysics is itself already value-laden, or should we say, value-compromised? Or does he have in mind some version of Aristotle's notion of the 'manifold sense' of 'being"? What kind of ontological 'unity' would he then have in mind?

Is it possible to extend his claim that moral values are grounded in natural facts about 'pieces' *of* the world to the further claim that what Wittgenstein called 'absolute' values are similarly grounded in the 'absolute' fact of *(the world's) existence itself*? If, that is, the truth or falsity of moral propositions is determined, hence explained, by facts *within* the world (including the *totality* of such facts, the world-*as-a-whole*), does that mean that our feeling-responses to the world's *existence*, to *the fact of existence itself*, are similarly cognitive? If so, does that mean the alleged *'mystery'* of (the world's) existence is thereby dissolved?

In turning to his next chapter, on the relation of values to worlds, perhaps we can get further purchase on what his answers might be to some of these questions.

Values and Worlds

Post opens this part of his discussion with what seems at first glance a surprising reversal of his physicalistic metaphysics. He admits that the philosophical vision governing his analysis to this point had been "limited," especially when it came to dealing with "non-discursive" realms of human experience that point to "many other ways for us to be and to represent and change ourselves and our world or worlds." Thus he proposes to "broaden the vision"– at least "to some extent"– to include other than propositional forms of truth, types of expression, modes of truth, ways "to live and be," that may on occasion even "enjoy some sort of priority" (Post, 284-5).

Nor is this all. Though philosophers traditionally have tried to "unify all things in relation to a particular domain of truth," they often ignore that "there are many other ways of seeing things whole," no one of which represents "the way things are in themselves, the way the world is, the meaning Being, the ultimate nature of existence." Post thus introduces a radical pluralism into his metaphysics. What accounts for this manyness of "worlds," he says, is that the variety of our ways of representing 'the world,' of 'what there is,' is grounded in our prior choices, that is, our prior values: "Characterization of something as the real, or as 'reality,' reflects a prior choice of vocabulary-cum-metaphor. These choices in turn reflect value judgements... In a sense, therefore, valuing is prior to characterizing something as 'real,' and thus prior to metaphysics and ontology." When we see things this way, he says, "metaphysics and ontology become more a matter of values than of what there is" (Post, 286-287). Not only do values "supervene" on facts, facts themselves, reality itself, turns out to be, dialectically, an expression of prior values. Obviously something very interesting is going on here in the heart of Post's "physicalistic but non-reductive" metaphysics. It seems to have undergone a reversal from a metaphysics-cum-values to an axiology-cum-ontology.

This raises two important questions for his metaphysics and for our inquiry. First, what does Post understand by the 'the world' or, another expression he uses, 'the way of the world'? Second, what does he mean when he speaks of the 'priority' of some ways of valuing 'the world,' or '*seeing* the world *as*,' over others? The two questions are not unrelated. Post suggests the direction his argument will take on the first question with a citation from Nelson Goodman: "And if I am asked what is the way the world is, I must likewise answer, 'none.' For the world is in many ways" (Post, 293). Clearly this impacts the second question. What is at stake is that upon our answer to 'what is the way is the world is? what is the world for us?,' different moral values, different 'ways to live and be' will follow. If there is no one way the world is, no '*the* way' the world is, what would this imply for establishing priorities as to how one *ought* to live and be?

Post canvasses a number of ways that have been proposed for 'the way the world is,' finding each of them wanting, concluding that "the way the world is cannot be the way it is to be seen, pictured, given, described objectively, explained, understood, interpreted, accorded meaning, or accorded an essence." There seems to be "no non-questing-begging" way of deciding among the proposed alternatives. Better to conclude of "the very idea of the way the world is" that "there is no such thing" (Post, 296). But if so, what is "our place" in this multi-perspectival 'world'? "No one place, surely, but many–at least a many as there are ways the world is." Each way of representing the world, of "picturing, seeing, describing, understanding, interpreting, feeling" is a 'map' of the way the world is. Each way of depicting the world is, and the title of his study indicates, one of the many 'faces' of existence, each 'face' an expression of our prior choices, our priorities as to 'ways to live and be' in a world thus seen, a world thus felt. (Post, 297)

This raises a question. Are some of these choices, these priorities, these values more important, more fundamental, than others? Faced with a plethora of possible ways to live and be, can one argue that "a certain sort of interest or purpose is unconditionally more important than all the others, and that a corresponding priority attaches both to our map and to the way of the world it represents?" This, he says, is "the hidden agenda" of many of the monopolistic philosophies that have characterized the metaphysical and theological traditions of the West. Each claims not only a monopoly on describing what there is but also on prescribing what our 'deepest values' ought to be. There is some truth in such monopolistic claims, says Post, but also some untruth too (Post, 297-298). Given the plurality of ways the world is, is it nevertheless still possible to defend "the very idea of ultimate priority"? The answer to this question could have an important bearing on the 'absolute' nature of feeling-responses to the Why question.

Addressing this question, Post makes several distinctions. To argue that one value is unconditionally more important than another is, first, not to say that it alone has intrinsic value.

For many things may be intrinsically valuable "beautiful, desirable, good, worthwhile" and none of them more valuable that all others. Second, for something to be unconditionally or absolutely more valuable is, he says, "either (i) that it is more valuable in every respect, (ii) that it is more valuable everywhere and everywhen, (iii) that there is no circumstance in which may be overridden by the other, or (iv) or some combination of (i-iii)" (Post, 298-299). After considering each of these possibilities, he concludes that none of "the ways the world is...can pretend to be unconditionally more important or valuable than the rest" in all respects, times and places, or circumstances: "talk of unconditional primacy proves after all to be talk of primacy in some respect, in circumstances where that respect is deemed urgent" (Post, 300-301). It would seem, therefore, not possible to make sense, for example, of Wittgenstein's notion of 'absolute values' or 'absolute experiences' when confronted by the mystery of (the world's) existence itself.

Of course, Post recognizes, often "interests are at stake in these struggles" among metaphysicians (and theologians), arguments about the way the world is often being disguised or even open disagreements about the way we ought to live, the right way to be and act as human beings. So it is that "many a dispute among metaphysicians is more a matter of values than of what there is. Frequently, this fact is disguised by uncritical talk of priority, primacy, ground, foundation, primordiality.... With each new insights into ourselves and our world or worlds there comes a powerful temptation to say, 'Here at last is the key to human and other being.' Such insights have included reflections on intentionality, will, dread, boredom, hope, becoming, death, caring." In other words, at stake are the most fundamental truths, the most powerful emotions, the most profound values that describe our world and motivate our lives. "No wonder," Post says, that calling into question the claim that there is only *one* unconditional way the world is, only *one* unconditional truth abut the way we ought to live or be, that "such a threat to my values can provoke an absolutist reaction" that have characterized monopolistic philosophies (and theologies) of the West (Post, 302-303).

There is, however, Post contends, "no such thing as *the* way we are. We are at least as many ways as there are domains of truth about us.... And some will find it consoling even that there is no such scheme, that here is an art, a matter of wisdom, forever safe from attaining the secure path of a science–safe also, one should add, from hierarchical schemes of valuation based on some ultimate face of existence of which the other visages are but masks. For there is no such thing" (Post, 304).

It may be as Post says. However does not so much emphasis on the pluralism of worlds and values run the risk of collapsing into out-and-out relativism, a subjectivism lacking in any sort of rational criteria whatsoever, an "anything goes" frame of philosophical mind? More to the point of Post's project, does it not undermine his previous and rigorous defense of a specifically physicalist ontology? Post himself sees the "perils of pluralism," as he puts it. In fact he cites two philosophers who have posed the same question: "Yet, after everything has been seen from each dimension's perspective, we still want all these pictures to be woven together into one unified patterning" (Robert Nozick). And: "A willingness to welcome all worlds builds none... awareness of varied ways of seeing paints no picture. A broad mind is no substitute for hard work" (Nelson Goodman). (Post, citations, 305).

Post's defense against the charges of relativism and subjectivism rests on reminding us that his physicalism, unlike monopolistic versions of naturalism, is 'non-reductive' and hence compatible with the 'explanatory autonomy' of other domains of discourse, including the valuative. Values are "grounded in the physical, in the sense of being nonreductively determined by it." But at the same time, as he also noted, the physical, dialectically, is grounded in the moral. "Grounding," Post reminds us, "like priority, is always in some respect." In this sense even his physicalistic metaphysics is not, ontologically, 'absolute' or unconditional. "Because physicalism is not (or need not be) monopolistic, we pluralists can have no quarrel with it, despite the fact that physicalism involves a monism of entities. For...the monism is combined with a pluralism of properties, of faces of existence, and of irreducible, autonomous, equally privileged ways of representing and changing ourselves and our world or worlds." Post concludes: "The real drama in philosophy remains where it has always been, in paring the rage for order with delight in near chaotic variety...by harmony of argument and metaphor, of logic and passion, so that we may understand and respond with all that is best in us" (Post, 306-307).

It is a delicate balancing act to untangle and then 'weave together" these two 'entwined' strands in a physicalistic but non-reductive metaphysics. Especially challenging for a physicalist 'monism of entities' is how to locate, ontologically, the emotions, the 'chaotic variety' of the 'passions,' how to defend the reasonableness and objectivity of our choice of priorities in ways to live and be. The emotions typically have been relegated to the status of second-class citizens in the metaphysician's catalog of what there is. Are the emotions, asks Post, 'faces' of existence too, so-called 'primary properties,' or are they simply 'masks' for something ontologically more fundamental, what are called 'secondary properties'? By way of response Post cites J. N. Findlay's observation: "To feel about something may in certain privileged cases be the last, most penetrating way of knowing what the thing is" (Post, 308). If we must retain the traditional distinction between primary and secondary properties, it should at least be made clear, says Post, that a thing's primary properties may be distinguished from its objective properties. One of Post's main theses, as we have seen, is that moral properties, inasmuch as they are 'determined' by (though not reducible to) physical facts, are objective, even if, in the traditional scheme of things, they are regarded as the primary properties of physical entities (Post, 310).

Well, then, asks Post, "what about somberness, cheer, and all the various moods, emotions, desires, and passions generally?" Do they, then, refer to 'faces' of existence? The first thing to note is there are in fact things which typically serve as the objects of such emotions, however else we describe that link. As with moral values, they serve to anchor the emotions in the world of natural fact. These "functional-intentional roles" of things, says Post, are "irreducible to the structural-physical state" of things. If they play their "appropriate roles," then it can be said, he argues, that "it is an objective truth that they are somber, cheery, offensive, lovable, fearsome, awesome, nauseating, boring, sickening, inspiring, or whatever." And in fact, in the appropriate circumstances, it can then be said, following Findlay's observation, that the most penetrating way of knowing what things are is "in terms of emotion" (Post, 315-316).

There is one stumbling-block, perhaps the major one, to this positive view of the grounding of values and emotions in the physical or natural facts of the universe, and that is, whatever partial meanings can be wrung from it, the universe, existence itself, is ultimately absurd, meaningless, *period*. How does Post think to rebut this hoary charge that threatens to reduce the central thesis of his non-reductive physicalism to nothing?

To do so he adopts a multi-pronged strategy matching what he notes is the multiple ambiguity of the question. The word 'existence' can have several different meanings. The word 'absurd,' insofar as it conjoined with 'existence,' is similarly hydra-headed. Among the several meanings of 'existence' the most important for this stage of our inquiry are perhaps two that Post cites: 'existence' can mean "the activities that make our lives;" but it can also mean "the whole of what there is" (Post, 317). The notion of the 'absurdity' of existence would seem to link the two senses.

Clearly Post has to rebut the charge that somehow a scientific view of the universe, as one philosophical critic alleges, "robs us of meaning in the sense of a purpose given us by some nonhuman source" (Post, citing Baier, 318). Post's answer is "emphatic": Not so, he says. "Neither science by itself nor naturalistic or even physicalistic interpretation...implies that the universe is pointless, or that it can supply no purpose or meaning" (Post, 318). How so? Let us assume that there is in fact no reason for the existence of the universe, for "the whole of what there is." Does it follow that therefore there can be no reason for our existence either? Post's reply is withering: "This is a slovenly line of thought from start to finish." (Post, *ibid.*) Again, how so? Simply because some natural facts *within* the universe could suffice to determine our values, to give us a sense of purpose or meaning, even if the universe as a *whole* has no explanation. Secondly, as concerns the alleged absurdity of the universe itself, to say as regards 'ultimate explanations,' that something is "absurd, irrational, brute, gratuitous, inconsequential, or an accident" is to invoke "some norm of rationality–in particular, some version of PSR." But this, as we saw him argue in the first part of this study (Post, 129), is simply to "betray an erroneous or obsolete conception of rationality." Thus, it simply does not follow from the fact that the universe itself has no explanation that the existence of the universe is therefore in some further sense absurd (Post, 319).

The distinction between facts *within* the universe and the universe *itself* or the universe as a *whole* leads Post to add a third sense to the previous twofold sense of 'existence.' So far, he says, we have been talking of existence "mainly in two senses: existence as the sum of activities that make up our lives, and existence as the totality of natural fact. But what about existence in the sense of the whole spatiotemporal universe?" (Post, 324). In light of the unclarity if not ambiguity we saw in Post's use of the term 'universe' in Part One of this study (the 'true' universe? the 'manifest' universe?), we must query whether this introduction of a new sense of 'existence' moves the discussion forward, or whether once again it brings into focus a deeply problematic aspect of his metaphysics. The question he is now asking us to consider is whether his thesis that values are grounded in facts within the universe can be extended to an argument that values can also be grounded in the universe itself.

How does he propose to make his case? His claim is that the universe, even though its existence lacks an ultimate explanation, nevertheless might have a meaning or meanings, a purpose or values, "in virtue of something else." What might that 'something else' be, however, if by 'universe' is meant 'the whole spatiotemporal universe'? Well, he says, it might be, "[f]or example, the totality of natural fact." Perhaps that 'totality' would be sufficient to "determine that certain value terms are true of the universe–say, that is is beautiful, terrible, awesome, eerie, intriguing, astonishing, and more. The universe then would have meaning at least in the sense that it objectively has value properties" (Post, 324).

Further, he says, the universe could also have meaning as "the appropriate object of certain emotions–not only, on occasion, of terror or awe but of acceptance and even reverence. Even though the appropriateness of these and other emotions could not be read off from a mere description of the universe, in the sense of being derived from or reduced to such a description, still the appropriateness could be nonreductively determined by the description" (Post, 325). This appears to suggest that in addition to the descriptions we have of natural facts within the universe, there are factual descriptions about the universe itself (*pace* the ambiguity of reference) that would entitle 'certain emotions.'

This is a strong claim and one that, in fact, could possibly provide for a solution to our basic question about the link between those 'certain emotions' and the fact of (the world's) existence. This makes it all the more important, therefore, that we be clear about how Post understands the reference of the term 'universe.' In particular, does it respect, or does it elide, the distinction, upon which we insisted in Part One, between talk about the existence of the world (universe) and the fact that there is something rather than nothing at all? If not, it may not yet provide the solution we are seeking.

Post sharpens the urgency of our concern when he then goes on to specify still more, multiple ways in which the 'universe' could be said to be meaningful. The universe he says could be seen as "the symbol and source of truth, beauty and goodness, if only because facts about its aspects or parts determine such matters." Or again, recalling his argument in Part One, we might say that the universe is "also the eternal, immutable, uncreated, independent, self-existence, explanatorily necessary First Cause of all that is." Further, for many that would already suffice "to justify according the universe the role of divinity.... to justify asserting that the universe *is* the divine." Finally, "if we conclude that only the True universe, not the manifest, is strictly the bearer of these properties, then we may treat the manifest universe as related after all to something transcendent, with respect of which we must refrain from positive predication... we could treat the manifest universe as a kind of God-marker, representing our present best attempt to limn certain aspects of the Universe beyond the universe." That would then be "the purpose or point of the universe."

Thus "naturalism in general and physicalism in particular, so far from implying that the universe is nothing but a collection of motes in the void, can treat it as divinity--in the spirit at least of Spinoza-- or as a marker of such divinity." Post concludes that "the determinacy of valuation licenses comprehending the universe in irreducible value terms, in which we rightly express the meanings and purposes of and in the universe." Because we can view natural facts and human values *sub specie aeternitatis*, "the description of things under the aspect of eternity determines meaning, value, purpose, and point" (Post, 325- 326).

In these remarks we clearly see the slippage among uses of the term 'universe' that are not always clearly disambiguated: the universe as 'the totality of natural fact,' 'the universe as a whole,' 'the whole (spatiotemporal) universe,' the 'true' universe 'beyond' the 'manifest' universe. In what sense, for example, is 'the totality of natural fact' different from 'the universe as a whole'? Is the latter the same as or different from 'the whole (spatiotemporal) universe'? How does he intend to fit his earlier distinction between the 'true universe' and the 'manifest universe' into the argument? Is the 'manifest' universe the 'universe' he has been speaking up to this point in his preceding argument? What discursive place or space do these various ways of referring to the universe inhabit? To what extent do they overlap? In what respects do they differ? What legitimates the move from facts within the universe, to the 'totality' of facts, to facts about the universe as a whole, to the whole (spatiotemporal) universe, to the Universe beyond the universe?

Further, do values undergoing a corresponding shift? If so, how? Why is it that 'certain emotions' (terror or awe, acceptance, even reverence), not others (nausea, boredom, despair, hopelessness) are linked, 'grounded,' in the fact of the existence of – what? – the totality of facts, the universe as a whole, the whole spatiotemporal universe, the true Universe beyond the manifest universe? As Post earlier remarked, there is more work to be done, not only, as he said, in axiology, but still in metaphysics too.

We will take these concerns with us into the final section where Post proffers a physicalist but non-reductive defense of specifically theistic values in a universe in which, unlike in traditional theism, there is no appeal to a transcendent entity other than, if it be such, the Universe beyond this manifest world.

Values and God

Post's defense of a naturalist theism proceeds in four steps: First, he dispenses with traditional, supernaturalist theism based on the existence of a meta-physically transcendent being, thus opening the way for the possibility of a revisionary theism compatible with his non-reductive version of a physicalist metaphysics. He then argues that religious predicates, and not just moral predicates, can be true and objective. Having established that general proposition, he argues that theistic values in particular can likewise be shown to be true and objective. He concludes by advancing the admittedly more tentative, because normative, hypothesis that theistic values are better than all other constellations of religious values.

The guiding question of our own critique will be the one that has guided us throughout this study: If, as I have argued, there is a cognitive difference between the fact that the universe exists (on whatever interpretation Post assigns to the term 'universe') and the fact that something exists rather than nothing, can Post's hypothesis of a physicalist but non-reductive theism be sustained, or will it in turn have to be dispensed with in favor of a still more radical hypothesis?

From Traditional to Revisionary Theism. Post begins by reminding us that his metaphysical thesis that what exists are physical entities does not carry the further reductive implication that things are nothing but physical entities. There, for example, moral facts that are equally objective and true. The question for theists then is whether God is included in what Post calls "the inventory of what there is." And yet, he says, even for 'certain theists,' this question already contains a mistaken assumption. What they would contend, rather, is that "theism is a matter not of what there is, but of how ought to talk about it, and how ought to see it." In other words, for such (unnamed) thinkers, theism is not so much a matter of what there is as it is an issue of values. "If so, looking for God in any inventory is misguided, as is supposing that Occam's razor had very much to do with ascertaining the truth of God-talk." Post's strategy will thus depend on the assumption that insofar as metaphysics does not locate God in the ontological inventory of a physicalistic metaphysics, it will be "of no direct use to theists" (Post, 329-330)

Of course some of the 'certain theists' Post has in mind may be those who argue that they are not interested in metaphysics because belief in God is not a matter of rational argument but of something more 'existential,' namely, faith. Post will have none of this. He is willing to concede that there may be more to theism than propositional belief. In fact he himself insists that faith surely includes as well an attitude to trust and a commitment to live a certain way. But having granted this, he insists that "one's faith, if it is to be true, must satisfy the logical prerequisites for truth.... One's faith, however fervent, must be well-formed, be non-empty, have no false presuppositions, be self-consistent, be consistent with all other truths, have no false implications, and satisfy the objectivity or invariance prerequisite. Otherwise, it is not true." We might add, as he sometimes does, it is not true *"period"* (Post, 331). Given Post's belief that theism need not involve belief in the existence of a transcendent deity, it will be interesting to see how the theism he proposes in its place meets these stringent logical criteria.

Post lists four logical possibilities for theists to respond to conflicts with "naturalism in general or physicalism in particular." They can reject theism. They can reject naturalism. They can argue that theism and naturalism are not logically inconsistent with each other, the so-called 'compatibility' hypothesis. Or they could attempt a 'synthesis' of the two (Post, 332). The first two options clearly represent traditional theism and reductive naturalism, both of which Post has already rejected. The latter two offer more possibilities of interpretation, including the possibility of a modified if not revisionary concept of 'theism' adapted to Post's revisonary, non-reductive version of physicalism.

The third option, what might seem a modern, post-Kantian 'compatibility' solution, falls short in his view. It is one with which "all of us ought ultimately to be dissatisfied." To say simply that there is "no logical inconsistency between theism and naturalism" does not answer the question "*why* they are consistent, despite so many appearances... We crave coherence and unity, a craving that can never be satisfied by mere logical consistency but ultimately only by some sort of synthesis." Unless theists present "a rational apologetic that incorporates an austere contemporary naturalism," they will never gain a hearing for their views or values "in an increasingly secular world." Thus Post opts for the fourth position, a version of the medieval unification of science, philosophy and theology in Aquinas, but updated to synthesize contemporary science and physicalist metaphysics in a naturalist theism (Post, 332-333).

In what follows, therefore, Post he will be making, and defending, the normative assumption that "objectively correct values include certain theistic values...together with the theistic ways of seeing and experiencing that they give rise to." Because this revisionary theism is not a matter of "the inventory of what there is," it is "not a matter of metaphysics or ontology." Rather it is a question of our decisions, our choices as to the values, the priorities, by which, ultimately we ought to live and be – values which are, "thanks to the determinacy of valuation," not merely subjective or 'existential,' but objective and true (Post, 336-337). Post has set himself a daunting task, but one for which he has prepared solid ground.

Before we move on to consider his analysis of religious predicates, we should note a few questions about the foregoing. Post suggests that some theists would agree that theism is not a matter of what there is, but rather of how we should live and be. Certainly it is true that many theists might put stress on the practical implications of their belief, but it is hard to believe that they would think such values made sense unless grounded in some sort of ontological reality beyond the natural facts about entities within the universe. What is fascinating about Post's approach to a revisionary theism is the extent to which it resembles the "existential" approach to theism of such thinkers as Paul Tillich. And yet, unlike Tillich's existentialist theology, in articulating his theism Post's focus from here on will be on axiology, whereas Tillich always insisted on the ontological underpinning of our existential concerns. What that transcendent reality might be is, of course, another matter. In fact, as we shall see, Post himself will end up defending a version of ontological transcendence.

For this reason Post's insistence that religious *faith*, whatever fervor it might also involve, must be grounded in a rigorous, rationalist notion of propositional *belief*, is similarly problematic until the question of the nature of the transcendent reality underpinning religious belief is clarified.

Finally, Post's grand project, his 'meta-narrative,' of a 'synthesis' of science and religion rests on an underlying rationalist concept not only of metaphysics in particular, but of the nature of philosophy in general. Despite his talk of the many 'faces' of existence, Post's 'revisionary' project, with its "craving for coherence and unity, a craving that can never be satisfied by mere logical consistency but ultimately only by some sort of synthesis," breathes the air of, remains committed to, the traditional totalizing passion of the post-Aristotelian project of a 'scientific' philosophy (Post, 52, 297, 339). This raises the fundamental question whether such a project can adequately grasp the link between our deepest emotions and the fact of (the world's) existence.

The Truth and Objectivity of Religious Predicates. Previously Post has argued that moral values, while not reducible to natural facts, nevertheless enjoy objective truth because of their determination by the latter. He now extends this argument to include the religious emotions as well. He cites once again Findlay's observation that sometimes "to feel about something may be the most penetrating way of knowing what a thing is." Scientific facts are not always prior in our understanding of things, Post says. Sometimes not only moral values but also religious feelings take priority as a source of truth. "From the fact that on analysis a predicate proves to contain some reference to human emotions, it does not follow that the predicate cannot express an objective truth, or a way things are, or a face of existence. For example, predicates that express the holiness of certain places and events, or the blessedness of certain persons and acts, or buoyant confidence in the goodness of creaturely existence despite all suffering, or the redeeming power of *agape* – all these predicates and more, (if construed...as predicates...for what things are like for a particular subject), could be true and could express a face of existence, one that smiles only on religious persons in response to their in these ways of seeing and feeling" (Post, 338). The qualification, 'for a particular subject,' does not open the door to subjectivism or relativism because, again, even then it remains the case that the cognitive value of such religious emotions is determined by descriptive truths about the 'places and events,' 'persons and acts,' 'creaturely existence,' or the 'power of love' to which the emotions are a response. "Even if everything is identical with some mathematical-physical entity or other – as the physicalist contends – nevertheless, everything is describable by some subjunctive religious predicate, and in that sense is a religious entity" (Post, 338-339).

Nevertheless, the question remains, "Why use religious predicates, subjunctive or otherwise?"

Because, Post argues, "there are purposes for which...other kinds of discourse do not adequately serve." Post lists some examples of such discourse: "parable, prayer, creeds, poetry, and more." They serve various purposes, "dimensions of meaning," such as: (i) "ways of interpreting certain experiences in light of a vision of meaningful existence; (ii) express ideals which, if lived up to, will save humankind; (iii) express answers to 'Why am I here?'; (iv) provide patterns for human action –not just abstract ideals, but vivid, actual exemplars; (v) use compelling, unforgettable imagery; (vi) arrest our attention by their strangeness, leaving us in sufficient doubt about their precise application to tease us into active thought, and also into active commitment and works; and so on." Post's point is that "theologians need no longer be bullied into holding that the decision to use some such language game or form of life is a matter ultimately of subjective preference or 'faith' on the ground, say, that this decision is neither derivable from nor reducible to any totality of natural fact." Instead, because of the 'determinacy of valuation,' they can argue "this decision corresponds with the facts" (Post, 339).

Further more, because, like moral values, religious emotions 'correspond with the facts,' it is simply the case that some of those religious language games and forms of life are "better" than others. That is, there are, says Post, "better and worse ways of spreading such imagination on external objects, and some ways correspond with the facts, while others do not. Religious names for the whirlwind ultimately are no arbitrary affair." Some theists might reply that "there is...no such thing as the way God is but many ways, and each domain of true discourse about God expresses a way God is." Post recognizes there is some truth in this claim, but contends that in the final analysis, because "facts are not neutral but laden with value," it is simply the case, regardless of "our subjective response to the facts...whatever our interpretations of or projections onto them," some moral values and some religious emotions "are correct instead of others." In other words, "in principle, at least, normative arguments can count against world-views," including competing religious ones (Post, 342-343.) While this might appear to be simply another version of the argument from morality, it is rather, says Post, simply a matter of "inferring from what...are the requirements of a correct and fully adequate morality to the correctness of a certain way of seeing and talking," namely, a theistic way. If so, then unlike the traditional argument from morality to ontology, "the truth of the theist's discourse, and the correctness of the theist's seeing-as, would not be a matter of extra entities." It would simply be a matter of 'existential' truth about a way to live and be grounded in facts of or about the world (Post, 344).

Post considers one last objection to his argument in this context: "But how would theologians be entitled to infer that their seeing-as is correct or true? Indeed, insofar as it is based on values, is it not 'merely a seeing-as', with no basis in reality?" This objection, Post acknowledges, is "nearly unstoppable so long as values cannot be appropriately grounded in facts." But of course his entire argument rests on the claim that in fact "moral values are appropriately grounded, via their determinacy." Ergo. (Post, 344).

This portion of Post's argument for a revisionary theism is both the richest and the most problematic. If he has succeeded in making the general case for the objectivity and truth of religious predicates, then the rest will be simply a matter of drawing out its implications for theistic ones in particular. For that reason it behooves us to pause and comment on some aspects of the foregoing claims.

Post's claim that every entity describable in the language of physical science can also be described by a religious predicate is fascinating for its implications of our attitude to everything that exists. It suggests that every entity within the world can serve, if viewed *sub specie aeternitatis*, as a witness to the miraculous fact not simply that the world exists, but that anything exists at all. It reminds one not only of the Jewish sense of the hallowedness of this world, or the Christian doctrine of the goodness of Creation, but also of the Zen Buddhist sense of the 'Buddha nature' inherent in even the simplest natural object or human activity. It is profoundly suggestive of one way to understand the link between our deepest emotions and the fact of existence itself.

Post's observation that religious discourse serves "purposes for which other kinds of discourse do not adequately serve" also reminds one of the observation of the existentialist theologian Tillich that symbols, the mode of discourse that characterizes much of religious language, says things, opens up 'dimensions of meaning,' levels of truth and reality, in ways that are otherwise impossible and not reducible to more literal forms of discourse such as that of natural science.

Nor is such figurative discourse found only in religion. It also serves the purpose of disclosing non-literal truth in such often related domains of discourse as art, music, politics and history. Once again, Post's non-reductive physicalism proves itself remarkably hospitable to a pluralism of discursive domains, forms of truth, types of reality, to what he calls the many 'faces' of existence.

That being said, there are other aspects of Post's argument that we may want to consider again. He speaks of "spreading the imagination on external objects" and "projections (of "subjective responses") onto them." The metaphors of external/internal and subjective projection/objective reality could be just infelicitous ways of referring to his distinction between natural facts and the values that 'supervene' upon them ('supervene' being itself a metaphor but a less metaphysically loaded one), but they could also be a philosophical 'Freudian slip' revealing a lingering bias in favor of a monopolistic or at least hierarchical metaphysics (something against which he himself inveighs), despite his staunch defense of the plurality of objective faces of existence, of the many and equally valid ways things are, expressed in the irreducible autonomy of various domains of discourse. It suggests that beneath his project there lies the unquestioned assumption of a tradition in Western ontology going back to Plato and Aristotle grounded in not only different, but differently ranked, domains of being, truth and discourse.

This is perhaps reflected in his response to the claim of those theologians who argue that "there is no *one* way God is but many ways, each domain of true discourse expressing *a* way God is." He seems prepared to argue that, in the final analysis, there *is* in fact only *one* way of talking about God that is true, that is 'correct.' He does not seem to be ready to allow that the criteria of religious truth and objectivity may form at most a set of rational minima, satisfaction of which could permit a plurality of 'correct' religious world-views, though not every such candidate might pass the criteriological test. The claim that there can be one and only one correct religious world-view seems on the most generous interpretation a normative judgment requiring further proof.

Post bases his claim on the legitimacy of comparing the moral consequences of a particular religious world-view. Negative moral consequences would render a religious world-view unworthy of belief. It could be argued, however, that this makes religious values dependent on moral values. Some theists would say that moral values follow from religious beliefs, not vice versa. *X* is right because it is God's will, God does not will *x* because it is, independently, correct. This would give Post the willies! But it reminds us of Wittgenstein's riposte to his positivist interrogator. Of these two conceptions of moral values vis-a-vis religious belief, the critic says, and presumably Post would agree, that "the more superficial interpretation" is that "the Good is good because God wills it." Whereas on "the deeper interpretation, God wills the Good because it is good." Wittgenstein strenuously disagrees: "I think that the first conception is the deeper one: Good is what God orders. For this cuts off the path to any and every explanation why it is good, while the second conception is precisely the superficial, the *rationalistic* one, which proceeds as if what is good could still be given some *foundation*. The first conception says clearly that the essence of the Good *has nothing to do with facts and therefore cannot be explained by any proposition*" (Wittgenstein, 1965,15, my emphasis). Whatever we think of Wittgenstein's rebuttal, in particular whether it can be defended in some other way, it is clear that, on this score, Post is clearly aligned with the positivist's camp.

This raises the following question. If, following Wittgenstein, the truth and objectivity of religious emotions cannot be 'founded' in a prior set of moral values and cannot be 'explained' by, 'has nothing to do with facts,' then is there still any sense in which they can be believed to be cognitively valid and support a set of moral values by which we can live and be? This is a question which, eventually, we must address head on. However, for now it is important to grant Post's argument to this point and see what it implications it has for the nature of talk about God..

The Objective Meaning and Truth of God-Talk. Assuming he has demonstrated that *religious* discourse is objectively true because determined by natural facts of or about the world, Post now proposes to show that one mode of religious discourse in particular, the one most central to *theistic* discourse, 'God-talk,' is also *objective* and *true* for similar if not exactly the same reasons. In doing so he will move from interpreting 'God' in as a non-referential term ("God is not the value of a variable") to interpreting 'God' as a "partially referential" term ("God is partly the value of a variable"). In other words, though he interprets 'God' primarily vis-a-vis moral or religious values, this is grounded in a view of 'God' as also having *meta*-metaphysical or ontological significance, though not as referring to a physical or metaphysical 'entity.'

A philosophical skeptic poses the metaphysical or "referential" problem for Post's revisionary theism as follows: "Do we have in theistic experience mere projection? Or do we have a projection matched by an objectively existing God?" We recall Post's 'certain theists' who would not see this as a problem. For them there is no conflict between science and religion of the sort underlying the skeptic's question. For them Occam's metaphysical razor is not relevant. But we already know that Post rejects this post-Kantian attempt to dodge the question. For him a revisionary theism must provide a 'synthesis' of science and religion, of metaphysics and God. And so he now takes up the challenge but – and here he is sympathetic with the anti-metaphysical theologians – without engaging in "abstract metaphysical disputes" (Post, 345-346).

Post's first task is to show that God-talk is *objectively meaningful*, that it has an '*object*' to which it refers even though that 'object' is not a physical or metaphysical 'entity.' His strategy is to reinterpret 'God' as a way of referring to what in Part One he labeled the 'True Universe,' the Universe 'beyond' the 'manifest universe. If we are permitted to make this equation, then in appropriate contexts we may think of the Universe beyond as 'divine,' if not as 'a divinity.'

To understand this claim better, let us first recap the nature of the distinction he made between the 'true' and the 'manifest' universe. The 'manifest' universe is "the known universe...the universe as conceived through our present scientific categories" as contrasted with "the true physical universe, or the Universe that lies 'beyond' the manifest universe." We must assume, he says, that whatever the state of our current knowledge, "the Universe is there to be characterized" (Post, 116-117). It is not entirely clear, however, what this notion of 'the Universe' really means beyond saying that it does not mean or refer to the physical universe as presently known or conceived. In other words, we can say what it is not, but not what it is. "The Universe is the unknown (or incompletely known) whole about whose part physics attempts (or ought to attempt) to give us descriptions that are true and complete." But as he admits, "There is not much one can do to make this intuitive idea more specific....we do not know specifically what we mean when we speak of the whole that is the Universe, or of its parts..." Post even qualifies this qualification still further when he adds that, though we have only an intuitive idea of the 'true physical Universe,' our current physical descriptions do refer, if only incompletely, to something that really exists. Therefore, "the Universe is not to be thought of as some completely uninterpreted reality, a thing-in-itself outside all conceptual schemes." It is not "ineffable" (Post, 156-158).

Now assuming this distinction, Post says, "We might even try assigning the role of the undisclosed ground – or Heidegger's 'Being itself' (on one reading) – to the Universe beyond the universe." And of course, as we recall, for Post a distinguishing feature of this Universe is that it is not known or describable in terms of *positive* physical predicates. It can only be pointed to by *negative* predicates, as in the Hindu *neti neti*, 'not this, not that.' "The Universe beyond, after all, is a unity not known through any positive prediction; and it is without beginning or end, neither coming to be nor passing away, eternal and immutable. Hence it is hardly a being or a thing in the usual sense..." (Post, 292). In a carefully qualified sense (so as not to be misleading) it could be considered the 'transcendent ground' of the visible universe. As the 'First Cause,' "the Universe beyond satisfies the key negative predicates...being immutable, not in time, tenseless, without beginning and time, not created, not explanatorily dependent on any being...so that in a sense it 'transcends every form which our intellect attains'" (Post, 361, citing a phrase from Aquinas)

It is because the True Universe can be descriptively characterized by these negative predicates that we cannot "plead on grounds of indeterminacy of valuation that there is no fact of the matter as to what choices we ought to make. Purely descriptive aspects of the Universe beyond the universe (of 'Being itself,' if we may equate them) determine our obligations here as elsewhere" (Post, 292). Further, because the observable universe is the visible manifestation of the Universe beyond "it can be accorded the role of, say, (a) the symbol and source of truth, beauty and goodness, if only because facts about its aspects or parts determine such matters." We can say even more. If we recall that the Universe beyond is also (b) "the eternal, immutable, uncreated, independent, self-existence, explanatorily necessary First Cause of all that is," that in itself can justify us in "according the universe the role of divinity;" it can even justify us in "asserting that the universe *is* the divine." And if we say that (c) "only the True Universe, not the manifest, is strictly the bearer of these properties of divinity, then we may treat the manifest universe as related after all to something transcendent with respect to which we refrain from positive predication" (Post, 325). If so, "we could treat the manifest universe as a kind of God-marker of the Universe beyond the universe" (Post, *ibid.*).

The claim that 'God' refers to the Universe beyond this visible universe is not as unprecedented as might first seem. There are, Post observes, traditions in which "the name 'God' would be given, unhesitatingly, to the eternal, self-existent First Cause, *whatever* it should turn out to be, especially if we refrain from positive predications of it, and if nonetheless, truths about it or its aspects determine all value and meaning." On any such view "the Universe beyond the universe is God" (Post, 337). Thus, at least revisionary theists can feel comfortable with the notion that "'God' and 'the divine substance' are names of the beyond that on occasion ought to take precedence; the beyond is not nothing but a mathematical-physical abstraction" And so, "If we must call 'the Universe beyond' a physical thing on the ground that physics takes a certain interest in it, then we must also call it a theological thing on ground that theology takes an interest in it" (Post, 363).

Having thus argued that God-talk is *objectively meaningful* insofar as it refers to an 'object,' the 'true' Universe (though it is "not a being or a thing in the usual sense"), Post's second task is to show that God-talk is *true*. His argument can be encapsulated as follows: "the content of such talk [God-talk] is the content of those [objectively correct] values." (cf. 352).

Post asks: "Is there way a theologian might try to argue that God-talk is objectively true, even though 'God' not only has no clear referent but has no referent at all?" Post gives three reasons for thinking so. First, there is no logical need for the subject-term of a proposition to be a referring term for the proposition to be true. Invoking a distinction from the tradition of linguistic analysis, Post notes that the surface grammar of God-talk could be one thing while its depth grammar could be something different (Post, 346-347)

Second, to interpret God-talk in terms of its surface grammar in subject-predicate form is, says Post, "a form of literalism." To resist "subject-object predicate literalism" would not undermine but would in fact support theists in their efforts "to resist identifying God with this or that, would thereby help thwart idolatry, would thus emphasize powerfully divine transcendence, would help account for key differences between science and religion, would bypass abstract metaphysical disputes about what must be in the inventory of what is, and would thereby pave the way for theologians to argue for the objective truth of God-talk." Significant benefits indeed, to which we shall have to return (Post, 351-352).

Third, what then would be the depth grammar of God-talk? The truth of God-talk would not have to do with reference to some transcendent entity, but rather with (to use Heidegger's expression) our being-in-the-world or (to use Post's earlier expression) our way of living and being: "ultimately its truth consists in or at least is based on the objective correctness of certain values and of a way of life. God-talk could express a unified complex of seeings-as, whose objective correctness is based on the objective correctness of the values and of the way." Thus, for example, the propositions 'God created the universe' and 'God is love,' two propositions central to the theistic tradition, could be objectively true if understood as standing for certain objectively correct values and a matching way of life, even though the subject-term 'God' fails of objective reference (Post, 347)

However, there is still that niggling little ontological question that refuses to go away: "What about the very assertion that God *exists*? Or that *there is* a God?" On Post's line of reasoning, one very strong possibility, he says, is "to treat 'God exists' ('There is a God', 'God is', etc.) as a kind of *meta*-assertion, to the effect that the theist's God-talk *is true* – namely, that God-talk expresses the experiencing, seeings-as, and values required by the form of life to which the theist belongs. And as noted, provided the form of life and values are correct, the God-talk is indeed true, and objectively so" (Post, 348, author's emphases). Post emphasizes the word 'correct' and its link to claims of truth because of his basic 'realist' thesis, that values are objective if they can be shown to be 'determined' by (though not reduced to) natural facts of or about the world.

This argument, he cautions, must not be mistaken for a post-Kantian 'philosophy as if' – as if God-talk were simply a "pragmatic fiction" supporting an independently arrived at set of values or way of life. Nor is theistic experience or talk of God a matter of "*mere* projection." Rather, Post strenuously insists, "God-talk is true, meaning true *period*, objectively true...'God exists' [is] not as a meta-assertion to the effect that it is good for us to see world as if there were a God, but rather it is a meta-assertion that the God-talk is true, hence that it is objectively correct to see the world as appropriately related to God" (Post, 349-350). The 'absolute' nature of Post's language here – God-talk is true *period*, theists values are not values *relative* to our self-interests – reminds one of Wittgenstein's insistence on the *absolute* nature of certain ethical (and religious) values.

Post agrees that there is still work to be done in fleshing out his case for a revisionary theism, but, he says, it would be "work in value theory or axiology, not in metaphysics or ontology, let alone in cosmogony." And so, if he has succeeded in establishing both the objectivity and truth of God-talk, he says, then "the rest is a matter of our will, a matter of resolve or commitment, hence in that sense a matter of faith" (Post, 355). However, before we move to the concluding part of Post's argument in which he argues for the superiority of theism to other religious world-views, we need ask a few questions about his argument for the objectivity and truth of theism.

Post argues that because his revisionary theism reinterprets God-talk primarily in terms of values, he, like faith-based thesists, can avoid 'abstract metaphysical disputes' (Post, 345-346). This position rests on, while appearing to reject, a traditional understanding of metaphysics, what Heidegger calls an 'onto-theo-logical' view that claims to provide a rational account of the structure of being, in particular of the cosmos, along with its grounding in a highest being. It is not clear, however, whether Post's and the theist's critiques would apply to a differently conceived, 'existentialist' ontology of the sort proposed by, among others, Heidegger. That is a position we will return to examine in a later section of this study. It needs at least mention here, since if there is an alternative approach to ontology that would meet the criticisms of traditional metaphysics made by Post and faith-oriented theists, it could call into question the (unexamined) assumptions on which their positions rest.

Post's defense of the *objectivity* of God-talk rests, as we have seen, not only on his thesis about the objectivity of 'correct' values, but also on a concept of the 'true' Universe, the Universe *beyond* the 'manifest' universe. Part of the difficulty of understanding his thesis, in addition to the fact that it is not always clear which of these two 'universes' he is talking about, is that it is not clear how 'correct' values are 'determined' by features of the Universe beyond the universe. These features are always given in the form of *negative* predicates, whereas when he speaks of the 'determination' of values by 'natural facts' he has in mind *positive* features of or about the ('manifest') universe. There could be several reasons for this lack of clarity. One is that, despite its being 'describable' only by *negative* predicates, Post in fact is still assigning a *positive*, i.e., very traditional metaphysical role to his concept of the 'true' Universe as the First Cause, that 'highest being' of the sort whose lineage traces all the way back to its role in the foundation of Aristotle's metaphysics. As he said, "the name 'God' would be given, unhesitatingly, to the eternal, self-existent First Cause, *whatever* it should turn out to be, especially if we refrain from positive predications of it, and if nonetheless, truths *about it or its aspects* determine all value and meaning" (Post, 337, my emphases). Assuming he is talking of the true Universe here, not the manifest universe (and again it is not always clear), it is hard to see just what the positive truths "about it" would be since it can only described via negative predicates. Nor is it clear to what the phrase "or its aspects" is meant to refer. Is the 'manifest' universe and *its* aspects one of the 'aspects' of the true Universe? Moreover, to say of the true Universe that 'correct' values could be 'determined' by it "*whatever* it should turn out to be" simply compounds the unclarity. Would the "truths about *it*" be the same whatever "it" turned out to be?

Finally, and this brings us back to the question of ontology, Post says "If we must call 'the Universe beyond' a physical *thing* on the ground that physics takes a certain interest in it, then must also call it a theological *thing* on ground that theology takes an interest in it" (Post, 363, my emphasis). We recall that Post offers as one of the advantages of his revisionary theism that, unlike the position that claims religion and science are 'merely consistent' with each other, his position proffers a 'synthesis' of science and religion, metaphysics and God – in short, of fact and value. The question we raise, as we have before, is what exactly the concept of 'thing,' that is, of 'being' is that would make possible such a 'synthesis'? The concept of 'being' as 'physical entity' upon which 'values are said to 'supervene' (and 'supervene' might be, as one philosopher noted, simply 'disguised reduction') raises the question, first, what is the 'being' of values, and second, what is the relation of the kind of 'being' that characterizes 'values' with the kind of 'being' that characterizes 'physical entity'? Absent that, it is hard to know what kind of ontological 'synthesis' could support Post's revisionary theism. Again, this suggests the possibility that a different understanding of 'being,' of metaphysics or ontology, an 'existentialist ontology,' might offer an account of 'physical entity' and 'value' that would put the discussion on a different, more conceptually clear and intelligible foundation.

Post's case for the *truth* of God-talk is not cast in terms of the true Universe but rather in terms of a notion of 'objectively correct' values. And yet, in the final analysis, as we have already alluded to above, the two topics cannot be separated, nor does Post wish them to be. That being the case, the problems we have noted in (i) reappear at least indirectly in (ii).

In arguing that the truth of God-talk primarily involves values rather than 'abstract metaphysical disputes,' Post anticipates the skeptical critic who asks how "God-talk is objectively true, even though 'God' not only has no clear referent but has no referent at all." As we saw, he gave three reasons for defending the claim. But this is puzzling, because he has already said that in fact God-talk does carry objective heft insofar as it refers to the true Universe, the Universe beyond the manifest one. Maybe this is a kind of meta-heft, but it is heft nonetheless. So why at this juncture would he suddenly abandon such a substantial foundation for God-talk, one which could, and in fact does, provide him metaphysical justification for the 'correctness,' i.e. truth, of theistic values?

In appearing to forego a true-Universe based defense of 'God exists,' Post interprets the proposition as "a kind of *meta*-assertion" about values. To say "God-talk is true" is to say that "God-talk expresses the experiencing, seeings-as, and values required by the form of life to which the theist belongs." This presupposes that the values required by a theistic form of life are themselves objectively true. But how is it established that the 'theistic form of life' or the 'theistic values' which call for that form of life are themselves true apart from their 'determination' by some metaphysical foundation or other? This brings us back to our immediately preceding puzzlement. Absent such a prior grounding, Post's 'meta-assertion' seems either a circular argument, a petitio principii, or a tautology. God-talk is true means God-talk expresses theistic values, but theistic values are only true if God-talk is true.

One reason Post gives for resisting 'subject-object predicate literalism' is a desire to support theists in their efforts "to resist identifying God with this or that," "thwart idolatry," "emphasize powerfully divine transcendence," and "bypass abstract metaphysical disputes about what must be in the inventory of what is." The payoff is that this would "pave the way for theologians to argue for the objective truth of God-talk" in the non-metaphysical or anti-metaphysical language of values (Post, 351-352). We see here Post's (legitimate) concern to avoid identifying the meaning of 'God' with traditional metaphysical talk God as a 'highest being (or entity),' talk which, in literalist hands, could easily end up, and has done so, in subsuming God under the metaphysical categories that limn 'this or that' entity *within* the world. But again we must ask, what of his concept of the Universe beyond the universe of this manifest world? He does not interpret it as a being or entity "in the usual sense" of those terms. Then is it not available as an ontological foundation, via his own thesis of 'determination,' for the objective truth of values and thus of God-talk?

Post argues that while there is more to be done in fleshing out the details of a revisionary theism, it would be "work in value theory or axiology, not in metaphysics or ontology, let alone in cosmogony" (Post, 355). In light of our foregoing questions, it would seem, however, that in fact there remains more to be done in matters ontological as well, as his concept of the true Universe beyond the manifest world seems to warrant.

Finally, in his conclusion he says that if he has succeeded in establishing the objectivity and truth of God-talk, "the rest is a matter of our will, a matter of resolve or commitment, hence in that sense a matter of faith" (Post, 355). This comment splits the cognitive aspects of God-talk from its volitional aspects, reducing faith, insofar as it is not a matter of propositional belief, to a matter of will. It thus betrays the underlying traditional rationalism of Post's metaphysics, the characteristic reduction of the volitional to secondary, subjectivist status in the hierarchy of meaning and truth. But is this necessary? Again, would an alternative, "existentialist" understanding of the link of the co-primordial relationship of the cognitive, emotive and conative provide a different understanding of the nature of faith and its relation to metaphysics or ontology?

To conclude, it seems there is in Post's revisionary theism a basic disconnect between the two aspects of his account of the nature of God-talk. On the one hand he finds in the notion of the 'true' Universe an objective basis in metaphysics for God-talk. On the other hand he finds in values the objective basis for God talk. However, the link, if any, between these two remains unclear. It is not clear what 'facts' about the *true* Universe (if we can speak of 'facts' in connection with something characterized solely by *negative* predicates) provide the objective basis for 'correct' values. It is not clear what, or how, religious emotions or theistic values 'correspond' with any such 'facts.' Post's non-reductive metaphysics, however, does provide a basis for an analysis of how certain emotions and values at least analogous to religious emotions and values could be grounded in facts of or about the *manifest* universe – "somberness, cheer, and all the various moods, emotions, desires, and passions generally" (Post, 315-316), or "the holiness of certain places and events, or the blessedness of certain persons and acts, or buoyant confidence in the goodness of creaturely existence" (Post, 338). But for an in-depth analysis of those possibilities we will have to turn elsewhere. In the next section of our study we will look at Quentin Smith's detailed phenomenology of the 'felt meanings of the world' which provides just such an account on the basis of a naturalist non-reductive metaphysics similar to Post's. Before we do, however, we must conclude our discussion of Post's account of the link between our emotions and the world's existence with a brief look at his claim that theism is superior to other metaphysical-cum-religious world-views.

As a coda to his argument, Post devotes the last pages of his study to the thesis that because revisionist theism is objectively true, not only does it replace traditional theism it is also "better" than monist or pantheist alternatives. Post offers several reasons for his belief, but admits that it is at best a tentative hypothesis, not strictly speaking a metaphysical claim, since it rests on "a further assumption" which, he says, "is problematic." In fact it is an assumption which has underlain his entire argument on behalf of God-talk to this point: "It is a normative assumption that the objectively correct values include certain theistic values together with the theistic ways of seeing and experiencing that they give rise to.... The crucial normative assumption is perfectly consistent with the minimal physicalist theses and, when conjoined with them, forms a synthesis of physicalism and theism in which each enriches the other while correcting the other's occasional extremes" (Post, 336-337). If this assumption is true, and it is a legitimate *if,* Post grants, then traditional forms of theistic metaphysics in Judaism, Christianity and Islam will be hard pressed to meet it. Post explores in further detail the implications of the assumption.

Given this normative assumption, the objective truth of God-talk entails the further claim that revisionary theism is superior to all other contenders. How so? First, the metaphysical implications of the claim. A revisionist theism, says Post, "is neither pantheist nor monist. For it does not identify God with anything, not even with the universe as a whole" (Post, 350). Indeed, if "the physical universe, whether manifest or true, ... the universe as a whole were called God," that would more likely be "pantheism, not theism." Why? Because it "seems most unlikely to have the personal attributes of divinity, however admirably it may exhibit such abstractions as eternity, immutability, self-existence," etc. (Post, 117). The point, says Post is that even on a revisionary interpretation, the objective values which prove the truth of theism entail a *dualism* incompatible with either pantheism or monism. Because Post's version of theism, like its traditionalist counterpart, "assigns truth to the theist's characteristic creedal sentences," for example the religious affirmation that "God is the maker of heaven and earth," it perforce assigns falsity to the pantheist's identification of 'God' with the universe as a whole (Post, 350).

What normative reasons, that is, what objective values does Post cite in support of his claim that a revisionary theism, which rejects any metaphysical ground in a transcendently existing being "outside the universe," can nevertheless be considered a species of dualism, can nevertheless subscribe to the doctrine of creation *ex nihilo*? Theistic belief is grounded in and an expression of a certain set of values, not a claim as to what is contained in 'the inventory of what is.' Therefore "to see the universe as created *ex nihilo* is, among other things, to see what there as essentially good, not as meaningless or absurd, and to see our lives as having a certain meaning and destiny dependent not on our transient purposes but on invariant and irreducible if sometimes mysterious imperatives about faith, hope, and love" (Post, 350). In other words, theistic belief, as expressed in these "seeings-as," is grounded in a constellation of objectively true or 'correct' moral values. In turn, a "correct and sufficiently subtle morality requires a certain sort of 'seeing-as,'...a seeing-as that involves, among other things, seeing us and the world as created, for a purpose, by a loving and transcendent God. Persons, the world, and morality thus become a kind of 'God-marker.' They are not nothing but natural and secular phenomena." For this reason, the revisionary theist believes, like his traditionalist counterpart, that "only theistic vision of world do justice to the uniqueness and sanctity of each individual life, to the tensions between duty or virtue and the pursuit of own happiness, to the necessity of love and forgiveness, and to much more, including the felt objectivity of these and other imperatives" (Post, 343-344).

Post anticipates objections, two in particular, to his claim that since it is objectively true, "a theistic complex of seeings-as" is superior not only to traditional theism but also to the seeings-as of other religious traditions.

The first objection, which in the context of this inquiry is less significant, is that "any normative justification for a theistic seeing-as heavily outweighed by various side effects [such as] "an authoritarian, patriarchal morality; ... an archaic sexism, tribal arrogance, and species chauvinism." Despite the best efforts of the revisionary theist to the contrary, the so-called "ordinary believer," habituated to "subject-object literalism," must inevitably fall into "the wrong sort of supernaturalism [which] seduces the believer into irrationalism and superstition" (Post, 354).

The second, more relevant and more weighty objection is that "*other religious varieties of seeing-as might well be normatively justified too, or instead.*" Why, it might be asked, should the varieties of Western theism be judged superior to, say, Asian varieties of theism or, for that matter, nontheism? They too offer "forms of life and complexes of seeings-as that rival the best of ours and indeed seem superior in some respects, as for examples in the attitudes they encourage toward animals, plants and the environment as a whole" (Post, *ibid.*, emphasis the author's)

In reply Post says that these objections simply show that the revisionary theist has more work to do – to point out in the first case that the negative side-effects "really do not follow from theism properly understood or properly revised," and in the second case to challenge other religious traditions to show whether, and if so how, they incorporate the objectively true, 'correct' values embodied in theistic seeings-as. In short, Post reiterates consistent with his revisonary view, it requires work "in value theory or axiology, not in metaphysics or ontology, let alone in cosmogony" (Post, 355).

However, the metaphysical and normative assumptions supporting Post's claims for the superiority of a revisionary theism need themselves to be challenged. We have already indicated what some of these problems are: the continuing ambiguity of reference of the term 'universe,' including its relation to the term 'God'; the resulting unclarity about the relation of metaphysics to value; and the problematic nature and scope of the criteria of rationality applied to religious, and in particular, theistic values and beliefs.

The *ambiguity of reference* of 'universe' and its relation to 'God' shows up at several points. Post says his revisionist theism "is neither pantheist nor monist" because "it does not identify God with anything, not even with the universe as a whole," for if "the physical universe, whether manifest or true, were called God," that would more likely be "pantheism, not theism." And yet we have already seen him willing earlier to equate 'God' with the True Universe. It is not clear, therefore, despite the 'dualist' nature of the values associated with the theistic tradition, why his revisionary 'theism' could not just as easily if not more rightly be seen as a version of pantheism or monism. And in fact one philosopher sympathetic to Post's project has seen it just that way (Smith, 1998, 230-234)

This ambiguity in reference impacts upon *the relation of metaphysics to values*. Post says that "to see the universe as created ex nihilo is, among other things, to see what there as essentially good," etc. He does not say what he has in mind with that phrase, 'among other things,' but we would not be amiss to think that 'created ex nihilo' involves certain metaphysical claims as well, not only a reference to certain values. If Post is willing to reinterpret the term 'God' in his revisionary theism in a way that equates it with the concept (the negative predicates) of the 'True Universe,' then it seems the further work to be done in defense of his revisionary theist hypothesis must include further work clarifying the exact nature of the relation between metaphysics or ontology and value theory or axiology. This means, of course, in clarifying the link between our emotional or evaluative responses and the fact of (the world's) existence. Why should theistic values vis-a-vis the True Universe be more true, more correct, than others?

Post argues for the superiority of theistic values to those of other religious traditions on the grounds that they are objectively 'correct' values by virtue of their 'determination' by facts 'of or about the universe.' The fact that his use of 'universe' is already problematic makes this claim equally question-worthy. It suggests a need to revisit the question of the ground, nature and scope of the criteria of rationality applied to theistic values and beliefs. Otherwise the claim that "only" a theistic vision does justice to theistic values is either a tautology or circular, a *petitio principii*. Should we not explore the alternative hypothesis that the criteria of truth for religious discourse can indeed yield normative verdicts in favor not only of theistic discourse but also of other religious 'seeings-as' which also meet a set of rational minima satisfaction? This would permit the possibility of a plurality of 'correct' religious world-views, though not every such candidate might pass the criteriological test. Must we feel rationally compelled to postulate a maximal set of criteria which would narrow the scope of truth to "only" one such constellation of values and beliefs? Would not the very notion of the True Universe, or 'God,' beyond the reach of all of our positive predicates not argue for such a hermeneutic generosity?

Post concludes that "persons, the world, and morality thus become a kind of 'God-marker.' They are not nothing but natural and secular phenomena." This is a powerfully moving and, it seems to me, profoundly true statement. But it also seems to me (observing the quote marks around 'God-marker') to be one that not only is equally at home in a number of other philosophical-cum-religious traditions, but could even be said to constitute a summation of the essence of the religious vision itself even despite the infinite varieties in which it has found expression among the religious traditions of the world.

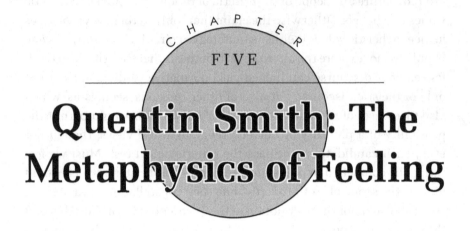

Quentin Smith: The Metaphysics of Feeling

"Without need to be theoretically instructed, consciousness quickly realizes that it is the site of variously contending discourses." – Seamus Heaney, "Crediting Poetry," 1995 Nobel Lecture

"Poetry can make an order true to the impact of external reality and sensitive to the inner laws of the poet's being" – Seamus Heaney, "Crediting Poetry," 1995 Nobel Lecture

Introduction and Overview

Post has put forward a comprehensive metaphysical account of the link between the emotive and cognitive elements in the Why question. His non-reductive metaphysics offers an explanation of why and how certain emotions and values analogous to religious ones could be grounded in facts about the (manifest) universe, emotions such as "somberness, cheer, and all the various moods, emotions, desires, and passions generally" (Post, 315-316), and values such as "the holiness of certain places and events, or the blessedness of certain persons and acts, or buoyant confidence in the goodness of creaturely existence" (Post, 338). But his case for a metaphysically-grounded link between the emotive and cognitive elements in the Why question, though comprehensive and many-faceted, left unanswered questions about the basis and nature of such a link.

Quentin Smith provides a more detailed phenomenological analysis of this link also based on a naturalist metaphysics of (the world's) existence. In an evocatively rich yet exacting phenomenological study, Smith puts forward a metaphysics of 'felt meanings' that proposes to offer just such an account of the link between such emotions and features of the world, an analysis that makes possible a radical reinterpretation of and answer to the Why question itself. His approach differs from Post's in a crucial respect. He grounds his analysis in what he calls a 'metaphysics of feeling' rather than a 'metaphysics of reason.' In that difference lies his claim to have provided a new and definitive solution to the Why question. As we turn to Smith's analysis we will be looking for answers to some of the questions left unanswered in Post's account, two in particular: Does Smith's phenomenology of 'felt meanings' account for and fill in the gaps in reason-based accounts like Post's as to why and how the world 'determines' our emotive or evaluative responses to the problem of existence? Does his phenomenology and the metaphysics on which it rests distinguish between responses to the fact that *something* exists rather than nothing and the fact that the *world* exists?

Smith's Thesis

Smith argues that traditional metaphysics has failed to accomplish its goal of demonstrating, on the basis of rational arguments, the existence of a divine cause and moral purpose of the world. In other words, it has failed to prove that the world's existence has any *rational* meaning. He proposes to build an alternative metaphysics on the idea that it is our intuitive feelings, specifically moods and affects, that make manifest the world's *felt* meanings. Each feature of the world can be shown to be a 'felt meaning' in the sense that it is a 'source' of a correlated feeling-response. While these feelings may be non-rational in the sense of grounded in a causal or teleological explanation, they are not non-cognitive. They are distinctive, 'extra-rational' phenomena that provide our fundamental and primary mode of access to the meanings of the world's nature and existence. Felt meanings are the ways in which the world actually is for us. In the absence of 'rational meanings,' i.e., reasons for the world's existence, felt meanings are the only kind of meanings the world can be known to have.

Thus, for example, Smith discusses such features of the world and emotional responses to them as: the very existence or 'happening' of the world, responded to or 'appreciated' in joy; the purposeless nature of that existence, responded to or 'appreciated' in despair; its being the greatest 'whole' there is, appreciated in awe; its being composed of contingent, unpredictable 'parts,' appreciated in dread; its perspectival appearance, its 'closeness,' to its human 'parts,' appreciated in love; and its independence of, i.e. non-dependence on, the human 'parts' to which it appears, appreciated in reverence. Of course such a list of felt meanings brings problems with it. Can a descriptive phenomenology determine which particular feeling-response is the appropriate appreciation of any given feature of the world? Can it determine the relationship among the different feeling-responses? Do joy, despair, awe, dread, love, reverence stand on the same level vis-a-vis one another, or does the metaphysical nature of the project dictate that one feature be judged more fundamental than others, or that some features be more simple, others more complex than others?

Smith's Method

Smith argues that these issues are resolvable once it is realized that knowledge of the world's features is not achieved solely through exact analyses or solely by poetic evocations but by the synthesis of the two. The phenomenological excavation and description of these two-sided felt meanings involves a two-step methodology. The evocative expressions to which feeling-responses to the world's features initially give rise must be supplemented by more exact analyses of the feeling-responses to decide which mood or affect is the appropriate appreciation of any given feature of the world. Each feature of the world, Smith argues, is exactly analyzable in a unique way. In turn, each feature of the world as exactly analyzable is evocatively describable in certain ways. Finally, each feature as evocatively describable corresponds to a specific type of mood or affect. The major task of the metaphysics of feeling, then, is to give evocative and exact explications of the principle features of the world as these features appear in the appropriate feeling-responses or 'appreciations.' Smith's

THOMAS DEAN

thesis, then, is that what is made manifest in these feeling-responses, these 'moody' or affective 'appreciations' is not something subjectively relative or something mystical that must be taken on faith. Rather, the felt meanings of the world can be 'evidentially known' in accordance with criteria of truth applicable to both the 'felt' or intuitive 'appreciations' and the corresponding conceptual analyses of those features of the world which are the 'source' of those feeling-responses.

Smith's Target

Along with the positive thrust of his project, Smith has a critical target in mind. His proposed metaphysics of 'felt meanings' is advanced against what he calls the 'metaphysics of rational meaninglessness.' The latter characterizes the 'degenerate' situation of metaphysics in the modern (post-Kantian) and post-modernist epoch. Reason, incapable of rationally discerning the meaning (cause or purpose) of the world's nature and existence was compelled to arrive, sooner or later, at the 'nihilist' conclusion that the world is rationally meaningless. In fact, not only the metaphysics of 'rational meaningless' but the very notion of the 'metaphysics of reason' itself rested on the founding assumption of Western metaphysics from Plato on – that the answer to the question: How are we to understand the existence and nature of the world?, Why is there something (the world) rather than nothing?, is to be found in a rational account of the ground – cause and/or purpose – of the world's existence, in the absence of which the world's existence must be judged to have no rational meaning at all. Smith's reply is that the world's having a reason for existing *matters* to us only because it has a *felt* meaning. If the world lacks a reason for existing, as the contemporary metaphysics of rational meaninglessness has it, this is of *interest* to us only because the feature of the world's 'groundlessness' has itself the *felt meaning* of emptiness. Says Smith, it falsely seems to matter whether the world has a reason for existing or not. What really matters is our experiencing of the world's felt meanings, joy at its happening or emptiness at its purposelessness. Further, there are many other felt meanings of the world, some of which have nothing to do with whether it has or lacks a reason for existing, such as awe when we experienced it as the greatest whole, or reverence when we experience it as independent of its appearance to us. Philosophers from Plato onwards have searched for the rational meaning of the world's existence, when what really matters to us are the felt meanings we experience in relation to its various features.

Smith's Terminology

An exposition of Smith's metaphysics of felt meanings will entail not only clarifying his thesis and supporting analyses, but also wrestling with his vocabulary. Like Heidegger, a thinker who was also trying to articulate a new way of formulating traditional philosophical problems, Smith employs a distinctive technical terminology of his own invention. His philosophical vocabulary includes familiar-looking words which have been given decidedly unfamiliar interpretations. He gives words unusual and extended meanings beyond or other than their ordinary usage, trying to jar us out of our accustomed ways of thinking. This can lead to confusion and misunderstanding unless we make the effort to follow him on the new linguistic and conceptual tracks he has laid down. To give a critical assessment of Smith's metaphysics of feeling it will be necessary, therefore, to come to terms with his novel terminology Already at the outset he confronts us with an unexpected use of the notion of 'feeling' around which he gathers a cluster of other provocative neologisms. In tandem with that he introduces a novel use of the term 'world,' particularly in his coinage, 'world-whole.' His use of 'feeling' and 'world' or 'world-whole' leads in turn to a reinterpretation of the notion of 'metaphysics' itself. Our task, therefore, will be to try to understand the new meanings he assigns to these three terms – *feeling, world* (*world-whole*) and *metaphysics* – and to the 'metaphysics of felt meanings' he constructs upon them.

Smith's Challenge

What gives Smith's metaphysics of felt meanings its philosophical interest and promise is that it challenges us to reverse the normal assumptions of metaphysical argument by giving feeling pride of place rather than reason. It upends reason-based and science-oriented metaphysics, making central instead the analysis of emotions, phenomena usually given a secondary, and usually negative role in matters epistemological, metaphysical and perhaps especially cosmological. Not only are we forced to learn new a new battery of psychological concepts, we are no longer able to rely on the ususal conceptual dichotomies of metaphysical explanation – cause and effect, facts and values – and the traditional types of explanation – efficient, formal, material, teleological. We are told we have to approach the inquiry the other way round, that we must proceed from feelings to cognition to the nature and reality of the world. We are told that the answer to the Why question will be found not in rational arguments or scientific explanations but in feelings, a source traditionally viewed as if not irrational then nonrational or, in Smith's word, 'extra-rational.' We are told that the answer will not be found in the 'rational meanings' and dichotomies of traditional metaphysics, concepts like cause/effect, means/end, values or purposes, nor in the modern or post-modern dismissal thereof. We are told rather that the answer to the Why question will be found in the philosophically unfamiliar yet ordinary everyday phenomena called the 'felt meanings' of the world.

In summary, Smith's metaphysics of the felt meanings of the world proposes to offer a descriptive phenomenology of feeling-responses to features of the world together with a systematic analysis of their interrelations in a unified hierarchy of 'appreciations.' Further, he intends his description of the cognitive links between these feeling-responses and corresponding 'importances' of the world to provide the philosophical basis for a positive 'spirituality' that overcomes the 'nihilism' of the metaphysics of 'rational meaninglessness' that characterizes our current world-epoch. As we move to a detailed look at his argument, we will have in mind Witherall's criteria: Does Smith's 'metaphysics of felt meanings' provide a philosophically satisfactory account of the link between our emotional responses and the fact of (the world's) existence? If it does, does it make possible a new and better way of understanding and answering the Why question itself?

The key to Quentin Smith's innovative approach to his 'metaphysics of felt meanings' is his claim that it is our *feelings*, not *reason*, that provide our fundamental mode of access to the existence and nature of the world. In fact his thesis is even stronger. It is not simply that our moods and affective responses disclose, provide a *cognitive link* to, that reality. Our feelings are already in themselves the *embodiment* of that reality. Our feelings *are* the 'reality' of the world. But if this is not to be just another form of subjectivism or Wittgensteinian solipsism run amok, clearly what

Smith means by 'feeling,' and for that matter 'world,' must be rather different from what we ordinarily understand by those terms and even from what philosophers traditionally have taken them to mean. We will begin by looking more closely at his interpretation of the phenomenon of feeling, although unavoidably, given his radical thesis, we will have to make reference to his understanding of 'world' as well. We will examine in turn his views on the nature of *feelings*, the nature of *'global'* feelings, the *hierarchy* of global feelings, and the *truth* of global feelings.

Critique

We face an immediate problem. As Smith himself recognizes, we cannot discuss one of these three topics – *feelings, world,* and *metaphysics* – completely in disjunction from the others. They are intrinsically bound up with one another as fundamental aspects of a prior phenomenon which, though unitary, is nevertheless internally articulated. Thus much of what pertains to an analysis of 'feelings' can and indeed must be also be discussed again under the heading of 'world' or 'metaphysics'– which means that those latter topics are already inherently present in a discussion of 'feelings' as well. An analysis of Smith's metaphysics of feelings must take this complicating factor into account; in fact, as we shall see, it provides the key to the critique that follows. Smith never clearly articulates the underlying phenomenon that gives unity to his work, though it is the unexpressed foundation of what is revolutionary in his revisionary metaphysics. This lack is the source of the criticisms that can be and indeed have been lodged against his project. It may also provide the key to answering a prior question that might seem too obvious to ask: *why* are our feelings vis-a-vis the world 'meaning-full' in the first place, *why* do the felt meanings, the 'importances' of the world 'matter' to us at all?

To anticipate, we can apply to the unitary-but-articulated underlying phenomenon that links these topics the hyphenated Heideggerian term, 'being-in-the-world,' a move that is appropriate insofar as Smith himself acknowledges his debt to Heidegger's notion in his book and defends it in his article, "On Heidegger's Theory of Moods," written while his book, which at the time he viewed as a "*phenomenology* of feeling," was underway. The problem, I shall argue, is that though Smith bases many of his key insights on this phenomenon, he does not fully explore its revolutionary implications for his own metaphysics. He falls back instead upon the traditional vocabulary of 'feelings' and 'world', however revised, of the metaphysical tradition which it was his intention to critique. Thus his vision of 'metaphysics' itself falls short of the radical potential implicit in the project of a phenomenology or 'metaphysics' of feeling.

What Smith appears to provide, therefore, is a new approach and vocabulary, but an old concept of metaphysics – new wine, as it were, but in old wineskins. However, this may seem a bit harsh, since even his critics agree that Smith's metaphysics of feeling is "the most important work in phenomenology yet written by an American," that it "presents a picture of our cognitive relationship to the world that is radically different from virtually all other such pictures," that it is a "radically new revisioning of metaphysics," and that it is "original enough to be counted as entirely new" (Allen, 1996). And yet we should also remember the qualifying phrase used by another critic appreciative of Smith's phenomenological metaphysics: while it may in one sense be 'adequate,' that does not necessarily means it is 'correct' (Witherall, 2002).

So, does Smith's phenomenological analysis liberate feelings from the metaphysical tradition, or does it, for all its newness and radicality, remain trapped in the parameters and problematics of that ancient path? I shall argue that, despite his radical redefinition of key terms, Smith's project is not free of the old problems the metaphysical tradition has in dealing with feelings and their relation to the world, and that therefore his project needs an even more radical re-interpretation, a totally different 'metaphysical' setting, in an 'existential-ontological' foundation such as Heidegger's from which Smith himself drew much, yet whose underlying thrust he may have missed. Crucial for deciding this issue is Smith's analysis of the basic phenomenon of 'feeling.'

We noted in introducing Smith's understanding of the nature of feelings that he had something totally different in mind when speaking of 'feelings' and 'world.' We reserved judgement, however, as to whether he had sufficiently made the case for his different understanding of these phenomena. That is the issue we must now consider. Does his analysis of 'feeling' succeed in making the case for a *cognitive link* between feelings and the features of the world to which they are a response? Or are feelings, on his account, in some sense the *embodied reality* of those features of the world? To determine these matters we will look first at his *ontology* of feelings – his answer to the question, *what* are feelings? This will include revisiting his notion of *global* feelings. We will then consider his *epistemology* of feelings – his answer to the question, what is the *cognitive* nature of feelings? In doing so we must remind ourselves that in the final analysis a discussion of his understanding of *feelings* cannot finally be separated from their intrinsic involvement in his view of the *world* and the nature of *metaphysics*.

Feelings

The Ontology of Feelings

What are Feelings? As a philosopher asks, "What, in the end, *are* emotions?" (De Sousa, 2013; I shall use the terms 'feeling' and 'emotions' interchangeably except when indicating otherwise. Each term has broader or narrower connotations than the other depending on context and definition.) He goes on to note that "A variety of possible answers to this 'ontological' question suggest themselves: physiological processes, or perceptions of physiological processes, or neuro-psychological states, or adaptive dispositions, or evaluative judgments, or computational states, or even social facts or dynamical processes." In other words, there may be no one simple answer; perhaps there is no one single thing that emotions "are." And yet, while the answers may differ, it is not clear that they are for that reason necessarily incompatible. The ontological question may be related to levels or types of explanation. For example, the so-called "higher-level emotions" of the sort with which we are concerned embrace not only physiological but also behavioral, expressive and phenomenological aspects. In fact, historically the locating of emotions within their distinctive ontologies was an important, but sometimes challenging task. (De Sousa, *ibid.*). And so it will prove for us too.

To take just one example: Each ontological account of the nature of the emotions can be seen to reflect different types of what Habermas calls "human interests." Habermas catalogues three: scientific-technical, cultural-hermeneutical, and critical-emancipatory. Each reflects a different model of knowing: the model of technical control, the model of hermeneutical understanding, and the model of emancipatory critique. We can see how an ontology that sees emotions as primarily physiological, physio-perceptual, neuro-psychological or computational states reflects the first of these interests or world-views. An ontology of emotions as primarily adaptive dispositions or social facts or processes could fit either the first or second, scientific or hermeneutical, interests, depending on the further definition of emotions. Whereas an ontology of emotions as evaluative judgments could fit either the second or third, hermeneutical or emancipatory, interests, again depending on the further specification of emotions.

Where might one locate Smith's ontology of feelings and felt meanings of the world on this ontological spectrum? It is pretty clear that he does not wish to see feelings reduced to the sort of physicalist metaphysics implied by the first of the above categories, the scientific-technical. Nor, insofar as he clearly indicates that such phenomena are not to be understood as 'values,' that is, as primarily *moral* phenomena, in particular values serving a *critical* function, would he see feelings and the felt meanings of the world as falling under the critical-emancipatory category. Insofar as feelings and felt meanings, though initially sensed intuitively or only implicitly, can nevertheless be expressed in the form of explicit evaluative (his term is 'appreciative') judgments – and indeed must be as the elements of a *metaphysics* of feeling – it would seem that, if we use Habermas' three categories, Smith's ontology of feelings falls under the rubric of a cultural-hermeneutical interest or world-view, that is, an ontology concerned with *the meaning(s)* of human existence vis-a-vis the world-as-a-whole. The question, then, is what exactly is the nature of a ontology that grounds, conceptually, the emotional link between human existence and the world-whole, the link that makes intelligible epistemological access via feelings to the world's felt meanings for our existence? In particular, can Smith's concepts of *feeling* and *world* serve to ground such an ontology? If so, how, and if not, why not? That is the critical question we must now consider.

Philosophers interested in this question have listed a number of different aspects of the phenomenon/a of *feelings* and/or *emotions*, discussing in detail such features as their intentional ('as') structure and content; their identity; the different types, kinds and levels; their inter-relations; their explanations; the differences between states and dispositions; the linkage between internal stimuli and external causes; whether they are subjective or objective, irrational or rational; etc. Presupposed in such analyses are always the different interests, world-views and ontologies with which philosophers have approached such discussions. As we have already mentioned, Smith's terminology involves his own novel set of distinctions on the basis of which he prosecutes his analyses. The question we are now considering, however, is whether the ontology that appears to support his phenomenology is adequate to the task, or whether it undermines the radical nature of his own effort. Let us therefore review his terminology once more, this time trying to probe its underlying ontological assumptions.

The Manifold Sense of 'Feeling.' As we have already noted, it is no easy task to say what Smith means by 'feeling,' especially if we are trying to determine its ontological grounding and implications. Never occurring as a single term, it appears instead in a variety of often novel, as it were, hyphenated combination forms. Smith speaks of some of these hyphenated feelings as occurring "On the side of the 'I,'" while others, said to be "corresponding," occur "on the side of the world." Further, feelings on each "side" are said to occur at two different *levels* – the level of *sensation* and the level of *awareness*, correlated with the level of *tonalities* and the level of *importances* 'emanating' from the side of the world. This distinction at the outset between two "sides" "correlated" with each other is already metaphysically problematic for Smith's position, not so much because it reflects a traditional position in metaphysics which has given rise to controversy for millenia, though that is the case too, but because it would seem to contradict his critique of that traditional view and undermine the radical ontological implications of Smith's own phenomenological analyses.

As a way into this problematic, we begin by looking at some of the issues in his understanding of the notions just mentioned: the *emanation* of felt meanings from the "side" of the world, the *levels* of feeling, feeling as a form of *awareness*, along with questions these raise about what underlies them, namely, his *extended use* of the term 'feeling' and the *phenomena* of feeling whose 'extended' meanings are central to a metaphysics of 'feeling' – 'importances,' 'appreciation' and 'world.' With these in hand, we will then return to a first look at our central topic, the *ontology* of feelings.

Emanations of felt meanings. Smith describes the 'feeling tonalities' on the "side" of the world as 'sensuously' felt *emanations* of features of the world that correspond to certain 'flows' of feeling on the "side" of the I. As noted previously, this notion is one that is important to clarify given the long philosophical tradition of distinguishing feelings as subjective phenomena 'internal' to the subject over against objective features of the world 'external' to the subject. Smith argues that his use of 'feeling' and 'world' does not involve this internal/external, subject/object dichotomy. Emanations of felt meaning are rather *relational* phenomena, he says features the world possesses *through being felt by* the I. In other words, he seems to be saying, these 'feeling-tonalities' or 'emanations' are *double-sided* phenomena playing a *mediating* role between the I and the world, *embodied realities* that join the two "sides" together – the *ontological link* between our emotional responses to the world and the features of the world's existence that we have been searching for.

On one hand they constitute the link to the I which '*imbues*' an entity as, say, looming over and threatening me. But this feeling of a threatening emanation is not merely a subjective phenomenon. The *source* from which it is felt to flow, the feature of the world that seems to loom over and threaten me, cannot simply be reduced to the I that imbues the world with that tonal-flow. My feeling of being threatened is my response to an entity that is actually threatening me. As Smith puts it, such emanations not only *seem* to be features possessed by the world dependent upon and in relation to the I, they *really are* such features.

But now we have to ask: What is Smith really saying? If world's emanations depend upon, are felt *meanings*, only in tautological relation to the I that feels them, are such 'meanings' not, in the final analysis, 'realities' only on the "side" of the I? Would the world have such 'features,' such 'felt meanings,' in the absence of the I? Is not the 'world' thus understood in fact reducible after all to what Wittgenstein called '*my* world'? But if so, is there another way of grounding such phenomena ontologically that could avoid this danger of this apparently Wittgensteinian lapse into what Heidegger calls metaphysical subjectism? It is not clear that a metaphysics based on an *ontology* of 'feeling' can supply the answer.

Levels of feeling. In his analysis of the relational character of feeling, Smith further divides the 'horizontal' "sides" of I and world into correlated 'vertical' levels as well – a first-order level of 'sensuous' intuition and a higher, second-order level of cognitive 'awareness.' Although, as we noted, he grants that in the *concrete experience* of feeling, these *intuitive* and *cognitive* aspects "never occur in reality apart" from one another, "they can for purposes of descriptive explanation be considered separately"

(Smith, 1986, 33). This methodological observation has problematic implications for positions he later adopts in his phenomenological analysis, in particular his claim regarding the priority of the 'direct,' 'pure' and 'immediate' nature of our intuitive feelings over against the linguistically and conceptually mediated nature of our feelings on the level of cognitive awareness. Again, while this is a controversial distinction of long standing not only in Western but also in Asian philosophical traditions of epistemology, it too is grounded in a problematic distinction on the level of ontology involving the nature of the relation of the I to the world. Is there such a thing as a non- or at least pre-linguistic experience of and relation to the world? If not, in what way can language be said to be always already present, implicated in constituting our so-called 'pre-linguistic' feelings and experience of the world? It could be argued that Smith's intuitive feelings have what cognitive implications they have only because they are already linguistically embedded in, shaped by, articulated from within a very particular metaphysical view of the world. So our critical question must be: is *language* in some sense ontologically 'co-primordial,' to use Heidegger's expression, with our *intuitively felt relation* to the world, on the one hand, and our *understanding awareness* of that felt relation, on the other? If so, in what ways, and with what implications Smith's metaphysical program?

Feeling as awareness. Feeling-awarenesses are *cognitive* awarenesses of what Smith calls the '*importances*' of the world-whole. Smith makes several points about them that are relevant to our concern. Already at the outset he tells us that they are to be distinguished from the 'feeling of *values*.' Against Scheler, for example, he wants to make clear that they are not primarily or even necessarily moral or ethical in nature. Since they are grounded in sensuous intuitions, they would seem rather to be basically aesthetic, or what he terms 'evocative' or "poetic" phenomena. This raises the question, however, what if any relationship these fundamental feelings have not simply to the ways the world is, but to the ways to be in a world thus disclosed. Can a metaphysics of feeling simply set the ethical question aside?

Among feeling-awarenesses Smith singles out two in particular for attention, *moods* and *affects*, specifically 'moody awarenesses' and 'affective-awarenesses.' These have several features that distinguish them from other kinds of awarenesses. Both moody awarenesses and affective awarenesses are '*global*' feeling-awarenesses. But whereas moody awarenesses are intuitive, non-inferential, 'extra-logical,' immediate' or 'direct,' indefinite or indeterminate, unfocused awarenesses of the importances of the world-whole that elicit them – "diffuse feelings about everything in general," on the other hand affective awarenesses are comparatively more determinate, more focused, veridical awarenesses of the world-whole – "consciously directed responses to the importance that elicit them." That is, unlike moods, each affect refers to a unique respect in which the world-whole is important, each discloses a specific 'region' of the world-whole. Here again of course we return to the question of the relation of language to feelings. Moody feeling-awarenesses are said to be immediate and intuitive in the sense that they are entirely innocent of language, allegedly 'pre-linguistic,' whereas affective feeling-awarenesses, insofar as they are conceptually more determinate, thus presumably involve language. The question, then, is how language came suddenly to be present in affective awareness when the 'correlated' level of moody awareness was said to be a 'pure' feeling-awareness, linguistically uncontaminated?

Finally, higher-order feelings, 'awarenesses' are also cognitive. They tell us something about the nature of the world, its features, the ways it is. What is interesting in this regard is that, unlike the tradition, Smith does not set feeling-awarenesses off against what might be considered phenomena of a different if not even higher epistemological order. Rather, he argues, such cognitive phenomena as perceiving and thinking, usually distinguished from feeling in traditional philosophical accounts, are in a metaphysics of feelings to be viewed themselves as sub-species of feeling-awareness itself. In fact, says Smith, *all* modes of awareness – thinking, willing, even valuing, not just feeling, are feeling-awarenesses (Smith, 1986, 71). It's almost as if he were returning to a Cartesian sense of *cogitationes*: *cogitatio*, i.e., in this case 'thinking,' thought of as awareness/consciousness more generally. For Descartes any mode of 'thinking' would be sufficient to qualify for the title, whether doubting, affirming, denying, willing, understanding, imagining, and so on. The term becomes so broad, so extended in meaning, that it threatens to lose its distinctive meaning, and thus its ontological underpinning, altogether. Thus one wonders, in Smith's case, whether another term than 'feeling' would be more useful, more apt, less misleading both to capture the phenomenological and epistemological variety he wants it to cover as well as the metaphysical or ontological foundation he wants it to provide. Could one substitute here, for example, William James' concept of 'experience' – thus, experienced feelings, experienced thinking, experience willing, etc? But what would be the ontology of that? James does not really say.

Obviously, here we confront a mare's nest of complexities. What exactly is the relation between sensuous intuitions, not of empirical phenomena but emotional phenomena, on the one hand, and the objects of empirical perceiving – whether so-called 'sense-data' or full-blown material objects, and the varieties of ratiocination that make up the general notion of thinking – from scientific hypothesizing and mathematical analysis all the way through to logical argumentation and metaphysical speculation? Is the relation one of derivation, reduction, extension? Smith does provide a brilliant analysis of some of these relationships – how, for example, the notions of causal and teleological explanation can be derived from the feeling-awarenesses of the world's importances, but it is a partial account at best, and leaves many other species of 'awarenesses' unaccounted for. On the other hand, again, would another metaphysics fare any better? And so we are left with our ontological conundrum.

Extended use of 'Feeling.' Smith defends himself against such critical cavils by reminding us that he is using the term 'feeling' and the other terms systematically related to it in a technical or non-standard sense. Thus such terms as 'phenomenon,' 'awareness' and 'importance' are being deployed in an "extended usage." Nor, having made this linguistic stipulation, does he rest there. His extended use of 'feeling' and related terms represents, he says, a deliberate philosophical challenge, indeed a critique, of the ordinary use of these terms as reflected in the metaphysical tradition. Why? Because, he contends, the ordinary usage of these terms reflects a restricted range of phenomena and a stunted idea of feeling-awareness. In short, it embodies an 'erroneous world-view' that expresses itself in the hoary but false dichotomies that stud the philosophical tradition – the opposition of fact and value, the 'neutral/important' distinction, the differentiation in theories of human nature between 'feeling' and all other kinds of awarenesses – cognitive, volitional, evaluative. All these dichotomies are rooted in what Smith calls a 'rational-spiritual perspective on reality' (Smith, 1986, 77). The epistemological consequence, he says, is that the ideas of fact, value, cause, effect, purpose, means and ends are 'degenerated' concepts 'unverifiable' in reality. "They do not signify any reality that can be discovered in intuitive feeling... What are discoverable are not facts and values, and causes and telic reasons and consequences, but *importances* in the nondegenerate sense" (Smith, 1986, 106). Whereas if we reinterpret such terms in a "new and nontraditional" sense, we can make explicit *holistically* how felt meanings such as "magnetizing importances, enhancing and detracting importances, and configured importances" can give rise, derivatively, to such notions as, for example, values, causes, etc. (Smith, 1986, *ibid.*). This is a a philosophically important and potentially revolutionary claim, and, as noted above, Smith does demonstrate how such a derivation of traditional metaphysical concepts might proceed – how, for example, notions of cause and purpose can be derived from feeling-awarenesses of the world's importances. But once again, the question is whether he has provided a sufficient basis in an *ontology* of feelings for his *phenomenological* analyses of these *conceptual* transformations. Our critical question, in brief, concerns the ontology underlying his (extended) vocabulary of 'feelings.'

Phenomena of Feeling. To try to get added purchase on this issue, let us look again at phenomena referred to in Smith's 'extended' vocabulary central to his metaphysics of 'feeling' – 'importance,' 'appreciation,' and, since we cannot avoid it, 'world,' whose 'importances' are the object of 'appreciative' feelings. The question we are asking in the case of each of these is what light, if any, they might shed on the ontology underlying Smith's extended notion of 'feeling.'

Importances. Something is said to be 'important' if it is of great significance or value, highly meaningful, matters greatly. The implication is that it is significant to, valued by, meaningful for, matters to someone – that it resonates, as Smith might put it, on the 'side of the I.' But this also implies that the object of such importance has features that justify attributing such value to it, that there is something on the 'side of the world' that appropriately elicits such a response from the side of the I. So far both Smith and the philosophical tradition are in agreement. However, for Smith, and for us, everything depends on how this double-reference is interpreted ontologically. As have seen, Smith's concern in making this double-sided phenomenon central to his metaphysics of feeling is to rebut the move in traditional metaphysics that reduces feeling to an 'inner' or 'subjective' sensation whose 'source' is an 'external object,' one that lacks *in itself* any meaning or significance. In that tradition the only 'real,' 'objective' property of an entity is being the 'cause' of feeling; being the external source of subjective feeling is only a secondary, 'neutral' aspect of its true nature, its essential being. For Smith, on the other hand, having meaning or significance, 'mattering,' constitutes ontologically the very *being* of an entity.

Clearly for a philosophy concerned to make sense of the link between our emotions and the fact that something (the world) exists, particularly in the context of the claim that the Why question cannot be answered by any metaphysics grounded in causal or teleological argument – a position we share with Smith, an ontology grounded in a traditional dichotomy of inner/external, subjective/objective, value/fact is a non-starter. We have to look elsewhere for an ontology, and epistemology, that can found such a link. The problem with Smith's phenomenological analysis of this link, however, is that, as we have suggested in previous sections, it is not clear what ontology, if any, grounds his concept of 'feeling,' and thus of the 'importances' of entities. Is there an ontological alternative to traditional causal/teleological metaphysics implicit in his analysis of 'feeling' and the double-sided phenomenon of the 'felt meanings' (importances) of the world, or is he still laboring, as it were reactively, under the negative influence of the metaphysical tradition? Perhaps we cannot answer this question until we look again at his concept of 'world.' In the meantime, we need to set this out as a fundamental conundrum.

Appreciation. For Smith the notion of 'appreciation' is correlative with that of 'importance.' Entities as 'importances' call forth 'appreciative' feeling-flows from the side of the I. Such feelings are appreciations of things as being important, as 'mattering' to us. Here too Smith points to the central fact of the double-sided nature of our engagement with the world. But as the 'correlative' aspect of this phenomenon from the 'side of the I,' the notion of appreciation presents us with the same ontological conundrum as does its partner concept of 'importance.' Why cannot we say that our appreciations are simply physiologically conditioned behavioral dispositions – admittedly of a 'higher' socio-culturally mediated sort expressed in evaluative judgments – responding to stimulus by external objects which, *in themselves*, have no intrinsic 'meaning'? Clearly Smith wants to reject this conclusion with its nihilistic implications – as do we – but on what alternative ontological basis can he do so – or can we? That is the question.

World. When we turn to the third of the concepts central to his metaphysics of feeling, the phenomenon of 'world,' we can perhaps begin to catch a glimpse, a hint, of another ontological direction that could be taken. Smith's metaphysical thesis, positively expressed, is that "the nature of human beings is appreciation...and that the world is a whole of importances." With this reference to the 'nature of human beings' in conjunction with that of 'the world as a whole,' Smith can be taken as alluding to an alternative ontology. The 'nature' of human beings, their essence, their very being, is that of 'appreciation.' If so, the challenge is to figure out how to interpret, ontologically, what it means to say that the *being* of human beings is 'appreciation.' As just noted, Smith does not do this. But he has here provided us with an important clue. For in this remark there is the suggestion of a philosophical anthropology that is neither physicalist nor behaviorist, an anthropology with corresponding implications for a cosmology grounded neither in causal nor teleological thinking. It is on the basis of such an anthropology, and its implicit ontology, that we can then move to interpret his thesis that the world is not a world of cause-effect or means-ends relations, but rather "a world that tonally flows in a certain direction and manner," in other words, that the 'world' is a 'whole' of 'importances' (Smith, 1986, 53).

Ontology of Feelings. We may not yet be in a position to suggest what an ontology that supports Smith's phenomenological analyses of feeling, importance, appreciation and world might look like, but he has given us important clues as to the direction we should look. On that basis perhaps we can push our inquiry bit further. As we do so, a question we should keep in the mind, one suggested but not answered by Smith's reference to the 'nature of human beings,' is this: *Why* do the 'importances,' the felt meanings of the world, 'matter' to us? The answer may seem obvious, but Smith does not provide it – and yet it may contain one more clue as we search for an ontology of feelings.

William James' concept of 'experience' as a *double-barreled* phenomenon, that is, an ontologically and epistemologically primordial notion that precedes its splitting off into correlated notions of subject and object, may be helpful here. What is attractive about James' concept when compared to Smith's metaphysics, is that it hints at the possibility of an underlying ontology that precedes not only the traditional metaphysical distinction grounded in the subject-object dichotomy, but also Smith's distinction between appreciations 'on the side of the I' and importances 'on the side of the world,' the unexamined ontological duality, however 'correlative,' between 'I' and 'world.'

When we asked 'what are feelings?' it seemed our emphasis was on the term 'feelings.' But perhaps what we need to focus on is the 'are' – what *are* feelings, what is their nature, their essence, their *being*? 'Feeling-sensations,' 'feeling-tonalities,' especially 'feeling-awarenesses' – these are ontologically awkward expressions. With them Smith is trying to say something, but what is it that he is trying to say? As a phenomenologist, Smith is committed to the claim that feelings have an 'intentional' structure, an 'as'-structure. They contain' an intrinsic reference *to* ... something. So they are, to invoke James' term, in some sense double-barreled phenomena, relational phenomena, bearing an inner reference both to the 'subject' who intends them and to that which is their intentional 'object.' But what is the ontology of that relational phenomenon? It is not simply on the side of the subject, nor on the side of the object; rather it is, as it were, somewhere 'in between.' But what is the ontology of that 'in-betweenness'? It can be neither the ontology of the subject nor of the object, but the ontology of the relationship of being 'in-between' itself. It cannot be an ontology of the I, nor can it be an ontology of the world. It cannot be the ontology of appreciation, nor can it be the ontology of importances. Neither can it be an ontology of feeling *tout court*, of feeling in some ontologically absolute or fundamental sense. As we have seen that phenomenon has already been divided up and parceled out to the sides of the I and the world. So if, *contra* Smith, 'feeling' is to be seen, in analogy to James' notion of 'experience,' as an ontologically primordial phenomenon, we are left with the task of making sense of it not, as Smith does, in terms of the relata (I, world) that form the two poles of a relation, but rather as the phenomenon of relationality itself. But how can something so concrete-sounding as feeling be ontologically understood as something so insubstantial-sounding as a 'relation'? To repeat: what is the ontology of that 'in-between-ness'? What a strange ontology it must be!

Whatever it is, however we are to understand it, this fundamental relation is none other than the link for which we have been searching, the link between our emotions and the fact that something (the world) exists. Of course the relation between the I and the world is in some sense in us, but it is so only in a derivative sense. In a more fundamental sense it is not "in" us at all. It is neither on the side of the subject viewed as its inner locus, nor it is on the side of the world viewed as its external cause or ground. The relation is neither subjective nor objective in those traditional senses. Rather the link is double-barreled in James' sense, that is, while it grounds and gives rise to the split of subject and object, ontologically it is prior to both. The link always already exists 'before' either I or world, is always already 'there' *in between* us and the world. It is not that we *are* that link or that we *embody* that link, it is rather that we find ourselves already existing *within* the link, as it were *dwelling in* the link, inhabiting a strange ontological space 'in between' I and world.

An understanding of that 'space' will not be cast in the language of a metaphysics of causal explanations. But neither will it be accounted for in a metaphysics of feeling. Smith's concept of feeling is already compromised by its associations with the tradition it is trying to overturn. Having narrowed the concept of 'reason' to causal and/or teleological reasoning in metaphysics, he resorts instead to an expanded notion of feeling to pursue what is nonetheless a rationalistic, metaphysical-explanatory project no different from that pursued in the metaphysical tradition before him. But the nature and priority of the ontological 'in-between' is what neither the vocabulary of metaphysical reason nor the vocabulary of feeling in either its traditional or extended senses is able to comprehend. And so the stakes are high. For if we can uncover the non-metaphysical ontology of that 'space,' it could provide the basis for a non-metaphysical answer to the Why question itself.

What are 'Global' Feelings? With these preliminary concerns about the ontology of Smith's extended notion of 'feeling' in hand, we turn for a closer look at his concept of 'global' feelings, a notion which will bring us closer to the implicit metaphysical assumptions underlying his phenomenology. As we asked of his notion of feeling, so here too we can ask about the ontology of global feelings: just *what are* 'global' feelings? *What* are they really feelings *of*? What Smith calls 'emanations' of the world-whole transport me, through global feelings, into "the great *sensuous-metaphysical regions* of the world." Each of these 'broad and deep' emanations, or 'global' feelings, discloses to me one of our fundamental ways of being vis-a-vis the world-as-a-whole. Our moods and affects are modes of existence grounded in these metaphysical 'regions' of the world-whole. But what exactly is the ontological nature of this *link* between moods or affects and the multiple ways the world, as it were, 'worlds'? We cannot give an entire answer at this point without looking more closely at the alleged 'object' of global feelings, the *world-whole*. But we can make an initial foray into the question.

To begin with, global feelings are a species of feelings. They bring with them, therefore, the ontological problematic we have just raised regarding Smith's account of feelings. But with the additional feature that they are said to link our emotions not to inner-worldly realities, but to the reality, including multiple 'regions,' of the world itself as a whole. This makes their metaphysical burden even heavier, raises the ontological stakes even higher.

Smith bases his argument on the claim that moods and affects are epistemologically privileged 'metaphysical' feelings, that is, feelings that refer to and bring us into emotional relation with the world *as a whole*. His argument takes advantage of one particular feature of moods, its *indeterminacy*, that is, the fact that moods seem to refer to nothing in particular but everything in general. They do not refer to inner-worldly things either individually or in some collectivity, therefore they must refer, holistically, to the totality of things as such, to the very being of things-as-a-whole. They are elicited by, if not projected upon, 'the world-as-a-whole,' 'the world-in-itself' – not, it should be noted, to something transcendent to the world, but rather to the 'world' simply as itself, the world reduced to the bare fact of its existence – but, a 'bare' fact laden, emotionally, with ultimate 'importance.'

It is fair to observe that at this crucial point in his argument Smith's allegedly pure, direct, linguistically unmediated 'global intuitions' are in fact also heavily laden with certain highly articulated metaphysical presuppositions. These include on the one hand his previous dismissal of a 'metaphysics of rational meaning' with its assorted 'proofs' of the existence of a being transcendent to the world, as well as his critique of a 'metaphysics of rational meaninglessness' with its nihilistic pessimism about any positive 'importances' of the world. One has to ask, therefore, just how epistemologically disclosive his 'global feelings' really are. What if in fact we ask about the 'global intuitions' of a theistically committed metaphysician? Certainly we have ample evidence in the writings of philosophers like Nietzsche or Sartre what the 'global intuitions' of a so-called 'atheistic' metaphysics would lead us to think. To take just one example, would 'global intuitions' of the 'purposelessness' of the world's existence come out the same in those two other cases? Presumably in one case it would be epistemic evidence of the unfathomable gulf between the ways of God and the ways of man; in the other it would confirming evidence of the ultimate meaninglessness of life itself. Smith claims to present his global intuitions as evidence for a realist metaphysics of feeling, feelings disclosive of, because elicited by, the objective importances of the world. But in fact they appear to be a retrojection of a specific metaphysics along the tracks that were already laid down. In one sense this is unobjectionable. Can any epistemology be entirely innocent of some metaphysical underpinnings or other? The point is that this needs to be acknowledged as such, not claimed to be otherwise, as if global feelings offered pure, direct, unmediated access to a world otherwise untainted by the insidious snake of human interest and language.

What is of particular interest, in light of this critique, is that Smith's notion of global feelings, in particular moods, seems to be a reprise, but in a *metaphysical* register, of Heidegger's analysis of moods in *Being and Time*. Revealing here is his article, "On Heidegger's Theory of Moods" (Smith, 1981), published at the time he was already deep into his book-length analysis of what at the time he was still calling a 'phenomenology' (i.e., not yet 'metaphysics') of feelings. In this essay his insight that modes of 'feeling-awareness' like moods have a privileged role in world-disclosure clearly builds on Heidegger's analysis of four aspects of the essential revelatory features of moods: their disclosure of what Heidegger calls our 'thrownness' into the world, their disclosure of what Heidegger calls our 'being-in-the-world' as a whole, and their disclosure of the ways things and the world 'matter' to us, their being as what Smith came to term 'importances.' A fourth feature found not in *Being and Time* but in works Heidegger wrote shortly after, and one that proved of central importance to Smith's subsequent book, was the function of moods as disclosure of being(s)-as-a-whole. (Smith, 1986, 213; cf. 144-145).

Two points among others stand out in Smith's reading of Heidegger's account of moods. First and most fundamental is his choice to focus on moods as disclosing 'being(s)-as-a-whole.' The first is Smith's translation of Heidegger's expression for *das Seiende im Ganzen* (alternatively *Seienden im Ganzen*), as a singular term: 'being-as-a-whole' or 'the totality of what is' (or again, in Smith's *Felt Meanings of the World*, as 'the whole of being'), whereas a more accurate rendering of Heidegger's expression would be the plural: 'beings-as-a-whole.' Heidegger's expression makes clear, as Smith's translation does not, that for Heidegger the reference of moods in this case is not to that which is ontologically fundamental but rather to something that is, in Heidegger's usage, 'ontic,' that is, ontologically penultimate. Smith is not unaware of this distinction, however, in that he refers to Heidegger's differentiation between an 'ontic' totality (referring to being(s)/*Seienden*) and what he labels Heidegger's 'ontological' totality (referring to Being/*Sein*). It is not clear in his essay what Smith thinks Heidegger might mean by the latter term, but he is clear that by the former term Heidegger means to refer to the totality/whole (*Ganze*) of beings (*Seienden*), a 'whole' revealed in moods such as boredom, anxiety, joy, etc. (Smith, 1981, 216). Smith maintains this reading of Heidegger in his subsequent book as well. There, however, he recognizes that by anxiety (*angst*) Heidegger means to refer to something more than simply the ontic 'totality of what is;' it refers more primordially to an ontological totality. Smith's uncertainty about Heidegger's distinction can perhaps be discerned in his comment in his essay that Heidegger's expression, *das Seiende im Ganzen* (alternatively *Seienden im Ganzen*) "in many respects is analogous to Heidegger's term for '*In-der-Welt-sein*' or '*In-der-Welt-sein als Ganzes*,' 'being-in-the-world (as a whole)" (Smith, 1981, 217). It is not clear, however, precisely how Smith understands the differences underlying the analogy. What is interesting about this in any case is that for Heidegger it is clear that feature of moods is a penultimate one, one that depends ontologically on the 'earlier,' i.e., more fundamental feature of moods, i.e., their disclosure of 'being-in-the-world' as a whole.

The question now is, having arrived at this additional understanding of Heidegger's distinction, what does Smith then make of Heidegger's ontic/ontological distinction, in particular Heidegger's (alleged) notion of an 'ontological' totality? Is the 'totality' in the ontic sense the same as the 'totality' in the ontological sense? Does Smith think they can finally be subordinated to a still greater sense of the world as a 'totality,' or would that represent a fundamental failure in understanding the radical impact of Heidegger's distinction for an understanding of the notion of 'world'? To answer this we must look at the offending passage in full:

> Heidegger's *angst*, as an essential or *a priori* effect, is mundane. Consider that *angst* is about an ontological or *a priori* whole, Being-in-the-world-as-a-whole (*In-der-Welt-sein-als-Ganze*). This whole differs from the *a posteriori* and ontical whole, which is the whole of being (*das Seiende im Ganzen*). The ontical whole is disclosed in boredom (for example): 'This boredom makes manifest being as a whole." Now we must think in a more fundamental

and unrestricted sense than Heidegger, beyond the confines of his absolutized ontological/ontic dichotomy, to recognize that the ontological and ontical wholes *are both parts of the whole composed of the ontological and ontical wholes*. It is this transontological and transontical whole that is the world-whole in the unrestricted sense and is that to which global affects relate. If the whole of the *a priori* and the whole of the *a posteriori* are *parts* of the world-whole in the unrestricted sense, then an anxiety that relates merely to the whole of the *a priori* must be a mundane anxiety. (Smith, 1986, 144-145, italics in original; also, 339 n. 94, ref. to Heidegger, *SZ*, 137; 339, n. 95, refs. to Heidegger, *VWW* sections 4-6; *WiM*; and *VWG*, chs. 2 & 3; 339, n. 96, ref. to Heidegger, *WiM*, 31; 339-340, n. 97, ref. to Heidegger, *SZ* 53, regarding which Smith says, "Strictly speaking, however, Heidegger's *angst* is not even fully revelatory of the ontological whole, for Being-in-the-world as a whole does not even exhaust *Dasein*'s ontological constitution: Being-in-the-world is of course a necessary *a priori* constitution of *Dasein*, but it by no means is sufficient for completely characterizing *Dasein*'s Being.'")

This is, to put it gently, not only an astonishing reading of Heidegger, but is a tendentious piece of philosophizing as well. To unpack all the confusions and misrepresentations it contains would take an essay in itself. For our purposes it suffices to make a few observations. To refer already in the opening sentence of the passage to Heidegger's notion of *angst* as 'mundane' is already a serious misinterpretation of Heidegger's understanding of the phenomenon. By 'mundane' Smith means 'referring to inner-worldly beings,' including 'the totality of beings' – what Heidegger would consider ontic entities or an ontic totality. To further confound matters, in the very next sentence Smith appears to take back what he has just said in the previous sentence, for it now turns out that *angst* is about an *ontological* 'whole.' But then in the third sentence, apparently collecting himself, he goes on to correctly distinguish between the two sorts of 'wholes' under discussion – the ontic whole of being(s) as a totality (*das Seiende im Ganzen*) and the ontological whole of being-in-the-world (*In-der-Welt-sein-als-Ganze*).

But now comes the real problem. For Smith proceeds to dismiss Heidegger's fundamental, i.e. "absolutized ontological/ontic dichotomy," which he has already bowdlerized in the previous sentences, inviting us instead to "think in a more fundamental and unrestricted sense than Heidegger" and "to recognize that the ontological and ontical wholes *are both parts of the whole composed of the ontological and ontical wholes*" (Smith's emphasis), a 'whole' he characterizes as a "transontological and transontical whole that is the world-whole in the unrestricted sense ... that to which global affects relate." How Heidegger's notion of 'being-in-the-world' is transformed by this feat of linguistic legerdemain into a mere 'part' of some 'transontological and transontical' or 'unrestricted' notion of the 'world-whole' is never made clear. It appears simply to be stipulated, for otherwise Smith's metaphysical notion of the 'world-as-a-,whole' would face of threat of being undermined by Heidegger's radically anti-metaphysical notion of 'being-in-the-world.'

The second point, related to the first, is that by construing the world-whole as 'being(s)-as-a-whole' or 'the totality of what is,' Smith interprets the phenomenon of 'world' *metaphysically* as the objective referent of 'global' feelings. He thus fails to realize the revolutionary *anti-metaphysical* implications of Heidegger's interpretation of the mood of anxiety (*angst*), the primordial mood which forms the main focus of Heidegger's analysis in *Being and Time*. For Heidegger, anxiety is not the disclosure of a hybrid 'world' mixing existential-phenomenology with cosmological-metaphysics; rather it is the disclosure of the prior existential-ontological phenomenon of 'being-in-the-world.' Smith's metaphysical mix reflects a fatal ambiguity in his concept of 'world,' about which we shall say more in a following section. Here we can simply observe that his 'world-whole,' conceived primarily as a 'totality of felt importances' (an 'existential-phenomenological world,' as it were), always teeters on the edge of back-sliding into the comforting embrace of a more traditional concept of the world as, in an 'unrestricted sense,' the 'totality of what is' (a 'cosmological-metaphysical world'). What is needed, therefore, is to disambiguate these two concepts of 'world.' In that way perhaps we will be able to focus in a more radical way on what it is that moods and affects disclose, not about the world of traditional metaphysics, to be sure, but also not about a strange hybrid that slips back and forth between traditional cosmological and more genuinely phenomenological concepts of world. Perhaps we will be able to uncover an ontology that explains why and how it is that moods such as anxiety, boredom or joy can disclose, can *link* us to, perhaps *are* the 'in-between' link of the primordial phenomenon of 'being-in-the-world (as a whole).' If so, perhaps we can then uncover the radical *truth* of such phenomena.

The Epistemology of Feelings

Pilate asked, "What is truth?" (John 18:38). Quite a question to ask of a man about to die. Truth – a matter of life or death? Raises the stakes. Falsehood is easy, but truth is difficult. Jesus said, "You shall know the truth, and the truth shall set you free." (John 8:32) Free *from* what? From falsehood, from death? Free *for* what? For life, for love? For existing *truly*. For the truth of our *being-in-the-world*.

It is Smith's claim that our moods and affects *disclose* the felt meanings of the world. These meanings are *actual features* of the world and our feelings are *appropriate responses* to them. Put another way, these feelings are *objectively true*, however paradoxical that may sound to philosophical ears used to dismissing them as *subjective* reports on inner phenomena. It is our feelings that are our fundamental *mode of access* to the existence and nature of the world. Smith puts forward an analysis of the *criteria of truth* to support his claim. This claim and these criteria are what we must now revisit.

What could it possibly mean to say of global feelings, and of the felt meanings or importances we ascribe to the world, that they are 'true' other than to say that, yes, it is true we do *experience* such feelings, and yes, it is true we do *ascribe* such meanings to, or *project* such importances upon, the *world*. But if this all 'truth' of feelings means, what prevents the richness of Smith's descriptions of global feelings from falling into the solipsism of a subjectivist phenomenology that fails to contact the objective 'world' of being and truth? Does the world *really have* the felt-meanings, the 'importances,' he says it does? Are the feelings in *response* to those importances *appropriate*? If so, by what *criteria* of truth, by what *method* for establishing their truth, can he show this? Smith tells us that the felt truths of the world are *multiple*. But this only exacerbates the question. In that case, if there is more than one truth about the world, then whether *conflicting or compatible*, in what sense can *any* of them be *true*? We will begin therefore by asking what Smith understands the *nature* of the truth of feelings to be, what he takes it to mean when he says of a feeling that it *is true*. We will then we ask whether his understanding of the *criteria* of the truth of feelings, the *method* for proving them, makes sense. Finally we will ask how there can be *conflicting and/or compatible* truths about the existence and nature of the world.

Truth. The first question to ask is not what are those phenomena that Smith thinks are *true*. We know the answer to that: for Smith feelings are what are fundamentally true. Rather we must ask what he means when he speaks of the *truth* of feelings. Only then can we consider his claim that it is emotions which are fundamentally true. This first question involves several subordinate ones.

Theories of truth. The basic question is this: how does Smith understand the *nature* of truth, that is, what is his *theory* of truth, and how does he see it applying to the phenomenon of feelings? Smith speaks often of feelings being *appropriate* responses to the importances of the world. According to the dictionary, to be 'appropriate' means in a general sense to be suitable for, congruous or compatible with, correspond in nature or kind to, a particular situation or condition, occasion or use. We can therefore gloss 'appropriate' as a kind of catch-all term for 'true,' but precisely because of its very generality it lacks the specificity we require. Philosophy traditionally has provided more exacting interpretations of 'appropriateness' or 'truth' in matters epistemological. The major candidates have been a correspondence theory of truth, a verifiability theory of truth and, more recently, a pragmatic theory of truth. Can any of these help us to unpack his understanding of the notion?

At different places in his argument Smith seems to employ the first two of these theories, correspondence and verifiability, but apparently not the third for reasons to which we will return. Each of these theories offers an *explanatory* account of truth that focuses on a single positive feature. In addition, at one place, referring to truth as 'presence,' Smith seems to hint intriguingly at a rather different idea of truth to which we shall also have to return, one that suggests a rather different, *non-explanatory* 'account.' On the assumption that traditional epistemologies are metaphysically-based accounts of knowing and truth, we might term the latter a *non-metaphysical, ontological* interpretation of truth. We will look at each of these in turn.

THOMAS DEAN

Correspondence theory of truth. Again, according to the dictionary 'correpond' is a two-termed, i.e., *relational* predicate meaning that some 'things' (*a*) are said to be similar to or consistent with, to coincide in its basic features or characteristics with, to be equivalent or parallel to, to agree with, some other 'things' (*b*). The notion requires that whatever sort of 'thing' *a* is (proposition, statement, belief, 'meaning,' feeling-sensation), it must be thought of as a 'what' distinct from the 'what' (fact, actuality, reality, state of affairs, 'importance') to which it must be shown to stand in a relation of 'correspondence.' *a* is thought of as a 'what' on 'the side of the subject' whereas the *b* is a 'what' on 'the side of the world.' *a* is thought to possess some quality, feature, property that 'accords' with some answering quality, feature, property of *b*. In logic or mathematics, for example, it might be said that *a* corresponds with *b* if and only if (*iff*) for every element of set *a* there is a unique element of set *b*. (This is a notion of correspondence like that worked out by Wittgenstein in his early work, *Tractatus Logico-Philosophicus*, an idea which, famously, he later came to reject as an inadequate account of how in fact language works.) At this point we might ask, given the above understanding of the two terms, *a* and *b*, what is the nature of the link between them, the *relation*, the 'correspondence' itself? Here things get murky. It seems hard to be more specific. 'Correspond' appears to be some sort of abstract idea lacking any further content postulated to 'account' for the fact that *a* can be said to refer to, be 'true' of, point truthfully to *b*. But *what* constitutes the 'referring,' *how* it 'points' – ahh, there's the mystery! As one encyclopedia account of the correspondence theory concludes: "what it is for a belief to *correspond* to a fact, if it is to be more than merely a picturesque way of asserting all instances of 'the belief that *p* is true if and only if *p*', is a problem on which the correspondence theory has foundered" (Horwich, 812). And if the correspondence theory, based as it is on one or another of the subject/object dualisms of metaphysics, has run aground, then any claim that feelings 'correspond' with importances must be similarly problematic.

Verifiability theory of truth. However, it is not clear that by itself this problematic poses an insuperable obstacle to Smith's account of the truth of feelings, at least not yet. For the main emphasis in his account would seem to be an analysis of the *appropriateness* of feeling-responses in terms of a *verifiability* theory of truth. This approach to truth would appear to avoid the metaphysical assumptions upon which, we have suggested, the correspondence theory of truth is dependent. Instead it tries to account for the close link between *knowability* and truth.

There are at least two versions of the theory. On the one hand there is a *holistic* version which involves the claim that *a* (proposition, belief, feeling, etc.) is verified iff it can be shown to be part of an entire system of *a*'s that is consistent and 'harmonious,' a so-called *coherence* theory of truth. On the other hand, there is an *intuitionist* approach to truth holding that for every *a* (proposition, belief, feeling, etc.) there is some specific *procedure* for determining whether it should be believed or not. Truth, here identified with *provability*, is discovered via the application of an *appropriate* procedure leading to direct intuition of *b* (fact, state of affairs, 'importance,' etc.). A problem with this approach to truth is that, as one commentator notes, it appears "to overstate the intimacy of that link" between knowability and truth because one "can easily imagine a statement that, though true, is beyond our power to establish as true" (Horwich, 812). However, whether this linkage issue would be a problem for a theory of truth based on feelings rather than statements is something we will have to consider. It is possible that behind even a verifiability theory of truth the spectre of metaphysics still looms.

In the meantime, it seems clear that Smith's approach to the verifiability of feelings, even global feelings, is not an example of a holistic or coherence theory of truth, even in the case of so-called 'global' feelings. Rather it appears to be a version of an intuitionist approach to verifiability. As Smith says, it is possible to *verify* whether a particular feeling-response is true, i.e., does in fact 'correspond' with a felt importance of the world. For Smith a verifiability approach to truth involves the claim that the truth of feelings is verifiable (knowable) only if they can be shown to refer to something "discoverable in intuitive feeling" (104). As he adds: "That this is so cannot be 'conceptually proven'; it must be experientially verified ... The criterion for verifying these (or any) significations is the discovery of the intuitively felt phenomenon they putatively signify...in one's own experience" (Smith, 1986, 179). This is a preliminary glimpse of what the verification theory of truth might mean for Smith, but as the mention of 'criterion' indicates, for a fuller answer we will have to wait until the following discussion of the *criteria and method* of truth..

Whatever the case in applying an intuitionist theory to feelings, it is possible that a version of the holistic notion of truth could be applied despite Smith's failure to avail himself of that option. Perhaps feelings, even global feelings, are not *in themselves* true, but *become* true when situated in a larger context of 'revelation.' If regarded as 'atomic' feeling-sensations, true in and of themselves, they would not, absent that prior setting, be true in any but a minimal descriptive sense, one having no bearing on what may or may not be the case in the world. In that case, Smith's analysis would have to start not from feelings as epistemological building-blocks, but rather from an analysis of the a priori 'field' or 'world' of experience, that 'open space' or horizon of experience within which they would then find purchase. But if so, what would it mean in that larger context to say of a particular feeling, even a global one, that it is 'true'? Would it have to be shown that the feeling was, as the coherentist theory has it, 'consistent and harmonious' with our other feelings? That might work in the case of propositional beliefs, but would that be possible in the case of feelings with all of their well-known complexities? If we are to suggest that a holistic approach to truth might be a way out of Smith's dualistic dilemma, it would appear not to be a coherence theory of truth in any classical, i.e., metaphysical sense.

Pragmatic theory of truth. What about a pragmatic approach to truth? This does not seem to be an alternative that Smith draws on, but should he have? Would it have helped him to avoid that ghost of metaphysics? A pragmatic theory of truth, associated with the radical (i.e., non-dualistic) empiricism of William James, was specifically formulated to avoid the assumptions of a metaphysical subject/object dualism. Thus, to say that *a* (proposition, belief, feeling, etc.) is true is not to refer to an alleged link between something 'on the side of the subject' and something 'on the side of the object.' It is rather to say that *a* is 'a good basis for action.' "True assumptions are said to be, by definition, those that provoke actions with good results" (Horwich, 812). To say that *a* (proposition, belief, feeling, etc.) is *true* is to say that it has the *value* of enabling the *fulfilling* of some desirable end or goal. In brief, if *a* is true, it has *practical* value. Of course, even this theory of truth has its problems. Like the preceding two, it too can be said to be an 'explanatory' account focusing on just one particular aspect of a more complex phenomenon. Then is a satisfactory account of the truth of *a* (proposition, belief, feeling, etc.) one that combines all three of these theories in a mega-theory, hoping thereby to avoid the problems associated singly with each? Or is it perhaps, as the pragmatic theory itself suggests, that the notion of truth, and in particular the truth of feelings, has to be recast on a different, non-metaphysical foundation altogether?

One possibility suggested by a pragmatic approach is to see truth or being-true not as an adjectival quality or property of an *a* (proposition, belief, feeling, etc.), but as having an adverbial force referring to a *mode* of activity, to a 'how.' The traditional theories of truth have taken truth to be the 'what' of an *a* (proposition, statement, belief, 'meaning,' feeling-things) seen as a 'thing' that needs to be brought into relation with another 'thing' distinct from it though in some sense (not spelled out) 'like,' 'corresponding' to, it. But what if 'truth' meant to refer to the 'how' of an activity, to a *mode* of speaking, saying, doing – in short, to a *way* of being-in-the-world, to being-in-the-world *truly*. What would it mean to conceive of truth in that way? Would a dualistic metaphysics of subject and object be able to accommodate it, or would we need a totally different, ontological analysis of being-in-the-world via feelings?

Truth 'on the side of the subject.' If we could interpret the 'truth' of feelings in an adverbial, activity-oriented way, would that mean for Smith's understanding of the concept of feelings? On the face of it, it would seem to call it into question, both 'on the side of the subject' and 'on the side of the object.' For example, what is implied in Smith's notion of feelings 'on the side of the subject.' What does he take the *reference* of truth to be, what is *that which* is said to be true? Traditionally there have been a variety of answers: sense perceptions, ideas, propositions, even sentences, all couched in a theory of correspondence or verifiability, but in any case not feelings. What is novel is that Smith wants to extend these theories of truth to cover the truth of feelings as well. In what sense is a feeling a 'thing' that can be said to be 'true'? Witherall says that Smith is a *'realist'* about feeling-intuitions, though such intuitions are not about the relation of sense perceptions or ideas to physical entities or metaphysical realities as traditionally conceived. They are about the relation of sensuous feelings to real features ('importances') of the world. Feelings are not just subjective reactions, they veridically *reveal* the actual features of the world-whole. They are *direct awarenesses* of those features. Our 'appreciations' of those importances are a form of knowledge and, in the case of global feelings, reflect our ability to directly feel the world as a meaningful whole. (Witherall, 47). The problem with Witherall's reading of Smith is not that it is not accurate, but that it shows that, despite the novelty of Smith's position, his concept of the truth of feelings continues to rely on the traditional theories of truth. Thus, the relation of 'revealing' or 'direct awareness' remains trapped (on the side of the subject) in the problematics of the theories of correspondence and verifiability that we have noted above.

Truth 'on the side of the object.' We can expect to find the same problem on the flip side of the 'reference' relation. What is implied in Smith's understanding of feelings 'on the side of the object'? What does Smith think is that which true feelings are said to be true *about.* What is that *to which* true feelings are said to refer? Smith says they are real features of the world, what he calls the world's 'importances.' What sorts of 'things' are importances? They are not the sort of physical entities or metaphysical realities traditionally conceived of as the 'objects' of sense perceptions or ideas. Rather they are the many different *ways* the world *matters* to us. They are what we might call, were it not that Smith abjures the term because of its narrowly moral connotations (as in Scheler's use, for example), the world's *values* for us. But what sort of 'objects' are values? In what sense can values be said to be 'facts,' states of affairs,' or 'what is the case' – the usual candidates as the 'objects' of propositions, beliefs, etc. Smith would reject this way of formulating the question because it seems to presuppose the very fact/value duality of traditional metaphysics that he wishes to replace by talk of feelings and importances. The problem, however, is that again his understanding of the relation between feelings and importance nevertheless rests on two theories of truth – correspondence and verifiablity – that come trailing clouds of metaphysical assumptions with them.

But what if we adopt an *adverbial* approach to the truth of that which is disclosed in feelings, as we did above. We might then say that what is disclosed in feelings are not *subjects* and *objects* held together in a mysterious relation of *correspondence*, but rather *ways* of speaking, acting, existing. Put another way, we would be saying that what is disclosed in feelings is not the *world*, its existing features, but rather *ways of being-in* the world, an adverbial reality, if you will, that always already exists *within* the field or horizon, the open space in which their 'relation' can then be understood *prior* to the separation of feelings and importances. This, at least, might make possible a way of understanding of the truth of feelings and importances that is non-metaphysical, that is, which does not presuppose the subject-object duality to be ontologically primordial.

Truth as 'presence.' As we noted above, at one point Smith refers to truth as 'presence.' An 'importance' of the world-whole has 'felt' evidence, he says, in that it is "immediately present in intuitive feeling." The remark is not further clarified, but it could be taken, though he does not, to suggest a rather different, *non-explanatory* 'account' of truth. On the assumption that traditional epistemologies are metaphysically-based accounts of knowing and truth, we might term the latter a *non-metaphysical* or *ontological* interpretation of truth. Why 'ontological' but not 'metaphysical'? Because it hints at the possibility of a concept of truth that rests not on the primacy of a metaphysical subject-object duality but on something that precedes such a duality, something that 'presences' and in so doing makes that epistemological duality possible – an 'older,' i.e. prior notion of *ontos*, 'being' and its relation to the phenomenon of truth.

In Book Six of the *Republic* Plato draws an analogy between the concept of truth and the light of the sun that makes possible 'vision' (seeing 'on the side of the subject') and 'the visible' (the seen 'on the side of the object'). Starting with the first part of the analogy Plato has "Socrates" say:

> Do you not observe that vision and the visible have this further need? Though vision may be in the eyes [*i.e., 'on the side of the subject'*] and its possessor may try to use it, and though color be present [*i.e., on the side of the object'*], yet without the presence of a third thing specifically and naturally adapted to this purpose, you are aware that vision will see nothing and the colors will remain invisible. That thing is what you call light...the bond that yokes together visibility and the faculty of sight is more precious (Plato, *Republic*, Book VI, 507d-508a).

It is the light of the sun that, on the one side, enables the subject to 'see,' to respond to the 'object,' and that, on the other side, allows the 'object' to 'be seen.' Should that light be *absent*, though the eye and object exist, the bond that yokes them, the epistemic link that *makes it possible* for the one to 'co-respond' to, to enter into 'relation' with the other, would fail to occur.

"Socrates" (Plato) then spells out the analogy of the light of the sun to the truth of being:

As the good is in the intelligible region to reason and the objects of reason, so is this [*the sun*] in the visible world to vision and the objects of vision. How is that? This reality that gives their truth to the objects of knowledge and the power of knowing to the knower is the idea of the good, and you must conceive it as being the cause of knowledge and truth in so far as it is known. Yet fair as they are, knowledge and truth, in supposing it [*the idea of the good*] to be something fairer still than these you will think rightly of it. But as for knowledge and truth, even as in our illustration it is right to deem light and vision sunlike, but never to think that they are the sun, so here it is right to consider these two in their counterparts as being like the good, or boniform, but to think that either of them is the good is not right. Still higher honor belongs to the possession and habit of the good (*ibid.*, 508b-509ab).

Plato extends the analogy still further, making the startling claim that:

The objects of knowledge not only receive from the presence of the good their being known, but their very existence and essence is derived to them from it, though the good itself is not essence but still transcends essence in dignity and surpassing power (*ibid.*, 509b).

There is a lot to unpack in these statements from the pre-Aristotelian stage of Western ontology, but much of relevance to a non-metaphysical concept of the truth of feelings and their link to the 'importances' of the world. First, we note the analogy between light and truth as that which *makes possible* and *links*, respectively, the seeing of the objects of 'vision' with the knowledge of the objects of 'reason.' Light banishes the darkness which makes it impossible for eyes to see and things to be seen. Similarly, truth overcomes its opposite, the 'untruth' that makes it impossible for our feelings to 'see' (feel) and for 'importances' to be 'seen' (felt). But second, we note that just as for Plato the light is not the same as its source, the sun, so too truth is not the same as its source, what Plato calls 'the (idea of) good.' It is the good that gives meaning, *value* and indeed *being*, to those features of the world that 'matter' to us, but that in itself, in its own being, 'transcends in existence and essence,' in 'dignity and surpassing power,' not only the importances of the world but even that something 'more precious,' the truth, the 'bond' that 'yokes' subject and object, i.e. feelings and felt meanings, together.

Before we go further in applying these passages to our inquiry, we need to return to an earlier passage to note the stakes involved. As Plato observes:

> You are aware that when the eyes are no longer turned upon objects upon whose colors the light of day falls but that of the dim luminaries of the night, their edge is blunted and they appear almost blind, as if pure vision did not dwell in them. Apply this comparison to the soul in this way. When it is firmly fixed on the domain where truth and reality shine resplendent it apprehends and knows them and appears to possess reason, but when it inclines to that region which is mingled with darkness, the world of becoming and passing away, it opines only and its edge is blunted, and it shifts its opinions hither and thither, and again seems as it lacked reason. (*ibid.*, 508c-508d)

In these passages, taken together, Plato leaves us with questions but also provides a clue how to transpose his language and insights into the present context and a direction for taking it further. Some of the questions: What is the 'darkness' (opposite? absence?) of truth to which he refers? How is it related to his distinction between knowledge and belief ('opining')? How it is related to his concept of 'the (idea of) the good'? In what sense is the idea of 'the good' the source of the reality of truth and/or the truth of reality? What implications does his idea of 'the good' have for an understanding of feeling as truthfully disclosing the 'importances' (goods, values) of the world, the ways the world 'matters' to us? And what does it mean to say that the 'idea' of the good, as the source of truth, 'transcends' in its *being* not only the being of the 'importances' of the world but the being of truth itself (if we can speak of the 'being' of truth)?

The clues: whatever our answers to these questions, and answer them we must, what does seem clear is that Plato sees philosophy as an activity that has an intimate relation with, and fundamental importance for, something called the 'soul.' Philosophy involves a kind of 'seeing' that goes beyond seeing the 'visible' world; it is not a 'seeing' confined to the colors of the world of empirical sense-perceptions, it is a 'seeing' that is a way of *being* in the world, the world of feelings and felt importances, but also of the life to which they lead. For what is at stake in philosophy is the 'matter' of *existing* 'in the truth.' For Plato, philosophy is not simply an *aesthetics of 'seeing,'* though it is that too – truth and the good 'shine resplendent,' it is also an *ethics of existence*, a hermeneutics of the 'boniform' soul.

But that is not the only clue we can take away from these passages. If we pursue the analogy of truth to light, we have to ask what is the not simply epistemological (i.e. metaphysical) but ontological nature of truth? What is the nature of the 'intimacy' of the relation of truth to its source, the source of truth and being that transcends them both in 'dignity and power'?

This section began by noting that Smith offered the tantalizing hint the truth had something to do with the 'immediate presence' of the 'importances' of the world to 'intuitive feeling.' In the light of the passages from Plato perhaps we can perhaps venture an alternative interpretation of Smith's phenomenology of truth as 'presence.' What if we understand the truth of feelings vis-a-vis felt meanings not as a mysterious link on the same 'level' as they, but rather as that prior 'presence' or rather (to capture the verbal sense contained in that word) 'presencing,' the event or happening of a 'light' – the 'opening' of a 'space' or 'field' or 'horizon' of experience – which makes it possible for such a link to occur in the first place? Prior to the subject functioning as a subject and the object serving as an object would be the opening of the world of experience itself in the ontologically primordial 'phenomenon' or 'event' of being-*in*-the world. Prior to the 'I'-as-subject and the 'world'-as-object would be the happening of the 'world' in an ontologically more fundamental, 'horizonal' sense. Truth would be that happening or opening up of that horizon of experience which we call, in a prior sense, 'world' and that makes possible in turn the coming into being of the 'link' between subject and object, the ability of the one to 'see' ('feel') the other and the other to be 'seen' ('felt') by the first.

If we limit ourselves to Smith's metaphysics of feeling, we will not be able to make further sense of this suggested alternative reading of truth.

And yet unless we try, we will not be able to make a final assessment of the many virtues of Smith's phenomenology of feelings and the felt meanings of the world. For now, however, we must leave it there – with questions unanswered but also clues to be followed.

Criteria. In the previous section we briefly touched on Smith's use of a verifiability theory of truth to defend the cognitive significance of feelings. We now need to pursue Smith's notion of the verifiability a bit further. He claims that the truth of feelings is verifiable because feelings refer to something, namely, an 'importance' "discoverable in intuitive feeling." He adds that while this cannot be "conceptually proven," it can be "experientially verified." Feelings are therefore not subjective. They meet the test of a criterion of truth. The notion of a criterion is closely related to that of *evidence.* For Smith the evidence that intuitive feelings provide is 'extra'- or 'pre-rational' in the sense of being immediate, direct, non-inferentially felt. A global state of affairs, "the world-whole *qua* possessing some feature ... has felt evidence in that it is immediately present in intuitive feeling" (Smith, 1986, 28; cf. 330, n. 88). "For example, a person experiencing an affect of awe tacitly and nonpropositionally feels it to be evident that the world is stupendous and immense" (Smith, 1986, ibid.). Thus the criterion for the truth of feelings is "the *discovery* of the intuitively felt phenomenon [feelings] in one's own experience" (Smith, 1986, 179). The felt meanings, the importances of the world, really are 'there' *in* our intuitive experience, and we can *point* to them. This criterion ensures that feelings are not subjective, that "there are criteria specific to intuitive feelings...that enable us to determine which appreciations are veridical," which feelings truly disclose the world's felt meanings" (Smith, 1986, 28). In short, as Witherall observes, Smith is a 'realist' about our intuitions, they are decisive evidence for the existence and nature of the 'importances' of the world. They constitute direct, cognitive awareness of those features. In our intuitive feelings we directly feel – and know -- the world to be a meaningful whole (Witherall, 47).

There is a problem, however: Has Smith really made ir clear *how* we know that our intuitions are true? *How*, by what *procedure*, can we verify them? It is all well and good to talk about 'discovering' phenomena to be 'present in' our intuitions, but exactly how do we go about doing that? How can we recognize or identify the alleged phenomenon as an instance of an importance or feature of the world? Smith's answer is that *what* an intuitively felt importance is can only be *defined ostensively* by

THOMAS DEAN

pointing to what intuitively appears in one's feeling. Further, the fact that a feature of the world can be "purely intuitively felt" *as* an importance can also only be *shown ostensively* by pointing to an actual instance of the appearance of that world-feature in one's intuitive feeling. Without that feeling-experience, one cannot have cognitive access to that world-feature to which the intuitively felt phenomenon or importance refers. Again: "One must discover this intuitively felt phenomenon in one's own experience." An outside observer like Smith can assist in that discovery "indirectly...through evocative and exact descriptions [that] attempt to evoke an ignited thinking-feeling" that elicits a memory of one's own intuitive feeling (Smith, 1986, 179). That may be true. But the problem is: how can *I* 'discover' by 'pure' introspection, as it were, that my intuitions are not deceptive? Smith's view of the criterion of, and procedure for verifying, the truth of our feelings raises a number of questions which need to be examined further. We can break them down into issues about feelings /intuitions, criteria/evidence, and the procedure of verification.

Feelings/Intuitions. Smith says we discover in our intuitive feelings the *presence* of important features of the world. If we are challenged to prove *that* it is there, in particular to identify *what* one it is, we cannot do so by rational argument, all we can do is point to it, 'show' it 'ostensively.' What makes this cognitivity of feeling possible? There appears to be an ambiguity. First, it is not clear whether Smith is saying that a reality of the world itself is in some sense *present in* our intuitive feelings, or rather that our intuitive feelings constitute *evidence* that *point to* a phenomenon *other* than, however closely 'linked' to, our intuitive feelings? In the former case, Smith does not provide us with an ontology of 'presence' that would enable us to understand how that can be. If the latter, in what sense can intuitions be said to be pure, unmediated, direct, or nonpropositional?

Perhaps we need to step back a moment and ask, what exactly does Smith say is contained in our intuitive feelings? What are the *contents* of our intuitions? What is the *structure* of our intuitions? In the case of global feelings, the *contents* are said to specific felt meanings or 'importances' of features of the world-whole. Let us take the example Smith uses. He says the *content* of the feeling of awe is *the stupendous immensity of the world-whole* 'immediately present' in that intuition. But look more closely at what Smith actually says: "For example, a person experiencing an affect of awe tacitly and nonpropositionally feels it to be evident that the world is stupendous and immense" (Smith, 1986, 28). Clearly the intuitive *content* of the feeling of awe has a very specific *structure*, that of a *proposition*. The affect of awe is not an unmediated, nonpropositional intuition but a structured. propositional feeling. Thus we can rephrase Smith's sentence to read: "a person experiencing an affect of awe tacitly and feelingly *believes that*: 'the world is stupendous and immense' is true."

In other words, it would seems that the content and structure of the 'metaphysical' feelings that form the basis of Smith's metaphysics of feeling are not phenomena directly, immediately, nonpropositionally – mysteriously – 'present in' intuitions. Rather they are feelings with propositional, cognitive import (whether tacit or explicitly acknowledged as such), and as such already theory-laden by the metaphysical context in which they are 'felt.' Our intuitions are 'seeings,' ways of seeing, paths, tracks always already laid down culturally and, in the case of a philosophical project like Smith's, along a specific conceptual-metaphysical *Denkweg.* Thus Smith's 'intuitive feelings' are in fact highly sophisticated, theory-laden, culturally encoded ways of seeing and appreciating the world. They are not 'atomic' intuitions from which we start our philosophizing in order to build up the edifice of metaphysical knowledge. Rather they are the end-products of a metaphysical world-view that first constructs them in order to then claim to 'discover' in them 'evidence' confirming what in fact had already been put in them. To see this we need only ask whether a theistic metaphysician would find the same 'felt meaning' in awe that a 'deflationary' metaphysician like Smith finds in it. For the theistic thinker, awe vis-a-vis the stupendously immense universe would bespeak the unimaginable creative power of a Creator, whereas for Smith it is testifies to the stupendous immensity of the world-whole *tout court*. Of course, it may not be a case of the same intuitions having different references – God or the world; it may be, despite the similarity of the feelings, they are not the same feelings at all. In either case, it would simply beg the question to argue such feelings are direct, unmediated or nonpropositional.

It should be clear what this argument is not saying. It is not saying that Smith's phenomenology of global feelings is simply a 'subjective projection' of alleged 'importances' upon an otherwise objective world of 'neutral facts.' It is not saying that the rationale of such feelings is a circular one, reading a world of projected meanings back into our intuitions. That would simply be to repeat the subject-object metaphysics and fact/value epistemology that Smith's metaphysics of feelings is designed to overcome. It is saying, in agreement with Smith, that the 'world' is first and foremost a world of what he calls 'felt meanings.' However, it is also saying that the way to understand the truth of our felt sense of those felt meanings will require an epistemological starting point and an ontological understanding rather different than the ones presupposed by Smith. Within Smith's understanding of the features of the world-whole the ontology is unclear. The features of the world-whole to which global feelings refer are not all of the same ontological sort. Some features of the world-whole are conceived in physicalist terms, some are conceived in abstract metaphysical terms, and still others are conceived in the 'existential' terms of an ontology of the world-whole whose features are neither physicalist nor abstract.

The above comments points up once again a fundamental problem with notion of feelings or emotions, one that is not entirely Smith's fault. As William James points out, feelings or emotions, like experience itself, are a kind of hybrid phenomenon, a double-barreled creature: they are neither fish nor fowl, neither totally on the 'side' of the 'subject' nor totally on the 'side' of the 'object.' It is as if cannot talk about them without talking about both 'sides' simultaneously. In a sense, however, Smith is capitalizing on this ambiguous nature of the phenomenon. In the opening paragraph of Chapter I where he first introduces his concept of 'feeling' just after the Introduction in which he describes the metaphysical nature of his project he says:

> The first step is to understand the real nature of feeling-sensations and the world as sensuously felt. Each concrete experience of feeling consist of a feeling-sensation and a feeling-awareness, and the correlated world-as-felt consists of a sensuously felt aspect and an important aspect that is apprehended in the feeling-awareness. Although feeling-sensations and the sensuously felt aspects of the world never occur in reality apart from feeling-awareness and apprehended importances, they can for purposes of descriptive explication be considered separately (Smith, 1986, 33).

What he says is that the two levels of feeling on the side of the subject never really exist apart from one another, and that the corresponding two levels of felt aspects on the side of the world never really occur apart from one another. But what he does *not* say is that on each level the feelings on the side of the subject and on the side of the world never really occur apart from one another. Yet, as James insists, in the case of the hybrid phenomena of feelings or emotions not only can the two sides not occur apart from one another – even if "for purposes of descriptive explication they can be considered separately" – they cannot be even then be rightly understood unless they are set back in their underlying ground in the primordial unity of experience itself.

Another factor contributing to the complex hybrid nature of the phenomenon of feeling is that emotions are intentional phenomena, that is, they involve 'consciousness of (something).' This means that the intentional 'object' of an emotion is an intrinsic part of its two-sided nature. As De Sousa explains, the intentional or 'formal' object of an emotion is "a property implicitly ascribed by the emotion to its target, focus or propositional object, in virtue of which the emotion can be seen as intelligible." It is a criterion specifying the "characteristic that must belong to [an emotional state] if it is to be possible for the state to relate to it." The specific nature of the formal object of an emotion is a decisive factor in the appropriateness of my appraisal of and response to a situation. "My fear of a dog, for example, construes a number of the dog's features (its salivating maw, its ferocious bark) as being frightening, and it is my perception of the dog as frightening that makes my emotion fear, rather than some other emotion." On the other hand, "if the dog obstructing my path is a shitzu, my fear is mistaken: the target of my fear fails to fit fear's formal object. The formal object associated with a given emotion is essential to the definition of that particular emotion. This explains the appearance of tautology in the specification any formal object (I am disgusted because it is disgusting); but it is also, in part, what allows us to speak of emotions being appropriate or inappropriate. This implies an excessively strong logical link between the state and its object's actual possession of the characteristic in question. Nevertheless it points to an important condition on the appropriateness of an emotion to a given object." The formal object of an emotion thus, by definition, provides a criterion for the truth of that feeling (De Sousa, 2013).

De Sousa's analysis of the intentional object of an emotion or feeling highlights another problematic aspect of Smith's phenomenological-cum-metaphysical project. On the one hand, in a phenomenological analysis of an intentional state such as an emotion, the *formal* object of that intentional state is *present in* that state. It is what *identifies* the state *as* being the state it is – fear, awe, etc. In this sense, as Smith's phenomenological analysis brilliantly describes, the stupendous immensity of the world-whole can be said to be 'immediately present' in the global feeling-state of awe. But, as De Sousa adds, the 'discovery' of the 'immediate presence' of the stupendous immensity of the world-whole in the global feeling of awe is not by itself a sufficient criterion for the truth of that feeling, it is not by itself decisive evidence for the actual reality of that feature of the world. To restate De Sousa's point: if evidence other than that contained in the emotion of awe fails to conform to the formal object of awe (if that 'fearsome' dog is a shitzu), then my awe (my 'fear) is mistaken. What is it about the world that strikes one as stupendously immense? If one can independently verify those features, then my global feeling will be true. If not, then I must have been mistaken in my feeling.

This critique tacitly rests on a subject-object metaphysics, however complicated by the method of 'bracketing' existence that takes place in a phenomenology of intentional states. The dilemma of Smith's project is that, for all its phenomenological brilliance, it never really breaks out of the methodological bracket within which it labors. If De Sousa's explication of the criteriologically necessary but evidentially insufficient relation of 'formal' objects of emotional states to the actual objects of experience is correct, as we are suggesting, then Smith's concept of feeling remains imprisoned within the framework of a dualistic metaphysics of experience. Once again then we must ask, perhaps having James, Heidegger or Merleau-Ponty in mind, is there not an alternative ontology of experience or existence that would enable us escape that metaphysical framework without sacrificing Smith's phenomenological insights?

Criteria/Evidence. How do these reflections bear on Smith's view of feeling-intuitions as criteria for and evidence about features of the world? We have just noted the tautological nature of the relation of an emotions to the formal objects that defines them, in other words that serves as the necessary criterion for their identity and the possibility of their truth. But we have raised the question whether this criterion is enough to ensure that feeling-intuitions in themselves constitute sufficient evidence to ensure the certainty of their truth.

There are several additional reasons for thinking that Smith's criterion of the truth of feelings – the 'discovery' of the 'immediate presence' of the importances of the world-whole in feeling-intuitions – will not help him to escape the metaphysical bracket in which he has placed his phenomenological analysis.

Criteria provide the standard, principle, test or rule for evaluating certain phenomena by the application of which those phenomena – propositions, statements, beliefs, feelings etc. –can brought into or can be said to stand in relation with other phenomena in such a way that correct judgments, knowledge, about those other phenomena can be obtained. A criterion provides or states the evidence for the correct judgment that a property of a thing (fact, state of affairs) is present, or that a proposition about that thing (fact, state of affairs) is true. They offer a way (method, procedure) for settling a matter of fact or truth with certainty. Sometimes, as in the case of Smith, for example, a criterion can rule that a certain state of affairs, say a feeling-intuition, is direct, unmediated, non-inductive evidence for the truth of a belief about an actual state of affairs of the world. In any case, a criterion should state what would constitute *decisive evidence* for the belief that something is the case, that it is true.

Can we say that Smith's criterion – that the truth of feelings can be determined by whether one can discover the immediate presence of realities of the world in one's feeling-intuitions – itself meets the criterion of being a 'criterion'? Certainly *formally* it would seem to do so. It says, do you want to know whether your feeling of awe *in truth* puts you in the presence of the stupendous immensity of the world itself? There is a way (method, procedure) to do so. You may not be able to prove it conceptually to me, but you can prove it for yourself by discovering it directly in your own experience. You can, as Smith says, 'show' it to yourself 'ostensively.'

There are problems with this answer. First, there is the matter of "the problem of the criterion" itself. This is not a problem peculiar to Smith himself, it is a dilemma endemic to epistemology, but as such it applies to Smith as well. "The problem," as one philosopher points out, "is generated by the seeming plausibility of the following two propositions: (1) in order to recognize instances, and thus to determine the extent, of knowledge, we must know the criteria for it. (2) In order to know the criteria for knowledge (i.e., to distinguish between correct and incorrect criteria), we must already be able to recognize its instances." If both are true we are stymied; trying to know the truth of a matter would be like a dog engaged in the futile activity of chasing its own tail. Nor does it seem to help if we say neither are true. There are then two choices. A 'particularist' would say that one should we choose (1), because unless you begin with what counts as an instance of knowledge, any criterion you try to invoke will be ungrounded, arbitrary. On the other hand a 'methodist' would say one should choose (2), because any identification of an instance of knowledge that does not proceed on the basis of a prior criterion will be hopelessly dogmatic. (Steup, 653).

Where might Smith come down on this dilemma? At first it might seem that, as a 'realist' about the truth value of our feeling-intuitions, he would choose the 'particularist' option given his claim that the phenomena present in our feeling-intuitions are "individual and concrete features of the empirically existing world-whole" (Smith, 1986, 27). And yet, if our preceding remarks are on target, it would be closer to the truth to place him on the side of (2), the 'methodist' option. Apart from the prior methodological framework provided by his metaphysics of feeling, it is not clear how Smith can guarantee that the phenomena I 'discover' to be 'present' in my feeling-intuitions are in fact veridical and not simply subjective self-reports. To repeat our earlier point: despite his assertions to the contrary, as even the structure of his book indicates, Smith does not start his analysis of the phenomena of feeling with the feeling-intuitions themselves but with the metaphysical setting in which the phenomenological analysis will proceed. He does not *start* with the 'particularist' intuitions as if they were concrete empirical phenomena on which to build a metaphysics – as if they were 'atomic' intuitions like those of similarly-minded positivists, only substituting feelings for sense data or perceptual givens. Rather he *ends* with them, *reading back into* them, like a rationalist-minded philosopher, a 'method' provided a priori by his metaphysics supplying the criterion for their 'exact description' as truths about the world.

Procedure of Verification. This brings us to another problem with Smith's 'discovery' criterion for the truth of our feelings, and that is the problematic nature of the verification procedure to which he appeals. Here we can turn to Wittgenstein for a critical assist. As just noted, Smith asserts that although we cannot conceptually prove the truth of our feeling-intuitions, we can prove it for ourselves by discovering it directly, that is, *showing it ostensively* in our own experience. But *how* can we know for sure that our feelings are not misleading without some independent way of checking? The issue with 'inner' phenomena like feelings is that, as Wittgenstein observed: "An 'inner process' stands in need of outward criteria" (Wittgenstein, 1953, para. 580). To be clear, 'inner' does not necessarily mean 'subjective,' but in the absence of 'outward' criteria how can we know? As Wittgenstein points out, it is impossible to give a *private* ostensive definition of a sensation or feeling (Wittgenstein, *ibid.,* para. 258). What is required is a link with some sort of third-person observation statements differing from first-person reports of sense impressions or feelings. Even for ourselves, our ability to identify and verify our inner impressions or feelings is only possible if our self-understanding of them has always already been linked to an intersubjective context of behavioral evidence and criteria. Even if for us these 'inner' phenomena are directly observable, the evidence of their 'presence' in us lies not simply in our self-reports but in our observable behavior – what we say and do. The question then is whether or how Smith deals with what would seem to call into question his criterion for deciding the truth of our feelings – the 'discovery' of their truth by a method of 'ostensive definition' and 'ostensive showing'

As we turn to an examination of his epistemological method we need to have in mind these Wittgenstinian observations. When we speak of 'true, 'truth' do mean by these terms something adverbial rather than adjectival, something referring to the nature of our activities, what we say and do, rather than to the properties of inner phenomena or of propositions about them? If so, what bearing will this have on Smith's understanding of the method for determining the truth of our feelings?

Method. Smith's project rests on what he terms an 'appreciative method of metaphysical knowing' (Smith, 1986, 24). However, he does not develop this method as a result of the outcome of his *phenomenological analyses* of the various 'sides,' levels and types of feeling. Rather, he presents it already fully formed in his introductory remarks on the *metaphysical foundations* of those analyses. Thus, before we 'discover' what phenomena are 'immediately present' in those feelings, Smith has made it clear that the possibility and nature of that knowledge will have been determined *a priori* by a metaphysical world-view and the 'methodological feelings' grounded upon it. It is, as he says, a 'method of *metaphysical* knowing.' In other words, reverting to the distinction above, he opts for a 'methodist' not a 'particularist' approach to the truth of feelings. We are to begin not with a theory and criteria of truth that arise out of an analysis of empirical *instances* of feeling-intuition; rather

THOMAS DEAN

our conclusions will have been framed ahead of time by a metaphysical *method* for making sense of them.

If so, how does this impact on Smith's presentation of his metaphysical method for determining the nature and truth of feelings? Let us begin by recalling its features. The method involves three levels or steps. It begins with first-order feeling-intuitions said to exist prior to and unmediated by any thought-constructions or conceptual analyses. They constitute "a direct sense of [the world as] a meaningful whole." It then proceeds to a second-order description, frequently metaphorical, of the 'felt meanings' of the world evoked by the first-order intuitive feelings. Finally, because metaphorical descriptions are "vague in their sense but rich in connotations," they call for "a new and higher-level methodological feeling," an analysis whose task is to make conceptually explicit the implicit content of the second-order metaphorical expressions evoked by the first-order feelings. By this three-step method one can then determine which feeling is the *appropriate*, i.e *true appreciation* of any given feature of the world. In this way we can be certain that what is 'made manifest' in our 'appreciations' are not simply our own subjective feelings but the actual felt meanings of the world *that are the 'source'* of those first-order feelings (Smith, 1986, 25-26).

But how can we be so certain of this? Because, Smith says, this metaphysical method is not *imposed on* feelings 'from the outside,' it is '*found in* feelings themselves' (Smith, 1986, 24). Can we really credit this claim? How is it possible that our first-order intuitions, allegedly 'unmediated by any thought-constructions or conceptual analyses,' can turn out to have specific contents and structures after all? If it were not so, the two subsequent levels of description – metaphorical and conceptual – would in fact be just such a metaphysical-methodological imposition. However, this does not happen, Smith contends. Despite what initially appears in our intuitions to be a *unitary* phenomenon, higher-order metaphorical descriptions and conceptual analyses disclose *structural features* to be *already present* in our feelings: "In the intuitive feeling, what explicitly appeared was the *unitary phenomenon* comprised of the various aspects and structural articulations *inherent* in the global importance; the various structural contents themselves appeared only in a *tacit* way" (Smith, 1986, 26). Smith concludes that therefore this metaphysical method "does not distort or eliminate the original contributions" of the intuitive feelings that evoke them. A three-step method based in and called forth by feeling-intuitions themselves permits him to develop "a metaphysical theory of the felt meanings of the world" (Smith, 1986, 27).

Smith would thus seem to have protected himself from our suspicion that his method for establishing the truth of feelings, rather than providing the evidentiary basis for a metaphysics of feelings, is in fact simply an imposition of that metaphysics on those intuitions. Nevertheless, our reservations remain. We will focus on his three primary claims: that his method does not *impose* itself upon feelings; that phenomena, i.e., features of the world, are *present* in feelings; and that intuitive knowledge of the (tacit) structural contents of these phenomena is a form of *pre-conceptual* knowledge "unmediated by any thought-constructions."

Smith's fundamental and indeed crucial claim is that his method does not *impose* 'thought- constructions or conceptual analyses' on feelings 'from the outside' but rather is *found* 'in feelings themselves." The method 'originates' from them in that it is not only *based* on feelings, most importantly it is *called for* by them. Not only *phenomena* but the *method* itself is 'discovered' in feeling-intuitions. In brief, his claim is that the method *begins* in feelings; it does not, as we have suggested above, *end* in them. To test this further, we will look at two of its supporting claims. The first is that the features of the world described by the higher-order analyses are *present* in feeling-intuitions. The second is that the structural features, i.e. *conceptual contents*, of those phenomena uncovered by subsequent analysis are already (tacitly) present in those phenomena and are what 'call for' that analysis.

We have already mentioned the problem involved in the claim that certain features of the world are themselves in actual fact *present* in feeling-intuitions. But since it is central to supporting his methodological claim, we need to review it again. It is the problem inherent in at least some versions of 'phenomenology,' one that inheres in Smith's analysis too – the problem posed by the phenomenological method of 'bracketing' out any reference to what actually exists in order to focus on an analysis of the intentional 'object' as it *presents* itself 'as it is in itself' in the particular intentional 'state,' here in feeling-states. In other words, it is the distinction between the 'formal object' of phenomenological analysis and the actual object that exists external to intentional states. So when we ask, just what is the phenomenon that is present in feeling-intuitions, we have to say it is simply a 'formal object,' that is, the intentional object of an intentional state. That is not nothing. It can be, as in Smith's work, the object of many and rich descriptive analyses, but given the prior 'bracketing' called for by the phenomenological method itself, to go from *phenomenological descriptions* to *metaphysical speculations* about actual features of the 'external' world is a step, nay a methodological leap too far.

Here we meet once again with the basic ambiguity in Smith's concept of feeling – the difference between feeling as an *intentional state* whose intentional 'objects' can be said to be objectively 'present' and available for phenomenological analysis, and feeling 'on the side of the subject' as an *empirical awareness* of and *evidence* for states of affairs external to it 'on the side of the world.' To be clear. This is not to reject Smith's claim that in feeling we are aware of a feature or importance of the world. But that *epistemological* sense of feeling as an *empirical* phenomenon has to be distinguished from a *phenomenological* concept of 'feeling' as an *intentional* state in which the 'object' or 'phenomenon' said to be *'present'* in 'feeling' is a *phenomenological* 'object,' not a concrete *empirical* object of the sort to which *empirical* feeling refers, about which a feeling can be 'true.'

If we were to reject this distinction, as in a sense Smith wants to do, we have to turn to an entirely different metaphysics of feeling than the one resulting in the above ambiguity. For example, what James does in his 'radical,' i.e. non-dualist metaphysics of 'experience' is something Smith could perhaps do with his metaphysics of 'feeling.' Like James, Smith could view feeling as a unitary phenomenon – not the unitary phenomenon that appears in feeling, but feeling itself – feeling as a primordial reality that is *unitary in form*, formally *monistic*, but *pluralistic* in *content*. Feeling could then be taken in two 'derivative' directions – *metaphysically* as having an 'objective' reference or *phenomenologically* as having a 'subjective' reference (cf. Lamberth, 25, 29 -30). This alternative itself, however, may not be entirely feasible. Perhaps it too smacks of metaphysical dualism. But if with Smith we want to say that in some sense the features of the world *really are* 'present' in our intuitions, it will not do to continue to construe feelings as 'intentional' acts, as 'consciousness-*of*(something).' We will need to find a completely different ontology to understand what such a claim of 'real presence' could possibly mean.

This bring us to the second point. What could it mean to say that the *structural features* of the phenomena uncovered by phenomenological analysis are already tacitly present in feeling-intuitions, and that further it is precisely those *conceptual contents*, "unmediated by any thought-constructions or conceptual analyses," that 'call for' explicit analysis? This question points up an ambiguity in the notion of the 'pure' – direct, unmediated – nature of feeling-intuitions. By definition it is true, tautologically true, that 'intuition' is a 'pure,' i.e. pre- or non-conceptual *mode of awareness*. This does not mean, however, that the *contents* of intuitions are similarly 'pure,' i.e. conceptually unstructured. Of course Smith sees this point. In fact he builds his entire higher-order analyses upon the latter fact. But that is not the gravamen of our critique. Our counter-suggestion is that it is only possible for Smith to find these conceptual contents in our feeling-intuitions because he has already introduced into his 'phenomenological' analyses of them the structural features of a specific metaphysical world-view. If anything is already *tacitly present* in feeling-intuitions waiting to be 'discovered' and 'explicitly articulated' by higher-order reflection, it is not the structural features and conceptual contents of *phenomena* (to paraphrase Smith) "unmediated by *metaphysical* constructions or *metaphysical* analyses," "unmediated by any thought-constructions or conceptual analyses," it is rather the structural features and conceptual contents of *metaphysics* itself.

Smith wants to urge the opposite for epistemological reasons that are as 'old' as metaphysics itself – to satisfy the ancient quest for the fundamental building blocks of knowledge on which the imposing edifice of metaphysics can be built. The concept of pure feeling-intuitions, free of prior metaphysical imposition, were brought in by Smith to fulfill that search. Since the metaphorical descriptions of those intuitive building blocks are, as Smith say, "vague in their sense but rich in connotations" and "express neither precise and rigorous descriptions nor complicated theoretical analyses," we are therefore justified methodologically in 'calling for' "a new and higher-level methodological feeling" whose purpose will be to "make explicit the implicit content" of the second-order metaphorical expressions "evoked" by the first-order feelings. Here we see the whole problematic. Are these 'methodological feelings' really *new*? The conceptual articulation these 'methodological feelings' make possible is certainly of a higher, *reflective* level, the level of *thought*, than the conceptually unarticulated phenomena on the lower, *intuitive* level, the level of *feeling*. But our counter-claim is that these *methodological feelings* are only able to give 'exact explications' of the features of the world 'present' in intuitive feelings because of a *circularity* in the method itself. It 'discovers' in the phenomena present in feeling the conceptual structures his metaphysics has already put there. In brief, Smith's method involves a *petitio principii*.

If this line of criticism is correct, it has implications for other aspects of Smith's analysis of the phenomenon of feelings. For example, what does it imply for Smith's claim that our intuitive feelings, in particular our global feelings, involve "a direct sense of a meaningful *whole*, a whole to which I respond with sensations of feeling" (Smith, 1986, 25). This becomes an especially knotty issue not only when we ask what it could possibly mean to intuit the world as a *whole*, but also when we consider the possibility of *multiple* such intuitions of the world-whole.

Intuitions of the world-as-a whole are said to take the form of *appreciations* of *importances*, of features of the world that *matter* to us. But what does it mean to speak of the *truth* of 'importances,' the truth of their 'matterings' to us? We speak of the truth of empirical objects, or rather of the truth of statements about them; we say that they are as we say they are. But can we speak of the truth of importances in the same way? Can we say of the importances, the matterings-to-us of the world, that they "*are* as we say they are"? The 'being' of the truth of importances must be of a rather different sort than the 'being' of the truth of material objects.

Smith says that the truth of the importances of the world can be known *evidentially* in accord with criteria of truth applied both to our *appreciations* of them and to the *features* of the world that are the *source* of those felt-responses. But this implies that we know what it means to speak of the *truth* of 'appreciations.' And yet, again, the 'being' of appreciations must be rather different than the 'being' of empirical perceptions. Do we know how to talk about the truth of importances and their appreciations?

Further, what does it mean to say that certain features of the world are the *source* of such appreciations and importances? Smith maintains that this does *not* mean that they are their *cause*. Then, on the 'side of the object,' what is the nature of the *relation* between the features of the world and their importances? Or asked from the 'side of the subject,' how do we come to see, to appreciate the features of the world *as* importances?

Conflicting and/or Compatible Truths? We will keep these issues in mind as we turn to the last section of our critique of Smith's concept of feelings. The problematic concerns the *multiplicity* of our global or 'metaphysical' feelings. Do they represent *conflicting or compatible truths* about the world-as-a-whole?

Why global felt-truths are compatible. Smith's contends that, while there are *multiple* global appreciations and importances of the world-whole, they do not *conflict*. Rather they are *compatible* with each other, they *co-exist* in a *harmony* of 'metaphysical' feelings. His argument rests on two claims: the world-whole *cannot* have features (importances) that cancel each other out; and these features are appropriately responded to in *one* type of affect and not in others. These two claims are what we must now examine. The stakes for his metaphysical project are high, because if either of his two claims falls, then not only the *hierarchical* structure of his metaphysics falls, his basic concept of 'metaphysical' feelings, i.e., of *metaphysical truth*, will be seriously compromised. He himself recognized this, for he said that this question was for him '*the* metaphysical problem' (Smith, 1986, 122).

Let us first review his argument. Global moods, he said, posed the problem of "*the seemingly clashing ways in which the world-whole is felt to be important*" (*ibid.*). Why should this be a problem? Because there appears to be in moods themselves no basis or criterion for deciding which one – euphoria or anxiety for example – discloses the *true* importance of the world (Smith, 1986, 123). Since there is no internal epistemic marker to distinguish the truth of one from other, it would that our moody intuitions are 'unreliable and incoherent' and as such poor candidates as 'metaphysical data.' In the absence of other, more concrete data, there would appear to be no way to decide among competing emotions. Whatever mood we happened to be in, we would feel that the world just was that way ... until we happened to 'find' ourselves in a different mood. Left to the mercy of our shifting, mixed, notoriously unpredictable emotions, we would lack a clear, fixed metaphysical pole-star by which to steer. If we stopped to reflect on it, we might conclude with a bemused regret that life is after all a tragicomedy of incompatible emotions and that the best we can do is get on with it. In any case it would be impossible, even laughable to think of a *metaphysics* of feeling that could overcome such uncertainty and lead to an ultimate harmony.

Here Smith wants to draw a metaphysical line in the sand. The situation presented in the preceding paragraph would result, he says, in an ultimate nihilism, an implicit metaphysics of rational meaninglessness. As Aristotle suggested, one way or the other you cannot avoid doing metaphysics. So here Smith takes his stand, staking out his position with the first claim cited above: "*the world-whole* cannot *have features (importances?) that cancel each other out.*" There are two possibilities, he says: either some importances of the world-whole can be shown to be true and others false – for example, the world really is 'fulfilled,' not 'empty'; or, though the importances of the world-whole differ they are not incompatible – for example, the world really is both 'fulfilled' and 'empty' – because while "the world-whole really has *all* the ways of being important...it has them in different and nonclashing respects" (Smith, 1986, 124).

There are several things that can already be noted in this formulation. It is not clear what Smith means when he says some importances of the world can be shown to be false. Either they are importances of the world or they are not. What would be false is not the importance but the statement, for example, that the world is 'empty.' That may be a minor, perhaps semantic quibble. However, when he says that 'some' features, i.e., more than one, are true, he assumes, without further argument, that they do not clash. But is it at least possible that they might?

Another problem is Smith's introduction of the notion that the 'importances' of the world refer to the world in different 'respects.' There is a confusion here that needs to be clarified before we can know how to proceed. In the two options Smith above speaks of 'importances,' but in his basic claim he refers to 'features.' Does it matter? Perhaps he was simply careless, but it points up a problem. *Importances* of the world are, or refer to, specific *features* of the world *seen as* having certain felt-meanings. Staying with the above example, the *importance* of the world *seen as fulfilled* rather than *empty* is, or refers to, the *feature* of the world as *happening* rather than its feature of *being-empty*. This raises a further question. Where exactly is 'the metaphysical problem' located? Is it a problem of compatible or incompatible *importances* of the world, or a problem of clashing or nonclashing *features* of the world? Can we not have clashing feelings about the same feature of the world – its happening, say, or its emptiness – both of the feelings being in some sense true? Or for every feeling that clashes with another must we find a different feature of the world so that the clash can be defused?

It would appear that in fact Smith has not canvassed all the possibilities available to this problematic. Most consequentially, there is a third possibility: the world-whole really has a multitude of importances, some of them clashing but all of them true. Why does he not consider this possibility? Because it does not make sense within the framework of his metaphysical assumptions. But might it make sense in another ontological setting, one that would not land us back in the nihilistic metaphysics of rational meaninglessness? Is it not even possible that, while a nihilist reading of the ultimate meaning (i.e., meaninglessness) of the world might clash with one or another non-nihilist interpretation of the ultimate meaning of the world, nevertheless both could be *true*? On the face of it, there seems no reason why not. William James, for example, considers three possible 'global' feelings-responses to the world: the universe is friendly, unfriendly, or indifferent. Each global feeling meets the criteria for an 'appropriate' response to the world. Each could be true without necessarily rendering the others false. Or as James would put it, each option '*becomes true*' when one opts for it over the others. But that leaves those remaining as what he calls 'live options' for others. James' approach would call Smith's project into radical question. Whether James' view can be defended or not, it at least suggests that there are other alternatives that could have been considered.

Meanwhile, let us return to Smith's argument, because he is not yet done. There is his second claim: "*the features of the world are appropriately responded to in one type of affect and not in others.*" Unfortunately the same ambiguity occurs in this formulation as well. First, he has shifted from discussing the 'metaphysical problem' in terms of *importances* to addressing it in terms of *affects*. Global affects are responses to the world's *features*. There are several points to note here. *How* those features are seen, namely, *as* importances, is the corollary 'on the side of the object' to affects 'on the side of the subject.' Despite the change of focus, the two options noted above present themselves here too. Either some affects are true and others false, or all are true but respond to different features of the world. But in this case too, do we not confront the same possibility of a third option? Adopting the Jamesian approach we could argue that any number of affects vis-a-vis features of the world could be true without for that reason others being false. Opting for joy because the world is friendly would not rule out others opting for fear in face of the enmity of the world or despair at the emptiness of the world.

There is a second problem with his shift to talk of affects. Recall that the 'metaphysical problem' arose because of the 'unreliable and incoherent' nature of moods, their lack of an internal epistemic marker by which to determine which if any were *true*. To drive a second nail into the coffin of the nihilistic spectre, Smith introduces a distinction between moods and affects. His claim is that affects provide the determinate data needed to solve the 'metaphysical problem.' This distinction allows him to argue that the diverse importances inchoately revealed in our moods, when filtered through their correlated affects, do not conflict with one another but prove to be mutually compatible. However, given the notorious variety and complexity of types of emotions, this stipulated distinction seems highly questionable. Affects are said to be more consciously focused on, more clearly directed to their respective importances. But what is the source of their alleged conscious directedness? Though Smith lists three ways in which affects differ from their correlated moods, he offers no independent evidence to support this distinction. The alleged determinacy of affects vis-a-vis the indeterminacy of moods strongly suggests rather that prior metaphysical assumptions have been imported to guarantee the desired outcome.

How global truths are compatible. However, let us assume for the moment that Smith's distinction is valid. How does he use it to defend his claim that the truths of our multiple global affects are mutually compatible? By proving that each affect refers to a unique feature of the world-whole seen as important – that each discloses a different metaphysical 'region' of the world-whole; and by proving that their logical inter-relations call for a hierarchy of levels of affective truth.

Affects and Features. Let us first restate Smith's basic points. Though there are *several* possible ways of correlating affects and features of the world, they are not *arbitrarily* correlated. Thus, each feature of the world-whole is *appropriately* responded to by [correlated with]one affect and not in others," and vice versa: each affect is an *appreciation* of [correlated with] some feature of the world and not others. But each affect can be an appreciation of [correlated with] *more than one* feature, while each feature can have *different meanings* [have different importance] when correlated with different affects. Finally, in cases where two or more affects are similar, the importances [features?] of which they are the pure appreciations may also be similar, and indeed could be partly if not wholly 'interchangeable.'

Smith's argument works as a rebuttal of our above criticism if the metaphysics on which it is based has first been independently established. Otherwise what we see here is again the introduction of a metaphysics *ab extra* under the guise of a development of structural correlations said to be already contained, now explicitly, in affects. The correlations of affect and features (or importances) can be said to be 'not arbitrary' only because of those prior assumptions. In fact we have already seen another way of interpreting the relation of different affects to the world, based on a different set of metaphysical assumptions. We need only recall Wittgenstein's concise but pregnant observation: "the world of the happy is quite another world than that of the unhappy" (Wittgenstein, *Tract.* 6.43) The happy and the unhappy are not referring to *different features* of the *same world*, they are responding to *different worlds* altogether. Joy in the 'fulfilment' of the world and despair in the 'emptiness' of the world do not refer to *different features* of the *same world*. It is not the *same* world that is simultaneously full and empty, not the *same* world that embodies both features without conflict or contradiction. When my mood changes, it has not shifted to a different *feature* of the *same* world-whole, rather it is the world *as a whole* that changes: "In brief, the world must thereby become quite another. It must so to speak wax or wane as a whole" (*ibid.*). Wittgenstein also said: "the world is *my* world" (Wittgenstein, *Tract.* 5.62). Taken together these statements imply not only that our different global feelings ('happy,' 'unhappy,' joyful, despairing) refer to different worlds, but also insofar as the world is always my world, not your world, the differences in our respective global feelings refer to further differences in worlds, again not to different features of the same inter-subjectively constituted world. How we arrive at the conviction – or is it an illusory belief? – that nevertheless in some sense we inhabit the same world is another matter. It suggests that we will need to look more closely at Smith's concept of the world itself. The point here is that whether Wittgenstein's metaphysics can be defended any more than, say, James', it shows that there is a specific metaphysics already at work shaping Smith's theory of the truth of affects and their correlation with the features (or importances) of the world. Smith's metaphysics of feeling does not emerge from structures already present in our intuitive feelings, rather it imports those structures and their correlated objects into them.

Hierarchy of Affects. Smith maintains not only does each affect refer to a specific feature of the world, there are relationships among them that call for a hierarchy of levels of affective truth. For example, though they seem to exist on the same level, the affect of despair is, however paradoxical it may seem, logically dependent upon the affect of joy. The emptiness of the world depends upon the fulfillment-of-happening of the world, joy is the appropriate response to the happening of the world itself, thus despair is a dependent upon, i.e. *privative* or 'negative' mode of, joy. Smith builds a multi-tiered hierarchy of affective truths on a careful analysis of same-level and higher-level dependencies among affects and their correlated importances. Thus rather than being deterred by the multiple correlations of affects and importances, Smith exploits this *pluralism* of phenomena on behalf of a *unified* theory of global feelings, that is, a theory of *metaphysical* truth, or perhaps better, a *metaphysical* theory of truth.

Regarding the 'metaphysical' nature of his hierarchy of affective truth, we will save our comments for the section on 'Metaphysics' below. However, we can already enlist the critical objections we made above for they apply here too. We suggested that different affects (happy, unhappy; joyful, despairing) are not responses to different features of the same world but are different ways of seeing the world as a whole. In fact, even that way of characterizing the matter is misleading. It suggests that the world that is the 'object' of our affective responses is the same world, that it is only our 'subjective' responses to it which differ. Smith himself wishes to avoid the fact/value implications of that way of viewing things. That is why he tries to guard himself by saying that our affects are responses not to the world *as such* but to different *features* of the world, albeit features of the *same* world. However, even this way of characterizing the situation inevitably leads in a dualistic direction. For 'behind' the 'phenomenological' world accessed through our affects there still stands the world-whole itself. Apart from the fact that in some sense it exists, it is for the rest an abstract Idea, a 'noumenal' world we can never directly experience in our 'metaphysical' feelings.

If then our affects are not different responses to (different features of) the same world, in what sense can they be said to constitute a hierarchy of responses to the world? If with Wittgenstein we say that there are as many 'worlds' as there are holistic feeling-responses to the world, as many 'worlds' as there are affective ways of seeing and being in the world, how are we to understand the logical relations among these different affects, these different 'worlds'? One thing seems clear: we cannot order the different worlds of the happy and unhappy, joyous and despairing, in any kind of systematic, hierarchical, or metaphysical structure. How can the world of the happy and the unhappy exist in that kind of relationship to one another? Can they and the many other moods in which we 'find' ourselves or affective attitudes we take toward the world be made 'compatible' with one another in that way? Can they be brought into some sort of overarching harmony in our emotional, not to mention our practical lives? If not, and it would seem not, then we may have to reconstruct not only our understanding of feelings but also our understanding of 'world' and metaphysics as well. That is the task to which we turn next.

Transitional Remark

With these comments on Smith's ontology and epistemology in mind, we are now ready to return to to an earlier question we temporarily deferred: Is this richness and multiplicity of feelings and felt-meanings compatible, as Smith claims, with a view of the *world* as ontologically a *unitary whole*? To answer this question we must turn from this discussion of feelings to consider specifically the notion that has been, if not always in the foreground, at least always present in the background of the foregoing remarks – Smith's concept of the *world*, specifically the *world-as-a-whole* or, the term he prefers, the *'world-whole.'*

World

We have suggested, drawing on Wittgenstein and James, the possibility that the happy and the unhappy, the joyful and despairing, live in *different worlds*, that their feelings are not simply responses to *different features* of the *same world*. Different global feelings, different worlds –in other words, a plurality of *worlds-as-a-whole*. Smith would disagree. It smacks of metaphysical Idealism, a 'subject-ism' ("the world is *my* world") that ill comports with the Realism of his theory of feelings. Rather, he insists, the *empirical plurality* of our feelings vis-a-vis the *empirical features* of the world taken as *all that exists* are compatible with a view of the *world itself* as a *unitary whole*. But does not this way of characterizing the situation also lead in an Idealist direction? 'Behind' or 'underlying' or 'making possible' the *phenomenological* plurality of feelings and features there is a unifying *transcendental* world-as-a-whole. Although in some sense it 'exists,' it does not exist in the *ordinary* empirical sense that its 'parts' do. Or, though transcendental, does it also exist in an analogous, meta-empirical sense, as a mega-empirical entity? Is it, as a *transcendental* 'world,' a 'world' that we never directly experience *in itself, as such*, in our empirically-grounded feelings, or are there, as Smith maintains, meta-empirical, i.e. 'transcendental' feelings, so-called 'global' feelings, by which we can access the transcendental world-whole directly? Depending on our answer to these questions, it is possible that despite his wish to disentangle himself from the snares of the philosophical tradition, Smith could still be enmeshed in the web of a dualistic (empirical-cum-transcendental) metaphysics. We shall explore this dilemma in terms of the *ambiguities* in Smith's concept of the world, and related problems in his characterization of the *features* of the world-as-a-whole.

Ambiguities of 'World.'

In examining the ambiguities in Smith's concept of the *world*, we shall look at his understanding of the *existing* of the world, two *worlds*, two *features* of the world *as existing*, and the world as a *whole*.

The Existing of the World. All along in this inquiry our subject has been the Why question. What is it that the Why question is about? Is it about the fact that the *world* exists? Or is it rather about the fact that *something* exists rather than nothing? Is there a difference between the two questions, or are they two ways of asking the same thing? The implications of the possible distinction between these two formulations can be seen when we look at Smith's comments about the *existing* of the world.

To review: For Smith, *that* the world *exists* is one of its 'important' *features*. This does not mean, however, that 'existence' is one of the *descriptive* features of the world's 'essence,' its '*what*.' If we mean by an 'essential' feature of a thing a feature necessary for *describing* it, then "existing is not an essential feature; it does not comprise *what* something is but *that* it is" (165). So Smith endorses the distinction between real or descriptive predicates that tell us something about 'what' a thing is, and the pseudo-predicate 'exists' that adds nothing to the *conceptual content* of a thing, but simply tells us of what is described by that concept *that* it exists. *What* the world is, in other words, is logically compatible both with its existing and its non-existing (Smith, 1986, 183). There is no contradiction in saying of the world that it exists but could just as well not have existed.

Now there appears to be a problem here. On the one hand Smith says that the *existence* of the world is *not a feature* of the *descriptive* sort that tells something about the *nature* of the world. On the other hand, he wants to say that the *existence* of the world *is* a *feature* of the world that tells us something about it. How can he hold both propositions to be true? Does the notion of 'feature' have the same meaning in both cases? Specifically, he says that the world's *existence* has the *feature* of '*being important.*' One of its *features* is the *importance* of its existing. Moreover, this *importance-feature* of the world *does* have *descriptive* content that can be spelled out, even though the *fact* of the world's existence itself is not one of the world's descriptive features. In other words, Smith wants to hold both the fact *that* the world exists does not add to a description of *what* the world is, and that it is an *important* fact *about* the world, one of the *features about* the world, that it exists, an importance-feature that can be described *prior to and apart from* any further importances the world might have by being the *kind* of world it is.

Smith's position, in other words, rests on the notion of an 'importance' of the world being a *unique* kind of *descriptive* feature that can apply to both the existence *and* the nature of the world. In fact, the importance-feature of *existence* seems to serve for Smith as a *meta-feature*, as it were a *transcendental* feature, one that grounds and makes possible all the other importance-features that describe the *nature* of the world. And of course this makes intuitive sense. If the world did not exist, it is importantly true that no other importance-features of the world would exist either. Whether existence is, in some impoverished sense, a 'descriptive predicate' or not, without it there can be no other predicates, descriptive or any other. Smith can in this way both accept and simultaneously finesse the distinction between descriptive predicates and 'exist' as a pseudo-predicate, because for him both the existence *and* the nature of world are first and foremost matters of 'importance.' As we have seen, Smith defines the world as "a whole of *importances*."

Thus far Smith. So let us focus on Smith's fundamental claim: the existence of the world is a feature, if not in the traditional metaphysical or empirical sense a 'descriptive' feature, then, in a metaphysics-of-feeling sense, an 'important' feature. But now we need to ask: What makes the otherwise descriptively empty fact of the world's existence a matter of importance? Is it the 'bare' fact of *existing* itself, or is it because it is the *world* that we are talking about as existing? In other words, is the importance-feature of the world's *existence* parasitic on what is already contained in the *concept* of world itself? Here we return to the distinction we have been urging throughout this inquiry – the 'cosmological fact' that the *world* exists is not the same as the 'ontological fact' that *something* exists rather than nothing. *Nor are the correlated emotions the same.* The fundamental 'ontological emotion' is not the same as the fundamental 'cosmological' emotion – similar perhaps, analogical maybe, but not the same. Smith's introduction of the notion of 'importance' as a feature of the world's existing elides the importance of this distinction between these two kinds of fact and their correlated emotions.

Ontology and Cosmology. To get at the implications, the 'importance,' of the distinction between the fact that *something* exists rather than nothing and the fact that the *world* exists rather than nothing – and differences of the feelings or emotions correlated with each – we need to introduce the underlying distinction that makes sense of it. We can do no better here than to draw on an essay on by Tillich, "The Types of Philosophy of Religion" in his *Theology of Culture* that distinguishes between the ontological and cosmological approaches to metaphysics. The classical discussion of the distinction occurs in 13th C. medieval philosophy between Franciscans and Thomists, but that discussion itself refers back to the divergence in ancient philosophy between the metaphysics of Aristotle and that of Plato. The contributions of the modern treatment of the two approaches, "in comparison with the classical answers, is small. These answers return again and again, separated or in mixture." To be sure, "the general trend is determined by the cosmological type and its final self-negation, though ontological reactions against it occur in all centuries" (Tillich, 1959, 20). (Tillich, like Smith, has in mind here the modern phenomenon of nihilism as the inevitable outcome of the cosmological type). Given the long and complex history of this distinction, Tillich's essay offers for our purposes the advantages of clarity and simplicity. It will be clear, as we proceed, that Smith's metaphysics of feeling, and in particular his claim that the *existence* of the world is an 'importance,' is simply a modern version of the ancient and medieval cosmological approach to metaphysics.

What are the implications of this distinction for Smith's claim? There are three: The most important is that the ontological approach is the foundation of the cosmological. Second, without its ontological foundation the cosmological approach has philosophically problematic consequences of which the threat of decline into nihilism is the most consequential. But third, if grounded in the ontological approach, the cosmological approach can avoid those consequences (cf Tillich, 1959, 10-11). Let us first develop these general theses a bit further, and then see how they apply to Smith's analysis of the *existing* of the world, his notion of two *worlds*, the two *features* he ascribes to the world *as existing*, and his concept of the world as a *whole*.

What are the implications of the ontological 'answer' to the Why question and how do they bear on a cosmological 'answer' to the Why question? Paraphrasing Augustine, the ontological 'solution' to the question, "Why is there being (something) rather than nothing?," is that the be-ing of being is itself the *presupposition* of the question. As Augustine might say, being can never be reached if it is made into the 'object' of a question and not its basis. For being is "the first truth, in the light of which everything else is known....[it] is the identity of subject and object. [It] is not a created function *of* our mind, but the presence of truth itself and therefore of being *in* our mind. Being itself [is] *primum esse*.... And this Being (which is not a being) is pure actuality. We always see it, but we do not always notice it; as we see everything in the light without always noticing the light as such....the certainty of Being itself." As in Plato's analogy of the truth of being to the light of the sun, this ontological knowledge is the expression of an immediate existential certainty, the fundamental 'ontological emotion' of *wonder* (Tillich, 1959, 13-16).

For Aquinas, on the other hand, the cosmological approach to knowledge, which is based on sense perception and conceptual abstraction, may provide the foundation for scientific explanations but can never account for the fact that something exists rather than nothing. "Immediate rationality... is replaced by an argumentative rationality...*the transcendentalia are not the presence of the divine in us, they are not the 'uncreated light' through which we see everything, but they are the created structure of our mind.*" (Tillich, *ibid.* 16-17). For the cosmological approach, being is no longer the fact of be-ing itself but becomes instead a particular being – for Smith, the world-whole as a transcendental Idea, or rather, an empirical *mega-entity*. "This is the final outcome of the Thomistic *dissolution* of the Augustinian *solution*" (Tillich, *ibid.* 19).

As noted above, if the world did not exist, obviously no features of the world, important or not, would exist either. The point goes further: If it were not for the fact that there is always already *something* rather than nothing, if it were not for the fact that *being* always and already just 'be's' (to recall Hawking), what Smith himself calls the 'nonnecessary' existence of the *world* itself would not have 'happened.' This is not the last word, however. It is important to to insist upon this fundamental difference between the 'ontological fact' of *being* and the 'cosmological fact' of the *world's* being. Nevertheless, it is also important that the ontological approach, though *distinct* from and *prior* to the cosmological approach, must be *reconciled* with the latter. The two philosophical *attitudes* and their correlative emotions "are not strange to each other but have been estranged from each other" (Tillich, *ibid.* 29). What we must do in the following, therefore, is show how Smith's descriptions of the *features* of the (cosmological) 'world-whole' and their correlative (cosmological) 'global' *feelings* are either grounded in and derivatives of the 'ontological fact' and 'ontological emotion' (as regards the *existence* of the world), or insofar as they refer to the specific cosmological *nature* of the world-whole, derive their global 'ultimacy' from their ontological ground. If not ontologically grounded, then the danger – which it is the main purpose of Smith's metaphysics of feeling to avoid – is that the cosmological fact and cosmological emotions will 'degenerate' into, prove powerless against, the reality and emotions of nihilism – 'the final negation' of a cosmological approach to metaphysical feelings that is uprooted from its ontological ground.

Two 'Worlds.' What implications does this distinction between ontological and cosmological approaches have for Smith's distinction between two different concepts of 'world'? To review: Smith differentiated the 'world' of a metaphysics of feeling from the 'world' of what he called a 'metaphysics of reason.' The latter is in fact the world as conceived by the traditional cosmological approach to metaphysics. It is a world-whole of physical cause-effect and teleological ends-means relationships. But the *existence* of that world is "a *brute fact*, an *intrinsically neutral* whole that cannot be known to be created for the sake of realizing value" (Smith, 1986, 106; my italics). Whereas for a metaphysics of feeling, the world is a whole of *importances*. Thus conceived, the *existence* of the world is not a '*brute* fact' but an '*important* fact,' a fact on the basis of which a metaphysical hierarchy of 'felt meaning' can be constructed. Here again we see Smith's determination to avoid 'the final self- negation' of metaphysics in a modern nihilisitic metaphysics to which he believes the traditionally-understood cosmological approach leads. Our question, however, is whether, without being grounded in the prior 'fact' of *being* itself, his own metaphysics of feeling, insofar as it is itself a cosmological metaphysics based on the existence of the *world*, can avoid that final self-negation. In other words, perhaps the place where the problem of the 'overcoming of nihilism' needs to be located is not in the distinction between the metaphysics of cosmological *cause-and-effec*t and the metaphysics of cosmological *feeling*, but in the question whether either metaphysics, insofar as it is a *cosmological* metaphysics, can overcome the threat of nihilism apart from a prior ground in the primordial *ontological* fact of being itself. (We shall come back to Smith's distinction between two 'worlds' as it bears on his notion of the world as a *whole*.)

Two Features of the World as Existing. We will try to illustrate this point by taking a preliminary look at the implications of the distinction between the 'ontological fact' (that *something* exists, that being 'just be's') and the 'cosmological fact' (that the *world* 'happens' *non-necessarily* to exist) for Smith's analysis of two feeling-responses to the fact of the *existing* of the world – *joy* at the *fulfillment* of its happening and *marveling* at (the miracle of) the *non-necessity* of its happening. Specifically we want to ask whether the metaphysical 'ultimacy' of these 'global' feelings is justified on *cosmological* grounds, or whether, however similar they at first appear, they are at best analogues of, and dependent upon, emotions grounded in the prior *ontological* fact of being itself.

To review: Smith's analysis of these two feeling-responses is based on on a distinction between the fact *that* the world *exists* and the *nature* of that world, its '*what.*' The Kantian distinction between the non-descriptive 'that' and the descriptive 'what' would seem to imply that the assertion *that* the world exists is not a description about *what* the world is. You cannot smuggle into the conceptually'bare' or 'brute,' i.e. descriptively empty assertion that something exists, even the world itself, such descriptive predicates as 'is a fulfillment' ('a plenum, a fullness, a positivity') or 'is non-necessary' ('neither necessary nor contingent'). To attribute to the mere fact of existence such '*as*' features – existence *as* fulfillment, existence *as* non-necessary – would seem to violate the

Kantian stricture. Smith's reply, as we have seen, is that for a metaphysics of felt meaning the fact *that* the world exists is not a *bare* or *brute* *(uninterpreted, meaningless)* fact, it is a conceptually-cum- emotionally pregnant *importance,* indeed the most important importance there is, upon which all other importances of the world rest and from which they proceed. "[T]he primordial phenomenon– that there *is* being and not nothing -- 'matters'" (Smith, 1986, 24)

There are two problems here. When Kant says that the assertion that something exists does not ascribe predicable content to the concept of that something, that it simply states that what the concept describes is instantiated, he grounds this distinction in the traditional *cosmological* idea of 'exist.' It is not so much this Kantian distinction but the underlying cosmological foundation of which it is an expression that Smith wants to reject. The problem, however, is that Smith does not provide a basis for his alternative claim that, though to say the world exists does not refer to a cosmological, i.e. *empirically descriptive* feature of the world, it does point to an *important* feature of the world. Here we return to our contention in the preceding section regarding Smith's two concepts of 'world': what accounts for the importance of the *existence* (the non-necessary happening) of the *world* is the fact that the existence of the world, the *kosmos,* is grounded in the primordial fact of *being (Grk: to on)* itself.

Second, Smith's statement – "[T]he primordial phenomenon– that there *is* being and not nothing -- 'matters'" – shows his awareness of yet another confusion contained in this ontological-cosmological distinction. The 'primordial phenomenon' is indeed 'that there is *being* and not nothing,' *not* as Smith everywhere else resorts to saying, 'that the *world* exists rather than nothing.' This means that we cannot credit his claim that it is the existence of the *world* that justifies our feelings of joy vis-a-vis its 'fulfillment of happening' and marveling vis-a-vis the 'miracle of its non-necessity' – unless, that is, these feelings can be shown to be analogues or derivatives of more 'primordial' emotions vis-v-vis the fact of being itself.

Absent that showing, it is not clear what it means to ascribe 'non-necessity' to a world whose existence is clearly that of an empirically contingent 'whole' (unless the 'whole' Smith has in mind is a 'transcendental' whole, a regulative *Idea* rather than a constitutive *mega-reality*), nor what it means to say that the world in its contingent happening is a 'fulfillment' or is 'fulfilled,' unless one is simply making the truistic observation that what is referred to in the concept of 'the world' is in fact 'instantiated.'

Rather, if we feel joy at the world's happening, if we marvel at the fact that it exists when it just as well could not have – and we do, rightly, feel these things – it is because these profound and authentic feelings are themselves rooted in and are expressions of – that in Tillich's phrase they derive their 'ultimacy' from – our emotional response of wonder to the primordial phenomenon of being itself. If we wanted to say of anything that it is a 'fullness' rather than an 'emptiness,' a 'positivity' rather than a 'nothingness,' it would have to be the primordial fact that there *is* being, that it 'just be's' – though it is not clear even then what that would mean. And if we wanted to say of anything that its existence was 'non-necessary' in the sense of being neither necessary nor contingent, again it would have to be the primordial fact that there *just is* being – though there too it is not clear what that would mean. In both cases, as we argued in Part I of this study, these would be odd ways of trying to talk about or say something 'descriptive' about the primordial fact that there is something rather than nothing.

But let us look more closely at these two 'importances.' There is, first, an additional problem in Smith's assigning the feeling-response of joy to the fact that the world exists, apart from any further description of its actual make-up. Chad Allen, in his review, "Smith's *The Felt Meanings of the World* and the Pure Appreciation of Being Simpliciter," critiques Smith's argument that joy is an appropriate response to the 'pure appreciation of being simpliciter.' While I believe he is wrong in the alternative he provides, his analysis serves to clarify further the issue at stake.

What is Allen's thesis? To summarize, he contends that the "most notable" problem of Smith's otherwise "viable" metaphysics of feeling is "Smith's conclusion that 'joy' is the proper affective response to the pure existence of the world, or Being simpliciter." Allen's claim is "not only that joy cannot be an affective response to Being simpliciter; but also that the metaphysics of feeling renders incoherent any notion of affective response to Being simpliciter." (By 'being simpliciter' I take Allen to be referring to what I have called the primordial fact that being 'just be's.')

What is Allen's argument? He begins by reviewing the lineaments of Smith's argument. For Smith each feeling is an, if not the, appropriate response to some feature of the world. The basic feature of the world is that it happens (exists). The appropriate feeling response to the happening of the world is joy in the fulfilment of that happening. An entire hierarchy of feeling-responses is then built upon this basic feeling of joy in the existence of the world (Allen, 71-72). Allen, however, contends that there is nothing in the *bare fact* of the happening rather than non-happening of the world-whole as such that would, in the absence of any *descriptive content*, justify the response of joy. This of course is a good Kantian observation. As he goes on to say, "Rejoicing is undeniably a moral reaction," namely, a response to something good that happens as opposed to something bad or without moral value. "Certainly I do not rejoice simply because something happens, without any consideration as to whether this thing is good or bad. Yet this is exactly what Smith contends about the happening of the world-whole – that I should rejoice merely because it happens" (Allen, 73).

Let us suppose this is correct. Then, Allen says, two questions follow: If joy is not a pure appreciation of the *'importance'* of being, *of what*, if anything, is it an appreciation? Second, if *joy* is not a pure appreciation of the importance of being, *what*, if anything is? (Allen, 76).

Joy, says Allen, is indeed a valid intuition of the world-whole, not of the world-whole 'purely,' but rather of the world *as* having the further, descriptive feature of being "the most fundamental *good* that exists." And it is the most fundamental good because, as Smith in this respect correctly observes, it is "the most basic condition for the realization of our adopted unconditional purpose, namely, the further appreciation of world-whole" (Allen, 78; citing Smith, 1986, 323).

It would seem, therefore, says Allen, that whenever we intuit the 'happening' of the world-whole, we always "intuit it *as* something," for the 'happening' of the world 'in and of itself' does not seem to elicit any affective response (Allen, 78)

Allen concludes: If the bare happening of the world-whole in and of itself cannot possibly elicit an affective response, then the world-whole as such cannot possibly 'appear' to us, since for Smith all awarenesses are feeling awarenesses. If so, then the 'happening' of the world fails to meet Smith's own criterion for being an 'importance.' In other words, "Being *simpliciter* is thus an anomaly within the metaphysics of feeling" (Allen, 78-79). But let us assume for a moment that, despite these critical remarks, we might still be able to find a place in a metaphysics of feeling for the 'pure' happening of the world-whole as an 'importance.' What place might that be? Perhaps, says Allen, it might have an epistemological status analogous to the 'brute fact' that some metaphysicians talk of. In any case, Allen agrees that as what Smith calls 'appreciative' beings we must acknowledge that "it is fundamentally good that the world continues to happen and that we may continue to experience it," that, as Smith says, the existence of the world 'matters,' that its happening has value.

There are two things to be said in rejoinder to Allen's critique, though neither applies to our own critique of Smith; in fact, both grow out of the latter. First, as his initial reference to "the pure existence of the world, or Being simpliciter" shows, Allen's critique rests on the same ambiguity we have pointed out in Smith, the apparent equating of, and hence shifting back and forth indifferently between, reference to the 'pure' existence of *the world* – the 'bare' fact that *the world* exists – and the very different phenomenon of the 'pure' existence of *being simpliciter* – the 'bare' fact that *being* just be's. We see this in his statement: "The happening of the world-whole...is Being *simpliciter*, it is the most basic way in which the world 'is'" (Allen, 71). This equivocation, which reflects Smith's own, does not augur well for the second part of his critique. Is it being simpliciter or is it the existence of the world to which, according to Allen, "joy cannot be an affective response"? Is it being simpliciter or the existence of the world to which he is referring when he says of Smith's metaphysics of feeling that it "renders incoherent any notion of affective response"?

Nevertheless, Allen's critique helps to clarify a sense in which, in spite of his own referential equivocation, Smith, unlike Allen, is correct in seeing a *valid link* between the phenomenon of existence and the response of joy. Where both he and Allen are mistaken is in thinking that the link has to do with the relating-or-not-relating of joy to the bare fact of the existence of the *world*. In other words, both Smith's claim and Allen's critique of that claim presuppose a Kantian, i.e. cosmological, rather than ontological understanding of what it is to which joy is a response. It is a response to being simpliciter, yes, but not being simpliciter confused with the 'bare existing' of the world, whether Smith's "happening of the world-whole" or Allen's "pure existence of the world," the "most basic way in which the world is."

What is the difference? It is the difference between a cosmological and an ontological understanding of the phenomenon of existence. How is it that one, the ontological, as Smith confusedly sees, elicits a response of joy while the other, the cosmological, as Allen clearly spells out, does not? Because, as we noted, the ontological understanding of being, unlike the cosmological, is the expression of an immediate existential awareness, namely, an experience of the fundamental 'ontological emotion' of wonder – in other words, of joy. In the history of Western thought the story of the cosmological-metaphysical understanding of the *world* since Aristotle is one of gradual displacement by scientific cosmology, a discipline which may be accompanied by the wonder and joy of scientific discovery and explanation. But this is not the existential wonder and joy that underlies the ontological intuition of the fact that there is *something* rather than nothing at all. That is a different, 'spiritual' attitude and response to the phenomenon that being "just be's," a something-rather-than-nothing which scientific discovery can never explain nor explain away. The strength of Smith's 'metaphysics of feeling' is that he, rather than Allen, has a grasp, however inadequately articulated, of that primordial ontological emotion. For Smith, as Allen notes, there can never be a 'mere factual' happening of the world-whole without a feeling response. That is the basic premise of Smith's whole program. What needs to be clarified in Smith's case, and what Allen's critique misses, is how an existential-ontological interpretation of the (alleged) 'bare fact' of the world's existence answers Allen's otherwise legitimate concern. That is what the distinction between an ontological and a cosmological interpretation of Smith's metaphysics of feeling offers us the resources to do.

As for the feeling-response of marveling, it follows from the preceding that the proper 'object' of marveling, the miracle to which it is a response, is not first of all that the *world* exists (rather than nothing), though the cosmos in itself is already an object worthy of our marveling, as philosophers from the beginning to the scientific cosmologists today richly attest. Rather, the more primordial marvel is that *anything* exists at all rather than nothing. Otherwise, a critic of traditional metaphysical cosmology, including Smith's updated 'feeling' version, can argue that marveling over the world's existence is, epistemologically if not emotionally, simply a case of wonderment at a fascinating phenomenon – the world in all its challenging complexity – but one that threatens to turn into nihilistic disenchantment the closer it comes to being completely explained. Remember that, for Aristotle then and Post today, the 'mystery' of the cosmos or universe is simply that which has not yet been explained but is in principle capable of being fully explained (away). How can cosmology protect itself against a modern-day Aristotlean debunking of the primordial sense of marveling, of wonder, at the world's existence? The fact is that, pace cosmological science or metaphysical realism, without a grounding in the prior, ultimately *inexplicable* fact that being 'just be's,' it cannot avoid the risk of degenerating into nihilism.

The World as a Whole. With these considerations of the ambiguities involved in Smith's analysis of the *existing* of the world, two *worlds,* and two *features* of the world *as existing,* we come to his concept of the world as a *whole.* Here we encounter the claim that goes to the heart, to the foundation, of his philosophical project: "To understand the precise sense in which the *world* is a *whole,* and specifically, an *important* whole, is a fundamental aim of the metaphysics of feeling" (Smith, 1986, 21). Why? Because upon this concept rests the corresponding foundational notion of 'global' feelings, and as he himself acknowledges, if there is no world-*whole* in a *transcendental* sense, "[if] the world-whole were absolutely identical with all existing things, this would entail that there would be nothing in which the various *global features* could inhere, and thus there would be no global features" (Smith, 1986, 203). This means, in turn, there would be no foundation upon which to erect a hierarchy of global feelings – in short, there would be no *metaphysics* of feelings. So the stakes are high. Upon this notion of the world-as-a-whole his entire metaphysical project stands ... or falls.

To decide this issue we must first look at the further implications of his concept of 'world,' for this will have a bearing on the sense in which it is possible, or not possible, to talk of the world-whole as a 'whole' that is more than, not just the totality of, all that exists. We will begin with a critique of his concept of the *world*-as-a-whole – that is, ambiguity in the kind of *world* he has in mind. We will turn to a critique of his concept of the world-as-a-*whole* – that is, ambiguity as to what kind of *whole* he has in mind.

World-as-a-Whole (I). Here we will look at the ambiguities in two aspects of his concept of world: his confusion of two different *concepts* of the 'world,' and his confusion of two different *contents* of the world in both its entitative/ontic and metaphysical/ontological dimensions.

Concepts of the 'World.' We noted above Smith's distinction between two different senses of 'world-whole': the world as a causal-cum-telology whole and the world as a whole of importances. We need now to consider this distinction more closely before examining whether, and if so in what sense, the world as a world of importances can or cannot be conceived of as a 'whole.' To do so it will be helpful to refer to a set of distinctions made by a thinker on whom Smith himself draws, Heidegger. In *Being and Time* (Ger: *Sein und Zeit*) Heidegger makes a similar distinction between two concepts of 'world,' each of which he breaks down into two sub-concepts resulting in four different 'world' concepts (Heidegger, *BT*, 93; *SZ*, 64-65). His analysis is useful for exposing the ambiguities of reference in Smith's usage.

Heidegger distinguishes, first, between two different concepts of 'world' similar to that made by Smith. One is an *empirical-transcendental* concept of 'world' analogous to Smith's cause-and-effect concept, the world of traditional metaphysics and contemporary scientific cosmology. The other is an *existential-ontological* concept of 'world' analogous to Smith's 'world of importances,' a concept of 'world' also closer to that of Wittgenstein or James. It is one that, for Smith too, represents a radical alternative to and critique of the traditional metaphysical concept. Heidegger, however, is very careful to keep the differences between these two concepts clear, not to confuse the sorts of things that can be said about one with what pertains to the other. As we will see, this is where the first problem occurs in Smith's account. Heidegger makes an additional distinction within both of these concepts of 'world,' and here we see another respect in which his analysis differs from and sheds light on the ambiguities in Smith's analysis. Within each of these two concepts of 'world' Heidegger distinguishes further between an 'ontic' or entitative sense and a corresponding 'ontological' or 'transcendental' sense. Thus, with regard to the first, empirical concept of 'world' [call it W1] he further distinguishes between a first-order or *ontic* use, 'world' as referring to the totality of concrete entities existing *within* the world – W1 in an *empirical-ontic* sense, and a second-order or transcendental sense of 'world' consisting of the abstract metaphysical concepts or *a priori* 'categories' which structure our first-order knowledge of entities within the world – W1 in an *empirical-transcendental* sense. With regard to the second, 'existential' concept of world [W2], he distinguishes again between a first-order or ontic use, what Heidegger calls the 'pre-ontological' sense of 'world' referring to the concrete *existential meanings* (what Smith would all 'importances') of the world 'wherein' we live, our *Lebenswelt,* Wittgenstein's '*my* world' – W2 in an *existential-ontic* sense, and its second-order or transcendental sense, the abstract ontological concepts or *a-priori* 'existential' categories which structure the 'worldhood' of the first-order realm of meanings or importances – W2 in an *existential-transcendental* sense.

To summarize, Heidegger's analysis of these four different senses of 'world' provides a helpful taxonomy that enables us to pinpoint where the ambiguities lie in Smith's account of the two 'worlds' and thus, as we shall see, in his account of the 'wholeness' of the world. Specifically we must ask whether Smith's analysis muddles the distinctions, first, between W1 in its ontic sense and W1 in its transcendental sense, and second, between W1 in both senses and W2 in both its ontic and transcendental senses. If he does, this will call into question his attempt to rest a metaphysics of global feelings on a concept of the world-as-a-whole.

Contents of the 'World.' To get further purchase on this matter, let us use Heidegger's distinctions to return once more to what it is that makes up the content of the two 'worlds' in Smith's account. First, having made a distinction between the world as a cause-effect totality and the world as a totality of importances, Smith then muddies the waters on the *ontic* level by including in his inventory of the world's 'parts' a whole range of phenomena that belong, on his own accounts, to two *different* 'worlds' and even then confusedly so. As he says, the world includes all sorts of 'things' in a 'very broad sense' (Smith, 1986, 255). Thus, for example, the 'world' in its 'unrestricted' sense is made up of a veritable grab bag of phenomena of every conceivable kind: not only all spatio-temporal things, but also mental things such as ideas, universals, relations, feelings, importances, etc., including all those 'parts' whose existence and/or nature we do not know about or of which we cannot even conceive (Smith, 1986, 255-256).

It is not clear how Smith sees these widely different kinds of phenomena to be related to one another, let alone fitted into a unitary sense of 'world.' Above all, how are the physical things and features of the spatio-temporal world to be brought together in a unified fashion with the existential 'importances' of the 'felt' world? One is also reminded of Post's distinction between two different senses of 'universe': the manifest universe, and the universe 'beyond' the manifest universe as including what we cannot see or do not know. Post's concept of the universe at least has the advantage of conceptual clarity: it is an entirely physicalist world, including a physicalist account of values or meanings. Of course Smith would reject Post's metaphysics as a cause-effect account that fails to capture the distinctive nature of the world as a whole of importances. The problem is that Smith's account rests instead on a conceptual confusion of the two worlds.

When we turn to the different ways in which the transcendental features of these two 'worlds' are to be understood, the picture seems even less clear. It is not that Smith is not explicit about the list of transcendental features that characterize his 'unitary' world; he is rather clear on that point. The world is: "the One Existent, Individual, Thing, Importance, and Whole" (Smith, 1986, 204, 192). Further, he maintains that this 'Existent' is not a Platonic or Kantian Idea but "the empirically existing world-whole" (Smith, 1986, 27). And yet he undermines his claim about the 'empirical' nature of this 'world-whole' with two further remarks. First, he tells us that this 'empirical Existent' is "the changeless condition of all changes," and that as such it remains "*unchangingly the same* through all the changes that occur to things *within* the world.... *the world* remains unchangingly *the world* throughout all alterations in features that inhere in *the world*" (Smith, 1986, 308-309). But in this use of 'world' the term clearly has a transcendental, not an empirical sense. If he insists nevertheless on using the same term to refer to an empirical existent, he must be using the term 'empirical' in an entirely novel sense, one, however, that he does not explain.

Second, he adds to this topsy-turvy confusion of attributes by assuring us, moreover, that *empirical* entities existing *within* the world themselves have *transcendental* attributes, that each thing has not only empirical properties but also the transcendental properties of "existing, oneness, thingness, etc." – that each existing thing is, like the world-whole itself, "singular, unique, individual, identical." Even ignoring for the moment the lumping together of Importance with Thing, one has to wonder whether he is using the term 'transcendental' in anything like its standard philosophical sense. If we are to bring the notion of importances into the picture, we have to ask whether the traditional philosophical concept of transcendental ideas, those formal categories that structure our experience of the objects of the empirical world (W1), can simply be carried over to describe the transcendentalia that structure the meanings or importances of the 'life-world' (W2) within which we exist 'existentially' as what Smith calls 'appreciative' beings.

But can the a priori existential-ontological structures of what Heidegger calls our "being-in-the-world" be interpreted via the transcendental categories that structure the empirical world in terms of 'thingness'? The felt importances of our being-in-the-world, our appreciations of the plurality of meanings and meaninglessnesses, are not empirical properties of W1, or if they are thought to be so, it is only insofar as they are parasitic on, derivative of, their primary reality in W2. At best we can speak of the a-meaning or non-meaning of W1 as conceived by the empirical sciences, for in W1 the dichotomy or question of meaningful/meaningless does not, cannot, arise. Though the parallel is not exact, the usage of 'a-meaning' or 'non-meaning' in this context is analogous to the usage of 'a-moral' or 'non-moral' – 'a-moral' meaning that which is neither moral nor immoral, that which lies outside the sphere to which moral judgments apply, or similarly, 'non-moral' meaning that which does not fall within the sphere of morals or ethics. Analogously, the notions of meaningful or meaningless do not fall within the realm of W1, with its transcendental features limned in the categories of traditional metaphysics, a metaphysics that Smith wishes, rightly, to reject as inadequate for expression the truth of felt meanings or importances, but to whose categories he resorts when it comes to defending the sense in which that world of importances is *both* an empirical *and* a transcendental *whole*.

World-as a-Whole (II). This ambiguity in his concept of the *world*-as-a-whole, its confused mix of the empirical ("things") and the existential ("importances"), carries over to his concept of the world-as-a-*whole*. But this is potentially fatal to his enterprise because, as he states, "To understand the precise sense in which the *world* is a *whole,* and specifically, an *important* whole, is a fundamental aim of the metaphysics of feeling" (Smith, 1986, 21, 53, 200, 203). This is not simply *a* but *the* fundamental proposition on which his whole metaphysics rests. The question we are asking is the one he himself sees as crucial to his project:"*what* is this whole?" (Smith, 1986, 256)

Whole as Empirical. Putting aside for the moment this conflict between an *empirical* and an *existential* approach to understanding the sense in which the world is a *whole*, there is is already a problem whether it even makes sense to talk of the world as an *empirical* 'whole,' as an Existent (whatever its mixed contents), by invoking the sorts of traditional metaphysical attributes that we have seen, for example, in Post's cosmological metaphysics: One, Unchanging, etc. Smith takes two *different* approaches to interpreting the world as a 'whole.' The first refers to the empirical 'parts' of which it consists: the world, Smith claims, is not simply an empirical *totality* of the things that exist, it is an empirical *unity* inasmuch as it is a '*one*' of 'many parts.' The second defines the 'wholeness' of the world by its *transcendental* features: One, Unchanging, etc. What is the relation of these two different interpretations to one another?

The Fallacy of Composition. The first claim, that the world is a one, a unity, of many parts, already involves Smith in a major logical blunder – it commits the Fallacy of Composition. The fallacy of composition arises when one infers that something is true of the *whole* from the fact that it is true of some *part* of the whole. But this is the inference Smith makes. The world whole, he says, shares the features of the parts of which it is composed; it is, like them, an empirical entity, albeit the greatest one there is. In the case of a wolf pack, he argues, the work pack is not itself a mega-wolf, whereas the world-whole of existent things is itself *an* existent (Smith, 1986, 204). His argument involves the assertion that "[t]here are not many worlds, but one world; the world necessarily has the feature of being one: the world is something unitary." Though the things that exist are many, we know the world as one (Smith, 1986, 202-203). Smith is very clear about the concrete empirical nature of that whole: the world is an 'existent,' not a Platonic Idea; it is "the empirically existing world-whole" (Smith, 1986, 27). There is a problem with this claim, however. What gives the world-whole its unitary character is in fact not an empirical feature, it is the transcendental categories that we bring to the ordering of our experience of the empirical 'parts' of the world. What gives the world its 'wholeness' is not its being the 'greatest' *existent* there is, a *mega*-thing, as Smith maintains. Rather it is that it is, as it were, a *meta*-'thing.' The unity of the 'world' is the unity of a transcendental a priori unity, not an empirical a posteriori unity. In fact, Smith's concept of the world-whole as a *unity* of *empirical* parts only makes sense if it is interpreted *a priori* as a *transcendental*, not an empirical whole. Its unity is not that of an empirical *existent* but of a *categorial* 'entity' defined by its 'transcendental' features: One, Unchanging, etc. Such transcendental features are precisely *not* features of its empirical parts. As Kant put it, the wholeness of the world is that of a regulative Idea giving unity to our experience of the parts of the world, not that of a constitutive (or descriptive) predicate of a mega-entity existing on a larger scale than any of the parts making it up. In other words, the world is a whole the way a wolf pack is a whole, conceptually not empirically.

The Whole of Importances. Smith might reply, rightly, that he is not thinking of the whole in such traditional, narrowly empirical terms. By interpreting the world as a whole of *importances*, he using the broader sense of 'experience' found in the Continental tradition of phenomenology on which he draws, in particular, the existential phenomenology of philosophers like Heidegger, Sartre and Merleau-Ponty. However, granting this, even if we do not apply the fallacy of composition in a narrower empirical sense, even if his concept of the world as a whole of importances employs a broadened or, in his term, "unrestricted" sense of the experienced 'parts' of the world, what would it mean to speak of such a world as a whole, given the plurality of felt meanings and felt importances of which it consists? That is, can he still use what are in fact the transcendental categories of traditional metaphysics (One, Unchanging, etc.) to characterize the world of importances as forming a whole? Is the richness and multiplicity of experiential importances compatible, as Smith claims, with a view of the world as a unitary experiential whole? Or does, in fact, the problem of the fallacy of composition apply even here to this broadened sense of the world as a whole of importances? Much rides on the answer to this question.

It appears legitimate to invoke the fallacy of composition here too, since Smith wants to claim that, just as the world-*whole* is not simply the *totality* of existents but is itself an *existent*, so too the world is not simply the *totality* of importances but is itself *an importance*. And not only that. Just as the world, because it includes all other existents, is the 'greatest' Existent, so too, because the world includes all other importances, it is the 'greatest' Importance. The world-whole is *more important* than all the other importances combined; it is the *most important* Importance that exists. Indeed, the 'parts' of the whole, even those lesser wholes that are themselves 'parts' of the larger world-whole, receive their (lesser) importance only "through being a part of the fulfilled whole" (Smith, 1986, 119-120). This is not only an important claim, it is an astonishing one, even an exhilarating one. For if true it means that even the most humble thing that exists acquires a shining significance by virtue of its inclusion in the 'fulfillment' of the 'happening' of the world-whole. But is it true? Even if it is true that the humble things of this world have a shining significance, is it only because they are 'parts' of the world 'whole'? The problem lies not only in Smith's again committing the fallacy of composition in violation of the empirical/transcendental distinction. A new problem enters at this point. It lies in his attempt to apply the part/ whole logic of a cosmological-metaphysics to the conceptually different world of an existential-ontology. Our different existential 'appreciations' of the 'global' meanings of our being-in-the-world are not, as he contends, felt responses to different importances ('parts') of the *same* world ('whole'), they are habitations of *different* 'worlds' altogether. As Wittgenstein observed, the world of the happy and the world of the unhappy are not two different takes on the same world; they are totally different worlds. The plurality of 'global' importances point to an ontological plurality of world-wholes, not to a metaphysical hierarchy of a unitary world-whole. As such they require a totally different way of conceptualizing the sense in which each of these existential-ontological worlds can be said to be a (transcendental) 'whole.'

Whole as Transcendental. Before we turn to that alternative possibility, we need to review where we have come so far. It would seem that whether he thinks of the wholeness of the world in narrowly empirical terms as a unity of its empirical parts or in a broader experiential sense as a unity of its felt importances, Smith's two attempts (the world-whole as an Existent, the world-whole as Importance) to bring the two different interpretations, empirical (or experiential) and transcendental (or categorial) together under the same conceptual roof violates the distinction, traditional since Kant, between the different kind of 'objects' in the realms of the Empirical and the Transcendental. Let us review that distinction once more as it applies in the present case.

The main point is a simple one. The 'wholeness' of which the transcendental speaks is not a 'wholeness' of existents, empirical, important, or any other; it is a 'wholeness,' a systematic unity, of meta-concepts, of categories by which we organize our experience of the things that exist, including felt importances. If we speak of the world as a whole, whether the world of existents or the world of importances, we will find ourselves landing in contradictions when we try to describe it in terms that apply to the things that exist within the world. Does the world of existing things have a beginning in time and space, or is it infinite in time and space? Both possibilities seems logically valid, yet neither is true, for each treats the world as an object within the world. (Nor does the Big Bang cosmology constitute an answer to that question.) When Smith talks of the world as a whole he is tempted to ignore this distinction, as we see when he treats the world as an Existent rather than as a transcendental concept that provides a framework for the ordering of our experience. In the case of his discussion of importances, he again tries to make his concept of the world do double duty – to stand as one among our many global feelings but also to give transcendental unity to our global feelings.

The fact is that Smith's concept of the world as a 'whole' in the sense of a 'one-of-many' does not sit on the same conceptual level as his list of the transcendental features (One, Unchanging, etc.) of the world, rather it *presupposes* the latter. The 'transcendental' *idea* of the world as a whole functions to *give unity to* his metaphysical scheme of the world as the 'whole' of the importances disclosed in our 'global' feelings. He is right in saying that the feature of the world's 'wholeness' refers to something *more than* just the *sum-total* of things or importances existing 'within' the world. In fact, absent this transcendental feature of 'wholeness,' we would be right to call into question, or at least radically reinterpret, the very existence and nature of 'global' feelings themselves. But when Smith argues that "[if] the world-whole were absolutely identical with all existing things, this would entail that there would be nothing in which the various *global features* could inhere, and thus there would be no global features" (Smith, 1986, 203), he commits the fallacy of composition by concluding, as he does not have to do, that therefore the world, which is a transcendental idea, is also an existing thing like all other existing things save for being the 'greatest' among them. When he concludes that "the world necessarily has the feature of being one," and goes on to include other a priori transcendental properties that make our experience possible, it becomes clear that that is not the world of empirical existents but the transcendental world of a priori properties which form the necessary conditions that make our experience of existing things 'within' the world possible – an *ideal formal* world, not a concrete existing one.

Whole as Horizonal. Now surprisingly Smith might agree with this entire line of criticism. He might say we were wrong to ascribe to him a view of the wholeness of the world of importances based on the transcendental categories that apply to a casual-cum-teleological understanding of the world. Rather, he might argue that the sense in which the world is a whole of importances does indeed involve a totally different way of thinking about its transcendental nature. For he himself has already advanced an intriguing third possibility which we have heretofore overlooked. Though his words may have misled us into thinking otherwise, he himself does not see the wholeness of the world as having the unity of an *empirical existent* or the unity of a *transcendental construct*. Rather, breaking with these terms for the cosmological-metaphysical tradition and in keeping rather with the implications of his alternative metaphysics of the "felt meanings," or "importances" of the world, he is suggesting that we should conceive the 'transcendental' nature of the world whole as the *existential horizon* of our meaning-experiences. In other words, here Smith could be seen as challenging our characterization of his project as reflecting confusion between a *cosmological-metaphysical* understanding of the world (W1) as a *Existent* 'whole' and an *ontological-existential* understanding of the world (W2) as an *Important* 'whole.' In other words, he might claim that in fact he is not confusing two different ways of understanding the nature of this 'whole' but rather introducing us to a new, third way of thinking. An added advantage of seeing the transcendental wholeness of the world in horizonal terms is that it then makes sense of the kind of evidence he draws upon in support of his claim that the world is a unified whole, namely, the evidence of our primordial moods. If he is correct, this would clear up a lot of the confusions that seemed to muddy the waters in his project. But once again we have to ask, does this fall-back interpretation really work?

We recall Smith, taking the idea from Heidegger, says that we are always in some mood or other. But usually and for the most part (Heidegger's phrase is *zunaechst und zumeist*) our moods are not in the forefront of our awareness. Rather they form the emotional background of our attention to the immediate objects of our concern. In that sense they can be said to constitute the 'horizon' of our awareness of the world as a whole. "[T]he world-whole is always 'there' in an immediate way on the horizon of my [everyday mundane] awareness" (Smith, 1986, 194). Moods thus supply a vague but all-encompassing felt meaning, an importance, to the things that appear 'within' the horizon of that awareness. So far, so good. Unfortunately, however, Smith once again falls prey to the temptation to place a transcendental weight upon these empirical moods that is more than the phenomena can conceptually bear. For as the horizon of my mundane awarenesses the world disclosed in moods is now said to be "the unvarying backdrop of all variations, the changeless condition of all changes. If the expression 'the world' is used to designate that in which the global features inhere, then it can be said that *the world* remains unchangingly *the world* throughout all alterations in features that inhere in *the world*" (Smith, 1986, 308-309).

But at most the world as the horizon of my awareness is changeless only in the *formal* sense that a *transcendental* regulative idea can be said to be 'changeless.' In that sense the 'world' may be unchanging, but it is also 'unreal,' not a mega-reality. The 'reality' of the world in that sense is the reality of a transcendental Idea/Ideal. But even in that transcendental sense, the fact is that the moods which form the *material* horizon, the world of our experience, are far from unchanging. Not only is the world of the happy a different world than that of the unhappy. The horizons of those worlds are not transcendentally or categorially fixed but shifting and plural. And that means the transcendental features of the world are shifting and plural as well.

Something and World: the Basic Distinction. But before we turn to consider how Smith's analysis of the 'global' features or 'importances' of the 'world-whole' are affected by these considerations, we must briefly address one other issue. How, if at all, does the distinction we have been making throughout this essay – between the fact that something exists and the fact that the world exists – bear on Smith's concept of the 'world-as-a-whole'? Can we speak of the fact that something rather than nothing exists as being a 'whole,' or can we use that expression only, if at all, in relation to the existence of the world? An answer to this question will have a direct bearing on what sorts of wholistic features ('global importances'), if any, can be ascribed either to the fact that something exists or to the fact that the world exists. As to the latter we have already called into question the various ways in which Smith believes we can speak of the world's existence as being a whole – empirical, transcendental, and horizonal. The question here, therefore, is whether we can apply the notion of a 'whole,' in any of those senses, to the fact that something exists rather than nothing – to what Allen calls 'being simpliciter' or what Hawking refers to as the fact that being 'just be's.'

It would seem we cannot. To begin with, the fact that there is something rather than nothing, being simpliciter, is not an *empirical* fact, that is, a *contingent* fact like the existence of something within the world or even the existence of the world itself, an existence which Smith himself says is 'non-necessary.' Nor is it a *transcendental* fact in the (Kantian) sense of a *necessary category* for organizing our thinking about the world of our experience. Then is it a *horizonal* fact? Can we not say of being simpliciter, analogous to what Smith says of the world-whole, that it is the *ontological* horizon of our experiences? Can we not say that it is not the contingent existence of the world but the fact that something exists rather than nothing that is *the* Important *horizonal* fact, the reality that lends importance to all else that exists within that ontological horizon, including the world itself,? Is it not this basic ontological fact, rather than the existence of the cosmological world-as-a-whole, of which it can properly be said that it "is always 'there' in an immediate way on the horizon of my awareness" (Smith, 1986, 194)? Is it not the fact that *something* exists, rather than the fact that the ever-changing *world* exists, that serves as the *ontological* horizon, "the unvarying backdrop of all variations, the changeless condition of all changes," that remains "unchangingly ... the self-same ... throughout all alterations in features that inhere in *the world*" (Smith, 1986, 308-309)? We said above of Smith's idea of the world as the *horizon* of my awareness that it is unchanging only in a transcendental, that is a *formal*, 'unreal' sense, that in a *material* sense its reality as the world of our experience is in fact an ever-changing, contingent and indeed plural one. Can we now say rather that it is being simpliciter that meets Smith criterion of being a 'whole' in a *horizonal* sense? And if not, why not? If the fact that something exists is not a cosmological fact in any of these senses, then how can we speak of the fact that something exists rather than nothing, the ontological reality of being simpliciter, as a 'whole'? Can we speak of the fact that something exists rather than nothing as in some *other* sense a 'whole' or must we conclude that the notion of being a 'whole' simply does not apply in this case?

The answer hinges on the various meanings of 'whole' and whether being simpliciter can fit any of the preceding definitions. As we have seen, Smith uses 'whole' in several ways. In its empirical use, it involves the distinction between a 'whole' and its 'parts.' However, the ontological fact that something exists rather than nothing does not, in and of itself, carry any implication of wholeness, of 'being a whole.' Rather the expression simply points to the 'bare' fact of being simplicter. In its transcendental use, 'whole' refers to the 'unity' of a set of trans-empirical 'Ideas' or categories. But the ontological fact that something exists rather than nothing is not an abstract category of unity. It is rather an immediate fact of our experience – that, in fact, there really is something rather than nothing. Finally, we cannot say of the fact that something exists rather than nothing that it is a 'whole' in the sense of the horizon, the 'unchanging backdrop' of our changing experiences of the world. All we can say of being simpliciter is, simply, tautologically, that 'it be's.'

Behind each of these attempts to characterize the fact that something exists rather than nothing as a 'whole' lies the same fallacy, the same Kantian stricture – trying to predicate of the fact that something exists, the assertion of *existence*, something more *about* it, to give it descriptive *content* – trying, as it were, to fill in the *ontological* 'that' with a bit of *cosmological* 'what' – to claim, in other words, that by the *bare* fact that 'something exists' we really mean the *content-laden* fact that 'the world exists.' The ontological 'emptiness' of these results leaves us with the question: then what sort 'fact' is being simplicter? To get further purchase on this question, we first need to say more about the subject touched upon previously, namely, the problematic nature of Smith's description of the *global features* of the world-whole understood as a whole of *global importances*. The distinction between the ontological fact that something exists rather than nothing and the cosmological fact that the world exists will have a direct bearing on our critique of his account of these features. That in turn will help us get clearer about the nature and importance of the ontological fact itself.

Problematic Features of the World

With this distinction between an ontological and a cosmological perspective in hand, we can move from a critique of Smith's definition of *world* to examine the problematic nature of the global features ('importances') of the world-whole, features of its *existence* (*that* it is) as well as features of its *nature* (*what* it is).

Before doing so, let us briefly review the problems we saw above. In trying to uncover the implications of the distinction of between the ontological fact of being simplicter and the cosmological fact of the world's existence for Smith's analysis of the features of the world-whole, we encountered an initial ambiguity in the ontological-/cosmological distinction itself. The *ontological* fact of being simplicter has itself been understood traditionally in *cosmological* terms, namely, as a descriptively empty or 'bare' fact. We saw this in Allen's critique of Smith, which was clearly based on this Kantian assumption. Allen charged Smith with trying to predicate of the fact that something exists, or the fact that the world exists (and he seemed to confuse the two), certain additional features, that it is a joyful and marvelous reality. Smith was trying to fill in the *ontological* 'that' with descriptive *cosmological* 'what.' Contra Allen, however, Smith was right to see a link between being simpliciter and the response of joy. It was by not being clear about the *non*-cosmological basis of his claim, however, that he opened himself to Allen's critique.

There was already a confusion, therefore, in both Allen and Smith between being *simpliciter* and the being (existence) of the *world*. This was further compounded by Smith's failure to clarify the distinction between an *existential-ontological* and a *cosmological-metaphysical* understanding of both 'being simpliciter' and the existence of the world. How is it, we asked, that an existential-ontological understanding of the fact that something exists can elicit a response of joy while the traditional cosmological-metaphysical understanding does not? Only if an existential understanding of being, unlike a non-existential one, is an expression of an immediate experiential awareness, or what Smith terms an 'appreciative' awareness, of being simpliciter. Such an awareness can give rise to, among other feeling-responses, the 'ontological emotion' of wonder or the response of joy.

We will return to a fuller discussion of what it means to speak of the ontology underlying such an existential awareness. For now, we will focus on the problematic way Smith's analysis of the various global importances and their correlated global feeling-responses shifts back and forth between an existential and what we might call an objectifying way of talking about the fact and nature of the world's existence. In the case of each importance/feeling pair we will examine whether it represents an objectifying or an existential understanding of being and the world, or, more likely, a mixed mode of understanding that results in a misleading account of the response. We will be building on the results of our previous analysis of the ontological basis of feelings and in particular our critique of Smith's descriptions of two of the importance-cum-feeling *features* of the *existing* of the world – the happening/joy and non-necessity/marveling pair. Our contention was that these global feelings were grounded in the existential-ontological awareness of the fact of being and the corresponding ontological emotions that arise in response to that awareness. They derive such 'ultimacy' as they have from that ontological ground. Insofar, however, as they are *cosmological* feelings, that is, feeling responses to the existence of the *world*, they refer not to the world's *existing* but, as Allen suggested, to specific features of the *nature* of the world.

To review the issue of Smith's problematic metaphysics of *feelings* as it bears on the metaphysics of the features of the *world*, we argued previously that we can apply the hyphenated Heideggerian term, 'being-in-the-world,' to the unitary-but-articulated underlying phenomenon that links these feelings to the world. The problem, I argued, was that though Smith bases many of his key insights on this phenomenon, he falls back instead upon the traditional vocabulary of 'feelings' and 'world' used in the metaphysical tradition which it was his intention to critique. I argued that, despite his radical redefinition of key terms, Smith's project is not free of the old problems the metaphysical tradition has in dealing with feelings and their relation to the world, and that therefore his project needs an even more radical re-interpretation, a totally different 'metaphysical' setting, in an 'existential-ontological' foundation such as Heidegger's. We suggested that in fact global 'feelings,' on his account, are the *embodied reality* of those features of the world. If so, then a full account of his understanding of *feelings* cannot finally be separated from his view of the *world* and *metaphysics*. It is to the 'world-side' of his metaphysics of feeling that we will now be concerned. Here we will confront once again the question we posed earlier: *Why* do certain features, or 'importances,' felt meanings of the world, 'matter' to us? What is the ontology of *world* features that can account for that? The features of the world give rise to 'global' feelings. We asked above: *What* are they really feelings *of*? Their alleged 'object' is the *world*, specifically, certain features of the *world-whole*. They are elicited by, if not projected upon, 'the world-as-a-whole,' 'the world-in-itself.' They have a privileged role in world-disclosure. Smith referred to Heidegger's analysis of the revelatory features of global feelings: they disclose our 'thrownness' into the world, they disclose our 'being-in-the-world' *as a whole*, they disclose the ways things and the world 'matter' to us, their 'importances.' To this list Smith adds: they disclose the fact and nature of being(s)-as-a-whole, the 'world-whole.' Heidegger's expression would be the plural: 'beings-as-a-whole.' Heidegger's expression makes clear, as Smith's translation does not, that for Heidegger the reference of moods is not to that which is ontologically fundamental but rather to something that is, in Heidegger's usage, 'ontic,' ontologically penultimate. Smith recognizes that by anxiety (*angst*) Heidegger means to refer to something more than simply the ontic 'totality of what is.' It refers more primordially to an ontological totality. For Heidegger ontologically the 'earlier,' i.e., more fundamental feature of the moods is their disclosure of 'being-in-the-world' *as a whole*. As we asked then, is the 'world-(as- a)-whole', the world as 'the totality of beings' in the ontic sense the same as 'being-in-the-world' as a whole,' the 'totality' of world in the ontological sense?

It is Smith's claim that our moods and affects *disclose* the felt meanings of the world. These meanings are *actual features* of the world and our feelings, he says, are *appropriate responses* to them. Indeed he maintains that these feelings are *objectively true*, however paradoxical that may sound to philosophical ears used to dismissing them as *subjective* reports on inner phenomena. But we must ask: what does Smith think true feelings are true *about*, what is that *to which* true feelings are said to refer? Smith says they are real features of the world, what he calls the world's 'importances.' What sorts of 'things' are these importances? They are not the physical entities or metaphysical realities traditionally conceived to be the 'objects' of sense perceptions or of ideas. Rather they are the many different *ways* the world *matters* to us. But if so, what if we adopt an *adverbial* approach to the truth of that which is disclosed in feelings, as we did above. We might then say that *what* is disclosed in feelings, that *to which* feelings are a response, are not *subjects* and *objects* held together in a mysterious relation of *correspondence*, but rather *ways* of speaking, of acting, ways of existing, ways of *being-in* the world. We would be saying that what is disclosed in feelings is not the world, its objective meanings, but rather ways of being-in the world, adverbial realities if you will, that always already exist within the field, within the horizon or open space of our 'being-in-the-world' in which their 'relation' can then be understood prior to their separation into (subjective) feelings and (objective) importances. They are, in James' sense, 'double-barreled' realities, embodied realities of the 'being-in,' the "between" that links the I-side and the world-side of the ontologically primordial phenomenon of being-in-the-world prior to their analysis into I-side and world-side. This then makes it possible to explain why and how cosmological feelings vis-a-vis the existence and nature of the world are grounded in and receive their truth from ontological feelings vis-a-vis the fact of being itself.

Let us, therefore, revisit Smith's analysis of the phenomena disclosed in our 'global' feelings to see if an adverbial approach can resolve the ambiguities involved in his hybrid concept of the world. We will look to see which of the feelings can be best understood as responses to the primordial fact that *something* exists (rather than nothing), not or not primarily as responses to the contingent fact that a *world-whole* exists, and which can be best understood simply as responses to the existence and nature of that world-whole itself. In the latter instance we need to keep in mind Smith's analysis of three different ways of viewing the world-whole – empirically, transcendentally and horizonally. We need to ask to which sense of the world-whole any particular feeling could be said to apply. It could also be possible that some moods can be viewed both in cosmological and ontological perspectives, as disclosing, in clearly distinguishable and exactly specifiable senses, both features of the penultimate reality of the world-whole and features of the ultimate reality of being itself. Finally, with each of these feeling/features pairs we will ask whether the global feeling in question was an *appropriate* response to its corollary world feature, but also, more consequentially for Smith's project, whether it was the *only* appropriate response or whether, contra Smith's claim that they are *metaphysical* feelings, *other* feeling-responses are also not only logically but existentially possible. If so, then as posited at the beginning of this section on World, following suggestions from Wittgenstein and James, the happy and the unhappy, the joyful and the despairing, will be shown to live in *different worlds*. For 'global' feelings are not simply responses to *different features* of the *same world*, they disclose the reality of *different worlds* altogether – not the reality of a single, hierarchically-structured world-whole, but the reality of a *plurality* of *world–wholes*. And because these 'world's and the feelings that disclose them, though analytically distinct, are yet interlinked 'moments' of the ontologically prior phenomenon of 'being-in-the-world,' they will be seen to be different *ways*, different *modes,* of 'being-in-the-world' itself.

With these qualifications in mind, let us look at what reality and what truth are said to be disclosed at each level of Smith's analysis of feeling/feature pairs, or at least a representative subset of each. Smith groups them into four levels: first-level feeling/feature pairs related to the *fact that* the world-whole exists; second-level feeling/feature pairs referring to the *fact that* the world-whole exists; third-level feeling/feature pairs that disclose *the nature, the what,* of the world-whole; and fourth–level feeling/feature pairs that reveal *the nature, the what,* of the world-whole. Though our analysis will proceed via these hierarchically arranged, metaphysically systematic levels, we should expect in light of our foregoing critique that they will collapse into an unhierarchical, unsystematic, "unmetaphysical" plurality of modes of being-in-the-world.

Our task in the following, as noted earlier, is twofold. First we must to show how Smith's descriptions of the *features* of the (cosmological) 'world-whole' and their correlative (cosmological) 'global' *feelings* are either grounded in and derivatives of the 'ontological fact' and 'ontological emotion' (as regards the *existence* of the world), or insofar as they refer to the specific cosmological *nature* of the world-whole, derive their global 'ultimacy' from their ontological ground. Second, we must show how, by undermining the hierarchical structure of Smith's cosmological metaphysics of the world-as-a-whole, this opens the way for an existentialist ontology of plural responses to the fact that there is something rather than nothing.

What is at stake in the critique that follows is the claim basic to Smith's metaphysical project that the existence of the world is not simply one of its 'importances' but is in fact its most important importance, its foundational importance, upon which the entire structure of all the world's other global importances are hierarchically erected.

The Ontological Ground of Global Importances. The basis of our critique rests on the claim we have already made that Smith's formulation of his metaphysical starting point, 'the existence of the world,' contains a fatal ambiguity. It conflates in one phrase the distinction between the fundamental ontological fact of what we can call 'existence-as-such' or in Hawking's phrase that 'being be's, namely the fact that there is something rather than nothing, on the one hand, and the cosmological fact of what Smith calls the existence of the 'world-as-a-whole' on the other. To which does Smith mean to refer? Is his understanding of the 'importance' of existence parasitic on his understanding of the 'importance' of the world, or is the importance of the world parasitic on the notion of existence? Depending on the answer further questions arise. Are the importances (feeling/features) of the world the same as or analogues of the importances (features/feelings) of being? Are the 'global' feelings of joy, marveling, wonder, awe different if their referent is being itself rather than the world-whole? Can the 'global' features of the world-whole be ascribed to being itself? Is the object bearing such features not the *existence* of the world but the particular *nature* of the world-whole? Is the importance of the world's existence grounded in the (different) importance of being itself, or does it refer to the particular nature of the world-whole? Can the notion of the 'whole,' fundamental to Smith's concept of the 'global' nature of feelings vis-a-vis the world-as-a-whole, even be applied to existence or being as such?

There is another problem we are going to have to consider in the analysis that follows. Smith's list of global feelings and features does not distinguish between two very different kinds of feeling states and their putative referents. On the one hand his list includes what we can call *intellectual* feeling states, states of the mind confronted with the fact of being and/or the existence and nature of the world-whole – such feeling states as wonder, awe, marveling, a sense of the mysterious, the miraculous, the marvelous, to which we can add such correlates as a sense of the amazing, the baffling, the stupefying, stunning, incomprehensible or inexplicable. On the other hand, and for the most part clearly distinguishable, are what we might call *emotional* feeling states that arise when confronted with being or the world-whole – feelings such as joy, fulfillment, love, peace, humility, tedium, desolation, sadness, despair, equanimity, dread, apathy, quietude, reverence, to which we might add heightened instances of these such as bliss (intense joy), ecstasy (overwhelming joy) and reverence (unqualified love). Complicating the picture further, as these last superlatives indicate, is that these 'global' feelings are not to be understood in a relative sense, as 'appreciative' responses to phenomena 'within the world.' Rather they are to be taken in an absolute or ultimate sense, as responses to 'meta-physical' phenomena that are themselves unconditional, unqualified – namely, the existence and nature of the world-*as-a-whole*.

Finally, as we will discover, while none of these 'global' feelings or features can be taken to refer exclusively to the fact that *something exists rather than nothing*, some will be discovered to refer to that fact as well as to the *existence and/or nature* of the world-whole, while still others will be found to refer solely to the *nature* of the world-whole. Among the former will be included intellectual feeling states such as wonder, awe, marveling, and stupefaction and such emotional feeling states as joy, despair, reverence, humility, quietude, and apathy. Among the latter will be such emotional feelings as, again, despair, but also peace, tedium, love, desolation, sadness, dread, equanimity, apathy and quietude. In the analysis that follows we will try to show why and how this is so.

Two Basic Importances. As draw out the critical implications of these remarks, we will see how it is that they constitute further reasons why in the end Smith's metaphysics of feeling cannot be sustained. We will begin by looking more deeply and specifically into the issues of what for Smith are the two foundational feeling/features pairs of importances: the feeling of *joy* in response to the *happening* of the world's existence, and the feeling of *marveling* at the *non-necessity,* the *miracle,* of the world's existence. As we see from the above remarks, while these two feelings respond to the fact of being and the world-whole both, they do so in different ways: the first as an emotional response to these phenomena, the second as an intellectual response. In the following we will see how and why this is so and what it portends for Smith's metaphysical project.

Joy in Response to the Event of the World-Whole's Happening. The ambiguity in Smith's phrase, 'existence of the world,' runs through and compromises his entire discussion of the first 'importance' of the world-whole – joy in response to the 'existence' of the world-whole, the 'fulfillment" of the fundamental 'event' of its 'happening.' As we saw earlier, there was already a confusion, in both Allen and Smith, between being *simpliciter* and the being (existence) of the *world.* This was further compounded by Smith's failure to clarify the distinction between an *existential-ontological* and a *cosmological-metaphysical* understanding of both being *simpliciter* and the existence of the world. How is it, we asked, that an existential-ontological understanding of the fact that something exists, or that the world exists, can elicit a response of joy, while according to Allen the traditional cosmological-metaphysical understanding of the 'bare fact' of existence, whether being tout court or the existence of the world, cannot? Joy, Allen argued, is an evaluative response to some particular feature of the world, something good that happens, but what features, what value, what 'good' can the bare fact of existence have? He asked: If joy is not an appreciation of the 'importance' of being *simpliciter* or the world's existence, *of what,* if anything is it an appreciation? But if *joy* is not an appreciation of the importance of being tout court or the world's existence, *what,* if anything is?

In answer to the first question Allen said joy is indeed a valid intuition, but not of the *existence* of the world, rather of the world *as* having the *nature,* i.e. the *descriptive* feature, of being "the most fundamental *good* that exists." The implication of Allen's second question, following Kant, is that no feeling that can be validly considered an appreciation of the importance of the existence of the world tout court. Smith countered, however, that for a metaphysics of feeling, inasmuch as we are appreciative beings, it is legitimate to talk of an appreciative response to the existence of the world. The world's existence is not a 'bare,' i.e. uninterpreted, meaningless fact: "the primordial phenomenon– that there *is* being and not nothing – *'matters'*" (Smith, 1986, 24). Indeed, as the *primordial* phenomenon, as the *fulness* of being, the existing or 'happening' of the world is the *ground* of all the other importances of the world: "'To be' in the sense of being present or existing is a fulness, a positivity, a plenitude...in comparison with nonbeing, nothingness. Since the world *is*, rather than *is not*, it is truly evocatively describable as being fulfilled rather than being empty" (Smith, 1986, 178). But Smith's answer will not do. Allen's questions still need an answer, and Smith's own reply provides the reason why.

World not Absolute. Several problems in Smith's account are fatal for his position. First, falling back upon traditional metaphysical language, he opposes the notion of the existence of the world to the non-existence of the world, the positivity of its being to the negativity of nonbeing, the fulness of its being to the emptiness of nothingness: "existing is the fullness of which nonexisting is the privation; existing is the positivity of being, of the Is, that is lacked by nonbeing of the Is Not." This dynamic structure of happen-ing, "more fundamental than either eternity or 'time'" in the traditional metaphysical sense, is "identical with Existing Itself." We must ask, however, whether this characterization of the world's existence is an ontological assertion, one that applies to the nature of being itself, as at first glance it seems Smith intends it to do, or whether it is a cosmological assertion in ontological disguise. Recall the absolute nature of the qualifiers he wishes to ascribe to the world's existence. Does he mean that the non-existence of the world is absolutely inconceivable? For contemporary cosmological science at least, this is not the case. It is possible that some world other than this one might have existed. Alternatively, it is possible that this world is only one world among a multi-verse of existing worlds. In other words, ontologically the existence of this world is not necessary, it is contingent. If in some sense the world-as a-whole can be considered 'absolute,' it would be so only *vis-a-vis* its parts or, as Smith would argue, *vis-a-vis* the totality of its parts as well. In other words, it would be only *relatively* 'absolute.' If one prefers, it would be *cosmologically* absolute, but not *ontologically* absolute

Happening as Contingent. The second point follows from the first. Smith claims that since the world *is*, rather than *is not*, it is truly "evocatively" describable as being *fulfilled* rather than being empty." But does the inference implied in 'since' follow? The world's existence, says Smith, is 'absolute,' *but only in the moment.* It is actualized in its fullness, its completeness, in a succession of presents each of which is absolute in itself – a series of, as it were, 'eternal nows.' Its absolute being in the present is surrounded before and after by absolute non-being: "the world-whole's fullness breaks forth into fullness from an emptiness and into an emptiness. The world-whole's fulfilment appears to be renewed again and again, as each new fullness arises from and vanishes into the emptiness.... The happening-not-yet and -no-longer are internally characterized as lacks or emptinesses of happening; happening is the fullness of which they are deprived in the mode of the not yet and no longer." But this means that the existence of the world is contingent, for there is no necessity in its continuance from moment to moment. It is the metaphysical equivalent of the theological idea of the continuous creation of the world by God. If for one moment God ceased his activity of creating, the existence of the world would collapse into absolute non-existence, into the nothing from which it is continuously created anew. The problem is that for Smith there is no metaphysical counterpart to the creative power that sustains the world in its being from moment to moment. The alleged 'fullness' of the existence of the world remains suspended in a more primordial absolute nothingness.

Double Reference of Joy. Joy, says Smith, is the global feeling that responds uniquely to a specific feature of the world, its existence as a fulfillment of happening. We need to explore two questions further. What exactly is this feeling, joy, and what makes it a 'global' feeling? What exactly is the feature, the referent, to which it is a felt response? Is it the fact that *something* exists rather than nothing, or is it the existence of this *world* in particular?

The Feeling of Joy. In its ordinary meaning synonyms for joy might be happiness, gladness, delight, pleasure. As Allen says, in such cases joy would be about something particular, some within-the-world referent that gives rise to that feeling response. But Smith is not talking about that joy at that *relative* level. The joy he has in mind is 'global'; its referent is something more than an inner-worldly thing, it is the world *as a whole.* It is joy raised to an *absolute* height, *intensified* to its *utmost.* Perhaps better words for the sort of emotional state he has in mind would be *bliss* or *ecstasy* or *elation* – *unqualified* affirmation, *ultimate* acceptance, *profound* thankfulness, *deep* gratitude – a *foundational* Yes to the phenomenon of the world's existence.

The Object of Joy. But if so, Allen wants to know, what feature of the world's existence can elicit such a response? What 'object' is joy a response to? It follows from what was said above that joy of an absolute sort, bliss, ecstasy, cannot follow from the relative fact of the world's existence, or rather it can, but only in a *relatively* absolute sense. Employing the same metaphysical distinctions Smith himself uses (though not to the ends he uses them), it can argued that there cannot be an absolute response to an object (the world) that exists only contingently, that exists, as it were, only relatively. But if so, Allen asks. then to *what*, if anything, can joy in an absolute sense be a response to? If the world exists only relatively, then relatively to *what*?

The answer cannot be a cosmological one, it can only be ontological. Absolute joy can only be a response to the absolute fact that something exists rather than nothing, that being just be's. The paradox is that, relative to the world's existence, being simpliciter appears to be totally abstract, undifferentiated, feature-less, possessing no 'feature' to which joy could be a feeling response. It is not any-thing in particular, it is a not-a-thing, it is no-thing, it is nothingness itself. If so, the very distinction, fundamental to traditional metaphysics, between being and non-being collapses into what one strand of Buddhist thought would call a "non-dual duality." We will return this point in the section on Metaphysics below.

In the meantime we are left with a conundrum. If being as such, in distinction from the world-whole with its various features, is itself feature-less, then how can joy be a feeling response to it? To what can it be said to be a response? At least in the case of the world's existence, Smith can argue that joy is a felt response to something specific – the 'fulfilment' i.e., the positivity, the fullness of the world's happen-ing. Why is this not enough? Again, because of the implications of the distinction between being simpliciter and the being of the world. It brings us back to Tillich's observation, that the existential- ontological understanding of being, unlike the metaphysical-cosmological, is the expression of an ontological intuition that there is something rather than nothing. With that intuition comes an immediate existential awareness, the fundamental 'ontological emotion' of wonder – of joy, bliss, ecstasy. Why is this different from our joy at the existence of the world? Because it is a wonder, a joy in response to something – the fact of being itself – which, contrary to Aristotle or the latest cosmological theory, no metaphysical explanation, no scientific discovery, can ever 'explain away.' That is the danger confronting a metaphysics of feeling that takes the existence of the world as an ontological absolute. It is the expression of a different 'spiritual' attitude – a joy, a sense of wonder, analogous to, but as Heidegger might say, 'earlier' than, prior to, more fundamental than, the joy or wonder that, rightly, expresses our response to the wondrous being of the world as well. The problem with Smith's metaphysics of feeling, as we argued earlier, is not that he is wrong to see joy as a response to the existence of the world. It is that he was not clear about the *non*-cosmological basis of his claim. That is why he opened himself to Allen's critique. His problem, as we argued then and have tried to expound here, is that in the case of joy he was trying to mix the *ontological* 'that' with a *cosmological* 'what.' Is there some other way, then, that the feeling of joy can be grounded in an ontology that supports Smith's claims on its behalf without 'mixing,' without confusing, the differences between the cosmological and the ontological 'object' of that primordial emotion?

Existential Ontology of Joy. Our claim has been that 'global' or 'absolute' feelings vis-a-vis the world are grounded in the existential-ontological awareness of the fact of being and the emotions that accompany that awareness. Given the distinction we have been insisting upon, how can we say, with Smith and against Allen, that joy is a valid response to the world's existence? Only by explaining how cosmological joy is grounded in ontological joy. Since Smith did not provide the explanation, that is what we need to do now. We will do so by appealing to an existential-ontological understanding of joy situated in an analysis of the primordial phenomenon of our being-in-world. An existential phenomenology of that sort can, I believe, explain the underlying insight of Smith's metaphysics of feeling that, in his articulation of it, was still struggling to emerge from a traditional cosmological-metaphysical framework.

We begin, then, by asking *why* do certain features, felt meanings or 'importances' of the world *matter* to us? What is the *existential*-ontology of the phenomenon of the *world* that can account for that? Smith has argued that certain features of the world, of the world *as a whole*, give rise to 'global' *feelings*. We asked above: *what* are they really feelings *of*? Their alleged 'object' is the *world*, specifically, certain features of the *world-whole*. They are elicited by, if not projected upon, 'the world-as-a-whole,' 'the world-in-itself.' They have a privileged role in world-*disclosure*. But these 'global' feelings are not simply 'object' oriented. As 'feelings' they exist on the 'subject' side as well. Our 'feelings' are, ontologically, *more* than that. They are in James' sense, 'double-barreled' phenomena, *embodied* realities of the primordial phenomenon of our *'being-in'* the world. They are the "between" that *links* what Smith calls the 'I-side' and the 'world-side' of our being-in-the-world *prior* to its analysis into the I-side and world-side. This means that our *cosmological* feelings vis-a-vis the 'world-side' – vis-a-vis the *existence* and *nature* of the world, its 'that' and its 'what' – are *abstracted* from that prior ontological linkage. They are grounded in, *derivative* of, our *ontological* feelings, those feelings that disclose the prior and primordial fact of our being-in-the-world itself. The primordial 'object' of joy, in other words, is not the *world-whole* to which our feelings are a response, it is our very *being-in*-the-world *as such*. That is what ultimately, absolutely, *matters* to us. It is because we first of all exist as *being-in*-the world that, derivatively, the *world* we 'are-in' matters to us.

We can now ask why and how *joy* can *matter* to us *ontologically*, and why and how the *existence of the world* in turn can be said to be the object of the 'global' *cosmological* feeling of joy. In answering this question, we will also be in a position to explain the many different ways in which other 'global' feelings, other 'appreciative' or *existential* moods and affects limned in Smith's metaphysics of feeling matter to us. Heidegger's brief discussion of the ontological mood of joy follows upon his more extended analysis of the ontological mood of another of 'global' feeling, the mood of *angst*, anxiety. What anxiety discloses about our being-in-the-world could be said to be the other or opposite side of what is revealed in joy. But is it the same 'world' that is disclosed? Keeping in mind Wittgenstein's observation that the world of the happy is not the same as the world of the unhappy, that the world of joy may not be the *same* world as the world of despair, let us see.

What are 'global' or existential moods and affects? They are our fundamental ways of being-in the world, what Heidegger calls our "basic factical possibilities" of being-in-the-world. These include, among others, the 'global' feelings catalogued by Smith. For Heidegger, while the existential-ontological mood on which he focuses in *Sein und Zeit* is "sober anxiety," nevertheless, he says, there *goes with it* an "unshakeable joy" (Heidegger, *SZ* 310). There are many other 'global' moods as well – hope, elation, enthusiasm, gaiety, boredom, sadness, melancholy, indifference, equanimity, depression or despair, some of which have been catalogued by Smith. Unlike Smith, however, who attempts to construct a metaphysical hierarchy of moods founded on joy, Heidegger does not present the mood of anxiety as *metaphysically foundational*, it is *ontologically disclosive*. It is a *methodologically distinctive* way of seeing into the nature and significance of alternative and what are in some cases incompatible modes of being-in-the-world. For Heidegger our 'global' moods (modes of 'being-in') disclose a *pluralism* of 'worlds,' not as for Smith the same One World-Whole. Thus, the world disclosed in anxiety may not be the same world disclosed in joy, though both moods express "basic factical possibilities" of our being-in-the- world.

But questions remain. Though the moods of anxiety and joy may appear to contradict one another existentially, to reveal different 'worlds,' Heidegger says that they *go together* (*mitgehen*) with one another. Then why is it anxiety, not joy, or even anxiety 'together' with joy, that for Heidegger paradigmatically discloses our being-in-the world, the world-as-a-whole? Why does he say that anxiety is the 'distinctive' mood disclosing our being-in-the-world, whereas for Smith it is joy that performs that role? And yet Heidegger says that the two moods 'belong' to one another. Do they, then, disclose the *same* meaning of our being-in-the-world? If so, why focus on anxiety rather than, like Smith, on joy? And what, for Heidegger, is the relation of anxiety and joy to our other 'global' moods? For Smith the answer to these questions is very clear: joy is our *basic* intuition of the existence and nature of the world and the *foundation* of all our other 'felt responses' to the world-as-a-whole.

In Smith's view, Heidegger's analysis of anxiety may indeed reveal the finitude, the 'nothingness,' the 'abyss' at the bottom of our being-in-the-world. But the phenomenon of anxiety vis-a-vis the world *presupposes*, metaphysically, that the world 'is there' in the first place, that its being is first of all a *positivity*. The revelation of the 'nothingness' of the world's existence fails to explain how it is that in joy we experience the world's existence as a positivity, a fulfillment, and how that mood can ground our other moods. If Heidegger is to have an answer to Smith, he must show not only how it is that anxiety and joy 'go together,' thus calling into question Smith's exclusive claims for joy, but also how that makes possible a non-metaphysical understanding of our 'global' moods in response to the existence of the world.

Specifically, then, what does Heidegger's analysis of anxiety do that Smith's analysis of joy does not – what does it disclose that joy does not? Why is the difference important for a critique of Smith's metaphysics of joy? Why nevertheless do the two moods 'belong' together? Are they ultimately, in some 'non-dual' or dialectical sense, 'one' – anxiety *sive* joy? What do they, 'together,' tell us about the meaning of our being-in-the-world that joy alone or anxiety alone do not? What is their relation to our other 'global' moods? Are they foundational or simply do they simply co-exist with other possible modes of being? To answer these questions, and in particular to show their subversive implications for Smith's metaphysical hierarchy of moods, we must take a short detour into Heidegger's analysis of anxiety *in Sein und Zeit*, the relation of anxiety to joy, and its relation to other ontological moods and 'factical possibilities of being.'

Excursus: Heidegger on Anxiety in *'Sein und Zeit.'* We begin with what anxiety discloses, how and why it does so. We then consider its relation to joy. Finally, we look at its relation to other moods and affects.

What Anxiety Discloses. For Heidegger anxiety (*Angst*) is only one of our basic possibilities of being-in-the-world, however it is methodologically a distinctive way in which the *primordial totality* of *being-in-the-world as such* – its *equi-primordial structural* totality as 'world,' 'Being-in,' and 'self' – comes to light (Heidegger, *SZ*, 140, 182, 297). This disclosure has existential and ontological consequences. Ontologically, our being-in-the-world shows itself, in comparison with things within the world, to be "completely indefinite." Existentially, the "totality" of things *within* the world "collapses into itself; the world itself has the character of completely lacking significance" (Heidegger, *ibid*.187). The indefinite nature of this meaninglessness means that "what threatens is *nowhere*. Anxiety 'does not know' what that in the face of which it is anxious is... it is already 'there,' and yet nowhere." In anxiety "the 'It is nothing and nowhere' becomes manifest ... *the world as such is that in the face of which one has anxiety*.... The 'nothing' [of things] is grounded in the most primordial 'something' – in the *world*. Ontologically, however, the world belongs essentially to one's existence as being-in-the-world. So if the 'nothing' – that is, the world as such – exhibits itself as that in the face of which one has anxiety, this means that *Being-in-the-world itself is that in the face of which anxiety is anxious*" (Heidegger, *ibid*., 186-187). In other words, by bringing one face to face with the world as world, not simply as the totality of things within the world, anxiety at the same time brings one face to face with one's *own* being-in-the-world (Heidegger, *ibid.*, 188). In anxiety is disclosed how and why the world 'matters.'

In what way does anxiety disclose that we are beings to whom the world 'matters'? What is it that anxiety discloses about one's being-in-the-world such that the world 'matters'? Anxiety, says Heidegger, brings one face to face with *thrownness* of our being, 'that it is there.' Specifically, in the mood [*Befindlichkeit*] of anxiety one *finds* oneself [*sich befindet*] "*face to face* with the 'nothing [*das Nichts*]; the possible impossibility of one's existence" (Heidegger, *ibid.*, 265-266). Anxiety discloses that one's being-in-the-world "has been thrown into the indefiniteness of its 'limit-Situation'... the 'nothing' with which anxiety brings us face to face unveils the nullity by which one is...in one's very basis, defined; and this basis itself *is* as thrownness into death" (Heidegger, *ibid.*, 308).

Anxiety and Joy. It is at this point that, having shown that anxiety is that mood that 'distinctively' bring us 'face to face' with death as the 'possible impossibility' of our being-in-the-world, the possibility which cannot be 'outstripped' of our own absolute nothingness, Heidegger now adds, in what might seem paradoxical if not contradictory, that "along with the sober anxiety which brings us face to face with our individualized potentiality-for-Being, there goes an unshakable joy in this possibility" (Heidegger, *ibid.*, 310). How so? Insofar as anxiety enables us 'resolutely,' courageously, to face and accept our being-toward-death as our final possibility, it 'frees' us, 'liberates' us for the 'existential positivity' of our being-in-the-world (Heidegger, *ibid.*, 298, 300). Thus, like Smith, Heidegger links the mood of joy to the positivity of being. There is an all-important difference, however. As we have seen, for Heidegger, unlike for Smith, there is no direct path to joy. To borrow a phrase from Dietrich Bonhoeffer, the German theologian who paid the ultimate price because of his participation in a plot to assassinate Hitler, there is no 'cheap grace.' Joy, yes, but at a cost that must be paid first. The way to the 'positivity' of joy must first pass through the 'negativity' of anxiety, of being-toward-death. One is reminded of William James' distinction between the 'once-born' and the 'twice-born.' The latter have had to pass through the valley of death, the "dark night of the soul," to experience the freedom and liberation of which Heidegger speaks. Yes, Tillich spoke of the the 'ontological emotion' of wonder" – of joy, bliss, ecstasy – in the presence of being, but he also spoke of the 'courage to be,' the existential resoluteness needed to face and overcome the co-primordial 'threat of non-being.' Heidegger is going against the mainstream tradition in Western metaphysics from Plato and Aristotle on that has privileged the priority of being over non-being, of joy over despair. In this respect, Smith's metaphysics of feeling, for all its differences with that tradition nevertheless remains in the mainstream. But for Heidegger, coming after the 'overcoming' *(Ueberwindung)*, the radical critique of that tradition by philosophers such as Schopenhauer, Nietzsche and Kierkegaard, and taken up later by Sartre, there can be no return to that metaphysics of being, to hierarchical metaphysics-as-usual.

Anxiety and Other Moods. Heidegger states, significantly, that while anxiety is particularly well-suited "to take over a methodological function *in principle* for the existential analytic.... of course it is essential to *every* state-of-mind that in each case being-in-the-world should be *fully* disclosed in all those items which are constitutive for it – world, Being-in, Self... undisguised by entities-within-the-world" (Heidegger, *ibid.*, 190-191; latter two italics mine). The problem here, however, is that in *Sein und Zeit*, unlike the rich phenomenological analysis Smith gives us, Heidegger does not further explore the link between either anxiety or joy and those other moods. His interest lies elsewhere. As he says: "the analysis of these... moods would transgress the limits which we have drawn for the present interpretation by aiming towards fundamental ontology" (Heidegger, *ibid.*, 310). We are left, therefore, to speculate as best we can what those links might be. In saying that every mood, not just anxiety, fully discloses the existential-ontological structure of our being-in-the-world, Heidegger does not seem to differ from Smith in seeing various moods as 'global' feeling-responses that disclose the world-as-a-whole. However, where Smith sees different moods as revealing different *features* of the *same* world, what Post termed that different 'faces' of the world, for Heidegger, like for Wittgenstein, each mood discloses a *different* 'world'– the world of anxiety *(Angst)*, the world of joy *(Freude)*. Though each mood reveals the same *formal*, i.e., existential-ontological *structure* of our being-in-the-world, namely, the co-primordial belonging-together of world, self, and 'being-in,' yet, as different *modes* of 'being-in,' each mood discloses a different *content* of the world with which it is ontologically co-primordial. In each linking mode of 'being-in' *we* exist differently, and we inhabit a different *world*. Thus, to cite the example on which Heidegger several times draws, 'indifference,' that "pallid lack of mood which dominates the 'gray everyday',", is also, analyzed structurally, an 'existentially positive' phenomenon; it too discloses the formal structure of our being-in-the-world (Heidegger, *ibid.*, 134, 345, 371). For Heidegger, therefore, there is no 'metaphysical' priority of one mood over another; anxiety may play a distinctive methodological function in his analysis, it may also serve to make possible a more dialectical, a more 'authentic' understanding of joy than we find in Smith. Despite his insight into the 'appreciative' nature of the 'I' in relation to the 'world,' Smith does not ground his metaphysics of feeling in an analysis of the underlying existential-ontological structure of our being-in-the-world. Heidegger's non-hierarchical, more pluralistic approach to a phenomenology of our moods makes clear the extent to which, as a result, Smith falls back upon a traditional, dualistic and hierarchical, i.e. 'metaphysical' understanding of the relationship between self and world and of our moods to one another.

It may not be entirely out of place to comment here on a related aspect of this problem which may have some bearing on our critique of Smith. Traditional Western philosophy, inheriting from Plato a three-fold division of the soul into intellect, will and emotion, has focused on the 'active' phenomena of intellect and will rather than the 'passive' phenomenon of the emotions. As a result, until the rise of phenomenology, it has presented us for the most part with a dichotomy, a choice between two epistemological-cum-metaphysical options regarding our relation to the world. Does the world have independent, objective features to which we subjectively respond, or do we subjectively 'project' the alleged 'features' upon the world in order to justify our 'responses' to them? What Heidegger and the phenomenologists, and Smith too insofar as he draws on them, offer us is a third possibility: We *find* ourselves (*sich befinden*) already and always *in* the world in a certain way, mode, mood (*Befindlichkeit*). Why? We don't 'know' why we are *thrown* (given, 'gifted') into the world in this way or that. If we did know, intellectually, we could, like Plato's charioteer, call upon the will to change our moods visa-vis the world. Like all our moods, however, what the mood of anxiety reveals to us is *that* we are so located, that we *are* and *have* to be; the rest, says Heidegger, is shrouded in nothingness: "The pure 'that is it' shows itself, but the 'whence' and the 'whither' remain in darkness" (Heidegger, *ibid.*, 134).

Heidegger's analysis of anxiety in *Sein und Zeit* may not yet be free of problems, however. Even if his analysis of anxiety can be defended against Smith's charge, there is still another problems, this one posed by the link between anxiety and that nothingness which Heidegger terms 'the Nothing.' Quite apart from the critical cavils of a logical positivist like Carnap, there are other philosophers, for example the thinkers of the 20th C. Japanese Kyoto School, who though thoroughly familiar with the Heidegger of *Sein und Zeit*, appeal instead to the Mahayana Buddhist insight of being-*sive*-nothingness, that what they term 'Absolute Nothingness' is dialectically identical (*sive*) with 'Absolute Being.' They argue, similarly to Smith but on different philosophical grounds, that anxiety cannot reveal the absolute positivity of being. This, they say, is because despite Heidegger's talk of 'the Nothing,' his analysis of anxiety in *Sein und Zeit* discloses only a nothingness *relative* to the existence of the *world*, not the *absolute* nothingness of *being* itself. Heidegger's analysis of anxiety as the portal into an intuition of nothingness does not really refute their claim that "'nothingness' cannot be encountered from a posture of anxiety... there is a nothingness that is not empty and meaningless, and that does not therefore summon in despair" (Waldenfels, 1-2.)

Whether Heidegger's ontology is less radical than the Kyoto School thinkers would like is another matter, one to which we will return when we undertake a further critique of Smith in the section on his metaphysics below. Here, restricting ourselves to the analysis of anxiety in *Sein und Zeit*, we can imagine Heidegger might say that insofar as anxiety reveals our being-in-the-world in its *contingent* totality, it discloses a nothingness 'beneath' it that is *absolute* in *relation* to the world's being. By disclosing the *relative* nothingness, i.e., the contingency of the world's being, it thereby discloses 'the Nothing' (*das Nichts*) that 'grounds' the existence of the world itself. Of course the existence of the world, if viewed *apart* from its disclosure against the 'un-ground' (*Abgrund*) of the Nothing, can in fact be 'grounded', i.e. *explained*, at least in principle, according to science and metaphysics. In that sense its existence is not a 'bare' fact, *pace* Kant. But according to Heidegger, what cannot be explained – what is *absolutely* 'absurd' – is the fact of being itself. It is in that sense that the existence of the world, too, is ultimately 'grounded' in *absolutely* nothing, in something that is *ultimately* absurd, something that is beyond any final, metaphysical explanation – the fact that there is something rather than nothing. And that means that along with the world's 'nothingness,' every entity *within* the world, including our own existence, is grounded in this 'Nothing.' Whether that constitutes a sufficient answer to the Kyoto School critics, or whether their talk of 'being *sive* nothingness' makes any better sense, we will put to the side for now. But in any case, it would seem that Heidegger's talk about 'the Nothing' leaves the mind, the intellect, language, logic, our very being, grasping at … nothing! Or does it?

Marveling in Response to the Event of the World-Whole's Happening. With this we turn to *marveling*, the second of what for Smith are the two foundational feeling/features of his metaphysics. The ambiguity in Smith's phrase, 'existence of the world,' that runs through and compromises his discussion of the first importance of the world-whole also infects his discussion of the second foundational importance, marveling at the miracle, the non-necessity, of the world's existence. The confusion pointed out above – between being *simpliciter* and the being of the *world* – obtains here also.

As we noted, for Smith, ontologically the existence of the world is not necessary but contingent. As we argued, though its existence may be *cosmologically* absolute vis-a-vis the totality of things *within* the world, nevertheless because of the non-necessity of its *being* it is not *ontologically* absolute. Further, because of the 'momentary' nature of the world's existence on Smith's account, the world-whole continually teeters on the edge of the abyss of a more primordial, an absolute, *nothingness.*

As we have seen, Smith tries to distinguish the referent of joy from that of marveling by appealing to the difference between 'is rather than is not' (as it were, the sheer being of the world) and 'is though it need not be' (i.e. the contingency of the world's being). For joy the world exists neither contingently nor necessarily, but *non-necessarily.* It simply and absolutely 'is.' His claim reflects the ambiguity of reference of these feelings between being (sheer is) and world (is though need not be) together with the added claim that second is *dependent* on the first. The problem, however, is that the notion of 'just is' legitimately applies, if at all, only to being tout court (by tautological definition, as it were), whereas if applied to the world's existence the distinction between 'just is' and 'need not be' simply collapses. If so, what he means by the *nonnecessity* of the world's existence becomes indistinguishable from the contingency of its being. Indeed, on Smith's account, the existence of *any existing thing within* the world is also a miracle. Of *anything* that exists it could be said "Even though it could not be, *it is!*" Its existence may indeed be a miracle, but not for the reason Smith gives. Not because its existence is a miracle within the more encompassing miracle of the world's existence, but because the *relative* miracle of its finite existence *and* that of the world-whole is grounded in the *absolute* miracle that *anything, including* the world-whole itself, exists rather than nothing at all.

It follows that as with joy here too, unlike Smith, we must distinguish between two kinds or levels of marveling – between marveling at the *relative* miracle that the *world* exists, and marveling at the *absolute* miracle that *anything* at all exists rather than absolutely nothing. The proper 'object' of marveling, the miracle to which it is primordially a response, is not first of all that the *world* exists (rather than nothing), though the cosmos in itself is already an object worthy of marveling, as philosophers from the beginning in metaphysics to the scientific cosmologists today richly attest. Rather, the more *primordial* marvel is that *anything* exists at all rather than nothing. If this were not so, a critic of metaphysical cosmology, including Smith's updated 'feeling' version, could argue that marveling over the world's existence is, epistemologically if not emotionally, simply a case of wonderment at what is indeed a fascinating phenomenon – the world in all its challenging complexity –a feeling that can easily turn into nihilistic disenchantment the closer the existence of the world comes to being completely explained.

There is another distinction between joy and marveling, however, one that Smith does not attend to in his analyses of these or other 'global' feelings and their correlate features, one that may clarify matters and also fit better with an alternative account of these moods – the distinction between feeling-responses that are primarily emotional and those that are more intellectual.

While marveling, like joy, responds both to the fact of being tout court as well as the existence of the world, it does so in a different way, with a different emphasis. Marveling, like joy, is of course an emotion, an dispositional attitude in response to something. As the phenomenologists on whom Smith draws point out, moods are not 'mere feelings,' merely 'subjective,' they too have an intentional structure, a cognitive reference, if only implicit. As Heidegger observes, moods are accompanied by an *understanding* of our being-in-the-world, they embody an *interpretive relation* to the world. In this regard, it may be said that the difference of marveling from joy is that, though joy too has intentionality, is a response to a 'feature' of something, in the case of marveling that intellectual or cognitive aspect is more prominent, the reference is more explicit, the belief-content is more clear and distinct, easier to see. In joy the emphasis falls on the *feeling*, on the *felt quality* of the emotion itself, whereas in marveling, though the feeling is strong, we are almost immediately directed toward the 'object' *to which* it is a felt-response. In that sense joy is a more 'intransitive' feeling-*state*, whereas marveling is a more 'transitive' feeling-*response.*

We will return to this distinction when it comes to cataloging the others of Smith's 'global' feelings, but before we do let us consider what bearing this distinction between joy and marveling has on a critique of Smith's treatment of these two fundamental feeling/features of his metaphysics. Perhaps the clearest implication is that it *reverses the order of dependence* between these two moods and the 'objects' they refer to. As will be recalled, Smith contends that marveling is *dependent* upon joy inasmuch as what marveling refers to, the *non-necessity* of the world's happening, *depends* on what joy refers to, the fact of the world's *happening* in the first place –as he puts it, that 'it *need* not be but it *is!*' *depends* on '*is* rather than is not.' The kind of 'dependency' Smith has in mind here appears to be *logical* or *propositional*, which is then elevated to the status of a dependency in *existence,*, a *metaphysical* truth.

But this will not do, for two reasons. First, Smith's claim proceeds from his confusion of being simpliciter with the being of the world – in particular, it tries to finesse the contingent nature of the being of the latter. For it can be said of the allegedly 'simple' happening of the world ('it just is') that it too 'need not have happened but it has' (in fact, on Smith's telling, it continues to happen, with no necessity, in every discretely separate moment!). On this score alone, therefore, it is not possible to discriminate the 'object' of joy from the 'object' of marveling. But there is a second reason. As we have seen, joy itself not as 'simple,' as straightforward an emotion as his argument requires. Even if Smith is able to reply to Allen's critique that the '*bare*' existence of the world does not justify an *evaluative* feeling-response of any sort, let alone that of joy, there is the problem we uncovered in the preceding analysis of joy. Joy is itself not a simple but a complex evaluative or (Smith's preferred term) 'appreciative' response, whether to the world's existence or to the phenomenon of being itself. As we have noted, its existential-ontological authenticity (for that is what Smith himself is talking about), not its metaphysical referent, is itself *dependent* upon its passing through, overcoming, and incorporating a prior feeling-response to the world's existence, that of anxiety.

Can we say that of marveling? Does marveling have, as it were, a dark side to it? To get at this question, let us first consider one of its cognate meanings – *wonder*. This is not a stretch (though Smith treats wonder as an entirely different mood), since one of the definitions of 'marvel' is 'wonder.' Indeed the word-etymology of 'marvel' discloses that it originates in the Greek verb for 'wonder.' The noun 'marvel' comes from the Old-French singular *merveille* (verb *merveiller*) taken from the Latin *mirabilia*, neuter plural of *mirabilis*, 'wonderful,' based on the verb *mirari, -are*, 'to wonder at' and the related adjective *mirus*, 'wonderful.' The other word Smith uses for the *object* of marveling, 'miracle,' stems even more visibly, via *miraculum*, 'object of wonder,' from the same root. Note that in both cases the transitive intentionality of the mood is explicit in its definition. To marvel *is* to feel wonder *at or about* something.

Replacing 'marveling' with 'wondering at' in fact helps to bring us closer to answering our question. It brings with it another advantage as well, to which we will return in a moment. But first, the phenomenon of wonder does, perhaps more clearly than marveling, have a dark side, it can have a double-reference, one negative, one positive; indeed, it can contain *both* in one and the same moment. We will examine that phenomenon further in the following chapter on Rubenstein's book *Strange Wonder*, whose title captures that duality – and more. For now let us just observe that the object of wonder can exert both a compelling force of attraction and a repelling force of fear, and if the object be something like Otto's sense of the Holy or Sacred, it can exert both at the same time. Assuming this to be true, how does this advance the argument? If both joy and marveling (aka wonder) are 'mixed' or complex moods in this manner, can we say that one is any more 'dependent' than the other? There is a significant difference. Joy in its authentic sense can only be reached by passing through its dark side. Wonder, on the other hand, like another cognate, awe (again, a feeling-response that Smith treats as an entirely different mood) need not undertake that existential journey since it already embodies, irreducibly, that 'strange' two-sidedness. Indeed, it is what evokes the 'dark' mood, anxiety, that joy for its part has to learn to face and take into itself. In that sense we can say that, despite the similarity of their double-aspect, it is wonder that gives rise to, that 'explains' – existentially, not metaphysically – the mood of joy. It is because wonder points, primordially, to an 'object' that harbors within it, indissolubly, the forces of both attraction and repulsion, that in its response to that 'object' joy can be said to 'depend,' in its struggle to achieve authenticity, on wonder.

Another advantage that replacing marvel with wonder brings with it is that it clarifies further in what sense joy can be said to depend on wonder. As Smith might agree, moods are not 'mere feelings' existing reductively on the 'side of the subject,' they are intentionally-structured 'appreciations' *of*, existential-ontological responses *to*, the nature of the world and being itself. Because its 'about' structure is more explicit than that of joy, and more clearly than does marveling, wonder pre-eminently discloses, existentially, the fundamental 'strangeness' of its ultimate referent. As anxiety pre-eminently reveals the nothingness of our finite being-in-the-world, so wonder pre-eminently unveils the 'strange' mystery of being itself. That is why Tillich speaks of wonder as *the* 'ontological emotion.'

For Smith joy and marveling are the two fundamental moods grounding a metaphysics of feelings understood as felt-responses to various features of the world-as-a-whole. We have called into question his analysis of these two moods and in particular their relation to one another. Specifically, we have argued that marveling cannot be viewed as metaphysically dependent upon joy; if anything the reverse is true. But the implications of this critique reach farther. They apply to Smith's analysis of other global moods and what they disclose about the existence and nature of the world. In turning to that briefly before we conclude with a critique of the metaphysical nature of Smith's project, in fact as a route into that critique, we will see how the reversal of the relation of joy and marveling (wonder) leads to a further undermining of the *hierarchical* nature of his analysis of moods and instead further opens the way to a *pluralist* way of understanding them.

Other Importances. For Smith joy and marveling are the two fundamental moods grounding a metaphysics of feelings understood as felt-responses to various features of the world-as-a-whole. We have called into question his analysis of these two moods and in particular their relation to one another. Specifically, we have argued that marveling cannot be viewed as metaphysically dependent upon joy; if anything the reverse is true. But the implications of this critique reach farther. They apply to Smith's analysis of other global moods and what they disclose about the existence and nature of the world. In turning to that briefly before we conclude with a critique of the metaphysical nature of Smith's project, in fact as a route into that critique, we will see how the reversal of the relation of joy and marveling (wonder) leads to a further undermining of the *hierarchical* nature of his analysis of moods and instead further opens the way to a *pluralist* way of understanding them. In doing so we will not discuss all of the moods Smith canvasses, rather we will again select some representative moods – intellectual and emotional, negative and positive – from each of the three 'levels' allegedly 'founded' on the two 'basic' importances, joy and marveling, assessing, as we do, whether they apply to being as such and/or the world-as-a-whole.

The first thing to be said is that these global moods, these global feeling responses, are not 'global' because they are different responses to different *features* of the same 'global' reality, the *same* 'world-as-a-whole.' Rather they are modes of 'being-in,' of existing within, the 'global' structure of 'being-in-the-world' *before* its analysis into 'self' and 'world.' Moods are analogous to James's notion of 'experience,' a double-barreled phenomenon that exists *prior* to analysis into self or world. Each experienced mood is a mode of reality that embodies and links the two ontologically *derivative* 'moments.' Each feeling-response is thus 'global' in the sense of being the actualization of a different way of being-in-the-world *as such, as-a-whole*. Each embodies the reality of a *different self* and *different world* (Wittgenstein), a different way of being of the self-as-a-whole and a different way of being of the world-as-a-whole. This means that the relationship of moods to one another cannot be understood by arranging them in a metaphysical hierarchy of 'levels' in which some are fundamental and others more or less dependent, in which some are metaphysically more 'pure' and others more 'impure' than others. Rather, as indicated in our discussion of the moods of marveling and joy, among the plurality of ways of being-in-the-world, though all are intentional in their in structure, for some, as in the case of marveling, the emphasis on an 'objective' referent may be more prominent, whereas for others, as with joy, the emphasis on a 'subjective' state may be more pronounced. Another 'horizontal' (and 'horizon-al') relationship we will now be seeing, is between moods that are positive, like joy and marveling, and at least in some cases a negative counterpart, e.g. in the case of joy, sadness, or in the case of marveling, apathy. With these observations in mind, let us take a 'de-leveled' look at examples at moods on the rest of Smith's 'levels.'

Positive Moods. We will begin by repositioning ('de-leveling') positive moods cognate with marveling that refer either to the fact of being as

THOMAS DEAN

such or to the fact or nature of the world's existence or some combination thereof: *awe, wonder, reverence.* In each of these cases Smith sees them as 'impure' or 'dependent' in their relation to the fundamental 'happening' of the world. But a closer look at this analysis of each shows that, in fact, they are equi-primordial, equally 'pure' as it were as the phenomenon of marveling. In each case too, as with marveling, they can be understood in both a relative sense, referring to the world's existence or nature, and an absolute sense, to the fact of being as such. Smith makes his case for their position occupying a more dependent level by emphasizing only what I am calling their relative sense. If, however, we can see them as having an absolute sense as well, this will problematize the 'metaphysical' character of his phenomenological description of them. Let's take them seriatim.

Awe. Awe is said to be a felt response to the 'immensity' of 'the world's existing.' 'Immensity' is said to be a feature of the world's existing "simply as such prior to any fuller consideration of the nature of the world." But clearly 'immensity' cannot be a 'feature' of the fact of existing as such, not without some further indication of *what* it is that is said to be immense, in other words, without some further description of the *nature* of the 'world' whose existence is said to be immense. And in fact Smith concedes as much. As he says, in the absence of the notion of the world's 'immensity' having any descriptive content, awe would revert to "a pure feeling of the world's fulfillment of happening, a feeling-of-fulfillment." In other words, awe would be another word for the 'pure' feeling-response of joy. There would be a difference, however, for as we have argued, whereas with joy the emphasis is the emotional state involved, for awe the intentionality is more pronounced. And what would the reference of awe be in that case? Not the world in its cosmological immensity, but the miraculous fact of being itself, the fact that something exists rather than nothing. Like marveling, then, awe would have a double sense: a relative sense related to the immensity of the world-whole, and an absolute sense related to the fact of being itself.

Wonder. We have already discussed wonder above as a cognate for marveling. But here too Smith, even more clearly, lends support to our argument instead. Wonder, unlike marveling, is said to be a response not to the 'that' but to the *what,* the *nature,* of the world-whole's existence. The feature of the world that gives rise to this response is its 'mysteriousness,' the uncanny sense of a 'hidden reality' behind its 'appearance,' an ineliminable 'otherness,' a strangeness. And what is that strangeness? Smith's answer: it is precisely this sense of the duality of the world's reality/appearance, it both beckons and thwarts me. How so: it beckons by suggesting a deeper reality, an underlying reason, for the world's existence, but it thwarts because *I have no way of knowing* what that reality, that reason, *really is.* There are problems with this answer. One is that its description of wonder is confused. Is it wonder at the 'accidental,' i.e. contingent existence of *this* world, that *this* world need not have existed, that it could have been *other* than it is? Or is it wonder in response to the absolute miracle of the fact that the world, this or any other, exists at all when there need not have been a world at all? If the former, then though the fact of other possible worlds indeed excites the imagination of many cosmologists and philosophers today, namely, scientific puzzlement or curiosity relative to the notion of this world or other worlds, it is a wonder to which it is not unreasonable to expect answers forthcoming. But if the latter, then it is a totally different phenomenon, it is wonder in the face of the absolute mystery that there is something rather than nothing at all. The otherness, the strangeness, is not that this world rather than some other(s) exists, it is that anything exists at all. Another problem with the answer is that, despite Smith's claim to have reinterpreted the nature of metaphysics, his notion of wonder falls back upon the very traditional metaphysical dualism of reality-and-appearance, thus undercutting the radical implications of his own notion of a metaphysics of feelings-and-features.

Reverence. For Smith reverence, like wonder, is a response to the *nature,* not the *fact,* of the world's existence. His characterization of it is problematic for not altogether different reasons. First, the mood is relative to the world-whole having certain specific features: it enjoys 'supremacy,' in particular, 'maximal greatness,' both by being 'the greatest thing of its kind and by having a 'positive, fulfilled' character. If the world were to lack one or more of these features, if it need not have had them, presumably it would not merit reverence. But as we have seen, it is not clear that the world is a 'whole' in the necessetarian, metaphysical sense required. Nor is it clear that the world, pace Leibniz, is the greatest thing of its kind (its 'kind'?), or that its cosmic nature is in any straightforward and unproblematic sense 'positive' or 'fulfilled.' Further, to speak of it as 'ontologically independent' of me and of my 'absolute dependence' upon it again shows Smith relapsing into a concept of world based on the categories of a metaphysics of cause-and-effect which he claimed to have abjured. What then is the intentional referent of the mood of reverence before which it takes its stance? It can only be that which is the object of marveling and awe: the mysterious, strange yet wondrous fact that being exists rather than nothing.

Negative Moods. The word for reverence in German is *Ehrfurcht*, a revealing word because more clearly than its English counterpart it combines the elements of 'honor' (*Ehre*) and 'fear' (*Furcht*). Reverence is a Janus-faced mood having both positive and negative valence: it points to a mystery that, as Smith also notes, is both stunning and ominous. It is analogous to the response to what Otto characterizes as the holy or sacred – a *mysterium* that is both *tremendum* and *fascinans*, forbidding-yet-beckoning. Reverence provides a segue into considering moods that respond negatively in a more one-dimensional way to the world's being: *despair, desolation, dread (anxiety)*. If joy and its near kin, bliss, elation, ecstasy, exaltation bespeak happiness in the extreme, then this bleak trio and their close relatives, sadness, depression, hopelessness, melancholy are mired in unhappiness to the nth degree. They are, as it were, the 'evil twins' of their positive counterparts, moods in which we find ourselves thrown into the abyss, the 'dark gulf' (Smith), the 'under-world' of being-in-the-world. But contrary to Smith's claim, however, they do not refer to different features *of* the world-whole. It is not only, as Wittgenstein observed, that the worlds of the happy and the unhappy are different *worlds*, mirror opposites. Rather, these unhappy moods disclose a 'black hole' into which the 'world-whole' *itself* vanishes. They reveal the heart of darkness, the absolute nothingness in the core of being itself. But how, and why?

Despair. According to Smith despair is a response to the ultimate 'purposelessness' of the world's existing. Not only is there is no reason or ground for its existence, it has no final goal, no ultimate telos. The world just 'is,' its existence just continues from moment to moment with no originating or teleological necessity This is true no matter what its other, more specific features the world might be. Now there are several problems with this account. Here again Smith confuses despair as a response to the world's existence with despair as a response to the mystery of existence itself. First of all, it is not true that the world 'just exists' in the absence of any cause or reason. That would come as a surprise to scientific cosmologists. Whatever the current status of their explanatory theories – Big Bang. Steady State, etc. – each involves the positing of a cause, a 'ground' or 'reason' for the existence of this world. Second, to say that the existence of the world is 'purposeless,' lacks any meaning, makes sense if the world one is talking about is the, literally, 'meaning-less' object of scientific cosmology. Science talks of the universe in terms of causes and effect, it does not trade in concepts of meaning or value except as phenomena 'externally' viewed. Rather, what despair discloses is something about the world of our lived experience, a world that has been plunged into an abyss of meaningless. In despair we yield ourselves and the world to that darkness and descend into a sadness that is absolute, a chasm, a chaos that is indeed bottomless and utterly devoid of hope. This utter meaninglessness is not, pace Smith, a *feature of* the world, for it is the world-*as-a-whole* that disappears into the dark pit of despond. What about this darkness, this absence of meaning, this nothingness on the other side of being? If we have in mind not the existence of the world but the fact of being itself, can we apply this cheerless prospect of purposelessness, of meaninglessness in some absolute sense to it? Or must we say rather that, in that dark realm of mystery, though it is not 'bare,' perhaps neither the notions of purpose nor purposeless, meaningful or meaningless apply? That the answer to that question is left to us?

Desolation. Desolation reveals that I am thwarted, not only by the fact the world-whole is ultimately unknowable in its totality, but also, says Smith, by the fact that it does not accommodate my desire for meaning and purpose. In its ongoing purposeless exist-ing, already disclosed in despair, it is now seen to be "utterly indifferent," "uncaring," "absolutely impersonal and unconscious," indeed as lacking any kind of awareness at all, let alone a positive disposition toward me; it is simply "an impersonal whole that blindly happens." It is this *negative meaning* that the metaphysicians of meaninglessness mistakenly understand as the 'brute fact' of its existence. Here, as above, there is the same confusion and accompanying problems. To talk of a world-whole, already a metaphysical construct, that is unknowable in its totality or exists 'blindly' – if by either of these is meant 'exists without any explanation, at least in principle' – are claims that would puzzle our cosmological scientists. In addition, such a world, as we have noted, is a world abstracted from our prior being-in-the-world. What is disclosed in desolation is, once again, not a *feature of* the world, but instead something about the ontologically prior phenomenon of our being-in-the-world *as a whole*. The world disclosed in desolation is a world destitute of joy, a wasteland of dreary emptiness, of profound sadness, a world emptied out of meaning and abandoned to the ruined vastness of a dark void in which, where there used to be a world of meaning, of joy, there has opened up beneath it the yawning abyss of an unrelenting meaninglessness, absolute nothingness.

Dread (Anxiety). Smith's account of dread owes a lot, of course, to Heidegger's analysis of anxiety, which we have described above. For Smith it is the world that reveals our existence to be 'precarious.' It outruns our cognitive resources insofar as it leaves me exposed to 'the strange and perilous unknown.' Most revealing, this parlous nature of my existence, what Heidegger terms our 'being-toward-death,' revealed in dread, is kin to the contingency of my existence disclosed in sadness, the indifference to of the world to my existence revealed in desolation, and the purposelessness of the world's existence which infects my existence with despair. What needs to be noted here, however, contra Smith, is that these negative moods do not so much refer to a *feature of* the world but to the more primordial phenomenon of the *whole* of my being-in-the-world as such – to the whole of my being *and* the whole of the world's being. The contingency of my being, revealed in dread (anxiety) is implicated in, is an expression and reflection of, the contingency of the world's own being, and vice versa. The contingency of the world's being is revealed not just through scientific cosmology or metaphysical speculation, but immediately, directly, in the contingency of my own being that is disclosed in dread (anxiety). In anxiety not only does the totality of things *within* the world collapse, the world *itself* is disclosed as having collapsed into nothingness. One *finds* oneself not only "*face to face* with the 'nothing [*das Nichts*]; the possible impossibility of one's existence," of one's being-in-the-world, but also face to face with the 'nothing' of the world itself, the non-necessity of its own existence. In dread, in anxiety, we experience a total annihilation of both self and world. We come face to face with absolute nothingness.

Faced with these polar opposites, the worlds of the happy, the worlds of the unhappy, how are we to understand the relation of these moods, these worlds? Smith's answer is clear. They are related to each other 'metaphysically' – that is, they are to be arranged hierarchically, two positive moods being 'foundational' – joy and marveling, the others, positive and negative, 'dependent' upon them in an ascending scale of levels of 'impure' moods founded on two intermediary positive moods – love and reverence. But, as our analysis of the relation of the moods of joy and anxiety to one another showed, in fact the relation of these two worlds and their respective moods cannot be understood *metaphysically-cosmologically* but rather must be approached *existentially-ontologically.* That is, these 'global' moods must be viewed 'horizontally' as alternative worlds, alternative ways of being-in-the-world as a whole; their relation to one another must be interpreted *dialectically*, not hierarchically.

Moreover, that dialectic is not just a one-way affair. It is not that a positive mood must incorporate and overcome a corresponding negative mood to be considered an authentic rather than inauthentic mood, as we saw in the example of the relation of joy to anxiety It is just as possible that the relationship, existentially, can go the other way, can be the reverse. Anxiety can swallow up joy, not only vice versa. Depression can negate every possible reason for celebrating existence; it can drag joy itself down into the pit of despond, the black hole of nothingness from which no light escapes. The same can be said for others of the negative moods Smith canvassed when they confront their positive counterparts. Tedium, boredom, sadness, apathy can, existentially, overwhelm love, peace, equanimity, humility, compelling those moods to give way to and be absorbed into their orbit. Negative moods too can be authentic rather than inauthentic modes of existence, can be permanent and abyssal rather than temporary and passing, when they overcome and incorporate their opposite numbers. Smith himself is aware of this possibility though his thesis compels him to reject it. He cites two examples of the unhappy world disclosed in authentically negative moods: Schopenhauer, who argues that "we have not to rejoice but rather to despair at the existence of the world; that is nonexistence is preferable to its existence; that it is something which at bottom ought not to be"; and Sartre, who describes "Existence – everywhere, infinitely, superfluous [*de trop*],for ever and everywhere ...[I am] stunned by the profusion of beings without origin; ... my very flesh ... abandoned itself to the universal burgeoning. It was repugnant."

Why does Smith resist this conclusion? For at least two reasons. First, as we have seen, he argues that there is only one type of affective response that a given feature of the world-whole 'truly deserves,' one only in which it is 'properly apprehended.' A version of Post's 'moral realism,' his claim is that only one such feeling-response can be 'correct.' Why? Because otherwise you are forced to conclude that all such feelings are 'individually relative' and, finally, 'arbitrary.' This is true above all of the very existence of the world itself. The world-whole's existence 'demands' only one such affective response, namely, joy. But as we have already argued, even that allegedly 'pure' and positive foundational affect is not a simple feeling-response but, to be authentic, must incorporate the global affect of anxiety into itself. In other words, Smith's claim seems based more on metaphysical fiat than actual phenomenological description.

He offers another rebuttal. Schopenhauer and Sartre, he says, are not talking about the world-whole in an 'unrestricted' sense. But this takes us back to the question: assuming the distinction between the existence of the world and the existence of something rather than nothing, and assuming for the moment it is legitimate to talk of the world as a 'whole,' can we use that expression in relation to the latter? Can we talk of the fact there is something rather than nothing as in any sense a 'whole'? If, as we have argued, 'global' phenomena such as joy or anxiety apply in the first instance not to *features of* the world or to the world itself as a *whole*, but disclose the more primordial phenomenon of our being-in-the-world, and of being itself, suspended over the possibility of an absolute nothingness, can we say of being simpliciter that it is in any sense *a something* that is a *whole*? Or must we say, analogously to what Smith says of the world-whole, that it is rather the *ontological horizon* of our experiences? It is, first of all, not the contingent existence of the world but the fact that something exists rather than nothing that is *the* horizonal 'importance,' the primordial ontological 'reality' that gives importance to all else that exists within that horizon, including the world itself. It is this basic ontological fact, rather than the contingent existence of the cosmological world-as-a-whole, of which it can 'properly' be said that it "is always 'there' in an immediate way on the horizon of my awareness."

As we have been arguing, the basic fallacy underlying Smith's analysis of the felt-responses to the features of the world-whole is that behind each of these attempts lies the same mistake – trying to fill in the *ontological* 'that' with a bit of *cosmological* 'what' – to claim that by the *bare* fact that 'something exists' we really mean the *content-laden* fact that 'the world exists.' The problem stemmed from his attempt to apply the part/whole logic of a cosmological-metaphysics to the conceptually different world of an existential-ontology. The richness and multiplicity of our experienced felt-responses to the world is not compatible, pace Smith, with a view of the world as a unitary experiential whole. Our different existential 'appreciations' of the 'global' meanings of our being-in-the-world are not, we have argued, felt responses to different importances ('parts') of the *same* world ('whole); rather they are habitations of *different* 'worlds' altogether. As such they require a totally different way of conceptualizing the sense in which each of these existential-ontological worlds can be said to be a (transcendental) 'whole.' The horizons of those worlds are not transcendentally or categorially fixed but shifting and plural. And that means the transcendental features of these worlds are shifting and plural as well. As we have found, it is therefore not surprising that Smith's hierarchical, systematic, metaphysical view of our global feelings has collapsed into an unhierarchical, unsystematic, 'unmetaphysical' plurality of modes of being-in-the-world.

If we are right, however, if we are confronted not by a hierarchy of moods dependent in a metaphysical manner on certain foundational moods, but by a fundamental conflict between two opposing modes of existence, between two different ways of being in the world in response to the mystery of being, each capable of absorbing the other, each claiming to disclose in an authentic way the 'truth' about our being-in-the-world and of being itself, how is such an existential-ontological impasse to be resolved? What seems clear is that it cannot be resolved metaphysically, only existentially, by resolving upon one way of being rather than the other. But how, in the absence of any compelling metaphysical argument, is one to do that? Moods are, by definition, not modes of being we have chosen, they are ways of being we always already find ourselves thrown into. It would seem there is no logical, no rational, no metaphysical way of answering the question. The unanswerable mystery of the fact that there is something rather than nothing seems to infect our own being as well.

The ontological 'emptiness' of these results leaves us with the question: then what sort 'fact' is being simpliciter? Can any metaphysics, even a metaphysics of feeling, answer this question?

We turn to the final task in a critique of Smith's metaphysics of feelings – the 'destruction,' the de-structuring, of the *metaphysical* structure of Smith's 'metaphysics of feeling' and what an alternative ontology might look like.

Metaphysics

As we have seen, fundamental to Smith's case for a *metaphysics* of feeling are three propositions: one of the global feelings and its correlated world-importance is the *foundation* for all the rest; the other global feelings form a *hierarchy*, a complex, carefully graduated, chain of further systematic dependencies; despite the multiplicity of these global feelings and their correlated importances, their mutual compatibility shows that underneath the manyness of the 'faces' of the world, the world itself is a *single, unitary 'whole.'* In the previous two sections, Feelings and World, we have criticized each of these propositions. Our overall point has been that Smith's metaphysics of feelings, despite his claim for its *radical* difference as grounded in feelings rather than reasons, is nevertheless a *traditional* metaphysics both in its intellectual assumptions and its spiritual motivation. Therefore, it does not provide a satisfactory *alternative* approach, an adequate 'deflationary' (Witherall), i.e. non-explanatory, non-metaphysical answer to the Why Question. In this section we must now flesh out this critique.

Already at the outset, however, their appears to a problem with such a critique. Smith would say that he never denied his project was metaphysical in nature. Further, he would remind us that he never claimed his metaphysics was designed to answer the Why Question. That question is in principle unanswerable and hence meaningless. The existence of the world has no reason, no cause or purpose, it just is; the world-whole is, as it were, sufficient unto itself. Rather, his metaphysics aims at discovering how and why the existence of the world matters to us, what its ultimate meaning is. On two counts, therefore, he would say that our critique is misguided from the start. It misses the whole point of a metaphysics of feeling. So what is our problem? Well, there are several, related to his metaphysical thesis, his metaphysical method, and his metaphysical motive.

Metaphysical Thesis

The underlying concern and motive of Smith's project is to overcome the intellectual and spiritual nihilism of the metaphysics of rational meaninglessness. Though in fact he accepts the intellectual part of their position, he rejects the spiritual part. Specifically, though he accedes to their argument that there is no reason for the existence of the world, that its existence is in that sense 'rationally meaningless,' he does not agree with the further claim that the world's existence lacks 'meaning' altogether. He see that, rightly, as a non sequitur. He himself concludes wrongly, however, that therefore it is necessary to distinguish a metaphysics based on reasons from one based on feelings. The reason why he thinks so is his failure to disambiguate the notion of 'existence of world,' to distinguish the fact of 'existence as such' from the existence of the 'world' in particular, that is, this world or any world. We must now see why and how this failure undermines his otherwise laudable attempt to 'overcome nihilism.'

We may begin by recalling, as he himself admits, that our felt responses to the world play "the same fundamental role in the metaphysics of feeling that causes and purposes have in the metaphysics of reason." In other words, as a *metaphysics* of feelings his project still subscribes to the traditional metaphysical search for a totalizing (wholistic) absolute, for an ultimate 'explanation,', a 'maximal' reason-why vis-a-vis the existence of the world. To be sure, not a 'reason-why' cast in causal or teleological terms, but nevertheless a 'reason-why' that, cast in terms of feelings, satisfies our intellectual-cum-spiritual urge for existence to have an ultimate meaning, that is, to have an ultimate *rationality*.

The problem is that Smith's attempt to distinguish between two different types of metaphysics, a metaphysics of reason and a metaphysics of feeling, muddies the water at the outset. It's a philosophical version of the shell game: now you see it, now you don't. His critique of a metaphysics of 'reason' and its search for the 'rational meaning' of the world's existence confuses and prejudices an understanding of both 'rational' and 'meaning.' On one the one hand his usage of 'rational' is restricted to the rationality of 'causes' or 'purposes.' But there are other, broader contexts in which we can talk about the reasons for, or rationality of, a subject-matter, as his own project shows. On the other hand, talk of 'meaning' is not usually thought of in terms of causal explanations but rather in contexts of semantics or values, hence Smith's use of the term in relation to 'importances.' For Smith, these importances, as the felt-meanings of the world are also a source of knowledge, above all metaphysical knowledge. As he says, "there is a unique kind of *knowing* proper to feelings" (his emphasis). So he rejects the "the nihilistic belief that the world *as a whole* has no knowable meaning" (Smith, 1986, 24). But this means there is a *'rationality' of feelings* too, that not just causes or purposes but feelings too can be 'rational.' Why, then, does Smith want to limit the notion of 'reason' and 'rationality' to the world of causes and purposes? Why does he not want to say that the existence of the world, though 'rationally meaningless' in one, restricted sense of 'rational,' is nevertheless 'rationally meaningful' in another, broader sense of the term?

If we reject his narrow definition of 'reason' and 'rational meaning,' then to say that, in this restricted sense, there is 'no reason' for the existence of the world does not necessarily mean that the existence of the world is *rationally meaningless* in a wider or deeper sense.. In one sense Smith agrees. He rejects the nihilist assumption that 'meaning' can only be 'rational' meaning." But he then appeals to what he calls the 'extrarational' meaning of feelings. By this he means that the criterion for the meaning or truth of feelings is not provided by reason in the narrow sense of causes or purposes: they "fall outside the sphere of rational evaluation altogether." They refer not "to reasons for the world but to its ways of being important." But if we argue, as he against himself shows, that the terms 'rational' and 'rational meaning' can be given an extended meaning, then we need not set feeling over against reason in that broader sense. If so, then it could be shown, contra Smith, that the existence of the world is rationally meaningful.

More, even the very claim that there is 'no reason' for the world's existence could be the basis, the 'reason,' for saying that the world's existence is therefore even *more* meaningful. To say of the world's existence that it has no 'reason,' no ultimate 'why,' could be a way of saying that the world's existence as such is a mystery, a miracle. Rather than having to choose between a metaphysics based on reason or a metaphysics based on feeling, we could say that 'no reason' opens the way for an even more extended rationality, *another* rationality, a 'logic' peculiar to the notion of mystery, miracle, wonder itself. The need would then not be for a metaphysics of feeling allegedly opposed to a metaphysics of reason, but rather for an alternative way of thinking, an ontology that shows how a 'rational' way of looking at the world whether in terms of reasons or feelings is a *derivative* mode of a deeper rationality in terms of which both the rationality of reasons and the rationality of feeling can be understood.

Smith of course does not go on to develop that ontological alternative. He does not do so because for him the ultimate locus of the meaning of the world's existence is not 'outside' or 'beyond' the world but is the existence of the world-whole itself. To make the distinction we have been urging between the fact of existence *tout court* and the existence of the world would require that one distinguish another sense of 'existence' that referred to something 'beyond' or 'outside' the existence of the world, that is, to a logic or rationality that exceeded that of the world itself, one that attempted instead to address the ultimate 'extrarationality' of the Why question itself, of the fact there is something rather than nothing. Smith's analysis of the global importances of the world, of the question why the existence of the world *matters* to us, does not, by his own admission, attempt to address this question.

Smith is very clear about his disinterest in the ontological Why question. But at the same time he seems to confuse it with its cosmological analogue. Thus, as he correctly reports, for Heidegger anxiety does not reveal the miraculousness of the *world's* existence, it discloses "the primordial phenomenon–that there *is* being and not nothing.... Anxiety awakens *Dasein* to the 'basic question of metaphysics, the question Why is there being at all and not rather nothing?'" Yet, Smith says, for both the traditional metaphysics of reason as well as his own metaphysics of feeling the basic question of metaphysics, contra Heidegger and Leibniz, concerns "the primordial state of affairs of the existence-but-possible-non-existence of the world." Again, commenting on Leibniz's posing of the question: "Why is there something rather than nothing? For nothing is simpler and easier than something," Smith says, "nevertheless there is something!...this miraculous existence of the world..." It is "the world's existing-even-though-it-could-not-have-existed [that is] miraculous and astounding." He thus segues, apparently without realizing the significance of the difference, between seeing the primordial phenomenon of metaphysics as the existence of something rather than nothing, on the one hand, and the existence of the world, on the other. But no matter. For Smith it is a distinction without a difference. For him the philosophically interesting and important question is not why is there being and not nothing, or why the world exists when it could not have existed, but rather, "In what way does it ultimately *matter* that there is being and not nothing?" Or was it: "In what way does the existence of the world ultimately matter?"

The fact is that for Smith the notion of global importances not only does not provide a reason for why there is something rather than nothing, it does not even provide a reason why the world itself exists. The fact that the world's existence matters to us is not an explanation for why it exists in the first place. And yet Smith wants to restore the world's ultimate meaningfulness over against a nihilist metaphysics and wants to do so in a traditional metaphysical way, not by appealing to the rationality of an ultimate cause or purpose, but by appealing to a different rationality employing an extended meaning of 'reason,' one based on the cognitive logic of feelings. Spiritually the attempt is praiseworthy, but intellectually it is compromised by the ambiguity of his initial metaphysical assumption. The fact is that the existence of the world *can* be explained as the variations on the Big Bang theory, string theory, etc, abundantly prove. What *cannot* be explained, why calls for an alternative, 'extra'-rationality, is the fact that there is anything at all rather than simply nothing –a rational 'surd' that brings us face to face, in a way the existence of the world by itself does not, with the question of the ultimate meaning of existence.

Metaphysical Method

The problems with his fundamental metaphysical thesis not surprisingly carry over to his discussion of the method of metaphysics as well. Or rather, more accurately, the method, the logic, of a systematic metaphysics, whether of reasons or feelings, is not suited to the method, the logic of a pluralism of equi-primordial ways of 'being-in' the world, the description and analysis of the plural 'worlds' we inhabit. Even more is it unsuited to the logic of wonder, mystery, miracle, the logic of being-and-nothingness, the logic of the Why question. For these ways of thinking also have their distinctive 'logics.' The logic of pluralism is not that of out-and-out relativism, the bugbear so often thrown up by those who would be metaphysicians, the logic of ontological wonder is not reducible, pace Aristotle, to that of scientific curiosity, the logic of being-and-nothingness is not an exercise in empty words void of substantive meaning. Like the method, the logic of metaphysics, these *alternative* logics too must satisfy criteria of experience, meaning and truth. But they call, as alternative ways of thinking, for different descriptions and analyses, different words and concepts, different logical 'grammars' – or, if we want to use his (misleading) term in a more appropriate way, for 'extra-rational' methods of thinking.

What is it about the method of metaphysics, of which Smith's metaphysics of feeling is a beautiful example, that makes it inappropriate for these alternative ways of thinking? The word 'method' itself, from the Greek *methodos*, a compound of '*meta*' (with, after) and '*hodos*' (way, road), perhaps offers a clue. A method lays down a track, prescribes a way, a mode, means or procedure for doing or attaining something beyond ('after') simply the multiple deliverances of raw, undigested experience. In a philosophical context it refers to a systematic way of doing this – proceeding in an orderly way, usually in steps or levels, usually as pre-determined by a theory, to provide a systematic description and analysis of phenomena, propositions and arguments in the investigation and exposition of some truth or truths of a higher or fundamental kind (think 'meta-physics'– 'after' or 'beyond' the realm of *ta physica*).

Clearly Smith thinks it was possible, by applying a *metaphysical* method to the description and analysis of global feelings, to articulate the structural elements of global importances in a precise and detailed way, and to integrate them into a systematic hierarchy of felt meanings constituting a body of theoretical knowledge of the world-whole. Why does he assume that such seemingly unitary phenomena as moods can be analyzed and expressed in exact and strict concepts? Because he presupposes that each mood is already intentional in nature, already structured by a theoretical content. Though only pre-theoretically implicit at the intuitive level, because that intentionality is already embodied in moods, its structure can now be made explicit and, what is most important for his argument, "can be done so without impairing or destroying but instead by harmonizing with" those intuitively felt meanings. The reason why this 'method' works so well is that the metaphysical structure that was said to have been proven by empirical appeal to pre-theoretical intuitions was itself already presupposed by the requirements of the method, was predetermined by the theory, was already 'present,' built in to the intuitions, thus making possible, *mirabile dictu*! the 'body of metaphysical knowledge' alleged to have been uncovered by the three-step method. The actuality was in fact the reverse; what was to be proved had already been pre-determined in the premiss. It was a vicious not a virtuous circle.

If the three-step method is already infected, then so is his statement, resolution and dissolution of the problem. The problem lies in trying to develop a systematic metaphysics of felt meanings in which the "the world-whole cannot possess features that cancel each other out." If such is not possible, the alternative would be that bugbear, relativism, even worse, arbitrariness, logical anarchism. But what if one is not trying to develop a systematic metaphysics, what if one is trying to develop an alternative logic of an equi-primordial plurality of worlds-wholes, or the even stranger logic of being-sive-nothing? Is it so certain that this cannot be done, that the only alternative to a systematic metaphysics, whether of reasons or feelings, is the nightmare of conceptual chaos?

The (allegedly) empirical data provided by moods, Smith argues, "show these importances to be *mutually compatible.*" But is it so clear that, for example, that the antagonists like joy and despair can fit together harmoniously? Can we reinterpret the Greek tragedians that way so as to ensure such a carefree outcome? Smith's sunny solution is premised once again on a foregone conclusion, that the world-whole "really is fulfilled, and really is not empty, although it deceptively seems to be empty in the deluded mood of depression." The different importances only appear to clash, says Smith, but in fact each refers uniquely to its own aspect, its own 'face' of the world-whole. The solution lies in showing the dependency, independency and interdependency of the various importances of the world-whole in a hierarchy of the world's felt meanings. More than that, our fundamental joy in the world's happening not only *resolves* the apparent clashing of the felt meanings of the world, it *dissolves* the question. But in fact, as the life-and-death struggle of joy and despair shows, as the irreconcilable divorce between the worlds of the happy and the world of the unhappy testifies, metaphysical myth, a secular version of the religious myth of the goodness of creation, may be powerless in the face of darker spiritual truth.

Metaphysical Motive

Smith's philosophical paean to joy brings us to the 'matter,' the desire, that drives Smith's entire project, his deep-felt concern to overcome the nihilism of post-rational metaphysics. Where the metaphysics of reason and the metaphysics of feeling agree, says Smith, is that each is "an expression of human spirituality...understood as a need for and quest after a meaning of the world." The existential need that underlies his metaphysics, that underlies *all* metaphysical systems, is not just 'philosophical' or 'metaphysical,' it is a *spiritual* eros that can be traced all the way back to Plato and his critique of the poets. The fact that Smith's metaphysics is based on feelings rather than on reasons, far from obscuring this link, only pays this desire deeper homage. The giveaway is his insistence that the felt meanings of the world be grounded in a transcendental experience, joy, that is 'pure,' 'direct,' 'unmediated' – *uncontaminated* by conceptual or theoretical dross – free, that is, of the dispiriting intuitions and grim arguments of nihilist metaphysicians. "Nhilism can be understood as a need for meaning of the world coupled with a conviction that such a meaning cannot be grasped." But while it may be that the Why question is ultimately unanswerable, Smith says, this does not mean we are condemned to the grim philosophies of the nihilists. Who except for a few misanthropes would willingly side with such dour thinkers, such long-faced philosophers, if it can be shown that "joy is the appropriate response to the world's existence," if the dark thoughts of kill-joy nihilists can be 'dissolved' in a 'pre-theoretical' intuition of the meaning-full 'gift' of existing itself? It is joy that is "the primordial importance ... that answers the spiritual need that underlies and motivates the metaphysical quest."

There may be problems with Smith's metaphysical theses or his metaphysical methods, but how can there be any critical cavils with his metaphysical motive? The desire, the deep spiritual need, surely all human beings share. However, must it necessarily eventuate in a metaphysical quest, or for those for whom it does, can it only be satisfied by a metaphysical solution? So there are at least two problems:

The first is, to what is this spiritual desire 'appropriately,' or better, rightly directed? The wish for ultimate meaning, being moved by an ultimate concern, is not in itself necessarily wrong. The problem is whether, in Smith's case, it is directed to the wrong, or better, to a penultimate object, the existence and nature of the world, rather than to the miracle that there is anything at all, world or not, rather than nothing. It is the latter, the mystery of being itself, that makes the world itself and everything within it the object of wonder.

The second problem, how is one to realize this desire, how embody it in one's being-in-the-world? There is a risk in trying to realize it. The threat of a nihilist response is all too real. There is of course a paradox in nihilist spirituality. Its avowal of the bleakness, the impossibility of realizing any ultimate meaning, is seemingly self-contradictory, absurd, because the experience of meaninglessness is itself a meaningful experience. One cannot, by taking the nihilist route, avoid, as beings for whom existence 'matters,' being 'condemned to meaning,' as Merleau-Ponty put it. The problem with this apercu, however is that some meanings can be overwhelmingly negative, death-dealing. If so, the paradox – meaninglessness is meaningful – offers intellectual cold comfort, existential thin gruel. As anyone in the depths of depression can testify, Heidegger's 'unshakeable joy' is easily countered by Tillich's 'shaking of the foundations.'

The problem is that Smith wants to overcome nihilism by metaphysical argument based on 'extrarational' intuition. But apart from the fact that he thereby cedes rationality and rational meaning to the nihilists, his appeal to feeling is a dangerous strategy. Nihilists can make the same appeal. That is why it is important for Smith to base his case on a *positive* experience that is *the* ground of all other experiences, including negative ones. But this is a transparent ploy doomed not to work against very *powerful* negative experiences. Tillich argues that the only way a positive experience can overcome a negative experience of meaninglessness is by taking it into itself. The existential question is, how much non-being can our being take. Tillich says that the more non-being we can take without being overcome by it, the more we gain in being. But the danger is that this gambit can be reversed. One could argue, on that contrary, that the more being one can take in to non-being without being seduced by it, the stronger becomes the sway of non-being. The negative experience can become a black hole swallowing up the positive, the 'world-whole,' as in Heidegger's experience of 'the Nothing.' A metaphysical argument that appeals to feeling, not thought, therefore, can end up being a double-edged sword. A metaphysics based on feelings alone harbors a fatal flaw. If nihilist intuitions are to be 'overcome' by countervailing experience, it cannot be by metaphysical argument of that sort, or of any sort, therefore, but by considerations of an altogether different kind.

So what to do, what is the solution to this existential impasse? Smith himself points in the direction of a different resolution, but interestingly it is not a metaphysical one. It is instead an ethical one. If the 'answer' to the nihilists is the fundamental experience of joy, it is not because of any metaphysical presuppositions or stipulations, but because, as Smith says seemingly following Heidegger, it is through an ethical act, the adoption of an existential posture of 'resoluteness' in response to an ethical exigency, what Heidegger labels the 'call of conscience,' what Smith characterizes as a 'global summons,' or sounding like Kant, an 'unconditional demand.' For Smith this call is for 'global resoluteness,' "a global feeling of a different kind," "not one global affect among others," rather one that "interconnects and unifies all my global affects, moods, and strivings." It calls me to a 'global mission,' gives rise to a sense of a 'global purpose.' However, here at this critical juncture Smith compromises his ethical insight. He falls back on the claim that the source of this demand is the world-whole. It is an ethics that validates itself metaphysically. But, contra Smith, the 'solution' is not found in a metaphysical argument. We cannot say afterwards, at some 'second' or 'third' methodological 'step,' that this ethical response, this existential resoluteness, was in the cards, was there, metaphysically, all along. Rather, as Levinas, even Plato himself would have it, the ethical, the Good, is 'beyond' being. To respond to the fact of being in joy, not despair, calls for an ethico-existential resolve that takes into itself, but not through metaphysical 'necessity,' the negativities of existence – not only the doubts of the rational intellect but also the darkness of moods such as despair. If such a resolve 'overcomes' those doubts and negativities, it does not remove them, it faces them, it allows them, it does not fear them. Yet they are always there, waiting their chance.

Conclusion

Smith wants to imprison the legitimate experience of our basic global feelings such as wonder in the systematic structure of a foundationalist metaphysics. So while he (and we) agree with nihilist metaphysicians who argue that in traditional metaphysics there is no 'answer' to the Why question, he draws from that the wrong conclusion. He instead takes the experience of ontological wonder and sets it back within a metaphysical structure. It may not be the structure of a metaphysics of 'reasons' (in his question-begging understanding of that term), but it is placed in a systematic structure nonetheless, the hierarchical arrangement of a metaphysics of feelings. By his stress on *feelings* we are tempted to overlook the fact that it is a *metaphysics* of feelings (though he is quite clear about his intentions), that is, feelings interpreted at the 'third step' in a traditional metaphysical way, in foundationalist metaphysical terms. Why does he do this? Why does he not follow out the logical implications of the experience of wonder itself? Because he is afraid of the bogey of relativism, of nihilism. We are left with the question, is there an alternative way of understanding experiences like wonder, mystery, miracle, like joy, love, and reverence, that is not 'metaphysical' in that sense, that is 'existential-ontological' instead, another way of thinking that avoids the twin pitfalls of nihilism or relativism, on the one hand, without relapsing into the dead-end of metaphysics, on the other?

Smith's strength lies in his rich, nuanced and persuasive phenomenological *descriptions* of our basic feeling-responses to the existence and nature of the world. But his work is compromised by a failure of philosophical nerve. The aesthetic beauty and compelling power of his experiential analyses end up to being forced into a pre-determined hierarchy of feelings, subjected to the strait-jacket of metaphysics. His is the *soul of a poet* trapped in the *mind of a metaphysician*.

Transitional Remarks

The positive contribution of the cosmological-metaphysical analyses in Part One lay in the preservation of our primordial sense of the mystery of existence, insistence upon the cognitive significance of the Why question, and refusal to reduce it to the feelings to which that awareness gives rise. That left open the possibility that the Why question does make sense insofar as it points to the ultimate limits of reason in a way that calls for an existential response to the cognitive situation of not-knowing in the face of the just be-ing of the world. The weakness was a lack of clarity about the distinction between the existence of the world and the mystery that something exists rather than nothing, and how that distinction might bear on the link between our cognitive awareness and our feelings about that mystery.

The positive contribution of Part Two has been a more explicit focus on those feelings and their link to our awareness of the universe or world. The weakness has been their inadequacy as philosophical responses to the original Why question. What is common to all the efforts we have canvassed so far is that while each of them tries to relate our fundamental feelings to facts, they refer them to facts about the existence or nature of the world, not to the fact that something exists rather than nothing. It is not just the existence of the world that 'matters' to us. The Why question 'matters' even more fundamentally because, unlike questions about the existence of the world, it puts our own existence in question. What is lacking, therefore, what we still need, is not a cosmological metaphysics but an existential-ontological answer, an analysis of the link between our cognitive awareness of the mystery of existence as experienced in *ontological* wonder and the *existential* response of joy and gratitude to which that awareness can give rise. That will entail drawing on a way of thinking and linked feeling-responses that are as unique as the mystery that there is something, rather than nothing at all – the mystery of existence itself.

SIX

Milton Munitz: The Mystery of Existence

To illustrate the difficulties in trying to give an answer that grounds the affective or existential responses, negative and positive, in aspects of the cognitive situation vis-a -vis the mystery of the world's existence, we shall begin by looking at what I shall call two 'transitional answers' which, while not satisfactory as explanations of the link of the affective to the cognitive dimensions of the Why question, nevertheless introduce important aspects of the problem and indicate the directions we need to go in order to arrive at more satisfactory analyses. We will return first for another look at Munitz's views, and then consider the widely commented on views of Wittgenstein in *Tractatus Logico-Philosophicus* (1922), "Lecture on Ethics" (1929-1930), "Lectures on Religious Belief" (1938). and *Culture and Values* (mostly in the 1930s and 1940s).

As already noted in Part I, Munitz does think there is an emotional element contained in the idea of 'the mystery of the existence of the world' along with its cognitive elements: awareness of the world's existence, the Why question itself, and the claim that the question cannot be answered, that the existence of the world cannot be explained. The question we must now look at more closely is how he explains the inclusion of that emotive element in his overall understanding of the mystery of existence. How does he relate the emotive element to the cognitive elements in more than simply a causal or psychological manner? Can he demonstrate in a phenomenologically and philosophically rigorous way the logical and epistemological link between the emotive and cognitive dimensions of the mystery of the world's existence? With these new questions in mind, we must re-examine his views on mystery and metaphysics and their relation to emotions. Specifically we must examine the relation between his claim that metaphysics cannot answer the question of the world's existence and his view of the relation between cognition and emotion at the point where thought has reached its limits. We look first at his concept of mystery, then his view of metaphysics, and then the place of the emotions in relation to each.

Mystery

Munitz is keen to reassure us from the outset that while his use of the concept of mystery does not, like the Aristotelian notion of 'wonder,' point to a soluble scientific problem, neither does it merely express a dissoluble puzzle. It is "a *sui generis* question," "a genuine intellectual problem," that expresses "an ineradicable feature of the human response to the world" As such the philosopher should not "seek to remove it, or to reduce it to something else" (Munitz, 1965, 5). What we notice already at the start is that Munitz seems to perform a reductive move of his own, namely, narrowing the meaning of the phrase "human response" down to its "intellectual" component only. But are there not other dimensions to the "human response" to the mystery of existence? If there are, is their role only subordinate; are they not central or basic to the kind of "response" in question?

Munitz alludes to this problem: "perhaps we need to consider whether the phrase 'the mystery of existence' serves merely to express an emotional response to the awesome magnitude" of world." And since people "vary in their capacity to make this response... are we not obliged to say the the phrase 'the mystery of existence. Does not have a genuine cognitive content at all?" (Munitz, 1965, 6-7) If instead of considering this possibility in a context of concern with what an Anglo-American positivist might say, we were considering this matter in the context of Continental thought, substituting the term 'existential' for 'emotional,' would the question have the same negative implications?

But Munitz clearly wrestles with the *sui generis* nature of this 'ineradicable' situation in which human thought finds itself. He agrees that the 'sense' of the mystery of existence is "an important starting point for philosophical inquiry," on the one hand, while immediately going on to add, that he would "reject the attempt to remove the mystery by trying to solve it" (Munitz, 1965, 11). Then what is the force of that little word 'sense'? It could be replaced by the word 'meaning.' But the ambiguity would in either case remain. It hovers precariously, especially in this limit situation of human "response," between the cognitive and the emotive, between, say, the intellectual and the aesthetic.

Munitz defends his particular use of 'mystery' in the phrase 'the mystery of existence' by saying that it is only normal to want to 'solve' the mystery. But in this non-normal situation, this would be an 'inevitable mistake.' Why? Because "this is the very meaning and irremovable character of the mystery" – that it cannot be solved! And then comes a most revealing passage for our guiding question. It turns out that one of the 'ineradicable,' 'inevitable,' unavoidable features of the concept of the mystery of existence is:

> "the *feeling of frustration* that is an *essential and ineradicable component* of the *sense* of mystery when the latter has been properly isolated and correctly identified for what it is. The latter *feeling must always remain as long as we are at all sensitive* to the mystery of existence, the mystery is never dispelled, and *expression* of this mystery can only succeed in stating our *feelings of frustration and awe.*" (Munitz, 1965, 11-12, emphasis mine)

In other words, despite his initial presentation of the mystery of existence in purely intellectual terms, he has gone on to add that nonetheless there is a 'essential,' i.e, permanent, emotional element to the awareness, and presumably the resulting (insoluble) question, as well.

Having said this, Munitz is now in a position to specify the defining features of his concept (the "logic") of mystery (Munitz, 1965, 12-13):

1. awareness that world exists [*happens*]
2. asking of the Why question
3. conviction that the question, though meaningful, cannot be answered, that the existence of the world cannot be explained

4. "feelings of astonishment, awe, perplexity that arise from, and accompany the awareness of, the incomprehensibility of the world's existence," feelings that "persist and cannot be removed"

For our purposes the most interesting aspect of this list is the nature of the link between the first three features and the fourth, between the "cognitive" ones and the "emotional" one. Munitz says the feelings "arise from" and "accompany" the first three. He has already told us that feelings are an "essential and ineradicable" component of the first three. But he does not, or at least has not yet, provided us with a philosophical framework for understanding the nature of this link. And that is what we need if we are to give a fully satisfactory answer to the Why question.

But is this an unreasonable request to making of him? After all, he has granted the point that the Why question cannot be reduced to an intellectual problem alone, that it necessarily has an emotional dimension as well. Further, by spelling out the phenomenological "logic" of the term in this way, he has accomplished two very important things. He has "rehabilitated" the term for legitimate philosophical analysis, while ensuring that, though it commits philosophical reason to admitting its own limits, it cannot be mis-used as an excuse to appeal to a transcendent source of revelation or faith (Munitz, 1965, 27).

Perhaps before trying to go further with this question further, we should first look at Munitz's understanding of the nature and limits of the metaphysical use of reason in particular. Perhaps it is not reasonable to push Munitz further on the relation of cognition to emotion in his concept of mystery if his view of metaphysics does not provide a framework that can accommodate it.

Metaphysics

It will be recalled that, at the conclusion of his defense of metaphysical agnosticism vis-a-vis the Why question, Munitz replied to two anticipated objections.

In reply to the first objection – that despite his claim that his agnosticism is philosophically grounded, what his sense of mystery in the final analysis amounts to is "simply a sense of astonishment, an emotional reaction, and nothing more" – Munitz argued that the very *asking* of the

Why question together with the fact that we *know* that it is unanswerable by any rational method "*is as essential* to what the mystery is*, as the feeling* that *accompanies* it." Thus we are not "reducing" the awareness of the mystery to "nothing more than an emotion of astonishment" (Munitz, 1965, 256-257; emphasis mine).

In reply to the second objection – that he locates the mystery in the wrong place, that it is the existence of the world, not the human inability to answer the Why question, that is the primary fact in analyzing the mystery of existence – he agreed that it is the *fact* of "the existence of the world which arouses our sense of mystery" and that, "if mystery were nothing more than statement of human ignorance – a fact about *us* alone -- and not, also, about the world, *the analysis would be faulty*." But on the other hand, "it is not the existence of the world, alone, that is the mystery; it is the fact that *we,* who are aware of the existence of the world, ask the kinds of questions we do.... The mystery, so to speak, is in the *relation, or interaction*, between the puzzled *mind* and the existence of the *world*, not in either one, taken separately." That the Why question is unanswerable "*tells us something about ourselves responding* to the existence of the world *in a special way*, in terms of an unanswerable question" (Munitz, 1965, 256-257 258, emphasis mine).

What is of interest in his two replies are the elements that refer either directly or indirectly to emotions, specifically whether they clarify the nature of the link between the cognitive and emotional elements that is our particular concern in this context. His concern, clearly, is to protect himself against his hard-nosed critics by defending the *cognitive* meaningfulness of his metaphysical agnosticism. The 'we,' the 'us,' the 'ourselves' who are 'responding' to the cosmological mystery are not 'reduced' to 'nothing more than an emotion', true, but it would appear that we are, for all *philosophical* purposes, reduced to 'minds' in the face of this mystery. To be sure, he admits the presence of an 'accompanying' *emotional* element as well, one that is as 'essential' as the cognitive element, but he does not really assign it the same level of *philosophical* importance, and thus does not seem interested, or perhaps even able, to further explain its relationship to the "principal' element of the cognitive.

He speaks of "the feeling that accompanies" the sense of the mystery of the world's existence. He mentions such feelings as awe and astonishment. Certainly those are feelings that many have vis-a-vis the vast universe surrounding us. But what is the precise nature of the relationship between the mystery of the world's existence, in particular, philosophical agnosticism in the face of that mystery, and the feelings that might or might not accompany that awareness? Do these feeling *necessarily* accompany that awareness? If so, why? Would he be willing to say, for example, that the statement that the existence of the world is a mystery is a cognitively meaningful statement that *logically entails* a feeling of awe or astonishment and a matching existential response? If not, why not? Is it because there are other feelings that are equally possible? Are there any cognitive restraints on which feelings might or might not qualify as legitimate responses to that mystery? How do such feelings bear on related responses to that mystery – moral, ethical, aesthetic, religious responses?

His replies do not explicitly address such questions nor do they offer any hints as to how he might address them if he were interested or able to do so. If so, why? Is it simply because his rhetorical focus was elsewhere, for example to rebut a potential positivist critic? Or is it because there is a problem at the very beginning of his inquiry with his 'cosmological' (re-)definition of the mystery of existence as the (conceptually 'determinate') mystery of the world's existence rather than the (conceptually 'indeterminate') mystery of being as such? If so, how what would this difference in initial formulation of the question imply for an analysis of the link between cognitive and emotive elements in answer to the question, 'Why is there something (the world), rather than nothing?'

Mystery, Metaphysics and Emotion

Munitz does not explicitly address this question, but perhaps by way of an indirect acknowledgment, he does turn at the end of his inquiry to a consideration of the implications of the mystery of existence for a more comprehensive, metaphysical world-view, one that embraces our deepest emotions as well. He does this, namely, by explicitly relating the mystery of existence and the fact of death:

> Each, in its own way, marks the impenetrable boundary
> that defeats our deepest longings: the one marks the limit
> to any hope of understanding the existence of the world;

the other marks the limit of our hope of finding endless satisfaction in all that we achieve in life. Out of the refusal to acknowledge the first type of limit are born on the one hand those metaphysical schemes that would – in one way or another -- penetrate the abysmal mystery of existence and solve it. Out of the other, are born all those religious schemes that promise eternal salvation or immortality to the person. Such systems of thought betray, all too clearly, the attempt to circumvent the genuine limits to human knowledge and aspiration, by indulging in what is, after all, only a fancied perfection and a false idealism. They cannot inspire confidence in their solutions. A more responsible and candid philosophy would start by acknowledging the facts of the mystery of existence, and the final *defeat* that awaits us in our personal death. To do so requires courage, clearheadedness, and *resignation* in the face of the inevitable. [These phenomena] set the limits within which man must pursue rationally (Munitz, 1965, 262-263).

Of course this view of the "existential" implications of the mystery of existence is, as he would be the first to admit, merely one way of interpreting the significance of that mystery for human life. If his choice to compare our sense of the mystery of existence to our awareness of death leads to conclusions that sound a bit negative, a bit pessimistic, a bit 'realistic' a la Freud, that does not mean, as our questions have already suggested, that those are the only feelings, the only existential response, possible to that mystery. It could be argued that the claim that death marks the limit of our hope of finding endless satisfaction is either an empty tautology or simply false.

Did he himself not say awareness of the mystery of existence is accompanied by feelings of awe and astonishment? Could it not also be argued therefore, each of those "impenetrable boundaries" also makes possible a sense of joy and gratitude, feelings that satisfy "our deepest longings" in the face of ultimate mystery?

As we noted at the end of the first part of this study, the positive contribution of Munitz's analysis lies in his preservation of our primordial sense of the mystery of existence, and in his insistence upon the cognitive significance of the Why question, his refusal to reduce it to emotions alone. However, what is lacking and what we still need is a more explicit analysis of the nature of the link between that cognitive awareness and the feelings of awe and astonishment and existential responses of joy and gratitude to which it can give rise.

Excursus: Munitz on Otto and Marcel

Munitz does consider, but only to reject, two alternative ways of understanding the relation of metaphysics, mystery and emotion. One is Otto's phenomenology of religious experience, the other is Marcel's analysis of the mystery of being. I am not concerned with the accuracy of his summaries of their views but with his use of them for forwarding his own position. A discussion of his critique of these alternative views will serve to further illustrate our conclusions about Munitz's failure to provide a satisfactory philosophical analysis of the mystery of existence, one that unites the cognitive and emotional dimensions of the Why question. This will serve in turn as a segue to our discussion of Wittgenstein's consideration of these matters.

Otto on Religious Experience. Otto's analysis of religious experience can be seen as a way to get around the strictures on meaningful experience laid down by logical positivism, in particular the views of Schlick. On this point Munitz agrees with Otto. He too rejects Schlick's positivist analysis of experience. But he does not see this as opening the way to Otto's alternative. And yet, as we shall see, his critique of Schlick would seem to provide an opening for a defense of Otto's view as well, if not precisely as Otto stated it, at least in a recognizably and appropriately modified form.

Schlick. Schlick's critique of the Why question and any accompanying emotions is based on his logical positivist theory of meaning, which includes not only the Principle of [Empirical] Verifiability, but also what Munitz calls the Principle of Answerability. Schlick argues that since the Why question does not admit of a meaningful answer, it is not a genuine question. Conversely, it is logically impossible to give an answer where there is no question. Thus, while the Why question might give rise to non-cognitive emotions such as wonder, frustration or despair, these feelings cannot in any sense be regarded as cognitively meaningful. (Munitz, 1965, 37ff; Munitz cites Schlick, 1962, 26).

Munitz contends, however, that while the Principles of Verifiability and Answerability may formulate a definition of scientific (or more broadly, empirical) questions, they cannot rule out the possibility of asking other types of meaningful questions (Munitz, 1965, 41). He thus views the positive theory of cognitive meaning as irrelevant, as "wholly inappropriate" for identifying the uses of language of the type "proper" to the question of the meaning of the world's existence (Munitz, 1965, 43-44). "Such use of 'cognitive' is too narrow. In a sufficiently broad use of the term 'cognitive,' even a philosophical question of the kind we are examining, would be classed as being 'cognitive' in character" (Munitz, 1965, 44) Thus we need a broader sense of meaning, of reason, of 'logic' if are to make sense of the Why question.

If so, then contrary to Schlick's reduction of metaphysical (what Munitz here calls 'philosophical') propositions to expressions only of emotion, the Why question involves "a use of language that...is not simply emotive." This is not, Munitz says, to deny that "there is an emotive component (connected with feelings of awe and cosmological astonishment) in the statement of the mystery of existence." But he hastens to add, and this is the main point, "I deny that this is *all* there is to it, or even its principal feature. These are feelings derivative from the realization of the unanswerability of the question" (Munitz, 1965, 44).

Before we pass on to Munitz' critique of Otto's theory of experience, we need to stop and ask a few questions about his response to Schlick. It may give us critical purchase not so much on what he says about Otto as on our more general question about what Munitz's understanding of the relation of mystery, metaphysics and emotion might be.

Munitz says there is an emotive 'component' to the mystery of existence. Is it a 'necessary' component? Or does it only 'accompany' the question in an adventitious, not necessary manner? If is a necessary component, wherein lies the 'necessity? Is it causal, logical, epistemological, ontological? It is said to be 'derivative.' Does this means its status is in some sense 'secondary'? In what sense? Is it logically dependent on the cognitive components? Or causally dependent? What is nature of this link? And what of the cognitive components? They are said to be the 'principal' features. How does Munitz determine the scale of 'importance' that allocates this priority of the cognitive elements over the emotional ones? On what does this relative evaluative weighting of the components rest? Presumably he understands the cognitive elements to be 'necessary' features of the Why question. Is that why they are the 'principal' ones? Could they also be 'sufficient' conditions, able to stand on their own feet, as it were, without 'needing' (the 'necessity' of) the emotional ('derivative') aspect as well? It not, why not? What does this priority of the cognitive say about the relative value of mind versus emotions in his philosophy? What does this say about the presuppositions of his view of ('cosmological') metaphysics?

Is it even possible that the situation is the reverse – that the initial 'awareness' of the mystery of existence is a *pre-cognitive* 'sense' or feeling of awe or astonishment *gives rise* to the question of the mystery of existence and to the sense that the question is unanswerable? If so, it would be the question that 'derives' from the feeling. How would one decide one way or the other? Perhaps the link of the emotive and cognitive elements points to a fundamental, primordial phenomenon, what in Buddhist terminology we might call the inter-dependent co-arising of the awareness and the question of the mystery of existence, the mutual interaction of the cognitive and emotive elements. If so, then the question is, does Munitz provide an adequate philosophical framework for such a co-primordial phenomenon? Or would we have to look elsewhere for an ontology that could account for it? At the very least we need further clarification from Munitz on these points.

Otto. With these questions in mind, let us re-examine his account of Otto's analysis of religious experience to see what clues it might offer us as to his resolution of the relation of mystery, metaphysics and emotion.

To review: for Otto, in his book, *The Idea of the Holy*, such experience, though non-inferential and immediate, is nevertheless a species of awareness in which both cognitive and emotive aspects are inextricably linked together. Furthermore, it is said to be a unique experience, "wholly different in character and subject matter from other modes of experience" – in particular, scientific experiences that meet positivist criteria of meaning and verifiability (Munitz, 1965, 223). It is not describable in 'rational concepts.' Rather, at its core is "an attitude of worship and a feeling of awe toward the Wholly Other." It points to "a *mysterion* – a profound mystery that baffles and defeats all attempts at rational, conceptual understanding." (Munitz, 1965, 224)

Now recall Munitz's response. On the face of it, Otto's description of this awareness of the *mysterion* and its accompanying feeling of awe would seem perfectly matched to Munitz's own description of the main elements of the experience of mystery: the awareness of mystery, the rationally unanswerable question to which it gives rise, and the accompanying emotion of awe. So why does Munitz not take the opportunity to explore it further for the clues it might offer to a more integrated view of the relation of the cognitive and emotive elements in his own sense of cosmological-metaphysical astonishment?

How does he frame the issue? "The important, central question is what *cognitive* value these experiences have, what epistemological worth they possess. Are they nothing more than feelings and attitudes belonging to individuals undergoing the experiences in question, or are they, on the contrary, revelations of some independently existing objective reality?... One cannot appeal to the experiences themselves to establish this; they are not self-authenticating."

Munitz's formulation of this critique rests on two assumptions, one epistemological, one metaphysical.

His epistemological assumption, which we already noted, is that there are no supporting public tests, no independent criteria for corroboration of such experiences (Munitz, 1965, 25-26). There are two problems with this assumption: first, as previously noted, it is simply false: in fact such tests and criteria do exist for alleged religious experiences (whether Otto would subscribe to this or not), for all such allegedly 'pure' experiences already come 'theory-laden,' nested in their respective discursive contexts. But second, even if it were correct, does it not mean Munitz is giving in to the very sort of narrowly positivist, anti-metaphysical view of experience limited to entities *within* the world that he has just criticized Schlick for holding?

His metaphysical assumption is that the "Wholly Other" of which Otto speaks, to which this experience points, i.e., for which it is "evidence," is a transcendent reality existing, as it were, 'outside' or 'beyond' the world, namely, "the divine source and creator of the world," in a word, "God." The question, however, is whether such an experience entails such an 'other-worldly' metaphysical assumption (whether Otto holds it or not)? And if not, why does Munitz not push this alternative metaphysical possibility further?

In my previous conclusion to his discussion of Otto it was suggested that Munitz was perhaps too hasty to dismiss the possibility that something like 'religious' experience, for all its emotive and attitudinal content, may also have cognitive import. In light of the above remarks, perhaps we now need to conclude, on the flip side, that precisely because of his 'principal' stress on the cognitive content of the experience of the mystery of existence, he fails to provide an adequate philosophical foundation for an integrated account of the emotive elements that 'accompany' it.

Marcel on the Mystery of Being. Gabriel Marcel, in his books *The Mystery of Being, The Philosophy of Existence* and others, is well-known for drawing a philosophical distinction between a 'problem' and a 'mystery,' between a scientific puzzlement about phenomena within the world and the wondrous mystery of the existence of the world itself. In his discussion of Marcel's concept of mystery, Munitz focuses on Marcel's notion of 'man's ontological need" (Marcel's phrase, cited by Munitz, 1965, 28). This ontological need, as the term 'ontological' makes clear, is a need for Being, which Being must in turn be, as the term 'need' makes clear, "a center of value." "To satisfy an ontological need," says Marcel, "it to find an appropriate target for awareness in something that could be a a *presence*, a radiating source of concern and love, and to which we can respond in an appropriate way, namely, with appreciation, love, and fidelity." (Munitz, 1965, 29)

The 'prototype' for this kind of experience of Being is, says Marcel, the experience of love. To view such a relation objectively, reductively, scientifically as it were, is not to *be* in that relation. Therefore, to experience the being of that relationship is to participate, at least on a finite level of existence, in 'a mystery.' (One is reminded here, though he does refer not to it, of Buber's similar distinction between an I-It relationship and the I-Thou relationship in which the Eternal Thou is co-present.) The fact that human love is but an analogy of the relation to Being is a reminder, says Marcel, that the 'ontological need' is "only partially satisfied in finite centers of response" (Munitz, 1965, 30-31). Only a 'source' of being and value which is 'infinite and unconditioned' can provide "a source of love, hope and faith that transcends all human limitations." Only such a 'source' can be "the true source of mystery... a mystery that lends purpose and meaning" to existence (Munitz, 1965, 31).

Munitz focuses his critique of Marcel's view of mystery on the claim that this "half-hidden religious orientation" is not a description of the sense of mystery he is talking about. For Munitz the contrast between a 'problem' and the 'mystery' is "a contrast between two kinds of questions that the human mind can raise" (Munitz, 1965, 31), whereas Marcel's 'mystery' "is not a *question* at all." It is a form of faith. Marcel, says Munitz, "nowhere raises a question about the existence of the world. For him, the ontological mystery is not a cosmological mystery.... It has, as its locus, some center of value, affection, and concern." (Munitz, 1965, 31). Whereas the 'mystery' with which Munitz is concerned is the 'cosmological' mystery, "a special type of unanswerable question about the existence of the world. It has nothing to do with the presence of a center of value, or a source of personal support and encouragement for the pursuit of value. It has nothing whatever to do with rescuing life from futility. The sense of mystery is brought into focus by the confrontation of the mind with the fact of the existence of the world about us... the mind's struggle with a question, namely, 'Why does the world exist?' The mystery consists in the mind's inability to find an answer to that question" (Munitz, 1965, 31-32).

Reading these comments one has the sense Munitz is drawing questionable conclusions from distinctions of his own, based in part on a standard of evaluation he rejects elsewhere (see his comments on Schlick above), which undermine any constructive effort of his own to link the cognitive and emotive aspects of the mystery of existence in a philosophically felicitous way.

The basic issue resides in his distinction between two types of mystery – cosmological, the mystery of the world's existence, and ontological, the mystery of being itself. The latter, he says, does not involve a (cognitive) question, but is simply a matter of (emotive) faith. But is this true? The former, he says, has "nothing to do with" the question of values. But is this true?

Munitz's distinction between a cosmological and ontological approach to the mystery of (the world's) existence has a long pedigree, whether he is in mind of it or not, that goes back to the beginnings of Western philosophical reflection (for an overview of this history on which the following comments draw, cf. Tillich, 1959.) There are indeed two different approaches to this ultimate metaphysical question that can be described as 'cosmological' and 'ontological.' So it is not his making of the distinction that is troublesome, it is how he interprets it – namely, as pitting a cognitive versus a non-cognitive, a value-oriented versus non-value oriented approach, as if these were ultimately incompatible.

Here he seems to be reflecting the modern, specifically positivist distinction between cognitive and emotive meaning that, in his comments on Schlick, he stoutly rejects as inappropriate to questions relating to the mystery of existence. This suggests that his approach rests on a underlying assumption about the nature of metaphysical inquiry that, in the end, whatever its acknowledgment of the emotional element 'accompanying' the awareness of the mystery of the world's existence, is unable to bring the cognitive and emotive elements together in a fully satisfactory way.

In fact a brief review of the history of this distinction in the history of Western philosophy shows that it is not true that the ontological approach does not involve a question and that therefore it lacks cognitive import. Nor is it true that the cosmological question has only cognitive, and no emotive import. In fact, the two types of thinking can and have been seen as two different approaches to, two different ways of thinking about, the same mystery of (the world's) existence. Not only that, it can and has been argued that, in fact, the cosmological type of philosophy is dependent upon the ontological type, and that without it, it leads, and in fact has led, especially in the modern period, to a destructive splitting off of the cognitive from the emotive dimensions of human thought and existence. This has resulted in a separation of the psychological ('existential') elements of intellect ('mind'), will ('moral') and emotion ('feeling') that, though inevitably in tension, are nevertheless co-primordial elements of the human 'soul.'

In both the cosmological and ontological awareness of the mystery of (the world's) existence, what is involved is an awareness of something that is, as it were, 'unconditional,' something 'other than' and 'beyond' the types of awareness, object and subjective, intellectual and emotional, of entities within the world, an awareness in which such distinctions either have not yet arisen or in which they find an 'original' primordial togetherness. This means that *all* of these elements must be co-primordially present in the awareness of, and question about, that mystery, whether phrased cosmologically (the mystery of the world's existence) or ontologically (the mystery of being itself). To call this awareness 'existential' is not to 'reduce' it to the level of the 'subjective,' the emotive only; rather, it is to point to an underlying, pre-existing and co-primordial way in which the entirety of our existence, not just our 'mind,' is touched by, caught up in, participates in, indeed can itself be "called into question," in the awareness of, and question about, the mystery of (the world's) existence.

To the extent Munitz's reductive understanding of the cosmological question sees the emotional element as merely 'derivative' rather than as a co-'principal' element in the question of the mystery of existence – and this seems clearly to be the case in his dismissive remarks about Marcel's ontological approach to the mystery of being – to that extent, again, Munitz's own 'cosmological-metaphysical' position must be judged to be an unsatisfactory answer to the question, "Why is there something rather than nothing at all?"

Ludwig Wittgenstein: The World/My World/ Ethical World

"The world is all that is the case, the totality of facts, not things." (*Tract.* 1.,1.1)

"Not *how* the world is, is the mystical, but *that* it is." (*Tract.* 6.44)

"The world is *my* world. I am my world. (The microcosm.)" (*Tract.* 5.62, 5.63)

"The world of the happy is quite another than that of the unhappy." (*Tract.* 6.43)

In turning to Wittgenstein's reflections on the experience of the mystery of the world's existence we will be looking for a philosophical framework and analysis that meets Witherall's criterion: a satisfactory philosophical answer to the question of the mystery of existence that gives an *integrated* account of the cognitive and emotive elements of this awareness. Wittgenstein shares something of Munitz's view, but with features that suggest further dimensions (e.g. ethics, aesthetics and religion) of that awareness.

From the outset, however, we immediately run into a serious, perhaps fatal problem. For the first thing to be said is that looking for any kind of "philosophical framework" in Wittgenstein, let alone one designed to provide "an integrated account" of the experience of the mystery of existence, appear to be pursuing a fool's errand. Wittgenstein made it very clear from the beginning to the end of his philosophical career that he completely rejected any and all attempts by philosophers to say anything metaphysical. Already in the *Tractatus Logico-Philosophicus* he said: "always, when someone wished to say something metaphysical, demonstrate to him that he had given no meaning to certain signs in his propositions" (*Tract.* 6.53). This is an "ascetic" (Hargby) view of philosophy he never relinquished. Indeed as the title of a recent book has it, Wittgenstein's philosophy would seem to be an "anti-philosophy" (Badiou), presumably meaning by 'philosophy' something like an attempt to provide a systematic account of the universal truths of reason that provide the foundation for all that we know, and do, and feel. That would certainly seem to encompass what we are seeking here: "a philosophical framework [*a metaphysics*]" that provides "an integrated [*systematic*] account" of the our knowledge and feelings about the ultimate questions of existence itself. Nothing would seem more 'philosophical,' more 'metaphysical' than that. So it would seem that looking to Wittgenstein for help in advancing our inquiry is doomed from the start to come up empty. He would have brusquely dismissed it with an peremptory wave of his 'anti-philosophical' hand.

And yet, and yet, Wittgenstein does have interesting and important things to say that have a direct bearing on a link between cognitive and emotive dimensions of the question of the mystery of (the world's) existence. Support for this intuition, his anti-metaphysical comments to the contrary notwithstanding, may be found in Ray Monk's biography, *Ludwig Wittgenstein: The Duty of Genius.* Monk tells us that his primary purpose in writing the biography was to show "what the connections are between the spiritual and ethical preoccupations that dominate [Wittgenstein's] life, and the seemingly rather remote philosophical questions that dominate his work... to show – what many who read Wittgenstein's work instinctively feel – the unity of his philosophical concerns with his emotional and spiritual life" (Monk, xviii). In fact I shall argue that there is a link between the cognitive and the emotional not only in the relation between Wittgenstein's life and work, but within the work itself.

So with these cautionary remarks and that promissory note in mind, let us begin. Although Wittgenstein's basic anti-metaphysical stance remains unchanged from his early through his later work, the contexts and ways in which it is expressed and its significance for our inquiry do change, and radically, between the *Tractatus* and his later work from 1929 on. We shall look first at his early work, the *Tractatus*, including notes for the *Tractatus* found in his *Notebooks 1914-1916*. We shall then turn to his work in the transitional stage represented by his "Lecture on Ethics (1929) and his comments on ethics to members of the positivist Vienna Circle (1929-1930). Finally, we will consider his later work beginning in the mid-1930's, in particular the collection, *Lectures and Conversations on Aesthetics, Psychology & Religious Belief*, based on notes taken by students from 1938 through 1946, and remarks scattered over the entire period of his later work, 1929-1951, collected in *Culture and Values*. We also draw on his comments in unpublished work cited in Monk's biography.

Early Wittgenstein: "Tractatus Logico-Philosophicus" and "Notebooks 1914-1916."

In the first part of this study we have seen how many-sided and difficult to pin down the concept of 'world' is. When philosophers, in particular metaphysicians interested in matters cosmological, talk about the 'world' do they mean: the manifest or the true universe? are they referring to an entity? the totality of entities? a whole? do they mean rather the 'experienced' universe as opposed to the universe of theoretical cosmology? do they conceive of its existence as necessary? contingent? are the attributes ascribed to it positive? or only negative? It would seem, in turning to Wittgenstein, that there is little more he could add to this plethora of competing characterizations than the ones we have already reviewed. And yet, in the work before us, the Tractatus, he does. In fact, he brings to his concept of 'world' what the Norwegian philosopher, Ingvar Harby, calls a '*double awareness*.' As we proceed, we may even want to expand on that notion – it may prove to be a triple awareness, or more – as if the concept of 'world' were not already complex enough. We shall review his comments under several heads: '*the* world,' '*my* world,' and '*ethical* world.' Even within these three, there are further divisions. As to the relations among them, that of course is our basic question.

The World

"*The world is all that is the case.*" (*Tract.* 1.). This is the very first of the numbered propositions that make up the Tractatus. At first glance it does not appear so different from the concept of the world as the totality of all the entities that exist. But, as if to put the brakes on such an obvious but over-hasty conclusion, Wittgenstein immediately follows this remark with a sub-proposition: "The world is the totality of facts, not of things" (*Tract.* 1.1). The world, says Wittgenstein, may be a 'totality' –but the 'all' is not made up of 'things,' i.e. existing entities, but of 'facts,' of 'what is the case.' What is the difference? Good question. It's one Wittgenstein's mentor in logic, Frege, asked as well. Wittgenstein goes on to say in a sub-sub proposition: "The facts in logical space are the world." (*Tract.* 1.13). And what is the case, the facts, is the existence of 'states of affairs' (*Tract.* 2). A 'state of affairs,' in turn, is "a combination of objects (entities, things)" (*Tract.* 2.1). And 'objects,' 'entities,' or 'things,' what are they? They are the underlying, irreducible 'substance' of the world. But what that 'substance' is, empirically or metaphysically, Wittgenstein does not say, nor does he feel he needs to say. As he observed in his *Notebooks 1914-1916*, "Our difficulty was that we kept on speaking of simple objects and were unable to mention a single one" (68e, June 21, 1915). The reason is that his concern when he speaks of 'the world' is with what he calls its 'scaffolding,' the structural features of the world as shown in the *logical* forms of the *propositions* in which we express the 'states of affairs' that constitute 'the world.' In other words, when he talks about 'the world' as 'all that is the case,' the first meaning of 'world' for Wittgenstein is 'the facts in *logical space.*' His concern about the world is thus not an *empirical* or *scientific* one, nor is it even a *cosmological-metaphysical* one, unless it is 'metaphysics' in a peculiarly *logical* or *linguistic* sense. It is almost as if he is not concerned with the world at all in any of the more robust senses in which we have been discussing it til now. It seems a very attenuated, 'ascetic' sense of 'world,' a world evacuated of its 'material' substance, empirical or metaphysical, and reduced to its merely 'formal' features. It would seem we are not going to get any help from Wittgenstein's reduction of metaphysics to logic in wrestling with the question, "Why does the world exist rather than nothing?"

If so far Wittgenstein does not seem to be helpful, things get even stranger. In one of the entries in his *Notebooks 1914-1916*, he says: "I know that this world exists" (72e, June 11, 1916). Here he seems to be talking of the world in very different, more substantive sense. The world is not just a logical structure, but something actual, something particular, a *this* that, in a more familiar sense, *exists* and can be *known* to exist. To unpack the meaning of this deceptively simple-looking statement and how it relates to the preceding formal or non-material sense of the world, let us begin by pairing it with another, equally simple-looking but baffling remark, this one from the Tractatus: "Not *how* the world is, is the mystical, but *that* it is" (6.44; an earlier version is found in his Notebooks: "the miracle [*Wunder*] is *that* the world exists. *That* what exists *does* exist" (86e, Oct. 20, 1916). Putting these two statements together, we have Wittgenstein saying that he *knows* the world exists, but that the world's existence is '*the mystical.*' But what can it mean to *know* something (the existence of the world) that, in one sense of the term 'mystical,' is said to be *unknowable*? Here we arrive at the heart of what may be termed Wittgenstein's 'double-awareness' of the world. In this statement from the Tractatus Wittgenstein distinguishes two different forms of knowledge or awareness of the world. There is the substantive (empirical or metaphysical) knowledge whose content is '*how* the world is,' that the world is *so-and-so*, that it has *such and such* describable features. But there is also a peculiar kind of knowledge or awareness whose content, if it can even be characterized as such, is limited to the seemingly 'bare' fact of the world's being itself, its mere or sheer, i.e. not further describable ("predicable") *existence-as-such*. It is this double awareness that we must now unpack, for here we seem to be on the edge, if not of an answer, at least of an awareness of (the question of) the mystery of (the world's) existence.

Hargby coined the term "double awareness" as a way of making sense of what he called Wittgenstein's 'that'-consciousness. Wittgenstein's 'that'-consciousness, as we have just noted, is a special kind of awareness based on the very particular and philosophically elusive experience of the 'that' of the world's existence – an awareness not of the 'how' or the what' of its existence. Wittgenstein's 'that'-consciousness is not a consciousness of entities *in* the world, nor even of the *totality* of such entities *in* the world, nor is it a consciousness of the *logical structures* of the world's existence as expressed in propositions about the states of affairs that constitute the world. As Wittgenstein says, "The 'experience' which we need to understand logic is not that such and such is the case, but that something *is*; but that is no experience"; *Tract.* 5.552. Wittgenstein's 'that'-consciousness is thus a strange kind of "experience." Indeed, by labeling it 'the mystical'

Wittgenstein is reminding us, whether explicitly or not, of the amazement, the wonder, in which, according to the Greeks, philosophy was said to be grounded. Wittgenstein's 'the mystical' is thus presumably a kind of *ontological* wonder – a wonder distinct from *cosmological* puzzlement about the 'how' or 'what' of the world that poses questions that can be answered or dissolved through scientific or metaphysical knowledge, as Aristotle (unlike Plato) proposed. By calling awareness *that* the world exists 'the mystical' Wittgenstein was trying to liberate such an awareness from any Aristotelian or modern temptations to provide a metaphysical or scientific *explanation* for the world's existence *as such*. His aim can be said to be one of 'purifying' the 'that,' of preserving a 'proper amazement' vis-a-vis the world's existence, of preserving the inexplicable wonder, the fundamental mystery, that something exists rather than nothing.

One way Wittgenstein expressed that liberating awareness and performed that act of preservation was by turning aside any effort to *say* anything about the fact that the world exists, rejecting not only any effort to *explain* it, but any effort even to pose it as a *question* for which it would make sense to seek an *answer*. This presupposes Wittgenstein's fundamental distinction between what can be *said* and what can only be *shown*, as seen in the following series of propositions:

6.5   For an answer that cannot be expressed the question too cannot be expressed.
        The riddle does not exist.
        If a question can be put at all, then it can also be answered.

6.51... a question only where there is an answer, and this only where something *can* be *said*.

6.522   There is indeed the inexpressible. This *shows* itself; it is the mystical. The right method of philosophy would be this: To say nothing except what can be said, i.e., the propositions of natural science, i.e. something that has nothing to do with philosophy: and then always, when someone wished to say something metaphysical, to demonstrate to him that he had given no meaning to certain signs in his propositions. This method would be unsatisfying to the other–he would not have the feeling that we were teaching him philosophy–but it would be the only strictly correct method.

7   Whereof one cannot speak, thereof one must be silent.

What can be *said* about the world, about its material 'how' and 'what' (not about its logical structure) are the propositions of natural science. But these, he says, have nothing to do with philosophy, in particular, with metaphysical propositions. To ask *meta*-physical questions about the world, as if these were about something other than its material 'how' or 'what' – for example, whether the world exists necessarily or only contingently, whether it has a beginning in time or exists eternally, and so forth – is to use concepts in ways that have no empirical or scientific meaning. It is an attempt to extend the meanings of such terms beyond their ordinary use in ways that go 'above and beyond,' 'outside' the world of natural science. Metaphysics asks questions that on their linguistic surface appear to make sense but which in fact have no conceptual meaning at all. 'Answers' to such faux-questions fail to make sense as well. Where a question cannot be meaningfully expressed, there is no point looking for an answer. Any such 'answer' would be no answer at all. Thus a metaphysical *riddle* about the world's existence does not exist.

And yet note what Wittgenstein is *not* saying. He is *not* saying *the mystical* does not exist. It is 'the riddle' that does not exist. But 'the mystical,' the mystical *does* exist: "There is indeed the inexpressible. This *shows* itself; it is the mystical." *That* the world exists is not a riddle, a puzzle to be solved scientifically or explained metaphysically, it is the fundamental mystery, the permanent wonder, that anything exists at all rather than nothing. Because the bare fact of the world's existence is not a proper subject for the explanations of natural science – in fact the existence of the world is the necessary presupposition for the enterprise of natural science – and because attempts to explain the world's existence in *meta*-physical terms lack meaning altogether, the fact *that* the world exists *shows* itself in and through what can be *said* about its *what* and *how*. But in itself its existence is the perduring ineffable 'something,' the 'that' which all the rest of our knowledge presupposes and on which it depends.

Here, at least, Wittgenstein seems to have come closer to the position Munitz defends, with one major difference. Wittgenstein would reject Munitz's stance of metaphysical 'agnosticism' insofar as the latter presupposes that it make sense to talk of 'knowing/not-knowing/doubting' in this context. Metaphysical *agnosticism* is still a *meta-physical* philosophy. Such philosophical skepticism is presumed to *make sense*. But Wittgenstein's concept of the mystical means even such agnosticism, such skepticism, must be ruled out as well. "For doubt can only exist where there is a question, a question only where there is an answer, and this only where something can be *said*" (*Tract.* 6.51) Wittgenstein thus concludes his discussion of the mystery of the world's existence, of the amazing, wondrous, ineffable fact *that* it exists, with his famous statement: "Whereof one cannot speak, thereof one must be silent." It is precisely at the point where language has reached the limits of what it can *say* about the world, that silence enables the wondrous fact of the world's existence to *show* itself to us.

My World

So far, Wittgenstein's philosophy, insofar as it could be called (his statements to the contrary notwithstanding) a kind of 'metaphysics,' would seem to be an *anti-metaphysical* metaphysics – either a minimalist exercise in an 'empty' *logic* of the world or an ascetic *mysticism* vis-a-vis the world, in either case a kind of *via negativa* that seems to deny more than it affirms when it comes to making any positive contribution to our search for a link between the cognitive and emotive elements in our experience of the world's existence. That is now about to change. Into Wittgenstein's 'double awareness' of the world – the world in its (presumably objective) 'how and 'what' and the world in its (presumably objective) 'that' – Wittgenstein now introduces two decidedly 'subjective' elements – one hinted at in an early and tantalizing phrase, not further elaborated upon, "The subjective universe" (*Notebooks*, 42e, April 17, 1915); and one addressed to an entirely new topic, "the meaning [*Sinn*] of the world" (*Tract.* 6.4). We shall begin in this section with a discussion of what he appears to have had in mind with the first phrase. In the next section we shall address his remarks about the 'meaning' of the world. Whatever the intent of these two new directions in his remarks, it is going to be increasingly difficult to avoid the conclusion that he is trafficking in some heavy-duty metaphysics himself.

"*The Subjective Universe.*" Wittgenstein now introduces us to a *third* concept of the 'world' in his philosophy (should we speak of a 'triple awareness'?) – the world as a 'subjective' world, the world as the metaphysical Subject's world. As he puts it in the Tractatus, "The world is *my* world. I am my world. (The microcosm.)" (*Tract.* 5.62, 5.63). The world which he seemed to be viewing from a distance, from the 'outside,'as it were – the world in its formal-logical structure, the world in its natural-scientific 'how' and 'what,' even the world in the bare 'that-ness' of its existence, seems suddenly to have been brought 'inside,' as it were, not simply to have become '*my* world' but somehow to have become identified with the 'I' itself. This seems a sudden and total inversion, an utter and complete reversal From what seemed an anti-metaphysical logicism-cum-positivism Wittgenstein's philosophy seems to have collapsed into a Idealist solipsism.

Before trying to make sense of this new twist in his thinking, let's look at some of the propositions he advances on behalf of his seemingly bizarre claim:

5.6   *The limits of my language* means the limits of my world.

5.61   Logic fills the world: the limits of the world are also its limits.
        ...otherwise logic must get outside the limits of the world: that is, if it could consider these limits from the other side also.
        What we cannot think, that we cannot think: we cannot therefore *say* what we cannot think.

5.62   In fact what solipsism *means*, is quite correct, only it cannot be *said*, but it shows itself.
        That the world is *my* world shows itself in the fact that the limits of the language (the language which alone I understand) means the limits of *my* world.

5.632   The subject does not belong to the world, but is a limit of the world.

5.633   Where *in* the world is a metaphysical subject to be found?

5.641   There is therefore really a sense in which in philosophy we can talk of a non-psychological I.
        The I occurs in philosophy through the fact that the "world is my world."
        The philosophical I is not the man, not the human body or the human soul of which psychology treats, but the metaphysical subject, the limit--not part of the world.

Wittgenstein drops these lapidary utterances into the midst of a dry discussion of logic as if they are stones from a higher place, or perhaps more precisely, from somewhere at the limits of what can be meaningfully said. Again, something that cannot be *said* is presented as *showing* itself at the limits of thinking and speaking – this time not the 'that' of the world's existence but the equally mystical-sounding existence of the 'I' – not the human being as a conjunction of body and mind, but a 'philosophical I,' a 'metaphysical subject' that exists not *in* the world, nor as 'part of the world,' nor as located 'outside' or on 'the other side' of the world, but at and as the 'limit' of the world itself – a metaphysical 'black hole' into which the existence of the world itself has seemingly collapsed: "I am my world. (The world microcosm.)." From a formal-logical view of the abstract structures of the world, or a natural-scientific view of the 'how' and 'what' of the world, or even a view of the world in its ineffable 'that'-ness, Wittgenstein seems to have changed his world-view midstream from what appeared to be an anti-metaphysical positivism to an Idealist solipsism of the first order. Talk about an utter and complete reversal, a sudden and total inversion–a philosophy turned upside down and inside out. It will not be the last of these surprises before we have finished with Wittgenstein!

Wittgenstein's switch in the *Tractatus* from a focus on topics of logic to a focus on the metaphysical subject is a reflection and distillation of a similar change that already occurred in his *Notebooks* when he moved from a focus on logic in his entries in 1914 and 1915 to a concentrated burst of entries about the metaphysical 'I' made in 1916 (apart from one isolated remark in 1915). These make their appearance at the same time he was assigned to a forward observer position on the front lines of the battle in WWI and began to ruminate about the possibility of his death and its implications for his philosophy. In particular he began to reflect on the link between 'the world' and what he meant by 'life.' Thus we find him saying such things as:

"*The limits of my language* stand for the limits of my world.
There really is only one world-soul, which I for preference call *my* soul and as which alone I conceive what I call the souls of others.
The above remark gives the key for deciding the way in which solipsism is a truth." (49e, May 23, 1915; cf. *Tract.* 5.6; 5.62)
"The World and Life are one." (77e, July 24, 1916; cf. *Tract.* (5.621).
"Physiological life is of course not 'Life'. And neither is psychological life. Life is the world." (*ibid.*)

"...the subject is not part of the world, but a boundary of the world.....not a part of the world but a presupposition of its existence..." (79e, August 2, 1916; cf. *Tract*. 5.632).

"Here the nature of the subject is completely veiled." (*ibid.*)

"The I is not an object." (80e, August 7, 1916)

"I objectively confront every object. But not the I. So is there really a way in which there can be mention of the I in a non-psychological sense in philosophy." (80e, August 11,1916; cf. *Tract*. 5.641)

"The I makes its appearance in philosophy through the world's being *my* world." (80e, August 12, 1916; cf. *Tract* 5.641).

"Mine is the first and only world! I want to report how *I* found the world." (82e, September 2, 1916)

"It is true: Man *is* the microcosm. I am my world." (84e, October 12, 1916; cf. *Tract*. 5.63)

"Now is it true (following the psycho-physical conception) that my character is expressed only in the build of my body or brain and not equally in the build of the whole of the rest of the world?

This contains a salient point.

This parallelism, then, really exists between my spirit, i.e., spirit [*Geist*], and the world." (85e, October 15, 1916)

"Is not my world adequate for individuation?" (89e, November 19, 1916).

Behind these remarks also lies Wittgenstein's return, under the existential stress of his battlefield situation, to the thought of the philosopher who made the greatest impression upon him as a youth during his highschool years. He had lost his Christian (Catholic) faith and in his search for a spiritual substitute was introduced to the magnum opus of Schopenhauer, *The World as Will and Representation*. It is in Schopenhauer's distinction between the world as an expression of 'Idea' ('representation') and the world as the expression of 'Will' ('Life') that we find the origin and basis for Wittgenstein's war-time reflections in his *Notebooks*, carried over into the *Tractatus*, on the difference between the 'worlds' of logic and natural science (the world as 'Idea') and the world of the metaphysical subject, the 'I' (the world as *my* world, the world as 'life,' *my* life). It is was Schopenhauer's metaphysical dualism that provided Wittgenstein the key for reconciling what at first glance seems his completely disparate interests in the abstract philosophy of logic and a concrete metaphysics of the self, between the conceptual

Realism of logic a la Frege and Russell and the transcendental Idealism of metaphysical solipsism. As Wittgenstein himself put it: "Here we can see that solipsism coincides with pure realism, if it is strictly thought out. The I of solipsism shrinks to an extensionless point and what remains is the reality co-ordinate with it." (82e, September 2, 1916; cf. *Tract.* 5.64)

Recapitulating his philosophical journey to that point: "This is the way I have traveled: Idealism singles men out from the world as unique, solipsism singles me alone out, and at last I see that I too belong with the rest of the world, and so on the one side *nothing* is left over, and on the other side, as unique, *the world*. In this way Idealism leads to Realism if it is strictly thought out." (85e, October 15, 1916; cf. *Tract.* 5.64)

What is notable about Schopenhauer's use of, and divergence from, the metaphysical dualism of Kant is relevant to understanding Wittgenstein's own philosophy at this point. In his approach to metaphysics Schopenhauer subscribed to Kant's limiting the sphere of what is knowable to our experience of the worlds of logic and natural science. But he differed from Kant in rejecting the latter's assigning of the transcendental 'I' to the realm of unknowable *noumena*. Instead, Schopenhauer argued, we have direct access, via introspection, to the 'I' itself, namely, in the felt experience of our own acts of will. Thus in place of a Platonic or Kantian metaphysical dualism he argues, in the spirit of the philosopher Spinoza, for a metaphysical psycho-physical 'parallelism,' a 'double-aspect' view of the reality that *links* the worlds of logic and science, on the one hand, to the world of our inner, subjective will, on the other. In fact, the inner 'will' is, not unlike Kant's transcendental ego, the metaphysical basis of the outer world of our 'ideas' as well. As one observer noted, for Schopenhauer "will and representation are one and the same reality, regarded from different perspective" (Wicks, 2017). More specifically, "the innermost nature [*Innerste*], the underlying force, of every representation and also of the world as a whole is the will, and every representation is an objectification of the will" (Troxell, n.d.). Thus the world as a whole has two sides, the world as 'will' ("for us") and the world as it "in itself." For Schopenhauer, then, "Man is the microcosm in which all that is fundamental to reality as a whole (the macrocosm) may be plainly discerned." (Gardiner, 328).

For Schopenhauer this metaphysical insight, paradoxically, itself finally rests on a spiritual transformation that transcends both the will and the world. "Such mystical insight, moreover, is necessarily incommunicable and indescribable; all knowledge, including that attainable by philosophy, here reaches its limit, and we are left with only 'myths and meaningless words' which express no positive content. 'The nature of things before or beyond the world, and consequently beyond the will,' Schopenhauer declared at the close of his main work, 'is open to no investigation.' The end of philosophy is silence." (Gardiner, 331). Here we begin to see how Wittgenstein *links* his two metaphysical claims: the 'that-ness' of the world– the mystical – that cannot be *said* but only *shows* itself, and the solipsism, the identity of the 'I' with the 'that-ness' of the 'world,' that likewise cannot be *said* but only *shows* itself. "On the one side [the side of the 'I'] *nothing* is left over, and on the other side, as unique, *the world*." For Wittgenstein too, as for Schopenhauer, this mystical insight into the transcendental identity of the self and the world has a more than merely 'philosophical' significance. For Wittgenstein as for Schopenhauer, it represents also an insight into the 'higher,' *ethical* significance of the 'I' and the 'world'. It is to this fourth meaning of the 'world' in Wittgenstein's thought, the world as an *ethical* world, therefore, that we now turn.

Ethical World

"*The meaning [Sinn] of the world.*" Wittgenstein's comments on Ethics in the *Tractatus* are linked to his Schopenhauerian notion of the metaphysical 'I' conceived of as will, a phenomenon that, as we have seen in his comments on the 'I', exists not *in* the world, not as a subject for psychology, but as a transcendental reality that *shows* itself at and as the limit of the world, or as he also says, as existing 'outside' the world of what can be *said*, paradoxically like the 'that' of the world's existence itself. He expresses this in another set of interrelated propositions in the *Tractatus*:

6.41   The sense [*Sinn*] of the world must lie outside the world. In the world everything is as it is and happens as it does happen. *In* it there is no value–and if there were, it would be of no value.

If there is a value which is of value, it must lie outside all happening and being-so. For all happening and being-so is accidental.

What makes it non-accidental cannot lie *in* the world, for otherwise this would again be accidental.

It must lie outside the world.

6.42   Hence also there can be no ethical propositions. Propositions cannot express anything higher.

6.421   It is clear that ethics cannot be expressed. Ethics are transcendental.

6.43   If good or bad willing changes the world, it can only change the limits of the world, not the fact; not the things that can be expressed in language.

In brief, the world must thereby become quite another. It must so to speak wax or wane as a whole.

The world of the happy is quite another than that of the unhappy.

6.4312 The solution of the riddle of life in space and time lies *outside* space and time.

(It is not problems of natural science which have to be solved.)

6.432   *How* the world is, is completely indifferent for what is higher. God does not reveal himself *in* the world.

6.44   Not *how* the world is, is the mystical, but *that* it is.

6.45   The contemplation of the world sub specie aeterni is its contemplation as a–limited–whole.

The feeling of the world as a limited whole is the mystical feeling.

There is a lot to be unpacked from these distilled statements. As before, we can turn for help to the lengthy series of notes on ethics and the will he was working on during the war year of 1916 that was so crucial for his later life and thought. His first entry, though it comes from the prior year, indicates the context in which to view the later remarks:

"The urge towards the mystical comes from the non-satisfaction of our wishes by science. We *feel* that even if all *possible* scientific questions are answered *our problem is still not touched at all*. Of course in that case there are no questions any more; and that is the answer." (51e, May 25, 1915; cf. *Tract*. 6.52).

In this comment we already see Wittgenstein distinguishing what can be *said* in the form of questions and answers about the 'how' and 'what' of the world as conceived in natural science, from an existential problem, the 'non-satisfaction of our wishes,' which *points to* [*shows, sich zeitigt*] something 'higher' than that world, something 'mystical' whose bearing is of a different, *ethical* nature. The problem of the ethical is not solved by the questions or answers provided by the sciences – "and that is the answer." But of course that leaves everything about the ethical still to be 'said'! Wittgenstein obliges:

"What do I know about God and the purpose of life?

I know that this world exists.

That I am placed in it like my eye in the visual field.

That something about it is problematic, which we call its meaning.

That this meaning does not lie in it but outside it.

That life is the world. That my will penetrates the world.

That my will is good or evil.

Therefore that good and evil are somehow connected with the meaning of the world.,

The meaning of life, i.e. the meaning of the world, we can call God.

And connect with this the comparison of God to a father.

To pray is to think about the meaning of life." (72e-73e, June 11, 1916; cf. *Tract*. 6.41; 5.621)

Here he gives us a list of 'propositions' linking a variety of 'limit' or 'boundary' notions: God, the purpose of life, the problematic of life, the meaning of life, 'outside' the world, 'life,' 'will,' 'good,' 'evil,' 'pray.' The answer to the question of the meaning of life, provoked by the sense that it is problematic, possibly meaninglessness, cannot be found within the world but lies at the limit, the edges, 'outside' that world. The problematic nature of life has something to do with my will, a will that penetrates the world but cannot be found *in* the world, a will that is a good and/or malevolent will. That will, my will, somehow determines the meaning of life, the meaning of the world itself, an ultimate meaning that answers the question about the purpose of life, an ultimate meaning which we can, if we wish, call 'God.' To contemplate the ultimate meaning of life in its connection with my will, good and/or evil, is to 'pray to God.'

"The world is independent of my will. Even if everything that we want were to happen, this would still only be, so to speak, a grace of fate, for what would guarantee it is not any logical connection between will and world, and we could not in turn will the supposed physical connection. If good or evil willing affects the world it can only affect the boundaries of the world, not the facts, what cannot be portrayed by language but can only be shown in language.

In short, I must make the world a wholly different one. The world must, so to speak, wax or wane as a whole. As if by accession or loss of meaning [*Sinn*]." (73e, July 5, 1916; cf. *Tract.* 6.374; 6.43)

On the one hand, the will determines the meaning of the world. But on the other, the world itself is independent of my will. If the events that transpire in the world happen to accord with my wishes, that is only a happy accident, a 'grace [*Gnade*] of fate.' It provides no evidence for an alleged link between my will and what happens in the world, nor can we will any such connection. Thus, if in any sense good or evil willing can be said to affect the world, it can only affect the world at its boundaries, the world as a whole, as it were, making my relation to it 'a wholly different one.' Its meaning will 'wax or wane as a whole,' as if it mysteriously gained or lost its entire meaning at one blow.

Wittgenstein asks: "But is it possible for one so to live that life stops being problematic? That one is *living* in eternity and not in time?" (74e, July 65, 1916) His answer follows immediately in what is the longest entry devoted to this question:

"To believe in God means to understand the question about the meaning of life.

To believe in God means to see that the facts of the world are not the end of the matter.

To believe in God means to see that life has a meaning.

The world is *given* me, i.e., my will enters into the world completely from outside as into something that is already there.

That is why we have the feeling of being dependent on an alien [*fremden*] will.

However this may be, at any rate we are in a certain sense dependent, and what we are dependent on we can call God.

In this sense God would simply be fate, or, what is the same thing: The world – which is independent of our will.

I can make myself independent of fate.

There are two godheads: the world and my independent I.

I am either happy or unhappy, that is all. It can be said: good or evil do not exist.

A man who is happy must have no fear. Not even in the face of death.

Only a man who lives not in time but in the present is happy.

For life in the present there is no death.

Death is not an event in life. It is not a fact of the world.

If by eternity is understood not infinite temporal duration but non-temporality, then it can be said that a man lives eternally if he lives in the present. [cf. *Tract*. 6.4311]

In order to live happily I must be in agreement with the world. And that is what 'being happy' *means*.

I am then, so to speak, in agreement with that alien will on which I appear dependent. That is to say: 'I am doing God's will.'

Fear in the face of death is the best sign of a false, i.e., a bad, life.

When my conscience upsets my equilibrium, then I am not in agreement with Something. But what is this. Is it *the world*?

Certainly it is correct to say: Conscience is the voice of God.

For example: it makes me unhappy to think that I have offended such and such a man. Is that my conscience?

Can one say: 'Act according to your conscience whatever it may be'?

Live happily!" (74e-75e; cf. *Tract*. 6.4311)

In these extended and fascinating comments we can see Wittgenstein wrestling with the relation between Schopenhauer's 'pessimistic' view of the will as suffering from embodiment in and dependence upon the happenings of a world 'alien' to its happiness, and Wittgenstein's own resolve to live a life of fearlessness and 'good conscience' in the face of his possible death at the front. We see him encouraging himself to make himself 'independent of fate,' so that by living fully in the present, by living 'happily,' he can face death with courage and equanimity, he can live an *authentic* life. In such a life the unhappy will has been overcome, and good and evil will no longer exist. His subsequent comments elaborate upon this theme: "I will call 'will' first and foremost the bearer of good and evil." (76e, July 21, 1916) "...it is also clear that the world of the happy is a *different* world from the world of the unhappy." (77e, July 29, 1916; cf. *Tract*. 6.43)

Wittgenstein asks himself the basic ethical question, "Suppose I do not do it? For there must be something right about the question after all. There must be a kind of ethical reward and of ethical punishment, but these must be involved in the action itself." He seems to imply that there is a question of absolute truth at stake here. Ethics involves a fateful choice, an up-or-down decision; it requires a response that must somehow be the true and right one. But what are the grounds for the response? He says: "I keep on coming back to this! Simply the happy life is good, the unhappy bad. And if I *now* ask myself: But why should I live *happily*, then this of itself seems to me to be a tautological question; the happy life seems to be justified, of itself, it seems that it *is* the only right life. But this is really in some sense deeply mysterious! *It is clear* that ethics *cannot* be expressed." And rightly so, for it is the logical expression of the transcendental status of ethics at the limits of the world, of the subject face to face with the mystical itself. "What is the objective mark of the happy, harmonious life? Here it is again clear that there cannot be any such mark, that can be *described*. This mark cannot be a physical one but only a metaphysical one, a transcendental one. Ethics is transcendental. Then the world itself is neither good nor evil." (78e-79e, July 30,1916; cf. *Tract.* 6.421)

So for Wittgenstein there is a right answer to the ethical question. There is also an equal and opposite wrong answer, one he came face to face with in the war:

"From time to time I was afraid. That is the fault of a false view of life." (May 6, 1916; Monk 138)

"A man who is happy must have no fear. Not even in the face of death." (74e July 8, 1916)

"Fear in the face of death is the best sign of a false, i.e., a bad, life." (75e July 8, 1916)

"I was afraid of death....This is precisely what 'sin' is, the unreasoning life, a false view of life....without the possibility of internal salvation.... Then an authentic life is unthinkable." (July 24, 1916; Monk,146)

"You know what you have to do to live happily. Why don't you do it? Because you are unreasonable. A bad life is an unreasonable life." (August 12, 1916; Monk, 146)

As Monk notes, in making these statements, Wittgenstein is speaking "not, this time, as a statement of a personal credo but as a contribution to philosophical thought" (Monk,141). At the opening of his chapter on Wittgenstein at the frontlines of the war, Monk cites a quote from Schopenhauer's *The World as Will and Representation* with which Wittgenstein was surely aware: "Undoubtedly, it is the knowledge of death, and therewith the consideration of the suffering and misery of life, that give the strongest impulse to philosophical reflection and metaphysical explanations of the world."

Of course it is one thing to engage in philosophical reflection about the true and the false, the right and the wrong, the reasonable and the unreasonable as regards one's ethical life, but it is quite another to conduct oneself in accord with one's ethical knowledge. Facing death on the frontlines of the war Wittgenstein was clearly aware of this too. The spiritual value of facing death heroically was touched on by another philosopher Wittgenstein read at the time. As William James says in *The Varieties of Religious Experience*: "if he be willing to risk death, and still more if he suffer it heroically in the service he has chosen, the fact consecrates him forever" (Monk, 112). To which, at the war's outset, Wittgenstein responded in his diary of the time: "Now I have the chance to be a decent human being, for I'm standing eye to eye with death" (1914; Monk, 112) Two years later, now at the front, "May I die a good death, attending myself. May I never lose myself." (Monk. 116) And again:"Perhaps the nearness of death will bring light into life.... I am a worm, but through God I become a man." (May 4, 1916; cited in Monk, 138). Monk comments: "What Wittgenstein wanted from war...was a transformation of his whole personality, a 'variety of religious experience' that would change his life irrevocably.... his a desire to 'turn into a different person' was stronger even than his desire to solve the fundamental problems of logic" (Monk, 112). Now, facing the horror of war for himself, "he needed, not only a religious faith, but also a philosophy" (Monk, 141)

The Russian offensive against the Austrian frontlines was launched in June 1916. Wittgenstein's unit took the brunt of the attack. "It was precisely at this time that the nature of Wittgenstein's work changed. It is as if the personal and the philosophical had become fused; ethics and logic – the two aspects of the 'duty to oneself' – had finally come together, not merely as two aspects of the same personal task, but as two parts of the same philosophical work." (Monk, 140-141) Already before the war Wittgenstein had imbibed from the work of Otto Weininger, *Sex and Character*, the idea that "Logic and ethics are fundamentally the same; they are no more than duty to oneself" (Weininger, cited by Monk, 24). Now, facing the Russian attack, Wittgenstein's earlier thoughts about logic and his thinking about his life himself became "but two aspects of the single 'duty to oneself,", a fervently held faith that influenced his work, eventually, transforming it from work on logic to "the curiously hybrid work [the Tractatus] which we know today, combining as it does logical theory with religious mysticism" (Monk, 116).

Wittgenstein's discussion of 'ethics,' cast in terms of the contrast/ conflict of good and evil, happy and unhappy, is grounded not only in this Kantian notion of duty but also in his Schopenhauerian metaphysics of the transcendental subject-as-will and its relation to the limits of the world, or at he also puts it, the world as a *limited* whole. Interestingly, Wittgenstein sees his switch to thinking about ethics, the metaphysical subject, and the world as a limited whole as not incompatible with, or unrelated to, his work on the logical structures of the world; rather, it is an 'extension' of that work. In this we see a reflection of the work which influenced Schopenhauer, namely, Kant's two treatises on 'pure' (transcendental) reason, one 'theoretical' (the a priori categories of the world), one 'practical' (the a priori categories of ethics). In Wittgenstein's mind there is a *link* between the two transcendental disciplines of Logic and Ethics, finding their unity in the transcendental Subject existing at the limits of the world:

"Good and evil only enter through the subject. And the subject is not part of the world, but a boundary of the world.

It would be possible to say (a la Schopenhauer): It is not the world of Idea that is either good or evil; but the willing subject.

Going by the above, then, the willing subject would have to be happy or unhappy, and happiness and unhappiness could not be part of the world.

As the subject is not a part of the world but a presupposition of its existence, so good and evil are predicates of the subject, not properties of the world.

Here the nature of the subject is completely veiled.

My work has extended from the foundations of logic to the nature of the world.

(79e, August 2, 1916; cf. *Tract.* 5.632)

The subject is not only not a *part* of the world, as, say, the object of a science of psychology; more, as *my* world it is the transcendental *presupposition* of the existence of the world. Further, as a subject whose existence is itself mysterious, it is *linked* to the mysterious character of the 'that-ness' of the world's own existence as a limited whole. As he says: "But now at last the connection of ethics with the world has to be made clear (84e, October 9. 1916):

"[T]he willing subject exists. If the will did not exist, neither would there be that center of the world, which we call the I and which is the bearer of ethics. What is good and evil is essentially the I, not the world. The I, the I is what is deeply mysterious!" (80e, August 5, 1916; cf. *Tract.* 5.631).

"The usual way of looking at things sees objects as it were from the midst of them, the view *sub specie aeternitatis* from outside. In such a way that they have the whole world as background. Is this it perhaps – in this view the object is seen *together with* space and time instead of *in* space and time? Each thing modifies the whole logical world, the whole of logical space, so to speak. (The thought forces itself upon one): The thing seen *sub specie aeternitatis* is the thing seen together with the whole logical space." (83e, October 7, 1916)

There is another implication for ethics in Wittgenstein's comment about the metaphysical perspective of seeing each thing *sub specie aeternitatis* and that is its bearing on the ethical attitude or virtue of compassion – an attitude that extends to all things in the world, not just to the human world. For as Wittgenstein, following Schopenhauer, says:

"The human body, however, my body in particular, is a part of the world among others, among animals, plants, stones etc., etc. Whoever realizes this will not want to procure a pre-eminent place for his own body or for the human body. He will regard humans and animals quite naively as objects which are similar and which belong together. *But now at last the connection of ethics with the world has to be made clear.* A stone, the body of a beast, the body of a man, my body, all stand on the same level. That is why what happens, whether it comes from a stone or from my body is neither good nor bad. Now is it true (following the psycho-physical conception) that my character is expressed only in the build of my body or brain and not equally in the build of the whole of the rest of the world? This contains a salient point. This [psycho-physical] parallelism, then, really exists between my spirit, i.e., spirit [*Geist*], and the world. Only remember that the spirit of the snake, of the lion, is *your* spirit. For it is only from yourself that you are acquainted with spirit at all. (82e Sept 2, 1916; 84e Oct 9, 1916; 84e Oct 12, 1916; 85e Oct 15, 1916; cf. Tract. 5.641; first emphasis mine)

With these remarks we can return to the distilled version we find in the *Tractatus*. The 'sense' [*Sinn*] of the world' that provides the 'solution' to the 'problem' concerning the 'riddle of life' in this world of space and time, cannot be found within this world of space and time, the world understood in its 'how' and 'what' via the aposteriori propositions of natural science (*Tract.* 6.41, 6.4312). Rather it must be looked for 'outside' the world so conceived, namely, at the apriori transcendental 'limits' or 'boundaries' of the world in the domain of the metaphysical "I", the willing subject, wherein we discover the transcendental presuppositions, both logical and ethical, that limn the world in which we live. The meaning of life is to be understood not in the propositions of natural science but in the propositions of ethics, which are transcendental. Those propositions ascribe properties to the willing subject – good or bad, good or evil, happy or unhappy. Such willing changes the world at its limits, making it 'quite another,' making it 'wax or wane as a whole.'

Here we see Wittgenstein's answer to our guiding question: what is the relation of the cognitive and emotive elements in the awareness of the mystery of (the world's) existence? For Wittgenstein, ethics is a felt response to an awareness of the 'the mystical' – 'not *how* the world is but *that* it is' (*Tract.* 6.44). As Wittgenstein says: "The contemplation of the world *sub specie aeterni* is its contemplation as a–limited–whole. The feeling of the world as a limited whole is the mystical feeling" (*Tract.* 6.45). 'Contemplation' or awareness of the 'that-ness' of the world is also a 'feeling' response to the 'that-ness' of the world. Wittgenstein's use of the expression, 'sub specie aeterni,' 'under the perspective of eternity,' in conjunction with the notion of a 'mystical feeling' indicates that for him awareness of the fact *that* the world exists, and exists as a *limited* whole, is not simply an awareness of the world as a quantitative whole but as as *qualitative* whole (Hargby, 241). It is a qualitative awareness because it draws the subject into the mystical, because it puts the subject's own existence in question. Here, in other words, there is no question of the 'that-ness' of the world's existence being a mere *factum brutum*. The that-ness of the world is never just a bare fact, for the world as a limited whole is the world of a subject, it is *my* world. Therefore the world is given to us, comes to us, already meaning-laden, value-laden in its 'facticity' (to borrow a term from Heidegger).

Therefore our response to the 'that-ness' of the world is never simply cognitive, it is also emotive; it is a 'felt' response. In particular, it is an *ethical* response. Awareness of the 'thatness' of the world as a limited whole, together with the existence of the subject at the limits of that world-as-a-whole, poses an ethical question, confronts us with a choice; it asks for an ethical response. What is the qualitative 'meaning of the world' to be? What is the 'solution to the problem of life' to be? Will existence, will the world viewed *sub specie aeterni* be seen in positive or negative terms? 'happy' or 'unhappy'? 'good' or 'bad'? 'good' or 'evil'? friendly or unfriendly? (William James)? useless (Sartre)? or absurd (Camus)? a life of suffering and compassion (Schopenhauer)? or a matter of indifference? (in the *Notebooks* Wittgenstein asks, "Is it possible to will good, to will evil, and *not* to will?") – in short, is it meaningful or meaningless? (even meaninglessness, says Tillich, is a mode of meaning; it only make sense against the background of meaning). Whatever the choice, whatever the decision, *my* world can never be simply a 'brute fact.'

As we have noted, Wittgenstein's reflections on ethics and the nature of the world came to the fore, replacing his focus on logic, when in 1916 he was posted to the front lines in WWII and had to come face to face with the possibility of his own death. Self and death, the two limits standing between which, from within the world, he became aware of, could point to, could 'show' the limits of the thinkable, the sayable. It is because of his 'double awareness' of these two boundaries that he could think of the world 'as a whole,' as a 'limited' or 'bounded' whole. (Hargby, 243). "[Philosophy] should limit the thinkable and thereby the unthinkable. It should limit the unthinkable from within through the thinkable. It will mean the inexpressible by clearly displaying the expressible. (*Tract.* 4.114, 4.115) It is in relation to the world-as-a-whole that the two levels or kinds of awareness show themselves" (Hargby, *ibid.*). There, at the limits of the world, in awareness of the thatness of the world's existence, is the place of wonder, where the metaphysical amazement arises, that something exists. Metaphysical wonder is only possible if the subject is drawn into the realm of the unthinkable and itself belongs to the mystical (Hargby, 244).

By clearing away false puzzles, Wittgenstein claims, like Kant, to be making room for the real 'riddle,' for the fundamental question of metaphysics itself: Why is there something rather than nothing at all? But paradoxically, it is there, at the limits of the world, with the discovery of the ethical solution to the problem of life, that the metaphysical question turns back on itself and is dissolved into the mystical whence it arose

(Hargby, 244). It is there, at the limits of the world, that philosophy returns to the wonder in which it began and in which its truth is preserved.

But what then is the truth of philosophy for Wittgenstein? At the end of the Tractatus he expresses a view of the nature and task of philosophy which, we shall see, he never really abandons, even though he later dismissed his early work on language in the *Tractatus* as mistaken:

6.53   The right method of philosophy would be this: To say nothing except what can be said, i.e., the propositions of natural science, i.e. something that has nothing to do with philosophy: and then always, when someone wished to say something metaphysical, to demonstrate to him that he had given no meaning to certain signs in his propositions. This method would be unsatisfying to the other–he would not have the feeling that we were teaching him philosophy–but it would be the only strictly correct method.

6.54   My propositions are elucidatory in this way: he who understands me finally recognizes them as senseless, when he has climbed out through them, on them, over them. (He must so to speak throw away the ladder, after he has climbed up on it.)
He must surmount these propositions; then he sees the world rightly.

The purpose of philosophy is not the discovery of scientific truths, nor even of metaphysical truths. The truths of science have nothing to do with the truth of philosophy, while the propositions of metaphysics, lacking meaning, do not even rise to the level of truth. The purpose of philosophy is to liberate us from the attempts of science or metaphysics to answer the Why question. Philosophy aims to free us for something more important. Its goal is to enable us to 'see the world rightly'– to see it in the right perspective, a perspective that is 'higher,' a view of the world *'sub specie aeterni.'* That awareness does not take the form of a better theory but of a transformed *attitude* toward the world. Wittgenstein says in his *Notebooks*: "The will is an attitude of the subject to the world" (87e, November 4, 1916). It is an *ethical* attitude. And so philosophy offers not a metaphysical answer but an ethical choice: You can condemn yourself to be unhappy because you cannot provide a cosmological explanation for the existence of the world. Or you can free yourself to be happy for the gift, the 'grace' [*Gnade*], of the world's existence. Wittgenstein's answer to the Why question: "Throw away the ladder and live happily!" Before we turn to the transitional and later phases in Wittgenstein's thinking about these matters, let us pause here for a critical observation on his early attempt to link the cognitive with the emotive elements in the awareness of the mystery of existence. In so doing we may simply be anticipating the direction of Wittgenstein's own later work. It seems clear that Wittgenstein's answer in the *Notebooks* and the *Tractatus* to our guiding question stands or falls on his reliance upon Schopenhauer's metaphysics of the Will and Idea. As Wittgenstein's biographer remarks: "Wittgenstein's remarks on the will and the self are, in many ways, simply a restatement of Schopenhauer's 'Transcendental Idealism,' with its dichotomy between the 'world as idea,' the world of space and time, and the 'world as will,' the *noumenal*, timeless, world of the self." However, Monk claims: "What distinguishes Wittgenstein's statement of the doctrine from Schopenhauer's is that in Wittgenstein's case it is accompanied by the proviso that, when put into words, the doctrine is, strictly speaking, nonsense." (Monk, 144) This suggests an interesting possibility. Wittgenstein himself remarked in a self-critical aside in the midst of wartime Schopenhauerian flounderings, "I am conscious of the complete unclarity of all these sentences" (79e, August 2, 1916).

What if, in the spirit of Wittgenstein's own critique of metaphysical propositions in the *Tractatus*, we withdraw that underlying support provided by Schopenhauer's metaphysics, would this undermine the intelligibility of Wittgenstein's attempt to link the cognitive and emotive, the logical and the ethical, in relation to the mystery of the world's existence? Or might it be that there is contained in his pre- or non- or anti-metaphysical reflections an independent, phenomenological or intuitive basis for a link between these two aspects of the Why question? If so, might that link appear again in his later work, even absent any resort to metaphysics? That is what we will attempt to discover as we turn to the transitional and later phases of his thinking about these matters.

Transitional Wittgenstein. "Lecture on Ethics" and "Notes on Talks with Wittgenstein" 1965

Wittgenstein broke off his work on logic with Russell at Cambridge University in 1914 and returned to Austria to volunteer for the war effort. After the end of the war, he arranged for the publication of the *Tractatus* in German (1918; English transl. 1921). He felt that in his book he had answered all possible philosophical questions, had said everything there was to say about such matters: "the *truth* of the thoughts communicated here seems to me unassailable and definitive. I am, therefore, of the opinion that the problems have in essentials finally been solved" (*Tract.*, Preface). Thus instead of returning to Cambridge to pursue philosophical research further (what would be left to ponder if all such questions had been answered?), Wittgenstein abandoned philosophy, seemingly forever, and trained to become an elementary school teacher in small villages in rural Austria. For the next ten years, from 1918 through 1928, Wittgenstein basically did no philosophical work.

During that interim, a "circle" of philosophers had emerged in Vienna called "positivists" for whom clarity in philosophy meant the elimination of metaphysics through the application of the scientific method. Thinking to have found in Wittgenstein's critique of metaphysics a kindred spirit in sympathy with their own rigorous and reductive scientific *Weltanschauung.*, they invited him to meet with them to discuss the Tractatus. They were sorely disappointed. They failed to grasp the nature of "the curiously hybrid work which we know today, combining as it does logical theory with religious mysticism" (Monk, 116). As Rudolf Carnap one of the leading members of the Vienna Circle (we will meet him again) rather revealing confessed:

> ...when we were reading Wittgenstein's book in the Circle, I had erroneously believed that his attitude toward metaphysics was similar to ours. I had not paid sufficient attention to the statements in his book about the mystical, because his feelings and thoughts in this area were too divergent from mine. His point of view, and his attitude...were much more similar to those of a creative artist...one might almost say, similar to those of a religious prophet or a seer. When his answer came

forth, his statement stood before us like a newly created piece of art or a divine revelation, as if insight came to him through a divine inspiration, so that we could not help feeling that any sober rational comment or analysis of it would be a profanation. (Carnap, cited in Monk, 243-244).

They had failed to consider the implications of something else that Wittgenstein himself had said in the Preface: "This book will perhaps only be understood by those who have themselves already thought the thoughts which are expressed in it – or similar thoughts.... the value of this work secondly consists in the fact that it shows how little has been done when these [philosophical] problems have been solved." What Wittgenstein was calling his readers' attention to, and what the members of the Vienna Circle had missed, is the link between logic and ethics that for Wittgenstein was central to the work – and, because of the war, to his life as well. As he told his friend Ludwig von Ficker, "the point of the *Tractatus* was ethical." In fact, as he also said, the religious [for him, indistinguishable from the ethical] point of view was how he saw every problem. In his letter to Ficker (November 1919) he said: "my work [the *Tractatus*] consists of two parts: of the one which is here, and of everything which I have *not* written. And precisely this second part is the important one. For the Ethical is delimited from within, as it were, by my book; and I'm convinced that, *strictly* speaking, it can ONLY be delimited in this way. In brief, I think: All of that which *many* are *babbling* today, I have defined in my book by remaining silent about it." (Wittgenstein, cited in Monk, 178).

Conversations during the war years with his friend Paul Engelmann also helped Wittgenstein to clarify "the connections between the mystical and the logical parts of the book." Wittgenstein said that "logic and mysticism have here sprung from the same root" (Monk, 150). Central to the book was his distinction between *saying* [expressing, uttering] and *showing* [making manifest]. Just as logical form cannot be expressed *within* language because it is the *form* of language, but makes itself manifest in *language*, so ethical and religious truths, though inexpressible in the propositions of natural science, make themselves manifest in *life*. (Monk, 142). For Wittgenstein this crucial distinction between what can be said and what can only be shown constitutes "The central thread that links the logic and the mysticism–the idea of the unutterable truth that makes itself manifest..." (Monk, 150). As Wittgenstein said to Engelmann: "And this is how it is: if only you do not try to utter what is unutterable then nothing gets lost. But the unutterable will be – unutterably – *contained* in what has been uttered!" (Monk, *ibid.*). Thus, as Monk insightfully points out: "The famous last sentence of the book – 'Whereof one cannot speak, thereof one must be silent' – expresses both a logico-philosophical truth and an ethical precept. The nonsense that results from trying to say what can only be shown is not only logically untenable, but ethically undesirable." (Monk, 156)

In fact Wittgenstein had already begun to move beyond the formal-logical view of language in the *Tractatus*. By the time he was finally persuaded to return to Cambridge, and to philosophy, at the beginning of 1929, he was, as his biographer put it, "prepared to overhaul all the conclusions he had reached up to now – prepared not only to consider new ways of thinking, but even new ways of life" (Monk, 263). An incident at the time neatly captured the change that was about to take place in Wittgenstein's philosophy. It happened during one of the weekly conversations he was having with Piero Sraffa, an Italian economist lecturing at Cambridge. Wittgenstein was defending the Tractarian claim that a proposition and the state of affairs it describes must have the same 'logical form' (or, his later term, 'grammar'). As Monk reports: "To this idea Sraffa made a Neapolitan gesture of brushing his chin with his fingertips, asking: 'What is the logical form of *that*?'" According to the story, this "broke the hold on Wittgenstein of the Tractarian idea that a proposition must be a 'picture' of the reality it describes" (Monk, 260-1). As Monk observed: "Sraffa had the power to force Wittgenstein to revise, not this or that point, but his whole perspective" (Monk, 260). Wittgenstein began to rethink his views from that point on, though the radically new philosophy that resulted from this gestural shock did not fully emerge until around 1932. In the intervening period his work was in transition. The work during this period that bears most directly on our particular concern was his "Lecture on Ethics."

It was in this transitional moment that, sometime between September 1929 and December 1930, he gave the only 'popular' lecture he was known to have composed or delivered: "A Lecture on Ethics." At the same time, in December 1929 and again in December 1930 he held private conversations on the same topic with two other members of the Vienna Circle, Moritz

Schlick and Friedrich Waismann. As noted, it was the "second part...the important one" of the Tractatus that the positivist philosophers of the Vienna Circle had missed – because, as Carnap confessed, "his feelings and thoughts in this area were too divergent from mine." Carnap and the other members of the Vienna Circle were not alone in this regard. Thus Wittgenstein used the occasion of his lecture "to try and correct the most prevalent and serious misunderstanding of the *Tractatus,* the idea that it is a work written in a positivist, anti-metaphysical spirit."

In the lecture "he reiterated the view of the *Tractatus* that any attempt to say something about the subject-matter of ethics would lead to nonsense, but tried to make clear the fact that his own attitude to this was radically different from that of a positivist anti-metaphysician" (Monk, 276-277). To the extent that the *Tractatus* adopted an anti-metaphysical stance, it could have been and was in fact mistaken as a form of 'positivism.' But in its concern with ethics and 'the mystical' it was clearly what could be called 'positivism-*plus*.' It was the ethical 'plus' that the Vienna Circle missed. It was that 'plus' to which Wittgenstein now addressed his remarks. However, while the body of the lecture and conversations with Schlick and Waismann show him still operating out of a Tractarian perspective on the ethical, more importantly they also hint at the new direction his work would eventually take in his approach to language, ethics, religion and the method of philosophy itself.

Wittgenstein's "Lecture on Ethics."

Our concern is with the links between the cognitive and emotional or evaluative aspects of the Why question. As we have already seen in Part I, this question is not a ordinary 'why' question of the sort that arises in a particular cognitive context, say, of a scientific inquiry, even a cosmological-scientific one. Instead it has the atmosphere of something 'absolute,' something 'metaphysical' or 'transcendental' about it, inasmuch as it arises precisely at the point where all 'relative' why questions arrive at the limits of their logical jurisdictions. In trying to explain to his uncomprehending interlocutors what I am calling, at this transitional stage of his work, the 'plus' aspect of his apparent 'positivism,' Wittgenstein draws upon a similar distinction between a relative and an absolute sense of 'the Ethical' in attempting to explain the relation of the ethical to the 'mystical' or mystery of the world's existence. In so doing he hopes to show in what follows "both the way and where it leads to."

He begins by noting that he is not using the term 'ethics' in its usual sense as 'inquiry into what is good,' but rather "in a slightly wider sense" that embraces what he considers "the most essential part" of what is usually considered 'Aesthetics' (Wittgenstein, 1965, 4). This is already a surprising move, an apparent departure right at the outset from what is usually considered 'Ethics.' Apparently Wittgenstein sees it as part of a more general inquiry into *values*. That in itself is perhaps not so unusual. But what particularly draws our attention is his, at this point unexplained, claim that this 'slightly wider sense' includes 'the most essential part' of aesthetics. What is that 'most essential part'? He does not say. But it alerts us to the presence of an element that may take us beyond the realm of that which is 'relative.'

Is this, then, his – expanded – definition of Ethics? Yes and no. And here we begin to get a hint of his later approach to 'philosophical investigations,' one that proceeds not by 'definitions' in the traditional fashion, but rather by giving of examples until one simply 'sees.' At this point it is not entirely clear, however, whether Wittgenstein has completely foresworn the route via definitions. He says he will give us 'a number of more ore less synonymous expressions each of which could be substituted for the above definition' of ethics in the slightly wider sense. His description and explanation of the procedure is fascinating, knowing what we know about his later work. By citing a variety of additional examples:

> I want to produce the same effect which Galton produced when he took a number of photos of different faces on the same photographic plate in order to get the picture of the typical features they all had in common. And by showing to you such a collective photo I could make you see what is a typical – say– Chinese face; so if you look through the row of synonyms which I will put before you, you will, I hope, be able to see the characteristic features of Ethics. (Wittgenstein, 1965, 4)

And so, he immediately gives us a list of those 'more or less synonymous expression." By 'ethics,' he says, he means to refer to an inquiry not into 'what is good,' but into 'what is valuable,' 'what is really important,' 'the meaning of life,' 'what makes life worth living,' or 'the right way of living' (Wittgenstein, 1965, 5). Do we find in these phrases "a rough idea" of what Ethics is concerned with? Do we begin to get a sense of what 'the most important' feature of Ethics is? If we do, is it because in such unqualified expressions as 'what is *really* important,' 'the *meaning* of life,' 'what makes life *worth* living,' or 'the *right* way of life,' we begin to get a whiff of that atmosphere of the 'absolute'?

Despite the apparent 'absolute' connotations of these expressions, Wittgenstein says that in fact they can be understood in "two very different senses...the trivial or relative sense...and the ethical or absolute sense" (Wittgenstein, 1965, 5). But immediately we note he limits the 'ethical' sense of the 'synonymous' expressions to their 'absolute' sense, leaving their 'relative' sense to mean what? Presumably something other than 'ethical.' But what other sense than ethical can such expressions as 'what makes life worth living' or 'the right way of life' have? His examples of relative uses of 'good' – a good chair, a good pianist, the right road – do not seem to capture even a relative sense of those 'synonymous' expressions. What these terms do involve, as expressions of relative value, are instead, says Wittgenstein, "mere statements of fact," of what we might call hypothetical, if-then judgments referring to what he calls "a certain predetermined purpose" or goal, or "a certain predetermined standard." Judgements of relative value can always be reformulated as judgments of fact, thereby dispelling the appearance of being a judgment of value. If you want to get to such-and-such a place, this is the right road to take, etc. Such judgments do not pose any "difficult or deep problems" (Wittgenstein, 1965, 5). Thus, he concludes, "although all judgments of relative value can be shown to be mere statements of facts, no statement of fact can ever be, or imply, a judgment of absolute value" (Wittgenstein, 1965, 6).

We have been now been led up to the edge of what Wittgenstein understands to be the absolute value of Ethics, that is, the absolute nature of its *negative* relation to the world of facts, to '*how* the world is' and its *positive* relation to the 'mystical' fact '*that* the world is' (*Tract*.6.44). He expresses this Tractarian metaphysical view with a dramatic reversal of the traditional moral view of the 'book of nature':

Suppose [a] man wrote all he knew in a big book, then this book would contain the whole description of the world; ...this book would contain nothing that we could call an *ethical* judgment... It would of course contain all relative judgments of value and all true scientific propositions and in fact all true propositions that can be made. But all the facts described would, as it were, stand on the same level... There are no propositions which, in any absolute sense, are sublime, important, or trivial... [T]here will simply be facts, facts, and facts but no Ethics.... [I]f a man could write a book on Ethics which really was a book on Ethics, this book would, with an explosion, destroy all the other books in the world. Our words used as we use them in science, are vessels capable only of containing and conveying meaning and sense, *natural* meaning and sense. Ethics, if it is anything, is supernatural and our words will only express facts... (Wittgenstein, 1965, 6-7)

The word 'supernatural' jars here, but presumably it is meant in the restricted sense of the Tractatus where the 'sense' of the world, the 'higher' or 'transcendental value' of the world, is said to lie 'outside' or at the 'limit' of the world seen *sub specie aeterni* as a 'limited whole' (*Tract.* 6.41, 6.42, 6.421, 6.45). In fact, what this description of the absolute nature of Ethics vis-a-vis the world of facts prepares us for are his unexpected – doubly so – introduction into the discussion of three examples of experiences of the Ethical – surprising, first, because they immediately put us into the context of the discussion by Munitz and then take us two steps further. But further surprising because, by invoking *concrete experiences*, Wittgenstein seems to be taking his first steps toward breaking the hold of the rigid logic of the Tractarian view of language, with its dismissal, in the context of a 'transcendental' inquiry, of the very notion of 'experience' (*Tract.* 5.552), gesturing instead toward the pluralistic and 'anthropological' (the term is Wittgenstein's) view of language that emerges in his later work:

[W]hat have all of us who, like myself, are still tempted to use such expressions as 'absolute good,' 'absolute value,' etc., what have we in mind and what do we try to express? Now whenever I try to make this clear to myself it is natural that I should recall cases in which I would certainly use these expressions... And there, in my case, it always happens that the idea of one particular experience presents itself to me which therefore is, in a sense, my experience [of absolute or ethical value] *par excellence*.... I will use this experience as my first and foremost example. (As I have said before, this is an entirely personal matter and others would find other examples more striking.) I will describe this experience in order, if possible, to make you recall the same or similar experiences, so that we may have a common ground for our investigation. (Wittgenstein, 1965, 7-8)

This is itself a 'transitional' passage *par excellence*. It is transitional because here we see one of the first examples of that case-method approach to analyzing the meaning of words in terms of their use that characterizes Wittgenstein's distinctive later *style* (a word he much liked to stress). But it is also transitional because, as we shall after he unpacks this 'experience' and the two others he goes on to cite, in the end he seems (it is not entirely clear) to fall back onto a Tractarian dismissal of the experience.

So, then, what is the 'particular experience' that is his 'entirely personal' experience '*par excellence*' and which serves, philosophically, as his 'first and foremost example'?

I believe the best way of describing it is to say that when I have it *I wonder at the existence of the world*. And then I am inclined to use such phrases as "how extraordinary that anything should exist" or "how extraordinary that the world should exist." (Wittgenstein, 1965, 8; his emphasis)

This is, of course, another way of stating his view expressed in the Tractatus:

Not *how* the world is, is the mystical, but *that* it is. The contemplation of the world sub specie aeterni is its

contemplation as a – limited – whole. The feeling of the
world as a limited whole is the mystical feeling. (*Tract.*
6.44, 6.45)

There are several interesting aspects of his remarks. First, he makes
clearer here what was already broached in the *Tractatus:* the 'mystical'
awareness of the 'that' of the world's existence is not simply a cognitive
awareness, it has an emotional component as well: it is also a 'feeling.'
Second, this experienced 'feeling' is now more specifically described:
it is a feeling of 'wonder,' or, as he says a bit further on, of something
'miraculous' (Wittgenstein, 1965, 10-11). Third, this feeling of 'wonder'
or the 'miraculous' is an *evaluative* feeling: it is an experience that
has 'intrinsic, absolute value' (Wittgenstein, 1965, 10). And so we see
Wittgenstein here explicitly *linking* the cognitive elements in the 'absolute'
experience of the mystery of the world's existence with a very specific
emotional, and indeed evaluative element. Not only that. Wittgenstein
is telling us that this particular experience, and the Why question to
which it gives rise, *cannot* be understood as simply a *cognitive* one; it
necessarily involves a *feeling-awareness* as well. In other words, it is an
experience, and question, that can *only* be expressed, and understood,
as a distinctively *total* experience, an experience that *personally* involves
the questioner both intellectually and emotionally as well.

Two comments before we pass on to two further examples Wittgenstein
gives of experiences of absolute value. First, while Wittgenstein insists on
the necessity of the link between the cognitive and emotive elements in
the experience of 'wonder at the existence of the world,' he does not really
tell us *what* the conceptual (logical, metaphysical) *basis* of this link is.
That it obtains, yes, but why? Here he takes us up the edge of the promised
land, as it were, but appears to leave it to us to find the way across.

Second, and this may be related to the first observation, it is not clear
that the two additional phrases he cites as giving expression to his feeling
of wonder – "how extraordinary that *anything* should exist" and "how
extraordinary that *the world* should exist" – are in fact expressions of
the *same* awareness, that is, have the *same* reference. Here we come back
to our earlier criticism of Munitz. There is, or so I have been arguing, a
clear distinction between taking the Why question to refer to the fact that
'the world' exists (the second phrase above, which reprises the position
in *Tract.* 6.44-6.45) and the more radical question implied in the wonder

that 'anything' should exist (the first phrase above). It remains to be seen whether the *basis* of the link between the cognitive and emotive elements in the Why question will prove to settle the issue of *what* the question is *about*.

Wittgenstein then cites two further (personal) experiences of absolute value: one is "the experience of feeling *absolutely* safe. I mean the state of mind in which one is inclined to say 'I am safe, nothing can injure me whatever happens'" (Wittgenstein, 1965, 8). This apparently was indeed a profoundly meaningful experience for Wittgenstein, because it goes back to an incident when he was about 21. As he told Norman Malcolm, "his previously contemptuous attitude to religion had been changed by seeing a play." In what was otherwise an unmemorable play one of the characters said that "no matter what happened in the world, nothing bad could happen to *him. He* was independent of fate and circumstances." This 'stoic thought' had a powerful effect on Wittgenstein because "he saw, for the first time, the possibility of religion. For the rest of his life he continued to regard the feeling of being 'absolutely safe' as paradigmatic of religious experience." As he told Bertrand Russell a year or so later, it was that experience, plus reading William James *Varieties of Religious Experience*, that helped him to cope with his *Sorge*, an anxiety that in fact plagued him the rest of his life (Monk, 51). The other experience he cited, which was "of the same kind," was that of "feeling guilty" (Wittgenstein, 1965, 10).

The common element among these three experiences is that, as Wittgenstein says, they are examples of what he, personally, means by an 'absolute good,' that is, an 'intrinsic, absolute value.' But beyond that does anything else *link* these feelings of wonder, safety and guilt to one another? Is there some implicit underlying metaphysical or 'existential' *basis* that allows to make sense of why just *these* three should serve as experiences of absolute value? Or, as intrinsic values, do they each stand on their own existential feet, with no relation to one another? Further, we have already raised the question of the conceptual (logical, metaphysical) ground of wonder as a response to the 'that' of the world's existence. Is there any such basis for a response of feeling absolutely safe or, even more oddly, guilty vis-a-vis the 'that' of the world's existence?

Wittgenstein does not say, but in this lecture on *ethics*, he goes on, interestingly, to relate these three examples to what he takes to be analogous *religious* ones. Thus, he says, the first experience, of wonder that at the existence of the world, of seeing the world as a miracle, "is, I believe, exactly what people were referring to when they said that God had created the world; and the experience of absolute safety has been described by saying that we feel safe in the hands of God." And of the third experience, that of feeling guilty, "this was described by the phrase that God disapproves of our conduct" (Wittgenstein, 1965, 10). This analogy of ethical terms to God-talk suggests one possible answer to our questions in the preceding paragraph. For Wittgenstein, personally, these three experiences are what one might call 'secular' substitutes for the faith of his Catholic childhood that he lost in his secondary school years. So, though not metaphysically reasoned out, and we shall see in a moment why they are not, nevertheless his resort to God-talk at this point in the lecture suggests the presence of an *unexamined basis* that would explain why he selected *just these three* particular experiences to exemplify what he meant by that which is 'absolutely good,' experiences that have 'intrinsic, absolute value.' What relates them is an *implicit* theism of a very particular kind, one that we might call an existential neo-orthodoxy of the sort that prevailed in post-WWI Europe at the time. It should not surprise us, therefore, if the name Kierkegaard should come up at some point in the lecture – and of course it will.

As I suggested, to this point in the lecture Wittgenstein seems to have given a hint of the method of linguistic analysis – the avoidance of definitions in favor of an assembling of examples – that he would later employ in his work. But he now reverts of the stance of the *Tractatus*. For while these three experiences have given us a sense of what he means by saying of something, an experience or perhaps a reality, that it has 'absolute value,' he introduces what is perhaps the real topic of his lecture, not the emotional power of such expressions, but their logical status:

> Now let me consider these experiences, for, I believe, they exhibit the very characteristics we try to get clear about. And the first thing I have to say is, that the verbal expression which we give to these experiences is nonsense! If I say "I wonder at the existence of the world" I am misusing language. Let me explain this: It has a perfectly good and clear sense to say that I wonder at something being the case... In every such case I wonder at something being the case which I *could* conceive *not* to

be the case.... But it is nonsense to say that I wonder at the
existence of the world, because I cannot imagine it not
existing. I could of course wonder at the world round me
being as it is.... One might be tempted to say that what I
am wondering at is a tautology.. But then it's nonsense to
say that one is wondering at a tautology. (Wittgenstein,
1965, 8-9)

Now the same applies to the other experience which I have mentioned,
the experience of absolute safety. We all know what it means in ordinary
life to be safe....To be safe essentially means that it is physically impossible
that certain things should happen to me and therefore it's nonsense to
say that I am safe *whatever* happens. Again this is a misuse of the word
"safe" as the other example was of a misuse of the word "existence" or
"wondering". (Wittgenstein, 1965, 9)

Wittgenstein is indeed interested in what links these three
experiences, or more particularly the expressions of them. However, he
is not interested in asking whether there is some alleged existential,
metaphysical or theological foundation that enable us to make sense
of them. Rather, "I want to impress on you that a certain characteristic
misuse of our language runs through all ethical and religious expressions.
All these expressions *seem*, prima facie, to be just *similes*.... some sort of
analogy" (Wittgenstein, 1965, 9). It is not that resort to simile or analogy
is, in itself, logically problematic. It is when these linguistic figures are
taken out of their ordinary context and given an absolute meaning that
the logical spectre of nonsense makes its appearance. Unfortunately this
confronts us with a dilemma. On the one hand the language of ethics and
religions (e.g, God-talk) does in fact express (describe or refer to) the sort
of experiences cited (Wittgenstein, 1965, 9-10). On the other hand, the
expression of such experiences involves speaking nonsense. What to do?!

Perhaps Wittgenstein is drawing an over-hasty conclusion. Perhaps
he is still under the sway of the earlier, 'positivist' parts of the Tractatus,
and following up on the 'plus' implications of his perspective on ethics
and the world *sub specie aeternitatis*. Maybe there are other possibilities
here for interpreting ethical language, for making sense of language
about that which is 'absolute'?

At first it would seem not. For Wittgenstein appears still to have a restricted view of the nature of figurative speech in ethical or religious expressions:

> Thus in ethical and religious language we seem constantly to be using similes. But a simile must be the simile for something. And if I can describe a fact by means of a simile I must also be able to drop the simile and to describe the facts without it. Now in our case as soon as we try to drop the simile and simply to state the facts which stand behind it, we find that there are no such facts. And so, what at first appeared to be a simile now seems to be mere nonsense. Now the three experiences which I have mentioned...seem to those who have experienced them, for instance to me, to have in some sense an intrinsic, absolute value. But when I say they are experiences, surely, they are facts; they have taken place then and there, lasted a certain definite time and consequently are describable. And so from what I have said some minutes ago I must admit it is nonsense to say that they have absolute value. And I will make my point still more acute by saying "It is the paradox that an experience, a fact, should seem to have supernatural value. (Wittgenstein, 1965, 10)

This is a fascinating passage both for what it says, or seems to say, and what it does not say. If a fact can be described by a simile, it can also be described without the simile. But are the experiences of absolute value experiences of facts? He describes them as if they are psychological experiences. But we already know from the Tractatus that the propositions of ethics are not psychological propositions. Rather, they are 'transcendental'; their locus is at the 'limits' of the world, not 'within' it as psychological experiences are. So if such propositions are understood to be about psychological experiences, i.e. facts, they will indeed be speaking nonsense. To call them a 'paradox' would be to go gently with them.

Clearly recognizing that and not wanting it to be the last word on the matter, Wittgenstein says:

Let me first consider, again, our first experience of wondering at the existence of the world and let me describe it in a slightly different way; we all know what in ordinary life would be called a miracle....For it is clear that when we look at it in this way everything miraculous has disappeared; unless what we mean by this term is merely that a fact has not yet been explained by science... This shows that it is absurd to say "Science has proved that there are no miracles." The truth is that the scientific way of looking at a fact is not the way to look at it as a miracle. For imagine whatever fact you may, it is not in itself miraculous in the absolute sense of that term. For now we see that we have been using the word "miracle" in a relative and an absolute sense. And I will describe the experience of wondering at the existence of the world by saying it is the experience of seeing the world as a miracle. (Wittgenstein, 1965, 10-11)

Wittgenstein is saying that an approach to interpreting the language of ethics or religion as if it were a 'supernatural,' i.e. meta-factual, super-scientific discourse (do we hear his Tractarian critique of 'meta-physics'?) would be a logical error. To try to understand such 'absolute' language as a meta-version of the fact-stating language of science would be to misunderstand it. But does this mean Wittgenstein thinks there is an alternative way of understanding such language – for example, talk of the existence of the world as, in an absolute sense, a 'miracle' – that would save it from being nonsense?

You will say: Well, if certain experiences constantly tempt us to attribute a quality to them which we call absolute or ethical value and importance, this simply shows that by these words we *don't* mean nonsense, that after all what we mean by saying that an experience has absolute value *is just a fact like other facts* and that all it comes to is that we not yet succeeded in finding the correct logical analysis of what we mean by our ethical and religious expressions. (Wittgenstein, 1965.)

To this we are tempted to say, yes, no, and maybe. Yes, the words even in their absolute use do have their own kind of sense. But no, this does not mean they refer to 'a fact like other facts.' *That* the world exists is not a fact like other facts, namely, facts about *how* the world is. To think otherwise simply seems to be a piece of a priori linguistic (positivist-inspired?) legislation. And so, maybe, we do indeed need to look yet further for 'the correct logical analysis' of ethical and religious terms. However, it seems at this transitional stage in this thinking Wittgenstein is not yet ready to consider such an alternative, one which will, however, come to mark his later work. For now he will have none of it. Or at least so it would appear.

> Now when this is urged against me I at once see clearly, as it were in a flash of light, not only that no description that I can think of would do to describe what I mean by absolute value, but that I would reject every significant description that anybody could possibly suggest, *ab initio*, on the ground of its significance. That is to say: I see now that these nonsensical expressions were not nonsensical because I had not yet found the correct expression, but that their nonsensicality was their very essence. For all I wanted to do with them was just *to go beyond* the world and that is to say beyond significant language. My whole tendency and I believe the tendency of all men who have ever tried to write or talk Ethics or Religion was to run against the boundaries of language. This running against the walls of our cage is perfectly, absolutely hopeless. (Wittgenstein, 1965, 11-12, his emphasis)

These remarks are very intriguing, paradoxical, if not riddling. The language of ethics and religion, the talk of absolute value, of the mystical 'that' of the world's existence, is not nonsensical in the sense that we have not yet discovered the alternative logic that would render them intelligible, rather 'nonsensicality' is their 'very essence.' But this is passing strange. This suggests that the nonsensicality of such language is not just, as it were, accidental, a matter of confusion on the part of its users that can be straightened out and dispelled by a little bit of linguistic therapy. Rather there is something about such 'absolute' use of language that belongs to their very 'essence,' that is, their very *logic*. And what is the logic of such absolute expressions? That it expresses something that goes 'beyond' the 'world,' that it transgresses the limits of the 'significance' of ordinary fact-stating language, language whose epitome is natural science. Such language finds its logical place there at the boundaries of fact-stating language. But if those who use such language persist in thinking they are describing some sort of meta-physical 'facts,' some sort of transcendent 'truths,' then their linguistic effort is 'perfectly, absolutely hopeless.'

Wittgenstein concludes his lecture in this way:

> Ethics so far as it springs from the desire to say something about the ultimate meaning of life, the absolute good, the absolute valuable, can be no science. What it says does not add to our knowledge in any sense. But it is a document of a tendency in the human mind which I personally cannot help respecting deeply and I would not for my life ridicule it. (Wittgenstein, 1965, 12)

If our gloss is correct, as his distinction between 'knowledge' and 'a tendency in the human mind' also suggests, and whether he would endorse this or not, Wittgenstein can be taken a la Kant as 'leaving room for faith.' That is, as with Kant, it is possible that Wittgenstein could allow ethical and religious language to have a 'significance' of another sort – at a price. If it is not to be dismissed as nonsense, it must forswear all claims to state meta-physical 'facts' and limit itself to the sphere of the 'practical,' the realm of feelings (wonder, safety, guilt) and their implications for ethical or religious behavior – what one positivist-minded critic dismissed as "morality tinged with emotion." Is this a price its users, so-called 'believers,' are willing to play? Maybe yes, maybe no.

In any case, there should be no doubt that Wittgenstein's respect for the language of ethics and religions is sincere. As he said in a remark a few years later: "Don't play with what lies deep in another person!" (Wittgenstein, 1984, 23, ca. 1932-1934). Wittgenstein's "Lecture on Ethics," like his *Tractatus*, seemed to its Vienna Circle listeners to breathe the air of a narrowly-conceived, scientifically-inspired, anti-metaphysical positivism. But in fact there was also a 'plus'-factor present that made such a reductive reading mistaken. While at this stage Wittgenstein continued to maintain that talk about ethics involved one in uttering nonsense, the *spirit* of his remarks, his *attitude* to such 'nonsense,' was radically different from that of positivist anti-metaphysicians. For Wittgenstein the language of ethics and its religious counterpart had a 'higher' meaning, an 'absolute value,' in comparison with which it was rather the language of facts that was without ultimate significance, that, viewed *sub specie aeternitatis*, was ultimately 'nonsensical.'

The paradox, the riddle, is that despite the absolute value such experiences had for him both personally and in his work, nonetheless in the early and transitional stages of his work Wittgenstein did not seem open to the possibility of an alternate 'logic' that would have allowed him to put into words their higher significance. Examples, yes, but a logic, no. He seemed still under the influence of the positivism of the time. As we turn to his later work, we will want to see whether he ever did look for or succeed to find a way to solve this apparent riddle. Such a solution would bear directly on our guiding question: what is the relation between the cognitive elements and the emotive or evaluative elements in the experience of the mystery of (the world's) existence?

"Notes on Talks with Wittgenstein."

While these two Notes do not represent any change in the transitional stage of his thought, they contain several remarks that merit attention: in the first, an intriguing reference to Heidegger; in the second, a surprising defense of theological ethics, a re-emphasis of an 'existential' point, and an apparent change in his view of language as a 'cage.'

Notes on remarks of December 30, 1929. The remarks read in their entirety:

> "[To be sure, I can imagine what Heidegger means by being and anxiety.*] Man has the urge to thrust against the limits of language. Think for instance about one's astonishment that anything exists. This astonishment cannot be expressed in the form of a question and there is no answer to it. Anything we can say must, a priori, be only nonsense [*Unsinn*]. Nevertheless we thrust against the limits of language. Kierkegaard, too, recognized this

thrust and even described it in much the same way (as a thrust against paradox). This thrust against the limits of language is *ethics*. I regard it as very important to put an end to all chatter about ethics – whether there is knowledge in ethics, whether there are values, whether the Good can be defined, etc. In ethics, one constantly tries to say something that does not concern and can never concern the essence of the matter. It is a priori certain that, whatever definition one may give of the Good, it is always a misunderstanding to suppose that the formulation corresponds to what one really means. (Moore). But the tendency, the thrust, *points to something.* [St. Augustine knew that already when he said: 'what, you swine, you want not to talk nonsense! Go ahead and talk nonsense, it does not matter!'**]" (Wittgenstein, 1965, 12-13)

The first and last sentences, enclosed in brackets, were omitted in the bilingual version published in *The Philosophical Review*, LXXIV 3-12. Apparently the positivist philosophers of the Vienna Circle with whom these discussions were held were so allergic to anything smacking of metaphysics or theology that they chose to eliminate them from the published version. Philosophy by censorship?

*The Heidegger reference is to *Being and Time* [*Sein und Zeit*] publ. 1927. Perhaps Wittgenstein had in mind a statement such as: "*That in the face of which one has anxiety is Being-in-the-world as such.*" (*BT* 230; emphasis Heidegger's). We will return to discuss the significance of this reference in the Excursus below.

**The Augustine reference is to a passage in Book I of the *Confessions* which, according to Monk, Wittgenstein was often fond of quoting. Interestingly, however, in his remarks here he has altered it. The original ran: "Yet woe betide those who are silent about you! For even those who are most gifted with speech cannot find words to describe you." In conversation with his former student and friend, Miles Drury, he preferred to render it still another way: "And woe to those who say nothing concerning thee just because the chatterboxes talk a lot of nonsense." Monk comments: "These free translations, even if they fail to capture Augustine's intended meaning, certainly capture Wittgenstein's view. One should put a stop to the nonsense of chatterboxes, but that does not mean that one should refuse to talk nonsense itself. Everything, as always, depends on the spirit in which one does it." (For the above, Monk, 282.) For 'spirit' one could substitute 'attitude.' As Monk observes: "St. Augustine, Heidegger, Kierkegaard – these are not names one expects to hear mentioned in conversations with the Vienna Circle – except as targets of abuse" (Monk, 283). Apparently the elisions suggest that if you do not want to talk about them, you simply omit them – a perverse use of Wittgenstein's "Whereof one cannot speak, thereof one must be silent."

Apart from the comment on Heidegger which introduces these remarks and the passage from Augustine which concludes them, a framing which apparently once again went over the heads of his positivist hearers but which should alert us, the most interesting thing about the passage for our inquiry is Wittgenstein's linking of the astonishment that anything exists – i.e., the first example of an experience of the Ethical or of absolute value which we already encountered in the "Lecture on Ethics" – with the explicit statement that such an experience or awareness "cannot be expressed in the form of a question and there is no answer to it." In other words, though Wittgenstein does not say so – but as we can, making use of his distinction – the Why question is a question in an 'absolute' sense which, if taken as a question in a 'relative' sense, cannot be asked and cannot be answered. Saying this is simply to make – to paraphrase Wittgenstein – an *apriori* comment on the 'grammar' of the expression of such astonishment. The Why question is, in a 'relative' sense, 'nonsense,' and yet it reflects 'the urge to thrust against the limits of ['relative'] language. It is a thrust against – to use Kierkegaard's logical term for it – 'paradox.' That logical thrust against the limits of relative, fact-stating language is *ethics*. The problem is that misunderstanding inevitably arises when this 'grammatical' – i.e., *logical* – distinction between the relative and absolute uses of terms is elided, so that philosophers start talking a lot of nonsense about ethical knowledge, values, definitions of the good, etc. But philosophical analysis that fails to observe this logical distinction does not reach to 'the [absolute] essence of the matter.' It is therefore 'apriori certain' that whatever they say about such matters will fail to express 'what one really means.' The paradox is that nevertheless such language really does '*point to something*'[*deutet auf etwas*]. But what is that 'something'? What is that 'essence of the matter'? What is it that one 'really means'? The riddle, the mystery, remains.

Notes on talks December 17, 1930.

Wittgenstein's comments are grouped by the editors into three parts. As each raises important issues for our inquiry, we shall look at them in turn.

On Schlick's Ethics: "Schlick says that theological ethics contains two conceptions of the essence of the Good. According to the more superficial interpretation, the Good is good because God wills it; according to the deeper interpretation, God wills the Good because it is good. I think that the first conception is the deeper one: Good is what God orders. For this cuts off the path to any and every explanation "why" it is good, while the second conception is precisely the superficial, the rationalistic one, which proceeds as if what is good could still be given some foundation. The first conception says clearly that the essence of the Good has nothing to do with facts and therefore cannot be explained by any proposition. If any proposition expresses just what I mean, it is: Good is what God orders." (Wittgenstein, 1965, 15)

This is a highly interesting but perhaps problematic way for Wittgenstein to defend his notion of Ethics as a concern with that which is of 'absolute' value. Wittgenstein's reply to Schlick certainly carries an unexpected shock value. It harks back to the famous discussion in Plato's *Euthyphro* where Socrates asks Euthyphro, a pious believer in the gods and by profession an interpreter of religion, what we might call a theologian, "Is that which is holy (or pious, Grk: *hosion*) holy because the gods approve it (or love it, Grk: *phileitai*), or do they approve (love) it because it is holy?" (Plato, *Euthyphro*, 10a) Though Plato's little dialogue ends inconclusively, the clear implication is that "Socrates" (Plato) would agree with Schlick, that the ethical content of religion can be understood in terms of a rational (not 'rationalistic') ethics. This appears to leave Wittgenstein saddled with Euthyphro's confused and indefensible position. What Wittgenstein wishes to argue here is clear enough. He wants to say, consistent with his views, that providing a rational explanation or foundation for a value which is 'absolute,' that transcends the realm of factual knowledge, is to mistake ethics for something it is not. And yet his equation of 'Good' with what 'God' orders itself appears to rest the absolute imperative of ethics on an absolute indicative (God, the ultimate Fact). This seems to entail the ultimate *irrationalism* of saying that whatever God wills, goes. Does he really want to say that ethics is non-rational? trans-rational? 'outside' or at the 'boundaries' of rationality? Here the term 'God' is indeed operating 'absolutely,' but in a different sense, namely, in a linguistic vacuum, abstractly (as is often the case in such philosophical disputes), apart from any context of its actual religious use. In his *Lecture on Ethics*, however, Wittgenstein presented his case more concretely, finding in examples of religious language taken from the biblical tradition analogies to what he meant by experiences of absolute value. Here we see once again the tension in this transitional stage of his thinking – between his narrow, 'logicist' view of language in the Tractatus and the broader, more pluralistic view of language (of logic and 'rationality') that begin to emerge at this time.

Value: "Is value a particular state of mind? Or a form inhering in certain data of consciousness? My answer is: Whatever one said to me, I would reject it; not indeed because the explanation is false but because it is an *explanation*.... At the end of my lecture on ethics, I spoke in the first person. I believe that is quite essential. Here nothing more can be established, I can only appear as a person speaking for myself." (Wittgenstein, 1965, 15-16; emphasis Wittgenstein's)

This is another interesting and at first glance puzzling set of remarks. The first part repeats his insistence upon the clear distinction between ethical propositions and factual propositions, in this case, propositions of psychology about 'states of mind' or 'data of consciousness.' But he then seems to turn around and link ethical propositions to psychological propositions that refer to himself – 'in the first person,' 'as a person speaking for myself.' What is more he declares this link to be 'quite essential.' This introduces, or rather as he says, repeats a point he made already in the Lecture on Ethics where he said of his example of an experience of absolute value that 'this is an entirely personal matter.' How to reconcile this apparent inconsistency? Perhaps he is alluding to the doctrine in the *Tractatus* -- and in more expanded form in his *Notebooks 1914-1916* – of the transcendental ('non-psychological,' 'philosophical,' 'metaphysical') subject of the ethical (*Tract.* 5.641, 6.423) as distinguished from the subject of empirical psychology. Possibly. But his repeated use of the word 'personal' suggests he is eschewing any Schopenhauerian doctrine and using the word in a more 'existential' or first-person, autobiographical sense. As he says, "I can only appear as a person speaking for myself." If so, and if this is not to be an inconsistency in his argument, then it points to the need to rethink the basis of his remarks about the ethical. Could he be moving here toward a more 'behavioral' or 'anthropological' understanding of the language of the ethical? What would this mean for the 'absolute' or *a priori* distinction he makes between the language of fact and language of value?

Religion: "Is speech [*Reden*] essential for religion? I can quite well imagine a religion in which there are no doctrines, and hence nothing is said. Obviously the essence of religion can have nothing to do with the fact that speech occurs–or rather: if speech does occur, this itself is a component of religious behavior not a theory. Therefore nothing turns on whether the words are true, false, or nonsensical. Neither are religious utterances *figurative*, for else they should be also expressible in prose. Thrusting against the limits of language? Language is not a cage. I can only say: I don't belittle this tendency; I take my hat off to it. And here it is essential that this is not a sociological description but that I speak *for myself.* For me the facts are unimportant. But what men mean when they say that '*The world is there*' lies close to my heart." (Wittgenstein, 1965, 16, his emphases)

Once again a fascinating set of remarks –for several reasons. Remember, they come a year after the earlier conversation and after the "Lecture on Ethics." Here we begin to see more clearly the sense in which his thinking is beginning to go through a transition. Some of his remarks seem to undo the proscriptions against ethical propositions he laid down in the Tractatus and repeated in the first conversation and even continued in the "Lecture on Ethics." The implications for his emerging post-Tractarian work are accordingly significant.

First and perhaps most striking, he now rejects the notion that language is a 'cage.' This seems to imply that the language of ethics and religion does not involve thrusting against the 'limits' of language, or if it does, it does not for that reason end up speechless, imprisoned as in a cage. If so, then perhaps the languages of ethics and religion have distinctive logics of their own other than the logic of fact-stating propositions. This new possibility is reinforced by his claim, again contrary to what he said in his previous conversation or in the Lecture, that religious utterances are not figurative (similes, metaphors, etc.), because, as he says, otherwise they could be reformulated in fact-stating prose. Perhaps a better way to state it is this: It is not that much religious language is not figurative, for in fact it is. It is rather that it is a mistake to think figurative speech is nonsensical unless it can be paraphrased in non-figurative terms. I think we see here further evidence that Wittgenstein is moving away from a

Tractarian view of language to the more pluralistic view of language that will characterize his later work.

Further evidence may be seen in his answer to the opening question: Is speech even necessary for religion? His answer, another shocker for anyone accustomed to thinking of religion in terms of the scriptural religions of the West, is that it is not. 'Obviously,' he says, speech has 'nothing to do with' the 'essence' of religion. But why? How is that so 'obvious'? Very simple. Because the 'essence' of religion – and we can imagine that he would say the same about the essence of ethics – is a matter of 'behavior,' of religious praxis, not 'theory,' e.g., 'doctrines.' And for religious praxis 'nothing turns on' whether the words that may (or may not) accompany that activity are cognitively 'true, false, or nonsensical.' Wittgenstein's new pronouncement is indeed shocking. Just when it appeared he opposed the reduction of religious speech to the something it is not, namely, non-figurative speech, he now seems to turn around and reduce it instead to something else, namely, a 'component' of *behavior*, speech as a kind of activity, not a statement of religious truth but something more like an expression of strong emotion, perhaps of a feeling of astonishment or guilt. This, as we will see, is a charge that will continue to follow him as he moves in the later stages of his work. Has he rescued the language of religion from reduction to statements of fact, only to assign it the 'reductive' function of expressing pious feelings or the 'speech-activity' of giving utterance to religious ritual? If so, how would his emerging position differ from the emotivist understanding of such language by his positivist-minded listeners? Further, by reducing the meaning of religious language to a mere accompaniment or expression of religious practice, is he not reducing the expression of absolute value to a psychological (or 'anthropological') matter after all?

It is after Wittgenstein concluded his shocking reinterpretation of the 'sense' of ethical and religious propositions previously held to be 'nonsensical' that Waismann, his interlocutor, perhaps shrewdly grasping the 'positivist' implications of these remarks, asked him: "Is the existence of the world *connected* with the ethical?" (my emphasis). Waismann's question goes to the heart of our inquiry. Is there a *link* between the cognitive aspect of the mystery of (the world's) existence and the emotive or evaluative aspects that are said to 'accompany' it? If so, what is its nature? If we can answer that, then perhaps we can understand as well the connection between the first experience of absolute value Wittgenstein cited – astonishment at the world's existence – and the second and third experiences – the feeling of absolute safety and the feeling of being guilty. This is a shrewd question, because if Wittgenstein says that there is a link, he would seem to be admitting there is some sort of *cognitive* dimension to ethical propositions after all, having just dismissed all such claims.

However, Wittgenstein's answer is equally shrewd if not evasive: "Men have felt a connection here and have expressed it in this way: God the Father created the world, while God the Son (or the Word proceeding from God) is the ethical. That men have first divided the Godhead and then united it, points to there being a connection here" (Wittgenstein, 1965, 16). To this fundamental question he chooses to make yet another analogy between the philosophical terms of the question and an 'answer' drawn from the figurative language of theology. Yes, there is a 'connection' between the 'that' of the world's existence and our ethical responses to that mystery, but perhaps it can only be expressed in the figurative language of doctrinal theology, not the 'nonsensical' propositions of metaphysics to whose terms, as the Tractatus stated, no meaning can be given.

What is not clear with this answer is whether, at this transitional stage in his thinking, Wittgenstein has abandoned the 'ontological' sense of the mystical found in the Tractatus for a kind of 'anthropological' understanding of ethical and religious language which sees it as the linguistic 'component' of behavior describable in the empirical language of the psychologist or sociologist of ethics or religion. From paying the price of silence in order to protect the reality and truth of that 'whereof one cannot speak,' we appear now to have reduced that truth and reality to the 'chatterboxes who talk a lot of nonsense' of whom St. Augustine spoke. When in 1929 Wittgenstein returned to Cambridge from his self-imposed exile from philosophy "prepared to overhaul all the conclusions he had reached up to now – prepared not only to consider new ways of thinking, but even new ways of thought" (Monk, 263), was *this* what he had in mind? If so, we may have to look beyond Wittgenstein for help with our guiding question.

In the meantime, however, perhaps we can gleam hints of another possibility by looking at Wittgenstein's few comments on some remarks of the 'existentialist ontology' of Heidegger.

Being and Anxiety. As noted above, Wittgenstein began his remarks in 1929 to the positivist-minded members of the Vienna Circle with the provocative statement: "To be sure, I can imagine what Heidegger means by being and anxiety" (Wittgenstein, 1965, 12). The reference is to Heidegger's treatment of these notions in *Sein und Zeit*. There is no record of whether Wittgenstein ever read Heidegger's book or whether he was simply responding to a quotation from the latter's work cited by one of his listeners, committed anti-metaphysicians all, for whom Heidegger was their favorite whipping boy. The statement to which Wittgenstein was referring was presumably the following:*"That in the face of which one has anxiety is Being-in-the-world as such"* (*BT*, 230; emphasis Heidegger's). The rest of the passage is revealing, if only as an indication of how Wittgenstein's remarks in the *Tractatus* and the "Lecture on Ethics" could be interpreted in another way. In any case, it will be suggestive for our later discussion. Heidegger continues: "That in the face of which one has anxiety is not an entity within-the-world. In that in the face of which one has anxiety, the 'It is nothing and nowhere' becomes manifest. The obstinacy of the "nothing and nowhere within-the-world" means as a phenomenon that *the world as such is that in the face of which one has anxiety*. The utter insignificance which makes itself known in the "nothing and nowhere," does not signify that the world is absent, but tells us that entities within-the-world are of so little importance in themselves that on the basis of this *insignificance* of what is within-the-world, the world in its worldhood is all that still obtrudes itself" (*BT*, 231; emphasis Heidegger's).

Later Wittgenstein: Lectures on Religious Belief; Culture and Values

Finally, in our consideration of whether Wittgenstein's philosophy can contribute to the resolution of our question concerning the cognitive and emotive or ethical dimensions of the Why question, we turn to his later work beginning in the mid-1930's, in particular the collection, *Lectures and Conversations on Aesthetics, Psychology & Religious Belief*, based on notes taken by students from 1938 through 1946 (published posthumously in 1966), and remarks scattered over the entire period of his later work (1929-1951) collected in *Culture and Values*, along with comments in his unpublished work cited in Monk's biography of Wittgenstein, *The Duty of Genius*.

Lectures on Religious Belief (1938)

Unlike the *Lecture on Ethics*, where he reinterpreted traditional religious doctrines in terms of experiences of absolute value – wonder at the miracle of existence, feelings of absolute safety or absolute guilt – or his subsequent comments to members of the Vienna Circle which appeared to further reduce religious doctrines to dispensable epiphenomena of religious practice, in his *Lectures on Religious Belief* (1938), as the title indicates, he returns to an analysis of religious doctrines themselves – in particular, his usual trio of examples: belief in the Last Judgment, the existence of God, and the immortality of soul – beliefs which at least traditionally have been thought to provide the intellectual foundation and cognitive support for religious values, religious experiences, and religious practice. At first glance, therefore, one might think to find here some Wittgensteinian suggestions for addressing the relation of the cognitive to the emotive or ethical dimensions of the Why question as well.

From the outset, however, it is clear that nothing of the sort if about to happen. Instead, Wittgenstein appears to have progressed even further in his new, "anthropological" approach to analyzing such beliefs and consequently to have moved even further away from any considerations of the cognitive or metaphysical dimensions of religious language. The basic thrust of his remarks, regardless of the religious 'doctrine' he chooses to analyze, is that religious belief is 'belief' in name only, that it shares nothing with our normal or ordinary sense of evidentially-based belief other than the word itself. In fact, one would be justified in thinking that he would say of the word 'belief' in the sphere of religion what he said elsewhere of other philosophically misleading concepts: "Sometimes an expression has to be withdrawn from language and sent for cleaning – then it can be put back into circulation" (Wittgenstein, 1984, 39). We might view his remarks in these lectures about the distinctively *religious* use of the word 'belief' as at least an initial attempt at such linguistic cleanup work

So how is it, then, with *religious* belief? In what respects is it not a matter of belief in any ordinary sense of the word, and to the extent it is not, then what is it a matter of? Does it have some alternative kind of sense, or does it, as his remarks earlier in the "Lecture on Ethics" sometimes seem to suggest, does it lack sense altogether? Is *religious* 'belief' just nonsense dressed up to look like belief?

Wittgenstein says that a closer inspection of religious belief shows a number of ways in which it not only diverges from ordinary belief, but is clearly not a case of belief at all in any of the usual senses of the term. The religious believer "has what you might call an unshakeable belief. It will show, not by reasoning or appeal to ordinary grounds for belief, but rather by regulating for in all his life... the man risks things on account of it which he would not do on things which are by far better established for him." Further, "he will treat this belief as extremely well-established, and in another way as not well-established at all.... this belief does not rest on the facts on which our ordinary every day beliefs normally do rest" (Wittgenstein, 1984, 54).

Here we see the basic outlines of Wittgenstein's understanding of the nature of religious belief and its characteristic difference from ordinary belief. Religious belief is subjectively "unshakeable." It does not involve "reasoning" based on appeals to objective "grounds." Rather, it "regulates" one's whole life in such a way that one would "risk" one's life on the basis of it in ways one would not do for beliefs based on empirical evidence. Wittgenstein summarizes the difference between the two kinds of belief: "How should we compare beliefs with each other? What would it mean to compare them? First, what you *say* won't be taken as the measure for the firmness of a belief. But, for instance, what *risks* would you take? An entirely different way of comparing beliefs is seeing what sorts of *grounds* he will give." (Wittgenstein, 1984, emphasis mine)

Wittgenstein goes on to say: "these controversies look quite different from any normal controversies. Reasons look entirely different from normal reasons. They are, in a way, quite inconclusive. The point is that if there were evidence, this would in fact destroy the whole business. We don't talk about hypothesis, or about high probability. Nor about knowing. In religious discourse we use such expressions as: 'I believe that so and so will happen,' and use them differently to the way in which we use them in science. Although, there is a great temptation to think we do. Because we do talk of evidence, and do talk of evidence by experience" (Wittgenstein, 1984, 56-57).

It would seem, in other words, that while religious beliefs do involve reasons, reasoning, of some sort, and do involve appeals to experiential evidence of some sort, such reasons are not "reasons" of any normal sort, nor can such experiences be considered "evidence" in any normal sense without, he says, "destroying the whole business." These remarks need further unpacking. Distinguishing in these ways between the two kinds of belief, reasoning and evidence, does not yet entirely clarify the matter. We want to know more clearly what the nature of these concepts is in their religious use.

The problem in gaining further clarity, however, is that, as Wittgenstein goes on to point out, "These people think entirely differently. Yet, so far, you can't say they believe different things. If you say: 'Do you believe the opposite?'–you can call it believing the opposite, but it is entirely different from what we would normally call believing the opposite... there is this extraordinary use of the word 'believe'. One talks of believing and at the same time doesn't use 'believe' as one does ordinarily" (Wittgenstein, 1984, 55, 59) Further, "they don't treat this as a matter of reasonability. You may say they reason wrongly. In certain cases you would say they reason wrongly, meaning they contradict us. In other cases you would say they don't reason at all, or 'It is an entirely different kind of reasoning.' You could also say that where we are reasonable, they are not reasonable – meaning they don't use *reason* here" (Wittgenstein, 1984 58).

This only raises new questions. What is this entirely different way of "thinking" that religious believers are said to practice? In what sense do religious believers believe opposite things, or do they not insofar as it involves an entirely different sense of "believing the opposite"? Do they use reason or do they not? Is that they use reason wrongly, or is that they use an entirely different kind of reasoning? Wittgenstein's remarks all seem very puzzling. Sometimes it seems as if Wittgenstein himself finds it equally puzzling.

Perhaps we can get further clarity if we look at what Wittgenstein views as the implications of these remarks for trying to understand the meaning of such religious doctrines as beliefs in the Last Judgement, the existence of God, or the immortality of the soul.

Of belief in *the Last Judgment* Wittgenstein observes, "one would be reluctant to say: 'These people rigorously hold the opinion (or view) that there is a *Last Judgement*.' 'Opinion' sounds queer. It is for this reason that different words are used: 'dogma', 'faith.'" Here he introduces new terms into the discussion. But does this clarify matters or only increase the need for linguistic therapy? Belief in the Last Judgment does not involve "talk about hypothesis, or about high probability. Nor about knowing. In religious discourse we use such expressions as: 'I believe that so and so will happen,' and use them differently to the way in which we use them in science" (Wittgenstein, 1984, 57).

So what then does it mean when someone says they believe in a 'Last Judgment,' that a Last Judgment "will happen"? Wittgenstein: "No induction. Terror. That is, as it were, part of the substance of the belief... What is the criterion for meaning something different? Not only what he takes as evidence for it, but also how he reacts, that he is in terror, etc." (Wittgenstein, 1984, 56, 62). Terror in the face of one's death? Because of what? Guilt? We are reminded of Wittgenstein's third example of an 'absolute' experience in his "Lecture on Ethics": "A third experience of the same kind is that of feeling guilty and again this was described by the phrase that God disapproves of our conduct" (Wittgenstein, 1965, 10). If belief in the event of a Last Judgment is the subjective expression an absolute guilt, then empirically-based evidence to the contrary, helpfully provided by, say, one's therapist, would not only be irrelevant, it would, as Wittgenstein says, "destroy the whole business." Here perhaps we have our first clue to the alternative nature of religious belief and something that distinguishes it from normal belief: the experience of "terror, etc." – and not just any fear, but angst, dread, terror in an 'absolute' sense. Wittgenstein has read his Kierkegaard.

Of belief in *the existence of God* Wittgenstein says, "If the question arises as to the existence of a god or God, it plays an entirely different role to that of the existence of any person or object I ever heard of.... If I even vaguely remember what I was taught about God, I might say: 'Whatever believing in God may be, it can't be believing in something we can test, or find means of testing'" (Wittgenstein, 1984, 59-60) Belief in God, as a religious belief, once again involves an "extraordinary" sense of believing. Nor can it be acquired in the way of ordinary beliefs. "If we ever saw this (Michelangelo's painting), we certainly wouldn't think this the Deity. The picture has to be used in an entirely different way.... You could imagine that religion was taught by means of these pictures" (Wittgenstein, 1984, 63).

We note two things here. The practical "role" of belief in the existence of God in one's life is once again "entirely different" from the role played by the objects of ordinary belief, and second, this role is often conveyed by pictures of one kind or another that express a distinctively religious feeling or experience. We are reminded here of Wittgenstein's first example of an 'absolute' or 'ethical' life-value in his "Lecture on Ethics": "When we speak of God and that he sees everything and when we kneel and pray to him all our terms and actions seem to be parts of a great and elaborate allegory... But this allegory also describes the experience which I have just referred to, [namely], if I want to fix my mind on what I mean by absolute or ethical value it always happens that the idea of one particular experience presents itself to me which therefore is, in a sense, my experience par excellence. I believe the best way of describing it is to say that when I have it I wonder at the existence of the world. And then I am inclined to use such phrases as 'how extraordinary that anything should exist' or 'how extraordinary that the world should exist.' (Wittgenstein, 1965, 8, 10). This "is, I believe, exactly what people were referring to when they said that God had created the world" (Wittgenstein, 1965, 10). And so here perhaps we have another clue to the alternative nature of religious belief and that distinguishes it from normal belief – the experience of 'absolute' wonder – again, not wonder that the world is *how* it is but *that* it is at all.

Finally, to illustrate the nature of belief in *the immortality of the soul*, Wittgenstein tells the story of "a great writer [who] said that, when he was a boy, his father set him a task, and he suddenly felt that nothing, not even death, could take away the responsibility [in doing this task]; this was his duty to do, and that even death couldn't stop it being his duty. He said that this was, in a way, a proof of the immortality of the soul – because if this lives on [the responsibility won't die.]" Wittgenstein comments: "The idea is given by what we call the proof. Well, if this is the idea, [all right]" (Wittgenstein, 1984, 70). While Wittgenstein did not cite this absolute sense of duty as one of the exemplary ethical values in his Lecture on Ethics, it is clear from his remarks elsewhere in *Culture and Values* and as reflected in the title of Monk's biography, "The Duty of Genius," that the sense of duty as an absolute value was something Wittgenstein himself personally felt. Here too, therefore, we have another aspect of the nature of religious belief distinguishing it from a belief in duties relative to factually-specifiable obligations.

A variation of belief in immortality of the soul is *belief in life after death*, a belief grounded for Christians in the doctrine of *the Resurrection*. Wittgenstein asks: "How am I to find out whether this proposition is to be regarded as an empirical proposition–'you'll see your dead friend again'?" Once again the criterion for what the believer means in this case too is "not only what he takes as evidence for it, but also how he reacts, that he is in terror, etc." (Wittgenstein, 1984, 62). In this case, however, instead of terror we might see in the "etc." the reality of love, an 'absolute' love whose power is stronger, more lasting than death itself. The words "not only" do give pause here. We might be tempted to think Wittgenstein is leaving room for some sort of objective factor in the case of religious belief. However, in keeping with the rest of his remarks, we should perhaps see in this simply a reminder that whereas ordinary belief involves the citing of evidence, religious belief does not, being grounded rather in something deeper and more primordial – what Pascal meant when he said "the heart has reasons that reason cannot know."

What should we conclude, then, of Wittgenstein's analysis of religious belief? Should we say, with the positivist critic and his opposite number, the literal-minded believer, that as regards religious belief "Wittgenstein is trying to undermine reason"? As so often, Wittgenstein's answer seems designed to provoke further thinking: "this wouldn't be false. This is actually where such questions arise" (6 Wittgenstein, 1984, 4).

Before we try to evaluate what this place might be "where such questions arise," let us review where we have come so far, where we stand. Wittgenstein distinguishes between two different kinds of belief/ believing, ordinary and religious. The former involves appeal to empirical evidence, the latter expresses a life-value. Thus belief in the existence of God expresses wonder at the miracle of existence; belief in the Last Judgment expresses a sense of profound guilt and anxiety; belief in the immortality of the soul or life after death expresses a feeling of safety no matter what happens in this life. In other words, what matters in the case of religious belief is not the content of the expression, what it is 'about,' but rather the fact of the expression itself – like a gasp of amazement or a cry from the heart – as the expression of absolute value, an attitude toward life itself, toward our ('my') existence in the world as a whole. In that sense it could be said to express an 'metaphysical' value, a 'transcendental' value that arises at the limits of language where the sense of the mystical also occurs – that place where, as Wittgenstein says, "such questions arise" or are silenced. If one rejects such religious beliefs, he says, one is not expressing a disagreement about matters of fact, one is not "believing the opposite" in that sense. Rather one is saying that such language does not "do" anything for one, that the value or attitude it expresses is not a 'belief' one shares.

Now there is a fundamental objection to Wittgenstein's analysis of religious belief, one shared alike by his positivist-minded critics and their opposite number, literal-minded believers. It is this. Wittgenstein's "anthropological" (the term is his) analysis of the form and function of religious beliefs rejects any attempt to provide a factual (whether empirical or metaphysical) reference for the 'objects' of religious belief. In fact it bears a striking resemblance to the movement of "demythologizing" and "existential" reinterpretation of theological doctrines that was taking place at the same time on the European continent. Like its Continental counterpart, Wittgenstein's "anthropological" reinterpretation seems a clear case of reductionism. If so, how can Wittgenstein avoid the charge of having relapsed into a version of Vienna Circle positivism, of a view of religion as simply "morality tinged with emotion"? Absent any transcendent referent, Wittgenstein's "anthropological" analysis of the emotive dimension accompanying, perhaps even motivating, religious belief amounts to nothing more than an exercise in the empirical psychology of religion, something Wittgenstein himself professed to abhor and certainly something no self-professed 'believer' would accept as reflecting his or her faith.

Even as sympathetic a commentator on (and former student of) Wittgenstein as Iris Murdoch in her richly textured magnum opus, *Metaphysics as a Guide to Morals*, appears to endorse this critique: "the *Lebensformen*, or 'language game,' contextual argument is, in my opinion, a wrong turn. It ushers in the 'soft' idea, already at large in both theology and ethics, that there is something called 'religious language' which is 'expressive' not 'descriptive.' This path favors structuralism, existentialism, and a renewed life for emotive theories of religion... This escape from the ubiquitous strictness of 'logic,' from the postulated unique and absolute nature of God (or Good) into the easier world of language-games and local meanings is a perilous excursion, not a solution" (Murdoch, 413). Murdoch continues: "Here, to speak of 'religious language' as something specialized, supposed to be expressive rather than referential, is to separate religion from the truth-seeking struggle of the whole of life... Praise and worship are not just expressive attitudes, they arise in very various cognitive contexts and are themselves a grasp of reality. In prayer we wait for God (or for the spirit and light of goodness) to be made manifest." (Murdoch, 418)

In other words, by this turn from the metaphysical 'asceticism' of the Tractatus or even the 'absolute' values of the "Lectures on Ethics," Wittgenstein in his *Lectures on Religious Belief* opened himself to critics, theist and atheist alike, who argue that this (alleged) view of religion is both 'empty' and 'blind.' Wittgenstein's new, "anthropological" view lacks the 'external' referent that gives traditional religious belief its metaphysical and theological substance and point. To paraphrase Kant's famous distinction – concepts without intuition are empty, intuition without concepts is blind. In other words, while it may be granted that a merely external (intellectual, 'proof'-based) faith without internal (emotive, existential) substance is 'empty,' nonetheless Wittgenstein's "anthropological" analysis, lacking any 'external' (metaphysical) reference, is 'blind.' To put this in another way, drawing on Wittgenstein's own 'linguistic turn,' the claim being made by the critic here is that what gives expressive meaning to the similes, pictures, symbols, doctrines, language etc. of religious belief is that these linguistic and non-linguistic means of expression are parasitic for their meaning on their ordinary, non-religious use. Absent that, religious belief lacks any basis in reality beyond the feelings of the believer. Of course this poses no problem for the atheist, who always thought as much, but the atheist would say that believers would never accept such a reductive reading of their faith.

Can anything be said in defense of Wittgenstein, or if not, can we at least extract from his comments elsewhere the elements of a possible defense of a 'Wittgensteinian' view? In fact it can be argued that there is if not an explicit at least an implicit metaphysical underpinning to his (apparently) "reductive" or "anthropological" analysis of religious belief. It is only implicit, however, and to that extent we have to look beyond his "Lectures on Religious Belief" to other remarks he has made for a "Wittgensteinian" solution to our guiding question. For this we turn to his comments collected in *Culture and Value* and others contained in Monk's biography, reflections that extend from the period just before the "Lectures on Religious Belief" up to the end of his life some fourteen years later. Here we may be able to shed further light on his views on religion from which we then might be able to extrapolate what a 'Wittgensteinian' answer would look like regarding the relation of the cognitive and emotive aspects of the Why question.

It has been said not only others but also by Wittgenstein himself that while he never committed himself to any formal religion, he saw every problem from a religious point of view. More than that. Throughout his career as a thinker he in fact continued to wrestle explicitly with ethical and religious dilemmas in his own life, values and attitudes reflected not only in the biblical language and doctrines he repeatedly returned to in his "Lecture on Ethics" and "Lectures on Religious Belief," but also, as we have already seen, as far back as his *Notebooks 1914-1916* and reflected in the last propositions of the *Tractatus*. These personal struggles motivated his philosophical reflections which, in turn, gave an intellectual foundation to his analyses of ethics and religion. His life-long struggle to resolve these existential and philosophical tensions may perhaps be seen as a post-Kantian, Kierkegaard-inflected version of Anselm's faith seeking understanding.

In highlighting some of his scattered comments on ethics and religion we should see them as containing several different but conceptually interrelated sorts of reflection. Some suggest a metaphysical foundation for his views on ethics and religion, some reflect his own personal struggles in relation to that ethico-religious absolute, and some indicate what he thought was required if those struggles were to be resolved.

Thus, in *Culture and Value* we find the following comments. The first two come from the transitional period of the "Lecture on Ethics." In them we hear clear echoes, if not the actual language, of the Tractatus (emphases mine): "...there is a way of capturing the world *sub specie aeterni*..." (Wittgenstein, 1984, 5). Again: "Perhaps what is *inexpressible* (what I find *mysterious* and am not able to express) is *the background* against which whatever I could express has its *meaning*" (Wittgenstein, 1984, 16).

The view of the world 'sub specie aeterni' refers of course to what in the *Tractatus* he called 'the Mystical' and what in the "Lecture on Ethics" he referred to as the experience of wonder – in both cases a reference to the 'extraordinary,' 'absolute' or, we could say, 'metaphysical' fact *that* the world exists rather than nothing at all – in other words, the 'fact' referred to by the Why question itself. But, in light of the criticism of the 'anthropological' turn in his later writings, the question is whether in the *Lectures on Religious Belief* and thereafter Wittgenstein drops his claims on behalf of this 'transcendental' foundation of ethics and religion. To answer that we turn to his comments from 1937 on (in the following cited passages, again the emphases are mine).

In 1937, the year before the "Lectures on Religious Belief," Wittgenstein filled a number of pages with his views on the three topics listed above. If we recall his comments on 'pictures,' one of the most interesting is this: "Religious similes can be said to move on the edge of an *abyss*" (Wittgenstein, 1984, 29). It is not clear whether the 'abyss' referred to is a transcendental, metaphysical abyss, the place where questions arise, or rather run out, or whether it refers to a personal, existential abyss given figurative expression in the language of religion. Probably both, suggesting there is an indissoluble link between them.

In any case, if we look at remarks made in the post-Lectures period up til near the end of his life, it is clear that Wittgenstein had not 'reduced' his view of ethical and religious reality to nothing more than a research topic for empirical psychologists. Some of these are embrace the second and third of our topics, but all are grounded in a reference to the first, to something foundational: "But don't we have the feeling that someone who sees no problem in life is blind to something important, even to *the most important thing of all*?" (Wittgenstein, 1984, 27).

For Wittgenstein there is a "problem in life," and it is "the most important thing of all" – the deepest, the most ultimate, it is the 'absolute' ethical and spiritual problems like those he cites in the Lecture on Ethics expressed in the language of religious belief. But, as with those who are tone deaf or blind to art, those who fail to see these problems, or to take them with absolute seriousness, may be said analogously to lack the eyes to see or the ears to hear.

"Religion is, as it were, *the calm bottom of the sea at its deepest point*, which remains calm however high the waves on the surface may be" (Wittgenstein, 1984, 53). For those who have found an answer in religion to the ultimate problem of life, for them it is as if they have plumbed the abyss of life and found at its utmost depth a calmness, "the experience of feeling absolutely safe" no matter what happens, a feeling that "nothing, not even death, could take away."

The problem is that: "One keeps forgetting to go right down to *the foundations*. One doesn't *put the question marks deep enough down*" (Wittgenstein, 1984, 62). "The problems of life are insoluble on the surface and can only be solved *in depth*. They are insoluble in surface dimensions" (Wittgenstein, 1984, 74). "When you are philosophizing you have to descend into *primeval chaos* and *feel at home* there" (Wittgenstein, 1984, 65). Or to vary the spatial metaphor: "Is what I am doing really worth the effort? Yes, but only if *a light shines on it from above*.... And if the light from above is lacking, I can't in any case be more than clever" (Wittgenstein, 1984, 57-58).

To be clever is not to be serious; to be clever is not to be profound; it is not to speak *de profundis*. One must have descended into the chaos of one's life, bottomed out in the abyss, one's cry must have originated from that primeval origin "where such questions arise." Then, if the grace of a light shines in the darkness from above, only then can one begin to understand and speak of the ethico-religious, only then can one give voice to that which is the deepest, the highest, "the most important thing of all."

Is there, then, a religious way of speaking, of seeing, of depicting religious belief? "Is there such a thing as *a metaphysical style* of drawing then? – *"Seen against the background of the eternal,"* you might say" (Wittgenstein, 1984, 75). *"What is eternal and important* is often hidden from a man by an impenetrable veil. He knows: there's something under there, but he cannot *see* it. The veil reflects the daylight" (Wittgenstein, 1984, 80). The light shines from above, but it is deflected by a veil, by a way of seeing that is blind to a religious view of the world, a way of seeing the world as the 'Creation' of God.

"If someone who believes in God looks round and asks 'Where does everything I see come from?,' 'Where does all this come from?,' he is *not* craving for a (causal) explanation; and his question gets its point from being the expression of a certain craving. He is, namely, expressing an attitude to all explanations. – But how is this manifested in his life. The attitude that's in question is that of taking a certain matter seriously and then, beyond a certain point, no longer regarding it as serious, but maintaining that *something else is even more important"* (Wittgenstein, 1984, 85).

The cosmologist asks about 'Creation' (the Why question) as if expecting a scientific or metaphysical answer. But for the religious believer the answer, "God," is not a causal explanation at all. Rather it is the expression of a belief that transcends all such "explanations," that no longer takes that approach seriously because it expresses the insight that the word "God" is a *pointer* to "something else [that] is even more important" – something, as Iris Murdoch says commenting on these passages, 'seen against the background of the eternal' in which the moral and mystical are fundamental (Murdoch, 422).

Murdoch's reference to the "moral and mystical' takes us back to the *Tractatus* where Wittgenstein, alluding to the matter at stake in these competing ways of seeing the world – the "something else even more important," "the most important thing of all" – said: "If good or bad willing changes the world, it can only change the limits of the world, not the fact; not the things that can be expressed in language. In brief, the world must thereby become quite another. It must so to speak wax or wane as a whole. The world of the happy is quite another than that of the unhappy" (*Tract.*, 6.43). What is amazing about this transformation of "the world" when the veil is removed, when one sees the mystery of the world's existence with the eyes of 'the happy,' that is, the eyes of faith, "what is incomprehensible is that *nothing*, and yet *everything*, has changed." (cited in Monk, 533; Wittgenstein's emphasis)

In the personal comments in his notebooks, in his letters to his friends, and in and between the lines of his lectures on ethics and religion Wittgenstein recorded his struggles with his inability to transform his own life from that of "the unhappy" to that of "the happy." He understood what was at stake in the issue of religious belief – the possibility of 'eternal' or 'absolute' happiness. He respected those who had been able to make the leap of faith. But he knew he had not experienced that light from above, that transformation himself. As he said of his own work: "What good does all my talent do me if, at heart, I am unhappy? What help is it to me to solve philosophical problems, if I cannot settle the chief and most important thing?'" (remark in April 1947; cited in Monk, 507). We can divine from his foregoing remarks what for Wittgenstein that most important thing was, what it was that was pointed to by "a certain attitude," by the attitude of "faith." I think we can be safe in saying, with his biographer, it was: salvation, redemption, "reconciliation with God" (cf. Monk, 573).

In a lengthy and remarkable passage from his comments in the year before his "Lectures on Religious Belief" Wittgenstein confessed:

> "We are in a sort of hell where we can do nothing but dream, roofed in, as it were, and cut off from heaven. But if I am to be REALLY saved, – what I need is *certainty* – not wisdom, dreams, or speculation – and this certainty is faith. And faith is faith in what is needed by my heart, my soul, not my speculative intelligence. For it is my soul

with its passions, as it were with its flesh and blood, that has to be saved, not my abstract mind... What combats doubt is, as it were, *redemption*. Holding fast to *this* must be holding fast to that belief. So what that means is: first you must be redeemed and hold on to your redemption (keep hold of your redemption) – then you will see that you are holding fast to this belief. So this can come about only if you no longer rest your weight on the earth but suspend yourself from heaven. Then everything will be different and it will be 'no wonder' if you can do things that you cannot do now. (A man who is suspended looks the same as one who is standing, but the interplay of forces within him is nevertheless quite different, so that he can act quite differently than can a standing man.)" (Wittgenstein, 1984, 33).

Reading these words it is all the more poignant that Wittgenstein's reported last words on his death bed were: "Tell them I've had a wonderful life."

Conclusion

We turned to Wittgenstein's reflections on the experience of the mystery of the world's existence to see if we could find there a framework and analysis that provided a satisfactory philosophical answer to the question of the mystery of existence, that gave an *integrated* account of the cognitive and emotive elements of this awareness. We noted that such a quest seemed doomed at the outset because of Wittgenstein's refusal, both early and late in his career, to offer a metaphysical explanation or indeed anything like a systematic philosophical account of either the fact that the world exists or of what our existential response to that fact could or should be. And in fact we have found it to be true that, as Murdoch noted, Wittgenstein "talked in a vaguer and more unsystematic way about religion and even God, sketching both logical arguments and appeals to experience" (Murdoch, 415).

And yet, as we have also seen in the above analysis of his works, from the *Tractatus* through the "Lectures on Religious Belief" and in remarks collected elsewhere, Wittgenstein did have important things to say that bear on the link between the cognitive and emotive (including ethical) aspects of the question of the mystery of (the world's) existence. In particular, we have found clear evidence that those critics are mistaken who claimed to see in the 'anthropological' turn in his later thought a 'reductionism,' the absence or abandonment of his earlier sense of the 'transcendental' foundation of ethics and religion. Indeed of Wittgenstein it can be said, as it was of an earlier unorthodox ethico-religious philosopher, that from beginning to end, both in his work and in his life, he was "ein Gott betrunkener Mensch."

Having noted that, however, can we say that in the body of his work Wittgenstein has given us something more than a "vague and unsystematic" answer to our initial question? Has he provided a clear and coherent account of the link between the "mystical" fact that the world exists, the ethical or existential life-problems that arise vis-a-vis that mystery, and the possible responses, intellectual and moral or religious to those limit-situations? Perhaps not. And yet it seems clear enough that for Wittgenstein there is a distinctively 'ethical' or 'religious' attitude, a 'transcendental' perspective, an 'absolute' mode of experience, that links these various elements. What makes it an 'ethical' or 'religious' is that it mediates between the 'metaphysical' and the 'existential' dimensions of our existence. It is in 'absolute' experiences of the 'ethical' – feelings of wonder, safety, guilt – and the actions which flow from them, it is in 'religious beliefs' and the practices which they embody and which give them meaning, that we find the link between the cognitive and emotive dimensions of the 'question,' between the mystery of the world's and, by extension, the mystery of our own existence. It is awareness of the stunning 'metaphysical' fact that the world exists that gives rise, at the limits of thought, to the 'transcendental' problematic of the 'ethical' or 'religious'– whether one accepts, intellectually and emotionally, the mystery of the world's existence, whether one sees oneself as living in 'the world of the unhappy' or 'the world of the happy,' in the world of the tormented or the world of the redeemed.

True, he does not explain how one is to be or become happy or unhappy, wretched or redeemed. Is it something one can choose by an act of will? He speaks of "good or bad willing" (*Tract.*, 6.43). Is it the result of an existential decision, a 'leap of faith'? Is it or is it not possible to provide a *rational* ground for one's specific emotional, ethical or existential response to one's situation in a world whose existence itself refuses rational explanation? Does that refusal bleed over into our own existence, rendering it too ultimately irrational, 'absurd'? Does he preserve the cognitive 'mystery' of the world's existence at the cost of the rationality of the ethical or religious? Is it finally the case that, as he imagines his critics charging, "Wittgenstein is trying to undermine reason"? He added: "and this wouldn't be false. This is actually where such question arise" (Wittgenstein, 1966, 64).

Precisely! Where then does Wittgenstein leave us in our quest? As a 'metaphysical ascetic' (Hargby), even an 'anti-philosopher' (Badiou), perhaps we should not have expected to find in his work the sort of clear and systematic metaphysics, ethics or religious philosophy that has long been a desideratum of Western philosophy. Perhaps we must be content with the substantial 'hints' he provided us over the long course of his career as a provocative and unorthodox thinker. As we turn to an examination of other philosophers who have addressed our Why question in a more systematic way, we may find that the 'ascetic' or 'anti-philosophical' nature of Wittgenstein's thought, together with the profound nature of his reflections on the ethical and the religious, nevertheless provide us with a helpful benchmark against which to assess the success of their own analyses. If so, for now let us conclude that Wittgenstein, though having advanced us beyond Munitz, has not taken us all the way to the promised land, has left us instead at the edge looking in, yet proves to have laid down some important markers to guide us on the rest of our way.

In continuing our search for an answer to the question about the link between the emotive and cognitive elements in the Why question, we have now considered, in addition to Munitz and Wittgenstein, two other philosophers, John Post and Quentin Smith, who brought a new phenomenological perspective to bear on these matters. Each of these thinkers has assayed to provide a philosophical account of the connection we are seeking. The question that now confronts us is whether the cosmological approach to metaphysics and realist approach to ethics of Post and Smith, or the suggestive but incomplete remarks of Munitz and Wittgesntein, can indeed provide the kind of integrated account we are looking for.

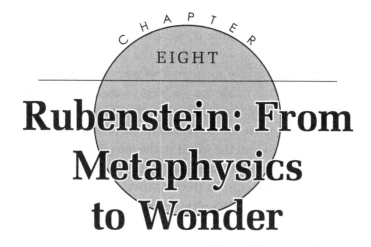
Rubenstein: From Metaphysics to Wonder

Review of Cosmological-Metaphysical Approach to Why Question

As we have argued, the analyses in Chapters I through III of Part One are all sub-types within one way of understanding the Why questions, one that presupposes a cosmological-metaphysical approach to the question. The problem is that while they do try to relate our emotional responses to certain facts, they relate them to facts about the nature and existence of the world, not the fact that *something*, a seemingly indeterminate That, exists, but facts, a determinate What, about the *world* that exists. But the That is not a fact in or of the world, nor it is the fact of the world itself, nor does it involve our relation to inner-worldly existents, at least not as these are understood in a cosmological way. Rather, the Why question, understood existential-ontologically, puts our own existence, the existence of the questioner, in question. By understanding how and why that is so, we will be able to understand why we must turn to an existential-ontological approach to "explain," to "answer," that is, to respond appropriately and adequately to the Why question, the question that arises when we become aware of the strange fact that something, rather than nothing, exists at all.

In other words, there are at least two ways the 'Why' aspect of the Why question can be understood. At first and for the most part (to use one of Heidegger's favorite expressions, *zunaechst und zumeist*), both seem to refer to the same thing, the existence of the world. On the one hand there is what we could call the 'objective' mode of posing the question, the *scientific* or *metaphysical* way of asking that looks for the cause for the world's existence – a First Cause, whether 'natural' or 'super-natural.' But there is another way of asking the question, what we might call a 'subjective' or *existential* mode of inquiry, that *links* the question of the existence of the world to the meaning of our own being-in-the-world. Curiously, a gesture in that direction crops up fleetingly in or as subjective 'moments' in the objectively-oriented treatments of Post, Rundle and especially Munitz, suggesting a repressed awareness of a more fundamental mystery lying underneath. We will address the peculiar nature of that 'repression,' if such it is, in the analyses that follow. And of course this 'subjective' aspect was, despite their philosophical inadequacies, a more prominent feature in the responses in Part Two of Wittgenstein and Quentin Smith.

But if, as we have been arguing, the various types of cosmological-metaphysical response to the Why question are unsatisfactory as regards the three criteria previously noted – preservation of our primordial sense of the *mystery* of existence, insistence upon the *cognitive* significance of the Why question, and refusal to *reduce* it to the feelings to which that awareness gives rise – then to approach the question so as to satisfy these criteria we must turn to another way of thinking, what Heidegger calls "another beginning" – another way of understanding both the Why question and our answers to it.

From Cosmological to Ontological Wonder

To do so we can begin by focusing on one of what Quentin Smith calls our 'felt responses' to the 'felt meanings' of the world, the existential response of *wonder*. Why choose this particular phenomenon? As will be recalled, for Smith wonder was not a 'pure' response to the 'fulfillment-of-happening' of the world-whole; that was assigned to the feeling of joy, of rejoicing, at the world-whole's existence. Wonder was not even a positively-toned first-order 'impure' response, like marveling at the miraculousness, awe at the immensity, or peace vis-a-vis the harmoniousness of the world-whole's existence, let alone a negatively-toned feeling like despair at the emptiness or tedium at the monotonousness of the world-whole's existence. Wonder was not even a 'pure' second-order response to the world-whole's revelation of itself; that was assigned to the emotion of love. Rather, wonder was consigned to the status of an 'impure' second-order 'appreciation' of the mystery of the world-whole's 'appearance' to us. So, again, why focus on wonder as the path into an existential-ontological answer to the Why question?

There are several reasons. First, Smith's hierarchy of felt responses to the world-whole collapses when we shift our focus from the existence of the world and its plurality of different ('determinate') cosmological features to the ontologically 'bare' ('indeterminate,' featureless) fact that something, anything, exists at all rather than nothing. Given this collapse, positive emotions such as joy, marveling, awe, peace, love, wonder, equanimity, stupefaction, humility and quietude, along with their negative or dialectical counterparts such as despair, tedium, sadness, desolation, dread and apathy, can be called into question too. Which, if any of them, can be seen as having any meaning or sense as responses to such a bare, indeterminate, featureless fact? If some of them do, how so, for what reason? Do they not all collapse into a potpourri of equally indeterminate, undifferentiated emotions? Can we even distinguish the so-called positive ones from the so-called negative ones among them?

Let us consider. If we do not surreptitiously reintroduce reference to specific features of the world-whole, we may nevertheless speak of wonder as a cognitive-cum-emotionally appropriate response to the overwhelming mystery of being. Even for Smith wonder was a proper response to the phenomenon of mystery, albeit that of the world's existence. Further, synonyms of wonder – awe, amazement, astonishment, marveling, stupefaction, again absent reference to specific features of the world, may be seen as equally appropriate responses to the mystery of existence. When we turn to the dialectically related negative side of the ledger, there too we find a cognitive-cum-emotionally appropriate response in the shock, the despair, when one comes face to face with the abyss, the 'without-ground' (*Abgrund*), the seeming bottomlessness and emptiness of the unfathomable mystery of being. Thus wonder or awe, with its Janus-faced twin, shock or despair are appropriate phenomena on which to focus our exploration of existential-ontological answers to the Why question.

There are additional supportive reasons as well. Philosophers and theologians who have approached the Why question from a non-cosmological perspective have also chosen to highlight the emotion of wonder as expressing an awareness of the mystery of existence. We recall that the theologian Paul Tillich, contrasting the cosmological with the ontological approach, spoke of it as 'ontological wonder.' And William James, capturing the Janus-faced, dialectical nature of the phenomenon, characterized it as 'wonder-sickness.' So it would seem that wonder is where we should begin our exploration of existential-ontological answers to the Why question, of responses to the mystery that anything exists at all rather than nothing.

The Ambiguity of Cosmological Wonder

First, however, it should be noted that the world, the cosmos, *is* an appropriate object of wonder, although a penultimate one insofar as it is not seen against the background of the primordial mystery. The cosmos in its order and beauty (Grk: *kosmos*) is a legitimate object of wonder. It lies behind teleological arguments for the existence of God. But for Smith at least such 'evidence' does not suffice or compel one to draw a theistic, let alone a metaphysical conclusion. Despite the appeal to such 'evidence' in support of a 'proof,' the world, in Hick's phrase, remains 'religiously ambiguous' – and, we might add, metaphysically too.

Hick, commenting on the teleological argument in *An Interpretation of Religion: Human Responses to the Transcendent,* observes: "We find [the universe] to be infinitely complex and to our minds infinitely *wonderful*. We are almost *stupefied* by it *immensity, awed* by the picture of the primal fireball exploding and the galaxies and worlds gradually forming; and *chilled* again by the thought of the fleeting character of life on a planet that must either burn up or become a frozen ball.... the *mystery* of the universe's existence and character can only evoke in any reflective mind a sense of *wonder*, and even *awe*, which if not taken up into a religious faith will most naturally find expression in mystical poetry" (Hick, 2004, 87, 91). The italicized words remind us of Smith's list of felt responses and features of the world-as-a-whole, its 'that' (*existence*) and its 'what' (*character*). Reminding us too of Smith's poetic descriptions of the world, Hick continues: "Nature is everywhere producing beauty – in the glory of sunrise and sunset, the colours and scents of flowers and trees and bushes, the grandeur of mountain ranges, the moving kaleidoscope of the clouds, the stillness of the desert, reflections on a lake, the strength and economy of movement of animals and the charms of their young" (Hick, 2004, 94) Hick concludes: "The postulation of a divine source of natural beauty is [however] optional; and once again the religious ambiguity of the world remains intact" (Hick, *ibid*.).

The problem with this characterization of the alleged ambiguity of wonder, however, is that both Smith and Hick's approaches rest on a fundamental mistake, namely, an appeal to cosmological 'evidence' in support, whether adequate or inadequate, of a metaphysical belief. But this approach (which is alright in a cosmological context) rests from the outset on a confusion, because it fails to probe the deeper, ontological source of cosmological wonder. As Tillich argues, the cosmological 'proof' itself rests on an 'argument' (Latin: *argumentum*) of an entirely different sort, one that does not appeal to (narrowly) empirical evidence, but to an wholly other awareness or 'intuition,' one that is ontological in nature. Hick dismisses the ontological argument, in the same way Kant and others since have done, as an attempt to prove the existence of a reality on the basis of concepts, thought, logic alone. He is right to do so insofar as the ontological 'argumentum' is *not* a 'proof' based on metaphysical concepts but rather an expression, in a 'mixed' mode, of a primordial ontological awareness, an awareness of the trans-metaphysical mystery that something exists at all, let alone a religiously or metaphysically ambiguous' universe. This is the object of that 'ontological wonder' of which Tillich speaks. It is that to which we must now turn as we move from metaphysics to mystery.

The Opening of Ontological Wonder

In contradistinction to Quentin Smith and the other thinkers discussed above, we have differentiated a cosmological from an ontological approach to the Why question and proposed wonder or awe, shock or despair, as phenomena that will provide another way, "another beginning," for answering the ontological question. We must now look more closely at the philosophical implications of this 'other way.

As just indicated, there will be two issues or dimensions, each involving a 'double,' to be considered: the *phenomenological 'double'* of the difference between cosmological and ontological wonder, featuring what Heidegger labels the 'ontological difference' between Being and beings; and the *existential 'double'* of response to the mystery of Being in an intrinsic dialectic of wonder/shock, awe/despair.

Taking each of these in turn, we encounter an obstacle at the outset. Attempts to describe, to provide a phenomenological analysis of ontological wonder, as free as possible of presuppositions, as the motto of phenomenology would have it, to go "back to the thing itself," face the problem that in fact no such "pure" description is possible. Even "description" in the realm of philosophy of the alleged phenomenon "itself" comes to us already theory-laden, already freighted with assumptions contained with a horizon of interpretation. The description already contains implicit questions we bring to the phenonemeon, the distinctions and comparisons we make, the concepts, terms, words we use, what Heidegger called the "grammar" of philosophical inquiry, a "hermeneutical circle" (another of Heidegger's terms) that we cannot escape. The best we can do, said Heidegger, was to attempt to get into that circle "the right way." Easy to say, hard if not impossible to do.

We see this hermeneutical dilemma, the underlying presuppositions, already at work in the very beginning of Western philosophy. For metaphysics down through the millenia, wonder, the wonder expressed in the Why question, has been understood, that is interpreted, first and foremost as the starting-off point in a quest for knowledge that must, if successful, end in a discovery of truth, that thereby transforms an initial sense of wonder into a settled sense of certitude. As Aristotle, following his teacher Plato, famously says "For it is owing to their wonder that men both now begin and at first began to philosophize." But, as Rubenstein, who will be our guide in these matters, notes, apparently departing from Plato, Aristotle quickly goes on to add, "Yet the acquisition of [knowledge] must in a sense end in something which is the opposite of our original inquiries.... we must end in the contrary and...the better state, as is the case in these instances too when men learn the cause..." (Aristotle, *Metap.* 982b, 983a; Rubenstein, 2008, 12).

But was Aristotle right? What *is* the 'thing,' the *Sache*, the 'object' of wonder? As we have seen, Smith distinguished two types or levels of 'objects' in addressing the phenomenon of the world's existence: that the world exists *rather than* does not – for Smith, the basic metaphysical fact, the proper response to which is joy, a purely positive feeling; and that the world exists when it *might not* have existed, i.e. the 'non-necessity' of its existence – for Smith a subordinate fact, the appropriate response to which, as we have seen, is a medley of 'impure' appreciations that embrace marveling at the miracle of its existence, despair at its emptiness, awe at its immensity, tedium at its monotonmousness, and peace at its harmoniousness.

The existential 'double' is clearly the 'object' of cosmological wonder, for it was not necessary that world as we know it, the structured cosmos, to have existed. It might have remained a chaotic fireball. There was no metaphysical, scientific or empirical necessity for the present world to have existed, to serve as the object of cosmological wonder of the sort that spurred Aristotle's metaphysical inquiries or that excite the cosmological imaginings of our day. There is a further problem: 'might not have existed' relies on the very traditional metaphysical distinction between possible existence and necessary existence. That leaves it very unclear what metaphysical status Smith assigns to the world's existence. Does that too rest on a hidden assumption that the world's existence *as such*, its 'pure' existence, its 'existence in and of itself,' its sheer 'presence,' possesses some kind of *aseity*? Can he really speak of the world's existence in the first sense without tacitly presupposing its existence in the second?

In these wonderings about wonder, then, that brings us back to the phenomenological double.. As we have argued, that harbors an ambiguity. It reflects Smith's confusion of and unclarity about the distinction between the proper object of cosmological wonder and the proper 'object' of ontological wonder. It could be interpreted ("experienced") in two different ways. Following Smith one could argue that, yes, the wonder is that the world exists rather than not, though as we have seen, it is not clear just what its metaphysical status is; but as we've argued, we could also, and better, see the cosmological fact of the world's existence as even more wondrous against the primordial background of ontological wonder – not just that *world* exists but that *anything, the world included,* exists rather than nothing at all.

This brings us to the core issue: whether it is possible to move beyond philosophy's originating sense of wonder and arrive at a knowledge of metaphysical or scientific truth, "something which is the opposite" (Aristotle), thus permitting philosophy to satisfy its desire for ultimate explanations (though, Post says, "we must never lose the gift of wonder"), or whether the sense of wonder points to an ultimate and irreducible mystery which, though frustrating philosophy's desire, may paradoxically protect and preserve the very existence and truth of philosophy itself. There is a third possibility, a 'middle' path, as it were, that wonder, understood as endlessly open questioning, is the essence of all genuine scientific inquiry, the strength of *science*, whose conclusions are always provisional, over against what seems the ineliminable temptation of *philosophy* to give definitive metaphysical, i.e. *meta*-scientific, answers to the question why there is something rather than nothing. Perhaps Aristotle's originary formulation of the issue opposing wonder to knowledge mis-stated the issue, perhaps more remains to be said. Let us turn, therefore, to a closer consideration of the phenomenon of ontological wonder in hopes of shedding further light on this issue.

To better be better prepared, however, we must briefly return to the second 'double' referred to above, the existential double of wonder-and-shock or awe-and-despair in response to the primordial ontological fact. It could be argued that a repressed fear motivated Aristotle's sense of the conflicted relationship of philosophy to its origin in wonder, a concern that, by surrendering to it, the sense of critical inquiry that lies at the origin of philosophy may be polluted by relapse into ignorance or worse, falling back into fascination with the "wonders of myth" from which philosophy in its beginnings struggled to free itself (Aristotle, *Metap.* 982b). As just suggested, this may not be true. Nonetheless, it is a further aspect of the core question that needs to be explored.

The existential tension at the heart of wonder does not pose a problem only for philosophy, it is even more obviously central to the paradox at the heart of religion. Rubenstein refers to the comments of the philosopher/theologian, Abraham Joshua Heschel, who speaks of 'radical amazement' at the mystery of being. Heschel argues that awe is wonder that has an understanding of its divine source; it is "mature wonder." As such, it is "compatible with both love and joy" (Heschel, 46, 74, 76-77). But, argues Rubenstein, this religious reading of wonder is one-sided, hence deeply problematic. It splits off fear, as an allegedly negative dimension of wonder, from awe, as a purely positive dimension, seeing fear as the antithesis of awe rather than that which gives wonder its depth, power and authenticity. To see awe as rendering fear null and void is a "reduction of wonder to a more manageable passion" (Rubenstein, 2008, 200, ftnt 27). We shall return to this question of the relation of awe to fear in the heart of wonder when we come to Heidegger's analysis of the phenomenon.

Our initial guide on this alternative, existential-ontological path will be Mary-Jane Rubenstein's provocatively-titled, thought-provoking book, *Strange Wonder: The Closure of Metaphysics and the Opening of Awe*. The title itself gives pause: Wonder may point to something strange, but in what sense could wonder itself be said to be strange? Or the double genitives in the sub-title: Metaphysics may strive for conclusive answers, but how could metaphysics itself be closed off? Awe may be an opening to what is wondrously strange, but what opens awe itself? Clearly a book that promises much to think about vis-a-vis existential-ontological answers to the question why anything exists rather than nothing at all.

The Opening of Wonder – a Dilemma

The opening of wonder, in both senses of the genitive – wonder in the objective sense as that which is opened up (by something) and wonder in the subjective sense as that which opens up (something) – first occurs in Western thinking, says Rubenstein, with what she calls "Socrates' small difficulty" put forward by Plato in his dialogue on knowledge, *Theatetus*. Socrates speaks of "an experience which is characteristic of a philosopher, this wondering [*thaumazein*]: this is where philosophy begins and nowhere else" (Plato, *Theatetus* 155d, Rubenstein, 2008, 3). The initiation of thinking lies in the sense of wonder.

However, philosophy does not necessarily end there. As we have seen, the opening of wonder can taken in two further, radically opposite directions. Thinking can be overwhelmed, immobilized by the awesome, indeed frightening power of a primordial experience that, paradoxically, immediately brings further thinking to a halt, finding itself confronted by a mystery that absolutely defeats it. Or it can be the exciting, indeed generous invitation to endless inquiry in the pursuit of knowledge that holds the promise of liberation from all that previously had shackled the human mind and imagination in the stranglehold of myth and superstition, including the possibility of finally achieving security from, control over, the terrifying forces and uncertainties of nature. Hence that "small dilemma" to which Socrates refers with his characteristic irony.

In the first section of her introductory chapter Rubenstein expands upon the first horn of the Socratic dilemma: "The philosopher's wonder marks his inability to ground himself in the ordinary as he reaches toward the extraordinary; it has rendered uncanny the very ground on which the philosopher stands. Standing in *thaumazein*, the philosopher stands exposed to that which he cannot master; that which, in turn, threatens to disable the sort of mastery one expects of philosophers" (Rubenstein, 2008, 4). Philosophy "clings to inviolable theories in order to take refuge from wonder's open sea of endless questioning, strangeness, and impossibility ... the frightening indeterminacy of wonder" (*ibid.*, 5,7). It would seem philosophy is not exactly off to a good start. Indeed, the experience of that 'frightening indeterminacy' would seem to constitute a strong temptation to fall back into, to take refuge in, that security-blanket of unexamined superstition from which it had been struggling to free itself. A dilemma indeed!

The Opening of Wonder – a Wound

But perhaps the description of the first horn of Socrates' alleged 'dilemma' overstates the paralyzing nature of wonder? What, after all, is paralyzed? Surely, as neither the evidence of Plato's thought nor that of his student and successor, Aristotle, go to show, it was not philosophy itself, not what came to be called the 'science' of metaphysics and the epistemology, the associated claim to 'scientific' knowledge, it entailed. Is there another way, then, to state the dilemma that does not result in such dire consequences for thinking?

The key lies in unpacking the double dimension of wonder. It is not only an epistemological phenomenon, it is an existential one as well. Wonder is, to use Smith's phrase, a 'felt meaning.' It has not only metaphysical significance but existential import too. Further, as the phrase 'frightening indeterminacy' suggests, the existential dimension of wonder is itself doubled. Noting the possible derivation of 'wonder' not only from the German *Wunder* but, more suggestively, from *Wunde*, cut, gash, wound,

Rubenstein says "Wonder, then, is inherently ambivalent" (Rubenstein, 2008, 9). It is two-sided, it harbors a duplicity. This doubleness is not ambiguity, however. Neither dimension of the primordial experience of wonder – as terror-*soku hi*-awe – is reducible to or eliminable in favor of the other, each belongs to the aboriginal *Sache selbst*.

One thinks in this connection of William James describing philosophy as the 'ontology of wonder-sickness' or Nietzsche characterizing Western metaphysics as arising out of a profound 'dis-ease.' For Rubenstein, however, following Heidegger, wonder, as an expression of the sickness, the dis-ease of philosophy, is simultaneously, however paradoxically, a profound affirmation, a health without which philosophy itself would succumb to a fatal illness. In a moment we will see how see the 'wound' of wonder can lead not only to the death but also the resurrection of thinking. But first we must look more closely at the phenomenology of the 'wound' itself. What exactly is the wound? What (or who) is wounded? Why?

Rubenstein begins by pointing out the 'tonal' difference (shades of Smith!) between two types of wonder, two types of what, following Smith, we could label its 'felt meaning.' One reveals the familiar as strange, the other assimilates the strange to the familiar. This distinction, she says, "can be roughly mapped onto the distinction between Platonic and Aristotelian wonder (Rubenstein, 2008, 198-199, n. 13): "There is an irreducible difference between a rigorous, investigative thinking that sustains wonder's strangeness and a rigorous, investigative thinking that endeavors to assimilate that strangeness." As to the former, Plato's, "This is because wonder wonders at the strangeness of the most familiar: at that which, *within the possibilities of determinate thinking*, still remains indeterminate, unthinkable, and impossible. Wonder wonders, therefore, at the opening in which all determinate thinking takes place. And insofar as Socrates tells us that wonder opens the possibility of thinking itself, we can risk the tautology: wonder wonders at wonder" *(ibid.* 8; emphasis Rubenstein's). This provocative Heideggerian tautology (*t'autos logos*, 'same-saying') needs to be unpacked lest philosophy descend once again into the logorrhea, the verbal mystification, from which Socrates/Plato tried to free it.

Rubenstein's emphasis on the context of this wonder that wonders, that it operates "within the possibilities of determinate thinking," itself gives reason to pause. Does that 'opening' which remains "indeterminate, unthinkable, and impossible" really point to an altogether different type of wonder that exceeds the curiosity that characterizes all scientific inquiry, or is it simply a mystified way of talking about the nature of scientific questioning itself? What, exactly, is the nature of this 'opening' if not simply that? Rubenstein, at least, following Heidegger, clearly thinks there is more to be said: "opening the question about wonder opens the question of opening itself" (Rubenstein, 2008, 8).

And yet when we try we immediately uncover another dimension of that Socratic dilemma. "What gives thinking pause when it goes about thinking wonder is that 'one will never be able to interrogate wonder philosophically except by way of a questioning that the operation of wonder will already have determined.' Any thinking of wonder is destined to miss its mark, and yet thinking cannot *not* think wonder, even if the difference between the thinkable and the unthinkable will never be closed, attempting to think the unthinkable *as such* will at the very least expand the limits of thought before collapsing back into them" (Rubenstein, 2008, 8-9). But this means that again we encounter that niggling little worry. What at first seemed a kind of breath-taking paradox – the attempt to think that which presupposes the operation of the very thing it's trying to think, a dog engaged in the self-contradictory effort of chasing its own tail, thinking *a la* Heidegger destined/doomed to thinking that which cannot be thought – proves in the end simply a post-modern exercise in "expand[ing] the limits of thought before collapsing back into them." An epistemological mole hill masquerading as a metaphysical mountain.

Or is it? "Opening the question of wonder, thinking opens the excess against which more 'proper' philosophy takes pains to secure itself." Rubenstein argues, "To the extent that it tries to resolve wonder into certainty, formulas, and clear and distinct ideas, ... philosophy that begins in thaumazein short-circuits its own genealogy" (Rubenstein, 2008, 11). This is clearly intended to bring us back to Aristotle, the philosopher who, on this Heidegger-*cum*-Post reading, was above all the thinker responsible for converting the wonder in which philosophy begins into that other type of wonder – wonder as the *curiosity* that opens up an "investigative thinking that endeavors to assimilate that strangeness." Thus begins the long travail of original wonder in the subsequent history of Western metaphysics. The strange wildness of primordial wonder is to be tamed, domesticated – not just overcome but forgotten altogether, any memory of its ever having existed buried along with the corpse itself. The wound of wonder that leads instead to its own death.

The Opening of Wonder – a Double Overcoming

Overcoming I: Metaphysics Overcoming

Rubenstein speaks of the fatal nature of the wound of wonder. It leads to the closing down, the closing off, the death of wonder in favor of the "certainty, formulas, and clear and distinct ideas" of the philosophical enterprise that it itself had spawned. The 'closure' of metaphysics represents what Heidegger, following Nietzsche, called the 'overcoming' (*Ueberwindung*) of original wonder in the subsequent history of philosophy in the West. But wonder cannot be so easily repressed. Metaphysics may be the death of wonder, yet wonder still haunts it as a ghostly presence. It is the dread secret, the awesome truth of philosophy's own birth. At the heart of metaphysics there lurks the specter of its own death.

But how, why, having given birth to something so wondrous strange, was wonder killed off in the first place, and by whom? What was (still is) the motivation for trying to forget, to overcome, something so wonderful as the opening of wonder that led to the birth of philosophy? The problem, says Rubenstein, lies in dread, awesome power of that opening itself. Philosophy tries to secure itself against 'the storm of indeterminacy' that is the very nature of primordial wonder. As the philosophical tradition progresses, wonder becomes something "not to be endured, but rather to be cured – or at least tranquilized." It already starts, as noted, with Aristotle: "It is Aristotle who first proposes a remedy for wonder in the knowledge of cause and effect." Thus, as for Post too, "wonder's function is not to expand its scope infinitely, but rather to eliminate itself…. Aristotelian thaumazein…seeks the very resolution that Socratic thaumazein struggles to resist; for, all the way up the ontological chain, causal knowledge gradually replaces the very wonder that sets it in motion" (Rubenstein, 2008, 12-13).

Though he reprises the metaphysics of Aristotle, his medieval follower, Aquinas, as a theologian, seems to preserve a residual sense of the two types of wonder. Thus he distinguishes between 'preliminary wonder' (natural causation) and 'permanent wonder' (divine causation)

(Rubenstein, 2008, 13). Here, too, however, a religious construal of primordial wonder is deeply problematic, for not unrelated but different reasons than Heschel's one-sided view of wonder as a wholly positive response to the mystery of being. The problem, as anyone familiar with Rubenstein's own guide, Heidegger, will instantly spot, is that Aquinas still remains embedded in what Heidegger calls the 'onto-theo-logical' framework of metaphysics. In other words, for Aquinas, permanent wonder is grounded in the highest *being*, the metaphysical First Cause of all other beings which, as dependent entities, are subject to natural causation, i.e., are the objects of 'preliminary wonder' or what Post, following Aristotle, calls 'curiosity.' But God, construed by metaphysics from Aristotle on as a being, the highest being, is not the object of primordial wonder. The highest being of metaphysics is not the mystery of being itself, the mystery that there is something rather than nothing at all. Aquinas' two types of wonder point rather to the sub-types of beings subsumed within a metaphysical hierarchy of beings, an overarching conceptual framework that leaves nothing unexplained.

The freeing of metaphysics and science from wonder, the death of primordial wonder, occurs with the rise of modern philosophy in Descartes. Though, true to the philosophical tradition, Descartes allows philosophy its initiatory role as a 'prod' to wonder, "we should ... try afterwards to emancipate ourselves from it as much as possible" by turning to the scientific method "as the most effective defense against wonder's attack on reason" (Descartes, *Les passions de l'ame*, A 76; cited in Rubenstein, 2008, 15). "For Descartes as for Bacon," Rubenstein notes, "causal knowledge of wonderful things disciplines and eradicates the ur-passion of wonder." By means of his famous method, "Decartes goes so far as to promise that once his method replaces all wonder, with comprehension, 'we' philosophers and scientists will become 'master of ourselves ... like God in a way'" (Descartes, *ibid.,* A152; Rubenstein, 2008, 15).

This seems, at first glance, a revolution in Western thought. It opens the prospect of metaphysics itself being replaced by the various sciences that have come to limn the modern era. But there is a fly in the ointment of the Cartesian hubris of modernity. Descartes has simply dressed up the old metaphysical tradition in fancy new garb. Like the philosophers of ancient and medieval times, Descartes has continued the metaphysical effort, as Rubenstein observes,"to put representational boundaries around the whole world." The problem, however, is that wonder, however repressed, refuses to go away. It lingers still, in the reluctant concession, from Aristotle through Descartes to Post, that wonder is needed to jump-start the enterprise of metaphysical and scientific inquiry.

It is more serious than that, however, for as Rubenstein, referencing Heidegger, argues, "wonder continually ungrounds the philosopher. [T]he task of thinking for Heidegger is not to make the thinker 'master' of himself or of others, but rather to return to the ground of being that ungrounds the thinking self. Since being remains unthinkable from the standpoint of metaphysics, however, this way will eventually open onto a way *beyond* metaphysics" (Heidegger, cited in Rubenstein, 2008, 16, 18). The 'overcoming' of metaphysics, therefore, is meant not in an objective but in a subjective sense of the genitive. It is not metaphysics that is to do the overcoming, it metaphysics that is to be overcome – the closure of metaphysics as the re-opening of wonder.

Overcoming II: Overcoming Metaphysics

There is, in other words, another, more positive way to interpret the founding experience of wonder, one that does not reduce it to a propadeutic to science or metaphysics. As the above citation from Heidegger suggests, it involves turning the tables on metaphysics, as it were, and subjecting metaphysics, indeed the enterprise of 'philosophy' itself, to what Heidegger calls 'another beginning' – what Rubenstein terms, in a word redolent with religious connotations, the 'resurrection' of wonder. It calls for re-opening the original opening of the 'strange wonder,' the 'wondrous primordiality,' that is the mystery of being itself (Rubenstein, 2008, 11).

This is not, however, a nostalgic return to a reassuring experience of mystery that swaddles the origins of philosophy at its infancy. Rather, as Rubenstein reminds us, "Awakening the perplexity at the heart of the everyday, Heidegger is effectively rousing the monsters of indeterminacy under the house of philosophy" (Rubenstein, 2008, 19; cf. Heidegger's citing of Plato's *Sophist* 244a in the opening of *Sein und Zeit*). In a series of inextricably linked dualities that recall Pascal's "abysmal awe," Otto's sense of "the numinous," or Kierkegaard's "*horror religiosus*," Rubenstein says, "Opening the question of wonder, thinking opens the fascinating/

repulsive, creative/ruinous, astounding/horrifying, heirophanic/ monstrous excess against which more 'proper' philosophy takes pains to secure itself" (Rubenstein, 2008, 11).

But why should this be so? Why does not the sense of the primordial mystery being, whatever upsetting consequences it might have for a rigorous science or metaphysics, nevertheless, as Aquinas or Heschel might argue, provide that ultimate existential reassurance that, as the poet opines, "God 's in His heaven/All 's right with the world!" What, then, exactly are the implications of speaking of 'the mystery of being,' and in particular, for distinguishing the phenomenon of being from the realm of metaphysical beings including God, the highest being? We recall that for Heidegger one of the features of metaphysics is that it does not let being be. It privileges beings over being and sets them within an explanatory framework that 'grounds' beings in a highest being, the goal being to eliminate any lingering elements of mystery. In the light of clear and distinct ideas it 'overcomes' the darkness of the disturbing sense of primordial mystery. As for being itself, Heidegger says, metaphysics reduces it to a matter of self-evidence; being needs no further clarification or explanation.

However, things are not so simple. Another dilemma raises its head. For, as Rubenstein observes, "Heideggerian wonder [is] a double movement. A certain shock or terror recoils at the sudden impossibility of the everyday, while awe goes on to marvel that the impossible nevertheless *is*." Here Rubenstein introduces a new theme – the shock of the ultimate mystery is not only that it awakens a 'monstrous indeterminacy' threatening the explanatory schemes of philosophy, or that it confronts us existentially with what Tillich calls the 'shock of non-being.' There is another dimension to the mystery of being – its "attunement to the strangeness of the everyday." It is the shock of marveling at and simultaneously recoiling from the "irreducible this-worldliness" of wonder, one that defeats metaphysical explanation (Rubenstein, 2008, 23). It is the problem of trying, and failing, to make sense, either philosophical or existential, of the relation of the mystery of *being* to the fact that *beings* exist, that 'the impossible nevertheless *is*.'

There are thus three dimensions to the shock administered to philosophy by the mystery of being:

Ontological – the shock of the fundamental question of the 'relation' of being to beings, what Heidegger calls the 'ontological difference' of being and beings: "Not knowing what being is, we cannot possibly know what beings genuinely are" (Rubenstein, 2008, 18);

Epistemological – the shock to philosophy's effort to reduce the meaning of being to a harmless concept vaguely sensed on the margins of the causal-explanatory framework of a metaphysics;

Existential – as the terms 'strange,' 'uncanny,' 'frightening,' 'terror,' 'recoil,' 'repulsive,' 'ruinous,' 'horrifying,' 'monstrous,' tell us, the mystery of being is not simply an knowledge-conundrum, a Wittgensteinian 'riddle,' a shock to our sense of epistemological mastery and self-esteem, it is a shock to our sense of the meaning of our existence. As Heidegger says, the question of the meaning of being puts the being of the questioner in question as well.

To explore the various dimensions of this three-fold shock further, Rubenstein turns to the phenomenology of wonder in Heidegger and three French philosophers influenced by his work – Emmanuel Levinas, Jean-Luc Nancy, and Jacques Derrida

The Phenomenology of Wonder

Double Transformation

For a closer look at the existential dimension of the shock administered by wonder, Rubenstein turns first to Heidegger, for whom to think the mystery of being it is necessary "to find another mood," one that resists the temptation to reduce the "uncertainty and irresolution" of wonder to the security of the explanations of metaphysic. For this it is necessary to *attune* oneself to "something like wonder" (Rubenstein, 2008, 28). What is striking, as just noted, is that paradoxically this wonder (*Erstaunen*) can present itself, surprisingly, unexpectedly, in "the everyday itself ... wonder reveals the strangeness of the everyday." As Heidegger puts it, "In wonder what is more usual itself becomes the most unusual" (Heidegger, 1994, 166/144). But this wondrous strangeness of the everyday cannot be reduced to the innocence and simplicity of everyday curiosity, nor is it a one-dimensional mood. Wonder is double-edged, it reveals "the profoundly disturbing force of the mysterious in the everyday. Dwelling in wonder is a kind of existential suffering, and it is a kind of suffering that metaphysics cannot ultimately endure" (Rubenstein, 2008, 30-31).

The 'duplicity' of wonder. Wonder is a mood or "attunement" constituted by *two* "equiprimordial comportments ... in perpetual tension: 'terror [*Erschrecken*] in the face of what is closest and most obtrusive, namely that beings are, and awe [*Scheu*] in the face of what is remotest, namely that in beings and before each being, being holds sway'" (Heidegger, 1994, 2/4). (One is reminded of the intrinsically double nature of the related mood of reverence, visible in the German *Ehrfurcht, Ehre* honor, *Furcht* fear.) If one of these two polarities is missing, it degenerates into enervating nihilism or empty curiosity. In revealing wonder in the heart of the everyday, *Erstaunen* "is not a simple wonder at the thatness of beings, but rather shock (*Schrecken*) and/or terror (*Erschrecken*) that, strictly speaking beings cannot be." Wonder exposes "the frightful 'nothing' that both transcends and constitutes beings themselves." The anxiety (Angst) to which wonder gives rise, in confronting us with the strangeness of beings, is a "double movement" by which one is "lifted out of beings and then back into beings. Its horror at the nothing gives onto a wonder that by virtue of this very 'nothing' beings are" (Rubenstein, 2008, 36-37). "For close by essential anxiety as the horror (*Schrecken*) of the abyss dwells awe (*Scheu*)" (Heidegger, 1998b, 103/234).

As Rubenstein interprets Heidegger, "Awe is the second, more enduring movement of this new wonder, a response to the shock of *Er/schrecken*. If Erschrecken registers that that which is cannot possibly be, then Scheu sees that it nonetheless is. While Erschrecken recoils at the abandonment of being, Scheu marvels that being nevertheless gives itself through this withdrawal" (Rubenstein, 2008, 38). Rubenstein's reading of Heidegger is interesting not only for its reminder of similar analyses of the experience of being – Tillich (being overcomes the threat of non-being) and Smith (marveling that beings need not exist yet nevertheless are), but also because it gives the impression that for Heidegger, as for Tillich or Smith, the positive side of the double mood of wonder – joy, awe (*Scheu*), in the end "overcomes," triumphs over, the negative side – shock, terror (*Er/schrecken*). It is not clear, however, in what sense awe can be said to the "more enduring" aspect of wonder since it is also said that both "comportments" are "equiprimordial, in perpetual tension." Whether this is Heidegger or Rubenstein speaking, we are confronted with a conundrum as to the ultimate meaning of this strange 'duplicity.' Does wonder in the end deliver us from the existential (and epistemological) suffering abhorred by the philosophers, or does it in require instead that we endlessly re-learn the painful wisdom of the tragedians? This is an issue to which we must and will return.

Wonder as transformative. What is clear is that the double-edged experience of wonder is, for Heidegger, transformative, one that "relates itself primordially to being [that] would also have to relate authentically to all beings" (Rubenstein, 2008, 40-41; Heidegger, 1998e, 251/179). Because wonder reveals the strangeness in the heart of the everyday, "everything that has been heretofore manifest to human beings, as well as the way in which it has been manifest, gets transformed" (Rubenstein, 2008, 57; Heidegger, 1998c, 124/168). It is the opening of wonder that calls thinking "to see the ordinary and the extraordinary in and through one another, thereby letting what is finally *be*" (Rubenstein, 2008, 59; Heidegger, 1994, 168/145). Rubenstein concludes her discussion of Heidegger with an observation that reminds one of Hargby's insight into "double-awareness" in Wittgenstein and Heidegger. For Heidegger, "The double movement of wonder takes us out of the world *only to put us back into the world* ... in order to reveal everything as different – as more itself – than it had been before." Everything depends, then, on not closing off wonder "but keeping it open" (Rubenstein, 2008, 60; italics in the original).

Heidegger's view of the duplicity and transformative nature of wonder, at least on Rubenstein's account, leaves us, as noted, with a question. Wonder is not only a revelation of the mystery of being, it also places a mystery in the heart of beings – and our own being. But what is the meaning of that mystery for our relation to beings and for our own existence? Does 'strange wonder' even have a final meaning, whether salvific or tragic? Where, as another philosopher will shortly ask us, are we supposed to go with that unsettling mood, that mystery? (Witherall, 90). To what – *by* what – are we ultimately 'attuned'?

Beyond Being

In searching for an answer to this existential dilemma posed by "the opening of wonder," Rubenstein turns next to Levinas, a thinker who locates the origin of wonder, in Plato's phrase, 'beyond being.' Though one does not usually associate ontology with the name of Levinas, rather ethics, in fact as Rubenstein's analysis makes clear, Levinas' comments on the phenomenon of wonder show a deep awareness of the *ontological* shock it presents to metaphysics. Levinas' phenomenology of wonder is grounded in his ontology of the *il y a*, the 'there is...' of being in itself apart from beings, the "sheer thatness" of being: "the anonymous, impersonal field of naked existence." In fact, the *il y a* is not even being; it is rather "neither being nor nothing but, like the *tehom* over which *Elohim* breathes in Genesis 1:2, personal flux that gives rise to their difference" (Rubenstein, 2008, 71). One thinks of the Creation Hymn of the *Rig Veda* 10.129:

> There was neither non-existence nor existence then; there was neither the realm of space nor the sky which is beyond. What stirred? Where? In whose protection? Was there water, bottomlessly deep? There was neither death nor immortality then. There was no distinguishing sign of night nor of day. Darkness was hidden by darkness in the beginning, with no distinguishing sign, all this was water. The life force that was covered with emptiness, that one arose through the power of heat. That one breathed, windless, by its own impulse. Other than that there was nothing beyond. Desire came upon that one in the beginning; that was the first seed of mind. Poets seeking in their hearts for wisdom found the bond of existence in non-existence.

However, Rubenstein sees a possible problem at this point. On the one hand, as the above remarks seem to indicate, Levinas "places the 'experience' of the *il y a* in the nonplace *beyond* being and nothingness." On the other, Levinas also insists, as did Bede Rundle in Part One of this study, that "no matter how hard the imagination tries, it cannot think away existence 'itself.' [S]heer thatness always returns to haunt even the starkest absence: even in the very insistence, or 'presence,' of that absence" (Rubenstein, 2008, 72, Rubenstein's emphasis). How to resolve this dilemma? And how does the experience of wonder fit in? Levinas explicitly links the experience of the *il y a* to Plato's locating of wonder at/as the origin of philosophical thinking: "like *thaumazein*, the *il y a* reveals the unfamiliarity of the most familiar. 'Its strangeness is due to its very reality, to the very fact that there is existence'" (Rubenstein, 2008, *ibid*; Levinas, 2001, 27-8/9). But then Levinas appears to reverse/revert himself by again locating the referent of wonder, the *il y a*, to a nonplace not only beyond beings, but beyond being itself. In wonder vis-a-vis the *il y a*, we encounter "indeterminacy itself, 'the absolute void, the "nowhere" in which the element loses itself and from which it arises.'" (Rubenstein, 2008, 80; Levinas, 1969, 21/147).

Rubenstein tries to resolve this apparent contradiction in Levinas' 'anti-ontology' by describing the *il y a* as in fact a *triadic* phenomenon involving being, nothingness and the *apeiron* (lit: indeterminate, infinite, indefinite) – for Anaximander the absolute origin, "the ur-elemental material out of which all things rise," for Levinas "the utterly formless, proto-creative stuff" out of which the differentiation of beings and nothingness arises" (Rubenstein, 2008, 79-80). Noting that for Levinas "the il y a was also characterized as 'neither being nor nothingness,' but rather the generator of the distinction between them," she concludes that "This peculiar triad (the apeiron as being, as nothing, *and* as the origin of their differentiation) is perhaps less inscrutable than it seems if one considers Heidegger's insight that from the standpoint of metaphysics ... 'being itself' is the same thing as 'nothing'" (Rubenstein, 2008, 81, Rubenstein's emphasis). It is not clear, however, in view of Levinas' strenuous efforts to distinguish his 'counter-ontology' of the *il y a* from Heidegger's Being, that appealing to Heidegger will rescue Levinas from this ontological dilemma. For Levinas "the *il y a* gives the lie to [Heidegger's] question: Why is there Being instead of simply nothing? Nothing, as pure absence, may be thinkable, but it is unimaginable. Indeterminate Being fills in all the gaps, all the temporal intervals" (Bergo, 2011).

Rubenstein has an additional reservation about Levinas' attempt to distinguish his ontology of the *il y a* from Heidegger's Being, especially in light of the latter's notion of the *Es gibt*, the giving of being (in both objective and genitive sense). Despite Levinas' critique of Heidegger, she says, "it is hardly clear that the il y a is distinct from primordial donation" (211, n. 53). However, Rubenstein's comment here too is problematic, since for Levinas the *il y a* as the *apeiron* is said to "give rise" to, is the "origin" of, the "generator" of the distinction between being and nothingness, is said, moreover, "to 'overflow with plentitude' from *beyond* being" (215, n. 135; Rubenstein's emphasis). Here, at least, Levinas seems to reprise Heidegger's *Es gibt Sein*.

There is another problem, one that Rubenstein does not touch upon but which goes to the heart of the distinction between a cosmological metaphysics and an existential ontology. And that is that Levinas' indeterminate flux, primal stuff – like Anaxamander's *apeiron*, Plato's *khora* in the *Timaeus*, the originating singularity of scientific cosmology, the primordial heat/desire of *Rig Veda*, and Chad Allen's critique of Quentin Smith's attempt to assign determinate attributes to the 'bare that' of existence – risks lapsing back into a pre-Heideggerian, metaphysical cosmology of Creation. Yet of course nothing is that simple. Similar to the claim that for Heidegger the 'duplicity' of wonder shows awe to be 'more enduring' than terror vis-a-vis the mystery of being, Rubenstein argues that despite the Vedic darkness of the il y a, existential nihilism is not for Levinas the last word. Wonder can also "allow thinking to pass from the horrifying opening of the elemental to the astonishing openness of ethics as responsibility" (Rubenstein, 2008, 96). This suggests a profound linkage between Levinas' 'anti-ontological' critique of Heidegger's Being, his apparent re-turn to a philosophy grounded in cosmology, and an ethics of openness to wonder. This important insight is one to which we will return in a later Part of this study.

There is a related problem. If wonder puts closure to metaphysics, renders it mute, speechless, before the mystery of existence, and if the *il y a*, further, gives the lie to the Why question itself, what further of substance is there for philosophy to say? We seem to have entered a Wittgenstinian moment: "Whereof one cannot speak, thereof one must be silent." Either philosophy is reconfigured as ethics, or it is replaced by one of the many sciences to which it gave birth. If the cosmological urge persists, one could return to its pre-philosophical efflorescence in the great cosmogonic myths or immerse oneself in the multiple scenarios of the multiverse, as Rubenstein herself has done in her follow-up book, *Worlds Without End: The Many Lives of the Multiverse*. And yet, the Why question still haunts in spite of its mythological or scientific rivals. The mystery of being is both older and ever-newer than all these.

Ever-New Surprise

Rubenstein turns to Nancy and his analysis of the *epistemological* dimension of the shock of wonder. Sounding a theme that will be central for Nancy, Rubenstein cites Luce Irigaray's comment on what for Descartes was "the first passion: *wonder*. This passion," says Irigaray,

"has no opposite or contradiction and exists as though for the first time ...
This feeling of surprise, astonishment, and wonder in the face of the
unknowable ... beholds what is sees always as if for the first time ... It does
not try to seize, possess, or reduce this object, but leaves it subjective,
still free" (Irigaray, 1993, 19-20/12-13; Rubenstein, 2008, 217-218, n. 28).
Describing Nancy's work, *Etre singulier pluriel/Being Singular Plural*,
Rubenstein says, as Nancy's title hints:

> when being is nothing but "just once, this time," each
> instance of existence is, in effect "the origin." If it is the
> case that "the world spring forth everywhere and in
> each instant, simultaneously," then the origin is what
> is most familiar, most ordinary, most common and in-
> common of all. Yet, precisely because it presences itself
> differently at each moment, this origin is unobjectifiable,
> unanticipatable, always coming as a complete surprise.
> (Nancy, 2000, 107/83; Rubenstein, 2008, 114)

What does this ever-new surprise of being disclosed in the mood of
wonder betoken for the existing knower? That "being itself is groundless,"
without Why; that "it is at the limits of thought...that thought must dwell."
In a note Rubenstein cites Kierkegaard: "This, then, is the paradox of
thought: to want to discover something that thought itself cannot think"
(Kierkegaard, 1985, 37; Rubenstein, 2008, 220 n. 64). For Nancy, as for
Derrida, "The unthinkable is the ethos of thinking." Again: "Thinking,
then, is a matter of freeing thinking for that which precedes it and
exceeds it – that which opens, and for that reason constantly slips away
from, philosophical discourse itself. [S]uch an ur-condition is 'the most
primitive layer of curiosity, the level on which we are primarily *interested*
by what is interesting par excellence (the origin)'" (Nancy, 2000, 39/20;
emphasis Rubenstein's, 2008, 112-113).

The epistemology of wonder is not an analytical, empiricist or any
other kind of metaphysical one; it is not a theory of knowledge reduced to
"finding a proof, launching a defense, providing a calculation, or securing
a determination." Rather it is existential, a matter of "holding thinking
within a certain original openness ... and in the furiousness with which
such groundlessness is denied" (Rubenstein, 2008, 114). The task of this
existential epistemology, opened up by the mood of wonder, is in a sense

to undo thinking, that is, "to undo the 'work' it will always be tempted to do," namely, to "erect some sort of edificial essence to guard against the vertiginous inessentiality, the ceaseless relationality, of existence itself. The work of thinking is, in other words, unworking" (Rubenstein, 2008, 115). As Nancy says of the 'aboriginal mood' of wonder, "in no way is this a blissful contemplation but, rather, a difficult, complex, and delicate set of decisions, acts, positions, and gestures of thought and writing" Nancy, 1997, 103/67):

> Wonder, as 'philosophy's virtue,' has something, rather, to do with keeping things difficult – with thinking at the limits of thinkability and making sense at the fault lines of sensibility. "In the final analysis, wonder is nothing other than that which happens or arrives at the limit. Wonder itself is a kind of sign without signification, and the sign – the index or the signal – that the signification is verging upon its limit, and that sense is laid bare.'" (Nancy, 1997,104/67; Rubenstein, 2008, 125).

Wonder, this most un- or anti-Cartesian "lucid" passion (one thinks rather of Camus) "that makes sense in and as the absence of sense" (Rubenstein, 2008, 126).

Thus for Nancy, "Exposed to the abandonment of sense, thinking runs up against a hardness at the limits of thinking – an unthinkability – a *resistance* to thought.... Such resistance, then, comes as a shock and gives rise to a kind of 'new awe.'" The mystery of being 'over-comes' thinking each time "as essentially surprising... Existence surprises us every time, so that, ultimately, there is no being at all without surprise. 'What makes an event an event is not only that it happens, but that it surprises.' In order to let beings come, thinking must therefore learn how to be astonished" (Nancy, 2000, 185/159; emphasis Rubenstein's, 2008, 126-127).

Nancy's epistemology of the ever-new surprise of wonder circles back to the existential and ontological themes in Rubenstein's analysis of Heidegger and Levinas and her introductory chapter on the phenomenon of wonder:

> If the movement by which the familiar becomes strange can be called shock (or surprise, anger, horror, or terror,

depending on one's situation), then the reciprocal, nonidentical movement by which this strangeness presents itself as *all there is* is indeed awe (or astonishment, marveling, etc. – but these terms can almost all be used in both of the senses we are attempting to distinguish here). In shock, thinking loses everything, and in awe, everything returns, at once more and less than thinking had thought it to be. (Rubenstein, 2008, 128)

The Gift of Wonder

In her Postlude Rubenstein returns once more to Irigaray. Wonder points us to the unthinkable, "the groundless ground," a fact that has devastating consequences for the fate of metaphysics. For, Irigaray says, "the groundless foundation of metaphysics amount to ruining metaphysics through and through" (Irigaray, 1999, 13/5; Rubenstein, 2008, 195). The destruction (or de-construction) of metaphysics, however, is not to be lamented. It is the painful but necessary price that philosophy must pay if it is to enjoy ecstasy, 'standing-out-in' (*ek-stasis*) the origin-al wonder that gave it birth: "only when there is the perilousness of being seized by terror do we find the bliss of wonder – being torn away in that wakeful manner that is *the breath of all philosophy*" (Heidegger, 1995, 531/366; Rubenstein, 2008, 234, n. 38). We have noted that for all three thinkers – Heidegger, Levinas and Nancy and indeed for Rubenstein herself – the 'negative' dimensions of the 'shock' of wonder bring about a dramatic conversion, an existential transformation, metamorphosing into their 'positive' partner in a dialectic of suffering and redemption. The shock of wonder translates into the ecstasy, the bliss of wonder. The double movement of wonder not only reveals, it *is* the gift of being.

There is a question, however, about the conclusion drawn from this existential dialectic. It is as if the dialectic, though painful and necessary to go through, unfolds almost automatically, as if once the terms of the equation are understood, the double-movement of the logic will drive to an inevitable telos. (As Rubenstein says, perhaps too revealingly, "these terms can almost all be used in both of the senses we are attempting to distinguish here.") There is a crucial factor missing, however. It is not a question of the meaning of terms. As the title of Rubenstein's chapter on

Derrida indicates, what is missing is the element of 'decision,' of choice, of, however limited, one's actual (as well as epistemological) freedom. For despite the logic of its dialectic, the shock of wonder could as easily eventuate in, leave us marooned existentially in, a sense of ultimate meaninglessness – the pessimism of a Schopenhauer, the nausea of Sartre's Roquentin, or the metaphysical nihilism that Smith was so anxious to overcome. Who or what is to say that it could not be so?

The shock of wonder, the question of the meaning of being, is not only a logical or epistemological conundrum, it puts the being of the questioner in question. It confronts us with a decision for which there are no guaranteed outcomes, a 'question' to which there are no certain 'answers.' There is only that perilous cliff over which we stare into the terrifying abyss of freedom. The Zen koan asks: "what do you do when nothing you do will do?" If we credit the thinking of these philosophers, and if we can find the courage within ourselves, the choice seems clear. The Hebrew Bible says, "I have set before you life and death, blessings and curses. Now choose life, so that you and your children may live" (Deut. 30:19). (Rubenstein, perhaps had this passage in mind, when she reminded us of "what Socrates told Theaetetus and what Heidegger, Levinas, and Nancy have all confirmed: the wonder philosophy opens is both a blessing and a curse.") Yes, a curse, a Kierkegaardian ditch seventy fathoms deep, which can only be crossed by a leap of faith. But because it can also be a blessing, it is a risk we must take. As Sister Helen Prejean adjures us in *Dead Man Walking*: "Choose life, seek justice; we are not permitted the luxury of despair." And so we must see the two-fold opening of wonder as a *gift*, indeed the *gift of being*.

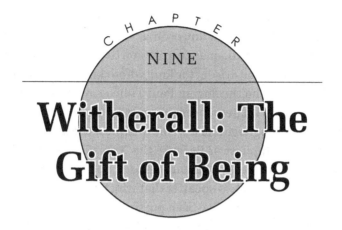

NINE

Witherall: The Gift of Being

Introduction: The Gift of Being

Arthur Witherall, the thinker discussed at the beginning of Part Two, discusses the gift-nature of being and our response to that gift in the last chapter of his book, *The Problem of Existence*. Examining his analysis, its insights and its problematic aspects, will lay the groundwork for looking at Heidegger's analysis of being, being as gift, and thinking as thanking in response to the gift of being.

Witherall introduces the existential-ontological nature of Being as gift at outset of his discussion. "The world does not exist for the sake of humanity. Rather we exist as outpourings of it" (Witherall, 121). As the 'beneficiaries' of this outpouring of Being, "the fundamental question of metaphysics, 'Why is there something instead of nothing?' ... confronts existence directly" (Witherall, 1, 121). What the title of his book calls 'the problem of existence' is thus "not a dry academic problem. It is not a question we can honestly treat as if it had no connection to our emotions and demanded nothing more of us than intellectual curiosity. It asks for the reason for existence, which is like asking for the absolute. It seeks for something which lies beyond our normal concepts and theories, and as such, it evokes absolute emotions" (Witherall, 121). The emotions evoked by the Why question, like those evoked by wonder – astonishment (*Erstaunen*), awe (*Scheu*), terror (*Erschrecken*) or reverence

(*Ehrfurcht*) – are '*absolute* emotions,' what Smith calls '*metaphysical* feelings.'

As *absolute* emotions or 'metaphysical' feelings, however, it is doubtful, says Witherall, that any ordinary concepts or technical terms of metaphysics can give adequate expression to the unique attitudes and emotional responses that arise at the limits of our knowledge and existence (Witherall, 122). As the theologian Paul Tillich says, absolute emotions (Tillich's term is 'ultimate concern') "must be expressed symbolically, because symbolic language alone is able to express the ultimate." Why not the concepts of metaphysics? Because the "transformation of concepts into symbols" when speaking about Being is due to the nature of that ultimacy – what it means to speak of that which is 'absolute.' In fact, the question is *not* the one we have been pursuing: 'Why is there something rather than nothing'?, which can be paraphrased as: 'Why *is* there *being*?' (an impossible combination of words, Tillich says). Rather, the question is: Which of the many possible *symbols or metaphors* for Being is *most adequate* to the meaning of Being? (Tillich, 1958, 47, 51, 54). For Witherall the answer to the Why question is found in exploring the metaphor of the *gift* of Being in both the subjective and objective senses of the genitive: Being is that which gives, and Being is that which is given. *The answer to the Why question is: Being is that which gives ... itself.*

Which, of course, is not an answer. To say that 'Being is ...' is, as Tillich says, an impossible combination of words, or at best a tautology, a '*t-autos-logos*,' a 'same-saying.' It is words just repeating themselves, chasing their tail in a hermeneutical circle. They seem to be saying something, but in fact they are saying nothing. What about this 'saying'? What about this 'nothing'? Not all hermeneutical circles are vicious, some can be virtuous if, as Heidegger says, we enter them "in the right way." So, if by focusing on 'gift' instead of 'Being' we take the above italicized statement not as an assertion of metaphysical fact but as an interpretive clue, a metaphorical pointer, it may be 'saying' something after all. If not only the 'answer' but even the Why 'question' itself are circular tautologies, perhaps resort to the metaphor of gift can shed light on how this particular instance of 'same-saying' may be saying something significant, something of deeper, profound, perhaps even abyssal importance.

Gift as Metaphor

Witherall analyzes three different dimensions of the metaphor of the gift of Being: the gift metaphor itself; its metaphysical content; its emotional or existential significance. In a conclusion he considers 'the meaning of it all,' serving as a transition from the *gift* of Being to thinking about *Being* as gift.

'Being gives Being (itself) to beings'

Witherall begins his exposition of the gift metaphor with a thesis statement that needs to be cited in full:

> The basic thought I wish to express is the thought that the existence of something instead of nothing is a gift. The existence of things, or the existence of the world as a whole, is given gratuitously. It is a bestowal of power and intelligibility, which is both free and unnecessary. This gift cannot be understood within a framework or economy of justification and reward, nor within the standard explanatory frameworks of reasons and causes, for it is asymmetrical. There is nothing 'beyond Being' which is not already involved in the transaction. Indeed, we may appropriately express the idea of the gift of Being by saying, not that there is some transcendent entity which acts or creates, but rather that it is Being which gives itself to beings. If we are to speak of anything which transcends the contingent world of finite entities, then it must be both that which gives and that which is given, somehow at the same time. Hence the question, 'Why is there something instead of nothing?' is answered by the proposition that Being gives itself to beings. That is, Being gives Being (itself) to beings such as ourselves, the things around us, and everything else which exists. Hence Being gives itself to the whole as a whole. This proposition is opaque as it stands, and requires a thorough exposition. If there is a transcendent source for all things which

exist, however, it is not a 'being.' It must be counted as Being itself. If there is no transcendent source of beings, then Being is identical with Nothingness, or with the absence of an ultimate. Yet, I shall argue, even in this case it remains true that Being gives itself to beings. (Witherall, 122-123)

This passage, packed with insights, provocations, and problematic elements, needs to be unpacked sentence by sentence. As Witherall says, "This proposition is opaque as it stands, and requires a thorough exposition." A preliminary analysis will prepare the way for appreciating the constructive aspects and challenging the more questionable aspects of his treatment of the gift of Being.

On the constructive side. Witherall says his 'basic thought' is that "the existence of something instead of nothing" is a gift. This metaphorical thesis has both ontological and existential import. Equating the term 'Being' with 'the existence of something instead of nothing,' he says that it is 'given to us.' Moreover, it is given 'gratuitously,' openly, abundantly, with no compulsion; it is 'free and unnecessary.' And yet as the 'to us' indicates, it ineluctably calls for a response: the gift of Being "must be evaluated as such when we try to understand it."

As the term 'understand' indicates, the thesis has epistemological and hermeneutical significance as well. How is Being, the gift of Being, to be understood? One thing is clear, how it is *not* to be understood: "This gift cannot be understood within a framework or economy of justification and reward, nor within the standard explanatory frameworks of reasons and causes, for it is asymmetrical." In other words, it is not to be explained or interpreted in terms of a causal or teleological metaphysics, nor can its logic resist any conceptual domestication whatever. Metaphysically the gift of Being is a sheer, fortuitous, gratuitous anomaly.

Then how *are* we to understand what apparently is resistant to all our usual modes of understanding, explaining or interpreting things? At this point Witherall makes an observation that will come back to give him trouble later. He says: "we may appropriately express the idea of the gift of Being by saying, not that there is some transcendent entity which acts or creates, but rather that it is Being wh gives itself to beings." On the face of it, this seems consistent with what he has just said about the resistance of the metaphor to any traditional framework, whether metaphysical or, as the terms 'acts' and 'creates' suggest, theological. As we shall see, however, his later comments will contradict this rather clear stricture, confronting us with the troubling question, why – why when he is so clear here does he take back his remarks when he turns to the details of his exposition? On what will he base the apparent *volte face*?

Toward the end of his opening remarks he makes a rather provocative observation that would apparently put the seal on his anti-metaphysical remarks. As he goes on to say, it we continue to wish to talk of something transcendent to "the contingent world of finite entities," on the one hand, but if there is no transcendent being on the other, this would mean that "Being is identical with Nothingness, or with the absence of an ultimate." It is not clear, however, how he means us to understand this rather sudden and dramatic ontological equation, because, in an apparent reversal of what he has just said, he concludes his opening statement by saying "Yet, I shall argue, even in this case it remains true that Being gives itself to beings." That Being gives itself to beings, that "Being gives Being (itself) to beings such as ourselves, the things around us, and everything else which exists," however tautological the proposition may be, nevertheless has an aura of meaningfulness about it. But to say that "Nothingness gives Being (itself) to beings such as ourselves, the things around us, and everything else which exists" would seem to be the total breakdown of meaningfulness altogether, a descent into complete and unintelligible ontological mystification, pure gibberish.

On the problematic side. Talk about Nothingness as giving Being to beings aside (it seems a temporary lapse in an otherwise consistent metaphysical thesis), there are other questionable propositions in Witherall's opening thesis statement that should be highlighted before we proceed. A problem arises already with Witherall's question concerning his own statement: "How does this proposition ['Being gives itself to beings'] explain why there is something rather than nothing?" Disregarding for the moment the idea that such a proposition does any 'explaining' at all, the difficulty continues in his two-fold answer: "Firstly, it is a metaphoric-metaphysical restatement of the fact of existence itself." As such, it is "a way of comprehending that there is something rather than nothing." First, how can the self-destructing phrase, 'metaphorical-metaphysical,' be used to explain anything? Further, how can this "impossible combination of words" be a used to 'restate the fact of existence'? It does not even qualify as an ingredient in a tautology. How can it be a 'way of understanding' something so resistant to comprehension as the fact there is something rather than nothing? Trying to force a metaphysical box into a metaphorical bottle is like trying to push a square peg into a round hole. It is saying, contrary to the sense of the two phenomena, that metaphors can be 'translated' into – reinterpreted by the concepts of – metaphysics without loss of meaning. As with poetry rendered into prose, what matters eludes the hermeneutical violence – its *experiential truth*. Witherall is going to have to work hard to get us to accept an 'explanation' plagued by an identity crisis – is it metaphorical or metaphysical? is it poetry-plus or science-minus?

Second, he says that the proposition ['Being gives itself to beings'] is "a schematic representation of the general form of explanation which has been employed throughout this essay." He seems to regard it as a metaphysically neutral or empty container hospitable to whatever concrete metaphysical explanations are inserted, an abstract formula which will "explain why our answers to the fundamental question succeed, when they succeed, in producing satisfaction" (Witherall, 123, brackets added). To be a general schema, it must be applicable to all three of the responses he will be analyzing (necessitarian, immanence, evaluative.) The formula is said to explain why a transcendence-based metaphysics, for example, theism, or a non-transcendence-based answer, for example, Smith's 'deflationary' metaphysics, make feelings of awe vis-a-vis Being or the world-whole 'appropriate.' By applying the formula we will be able to give "a complete answer to the fundamental question" (Witherall, 124) – this despite the fact that such answers may be refutable on other grounds. What about other 'explanatory relations,' for example, "creating or grounding or necessitating"? If Being can be "subsumed under" any of them, then they too, generously, can be included under the "umbrella relation of gift-giving." The relation of 'giving,' he says, has "deep evaluative significance and great explanatory power... it is at once personal, evaluative, mundane and transcendent." It would seem the gift umbrella can be opened up wide enough to shelter just about any relation under the metaphysical sun! Indeed his choice of the word 'schematic' to characterize this explanatory 'umbrella' is indicative of the underlying problem of his thesis – its inability to make up its mind. A 'schematic' form can be either a 'simplified' form or a 'symbolic' form. Therein lies the ambiguity that haunts his exposition.

There is a further problem. In interpreting the metaphorical proposition that 'Being gives itself to beings,' he falls back on metaphysical dichotomies that ground 'the standard explanatory frameworks of reasons and cause' he had just rejected as inadequate for 'explaining' the 'asymmetrical' question of Being. Thus he distinguishes, as in traditional metaphysics, between transcendent and immanent, necessary and contingent being. He says, "the capitalized word 'Being' denotes the transcendent source of the gift of existence, hence the origin of all finite beings. The uncapitalized word 'beings' means 'immanent entities." Again: "If there is a transcendent source for all things which exist, however, it is not a 'being.' It must be counted as Being itself. If there is no transcendent source of beings, then Being is identical with Nothingness, or with the absence of an ultimate." This appears on the surface to be saying that the explanatory framework of metaphysical causes is appropriate for capturing the 'asymmetry' of Being. Being can be brought under conceptual control after all; it proves to be nothing other than the familiar metaphysical 'source' or 'origin' of the world of contingent entities. This cosmological-metaphysical misunderstanding of the meaning of Being is confirmed when he conflates the two notions we have been trying to differentiate: the '*existence* of things ' (meaning the *Being* of beings) and 'the existence of the *world* as a whole' (emphasis added).

These critical observations would seem to undermine Witherall's use of the gift metaphor to understand the meaning of Being. The problematic aspect of his thesis, stemming from his impossible hybrid of 'metaphorical-metaphysical explanation,' will continue to plague the rest of his exposition. However, if we return to the constructive side of the metaphor, there may be more to be said. The above criticisms may prove useful in clarifying how the metaphor of gift, *properly* understood, can serve as an *appropriate* response to the mystery of Being, as an 'evaluative' answer to the question, 'Why is there something rather than nothing?'

The Metaphor of Gift.

Our metaphysical feelings, Witherall says, here in agreement with Smith and James, are two-directional. They "are not merely inner strivings of the soul, they are directed outward towards the immanent world, or at the transcendent source of immanent beings." The feeling of "confronting something vast and indigestible...is powerful." We encounter the existence of the universe, the world-whole, that 'strange wonder' (Rubenstein), as if "receiving a gift." We respond to it as "that which has given and that which is given." Our feelings of awe, joy and gratitude are intelligible, Witherall argues, "if we think of existence itself as a gift" (Witherall, 123-124).

What is an appropriate understanding of and response to a gift? A 'true gift' (Witherall is here using the word 'true' in an 'absolute' or unqualified sense) is "a gratuitous bestowal of something. It is not a measured exchange of objects with commensurate value, but something free and unnecessary, something which is given and received without any expectation of a return. All that expected of one who receives gift is that he truly (that word again!) accept it as his own, and appreciate it." If a gift was given, Witherall says, "only because a return was expected, the transaction has been reduced to an economic exchange" (Witherall, 124). The gift is no longer a gift, it's just a mundane trade-off. Of first importance, then, is the 'how' of one's receiving of the gift, one's attitude and comportment toward it. An appropriate response must be as "personal and intimate" as the gesture behind the giving. The assumption is that one who makes "a truly gratuitous bestowal...must lose something personal or intimate" (Witherall, 125). Though he does not cite him, Witherall's analysis is clearly in accord with the influential understanding of 'the gift' in Derrida and philosophers influenced by him. The anthropological ritual of sacrifice and the theological concept of *kenosis*, self-emptying, perhaps also lie behind his notion of the gift.

As Witherall points out, before the rise of philosophy, "many of the oldest cosmogonies, cast in the form of mythological stories, understood the origin of the universe in terms of the concept of birth." The metaphor of giving birth, of bringing about the existence of something, was how one gave expression to the *significance* of the event, a meaning that could not and, for all that, still cannot be expressed in the more 'neutral' words of the later cosmologies of the metaphysicians. As Witherall argues, "unless we speak in some such way, we will miss an essential aspect of the event. The origin of the world – this is not an everyday happening. It is the happening of all happenings, and it leads to everything, to all beings" (Witherall, 125). We remember Smith's use of the word 'happening' in this context, in particular its uncertain oscillating between a cosmological and ontological interpretation of existence. A similar hermeneutic instability seems to infect Witherall's presentation as well.

Witherall concludes his analysis of the metaphor of gift with a mix of phenomenological, metaphysical and theological observations. ""Existence is freely given, and freely presented to us. If this were not so, then it would be impossible to interpret existence as a gift of love" (1 Witherall, 26). We were prepared for this particular gloss of love as the motivation behind the gift by his previous comments on the personal, intimate and self-sacrificial nature of the act of bestowal.

Providing an example of how theism might satisfy the schematic formula of the gift of Being, Witherall cites the divine gift of Creation:

> Properly conceived, this is not merely an approximation
> to ontological giving, it is the real thing, or a least an
> example of the real thing. For 'God' is one of the names
> of Being, and creation is just the totality of beings. In
> the idea of the gift of creation have instance of complete
> emptying. God divests himself of his own Being, and
> gives it to beings, to the world. And yet, paradoxically,
> God remains what he always was. (Witherall, 127)

To justify this theistic construal of the 'gift of being' "without employing the standard, mundane concept of causation," Witherall invokes a non-standard interpretation of theistic metaphysics that verges on pantheism or at least something like Whitehead and Hartshorne's panentheism. "God acts on himself and hence, in a way, he 'becomes' finite." He further defends this hermeneutical departure from classical theism by referring to another metaphysical option: "Mystical theism asserts that God remains infinite even while becoming finite." Witherall is particularly attracted to this latter possibility because "This is a form of expression which is available to theists, but...is also possible to express...in terms acceptable to an atheist." How? Simple. By using "the religiously neutral words I have already employed: 'Being gives itself to beings.'" Of course if we do that, he says, we must understand "'Being' as signifying something extramundane" – for example, Smith's 'world-whole' or perhaps Heidegger's sense of 'Being' (Witherall, 127).

This hermeneutical sliding back and forth among the metaphysics of theism, pantheism, panentheism, mysticism, whole-world cosmology, and Heideggerian ontology is perhaps not the best way to do justice to the genuine insight offered by the metaphor of gift for responding to the mystery of existence. It only works it we accept Witherall's underlying premiss, that the metaphor, 'Being gives itself to beings,' is indeed an empty form that can be fleshed out by a wide variety of metaphysical applications, regardless of the merits of any independent arguments that lend or deny them support. This is an assumption, however, that will be challenged in the following remarks. That this critique calls into question the metaphor of the gift of Being in no way follows. Metaphors outlive metaphysics.

Gift as Metaphysics

"*Symbol gives rise to thought*" (Paul Ricoeur). Witherall's understanding of the metaphor of gift is apparently compatible with, can in Ricouer's mantra, "give rise to," a variety of metaphysical interpretations. In an ensuing catalog of traditional metaphysical attributes, what he terms the 'features of the gift of Being,' he gives this (alleged) hermeneutical adaptability of the gift metaphor free philosophical reign. The mixed nature of the 'applications of the explanation-schema' that result from the muddled notion of 'metaphorical-metaphysical explanation' is not unexpected, but it will be necessary to separate the metaphorical kernel from the metaphysical chaff.

Though using the metaphor of gift to imagine the relation of Being to beings, this does not, says Witherall, "specify the whole sense of the proposition that Being gives itself to beings. There are other significant features of transcendent Being, considered as a gift. These must also be specified if the proposed explanation-schema for 'something instead of nothing' it to succeed" (Witherall, 128). Witherall highlights three of these 'other significant features': metaphysical necessity, transcendence, and intelligibility. Notice the assumptions we are asked to buy into. The first is that an interpretation of the metaphor *as metaphor* is not sufficient for understanding 'the whole sense' of the (metaphorical? metaphysical?) 'proposition' that Being 'gives' itself to beings. The metaphor 'gives rise' to the necessity of a 'translation' into the categories of metaphysical 'thought.' But is this necessity('must') necessarily so? For Ricoeur the 'thought' to which the 'symbol' (here, metaphor) 'gives rise' does not escape from, go 'beyond' ('meta-') the realm of the metaphorical into the empyrean heaven of metaphysics; it remains embedded within the mundane, 'earthy' context of the symbol itself and interprets it from within the wealth of its own metaphorical resources. As Ricoeur says, "this articulation of thought [is] left to itself in the realm of symbols" (Ricoeur, 288). The second assumption is that we are looking for an 'explanation' of something – the mystery of Being – that is 'asymmetrical' to, antithetical to, any explanation whatsoever – that in particular is allergic to the hubris of attempts to domesticate it within a metaphysical 'explanation-schema.'

There is, in short, no need for a metaphysical *translation* of the metaphor of the gift of Being, nor for a metaphysical *explanation* of the mystery of Being. To think so suggests a misunderstanding of the nature of the metaphor and the mystery. But perhaps something can be rescued from the 'metaphysical features' and 'applications of the explanation-schema.' We can ask of each to what extent does it illuminate or detract from understanding the metaphor of gift as an *appropriate* response to the mystery of Being?

Metaphysical Features

Metaphysical Necessity. Of the three metaphysical 'features' Witherall gives the most attention to the 'necessity' of the gift of Being. We must too, accordingly. We begin, then, by asking what light, if any, the metaphysical concept of necessity (as distinguished from contingency) can shed on the gift of Being. Already at the outset there is a difficulty. How is one to reconcile this concept with Witherall's characterization of a 'true' gift as one that is 'free and unnecessary.' How can the gift of Being be both necessary and unnecessary? Does Witherall try to resolve this apparent contradiction, or does his explanation simply skirt it?

Witherall begins with a circular hypothetical. If there is a 'genuinely explanatory' answer to the Why question, then "it must truly function as an explanation." Though this looks suspiciously like a tautology – if A is A, then A is A – Witherall insists it cannot be reduced to an "empty tautology." This assumes, of course, that all 'same-saying' is 'empty,' an assumption we have already had cause to reject. His argument continues: "We must be able to say that something exists *because* Being gives itself to beings" (my emphasis). This again looks like words that amount to saying the same thing. He concludes, however, that these two statements are meaningful, that they do 'say something,' and thus entitle us to "exclude the possibility that speaking of 'Being' is unintelligible." Instead, "we must be able to speak of transcendent Being" (Witherall, 128). The hypothetical has been converted by a feat of logical legerdemain into a categorical assertion. The metaphor of gift has been magically transmogrified into a metaphysics of causality.

How can this surprising move be justified? Because, he says, already the Why question "presupposes that there is 'something' in virtue of which things exist. This something is Being, and it is transcendent. It is not reducible to the status of an immanent object within the contingent world" (Witherall, *ibid.*). On the contrary, the easy assumption, indeed the reduction of the asymmetrical notion of Being as a 'transcendent' resident *within* the house establishment of the metaphysics, dwelling in domestic partnership with its hoary opposite, 'the contingent world,' makes total nonsense of the radical discomfiture, the shock and estrangement, to which the Why question subjects the entire metaphysical tradition, by which it effects the *closure* of metaphysics. It assumes there is no way to talk of the 'relation' between Being and beings except in terms of the metaphysical dualism of transcendent versus contingent being and a *causal* relation between them. It assumes there is no way to understand the 'transcendence' of Being or its relation to beings *non-metaphysically*.

Operating on these highly questionable assumptions, Witherall draws a further, perfectly logical but equally *fragwuerdig* conclusion. "In claiming that Being gives itself, *and* using this as an explanation-schema for understanding the fact of existence, we are excluding the possibility that the presupposition fails" (Witherall, 128; my emphasis). The fly/flaw in the logical ointment is that the metaphorical nature of the first half of the sentence is negated by its reinterpretation in the second part as an explanation-schema that is metaphysical in nature. The allegedly 'excluded' possibility then logically follows. But the conclusion is invalidated by the hybrid nature of the premisses.

Before continuing his argument, Witherall makes what seems to be an aside, repeating a puzzling remark he made earlier, a dialectical observation that is even more provocative, if possible. He says there is a 'legitimate answer' to the Why question, "even if the answer involves an identification of (transcendent) Being with Nothing." Even here, he says, the explanatory schema may be applied: "That Nothing lies at the heart of things, that there is a *'creative'* Nothingness which *makes* beings be, is an occasion for marveling, and it is neither verbal trickery nor gibberish" (ibid., my emphasis). Again, though here his argument really does seem to verge on the edge of linguistic absurdity, he invokes the language of metaphysical causality ('makes things be') to talk about the (non-?) 'relation' of an allegedly 'creative' Non-Being to the realm of being-full things. It is best to leave this seeming double-talk in the already problematic world of metaphysical speculation to one side, returning to it later – if we must.

Returning to his argument, Witherall appears to acknowledge that the proposition (explanatory schema?) 'Being gives itself to beings' could be construed as a tautology after all. But, he hastens to add, this would be to misinterpret it. How? By "ignoring its relational form." But when he explicates the semantic content of the metaphorical gift 'relation,' he immediately lapses back into the jargon of a logic derived from metaphysics. To see 'Being gives itself to beings' as merely a tautology, he says, is to assert that it is "no more than the predication or instantiation of the property of 'existence.'" But this is a confusing way of uttering the empty truism that "things which exist have existence." It is to deny "that there is a transcendent Being which can be related to immanent things" (Witherall, 128). It simply returns us to where we started!

Interpreting the relation, 'Being gives itself to beings,' as a tautology is in any case, says Witherall, a 'misreading.' Why? Because, as the metaphor of giving a gift implies, "Being must give itself to that which is genuinely *other* to itself, to that which is immanent, or it will not be a real gift, for it will not involve the relation of giving" (Witherall, 129; my emphasis). We forget for the moment that Witherall has also said that the relation of giving can be interpreted self-referentially, solipsistically, as Being giving Being to *itself*. The critical point is that, given these assumptions, the gift-relation has to be interpreted as 'real' in *metaphysical* terms. For Witherall, there is no other *non-tautological, non-metaphysical* way of making sense of the metaphor of the 'gift' of Being.

Further logico-metaphysical distinctions accrue to the otherwise hapless metaphor. The allegedly 'explanatory' proposition, 'Being gives itself to beings,' is not only not tautological, it is also not contingent. Rejecting the "positivist dichotomy between tautologous necessity and empirical contingency," Witherall says "there is little sense here in speaking of either logical necessity or contingency." Why? Because the 'proposition' is a 'schematic' one. It turns out that 'Being gives itself to beings' not, in the ordinary sense, a logical or fact-stating proposition at all; it simply expresses the 'general form' of 'satisfactory' propositional, i.e., metaphysical answers to the Why question. If pushed, one could say the explanatory schema has a kind of 'metaphysical' necessity, but this should be interpreted to mean that 'Being gives itself to beings' is "'necessary' given that there is a fully satisfactory answer at all" (Witherall, 129). Of course that is precisely the devastating question that the shock of Being puts to the entire metaphysical enterprise. The first part of the conclusion Witherall draws from this logical-metaphysical situation at first looks the same: "There might be no such answer." But the second part of his conclusion goes beyond this, in itself already startling, possibility. If not, he says, "then it is either false or nonsensical to say that Being gives itself to beings." With this he has again painted himself into a corner from which, given his metaphysical assumptions, there appears no exit. For there is another possibility. Though there is may be no metaphysical answer to the Why question, there are other, non-metaphysical 'answers' that make possible an appropriate understanding of and response to the metaphor of the gift of Being. We will return to this point below.

Here Witherall introduces a new, tantalizing possibility, one that reminds of Heidegger's indecision about the relation of Being to beings. "Under the present interpretation," he says, "it is not metaphysically possible for there to be absolutely no beings at all." As Heidegger might have put it, Being is always the Being of beings. But why could there not be Being without beings? Because, says Witherall, "this would be equivalent to saying it is possible for the gift of Being to be permanently and universally withheld, so that no possible thing was actualized at all. This may be considered a bare logical possibility, but nothing more" (Witherall, 129). Ignoring for the moment the controversial distinction between metaphysical and logical possibility and the resort to Aristotelian metaphysical distinctions between possibility and actuality, there is another possibility – that Being is not always the Being of beings, not only 'not always' but 'not at all.' This might make no sense *metaphysically*, but it might be precisely what is meant by saying *metaphorically* that Being gives the gift of Being to beings. If there are beings, then yes, speaking metaphorically, not metaphysically, it is Being that gives them Being. But Being does not 'have' to grant Being to beings. If it does so, then as

Witherall himself has earlier said in interpreting the meaning of the metaphor, it is not out of metaphysical necessity but gratuitously. That Being gives itself to beings is metaphysically inexplicable, mysterious, without Why, 'free and unnecessary.'

That Witherall cannot free himself from the bewitching spell of metaphysical categories is even plainer in his follow-up defense. "Within the scope of the metaphysical possibilities allowed *under the assumption that there is a satisfactory answer to the question of existence*, there is no room for a situation in which there is *a transcendent Being* whose *role is to explain why* anything exists at all, and yet this role is *contingently* not performed. Such a supposition is self-defeating" (ibid., emphases mine). Of course if one subscribes to those ancient categories, then by definition the argument carries. Perhaps Witherall can be forgiven, however, for even Heidegger was immune from that old-time magic when he changed from thinking there could be Being without beings to saying that Being is [always?] the Being of beings. Perhaps Tillich was more alert to the difference between metaphysics and metaphor when he moved in a reverse direction from saying that 'God is Being' was a non-symbolic statement to saying that 'God is Being' was a symbolic expression. The point is, Witherall assumes that the *meaning* of the *metaphor* of 'gift' is that there is a *metaphysical* 'answer' to the question of Being, that the answer *refers* to a metaphysically-interpreted phenomenon of Being, that Being is in some sense 'transcendent' in 'relation' to a 'contingent' world whose existence it is 'necessary' to 'explain' metaphysically by reference to that transcendent Being.

In the absence of that assumption, Witherall says, repeating what he said earlier, the most one could say is that transcendent Being is 'equivalent' to Nothing, and that "this equivalence helps to explain why the world exists as a logically [*not metaphysically?*] contingent fact." To say that transcendent Being is 'equivalent' to Nothing, assuming we know whether this paradoxical equation is saying anything all, for Witherall "entails that the world's existence is a contingent fact, and thus satisfies the intuitions of the brute fact view, but even in this case we cannot say that the world is an absolutely brute fact. To say this would be to say that it is not merely logically contingent but also that it is utterly unintelligible, and thus make a satisfactory response impossible" (Witherall, 129-130). Witherall's statements here are rife with problems. To say, first of all, that the world's existence is a contingent fact, i.e, absent any metaphysical basis in transcendent Being, does not necessarily mean that its existence is a 'brute' fact. That is a misleading way of expressing the 'deflationary' position, and in any case is not Quentin Smith's view of the non-transcendently-grounded world-whole. Secondly, it does not follow from the absence of a transcendent metaphysical explanation, that therefore the world's existence is 'utterly unintelligible, unless, of course, the intelligibility of the world is, by definition, once again keyed to a metaphysical explanation rather than a metaphorical vision.

Even on Witherall's own chosen metaphysical grounds, he appears to concede that the brute fact, i.e., utter unintelligiblity of the world's existence does not necessarily not follow. One could, he says, "consider the possibility that no truly satisfactory answer can be given to the question, not even the answer provided by the brute fact view, that there is no reason for something instead of than nothing. This appears to be a logical possibility, there is nothing self-contradictory about it" (Witherall, 129-130). But it would be premature to think so. Rundle, as we saw in Part One of this study, rejected the logical possibility of the 'brute fact' view. It turns out that Witherall agrees: "we cannot seriously consider the idea." Why not? Because, returning to his default position, Witherall says, in that case once again we would not be able to say that Being gives itself to beings. For the 'brute fact' position would have implied an 'intelligible explanation' where in fact there was none. The alleged logical possibility, therefore, is not just false, it is totally meaningless (Witherall, 130).

Witherall concludes, "If this is clear, then it is also clear that the explanation schema, which is expressed by the gift metaphor, has *a certain kind* of necessity. This kind of metaphysical necessity will make more sense if the notion of transcendent Being is taken to be genuinely significant, and not *merely* a metaphorical or mythological concept" (Witherall, 130; emphases mine). A 'certain kind' of necessity? If not metaphysical, then perhaps metaphorical? Or would that be 'merely' a metaphor? Having offered us the metaphor of gift on the one hand, is he now withdrawing it on the other, replacing the 'merely metaphorical or mythological' with the 'metaphysical'? Alas! it would appear so. One is reminded of Tillich's comment about symbols: "Only a symbol? He who asks this question shows that he has not understood the difference between signs and symbols nor the power of symbolic language, which surpasses in quality and strength the power of any non-symbolic language. One should never say 'only a symbol,' but one should say 'not less than a symbol'" (Tillich, 1958, 52).

With Tillich's remarks in mind, perhaps, as we said at the outset of this section, we can rescue something from Witherall's discussion of metaphysical necessity that will illuminate, not confuse, the way in which the metaphor of gift can be seen as an *appropriate response* to the mystery of Being. What can we take away from the *metaphysical concept* that might help us to understand the *metaphorical symbol*? There may not be a metaphysical answer to Witherall's 'fundamental question of existence,' does that preclude there being a metaphorical 'answer'? If not, then there might still be sense in saying that Being 'gives' (itself) to beings, 'gives' beings their Being. The 'giving' of Being to beings may not involve metaphysical necessity, and yet the metaphor of a gift does express a 'necessity.' It is the 'necessity,' the need, to see, to experience, to be aware of, to think of and to respond to the 'relation' of Being and beings *in a certain way,* a way that is uniquely expressed in the metaphor of a *gift.* If so, then gift-metaphor is not a 'mere symbol'? Nor is the 'relation' expressed in the metaphorical statement, 'Being gives itself,' a 'mere tautology' simply 'restating' the 'fact' of Being. In fact, we will need to ask in what sense the metaphor of the 'gift' of Being points to a 'relation' at all.

At this juncture we need to remind ourselves of the nature of a metaphor, or symbol, and its difference from a literal word, whether an ordinary everyday word or the technical abstraction of a metaphysical concept. What, then, is a metaphor? It is a double-barreled term, and in this context, doubly so. First, it involves 'transferring' a meaning *forward* (from the Greek *meta-,* 'across, beyond' + *pherein,* 'to bear,' thus 'to carry across or beyond'), from the thing to which it literally applies, 'across or beyond' to a phenomenon that is different but analogous. The metaphor is said to re-present this phenomenon by virtue of some feature it possesses that resembles a feature of the source meaning. Thus the metaphor of the gift of Being is said to be appropriate if it expresses some feature of Being that is similar to a feature of gifts in their ordinary sense. The feature of the 'gift' of Being that Witherall highlights is its 'free and unnecessary' nature, similar to that of a 'true' gift. Note that this 'transferring' of meaning moves in precisely the *opposite* direction from the 'translating' of a metaphor *back* into literal speech. Such translation does not retain the concrete meaning of the metaphor stemming from the 'materiality' of its original source, but rather dims down its meaning, reducing it to the abstract 'formality' of metaphysical thought with an inevitable loss of meaning, of its *existential force*, its 'truth.'

When it comes to expressions of that which is 'ultimate,' there is a second 'duplicity' in the metaphor of the gift of Being. As an expression of what Smith insightfully termed '*felt* meaning, i.e. not literal meaning (which includes the technical terms of metaphysics), it is as much an expression of *our* existential relation to the mystery of Being and the beings to which it 'gives' itself as it is to the mystery of Being itself and its 'relation' to us. What Tillich observes of religious symbols, may, with a substitution ['Being' for 'God'], be applied to the metaphor of the gift of Being: "In the notion of God [*the gift of Being*] we must distinguish two elements: the element of ultimacy [*Being*], which is a matter of immediate experience and not symbolic in itself, and the element of concreteness, which is taken from our ordinary experience [*a gift*] and symbolically applied to God [*Being*]" (Tillich, 1958, 53). In the ordinary experience of receiving a gift, one that was gratuitous, we find an existentially powerful symbol for expressing our experience of something 'beyond' that, something we can only describe as an experience of the 'gift' of Being itself and what that means for our own existence.

In other words, the Why question should be 'demetaphysicized,' taken out of the 'language game' of metaphysical causes and cosmological origins, and inserted into a different 'form of life,' one that more adequately expresses its existential-ontological import. That is, it should not be seen as a metaphysical question looking for a metaphysical answer, as a puzzled query searching for and legitimating a metaphysical 'explanation.' Rather it should be interpreted as a metaphorical way of directing us to the mystery of Being, albeit in a mixed mode, in as it were 'metaphysical disguise,' a metaphorical expression whose grammatical function (its 'role' to use Witherall's word) is as a pointer to the mystery of being inviting our response. To paraphrase Tillich, the point is not to be misled into looking for a metaphysical answer to the Why question as if it were such a question. The point is rather to ask which symbols, which metaphors, are most appropriate to expressing the mystery to which that question points, and thus to indicate appropriately felt responses. Tillich says that symbols 'participate' in the reality of that to which they point; they 'open up' dimensions of that reality and 'unlock dimensions' of our being which 'correspond to' to those features (Tillich, 1958, 48-49). The question of Being is not asking for a metaphysical answer; it is asking which of the many symbols of Being are most adequate to the meaning of Being and its meaning for my being.

If we proceed on the basis of this existential-ontological understanding of the two-fold duality of metaphors in relation to the 'ultimate,' then Witherall's choice of the metaphor of a gift to express the 'necessity' of the Being makes eminent good sense. The 'necessity' is an existential one, but the 'necessity,' paradoxically is 'free and unnecessary.' On the one hand, there is no necessity to respond to the mystery of Being; we are not required, not compelled. On the other hand, the fundamental question of existence is compelling, unavoidable, inescapable. It poses a demand, an exigency, to which we must respond. And we do, but – paradox upon paradox – usually, *zunaechst und zumeist*, by various strategies of evasion. The gift of Being is an offer we cannot refuse, existentially, yet one we are free to refuse, epistemologically (Hick). An offer, a gift, that cannot and can be refused. It is a 'necessity' because, as beings whose being is an issue, the question of being puts our own being in question. Willy-nilly we 'find' ourselves existentially 'moved' by an ultimate concern, drawn by an 'existential teleology,' but that concern is expressed the most part in the disguise of a raft of penultimate concerns – as what H. Richard Niebuhr called an existential 'polytheism,' what Heidegger called an 'inauthentic mode of existing, a way of being not 'attuned' to the question of Being. The structure and dynamic of our existence is inexorably determined by that concern or 'care' (Heidegger). And yet we are 'free' to choose the among a endless variety of ways of actualizing that 'care.' We are free to delude ourselves that we need not confront the question of the ultimate meaning of our being, that we can avoid the question of the ultimate meaning of Being itself. To be sure, the question of the meaning of Being is not the same as the question of the meaning of *our* being – but it is inextricably linked to it. Ultimately, there is no escaping it, no exit. It is 'necessary.'

To conclude: On the one hand, Witherall's argument is that if there *is* a metaphysical 'answer,' a metaphysical 'necessity,' then Being's 'giving' of itself is *not* truly a gift. Being would have to 'give' itself to beings out of ontological compulsion – out of *necessity*. The necessity could be cast in terms of a metaphysical theory of 'emanation' or a theological concept of 'creation.' But whatever the metaphysical details, the point is that Being would *have* to 'ground,' *have* to 'create,' *have* to be the 'source,' 'origin' or primordial 'cause' of beings. Being would then no longer be a mystery, 'without why.' We would no longer be able to speak of the *gift* of Being. The metaphor of 'gift' would be reduced to the subordinate status of 'merely' a metaphor, 'only' a symbol, awaiting the 'translation' of its *true* meaning into the *non-metaphorical* vocabulary of metaphysics.

On the other hand, if we draw out the implications of his own initial description of the gift metaphor we see that the argument must be reversed. The non- or anti-metaphysical point of the metaphor is that if there *is* an answer, explanation, or necessity, then Being *cannot* be said to 'give' itself to beings. Clearly that would be is to reverse the meaning of the 'necessity' that Witherall professes to see in the metaphorical expression, 'Being gives itself to beings.' It suggests that perhaps he does not see the implications of his own use of the gift metaphor. If something is a 'true gift,' then as he says it is 'free and unnecessary.' In other words, there is *no* necessity for it, *no* explanation for it, *no* 'Why.' Otherwise it could not *truly* be a gift. That is the whole point of the metaphor of the *gift* of Being.

Transcendence. We come to the second 'metaphysical feature' that Witherall highlights: *transcendence.* Here too we shall ask what light, if any, the metaphysical concept of transcendence (as distinguished from contingency) casts on the metaphor of the gift of Being. To what extent does it make sense or create obstacles for understanding the gift metaphor as an *appropriate* response to the mystery of Being? What does Witherall think the concept of metaphysical transcendence means, and how does he think it applies to the metaphor of the gift of Being?

Something is 'transcendent,' he says if "it cannot be conceived as a concrete contingent thing amongst other things, falls under no category, and is dependent on nothing outside itself." But having said then, he then proceeds to list several definitional features of Being which, like the terminological catalog in Post, appear to have positive metaphysical substance, though negative in predicative form. Transcendent Being is said to be "infinite, ungraspable, and ineffable." Or theologically expressed, "God is Being itself. He simply and unqualifiedly is, without a beginning or end and without depending upon anything else for existence or for any other characteristic." Though this transcendent 'Something,' whether Being or God, "lies beyond our powers of comprehension," nevertheless we can "point"' to it. The very fact of "coming to realize that there is limit to our concepts can be a way of seeing beyond this limit" (Witherall, 130).

This conceptual back and forth --now you grasp it, now you don't-- though quite in line with the metaphysical and theological tradition, is nevertheless problematic as an interpretation of the metaphor of gift. Tillich, who also subscribed to the proposition, 'God is Being itself,' had, unlike Witherall, second thoughts about it. Having initially said, like Witherall, that it was a non-symbolic, straight-forward metaphysical proposition, the one non-symbolic statement in the systematic edifice he built upon it, he later reversed himself. 'God is Being itself,' he said, is a symbolic, metaphorical proposition; it cannot 'translated,' without loss of concrete meaning, into metaphysical terms.

What is interesting is that Witherall himself seems to have had some critical reservations about applying those negative predicates to Being. A few lines later he observed: "There are difficulties in understanding the very idea of that which cannot be grasped." And yet, nothing daunted, he bravely insists, "we must somehow continue to speak of Being, without knowing exactly and categorically what is meant." The problem is compounded by the fact that "we are also confronted with the problem of situating this in the context of gift-giving" (Witherall, 130).

But if so, how are we to proceed? How can we get out of the seemingly hopeless corner into which these conflicting hermeneutics have painted (not pointed) us? Witherall's response is provocative – both ingenious and suggestive. First, he says, we must understand the meaning of Being's transcendence differently. To say that Being is transcendent is to say that it "transcends itself, or 'goes beyond' itself, and thus gives itself or releases itself into immanence" (Witherall, 131). If this were an exercise in theological *kenosis* or Christological paradox a la Kierkegaard or what Jan van Bragt, an expositor of Kyoto School Buddhist dialectic, terms 'trans(de)cendence' – we might have some inkling of the conceptually murky waters into which we are being led. Witherall's mixed 'metaphorical-metaphysical' rhetoric – 'Being *releases* itself' – could be seen as pointing in this direction. But alas! those notions are nested in religious *metaphors*, not the *metaphysical* concepts Witherall has in mind.

Nevertheless, by reconceiving Being's transcendence in this paradoxical way Witherall clearly means us to understand that "the standard concept of identity is inapplicable to transcendent Being." This rethinking of transcendence has several important consequences. To say that Being gives *itself* to beings is to say, first of all, that "immanent beings have an aspect of transcendence." Among examples of similar metaphysical or theological doctrines, one thinks of the Quaker George

Fox's reminder that "there is that of God in everyone." But even more interesting, for Witherall this revised concept of Being's transcendence extends to the insight, at first sight not at all obvious, that all beings "are indefinitely connected with all other beings." Shades of Indra's jeweled net at every node of which a gem reflects all the other jewels in the web, Hua Yen Buddhism's metaphor for the interconnected co-arising of all beings. This is heady metaphysics indeed.

Nor is Witherall finished surprising us. Turning again, as he did earlier, to mysticism to salvage the case for a metaphysical interpretation of Being, he quotes a lengthy passage from Alan Watts' exposition of mystical theism. Witherall draws on it to defend his revision of Being's transcendence via an appeal to the mystical doctrine that "God, or Being, is everywhere, and can be apprehended in each finite thing... These statements are not intended to be grasped, nor are they capable of 'analysis.' They are simply expressions, in different contexts, of the idea that each finite thing has an aspect of infinity, as long as it *exists*, for its existence means that it is a gift of transcendent Being" (Witherall, 131, Witherall's emphasis). As Alan Watts says: "the creature may thank God for the free gift of life and being, not only because it might not have been given, but also because the gift *is* God" (Watts, 143; emphasis mine). My stress on the '*is*' is meant to draw attention to the radical implications of Watts' statement that perhaps go beyond what Witherall intended to say. In any case, both Watts and Witherall's 'mystical' interpretation of Being's 'transcendence' calls for further reflection.

We might wish to agree that each finite thing in some sense embodies, is a window into, the wondrously strange gift of Being. It is not at all clear, however, that statements asserting that fact cannot be 'grasped' or are incapable of 'analysis'. Not only does Witherall devote a book to explicating the meaning of 'the fundamental problem of existence,' he employs an 'explanation-schema' that presumably does 'grasp' and does provides an intelligible 'analysis' of just such statements via a variety of metaphysical 'answers' to the question. Further, though he does not say what are those 'different contexts' in which we are to understand those 'expressions,' perhaps we can take him to mean the contexts of those different fillings-in of the explanatory schema which give the statements their metaphysical substance and otherwise elusive plausibility. In any case, it would seem they are not the 'merely metaphorical' contexts in which they found their initial utterance.

Let us explore the interpretive possibilities of Witherall's revisioning of Being's transcendence, supplemented by Watt's radical 'is,' a bit further and perhaps in another direction. As we proposed with Witherall's analysis of necessity, so we can suggest with his analysis of transcendence, especially in view of the hermeneutical openings it provides. This will mean viewing transcendence, like necessity, as a metaphorical notion pointing to an existential-ontological, not cosmological-metaphysical reality, seeing it as *existential* transcendence analogous to the way we speak of a morally or spiritually 'higher' mode of existence that 'goes beyond' our ordinary modes of being. Being 'transcends' beings in the *existential* sense that to see Being as 'giving itself or releasing itself' to beings, or *as* beings (Watt's 'is'), is to see them in a different way, in an extra-ordinary light, unlike the way we ordinarily see them. To say that Being is the being of beings is thus not a metaphysical tautology, nor is it, if taken as stating a metaphysical fact, the truism that beings exist (pace Kant or modern logic's dismissal of 'exist' as a descriptive predicate); rather it is a profound existential affirmation of the mystery of beings themselves.

The affirmation of Being's 'transcendence' is an expression of an 'authentic' mode of being (Heidegger) or ultimate *concern* (Tillich) vis-a vis beings over against the everyday 'inauthentic' mode of losing ourselves in 'penultimate' concerns in relation to beings. Like necessity, so transcendence is not a metaphysical 'feature' of Being, rather it points to an existential mode of relation to Being, a relation expressed in metaphors as a response to the ultimate 'gift' of Being 'releasing itself' into/as beings. What is 'transcendent' is the mode of 'seeing as,' *the mode of seeing Being in and as beings.* To say that Being gives itself to/as beings is easy to say, but also easily misunderstood as a 'mere metaphor,' or worse, as an empty tautology. It is extra-ordinarily important but hard not only to see but even if intuited, to express in language appropriate to that way of seeing. It can only be articulated in symbols that 'go beyond,' transcend, our ordinary, habitual ways of seeing and speaking, metaphors that give appropriate expression to the ultimate truth of the 'absolute emotions' by which we respond to the mystery of existence as the 'gift' of Being itself.

There are many ways of 'seeing-as' vis-a-vis beings. Heidegger discusses several of these in *Sein und Zeit,* John Hick discusses several in *An Interpretation of Religion: Human Responses to the Transcendent.*

We can see things as 'bare things,' simply 'there,' mere objects, 'dimmed down' in their being, the 'things' of classical metaphysics, reduced to their Aristotelian or Cartesian 'properties'; or perhaps as the subject-matter of the modern counterparts of metaphysics described in the impersonal language of scientific study. Or we can see them as things of use to us, see them in their relation to our various human purposes – the forest as a 'resource' for lumber, animals as disposable fodder for medical experiments, or captive creatures in zoos, or pets for our amusement or non-human compansonship. Or we can see them 'in and for themselves,' for not any ulterior purpose, simple for their intrinsic aesthetic value (Smith): the beauty of the songs of birds or glorious sunsets, etc. Or 'highest' of all, going beyond, transcending these other ways of seeing them, we can see them ultimately, and responding to them emotionally, as embodiments of the mystery of Being itself, as gifts of Being itself. Indeed, if we are to credit the 'is' of Watts, we can see them *as* Being itself.

Thus to see the 'trans-de-cendence' of Being in the' im-manence' of beings is to see the 'in-dwelling' of Being in beings. But it is also to see imminent beings *in* their transcendence, *as* transcendence, *as* the Being of beings. In the paradoxical dialectic of Buddhist metaphysics, transcendent Being, immanent beings: same thing. Being *sive* beings, beings *sive* Being.

Intelligibility. We turn briefly to the last 'metaphysical feature' that Witherall highlights: *intelligibility.* What if any light does the concept of metaphysical intelligibility shed on the metaphor of the gift of Being? Does it clarify or confuse understanding the *appropriateness* of the gift metaphor as a response to the mystery of existence? What does Witherall mean by metaphysical intelligibility? How does he think it applies to the metaphor of the gift of Being?

Despite his assertion that Being is "ungraspable," Witherall maintains that "Being is intelligible in itself, and gives intelligibility to beings" (Witherall, 131). However, it is hard to see how, if Being cannot be 'grasped,' is not capable of 'analysis,' that is is nonetheless 'intelligible' – not only that, that it renders all other beings 'intelligible' as well. The empirical concepts and theories of the sciences are efforts to make finite things intelligible; the abstract categories of metaphysics are directed to the same end. But how are we to understand that that which cannot be grasped is the source of all intelligibility? Witherall's answer as before: by interpreting it as gift. "Being is intelligible because the world of beings is intelligible. That is part of the gift" (Witherall, *ibid.*). However, notice the reversal: it is not that Being lends intelligibility to beings, it is the other way around; because we can understand beings, they lend intelligibility to Being – as gift. A version of the cosmological argument, it would seem.

Witherall even makes a case for a secularist version, like that of Quentin Smith, of this disguised theological claim. Even if there is no transcendent Being, he says, "this absence is itself the source of order and meaning in the world ... miraculously." The "gift of intelligibility" can be seen in "the basic fact that the universe, which exists contingently and purposely, is gratuitously lucid." Gratuitously. But that means, as we have seen, 'free and unnecessary,' in other words, groundlessly, absent any reason, cause or justification, without Why. As Witherall himself spells out, in its non-theological version the totality of beings, the world-whole, "makes itself available to description and explanation, and does so without any particular reason, and without having any transcendent source" (Witherall, 132). But that means, once again, that the existence of beings, the gift of Being, ultimately *lacks* metaphysical intelligibility. It is beyond the 'grasp' of metaphysics, transcends explanatory 'analysis.'

If so, what can we take away from Witherall's attempt to say the gift of Being is in some sense, in some context, 'intelligible'? Perhaps we can turn to J. N. Findlay's 'logic of mysticism' for help. Findlay says in his article of that title, "The logic of a mystical absolute is the logic of a limiting case, and we must not expect a limiting case to behave in the same logical manner as a case which does not fall at the limit" (Findlay, 179). Clearly talk about the mystery of Being and the gift of Being are examples of what Findlay calls language at the limit of ordinary logic. Even Witherall admits that standard notions of identity do not apply in this case. Metaphysical intelligibility is thus not an instance of epistemological intelligibility. Epistemology, in it standard, metaphysically-based use, is not applicable here. And yet seeing the metaphor of gift as an *appropriate* way of pointing to the mystery of Being implies the presence of *some* kind of 'intelligibility' in the service of a different 'logic' – a different 'language game' giving expression to a different 'form of life.' What kind of intelligibility, what mode of existence? It is the *existential* intelligibility, the *existential* epistemology, of existence lived at the limits of its being. It is existence coming face to face with itself, knowing itself, existentially, as the embodiment, the gift, of Being itself.

Applications of the Explanation-Schema

We turn now to the two metaphysical 'applications' – immanental' (atheist) and 'necessitarian' (theist) – which Witherall claims fill in the 'explanation-schema' of the 'gift of Being' We will ask of each 'application' whether it illuminates or obstructs an understanding of the gift metaphor as an *appropriate* response to the mystery of Being. Our argument will be: each of these two metaphysical world-views must be rejected on independent grounds; this critique notwithstanding, they cannot, as metaphysical doctrines, be put forward as 'translations' of the metaphor of the gift of Being; consequently, the metaphorical proposition, 'Being gives itself to beings,' is not a 'neutral' explanatory schemata that somehow 'bridges' these two opposed and irreconcilable metaphysical doctrines. The gift of Being is not an invitation to metaphysics. It does not stand in need of metaphysical intervention, rescue, or 'translation.' It is a metaphor that points beyond itself, that 'participates' in, discloses, and makes possible an existential response to, the reality of that which transcends it. Despite these reservations, however, some aspects of Witherall's metaphysical 'applications' may be helpful for clarifying an alternative, existential-ontological interpretation of the gift metaphor.

We begin by asking what Witherall means by an 'application' of a 'explanation-schema,' and why he thinks metaphysical applications are necessary if we are to fully understand the metaphor of the gift of Being. To remind ourselves: an *explanation-schema* is "a general schema which can be instantiated by a variety of explanatory propositions" termed *"explanatory applications."* The fundamental question of metaphysics, 'why is there something instead of nothing,' transcends "all of the normal conceptual structures and standards, asking for an explanation beyond any explanatory framework." If we are to provide "an answer to it of a certain kind," it is necessary to resort to a more indirect, formulaic approach. While an explanation schema, by virtue of its generality, lacks "distinct information content,' it opens a space for more concrete metaphysical answers. Witherall's assumption from the outset of his inquiry is that the Why question can be and must be answered, and that it has a general answer which, though not a direct answer in and of itself, is hospitable to more specific metaphysical interpretations, or 'applications,' which "do not entirely form a closure, but which, taken together, form "a coherent and complete response, in at least the sense that the investigation has a distinct conclusion" (Witherall, 1). We can understand, then, why Witherall regards the particular explanation-schema he favors, 'Being gives itself to beings,' as an "incomplete application" that needs to be given metaphysical content "if it is to acquire the status of a full-blooded answer to the question of existence" (Witherall, 133-134). Without a metaphysical interpretation, "the metaphor of gift-giving transcendent Being" would remain a tantalizing tease, an imaginatively suggestive but explanatorily empty formula.

Not every metaphysical application will do. To be a "completely satisfying response" it must meet certain criteria. It must be not only "intellectually well-constructed," it must also be "emotionally adequate." In that latter regard, it must "make sense of our wonderment, our astonishment, our gratitude, and our feelings of awesome depth as we confront the fact that there is something real, instead of nothing" (Witherall, 134). If it does not, it will be pronounced unsatisfactory and will not apply to the explanatory schema, 'Being gives itself to being' Just as certain 'felt meanings' do not qualify for Smith as metaphysically adequate, so apparently for Witherall not all metaphysical applications are suitable either. In any case it would be difficult to canvas them all, so Witherall is perhaps wise to limit himself to some of the more obvious candidates. The list of emotional feelings sounds familiar. Witherall is, after all, a close reader of Smith. One could ask, however, whether any of them necessarily fit the metaphysical bill. We can after all wonder at, be astonished by, grateful for, or feel awe in the presence of phenomena that are less than metaphysical in size. They could be 'completely satisfying' not only emotionally but intellectually within the context of worldly phenomena that elicit them. What, then, would be the difference between such relatively 'mundane' emotions and their 'absolute' counterparts evoked by the mystery of Being itself? Will the metaphysical applications account for that?

Witherall considers three applications – deflationary, necessitarian, and value-based – which, "taken together, constitute a system of explanation." He is careful to sound two qualifying notes, however. These metaphysical worldviews, taken individually, are logically incompatible. This is not fatal, however, for "each invokes a specific interpretation of 'giving' as 'gratuitous bestowal', and as such they can be coherently combined under the general proposition that Being gives itself to beings." And yet this coherence is "shaken to some extent by the fact that they are motivated by opposing attitudes, which, rather than being reconciled in a grand synthesis, tend towards 'tension'." One might ask whether, if so, such attitudes as gratitude, wonder, astonishment and awe can mean quite the same when sited in incompatible metaphysical contexts. Once again, we are not to worry however, because such existential 'tension' can be 'creative' (shades of the conflicting 'felt meanings' that submit to a metaphysical hierarchy in Smith!) As Witherall observes, while it is necessary to apply metaphysics to the explanatory schema of the gift of Being, this must have relevance to our own existence "in some way" lest it degenerate into existentially inadequate "purely technical discourse." It is interesting that he sees the combination of these mutually incompatible philosophical standpoints as forming a 'system' of explanation ("in some way"), this despite the fact that the object of the inquiry, Being, is something that has been said to resist every such 'grasp' or 'analysis.' Once bitten by the bug, metaphysics apparently proves irresistibly addictive.

By way of summary, then, of the three metaphysical positions. The first, in a peculiar, almost question-begging choice of terms, Witherall labels 'deflationary' or 'immanence (brute fact)' view he associates with Quentin Smith. Here the focus is on contingent beings, not a transcendent Being, "so that existence becomes truly gratuitous, even to the point where it is 'inexplicable,' in the sense of having no rational explanation." The second, labeled 'necessitarian,' for example theism, focuses on a self-sufficient transcendent Being, and must "postulate a gratuitous gift in order to render immanent beings explicable in terms of transcendence." The third, termed 'evaluative,' encompasses the 'whole' of the being/Being relationship, and consist of specific attitudes or value-orientations, aesthetic and/or moral, which, as noted above, align them closely with one or the other of the first two positions, "depending upon how they are constructed." (Witherall, 134-135). In the end, Witherall says, speaking metaphysically there are really only two "satisfactory forms of explanation," the deflationary based on contingent beings or the necessitarian based on transcendent Being. Though, as we have seen, he said these two are in 'tension' with one another, "each one is reasonable on its own grounds." Note: this is a different claim. Previously he had said that, despite their 'tension,' i.e. their incompatibility, they could be joined together to form a coherent and complete system of explanation. That claim presupposes the prior, equally problematic claim that each is reasonable in and of itself. And even if that is so, does that mean that without them the metaphor of the gift of Being cannot be understood? Could the problem be rather with the effort to 'translate' the mystery of existence into a metaphysical meta-system, into *any* metaphysics, in the first place? Clearly there much that is problematic, if not question-begging, already in Witherall's introductory remarks, and we have not even begun examining the individual metaphysical applications yet.

Immanence (the Brute Fact View). The first of the two metaphysical applications that Witherall considers a satisfactory explanation of the gift metaphor and thus answer to the question of Being is what he labels variously as the 'deflationary,' 'immanence' or 'brute fact' view. It is based on entities "within the world of beings, that is the world containing all and only existent objects" (Witherall, 135). Already we note a divergence from Smith's statement of this metaphysical view. For Smith the 'deflationary' view distinguishes inner-worldly beings from the being of the world-as-a-whole; it is only the latter which is the appropriate focus of the metaphysical felt meanings. We see here already the question-begging implicit in Witherall's restatement of what he takes to be Smith's view. We see this even more clearly in his next assertion: "What is clearly and explicitly excluded from the world of immanent beings is Being itself" (Witherall, *ibid.*) Of course this is true, by definition, but only if one overlooks the 'transcendent' status of the existence of the world-whole in Smith's metaphysical system. Witherall admits that 'immanent' and 'transcendent' are definitionally 'relative' But this does not mean they can be used automatically to distinguish between 'Being' and 'world.' The confusion arises partly because Witherall, like Smith, is misled by the ambiguity of the phrase 'the existence of the world.' Each wavers between emphasis on the existence of the *world* and the *existence* of the world, that is, that something exists rather than nothing.

Given this traditional, 'deflationary' reading of the world as not only the totality of contingent beings but also, contra Smith, as a contingent being itself (space-time, says Witherall, is 'immanent,' metaphysically speaking), it is no surprise that Witherall can conclude that the "immanent world...gives us nothing which will answer the 'why' question" (Witherall, 136). Instead "[it] will naturally lead to the idea that existence is a brute fact, that is has no causal explanation, and no ultimate purpose or value" (Witherall, *ibid.*). However, not all is lost. A deflationary position can be satisfactorily formulated if and only if it satisfies two fundamental criteria: intellectually, it must explain *why* there is no ultimate explanation for existence, otherwise it is "nothing but a groundless assertion, and fails to satisfy the intellect;" emotionally, it must be able to "recognize and account for our feelings of wonder and awe" in our encounter with the Why question. But a paradox or irony, rather a *petitio principii* accompanies this proviso. If it satisfies those criteria, it will no longer be what it purports to be: "a deflationary thesis cannot be entirely deflationary."

On these grounds Quentin Smith's world-whole meets the first criterion. By a breath-taking metaphysical sleight of hand ("now you see it, now you don't"), though Smith's deflationary view is a form of "a priori atheism" which asserts "that there cannot be any cause or reason for the existence of the world and that the very idea of God is incoherent," nevertheless it can be "reconciled" with the explanatory schema, 'Being gives itself to beings.' How, you ask. Easy. Reprising an earlier move, Witherall says, simply recast it in the form of "the hypothesis that transcendent Being is identical with Nothing." But what is that dextrous maneuver supposed to accomplish? It creates "an empty place in the gift-giving relation" between beings and Being. This absence can be taken as a tacit recognition by the deflationary metaphysician that "there is a place for transcendent Being," although it happens that "it is an empty place" (Witherall, 136-137).

This piece of philosophical legerdemain is astonishing enough. But Witherall goes on to amaze the reader further when he asserts that "only if the place of transcendent Being is empty can we truly respond emotionally to this emptiness." It turns out that it is precisely this *absence* of an ultimate cause or reason for the world's existence to which we respond emotionally in the various metaphysical 'felt meanings' cataloged by Smith. For example, in the affect of 'godless desolation' we directly intuit "an absolute emptiness, a darkness and silence devoid of God ...the nonbeing of God" (Quentin Smith, 1986, 140, cited by Witherall, 137). But this only means that Smith's position, and Witherall's use of it, to support the coherence of a 'deflationary' metaphysics is in fact parasitic on the very metaphysics it claims to have dismissed as 'incoherent,' namely, talk of God, theism. Note, however, that in the lengthy quote cited by Witherall, Smith calls the affect of godless desolation a "seeming intuition ... I seem to intuit a *nothingness*..." (ibid., Smith's emphasis). Witherall, however, converting Smith's 'seem' to a 'can,' argues that "if there is an absence to which we can respond, then we must have implicitly recognized that there is a 'place' in our conceptual scheme which is empty," i.e., a place empty of but implicitly recognizing the (absent) presence of transcendent Being. In other words, responding to the absence of transcendent Being is no different from tacitly admitting the 'existence' of that very Being if only under the rubric of Nothingness.

On the basis of this feat of verbal gymnastics, Witherall then says that for Smith "existence is gratuitous. It is given to us for no reason, and without any cause. It is therefore truly a gift, and is truly bestowed miraculously upon beings." This is "a feature of the world-whole, a real feature, not a mere appearance." But Witherall may be too quick in imputing to Smith this restricted interpretation. For Smith say, it is "*one* of the felt meanings*" of the world," it refers to only *one* of the world's features (Witherall, 137; my emphasis.) For Smith, other features, other 'felt meanings,' negative ones, not only desolation but also despair, tedium, sadness, apathy and dread are also *appropriate* responses to the world-whole. For Witherall, on the other hand, it is *the* metaphor (gift) for *the* attitude (gratitude) that is *the* appropriate response to absence of transcendent Being *qua* Nothingness. Disregarding the negative emotions, Witherall interprets Smith as in agreement with his own reading of the deflationary position: "Being gives itself so completely that it is exhausted, and has thereby emptied itself in to beings. Hence transcendent Being is Nothing" (Witherall, 138).

This does not terminate the dialectical pyrotechnics, however. Though the existence of the world would seem to be hovering on the edge of an abyss, inasmuch as the existence of the world is contingent, it "avoids the abyss in each moment. [T]he abyss (Nothingness) can be said to 'relinquish itself,' and in so doing gives us the world." This, says Witherall, is "a clear exemplification of the gift-giving schema. We can recognize the gratuitous nature of "the world's existence" by the fact that it exists over "the abyss of Nothingness." Thus, though it appears to be denying that there is a transcendent Being, in fact "Smith's insistence that the notion of God is incoherent can be understood as a way of insisting upon the transcendence of Being" (Witherall, 138). Disregarding for the moment the hopeless conceptual tangles Witherall gets himself into because of his reliance on traditional metaphysical vocabulary – necessity vs. contingency, transcendence vs. immanence – with the resulting irony of being forced to substitute metaphorical imagery – Being 'bestows itself,' 'is exhausted,' 'relinquishes itself' – for metaphysical explanation, one can only shake one's head at the verbal prestidigitation he has to perform in order to see the transcendence of Being in the guise of Nothingness. The problem stems from seeing all these terms in the context of cosmological metaphysics. This will become even clearer when we turn to the next application, the metaphysics of the necessitarian view.

Necessitarian Applications. Witherall has already admitted that the necessitarian position is "a strange and perplexing doctrine" in which one sinks knee-deep into the quagmire of a "bizarre" mixture of ideas (Witherall, 84). We should be prepared, therefore, for equally strange, perplexing and bizarre metaphysical contortions in Witherall's attempt to salvage something coherent and meaningful in talk of a transcendent, necessary Being. In particular we should be alert to the dubious work that verbs like 'point' and nouns like 'paradox' are made to do.

Witherall begins by appearing to backpedal from a straight-forwardly metaphysical 'translation' of the gift of Being. He introduces his discussion of the necessitarian 'application' with the observation that, after all, "discourse about Being itself, or God, is always problematic." Worse than that, "such discourse must retain an element of metaphor and mystery, or it will descend into ordinary talk, which results in metaphysical confusion." Yet, despite the need to stay cognizant of its original source in 'metaphor and mystery,' talk about Being or God feels compelled to be "truly meaningful discourse, as opposed to babbling" (Witherall, 139). 'Meaningful discourse?' That means that once again metaphysics must ride to the rescue of 'mere' metaphor or mystery lest it degenerate into foolish superstition or utter gibberish. On the one hand, talk about a transcendent Being must continue to be and be seen as metaphorical and mysterious, for if it does not, if it is confused with literal speech, metaphysical confusion will result. On the other hand, it cannot be or be seen as *merely* metaphorical and mysterious, or metaphysical confusion will result. This may seem contradictory, but actually it is not. For, says Witherall, the metaphorical and mysterious 'element' while necessary is not sufficient to render Being itself, or God, meaningful and intelligible. For that metaphysics is required – if only in its own interest – to avoid being itself reduced to or exposed as a jumble of confusion.

Thus forewarned, we enter the weird wonderland of double-talk about transcendent Being. Witherall plunges right in, informing us at the outset that "it is inappropriate to talk of a 'perspective of transcendence'." Why? Because "transcendent Being does not provide us with a conceptual framework for understanding the world. Instead it provides a sense of meaning which cannot be obtained within our mundane discourse about beings" (Witherall, 139). Already questions arise. What does this mean for the just concluded discussion of Quentin Smith's metaphysics based on the perspective of immanence? Do not transcendence and immanence go together in the pantheon of metaphysical dualities? And before that, wasn't it the perspective of transcendence that made the contingent world 'intelligible'? Now it seems we are being told that there is no 'conceptual framework' by which to understand either transcendent Being or the contingent world of which it was thought to be the cosmological-metaphysical ground. Apparently there has been a serious misunderstanding. Being is not a conceptual foundation for understanding beings, it is only "an expression of the idea that there is a 'beyond' to which we may 'point,' even if we cannot state exactly what it is, nor find an immanent category under which it can fall" (Witherall, 140). What, we might ask, happened to the explanatory schema of 'gift' to which the notion of transcendent Being was supposed to give metaphysical content? What are we to make of this 'pointing beyond'? Point how? To what? What is its relation to the 'immanent categories'? But perhaps the situation is not as dire as Witherall's opening remarks suggest. There is one well-developed conceptual framework that may save transcendent Being from this unpromising opening after all –the necessitarian metaphysical application labeled 'theism.'

Theism. The notion of God, says Witherall, is "an ultimate explanatory postulate. He cannot be explained in terms of anything else, and his existence is necessary. In fact, God is Being itself, and has the same content as Being, which means he is self-existent, dependent on nothing else, and in a sense self-explanatory" (Witherall, 142). God is what Post would call an 'ultimate explainer.' Several things require comment here. First, what does Witherall mean by seeing 'God' as a 'postulate'? The notion of a postulate is derived from logic or mathematics and here taken over into metaphysics to mean something the existence, fact or truth of which is assumed or accepted (postulate) as a premise or starting point for logical reasoning, mathematical proof or, in this case, theological belief. In itself a postulate cannot be proven, but if it is necessary for what follows and if what it entails seems plausible, it is generally accepted as existing, factual, or true. In fact, as classically conceived, it is taken to be so evident as to be accepted as true without controversy. But is that what the heaviest term in the language, God, or Being itself, comes down to, a mere postulate? An 'as if'? Has the Creator of heaven and earth come to this?

Second, and more controversially, given Witherall's statement that the notion of a transcendent Being is strange, perplexing, bizarre, problematic, outside any conceptual framework, how are we to understand the list of apparently content-filled descriptive predicates – self-existence, non-dependence, self-explanatory – he goes on to ascribe to God-as-postulate? A strange, perplexing and bizarre mix of claims and terms indeed! Especially in light of his immediately following claim that God "has the same content as Being, which is to say that he has no conceptual content" (ibid.)! How does he propose to extricate theistic metaphysics from this bewildering maze? It would appear he proposes to do so only by leading us further into this conceptual bog.

"Whether or not he exists, it is a conceptual truth that God is unsurpassable, or infinite." How do we know that? It "is true by definition." That is simply how the word is used. If we mean anything by the word, that is what we mean and that is what it has always meant. After listing more of the familiar definers of 'God,' he concludes: not only does the divine Being transcend all beings, he even transcends all concepts. "The names that we use to denote transcendent Being are themselves bereft of conceptual content, and serve only to point to that which lies beyond, rather than to define it" (Witherall, 143). This stricture apparently extends not only to the so-called positive attributes of the divine, but to the negative attributes that feature in negative or mystical theologies as well. To take just one example: the notion of God as 'infinite' is, says Witherall, a "signification of transcendence rather than a positive concept." It is not a category under which beings fall; "it is rather a negation of finitude." Though it appears to have a affirmative function – God *is* infinite, the formation of the attribute by the grammatical act of negation – 'in-finite' – is a reminder not to be misled into thinking, though it is a 'signifier' that 'points' to the transcendent, that in so doing it *says* anything positive about the God-postulate. (Post, we recall, says something similar about negatively-formed predicates of God.) As Wittgenstein might have opined, is God-talk one of those instances where language cannot 'say,' whereof one cannot speak, but where perhaps, out of the silence of *das Mystische*, it can 'show'? Is this what Witherall means by describing God as a 'signifier' that 'points' rather than as a confusion of concepts that try, misleadingly, to 'say'?

As if this linguistic confusion of grammatical forms with semantic functions were not enough, Witherall has one more trick up his theistic sleeve. "Given that we have some notion [is a notion a concept] of God, it is a conceptual truth that he is absolutely unsurpassable. And yet paradoxically, he transcends all of our concepts" (Witherall, 143). Like the verb 'point,' Witherall brings in the noun 'paradox' when metaphysical language butts its head against its conceptual limits. Nothing if not deterred, Witherall grasps the nettle firmly: it must, therefore, "be possible to use the apparently inconceivable inconceivability of transcendent Being positively" (Witherall, *ibid.*). Shades of Donald Rumsfeld's 'unknown unknowns'! This is paradox upon paradox. The pointing seems to have ended up going in circles. Nor are we done.

Unleashed by paradox to speak positively about the God-postulate, we now descend from the empyrean of metaphysics to the hum-drum world of earthly analogies. In an effort to twist, though it looks more like abandoning, necessitarian concepts to fit the explanatory-schema of Being giving itself to beings, aka God's giving of himself to the world, Witherall is forced to fall back upon the rhetoric of metaphor which the concepts of metaphysics were supposedly to translate but now are apparently unable to do. God, we are told, does not give himself to the world out of logical or metaphysical necessity, but through "a free spontaneous decision to become finite." Because "this is a non-necessary decision [what happened to the feature of necessity?], we can legitimately speak of contingency, and thus we can say that there is truly a gratuitous bestowal, a genuine gift" (Witherall, 143). Clearly we have left the sphere of abstract metaphysics and returned to world of personal metaphor where theistic God talk found and finds its native home. Apart from mixing two different language games –contingency/necessity, freedom/ necessity (Tillich prefers to pair 'freedom' with 'determinism' to avoid the unnecessary confusion of using 'necessity' in two different semantic contexts), Witherall seems saddled with an awkward dilemma. Either one tries to make sense of the explanatory schema, 'Being gives itself' to being via one or another metaphysical applications, or, if ones wishes to make sense of the theistic schema, 'God gives himself to the world,' one must pay the price of giving up metaphysics in favor of ('mere') metaphor.

Witherall defends his determination, nevertheless, to translate the metaphor into metaphysics (since God is Being itself) by insisting that God must be able "to be both himself and other to himself." Though this might seem self-contradictory, "it need not be." He repeats his earlier claim: "The standard concept of identity, which entirely precludes this possibility, should be understood as applying only to finite immanent things, and not to God" (Witherall, 143). He thus proposes to avoid what previously appeared to be a paradox. On the one hand, because "God transcends thinghood, [he] may be truly said to be a non-thing." On the other hand, "he is Being itself, and gives Being to things." We can then make perfectly good sense of the doctrine of Creation (for that is what we are talking about). We can translate it successfully into the dialectical concepts of metaphysics without need to depend on personal metaphor. In language that reminds us of the fundamental question, 'Why is there something rather than nothing at all?,' the metaphysical theist can reply: "God created the world *ex nihilo* – that is, from nothing at all." Understanding this *nihil* this does not pose metaphysical obstacles. Rather, "'nothing' is simply the 'non-thing,' which is God. That which lies beyond our framework of understanding, as transcendent Being does, must appear to us as a nothing, a non-thing, or an emptiness ... God is the nothingness from which the world originates." Like the flourish of the magician's cape which detracts us from seeing what is really going on, Witherall's equation would hoodwink us into believing that the absolute nothingness captured in the phrase 'nothing at all' was really just a relative nothingness, and that the 'non-being' of God simply means 'not a finite thing.' Witherall would strain our credulity further when he concludes on an even more extravagant metaphysical-theological note: "It is even possible for God to incarnate himself as nothingness" (Witherall, *ibid*.). As with the language of creation, here too with the language of incarnation Witherall would seem, protestations to the contrary notwithstanding, dangerously close to backsliding from metaphysics to (mere) metaphor.

It is not surprising that, on first sight, this equation of God's Being and Nothingness would appear conveniently to support Witherall's irenic thesis that deflationary or immanental and necessitarian or theistic metaphysics can be housed together companionably under the one roof of the explanatory schema, 'Being gives itself to beings.' For, he says, "In making these claims, the theist appears to echo the deflationary position which claims that there is no transcendent Being. For if God appears to us as nothing, an emptiness or an absence, then theism parallels the metaphysics of felt meaning, which also is a response to the absence of an ultimate reason for existence" (ibid.). Unfortunately the situation is not that innocent. The fundamental assertion of theism is that there *is* a transcendent Being, that God *does* 'exist,' *pace* some theologians, for example Tillich. Thus, though in some sense "our concept of this Being is negative, so that it may appear to us as an emptiness, a non-thing," that is simply "a consequence of our own limited perspective."

The central difference, then, between the deflationary and theistic metaphysics is that the former in essence denies that there is an answer to the Why question, while the theist argues that the existence of the world cannot, as Smith would have it, be a 'brute fact' absent any further considerations. There *is* an answer, and that answer is: "there must be a necessary existent." Despite the 'negative' nature of the traditional attributes of God – infinite, non-immanent, non-thing, etc. – the theist holds, unlike the deflationary metaphysician, that "there is something there, and that it is necessarily so. It is not an empty place in the schema, however much it may appear to be" (Witherall, 144-145). If so, an ugly problem raises its head: how can such mutually contradictory worldviews be thought by Witherall to dwell together amicably in Heidegger's 'House of Being'? More problematic than that: can either one of them, as variations on a cosmological understanding of metaphysics, be thought to be satisfactory explications of the gift metaphor itself? Perhaps the third alternative Witherall discusses, the metaphor of the gift of Being understood not metaphysically but evaluatively, as an expression of an aesthetic or moral response to Being, will gives us as way out of the corner into which Witherall seems so far to have painted himself.

But we before turn to those evaluative applications, let us ask what, of constructive value, we might be able to take away from the two foregoing metaphysical applications? Specifically, if we are concerned to transfer the metaphor of the gift of Being from the concepts of a cosmological-metaphysics into an existential-ontological vocabulary, what elements of the immanental and necessitarian answers to the Why question can we take over into a possible non-metaphysical alternative? Further, how would such a conceptual transfer solve the even more difficult problem of preserving rather than replacing the unique force and truth of the original metaphor? This was the terminological problem that confronted Heidegger when he tried to break away from traditional metaphysics and develop a way of speaking ontology 'metaphorically,' one with which he struggled over his own multi-faceted philosophical career.

One final note before we proceed. We criticized Witherall for focusing on gratitude as the most appropriate response to the gift of Being when, as Smith showed, there are so many other felt meanings, both positive and negative, which were also appropriate responses to the world in one or more of its features. On the other hand, Smith himself chose to focus on one of those feelings as the fundamental felt meaning over against all the others, namely joy at the basic fact of the happening, the existence, of the world. Perhaps it is an occupational hazard of metaphysics to search for and claim to have found the secret key that unlocks the door to the Being of beings. Existentially we do choose, and must choose our response. But the question is, does the world-whole or the Being of beings validate this choice? Or rather, can the metaphysical 'translation' of 'Being gives itself to beings' justify the choice which the metaphor evokes? Can philosophy support with reasons what James called our will, our right, to believe?

Gift as Felt Meaning

The fourth metaphysical feature Witherall highlights, "intimate involvement," and its corresponding application, the "evaluative," are not strictly metaphysical in the narrow sense of explanatory, as Witherall himself admits. However, as with the two metaphysical applications of the explanatory schema, Witherall selects two evaluative applications to flesh out the metaphor of the gift of Being, each roughly parallel to its metaphysical counterpart: aesthetic value, with parallels to the metaphysics of immanence, and moral value, with parallels to necessitarian or theistic metaphysics. We look first at his analysis of the feature of intimate involvement and then examine the two applications put forward as evaluative interpretations of the gift of Being.

Intimate Involvement

To describe the significance of 'intimate involvement' for interpreting the metaphor of the 'gift' of Being, Witherall draws on Smith's phenomenology of the double-barreled phenomena of 'felt meanings' and Heidegger's analysis of 'world' (*Welt*) as our concern-ful environs

(*Umwelt*). "That we are given Being, that there is a universe instead of nothing at all, touches us deeply, because it is the primary fact of our lives, without which nothing would be meaningful." This 'gift' of Being, of the existence of the world, "allows beings to find themselves within a world, and thus to become involved in that world" (Witherall, 133). The metaphor of a gift expresses the meaning we feel, the existential facticity of, the world's closeness (Smith); the world is familiar, not strange, not alien, not uncanny.

And yet, there are different ways of interpreting this gift, this feeling of intimate involvement with the world that has been given to us, the world into which we 'find' ourselves 'thrown' (Heidegger's *Befindlichkeit* and *Geworfenheit*). If, with theism, we interpret it through a theological lens, we speak of God giving himself to the world in an act of intimate love. If, with Smith, we interpret it as the 'immanence' of the world-whole, we say it is a 'closeness' which evokes a response of intimate affection.

However we express this felt intimacy with the world as the gift of Being, on the other hand, the fact is that "[it] can only appear as wholly unintelligible to those who have felt nothing marvelous in the fact of existence." In words that remind us of the double-nature of Rubenstein's 'strange wonder' in the face of Being, Witherall says, "One may fail to feel the intimacy of Being if one is yet to awake to the wonder occasioned by the fundamental question of metaphysics, or one has not yet found a voice for it, or one is consciously avoiding it for fear of what it may mean." Intimacy is, as we know, a complex and mysterious affair: it can evoke love and affection, it can arouse fear or denial, it can reduce one to silence because one does not know what to say or how to respond, one can even try to ignore it, to pretend it doesn't exist, to avoid it altogether. As Witherall rightly observes, faced with the existential dilemma posed by this ambivalent gift, "Nobody chooses to exist, but we may choose to receive this existence as a gift, and appreciate it as such." Acceptance of intimacy as a gift necessitates what is, paradoxically, an act of abyssal freedom; it calls for what Kierkegaard might have called a 'leap of faith' into a yawning metaphysical void. The gift of Being asks not for a metaphysical explanation but for an 'evaluative' response – yes or no, in or out, to be or not to be?

Witherall concludes in a Heideggerian vein: "We are thrown into the world, and we have some comprehension of the world's wholeness. I can indistinctly refer to the totality of the world by directly referring to things in my environment. The whole is the totality of myself, the beings around me, and everything else which extends beyond them. But to say this, to successfully refer to the whole in this way, presupposes that I am totally immersed and intimately involved with beings, and thus also with Being. Hence if the gift of Being is to be taken as a serious metaphor, it must be as an intimate gift" (ibid.) Again the necessity, the 'must,' which faces us in the question of the meaning of Being. As Heidegger says, the Being-question puts our own existence into question. It demands an answer. The Why question will not let us go.

Evaluative Applications

As Witherall has, perhaps unintentionally, suggested, the fundamental question of existence may not need a metaphysical answer at all, it may be met by a particular 'evaluative' response, an interpretation of the gift of Being that expresses our fundamental attitude toward being-in-the-world. Evaluative applications "entail a certain response to the situation of existence is desirable or necessary. This response may be described as gratitude or some other form of appreciation, but it naturally evokes the idea of a valuable endowment, or in other words, a gift.... A truly satisfactory response to the question is a response which comes from the whole of life" in both its emotional and intellectual aspects (Witherall, 146). The 'ultimacy' of such an evaluative 'answer' is measured by its "relevance to the question of life itself. We may choose to live a life in response to the gratuitous gift of Being...in ethical or aesthetic terms" (Witherall, *ibid.*) One is reminded of Kierkegaard's analysis of these two life-options in *Either/Or*. One might consider a further existential option, the religious, the stance of faith, what Witherall describes as the theological.

Elaborating on the apparently non-metaphysical direction of these remarks, in fact veering back in the direction of metaphor, as Witherall now startles with what seems an explicit repudiation of his previous metaphysical speculations: "The mystery which is hidden in the fact that there is something instead of nothing cannot be totally resolved, not even by a fully developed system of explanation. Instead of being resolved by an answer, the mystery is unfolded by a metaphor, and the metaphor becomes a pattern of meaning into which we may fit ourselves"

(Witherall, 146). What is surprising about this statement is that, contrary to the main thrust of his book, it takes us entirely out of the realm of metaphysical 'answers' the Why question. It seems a clear admission that in fact the Why question *cannot* be understood metaphysically, that it can *only* be responded to existentially, a response which, as Tillich indicated, can *only* be expressed in the language of metaphor, symbol, *mythos*: "Man's ultimate concern must be expressed symbolically, because symbolic language alone is able to express the ultimate... In no other way can faith [i.e., ultimate concern] express itself adequately" (Tillich, 1958, 47, 51)

As Witherall's comment hints, however, there is a price to pay for thinking that replacing metaphysical explanation with an evaluative interpretation 'unfolded by metaphor' will somehow resolve the issue. Resort to metaphor does not 'answer' the question of existence, for, he argues, "it is irrelevant to consider which form of answer to the fundamental question is 'the best fit,' just as it is irrelevant to consider which is 'most true'." For example, both aesthetic interpretations and moral interpretations "are satisfactory, fit into the scheme ['Being gives itself to beings] in some way" (Witherall, 148). You make your choice and pay the price. When you plump for a 'pattern of meaning' that is 'absolute' for you, your decision in no way relieves you of the burden of that freedom with its attendant anxiety. Is there, then, no way to assess the 'fit' or the 'truth' of an evaluative response? Are aesthetic and moral 'answers' equally 'satisfactory'? Despite his preference for gratitude, a clearly moral response, Witherall seems to think that those who prefer an aesthetic response, if it meets certain criteria of life-'fit' and existential 'truth,' may with equal justification say their choice is just as good, just as true, just as right. It certifies their Jamesian 'will' or 'right' to 'believe.'

Moral Value. James' will to believe is a vote for the moral value of the universe, the belief or at least hope that in the long run the balance of the morally good will outweigh that of the morally destructive. It is an 'evaluative' orientation that says we have reason to think and a right to believe "that suffering need not be meaningless, and that cruelty is an affront to the order of the cosmos rather than an essential part of the system, that life is worth living" (Witherall, 148). It is a commitment, reflected in a feeling of gratitude, that existence is better 'explained' "by an ultimate moral value" than by Descartes' evil demon bent on wreaking havoc on the world. Those who hold this view, says Witherall, answer the Why question by "employing the value of the gift of existence as the focus of their explanation. Being has absolute value, or it is absolute value, and is given to the world of beings. Thus value itself explains why there is something rather than nothing" (Witherall, 146). As the British philosopher, John Leslie, argues (and perhaps this is Quentin Smith's view too), "something is *intrinsically* better than nothing" (Witherall, 149, my emphasis).

There is problem, however, and that is whether this attitudinal stance really constitutes an 'answer' to the Why question. It seems more like a restatement of the explanatory-schema, 'Being gives itself to beings,' than a concrete explanation. Above it was said moral value is often associated with a necessitarian metaphysics, usually theism. Perhaps moral value can be given a more full-bodied role if it fleshed out with a theistic supplement.

What values flow from a theistic view of Being? Worship (*Verehrung*) or reverence (*Ehrfurcht*) centrally involves thankfulness (*Dankbarkeit*). It is a primary way of expressing gratitude (*Dankbarkeit*) to God for the gift of existence. Theism spells out the schema, 'Being gives itself to beings,' by interpreting it as God's giving himself in an act of love. Reverence as the 'felt meaning' of the gift of Being, the gift of love, means seeing love as an absolute value, as the value of Being itself. Reverence is the expression of an 'absolute commitment' to 'intimate involvement.' In a Christian context that moral value is known by its Greek equivalent, *agape*. Gratitude is also what gives value to a moral way of life lived in accord with that love. Gratitude "is a way of loving God, and thus, in a way, feeling love for the entire cosmos" (Witherall, 145). If one asks, 'Why does God give himself in love?' it is like asking, 'Why does Being give itself to beings?' Being 'gives itself' to beings because that is what 'Being' means. Similarly, in the theistic appropriation of Plato's equation of Being with Goodness, God gives himself in love because God *is* love; that is what 'God' means. The 'because' simply draws out and makes explicit in the predicate what was already contained in the subject. In that sense, these "impossible combinations of words," when directed to the heaviest words in the language, words like 'Being' and 'God,' may seem like tautologies. But if they are, they are anything but 'mere' tautologies, they are examples of *t'autos-logos*, of 'same-saying,' that utter the most profound thoughts of which human speech is capable.

Witherall concludes this disquisition on the moral value of love with the observation that "A completely philosophical theism, which is formulated only to answer the fundamental question of metaphysics cannot address the question of how anybody should worship God" (Witherall, 145). We are reminded of the ancient adage, reprised by Pascal and Heidegger, that the God of the philosophers is not the God of faith. Perhaps part of the reason is the problematic relation, present from the first encounter of Greek philosophy with Biblical faith, and seen throughout this part of our study, between metaphysics, expressed in the concepts of philosophy, and metaphor, expressed in the symbols of religion.

Aesthetic Value. Another evaluative application of the schema, 'Being gives itself to beings,' interprets the metaphor of gift in aesthetic terms. For Witherall, Nietzsche provides a particularly illustrative case of aesthetic values grounded in an atheistic metaphysics. On Witherall's reading, Nietzsche's 'death of God' means "there is a vacuum, an absence of ultimacy, which affects not only our beliefs but also our feelings, and the way that we live" (Witherall, 151). However, it would be a mistake to conclude that this entails that existence has no meaning. Quite the contrary. Here too, as he said in his analysis of Being and Nothing, Witherall finds in Nietzsche's metaphysics a 'place,' a transcendent locus, "once filled by God, [that] should be filled again, if not by a deity then by some other form of significance." If it were not so, in the absence of any fundamental meaning of existence we would inevitably face 'ultimate despair' (Witherall, *ibid.*).

Over the course of his career Nietzsche described that 'place,' that source of ultimate meaning, in different ways. In his early work, *The Birth of Tragedy*, it is "not a rational meaning but a non-cognitive, aesthetic meaning" (Witherall, 151). Here, Witherall astutely observes, his position resembled that of Smith's metaphysics of felt meanings, as perhaps might be expected in a view that sees ultimate emotions as responses to various aspects of the world-whole. A quick perusal of Smith's list indicates that most are indeed 'aesthetic' in nature: positive feelings of joy, marveling, awe, wonder, stupefaction, equanimity, peace, quietude; on the negative side of the ledger, despair, tedium, sadness, desolation, apathy, dread. Later, Nietzsche came to reject a narrowly 'aesthetic' reading of existence in favor of a more robust aesthetics based on the metaphysical notion of the Will to Power. On Witherall's interpretation of this 'immanental' metaphysics, "[t]here is no ultimate 'why' here, for the world is just Will to Power, and that is all that it is. Nothing outside the world is postulated to explain why it is like this, or why it exists" (Witherall, 151-152).

As an immanental metaphysics based on the death of God, on the absence of a transcendent source of Being, Witherall says, Nietzsche's shows that an evaluative interpretation of the gift metaphor does not require a moral metaphysics based on theism. "Although it is no longer a gift of love for which we are to be grateful, it is a gift of creative power within which to see our own selves as manifestations of beauty." Being, as Will to Power, "gives itself to the world, or gives birth to the world, not in the spirit of love but in the spirit of an artist giving himself over to this work. It creates because it is overfull, it has too much beauty, and therefore it gives itself" (Witherall, 152). Of course, if one were theistically inclined, one could speak of the beauty of God and of God's Creation, one could even say, in a Platonic vein, God *is* Beauty. Witherall's (and Nietzsche's) point, however, is that one need not speak of Being's gift of the world in theistic terms, one can do so in non-theistic, aesthetic ways as well. Being, explicated as Will to Power, is *creative* power, it is the *gift* of creative power.

In other words, for Nietzsche although the death of God means the absence of any ultimate rational meaning or any ultimate ethical value, Being nevertheless has an overflowing positive meaning. If God is dead, if he is erased from the face of the universe, existence itself must be free and spontaneous, is itself nothing but gratuitous creativity, the gift of Being. For Nietzsche, "The world then becomes playful, artistic, and joyous" (Witherall, 152). True, in and of itself, an *aesthetic evaluation* of the world would not seem to answer the Why question by providing a *metaphysical explanation* for the world's existence. But for Nietzsche and Smith both, aesthetics is not a matter of mere subjective 'feelings,' it is a double-barreled phenomenon with its roots deep in the soil of the world-whole's reality as an expression of endless, over-flowing creativity. For Nietzsche, the world, Witherall says, perhaps having in mind the Hindu notion of *lila*, the universe as the playground of the gods, is a "playful gift of Being itself." Therefore, "if the ultimate value, in terms of which the fundamental question of existence is answered, is an aesthetic value, then we must also appreciate that our finite existence...is a spontaneous, creative, gratuitous gift" (Witherall, *ibid*). When Nietzsche speaks of *amor fati*, love of one's fate, that love must be understood aesthetically, nor morally. It is "a love of life as it is: contingent, gratuitously bestowed, and dazzling. It is also, clearly, an appreciation of things as... indeed gifts," gifts of Being, "even if this Being is an emptiness" (Witherall, *ibid.*).

Witherall's is a 'creative' reading of Nietzche, to which the latter might not have objected, since for him all truth was a matter of 'interpretation.' It raises a number of issues. For example, Witherall uses the traditional metaphysical dualism, transcendent/immanent, to characterize the 'place' filled by Nietzsche's concept of the Will to Power. Witherall clearly visualizes this 'place' as a transcendent locus even in the absence of a transcendent Being filling it. It is a 'place' of 'transcendence' that remains despite the alleged 'immanence' of Nietzsche's metaphysics. It questionable, however, whether Nietzsche, despite his own generous notion of hermeneutics, would have accepted such a traditionalist interpretation of his worldview. One might ask why the Will to Power is not a perfectly good answer to the Why question. Why cannot the gift of Being, the overflowing creativity of Being, be an appropriate metaphor for the underlying power of Being that explains why and how things are? Why should that creativity be called the gift of Nothing, just because an alleged transcendent locus was left unfilled, when it is clearly an expression of Being itself?

Witherall seems to be of two minds here. On the one hand, he sees Nietzsche's later aesthetic evaluation of existence as correlated to, if not grounded in, the creativity of Being celebrated in an immanental metaphysics of the Will to Power. On the other hand, as if returning to Nietzsche's earlier, non-metaphysical elevation of the aesthetic, Witherall says that this aesthetic evaluation is *not* metaphysically explanatory. It signifies, but does not explain, the 'playful gift of Being' as if its were a kind of poetry-plus. Which is it to be? There are two problems here. On the one hand, it seems clear that in his mature work Nietzsche does attribute explanatory power to his aesthetic concept of the Will to Power. On the other hand, while acknowledging this fact, Witherall nevertheless tacitly faults Nietzsche's concept twice over, first by giving it less than full metaphysical blessing – it does not really fill that transcendent 'place,' so its status must be ontologically downgraded to that of 'Nothing,' and in a second insult, by resorting to metaphor to interpret the original metaphor – the metaphorical 'gift' of Being is metaphorically described as the 'playful' gift of Being – Being, as it were, having fun, amusing itself in a sporting way.

Witherall raises a valid question, however, that can forward the discussion of both the moral and aesthetic approaches as interpretive (existential) if not explanatory (metaphysical) responses to the Why question. If, as Witherall suggests of Nietzsche, an evaluative interpretation is not grounded in a metaphysics, it is difficult to see how it could serve even as an interpretation, if not an explanation, of the fact of Being. In the absence of what T.S. Eliot called an 'objective correlate,' whether transcendent or immanent, theistic or mundane, moral and aesthetic values collapse into matters of subjective preference only, however complexified or gussied up in the latest theoretical novelties. Nietzsche himself, recognizing this dilemma, rejected his earlier aesthetic subjectivism in favor of his later metaphysics of the Will to Power. It was Nietzsche too who, more than anyone else, was fully aware of the threat nihilism posed to moral values in the absence of a theistic underpinning, faced by the death of God. The question is how a moral or aesthetic view of the world can gain purchase in reality if a metaphysics, whether dependent on a transcendent Being or wholly immanent in character, is not available to provide such a basis. In any event, whether on Witherall's or Nietzsche's interpretation, both theism and the Will to Power remain problematic ways of addressing the Why question precisely insofar as they are *metaphysical* answers, not because they do or do not ground moral or aesthetic valuations.

Witherall's decision to focus on two categories of evaluative worldviews, aesthetic and moral, remind one Kierkegaard's discussion of the existential option of the aesthetic and the ethical modes of being in *Either/Or*. Kierkegaard, however, did not see these as the only or ultimate existential choices facing the existing individual. A third option, the religious, subsumed them both, but it too was not conceived in metaphysical terms. Kierkegaard, before Heidegger, had already understood, in his anti-Hegelianism, that one had to go beyond the dualisms and dialectics of metaphysics. Instead all three were described in what he called his 'poetic' oeuvre. Metaphysics fell short when it came to an existential analysis. Going back further, there is Plato's tripartite analysis of the 'soul' in which the aesthetic and the moral may be seen as two of the three dimensions of a unified existence, the third being the rational or intellectual part. The 'just' life is one in which all three elements exist together in a harmony in which each mode of existence is given its due. Witherall does try to bring together these three, adding metaphysical explanation to his account of the two evaluative orientations. The question, however, as Kierkegaard and Rubenstein have asked, is whether, if metaphysics falls short, there is another way of supporting a moral and/or an aesthetic response to the Why question.

Gift of Being: Being of Gift

The last section of the last part of Witherall's study is titled "The Meaning of It All." Here he summarizes the argument of his book – his thesis that the metaphor of the 'gift of Being,' by its hospitality as "a general metaphysical structure," provides a satisfactory and adequate framework to several metaphysical and evaluative explanations for answering the question of Being. It offers itself as the "common ground" of each, meaning that the metaphor of gift points to a feature shared in common by otherwise mutually incompatible worldviews, theist and atheist, ethical and aesthetic. The claim that there is a 'common ground' among these positions should not be taken as saying they enjoy some "common propositional content." The 'metaphorical/metaphysical' structure of the gift of Being "is reflected in fundamental attitudes more than fundamental doctrines" (Witherall, 153). Key among those attitudes is gratitude, thankfulness for the gift of Being, however it is doctrinally understood.

This summary is quite helpful because it makes clear the problematic heart of his thesis. It is located in the peculiar hybrid construction we noted earlier – the conflating of two different language games, 'metaphor' and 'metaphysics' as it they could be made to fit together in one unambiguous conceptual framework that proves conveniently to be one thing when you want it to be but quite another when that is more suitable to one's purpose. Is 'the gift of Being' a metaphorical construct or is it a 'general metaphysical structure'? Does the fact that both theism and atheism can make sense of the gift metaphor on their own terms, that they can find room for this or that attitude in their own systematic frameworks, mean that these two incompatible metaphysical philosophies therefore share a 'common ground'? If that claim is permitted to pass, then almost any metaphor and any attitude can serve as a 'common ground' between them. The argument is a slippery one at best.

What Witherall sees as an additional plus in the metaphor of the gift of Being only bears this out. He says, insofar as the metaphor can "sustain the absence of one of the terms of the giving relation is a strength rather than a weakness" (Witherall, 153). In other words, if the 'giving' relationship is not grounded in a transcendent Being, not to worry, that's a good thing about the metaphor. Because, as Witherall has said more than once, "Being need not be given by a transcendent 'entity.' It can also be given by sheer nothingness, or by a 'non-thing.'" Here Witherall brings Heidegger to the rescue: "Being, as Heidegger emphasized, is not itself a being" (Witherall, *ibid.*). Apart from whether Heidegger would have endorsed the equation of the Nothingness of Being with the no-thingness of Being, one has to question what sense there is to a 'relation' one of whose terms is missing, is, as it were, 'not-a-term.' How can nothing 'give' something, or as the traditional query went, how can something come out of nothing? Nothing comes out of nothing. To think otherwise is either to be tacitly parasitic on an 'absent' transcendent 'place,' or it is to indulge in what Socrates called meaningless word-play, metaphysical sophistry.

Witherall follows up this claim that sheer nothingness can be said to 'give' existence by drawing the consistent yet nonetheless startling conclusion that, when all is said and done, not the traditional 'expansive' answer based on a transcendent Being, but rather the 'reductive' or 'deflationary' answer based on a rejection of a transcendent 'entity,' on the non-being of transcendent Being, is the template for assessing the satisfactoriness of all other answers. On what does he base this, at first glance, anti-traditional and counter-intuitive assertion? He offers two reasons. First, the basic insight of the deflationary position is that "reason cannot deal with the fact of existence." Each of the other answers discussed must in one way or the other must assume a similar stance (Witherall, 153).

By 'reason' Witherall apparently means in this context the activity of explaining metaphysically why there is something rather than nothing. This is puzzling, because both the necessitarian and the immanental positions are presented as metaphysical 'applications' (i.e., explanations, 'reasons') that fill in the metaphorical blank. The reason for the confusion becomes quickly clear. Witherall interprets the deflationary position as saying, "To an ultimate question there must be an ultimate answer, and this must refer to something which lies beyond reason." There a couple of problems here. First, the sentence itself is an example of metaphysical reasoning to which we are invited to give rational assent. Second, the two occurrences of 'must' give pause. The second part, which may or may not be the deflationary view, does not in any case follow from or lead back to the first part. To say that reason *cannot* deal with the fact of existence is *not* a way of referring to something *beyond* reason. Further, if we take Smith's metaphysics of the world-whole as illustrative of the deflationary view, it is clear that he would argue that his view is eminently reasonable, that it in no way refers to something lying beyond reason. Further, assuming the 'ultimate question' can be stated reasonably, it is in no way clear that it requires there be an 'ultimate answer,' or any answer at all. It may simply be a pointer to a mystery that, as Hannah Arendt says in *The Life of the Mind:Thinking*, invites pondering, not 'answering.'

Witherall's sense of a transcendent dimension in even the deflationary position carries over to his claim about the moral and aesthetic values. These 'ultimate values,' like their metaphysical counterparts, are also said to lie "beyond rationality." Therefore "we must [another 'must'] either adopt them or not. These things must be intuited, rather than rationalized, for they represent the end-points, the extremities of thought, beyond which there is no strictly logical path" (Witherall, 153). These claims too are puzzling. First there is the injection of the distinction between intuition and reasoning into the discussion, along with the sudden reduction of reason and rationality to the status of that which is 'rationalized.' Next, each of these evaluative stances, as we have seen, is capable of being readily accommodated by a cognate metaphysical stance, providing it with at least a modicum of rationality. Finally, there are criteria, presumably rational, by which the validity of the choice of moral and aesthetic responses to the gift of Being can be assessed, including, among others the way of life to which such choice of attitude leads. Witherall can succeed in making these claims only, it seems, if he is employing a very narrow or prejudicial sense of the term 'rationality' in the phrase 'beyond rationality.'

The second reason why the deflationary approach is said to be 'primary' is that "it is the natural origin of our thoughts about the fundamental question" (Witherall,153). 'Natural'? In what way? As Rubenstein also pointed out in her analysis of the double-aspectival nature of wonder, the Why question can evoke, initially, a sense of fear or anxiety. Any answer to it seems to lie far beyond us, and hence to defeat our desire to have an answer to the related question of the ultimate meaning of our existence. But, says Witherall, "if we are to overcome this fear, we must be reconciled with the question itself. The natural way of obtaining such a reconciliation is to be reconciled directly with the inexplicability of the fact that something exists." In this lies the second advantage of "the brute fact view, even if it pays the price of admitting that there is something astonishing, awesome or even joyous about the world itself" (Witherall, 154). Again, a bit of a surprise here. It seems unlikely that a sense that the universe 'just is' for no reason at all would lead to feelings of astonishment or awe, let alone joy. The notion that these positive emotions would be the 'price' that the brute fact would have to 'pay' suggests how implausible that scenario is. The 'natural' felt meaning of the 'brute fact' view would seem to lie more along the lines of the initial anxiety, perhaps provoking a Sartrean sense of nausea at the meaninglessness of Being, a sense that our own existence is *de trop*, too much, *une passion inutile*, useless, an excrescence in the implacable void of sheer nothingness.

Of course there is a way out of the apparent 'no exit' of the deflationary view, however 'primary' it is, unconvincingly, portrayed as being. The way to overcome the frustration at being unable to answer the question, to go beyond Sartrean nausea and despair, to be 'reconciled' to feeling that not only the answer but even the question itself is 'beyond' us, is to take refuge in that very Beyond. "[By] recognizing, *in one way or another*, the transcendence of Being, by adopting an interpretation of Being itself, we may answer the *question in a certain way* without destroying our sense of wonder at existence" (Witherall, 154; emphasis mine). If Witherall can explain how a metaphorical 'interpretation' of the transcendence of Being can be carried through without being 'translated' into a metaphysical 'explanation' that destroys our sense of wonder at Being, he will have redeemed the price paid by the deflationist metaphysician. Only if his 'answer' takes the ultimate form, paradoxically, of a non-answer, an anti-answer. But is he willing to go that far?

Summing up, he says, "So there are two basic approaches: the deflationary view, which offers reconciliation by way of facing the impossibility of answering the question, and the construction of an interpretation of Being, which reconciles us directly with the question by providing an answer. These two approaches result *in different ways* of expressing the gift of Being' (Witherall, 154). This nicely sums up also the problematic nature of his basic assumptions. First, he argues, asking us to set aside common sense, or what German perhaps more appropriately calls 'healthy understanding,' that we can find *positive* reassurance in accepting that *negative* fact that the Why question *cannot* be answered. Second, he contends, on the other hand, that the Why question *can* be answered and '*directly*' at that – at least 'in one way or the other,' 'in a certain way.' Third, he asks us to suspend disbelief by accepting that these incompatible answers (or non-answers), 'in different ways,' each satisfactorily 'translate' into the language of metaphysics the poetic metaphor of the 'gift of Being.'

At this point his summation veers off into another and unexpected direction. Apparently retreating from the reconciliation of the deflationist and necessitarian views under the umbrella of the gift metaphor, he now seems to fall back on metaphor itself. It would appear that taking a literal view of the metaphysical translation of the gift metaphor may, after all, fall short, way short, of capturing or doing justice to its symbolic truth. Why the return to metaphor now? "The reason we should use a metaphor in answering the fundamental question is connected to the sense of moving beyond the realm of reason ... beyond literal meaning." Backtracking a moment, he quickly adds, "this does mean that our answers become entirely senseless." Though we must use poetic metaphor to go 'beyond the realm of reason,' this does not mean that metaphysical answers cast in the form of literal concepts are rendered null and void. However, as Witherall argued at the outset of his study, answers to the Why question can only be judged satisfactory if they meet *two* criteria – the criterion of cognition, satisfied by metaphysics, but also the criterion of feeling, and "[m]etaphor can do this in a way that mundane literal usage cannot" (Witherall, 154).

What makes the gift metaphor especially appropriate is that "it emerges naturally [that word again] from our astonishment, and reflects the intensity of our feelings, as much as it supplies a resolution of the inquiry itself" (Witherall, 154). In fact, Witherall wants to go further. He wants to say that the gift metaphor 'has truth': "[The] proposition that Being gives itself to beings is correct, it is capable of endorsement, and reflects a genuinely explanatory proposal, albeit one that has various divergent expressions. The reason this is a true metaphor is that there is a genuine limit to rational construction" (Witherall, *ibid.*). On the other hand, if the metaphorical proposition, 'Being gives itself to beings,' were 'watered down' ['translated'?] into a literal 'equivalent,' it would run something like the following: "The reason that there is something instead of nothing is that there is a mysterious non-thing which we cannot describe, except by saying that it is Being itself, and this has gratuitously bestowed existence upon the less mysterious immanent things we encounter in the world." That proposition, he said, would "rightly reflect the oddity of existence. It claims both that the source of the gift is ineffable, and also that the gift is without justification" (Witherall, *ibid.*).

Again the same worrisome problem rears its double-faced head: the gift metaphor is true, but this is immediately qualified by labeling it metaphysically as an 'explanatory' proposal. It is not really true *as a metaphor* at all, it was a *metaphysical* proposition masquerading as what it is not and cannot be. What makes it 'true' is not some feature unique to metaphors but simply that it posits a limit to 'rational [metaphysical?] construction.' But does metaphysics need metaphor to point out those limits? Further, the alleged literal 'translation' of the metaphor is not so 'literal' after all; it trades on, is apparently unable to get along without, the metaphor itself: the 'mysterious non-thing,' equated with Being itself, '*gratuitiously bestows*' existence upon things. The literal translation finds it necessary to indulge in, to be parasitic on, the gift metaphor itself ...to make sense of the metaphor. A hermeneutical circle indeed!

Witherall continues to confront us with paradox. The answer to the Why question, he says, "can be formulated, but only when we understand that it cannot be an answer which leaves everything clear. It must be the kind of explanation which does not 'explain away' but instead invites us into a deepened appreciation of mystery" (Witherall, 155). In fact, Witherall here verges on what would be a more satisfactory 'answer', one appropriate to the 'oddity' of the question itself: an answer that is an 'answer' in name only, not an answer at all but a non-answer, an anti-answer, a pointer to that which evades all answers ... and questions. As he says, "such an answer will not make the fact of existence less awesome, but it can succeed in bringing human beings closer to the centrality of this fact." As in the book of Job, the metaphor does something that metaphysics cannot do: it "answers a mystery with a mystery. Job is confronted with riddles; but he is comforted" (Witherall, *ibid.*). Witherall proposes this metaphorical/metaphysical paradox as a solution: "A mysterious and metaphoric understanding of the fact of existence must therefore become the answer. It must be understood as an explanation."

Again he takes away with one hand what he has just appeared to give us with the other: Yes, the 'answer' is 'mysterious and metaphoric,' but for all that it is still an 'explanation,' not a metaphor, not a mystery, after all.

Having run metaphor and metaphysics together throughout his study, Witherall has one last surprise in store. In a stirring peroration, he ends on a high note of metaphor in which metaphysics is reduced to a mere appendage:

> The gift of Being is given to us here and now. It is the reality which unfolds before our eyes, within our bodies, around us in the world of immanent things. We should not forget that our question is deeply related to the question of what it is to be a thing, an entity, a 'something' which is not nothing. The idea that there are 'mere things' is an illusion. Each immanent thing is a gift, it is something miraculous, if only for its existence. It is the idea that we should respond to the world of beings with respect, with love and gratitude, and with a sense of the hidden meanings that lurk in the obscurity of the everyday. In moments of despair, when we call out 'Why is there a world?' the answer is forthcoming: this world is our gift. We can use it or neglect it, but it remains true that it is given to us. If we reel back, stunned by the realization that the world is spectacularly gratuitous, then we have at least come to a *final point*, a *true* realization which is a *completion* of thought and feeling. On the other hand, if all that we can see are 'mere things,' things which we take for granted, then we have lost the sense of existence. In the midst of the darkening of the world, when all is lost and when we can find neither ourselves nor the meaning of our lives, we should reflect that existence is given to us, and respond to this as a gift. (Witherall, 155-156).

Witherall said, in concluding his discussion of Nietzsche's aesthetic/atheistic metaphysics that it involved an "appreciation of things as gifts," gifts of Being. Perhaps in that observation we can find a key. Things are gifts of Being. So is Being. Being is both giver and gift, a gift that in giving beings gives itself ... by sacrificing itself that beings might be ... a giving and gift that, by 'concealing' itself, lets beings be. To unpack these perhaps unnecessarily paradoxical sounding metaphorical tautologies will take us beyond Witherall to Heidegger's thinking on Being and beings, to thinking as thanking ... for the gift of Being.

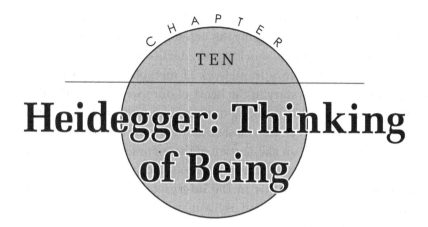

CHAPTER

TEN

Heidegger: Thinking of Being

In turning to Heidegger's 'answer' to the Why question, it will be helpful to summarize the positive results achieved so far. In Part One the positive contribution was preservation of an awareness of the primordial mystery of being, insistence upon the cognitive significance of the Why question, and refusal to reduce it to subjective feelings. In the cosmological-metaphysical and transitional sections of Part Two the positive contribution was a more explicit focus on feelings as links to our cognitive awareness of the universe or world. However, common to Part One and those first two parts of Part Two was that though they tried to relate fundamental feelings to facts, the facts to which they referred were the existence or nature of the world, not the fact that something exists rather than nothing.

It is not, of course, that the existence of the world does not 'matter' to us. The sense in which the Why question 'matters' more is that, unlike questions about the existence of the world, it puts our own existence in question. What was lacking in Parts One and the first two parts of Part Two, in other words, was an existential-ontological account of the link between our cognitive awareness of the mystery of existence and the felt responses to which that awareness gives rise. That awareness and response entails another way of thinking about the Why question and answers to it – a way of thinking as unique as the mystery of existence itself. It requires what Heidegger calls 'another beginning.' In this last part of Part Two we have started to explore that other way of thinking.

Rubenstein's phenomenology of wonder and Witherall's analysis of the gift of Being have prepared the way for understanding Heidegger's way of asking and answering the Why question. How does Heidegger address the *ontological* shock of encountering the 'ontological difference' of being and beings; the *epistemological* shock of the reduction of the meaning of being to the causal-explanatory framework of metaphysics; and *existential* shock of finding a mystery in the heart of our own being. Indeed, if as Heidegger suggests, his thinking of Being can be seen as an originary poetizing, perhaps it can also be seen as an originary *ethics*.

Before turning to an elaboration of these cursory answers, we need first to remind ourselves of the context of Heidegger's approach to the Why question. We find this in the interpretation of the existential-ontological structure of Dasein as 'being-in-the-world' set forth in *Sein und Zeit* (*Being and Time*). In our critique of Smith we previewed two of the elements of this articulated-but-unitary structure: 'world' and 'being-in.' It is the latter, 'being-in,' with its parallels to James' notion of the double-barreled structure of experience, that provides Heidegger's solution to the alleged problem of the 'link' between our cognitive awareness of the mystery of Being and our felt responses to that mystery.

As will be recalled, for Heidegger the existential-ontological structure of 'being-in' is the 'between' that links the 'who' element and the 'world' element of the primordial phenomenon of being-in-the-world prior to their being split apart into the ontologically derivative 'subject--side' and 'object-side' of traditional epistemology and metaphysics. For Heidegger, therefore, what Smith called our 'global feelings' cannot be understood by being reduced to our subjectivity, Rather, as aboriginal moods or affects, they disclose the prior and primordial fact of our being-in-the-world itself. They embody and constitute our "basic factical possibilities" of being-in-the-world: "it is essential of every state-of-mind that in each case being-in-the-world should be fully disclosed in all those items which are constitutive for it – world, Being-in, Self... undisguised by entities-within-the-world" (Heidegger, *SZ*, 190-191/*BT*, 235). Each embodies, as it were, the reality of a *different mode of being* and a *different world*. However, and this will prove important for our further analysis, no one mood has an ontological or existential priority over another. Each discloses in its own way the reality of our relation to being-in-the-world vis-a-vis the mystery of Being.

When we turn to Heidegger's analysis of the mystery of Being and responses to it, we must keep in mind this articulated-but-unitary structure in which both cognitive awareness of the mystery of Being and responses to it are primordially embedded – how they are justified as 'linked,' as equi-primordially 'belonging together.'

Two other cautionary notes: First, in the following two sections, we will try as much as possible to interpret the meaning of Heidegger's metaphors for Being in plain and simple language, as Heidegger himself frequently did in his later works, while observing Witherall's warning to avoid 'watering down' Heidegger's thinking into an inappropriate literalism. As Arendt observed, all philosophical terms began their lives as metaphors, extensions of their everyday counterparts. In this they reflected the originally (Heidegger would say 'originary') 'poetic' nature of metaphysical 'thinking' as it struggled to free itself from the concrete language of *mythos* and translate its insights into the new technical vocabulary of *philosophia*. As Tillich reminded us, theology still speaks – tells its *mythos* (*Geschichte*, 'story'/'history') in the language of symbol and metaphor. The abstract concepts of metaphysics, on the other hand, are metaphors that have died and forgotten their 'mythic' origins. That is why Heidegger, like Witherall, turned from the lifeless terms of metaphysics to metaphors that still had the power of living speech in them. That is why, as we shall see, he slowly left behind the language of metaphysics, drawing increasingly on the 'poetic' resources of metaphor – gift, call, appeal, speech, grace, sending, house, shepherd – to arrive at 'another beginning.' That is why already early on he seemed to be indulging in taking questionable, even off-putting liberties with the familiar language of sober thought. Compelled by the *Sache selbst*, Heidegger was *unterwegs*, taking hitherto unexplored paths in the thinking (of) Being.

Second, we will not be trying to analyze the totality of Heidegger's oeuvre or chart the changes he makes *unterwegs*. Others have done that, and in any case it is not necessary for our purposes. Instead we will limit ourselves to the central focus of this study, the Why question and its implications for the thinking (of) Being. We will select only those parts of his thought relevant to this topic – why the Why question is 'asked,' how it is 'asked,' and why and how it is 'answered.' We will look first at his views on the mystery of Being, its relation to beings, Dasein, and Nothing. Then, from the 'gift' of Being, we will turn to his thinking (of) Being as 'answering' the 'call' of Being, and the 'answers' of wonder, thanking, and piety as ways of 'protecting' the mystery and gift of Being.

Heidegger I: (Thinking of) Being

The Mystery of Being

From the beginning of his studies in philosophy Heidegger was captivated by the problem of *the meaning of Being*. This is reflected in the quote from Plato's *Sophist* (244a) with which he opened his first published work, *Sein und Zeit* (*Being and Time*): "For manifestly you have long been aware of what you mean when you use the expression 'being' (Grk: *'on'*; Ger: *'seiend'*). We, however, who used to think we understood it, have now become perplexed." Heidegger commented: "Do we in our time have an answer to the question of what we really mean by the word 'being' (*'seiend'*)? Not at all. So it is fitting that we should raise anew *the question of the meaning of Being*" (*SZ*, 1; *BT*, 21; emphasis Heidegger's).

Shortly after *SZ* (1927), Heidegger published a short work, *What is Metaphysics?* (1929) in which the 'being' question, compelled by a phenomenon Heidegger called 'the Nothing' (*das Nichts*), took the form of the Why question: "Why are there beings (*Seiendes*) at all rather than nothing?"("... *die Grundfrage der Metaphysik, die das Nichts selbst erzwingt: Warum ist uberhaupt Seiendes und nicht vielmehr Nichts?*") (1998g, 42/ 96). Apparently it had become clear to the young philosopher that the answer to the question of the meaning of being had first to go through the dark night of nothingness. It had to descend into an abyss (*Abgrund*) at the center of Being itself. Not only that. Because of the Nothing at its empty center the meaning of Being had to remain an open question, a mystery that repelled and expelled every metaphysical explanation or answer.

To understand these claims it is necessary to ask some questions. What does Heidegger's neologism 'the Nothing' mean? If it was intended to be taken literally, has it gone over the edge into complete nonsense, as logical positivists like Carnap and Quine argued? If instead it was to be understood as a metaphor, then what is it a metaphor of? Why does it the Nothing require that Being remain a 'mystery' (*Geheimnis*) defeating philosophical comprehension? In Heidegger's formulation of the Why question, what is the relation of the Nothing to 'beings' (*Seiendes*). To answer these questions will involve looking at two places where Heidegger introduces the notion of the Nothing: his existential analysis of Dasein as the being 'held out in the Nothing'; his ontological discussion of the concealment of Being as the revealing of beings.

But first, we must try to understand, at least provisionally, what Heidegger means by talking of Being as a mystery. We may begin by considering the ordinary meaning of 'mystery,' for, as with all technical terms of philosophy, ordinary usage is where such thinking starts. The term is primarily understood in relation to knowing. Something is a mystery if it is difficult or impossible to understand or explain, beyond human knowledge or comprehension, incapable of solution by human reason. It refers to something hidden or obscure about which we are "in the dark," something that resists illumination, resists being brought out "into the open." It could be a riddle (Wittgenstein: *Ratsel*), an enigma, a puzzle (though Marcel distinguishes a puzzle from a genuine mystery). In short, a mystery is something deep, profound, inexplicable, something that has not or cannot be explained.

Keeping this usual understanding of mystery in hand, what is Heidegger's philosophical understanding of the term?. Here, as seen, Rubenstein provides a helpful introduction in her discussion of wonder. For Heidegger, she says, wonder points to a phenomenon that thwarts philosophy's desire for ultimate answers. It is a primordial experience in which the attempt to explain being as a metaphysical concept runs up against a wall: "Standing in *thaumazein*, the philosopher stands exposed to that which he cannot master; that which, in turn, threatens to disable the sort of mastery one expects of philosophers" (Rubenstein, 2008, 4). There are other implications too, ontological and existential. The mystery of being not only threatens the explanatory structures of metaphysics, it discloses "the strangeness of the everyday" – the mystery that beings exist, that "the impossible nevertheless *is*" (Rubenstein, 2008, 23). As Rubenstein comments: "Not knowing what being is, we cannot possibly know what beings genuinely are" (Rubenstein, 2008, 18). The mystery of being also confronts us existentially with the 'shock of non-being' (Tillich). For Heidegger, the question of the meaning of being puts the being of the questioner in question as well. There is a mystery not only in the vital core of philosophy but in the heart of beings and human being as well.

Thus for Heidegger, *that* being is a mystery seems clear. As Richardson observes, "This Source remains questionable precisely inasmuch as it remains hidden, undeterminable by exact and certain knowledge, sc. mystery" (Richardson, 257). The question, however, is *why* and *how* that is so. The answer has several dimensions: *epistemological* – being eludes metaphysical explanation, but *why* and *how*? *ontological* – being discloses the strangeness of beings, but *why* and *how*? *existential* – being puts our own being in question, but *why* and *how*? In fact for Heidegger the meaning of the mystery of being for *metaphysics* cannot be grasped without considering its origin in the *experience* of being. To answer the question *why* for Heidegger being is a *mystery* for philosophy, therefore, we must first look at how and why that mystery is disclosed primordially in two phenomena: *Dasein* and the existence of beings as such. That in turn will lead us back to the question of how he understands the relation of being to the mysterious phenomenon of 'the Nothing.'

Being and Dasein: The 'There' of Being

What awakens us to the question of the meaning of being, to its mystery? Experience, as with other things. What experience? There could be many – wonder, dread, boredom, joy, anxiety, hope, joy, enthusiasm, gaiety, satiety, sadness, melancholy, desperation, elation, equanimity, even the pallid lack of mood – indifference (Heidegger, *SZ* 345-346/*BT* 395-396). As these terms indicate, for Heidegger the 'meaning' of Being, and hence the 'mystery' of Being is not meant in a narrowly semantic or epistemological sense, but is broadly existential and ontological. In the phenomenological analyses of *SZ/BT* Heidegger describes three ways in which Dasein experiences the meaning of Being. These also include a first sketch of Dasein's encounter with the phenomenon of the Nothing *(das Nichts)*, the manner in which, in Heidegger's metaphorical phrase, Dasein is "held out in the Nothing." Dasein comes face to face with the problematic meaning of Being and the disquieting reality of the Nothing in the 'originary fear' of anxiety (*Angst*) when it confronts the disappearance of the meaningful 'world' of beings-as-such, in 'being-toward' the "impossible possibility" of death itself, and in 'originary guilt' in relation to its own existence, the necessity of being the 'null' basis of its own non-necessary being.

Angst(Anxiety)

Although every mood discloses Dasein's being-in-the-world in one way or the other, for Heidegger the mood of anxiety (*Angst*) plays a phenomenologically distinctive role. It is the master mood of negativity. It is the key that opens Pandora's box. It sets everything in motion – guilt, meaninglessness, death. In each case it discloses Dasein's "primordial totality of Being" (SZ 182, 190-191/*BT* 226, 234-235). The anxiety of which Heidegger speaks is thus not ordinary fear directed to a particular object *within* the world. Angst is an 'originary' fear, that is, a fundamental state-of-mind or mood which has no object, whose 'object,' phenomenologically speaking, is "the nothing and nowhere" (*SZ* 188-189, 252/*BT* 233, 296). Heidegger is not saying that the object of anxiety is the totality of beings (*das Ganze des Seienden*), nor does it point to an absolute nonbeing of nothingness. Both of these are for Heidegger ontologically impossible notions: "Anxiety is anxious in the face of the 'nothing' of the world; but this does not mean that in anxiety we experience something like the absence of what is present-at-hand within-the-world" (*SZ* 343/*BT* 393). Rather in the experience of anxiety, the world-*as-a-whole*, beings-*as-such* (*das Seiendes im Ganzen*), collapse into the dark night of meaninglessness (*SZ* 186-7/*BT* 230-232).

Angst is the existential-ontological realization of what Tillich called the shock of 'spiritual' nonbeing – the experience of emptiness, despair, the lack of hope – the loss of "a meaning which gives meaning to all meanings." Existence is disclosed as "completely lacking significance." Moreover, it is "completely indefinite": "Anxiety 'does not know' what that in the face of which it is anxious is... it is already 'there,' and yet nowhere; it is so close that it is oppressive and stifles one's breath, and yet it is nowhere. In that in the face of which one has anxiety, the 'It is nothing and nowhere' becomes manifest'... In anxiety one feels 'uncanny'... the peculiar indefiniteness...the 'nothing and nowhere'... 'not-being-at-home'.... From an existential-ontological point of view, the 'not-at-home' must be conceived as the more primordial phenomenon" (*SZ* 188-189/ *BT* 233-234). Intriguingly Heidegger adds: "Here the disclosure and the disclosed are existentially selfsame." One can only speculate at this point how this primordial 'selfsame' of existence-as-nothing might figure in Heidegger's later reflections on the 'selfsame' of Being *sive/soku hi* ("or/is and is not") Nothing. For now it seems clear that angst not only puts the meaning of Dasein's 'being-in-the-world' in question, it gives rise in an existentially shattering way to the question of the meaning of being itself. It not only threatens to undermine, to destroy Dasein's own being, it risks reducing the meaning of being itself to a nothing, to a *nihil*. It raises the specter of an absolute nihilism.

Death

Angst not only confronts Dasein with the specter of the ultimate meaninglessness of its existence, it brings Dasein face to face with the possibility of the very end of that existence. Angst reveals what Heidegger terms 'being-toward-death' (*Sein-zum-Tode*), what Tillich calls the shock of 'ontic' nonbeing, dread in the face of finitude. We may not will or want our death, but in the grip of meaninglessness, death acquires a mysterious and compelling meaning. It discloses the ultimate 'nullity' (*Nichtheit*) at the bottom of Dasein's existence, and yet paradoxically, as such death is also the *basis* of Dasein's Being. Death is "the possibility of the impossibility of existence–that is to say, the utter nullity of Dasein." Yet death also discloses Dasein as "the thrown (that is null) basis for its death." (*SZ* 306/*BT* 354, cf. *SZ* 250, 258-259, 262/*BT* 293-294, 302-303, 306-307). It would seem death is a duplicitous, a double-dealing phenomenon. It appears to offer a choice. Descent into nihility or freedom *for* death: death *cum* resurrection. But does it?

Heidegger first offers a *formal* existential-ontological interpretation of the phenomenon of death. He then provides a phenomenological interpretation of '*authentic* Being-toward-Death.' Formally considered, "death signifies a peculiar possibility-of-Being in which the very Being of one's own Dasein is an issue." (*SZ* 240/*BT* 284) This echoes Heidegger's basic claim in *SZ* that the question of the meaning of Being is an issue for Dasein's own Being. Death is the primary example of how and why this is so. It will be recalled that for Heidegger a mood, or state-of-mind, brings Dasein "face to face with the thrownness of its 'that it is there.'" The mood of anxiety is existentially and ontologically fundamental in that Dasein finds itself "face to face with the 'nothing' of the possible impossibility of its existence ... The 'nothing' with which anxiety brings us face to face, unveils the nullity by which Dasein, in its very *basis*, is defined; and this basis itself is thrownness into death ... Thrownness into death reveals itself to Dasein in a more primordial and impressive manner in that state-of-mind which we have called 'anxiety' ... Being-towards-death is essentially anxiety" (*SZ* 251, 265-266, 308/*BT* 295, 310-311, 356; emphasis Heidegger's). In short, death is, formally speaking, Dasein's "way to be." It is not only inherent in but the 'very basis' of Dasein's mode of being-in-the-world. The kicker is, as Heidegger immediately adds, it is also a 'thrown' being "which Dasein takes over as soon as it is" (*SZ* 245/*BT* 289). It has no choice. Or does it?

Formally speaking, no. For this is an existential-ontological *description* of Dasein's way of being. But concretely, existentially, yes, for it confronts Dasein with the choice referred to above: not 'to be or not to be,' but *how* to be. What 'stance' to take vis-a-vis the anxiety of being-towards-death? How to 'take over' one's 'thrown' being given that the 'basis' of our existence is 'nullity,' the 'nothing'? How can one be *free* for one's death when death presents itself in anxiety as the unavoidable impossibility of an existence at all? And yet Dasein's being-towards-death calls for a decision, indeed counter-intuitively makes such a decision possible. As the 'possible' impossibility of its existence, death discloses to Dasein the *freedom* that characterizes its being-in-the-world. That death is unavoidable is a fact, but the attitude, the 'stance' one takes toward that fact is nonetheless within Dasein's limited (finite) power. The finitude of Dasein is not the finitude of a thing. "Only Being-free *for* death, gives Dasein its goal outright and pushes existence into finitude ... being free for death, in a possibility which it has inherited and yet has chosen ... the power of finite freedom." It this freedom, "which 'is' only in its having chosen to make such a choice," that enables Dasein to 'take over' its 'thrownness' in the face of the 'possible impossibility' of its own death. "Only an entity which, in its Being ... is free for its death and can let itself be thrown back upon its factical 'there' by shattering itself against death...can...take over its own thrownness" (*SZ* 384-385/*BT* 435-437, Heidegger's emphasis).

Thus Heidegger leaves us with a triple paradox/conundrum/koan: how can being free *for* death mean shattering oneself *against* death? how can being *free* for death mean *letting* oneself *be thrown back* upon oneself? how can *letting* oneself *be thrown back* be a *taking over* of being thrown? What is Dasein's *responsibility* –or *guilt* –in the face of its thrownness, its death, its nullity – in the face of 'the Nothing'?

Guilt

Taking over implies responsibility (*Schuld*). Another word with two faces. *Schuld* can also be translated/interpreted as guilt. Guilt for responsibility failed. Dasein was not responsible for being 'there,' yet has to take over responsibility for being 'there.' Another koan: How can Dasein be held responsible (*schuldig*) for something – its thrown being – for which it was not responsible? How can Dasein be held guilty (*schuldig*) for something – its thrownness – which it did not do? Thus angst reveals another aspect of Dasein's encounter with the Nothing, what Tillich calls the 'moral' (but in an originary sense) shock of nonbeing: Dasein's guilt-cum- responsibility as the null basis of its own null being: "Hence we define the formally existential idea of the 'Guilty!' as 'Being-the-basis for a Being which has been defined by a 'not'–that is to say, as *Being-the-basis of a nullity*" (*SZ* 283/*BT* 329, cf. *SZ* 305/*BT* 353; Heidegger's emphasis). Here too, as in its being-towards-death, Dasein is confronted with a fateful either/or: descent into the guilt of an inauthentic mode of being, into 'untruth', or resurrection into responsibility, into an authentic mode of being, into 'truth': guilt-*cum*-responsibility, death or resurrection.

Once again, Heidegger precedes an interpretation of *authentic* 'being-guilty' with a *formal*, existential-ontological analysis of guilt. Formally viewed, what is normally called guilt is grounded in an ontologically prior phenomenon of originary 'being-guilty.' This originary 'being-guilty' "lies in Dasein's Being as such, and ... does so in such a way that so far as any Dasein factically exists, it *is* also guilty" (*SZ* 281/*BT* 326-327, Heidegger's italics). Dasein's being-guilty is both a lack and a basis. On the one hand, inherent in the phenomenon of "Guilty!' is the conception of "guilt as 'having responsibility for'–that is, as Being-the -basis for..." On the other hand, guilt is "*Being-the-basis* for a lack of something...in such a manner that this very Being-the-basis determines itself as 'lacking in some way' in terms of that for which it is the basis" (*SZ* 282-283/*BT* 327-329).

As an entity, Dasein "has been brought into its 'there,' but *not* of its own accord ... Although it has not laid that basis *itself* it reposes in the weight of it, which is made manifest to it as a burden by Dasein's mood" – specifically, the mood of anxiety. Dasein, "which as such has to lay the basis for itself, can *never* get that basis in to its power; and yet, as existing, it must take over Being-a-basis.... 'Being-a-basis' means *never* to have power over one's ownmost Being from the ground up. This '*not*' belongs to the existential meaning of 'thrownness.' It itself, being a basis, *is* a nullity of itself. 'Nullity' [*Nichtigkeit*]...is rather a 'not' which is constitutive for this *Being* of Dasein–its thrownness.... This basis is never anything but the basis for an entity whose Being has to take over Being-a-basis" (*SZ* 284-285/*BT* 329-331).

Thus Dasein, "in its very essence, is permeated with nullity through and through ... Dasein's Being means...Being-the-basis of a nullity (and this Being-the-basis is itself null). This means that Dasein as such is guilty, if our formally existential definition of 'guilt' as 'being-the-basis of a nullity' is indeed correct" (*SZ* 285/*BT* 330-331). That is the issue that confronts Dasein in its thrown being, in its finite freedom; that is the specter that haunts its fateful either/or – Dasein, "in its uncanniness: primordial, thrown Being-in-the world as the 'not-at-home' - the bare 'that-it-is' in the 'nothing' of the world" (*SZ* 276-277/*BT* 321-322).

It is against the background of this formal-ontological characterization of Dasein's being guilty as such, of being the null basis of its own nonbeing, that Heidegger turns to the notion of re-solve or resoluteness, *Entschlossenheit*, to characterize Dasein's "self-projection upon [its] ownmost Being-guilty" (*SZ* 297/*BT* 343). The German noun comes from the verb *entschliessen*, literally to 'unlock' something, from the negative prefix '*ent-*' (English: 'un') and the verb *schliessen*, to shut, close, bolt sth. – in other words, positively viewed, to open sth. up, to disclose, to make manifest, to let sth. be – in the present case, to 'project' or affirm a possibility of Dasein's being. Resoluteness is an "authentic disclosedness" that modifies Dasein's Being in such a way its lets Dasein "be called forth to [its] ownmost *Being*-guilty. When Dasein is resolute, it takes over authentically in its existence the fact that it *is* the null basis of its own nullity" (*SZ* 297-8, 305-306/*BT* 343-345, 353-354)

Thus, as resoluteness, the anxiety of guilt *frees* Dasein *for* "the pure 'that-it-is' of one's ownmost individualized thrownness ....Anxiety merely brings one into the mood for a *possible* resolution." (*SZ* 343-344/BT 394-395), a decision one still has concretely to make. Dasein "harbors in itself both death and guilt equiprimordially.... Only if death, guilt, conscience, freedom, and finitude reside equiprimordially in the Being of an entity... can that entity exist ... in the very depths of its existence... Along with the sober anxiety which brings us face to face with our individualized potentiality-for-Being, there goes an unshakable joy in this possibility"

(*SZ* 306, 310, 385/*BT* 354, 357-358, 437). The choice, the responsibility, is ours.

And yet, more remains to be said, perhaps that which is most essential (*wesentlich*). As we now have seen, in *Sein und Zeit*, the character of the '*not*,' 'the Nothing,' is experienced, has disclosed itself, in three ways: as the *meaninglessness* of Dasein's being-in-the-world as such; the *finitude* of Dasein's being as 'being-toward-death,' and the *contingency* of 'thrownness' which Dasein is guilty-*cum* responsible (*schuldig*) to 'take over' in its 'finite freedom.' As Polt observes, Heidegger's 'nothings' have been interpreted in many different ways: as insubstantiality, negation, otherness, and meaninglessness (Polt, 60). The manifold nature of Dasein's experiences of these 'nothings' seems analogous to the manifold meanings of being in Aristotle and Brentano that launched Heidegger on his philosophical quest. Heidegger wondered whether there was a single, unified truth of Being. The same question arises with Dasein's multiple experiences of the nothing. Are these, finally, one or are they irreducibly many – or are they/is it neither? We have arrived face to face with "the ontological problem of clarifying existentially the *character* of this 'not' *as a 'not'* ... *[T]he ontological meaning of the notness [Nichtheit]* of this existential nullity is still obscure.... Has anyone ever made a problem of the ontological source of notness?" (*SZ* 283/*BT* 328-329, *SZ* 285-6/*BT* 330-332).

It would seem that we have not gotten to the bottom, or source, of Dasein's many-sided encounter with 'the Nothing.' More digging needs to be done. What bearing do these experiences of the 'not' that mark the entity called 'Dasein' have on the question of the meaning of the Nothing and the meaning of Being? Perhaps a consideration of how the phenomenon of the Nothing is expressed/expresses itself in the Being of *beings* will give us the clue we seek.

Being and Beings: The Ontological Difference

As observed, there are at least two ways in which for Heidegger the Nothing is revealed or reveals itself: First, existentially, in Dasein the 'not' is disclosed in/as the experience of anxiety vis-a-vis the meaninglessness of the world, in/as finitude vis-a-vis death, and in/as the contingency of thrown being disclosed in guilt. Second, ontologically, Nothing is disclosed in/as Being's 'hiding' itself in order that beings may be 'revealed' as beings, both *that* they are and and as *what* they are.

As we now turn to this second, ontological setting, the problem we will confront is that Heidegger, in his effort to eschew the concepts of metaphysics in his thinking about/of/on beings, Being, and the Nothing, relies heavily on the use of metaphors and paradox. The question is whether these can be translated, not into the language of metaphysics, but in the interests of intelligibility into a language that, while not metaphorical, is faithful to the content and intent of his metaphors – this despite the truth of Arendt's observation that the language of philosophy originated and lives from metaphor.

With this proviso, what are some of the issues we will need to consider in trying to understand Heidegger's 'answer' to the Why question? Perhaps the first and most basic is what Heidegger's formulation of the Why question tells us. For Leibniz the question ran: *"Pourquoi y a-t-il quelque chose plutôt que rien?"* ("Why is there something rather than nothing?"). In his first formulation of the question in *What Is Metaphysics?* (1929), Heidegger asks, *"Warum ist ueberhaupt Seiendes und nicht vielmehr Nichts?"* ("Why are there beings at all and not rather nothing?") (Heidegger, 1998g, 42/96). Unlike Leibniz, however, who was looking for an answer in the form of a First Cause, a metaphysical ground of beings in a Highest Being, what Heidegger wants to know in asking the question is how it is that beings come to be *manifest as* beings out of Non-being, how they come to *differ* from the Nothing. In his second iteration of the Why question in the later "Introduction" to *What Is Metaphysics?* (1949), he appears to focus even more on Being and the Nothing than on beings, introducing at the same time a new theme. He asks "How does it come about that everywhere beings have the primacy and lay claim to every 'is,' while that which is not a being, which is thought of as Non-being in the sense of Being itself, remains forgotten?" (Heidegger, 1998g, 42/ 96; cf. Richardson, 14, 169-170, 203-204).

Thus, for Heidegger the Why question serves a different and more complex goal, one quite unlike the one envisioned by Leibniz or subsequent metaphysical thinkers. Its purpose is two-fold. On the one hand, it is for Heidegger a point of access into what he terms 'the ontological difference,' the difference between Being (*Sein*)/ Non-being (*das Nichts*) and being/s (*Seiende/s*), a phenomenon he claims has not been and never can be addressed by metaphysics. At the same time the Why question serves to bring to light what he calls 'the forgetting' of Being and thus to explain why metaphysics falls short in its 'answers' to the Why question and how it is that, *zunaechst und zumeist* ('at first and for the most part'), Dasein 'falls' into an 'inauthentic' relation to beings. For Heidegger, therefore, the Why question assumes that we already have an implicit understanding of Being, being/s and the Nothing: "It is this comprehension of Being that first renders possible the 'why?'" (Heidegger, 1998d, 48/130). The Why questions functions not as a request for a metaphysical answer but to make explicit that pre-ontological understanding. In this sense his thinking of Being is true to its phenomenological origins: it is descriptive-interpretive, not causal-explanatory.

Before we examine in more detail his understanding of Being, beings and the Nothing, however, we must take account of what could prove to be a problematic aspect in his reformulation of the Why question, a possible ambiguity. It will be noted that Leibniz's formulation is in accord with the wording used throughout this inquiry. The operative phrase was *'quelque chose,' 'something,'* i.e., something unspecified, indeterminate, not necessarily a being or beings, whereas in Heidegger it reads *'Seiendes,' beings,'*which carries a suggestion of determinate realities. If so, what does *'Seiendes'* refer to – individual beings in general, beings-as-a-whole, the 'world,' even Being itself – rather than nothing? Or does it here simply refer, like the phrase in Leibniz, to something, anything, in general? For Heidegger is the Why question, 'Why does *something* exist?' or is it, 'Why do *beings*, or *the world*, exist?'? In the latter case, does it then still come trailing clouds of cosmological-metaphysical glory? In *WM*, his early post-*SZ* work, is he still asking the Why question 'metaphysically'? Has he not yet arrived at a fully existential-ontological interpretation of beings, Being and Nothing, or the 'ontological difference'? Does this apparent ambiguity matter?

Whatever the answer to these questions turn out to be, already in his analysis of the three types of 'not' in SZ there is a distinction that might help clarify the matter. The first part of SZ provides a *formal-structural* analysis of Dasein, a "preparatory fundamental analysis," in which the 'not' disclosed in anxiety is the 'nothing' of the *world* as such, the meaninglessness of *beings-as-a-whole*. Though it is an existential-ontological analysis, there is a 'cosmological-metaphysical' aspect to it in its reference to the 'world' of 'beings.' But in the second part of SZ, when Heidegger turns to a "primordial existential interpretation" of Dasein, anxiety is more clearly seen as disclosive in an *existential-concrete* sense in the 'not' of Dasein's finitude, its *'being-towards-death'* and in the 'not' of Dasein's contingency vis-a-vis its *'being-guilty.'* When Heidegger explicitly raises the Why question in *WM*, it is in the *formal-structural* manner of the first part of *SZ*, the difference being that, instead of focusing on the 'not' of beings in the context of Dasein's *being-in-the-world,* he is turning his attention to the 'not' of beings in the context of the *Being of beings.'* In turning to *WM*, we will therefore consider his views on the latter topic in three stages: what Heidegger means by *beings* and *beings-as-a-whole* (*das Seiende im Ganzen*); what he means by his thought-provoking neologism, the *'ontological difference,'* which links *beings* and *Being*; and finally, a first approach to what he means by the complex and many-aspectival phenomenon of *Being* itself.

Beings (das Seiendes)

What does Heidegger mean by 'beings'? What are beings? In the Why question he is asking what beings are *as such*. It is already clear from *SZ* that he does not mean 'beings' as *Vorhandensein*, beings 'determined' *as* 'present at-hand,' 'objects-merely-there,' nor does he mean 'beings' as *Zuhandensein*, beings 'determined' *as* entities 'ready-to- hand,' 'things-of-use.' Neither does he see them as beings that simply 'be' in some indeterminate sense, embodiments of the general, universal, empty sense that characterizes the traditional metaphysical definition of 'being.' Instead, in *SZ*, he see them in the context of Dasein's being-in-the-world, that is, as following from Dasein's pre-understanding of Being: "with [Dasein's] existence...comes to pass an irruption in the totality of beings of such a nature that now for the first time beings...in themselves, that is, as beings, become manifest" (Heidegger, 1962, 206/ 235). As Richardson comments: "What is the most fundamental characteristic of beings? The fact that they are revealed (*offenbar*) to There-being as being what they are" (Richardson, 42-43). Beings are correlated with Dasein's being-in-the-world, not as *vorhand* nor as *zuhand*, but 'as they are,' 'as such.' But what is the meaning of this *'as they are,'* *'as such'*?

When Heidegger goes on to ask in *WM*, "Why are there beings at all and not rather nothing?" he now interprets the Why question as Dasein's response to the primordial experience of beings against the background of their possible non-being. He is asking, what does it mean to say that beings are *as the 'other'* of the Nothing? (cf. Heidegger, 1998c, 15-16/144-145; cf. Richardson, 238). But this confronts us with a new question: What is the relation between beings as they are, as such, and beings as the other of nonbeing? Answer: Beings *are* 'as such' *as* the 'other' of the Nothing. But that does not answer the question. What *is* this sameness or identity between the 'as such' and the 'other' of the Nothing? What is the nature of beings such that they *'are' as* the other of the Nothing? Just what *are* beings?

Nor does the mystery end there. The question, 'what are beings?' presents us with another dilemma, two in fact. To answer the question we must clarify another distinction that has been left unclear. When Heidegger speaks of the fact that beings are revealed (*offenbar*) to Dasein, what is it that is revealed? It is not the 'that' of their being that is disclosed, rather it is beings in their 'what.' The question, 'what are beings?,' turns out be two questions: what does it mean *that* beings exist? and, *how* do they exist, as *what* do they exist? Here we encounter the first paradox: as Heidegger puts it, the problem is that for beings to be revealed in their 'what,' their 'that'– their being as such – must be concealed. It is a revealing is simultaneously a concealing. This is difficult enough to understand. But the alleged revealing-*cum*-concealing has an additional consequence. It is not that we do not see *that* beings exist. The existential paradox is that we *do* see, but because we take this being of beings for granted, we *do not* see it. The dilemma is that while the 'that' (being) of beings 'must' disappear so the 'what' of beings can appear, the almost inevitable result is that beings are then *not* seen as they *genuinely* are 'as such.' What happens is not just a 'concealing' of the 'that' of their being, but a 'forgetting' of their being *as beings* with the consequent 'fall' of Dasein into an '*inauthentic*' relation to beings now seen as 'reduced' to the everydayness of their 'what' as *vorhand* and/or *zuhand*. Forgotten is an awareness of the mystery 'that' they exist rather than nothing at all– the *mystery* of their being. Seeing them *zunaechst und zumeist* as *things vorhand* and *zuhand*, we do not see their *being* as mysterious. We do not see *them* as mysterious. As the 'other' of the Nothing, the mystery of beings *is* the mystery of Being itself.

Can the proposition be reversed? Can we say the mystery of Being *is* (nothing other than) the mystery of beings? Yes and no. Perhaps turning from 'beings' to the related notion of 'beings-as-a-whole' (*das Seiende im Ganzen)*, can shed light on the matter. Some passages in *WW* could be taken as suggesting the answer was Yes, Being could be conceived as simply beings-as-a-whole. But the essay ends with the clear indication that, No, Being is something other than beings-as-a-whole, in which case the proposition cannot be reversed (Heidegger, 1998c, 19-20, 23, 25/147-148, 150, 152; cf. Richardson, 245). It would seem the 'other' of the Nothing is operative here too: beings 'as-a-whole,' like beings 'as such,' are 'other' than Being. Though we are not yet in a position yet to say anything further about the relation of the 'other' of the Nothing to the 'other' of Being, we can take a brief look a Heidegger's alternative phrase for 'beings as such,' namely, 'beings-as-a-whole'.

Beings-as-a-Whole (das Seiende im Ganzen)

What does Heidegger mean by '*beings-as-a-whole*' (*das Seiende im Ganzen*)? One thing he does not mean. They are not 'the whole of beings' *(das Ganze des Seienden)*. As noted, for Heidegger this is an impossible notion. The two notions are easily confused by commentators, for example by Richardson when the mistaken phrase, 'ensemble ['whole']-of-beings,' is frequently used interchangeably with the correct expression, 'beings-in-ensemble' ['as-a-whole'; Grk: *katholon*]. For Heidegger the notion always refers to beings as experienced *within* the context of Dasein's being-in-the-world. There is no cosmological-metaphysical place 'outside' being 'in' the world from which the alleged totality (*Ganze*) of beings could ever be known let alone meaningfully posited.

This sheds additional light on another potential difficulty noted above. Is Heidegger's formulation of the Why question still partly dependent on a cosmological-metaphysical understanding of beings and the world? It would seem not insofar as Dasein's primordial access to the existence of beings-as-a-whole is via the phenomenon of anxiety. The being of the world is understood existentially-ontologically, not on the basis of an epistemic standpoint external to Dasein's being-in-the world. It is in the experience of the Nothing in dread that beings are first disclosed 'as-a-whole.' "[A]s the repelling gesture toward beings as a whole in their slipping away, it manifests these beings in their full but heretofore concealed strangeness as what is radically other– with respect to the nothing. In the clear night of the nothing of anxiety the original openness of beings as such arises: that they are beings – and not nothing" (Heidegger, 1998g, 34/90).

Here is the origin of the Why question, the experience of the mystery, the strange but wondrous fact that beings are: "The glimpse into the mystery...is a questioning – in the sense of that unique question of what beings as such are as a whole" (Heidegger, 1998e, 23/151). Heidegger's abiding fascination with the outbreak of philosophy with the Greeks reprises the originary wonder of a Plato in which the strange and mysterious question-worthiness (*frag-wurdigkeit*) of beings as beings (*on he on*) was first revealed. But beginning with Aristotle, beings were reduced to objects of 'science,' of 'knowledge,' the strangeness and mystery of their being "buried in obscurity," replaced by the explanations of metaphysics (cf. Richardson, 255-256).

With Heidegger, however, the mystery, the *frag-wurdigkeit* of beings to which the Why question points reappears. What are *beings*? What are *beings-as-a-whole*? What is *Dasein's* being? If Being is a mystery, then beings – the being of beings-as-a-whole, the being of the world, Dasein's own being – must also be, ultimately, mysterious. If so, beings are to be understood, and responded to, not as *vorhand* or *zuhand*, but *as they are*, as wondrously strange, as strangely wonderful – in other words, as mysterious as *Being* itself.

This double-mystery of Being and beings leaves some questions unanswered. What makes beings a mystery and not just something 'present-at-hand' or 'ready-to-hand' is their relation to the mystery of Being. But what exactly is the nature of that relation, and, for that matter, what is the nature of Being itself? To answer these questions we must consider first Heidegger's neologism, the 'ontological difference,' which describes the relation of Being and beings, and then his understanding of the nature, the 'essenc-ing,' of Being itself.

The Ontological Difference

What does Heidegger mean by his novel coinage, 'the ontological difference'? Is it just the difference between the fact that things exist and what or how they exist? Is that what he means by the difference between Being and beings? What gives rise to the ontological difference? Is it simply a product of grammar? of metaphysics? of 'the Nothing'? or of some 'third'? Richardson opines that it originates in the ambiguity (the "peculiar duality") of the original Greek word for being, *on* as duplicated in the phrase, *on he on*, 'being as being': "What is this ambivalence after all? Nothing else but the correlation in a single word of 'being' as noun and 'being' as verbal adjective, hence of that which is (manifest) and the process by which it is (manifest), of beings and Being"– in a word, the 'ontological difference.'" Yet it is a *grammatical* equivocality that carries *ontological* freight. It is grounded in the nature of Being itself: "Is it not the withdrawal of Being in its bestowal [*of beings*] that constitutes the ontological difference? ... it is this which constitutes the intrinsic ambivalence of *on*." Further, it has implications for the *thinking* of Being: "It is the ambivalence of *on* which is absolutely primary. By the ontological difference, we understand here the difference between Being and beings as the reverse side of the ambivalence of *on*, sc. the necessary coupling of Being and beings. It is this duality which is absolutely primary in the process of thought." (Richardson 12, 442, 606, 608). Thus it would appear that the ontological difference originates from several sources: the ambiguity of the word 'being,' its embeddedness in a doubleness in Being itself, and the consequent primacy of this duality for the thinking of Being.

But to list these themes is only the beginning of trying to understand what Heidegger means by the term. As he himself wonders: "What remains more of mystery, that beings are or that Being is? Or even by way of this reflection have we not yet succeeded in drawing near to the mystery that has occurred with the Being of beings?" (Heidegger, 1998b, 23/290). For Heidegger, thinking through this 'mutual dependence' of Being and beings upon each other is what it means to think the ontological difference as such (cf. Richardson, 563). Where does such thinking lead?

The first mention of the ontological difference occurs soon after *SZ* (1927) in *WG* (1929). Central to the oblivion that overtook Being and that characterizes the nature of metaphysics in the subsequent history of philosophy in the West is that the 'absolutely primary' difference of Being from beings – the ontological difference – has itself been forgotten, the duality that stems from the ambiguity of *on*. The problem is that the duality (*Zweideutigkeit*) "names both [*Being and being/s*] at the same time and neither as such" (*Holzwege*, 162). It this double sense of *on* from which the ontological difference arises. So when Heidegger reformulates the Why question – "How does it come about that beings take precedence everywhere and lay claim to every 'is,' while that which is not a being – namely, the Nothing thus understood as Being itself – remains forgotten?" – he is not only asking about Being and the forgetting of Being, he is asking about the prior forgetting of the ontological difference itself– a difference which, as we shall see, contains an even further doubleness of its own (Heidegger, 1998b, 23/290, (cf. Richardson, 12-14).

The ontological difference: the difference of Being and beings. Perhaps the simplest approach to the ontological difference is to say that it refers to the difference, the 'not,' between Being and beings, a difference which is at the same time an intimate togetherness – so 'intimate' that, as the ambiguity of the *on* suggests, neither'is' nor *can* be without the other. Thus in WG Heidegger insists that Being is always the Being *of* beings, never Being as such *apart* from beings: "The ontological difference is the 'not' between beings and Being.... Ontic and ontological truth each concern, in different ways, *beings in* their Being and the *Being of* beings. They belong essentially together on the ground of their relationship to the *difference between Being and beings* (ontological difference)" (Heidegger, 1998d, 5, 15/ 97, 105; cf. Richardson, 174). The ontological difference thus lies at the origin of the oft-repeated and at first seemingly innocuous phrase, the 'Being of beings.' Even in his later work, *Was Heisst Denken?* (1954), Heidegger continues to emphasize the central significance of this Janus-faced phenomenon. For in the phrase, the 'Being of beings,' the 'of' indicates a doubled 'difference': it points in *two* directions at the same time: "'If we say 'Being, this means : the 'Being of beings.' If we say 'beings,' this means: beings with regard to their Being. We speak always out of the duality (*Zwiefalt*)" – i.e., the duality of the ontological difference (Heidegger, 1968, 174/227; cf Richardson, 605). It is because of the ambiguous nature of the *on*, the *Zwiefalt* of the ontological difference, that Heidegger's 'thinking of Being' is compelled to be a thinking of the togetherness-in-difference, the *non-dual duality*, of Being and beings. Being is only and ever the *Being of* beings, whereas *beings* are only and ever *what* they are as the beings *of Being.*

The ontological difference: ontological and ontic truth. Mentioned was made above of the distinction between ontological and ontic truth. By 'ontic' truth Heidegger means the various truths about beings as entities-in-the-world, whether *vorhand, zuhand* or other. But how does he understand 'ontological' truth and how is it related to ontic truth? Though Heidegger later had reservations about the distinction as expressed in the transcendental-metaphysical terminology of 'makes possible,' it would appear to retain its value for explicating the ontological difference of Being and beings. His answer is not easy, though in WG it is stated in what appear to be intelligible enough (if metaphorical) terms: "*Unveiledness (Enthulltheit) of Being first makes possible* (ermoglicht) *the manifestness of beings*. This unveiledness, as the truth of Being, is called *ontological truth*" (Heidegger, 1998d, 13/103-104). Ontological truth is the truth of Being, truth in the sense of *a-letheia*, un-hiddenness, un-veiledness. It is what 'makes possible' or (another word from metaphysics) 'grounds' ontic truth, the un-veiledness or 'manifestness' of beings. It is what Heidegger refers to in his lapidary formulation: 'Being lets beings be.' Yet, as observed above, this 'letting be' in fact runs two ways, for without beings, Being itself 'is' not, can not 'be.' One could say, therefore, that it is also beings that 'make possible' Being, that 'let Being be.' Without Being, no beings; but without beings, no Being. But that is to say: without the ontological difference, neither Being nor beings.

The ontological difference: a double 'not'? In addition to the double reference of the ontological difference – Being and beings, there is what seems to be a doubleness in 'not' that constitutes the ontological difference itself. On the one hand, in *WG* the 'not' is characterized as the 'not' of the *ontological difference* that separates (while linking) Being and beings. Being is 'not' *a* being but the Being *of* beings. On the other hand, in *WM* the 'not' is *the Nothing* as the 'not' of *beings*: "The Nothing is the Nothing of beings and thus Being as experienced from [the perspective of] beings" (Heidegger, 1998d, 5/97) What is the relation of these two 'not's? One possibility: the 'not' of the ontological difference and the 'not' of the Nothing are the same but not identical, 'co-relative' in the linked togetherness of the Being- of-beings, a duality that is non-dual. What is common to both, Richardson notes, is the negativity 'inscribed' in Being: "Being as permeated with negativity" (Richardson, 564). He asks: "How comprehend this mysterious reticence which is mutual to both Non-being [*the Nothing*] and beings, each revealed by reason of what it is *not*? This 'not' which separates beings and Non-being [*the Nothing*] is difference, sc. the ontological difference. " This is where "the full weight of the Why question falls." Thus when Heidegger asks why are there beings rather than nothing, as over against Leibniz's understanding of the question, he is asking "what it means for beings to emerge out of Non-being [*the Nothing*], hence to be differentiated from Non-being [*the*

Nothing]" (Richardson, 203-204). In asking the doubly-negated Why question he is asking not about a First Cause or Highest Being but about the ontological difference.

The ontological difference: 'non-dual duality.' There have been two mentions above of the non-Heideggerian yet 'Heideggerian' notion of *non-dual duality* – a twoness that is not a simple twoness, but also not a simply oneness, a 'sameness' that is not an 'identity.' It refers, as noted above, to an ambiguity or ambi-valence in the concept of *on*, one that is 'absolutely primary' in the thinking of Being. The ontological difference of Being and beings holds a 'two' (duality) together (non-dual) in a 'co-relation.' In fact, as Heidegger goes on to say in *Unterwegs zur Sprache* (1959), the 'difference' of Being and beings is not a 'difference' or 'relation' in the usual metaphysical sense at all, that is, a relation between two beings. Being is not *a* being. Then how are we to understand the 'of' that links them? As, he says, a '*dif-ference*': the *cum* contained etymologically in 'co-relation' – 'Being-*cum*-beings' – is a 'non-duality' to which each, on the one hand, belongs but out of which, on the other, each emerges in an interlinked 'duality.' Heidegger hyphenates the normal German word for 'difference,' *Unterschied*, into its two verbal elements to make his point. The ontolological difference, the 'Being *of/cum* beings,' is the *Scheid* (separation) between (*Unter*) Being and beings "that refers both to each other by the very fact that it divides them into two" (Heidegger, 1975g, 24-25/202-203). The ontological dif-ference is thus the mutual belongingness-in-separation, the non-dual duality, of Being *cum* beings, out of which emerge Being *as* Being, beings *as* beings – the Being *of* beings (Heidegger, *op. cit.*, 29-30/206-208; cf. Richardson, 579-580).

Being (Sein)

So far we have asked how Heidegger understands beings and the ontological difference. But we cannot complete the discussion without finally asking, as Heidegger might, 'how is it with Being itself?' What is meant by *Being* in the phrase the Being *of* beings? What is Heidegger's understanding of that term, that phenomenon, which has been his constant companion ever since he first read Brentano on the many meanings of 'being'? Being, that spectral presence haunting metaphysics like an uninvited visitor who refuses every invitation to sit down and imbibe the certainties at the feast of the philosophers – yet refuses to go away. There are problems within problems when it comes to trying to unpack the meaning of Heidegger's interpretation of this many-meaning term. Two things are certain: Being is not the Highest Being among beings nor is it the First Cause of beings, *pace* metaphysics from Aristotle on; Being is not *a* being at all. But having said that, it is perhaps best to leave everything else unsaid – except that Heidegger's entire oeuvre is nothing but a thinking of and talking about Being – and thus we are condemned to the enterprise as well.

That is not all. As Heidegger gradually moved away from the language of metaphysics from within which, in his early works, by a 'violent' critique he attempted to wrest free a new kind of language for thinking and talking about Being, in his later works he turned more and more, almost perforce, compelled he would say by Being itself, to thinking of Being in what many dismissed as a 'poetic' manner of speaking. He resorted increasingly for philosophical inspiration to the pre-Socratic Greeks and German Romantic poets as well as images drawn from the landscape of Southwest Germany that surrounded him in his Black Forest refuge. The result, perhaps inevitably, was what looked like an effort to 'go back' to philosophy's mythopoetic origins – to thinking caught in the very moment of its emergence from the activity of mythopoesis – a 'story-making' halfway between *Dichten* (poetizing) and *Denken* (thinking) – before it had settled down in the 'scientific' language of metaphysics. The question is whether such language can be 'translated' into non-metaphorical terms without losing the truth of what it is trying to say – perhaps an impossible task. The problem is that the language, especially of the later Heidegger, is no longer the familiar third person language of 'objective,' scientific, explanatory thinking, the language of metaphysical *reasons* and *causes*. It is instead the first person language of 'subjective,' mythopoetic thinking, the language of existential -ontological *response*. Why? Because for Heidegger the thinking of Being in the last analysis is the language of *mystery* about which metaphysics one cannot 'speak.'

To illustrate this point, Witherall hazarded a guess as to what one such limping attempt at a literal translation would look like – with its all-too-predictable and painful results. If the Heidegger's thinking of Being were 'watered down' to something literal, he says, it would go something like this: "The reason there is something instead of nothing is that there is a mysterious non-thing which we cannot describe, except by saying that it is Being itself, and this has gratuitously bestowed existence upon the less mysterious things which we encounter in the world" (Witherall, 154). As an attempted paraphrase of Heidegger's thought even this rendition is a doubly limping one. Heidegger does not talk of the 'reason' why there is something except to reject the use of the term in this context; he does not ask about the existence of 'something' but rather about the existence of 'beings'; he does not say that Being is a 'non-thing' but that it is 'not a being'; and finally, he would not say of beings that their being was 'less mysterious' but instead that it was as 'strange' or 'mysterious' as that of Being itself.

Lest one be tempted by the foregoing to conclude that Being is the most questionable (*fragwurdig*) item in the philosophical armamentarium and thus, in the judgement of the metaphysical tradition, to be simply ignored as of no use or importance to the scientific task of thinking about beings, Heidegger resorts once again to the linguistic tactic of hyphenating a word whose positive potential might otherwise be passed over. Being is rather, he says, the most *frag-wurdig*, the most *question-worthy*, of all. And yet it is also precisely that which *cannot* be questioned, *cannot* be made to undergo an interrogation. Being is that which is most worthy of question, most worthy of thought, and yet that for which there is *no* answer– unless by 'answer' is meant an existential 'response.' But if so, how does Heidegger propose to make sense of Being? Can thinking of Being be understood in non-metaphorical words that nonetheless are appropriate to the mystery? Is 'Being' (*Sein*) simply a capitalized shorthand – reflecting the genius, or limitation, of German grammar – for the *That* of beings, nothing more than a way of pointing linguistically to the mystery *that* beings exist, a way of highlighting something other than the *What*, the *nature or how* of beings? Or does it refer, ambiguously, to both – or to neither, to some 'third' that precedes and gives rise to that distinction? (cf. Richardson, 245)

To get purchase on these questions we need to consider the many facets of Heidegger's thinking about Being: the grammatical distinctions it involves, the implications of the preposition 'of,' Being's relation to Dasein, thinking, the Why question, and 'the Nothing,' and finally, the positive predicates Heidegger assigns to it.

Grammar of Being. We have already mentioned this aspect in discussing the ontological difference, but it bears repeating. What is the significance of the grammar of 'Being'? As a noun used in a substantive, 'entitive' sense, it seems to refer to the *being* of beings – that *there are* beings, the *that* as distinguished from the *what* or *how* of their being. It seems to be a restatement of the traditional medieval distinction between the *existence* and *essence* of beings – a distinction which has fallen out of favor since Kant, the aspect of *existence* being reduced to the mental act of *positing* an '*x*' the features of which are confined to descriptions of the nature of beings. As a verb, the 'be-ing' or 'exist-ing' of beings, it seems acquire a temporal, processive sense. The question in that case is whether the entitive that/what distinction can be accommodated the verbal sense. What Richardson labeled the 'peculiar duality' of the term, contained already in the Greek *on*, is "nothing else but the correlation in a single word of 'being' as noun and 'being' as verbal adjective." The ambiguity of the ordinary term is then taken over and elevated into a metaphysical duality, the fundamental difference-in-togetherness of beings as that which is and Being as the mysterious cause, origin or process 'by which' beings appear (cf. Richardson, 12). Thus the notions of the 'Being of beings' and 'thinking of Being' are systematically ambiguous, harboring in both cases noun-like and verb-like aspects, and capable of being interpreted as both subjective and objective genitives: in the first case, the active source of beings/the generic feature of beings, in the second, thinking about Being or (metaphorically) Being's 'thinking.' One is tempted to say, in view of this thought-resistant conundrum, better just to leave the term buried in its runic obscurity and move on to matters more easily decipherable.

The Preposition 'of.' The insertion of the possessive/genitive 'of' into the ambiguous mix in the 'Being *of* beings' only compounds the confusion. The question is: what is meant by Being *as* the Being *of* beings? What kind of 'relation' is this supposed to be? Many of the relational expressions Heidegger uses have a causal or explanatory aura to them: Being is that '*by which*' beings are what (and how) they 'are'; Being is that '*by reason of which*' beings become manifest; ontological truth '*renders possible*,' therefore '*grounds*' ontic truth; Being conceals itself behind the beings '*to which it gives*' presence; Being has primacy over thought, simply because it *gives rise* to it (Heidegger, 1962, 214/245-246; *SZ*, 212/*BT*, 255; 1998d, 13-15/103-106; cf. 1998e, 24-25/150-151; 1998a, 58/242). And yet, as his critique of a metaphysical interpretation of these phrases makes clear, he does not intend them to be understood in a causal or explanatory sense. Being is not the *cause of* the existence of beings, nor the *explantion of* the fact that there are beings. What, then, does it mean, then, to say that Being 'lets' things be? In what sense is this 'letting' to be understood. Is it a metaphor, not meant metaphysically or ontologically? In fact, since Being is said to look 'both ways' in the phrase, it would seem that the 'relation' of Beings to beings is a *double* 'letting-be.' If *Da*-of-*Sein* or the thinking *of* Being are added to the relational stew, the directionality of the 'of' is only further problematized. Below we will see that, seemingly not thinking to have already made things difficult enough, Heidegger will add that it is in fact not Being but 'negativity,' the Nothing, which 'lets' beings be, 'by which' beings are.

Being and Dasein (There-being). The reference to Dasein as the Da-of-*Sein* is yet another instance of the duty the preposition 'of' is required to perform in Heidegger's explication of Being. His use of the hyphenated expression in his later work indicates he did not leave the relation of Dasein to Being in *SZ* entirely behind, if at all. As his comments in his prefatory letter to Richardson on the alleged distinction between the so-called 'Heidegger I' of *SZ* and the later so-called 'Heidegger II' make clear, the difference is more apparent than real (cf. Richardson, viii-xxiii). Dasein, as the Da-*of*-Sein, the 'There' *of* Being, is said still to be 'needed' by Being in order for Being to 'let beings be' and for Being itself to 'be,' and that means for the 'ontological difference' to happen or occur (*ereignen*). In that sense, as his characterization of Dasein as 'Being-in-the-world' also indicates, Heidegger may be appropriately seen in the line of post-Kantian critical idealism and post-Husserlian existential phenomenology. For there to be Being as the Being-of-beings, there must also, first, be Dasein as the Da-of-Sein.

The continuity, despite difference in terminology and emphasis (from Dasein to Being), between the early and later Heidegger can be seen when passages from *KM* and SZ are set side-by-side with ones from *EM* and *WM*. Thus, in *KM* Heidegger says: "The Being of beings is, however, comprehensible only under the condition...that There-being, by reason of its very nature, thrusts itself into Non-being" (Heidegger, 1962, 214/ 245-246; cf. Richardson, 38). We have already seen this 'thrust into Non-being' in the phenomena of the slipping away of the world and the experiences of death and guilt in *SZ*. In this dialectical 'of' it would appear that Dasein is only responding to the initiative of Being. Heidegger says that it is 'because' of Being that beings are revealed to There-being (*das, was Seiendes al Seiendes bestimmt*) (*SZ* 6/*BT* 25). However, it would also seem the relational directionality is reversible. Though Being is that 'by reason of which' beings are 'let be,' this is only possible because of the being of Dasein as the 'There' of Being. How so? Because, Heidegger says, "Only so long as Dasein *is*, i.e., the ontic potentiality of the comprehending of Being, 'is there' Being" (*SZ* 212/*BT* 255; cf. Richardson, 43).

When we turn to later works, like *WM* and *EM*, the same motif is sounded. The emphasis on Dasein's responsibility for the 'being' of the 'Being of beings' is, if anything, even more pronounced. Yes, the Being which 'discloses' itself to/in Dasein is not simply Dasein's being but that of beings as such. Nevertheless it is the task of Dasein as the Da of Sein to ensure that this disclosure happens *(ereignet)*. "[Dasein] assumes and brings to its achievement [his] stewardship over the dominating might of the Over-powering [*Sein*]." Richardson comments: Dasein's "task consists in opening-up a domain of non-concealment for beings by forcing being into disclosure, thus permitting it to be itself" (Heidegger, 2000, 22, 110, 132, cf. 135, 145/31, 153, 184; cf. 188-189, 203-204; Richardson, 281, 283). There is a kind of 'violence' required on the side of Dasein in this relationship if the event of the ontological difference is to occur, if the disclosure of beings as beings and of Being as Being is to happen. Though Being can appear to have the power and the initiative in disclosing itself to Dasein, in fact its 'dominating might' and 'self-disclosure' are only effectual if Dasein heeds the 'appeal' of Being. Otherwise, absent the cooperation of Dasein, Being remains obscured by virtue of an inner poverty or powerlessness. Being remains a lack, an emptiness, indistinguishable from the Nothing. Driven by an inner exigency, a *necessity*, Being *needs* Dasein to be the Da-of-Sein in order that Being can itself be and let beings be. "Being directs its appeal to [Dasein] for the sake of the truth of Being itself" (Heidegger, 1998g, 49-50/236-238; cf. Richardson, 477).

Thinking and/of Being. We turn to the other directional relation signified by the 'of.' That pesky preposition links Being with yet another phenomenon, this time in the hyphenated reality of the 'thinking-*of*-Being.' What is the nature of this 'relation'? What is the nature of the 'thinking' side of the 'of'? And how does the 'negativity' of Being fit into the picture? As in the case of Dasein as the Da-of-Sein, here too Being is said to have the agency: Being has primacy over thought, simply because it gives rise to it (Heidegger, 1998a, 58/242; cf. Richardson, 542). We have already had cause to note the 'casual' nature of that phrase, 'gives rise to.' So what is Heidegger trying to say? Richardson surmises that "the source of thinking must be Being itself, and...that phrase 'of Being' ('the thinking of Being') is perhaps a 'subjective' as well as an 'objective' genitive" (Richardson, 249). But again, that term, 'source,' has an uncomfortably causal ring.

Perhaps, therefore, it would be better to stress, as with Dasein, the contribution of the other partner in the phrase 'thinking of Being,' namely, thinking. And what form does this thinking take? The form of interrogation; it is to "think by question." To think the Being of beings is to think, i.e, to ask about, beings, beings-as-a-whole, in a questioning way, as essentially '*frag-wurdig*,'worthy-of-questioning: "This interrogation thinks...the question about the *Being* of beings." It is to ask "the only question worth posing, the Being-question itself." But this means to think beings vis-v-vis the *negativity* of their Being, the Nothing – "Why are there beings rather than nothing?" In other words, it is to let beings be by a thinking that is open to the mystery of their being – and the mystery of Being itself (Heidegger, 1998e, 15-16, 23-25/144-145, 150-151; cf. Richardson, 246). Such thinking "is at once both gentle and rigorous. It gentleness consists in a tranquil release, in docility (*die Gelassenheit*) toward the dominating mystery; its rigor consists in the re-solve [*re-solve understood as letting be*] that does not destroy the mystery but does force it into the Open of its own truth, sc. lets it come-to-presence *as mystery*" (Richardson 253; cf. Heidegger, 1998e, 26/152 : '*milden Strenge, strengen Milde*'/'gentle sterness, stern gentleness'). And so, with the 'thinking of Being,' we find ourselves returned to the mystery of the relation of Being and the Nothing presupposed in the Why question itself.

Relation of Being to the Why question. The Why question assumes a prior understanding of the relation of Being to the Nothing. How so? It issues forth from the ontological difference of Beings and being in which Being is *not*-a-being. Heidegger expresses this relation and difference that gives rise to the Why question as the tension of a positivity and negativity or, what is the same, of revealment and concealment. Being 'reveals' the positivity of beings by 'concealing' itself as a negativity, a non-being, 'the Nothing.' It 'hides behind' the beings to which it gives itself. "[Being] remains to that degree far-off as there belongs to itself an essential self-withdrawal.... Because a luminous hiding belongs to Being, Being shines forth in the light of a concealing withdrawal" (Heidegger, 1998d, 44-45/116-117; 1962b, 138/177-178; 1998e, 26/152; cf. Richardson, 170, 452). In other words, as Richardson observes, "[T]he entire problematic of revealment-concealment in Being is nothing more than the problem of the 'not' which constitutes the ontological difference as such" (Richardson, 565). It is clear that Heidegger does not mean the 'negativity' or 'concealing withdrawal' of Being to be taken, as it were, negatively. It is not to be seen as a privation of Being but, paradoxically, as of its very 'essence,' as its positive 'property,' if that metaphysical word may be used. Moreover, it is precisely that which constitutes, for Heidegger, the *mystery* of Being (Heidegger, 1998e, 19-20, 22-23, 25/147-150, 152; cf. Richardson, 240).

In the metaphysical tradition, as seen for example in Leibniz, the implication of the Why question was that if we went far enough back to a 'first' cause, or if we went deep enough to a primordial 'ground,' we could somehow finally reach or break through to an 'answer' that solved the mystery. This has been, as Rubenstein showed, philosophy's distinctive *hubris*. But for Heidegger this is fool's quest. It is Being itself, *as such*, that repels and expels all such attempted 'answers.' Being *as such* is that process of self-concealing withdrawal that gives rise to the being of beings. Thus, thinking of Being, thinking the ontological difference, asking the Why question is *not a search for an answer but a way of guarding and protecting the primordial mystery of Being* (Heidegger, 1963, 14, 23, 99, 109, 138; cf. Richardson, 446). To fully understand this darkness in the heart of Being (*Sein*), however, we must turn to its shadow companion, the Nothing (*das Nichts*).

Being and Nothing: the Same

Heidegger says he was 'ensnared' from his earliest days as a thinker by the question of Being. From early on he also introduced the theme of the Nothing into his thinking of Being. By his later years he had condensed his reflections into a 'guiding statement' – "Being: Nothing: The Same" – a formula, he said, that was "so simple that it is extremely difficult to explain philosophically" (Heidegger, 2012, 58, 72). Confronted by the maddening difficulty of thinking the ontology of Being and Nothing, he concluded: "It is better here to give up the 'is'– and to simply write: being : nothing" (Heidegger, *op. cit.*, 48). One can understand his frustration, yet how can he think this apercu solves the mystery? How can Being and Nothing, traditional metaphysical opposites even in the dialectic of a Hegel or the mysticism of an Eckhart, be said to be the 'same' without emptying out the conceptual content of Being altogether? Has Heidegger fallen into Hegel's 'night in which all cows are black'? Has he succumbed to Aurobindo's 'logic of the infinite' where all contraries collapse into identity? If not, how are to understand the 'sameness-not-identity' of Being and Nothing? What does Heidegger mean by this lapidary yet enigmatic equation? From what *place* can Heidegger make such a statement? (Heidegger, *op. cit.*, 57).

We have made an initial stab at trying to understand what Heidegger means by Being in reference to its grammar and its relation to Dasein, thinking, and the Why question. But we cannot go further in that direction without coming to terms with what he means by the Nothing. Not surprisingly the Nothing has as many dimensions as its corollary, Being. As we have seen, it too involves different aspects as related to Dasein, beings, the Why question and the ontological difference. As we consider each of these, perhaps we can gain clarity as to why and how Heidegger brings his thinking about Being and Nothing to a point of convergence in that simple yet strange formula: Being: Nothing: the Same.

The existential dimension of the Nothing from the perspective of Dasein was experienced as meaninglessness, guilt and death. But Heidegger concluded his analysis of these phenomena noting that the fundamental question about 'the Not' was left unanswered in SZ. It was left to be taken up explicitly in WM. "The ontological meaning of the notness [*Nichtheit*] of this existential nullity is still obscure. But this holds also for the ontological essence of the 'not' in general. Ontology and logic... have exacted a great deal from the 'not'...but it itself has not been unveiled ontologically.... Has anyone ever made a problem of the ontological source of notness, or, prior to that, even sought the mere conditions on the basis of which the problem of the 'not' and its notness and the possibility of that notness can be raised? And how else are these conditions to be found except by taking the meaning of Being in general as a theme and clarifying it?" (*SZ* 285-286/BT 330-332). These are questions Heidegger addresses in his post-*SZ* works when, seen from the perspective of Being, the Nothing appears as the (self-) concealing of Being in the un-concealing of beings. The question thus presents itself: how are these two perspectives or actualizations of the Nothing related? What is their commonality? If they are 'different' are they yet the 'same'? How do they bear on "the unthought, because still withheld, mystery of Being itself?"

It remained for Heidegger to link that mystery to the negativity in the heart of Being, to Being as the Nothing (Heidegger, 1977d, 244/109-110; cf. Richardson, 436).

The Nothing and Dasein Revisited

With the shift in the later Heidegger from Dasein to Being there goes a change in the meaning of the Nothing for Dasein. From the negativities of meaninglessness, guilt and death there is a transition to the positive significance of the Nothing in relation to Dasein. Heidegger has told us that Dasein in its essence "thrusts itself into the Nothing" (Heidegger, 1962, 214/245-246). But this being "held out in the Nothing" is now seen not as a privation but as a constructive 'making possible' owing, paradoxically, to the initiative of the Nothing itself. How so? What is this new perspective on the Nothing? Heidegger's definition: "The negativing element in Being is the essence of what I call the Nothing" (Heidegger, 1998a, 114/273). But how can this 'negativing' dimension in the guise of the Nothing have a positive function vis-a-vis Dasein? For Heidegger, since Being is 'not-a-being' that conceals itself in revealing beings, it cannot be grasped by Dasein except in the form of a 'nothing.' Thus it is as the Nothing that Being discloses to Dasein the fact that beings are (cf. Richardson, 534-535). As Heidegger argues in the third section of *Was ist Metaphysik?* (1929), it is the function of the Nothing to make beings manifest as beings. "Non-being repels attention from itself and directs Dasein's gaze towards beings." It is because of the Nothing that beings are revealed as "that which is not [the] Nothing." But this is the function of Being itself: "In the Being of beings comes-to-pass the Nothing in its very essence... the Nothing reveals itself as belonging to the Being of beings." We have encountered this 'not' that separates beings and the Nothing before – it is none other than the ontological difference (Heidegger, 1998g, 35, 39; cf. 38, 42/91, 94, cf. 93, 96; cf. Richardson, 201-203).

The Priority of Nothing in the Why Question

As we have seen, for Heidegger the Why question does not ask, as it does for Leibniz, about a First Cause or Highest Being, the metaphysical linchpin undergirding beings-as-a-whole. Rather it asks how the ontological difference between Being and beings comes to pass. The answer is that it comes to pass because of the Nothing. In other words, in answering the Why question it is not Being but the Nothing that has priority. As Richardson observes, "It is Non-being that 'forces' the question upon us. Does this not mean that the Nothing exercises a priority of sorts in the posing of the question? Dasein must yield, through a unique type of surrender, to beings-in-their totality, and abandon itself completely to Non-being. In practice, this will take the form of posing the question about the ontological difference" (Richardson, 204, 206, 244; cf. Heidegger, 1998g, 42/96). Thus, in his interpretation of the Why question, for Heidegger, in contrast to Leibniz, who emphasizes the primacy of Being, it is the Nothing that is *prior*, ontologically, to Being. It is because of this fundamental experience of the Nothing in the Why question that Dasein, struck by "the strangeness of beings and an appreciation of how wondrous it is that they 'are,'" comes to pose the Why question. It is the revelation of Non-being that lies at the basis of all wonder (*Verwunderung*), and, therefore, of every 'Why?' It is because of the Nothing that Dasein is freed for a true sense of beings as such, not as *vorhand* or *zuhand*, but as they 'are,' in their *be-ing*, as 'wondrous strange'" (Heidegger, *op. cit.*, 34, 41/90, 95-96; Richardson, 201).

The Nothing and Being: the Same?

And yet, Heidegger says the Nothing is the 'veil' of Being. From the perspective of Dasein, or beings, the Nothing is not Plato's *ouk on*, nothing in an absolute sense, but Plato's *me on*, the Nothing-as-Being viewed as a counter-concept to beings, as *not*-a-being, as the 'other' to beings: "This completely Other to all beings is the Nothing [and] the Nothing as the Other to beings is the veil of Being." In other words, the disclosure of beings by the Nothing is the activity of Being itself: "In the Being of beings comes-to-pass the Nothing in its very essence... The Nothing reveals itself as belonging to the Being of beings." The Nothing and Being are the Same (Heidegger, 1998d, 21-23, 35, 39; cf. 38, 40, 42, 45-47, 51/ 288-290, 91, 94; cf. 93, 95, 96, 233-235, 238; cf. 1958, 36-40/ 93, 95, 97, 99, 101; Heidegger, 1982, 108-109/19-20; cf. Richardson 474). What does this mean for our understanding of the *Nothing*? What does it mean for our understanding of *Being*? And what does it mean for our understanding of their 'co-relation' as the *Same*? The consequences, though startling, unexpected, are nevertheless consistent with his equation. Nothing is not a lack but an excess, whereas Being is not a being but an emptiness.

The Nothing. "What occurs with the nothing in 'What is Metaphysics?' The nihilation of the nothing 'is' being. But if Being and Nothing are the same, then the Nothing in question cannot signify a lack. Therefore, one should not understand negating in a privative-negative way. It is a matter of something other, completely specific and unique. We keep the guiding statement ever in view: Being : Nothing : The Same. Nothing is a characteristic of Being." But if the Nothing is not to be taken in a 'privative-negative' sense, then how *is* it to be taken? Heidegger answers: "what is decisive in all this is that the privation, the *a* of *aletheia*, corresponds to this excess. Privation is not negation" (Heidegger, 2012, 57-58). What, then, is the 'excess' to which he refers? Clearly, the excess of Being itself.

Being. But how can Being be an excess if it is an emptiness? Strangely enough, it is easier to understand how it can be the latter. Many if not most of Heidegger's remarks testify to that. In relation to beings Being is an abyss, an *Abgrund*, a 'groundless ground.' It has no 'being,' 'essence' of its own. Its 'being' is emptied out, negatived as the Nothing in letting *beings* be. The Being of beings is the mystery that beings are, but one cannot speak of the 'Being' of Being, for it 'is' (Heidegger's word is '*west*,' from '*wesen*') as the Nothing. As Richardson put it, Being is 'inscribed' with nothingness: "Being is permeated with negativity" (Richardson, 564). The 'essencing' of being, its *wesen* verbally understood, is the 'nihilation' of the Nothing. *Das Sein west insofern als es Nichtet.*

The Nothing and Being: Levinas' Critique

But this leaves us with a mystery. If, however counter-intuitively, the Nothing is an excess and Being is an emptiness, how can they be said to be the Same? This is the critical problem Levinas sought to address. To review: According to Rubenstein, Levinas' thinking is grounded in an ontology of the '*il y a*.' This could be taken as a translation of Heidegger's German '*es gibt sein*.' But that is not how Levinas interprets its significance for thinking of Being. Unlike for Heidegger, for Levinas the '*il y a*' refers to being *apart* from beings, "the anonymous, impersonal field of naked existence"; it is 'indeterminacy itself,' "the absolute void,

the 'nowhere' in which the element loses itself and from which it arises"
(Levinas, 1969, 121/147; 2001, 44/80; Rubenstein, 2008, 71, 80). One is
reminded of Sartre's distinction between being in itself (*l'etre-en-soi*)
and being for itself (*l'etre-pour-soi*), novelized in Roquentin's nausea
when confronted by the 'sheer thatness' of the chestnut tree root. But
Levinas goes even further. The '*il y a*' is not even the 'naked' presence
of being; it is "neither being nor nothing but the personal flux that gives
rise to their difference" (Rubenstein, 71). It is like the primal but fecund
chaos, the mysterious 'nonplace' out of which both being and nothing
arise in pre-metaphysical traditions: "There was neither non-existence
nor existence then. Darkness was hidden by darkness in the beginning.
Poets seeking in their hearts for wisdom found the bond of existence
in non-existence" (*Rig Veda* 10.129). Could this be the origin, shrouded
in mystery, of Heidegger's ontological difference? And yet, Rubenstein
says, Levinas seems to reverse himself, saying, like Bede Rundle earlier
in this essay, that "no matter how hard the imagination tries, it cannot
think away existence 'itself. [S]heer thatness always returns to haunt
even the starkest absence: even in the very insistence, or 'presence,' of
that absence" (Rubenstein, 72). There seems to be a tension, therefore, in
Levinas, but perhaps also in Heidegger, between ontology as the thinking
of Being and the anti-ontology of a primordial 'nonplace' prior to the
ontological difference of being and nothing.

Levinas' critique of Heidegger's notion of Being as always the Being
of beings as revealed to Dasein bears striking parallels to Chad Allen's
critique of Quentin Smith's metaphysics of feeling. As will be recalled,
Allen charged Smith with illegitimately importing a value, viz. joy, into
our consciousness of the 'brute fact' of the world's existence 'in itself' –
forgetting the basic distinction between fact and value, the bare fact of
the world's being and felt-responses to that feature-less fact. Any talk of
an affective (substitute: existential) response to that fact would therefore
simply be incoherent. One could not even speak of *angst* let alone joy in
response to the world's anonymous, impersonal existence. What might
Heidegger say to such a critique? To Heidegger, Levinas' Sartrean-looking
notion of being as indeterminate existence or Allen's reference to 'Being
simpliciter' would be a lapse back into the distinction between existence
(that) and essence (what) of the kind that characterizes metaphysics, that
is, a distinction abstracted from the prior 'being-in-the-world' of Dasein.
For Heidegger, Being 'is' only as disclosed to Dasein. There is no Being

without beings, nor is there an ontological difference of the two apart from Dasein. Being *as such* is always already understood as Being '*for*' Dasein. And Being is 'there' for Dasein only if Dasein in turn is understood as being-in-the-world, not a 'worldless' Cartesian ego confronted by an equally 'worldless' being '*in-itself*'.

But maybe Levinas and Allen have a point? How can one justify even anxiety let alone joy at the brute fact of the world's existence? Or is this the wrong question? Does it already prejudge/prejudice the issue? Should the question rather be: How can one justify anxiety or joy or the other moods Smith and Heidegger catalogue as responses to the 'fact' (Heidegger's term 'facticity') of Dasein's 'thrown' being-in-the-world? The issue between Allen and Smith, between Levinas and Heidegger, would appear to be joined: Which phenomenon is ontologically prior – the *world's being* or *being-in-the-world*? Intuitions seem hopelessly divided. On the one hand, it would seem, intuitively, that we cannot speak about something as abstract as Being 'in itself' apart from – as it were 'outside' of – Dasein's encounter with Being within the context of being-in-the-world. On the other hand, it would seem, intuitively, that Smith and Heidegger have lapsed into an affective/existential 'subjectism' vis-a-vis the 'objective reality' of a world that would exist even if there were no human observers. How can one understand that independent reality, let alone a 'something' beyond both being and nothing, if one is confined to the existential horizon of being-in-the-world?

In an attempt to answer these questions, we need to return to the distinction between an existential-ontological understanding of being (i.e. Dasein-based) and a cosmological-metaphysical understanding of being. The former, unlike the latter, is grounded in an immediate *existential*, not narrowly *epistemological*, awareness of being, what James called and Rubenstein analyzed as the 'ontological emotion' of wonder. The affect of ontological wonder has several implications. It is a *felt*-response to being-in-the-world, not a cognitive *reduction* to the (alleged) 'bare fact' of the world's existence. It is not wonder in the face of a *non-contextual* being 'in itself,' it is wonder, expressed in the Why question, at the disclosure to *Dasein* of the Nothing-cum-Being that lets beings be, that 'gives being.' The problem with the notion that '*es gibt sein*' or the '*il y a*' refers to in an unmediated way to the 'brute fact' of the world's existence is that it risks becoming a felt-response nonetheless, namely the experience of despair. In other words, such metaphysical 'purism,' such ontological asceticism, is in danger of falling into an existential nihilism. It is not surprising that Heidegger's description of Dasein's despair at the meaninglessness of the world's existence was interpreted just that way by many of his critics. It is a legitimate concern. How can Heidegger or Smith justify the assertion that joy is not only an appropriate but the most basic felt-response to the mystery of Being? As argued earlier, Smith did not really argue for the claim other than simply to assert that the happening of the world-whole was in and of itself a happy 'fulfilment.' How, then, can Heidegger, whose SZ seems considerably 'darker,' who gives a detailed and convincing phenomenology of anxiety, go on to claim that nevertheless the companion of anxiety is joy? How can he say that "Along with the sober anxiety...goes an unshakeable joy"? (*SZ* 310/*BT* 358; cf. *SZ* 308/*BT* 355)

There are perhaps two ways to understand this existential stance. The first is that Heidegger's analysis of Dasein's anxiety in face of the meaninglessness of being-in-the-world occurs in the first part of *SZ* titled 'preparatory fundamental analysis of Dasein.' The statement just cited, however, is found in the second part of *SZ* which deals with 'a primordial existential Interpretation' of Dasein. It occurs in the section in which Heidegger has finally arrived at an analysis of 'the way in which Dasein's potentiality-for-being-a whole' comes to have 'existentiell authenticity.' In other words, in a dialectically more rigorous analysis than that of Smith, Heidegger juxtaposes the 'authentic resoluteness' Dasein's 'unshakeable joy' with the 'inauthentic' response described in the first part of *SZ*. Joy is indeed a legitimate if not fundamental response to Dasein's being-in-the-world, but the summit of joy can only be reached if one has first passed through the dark valley of anxiety. We are reminded of James' twice-born' souls or Paul's notion of being 'born again' – Tillich's 'New Being.'

But there is a second dimension to Heidegger's claim, one that reflects the so-called 'turn' in his later work from a focus on Dasein to a focus on Being. Here too, as with Levinas' '*il y a*,' the specter of nihilism rears its head. If Being is emptiness and it is the Nothing that is excess, why doesn't that leave us mired in nihilism? We have been exploiting Heidegger's paradox. It is time to ask about its meaning – Heidegger might say, to bring it out of 'hiding' (*lethe*) and ask about its 'truth' (*a-letheia*). What does it mean to say the Nothing is excess if not that Being itself is this 'excess,' albeit disclosed first of all, in a paradoxical way, in Dasein's three-fold experience of the Nothing as the 'veil' of Being? If, however, in a dialectical reversal, the proper (Heidegger: 'authentic' or 'ownmost') response of Dasein to Being-as-Nothing, Nothing-as-Being proves to be anxiety's other 'face,' joy, what does this tell us about Being itself *beyond* the fact that it is first and for the most part, indeed *necessarily*, grasped as the Nothing?

Being Redivivus: Being as Excess

Being is that which lets beings be. It lets beings be by 'concealing' itself as 'not-a-being,' as the Nothing, – in order that beings may be 'revealed,' may 'be.' As Richardson says, "What is important to realize is that the Source [*Being*] *as such* is self-concealing.... This self-withdrawal in giving rise to beings, this bestowal that is also a withholding... [in this] consists its mystery ... an open domain that closes itself up, that reveals and conceals at once" (Richardson, 446-447, emphasis Richardson's; cf. Heidegger, 1963, 14, 16-17, 23, 99, 104, 109). Fine and good. But what of Being *itself*? Is its mystery such that its '*as such*' can only be grasped as a 'Nothing'? To the contrary. It turns out that for Heidegger, after this long slog through an interpretation of Being as the Nothing, there *are* positive predicates that can be affirmed of it after all – in fact some very traditional, metaphysical-looking attributes that resemble nothing so much as those listed by Post! How are we to understand this surprising reversal, indeed upending, of what until now we have been led to think? Are there Heideggerian texts that can support *this* unexpected 'turn'?

It seems there are, nor have commentators been slow to point them out. Most recently, for example, Capobianco, drawing on Heidegger's own terms, asserted that Being is not only the Being of beings, "this is the Simple, this is the One (*hen*), this is the *singulare tantum*" (Capobianco, 2010). Before that, Richardson in his *magnum opus* catalogued the numerous places in Heidegger's writings that evidenced the same or similar features. In Heidegger's Holderlin interpretations Being, poetized as the 'Source' or 'Origin' (*Ursprung*), is described as "an overflowing abundance, rather a superabundance, a continual overflowing." Here is the precedent for Jean-Luc Marion's later characterization of Being as 'saturation' or Quentin Smith's metaphysics of the world-whole as a 'plenitude.' Richardson says: "It is as if Being in its exuberance continually surpasses itself [*shades of Whitehead and Hartshorne!*], then flows back upon itself to make the experience of its own inadequacy to itself. This self-surpassing self-inadequacy is the very nature ['*essenc-ing*'] of Being-as-origin" (Richardson, 444; cf. Heidegger, 1963, 23). Nor is this the only such site. Richardson documents a raft of supporting texts that encompass most of Heidegger's post-*SZ* work. Collectively they seem rather conclusively to answer the question: "for Being 'itself', the *lethe* [*Non-being*] that is mystery, what is to be said of it now?" The answer: "It is Wealth, Treasure, a hidden Fullness. It is inexhaustible Wellspring – ineffable! – the Simple, the All, the Only, the One" (Richardson, 640; cf. Heidegger, 1975f, 220-221/70-71; 1996, 107, 171, 184, 188/60-61, 102,110-111,113; 1998f, 156/; 1966, 70; 1982, 103, 197/15, 91; 19753, 325/39-40; 1953, 4). But having diligently unearthed all these references, Richardson then says in what can only be a howling *non sequitur*: "Beyond this, we dare not say anything about Being 'itself' at all; we must simply leave it without name" (Richardson, 640). But if Heidegger really said all this, he has already said too much! How can he think to assign all these descriptors to Being 'itself' if Being is ultimately a mystery?

Now either Richardson has gone overboard, over-interpreting what may be simply an indulgence in poetic license on Heidegger's part, or Heidegger meant such expressions to be taken in all seriousness, whatever difficulty they might present to thinking of Being-as-Nothing, not to mention to his long-standing critique of such 'metaphysical' features being ascribed to Being. But it would seem that Richardson is fairly reporting what Heidegger himself thought. In his 1962 letter to Richardson on the occasion of the latter's book Heidegger said that Being "abounds in hidden plenitude" (Richardson, xxii-xxiii). Again, at the end of his career, in the *Four Seminars*, Heidegger reiterated these views, in striking accord with Rubenstein's account of the origin of philosophy in wonder. Being, said Heidegger in 1969, "is the *overabundance*, the *excess* of what presences. The Greeks name this thrust of presence *thaumadzein*. Consequently, it must always be emphasized that the dimension of the entirely excessive is that in which philosophy arises. Philosophy is indeed the answer of a humanity that has been struck by the excess of presence – an answer which is itself excessive." (Heidegger, 2012, 38, emphasis Heidegger's; cf. Plato, *Theatetus*, 155d). What a fascinating passage! Wonder (*thaumadzein*) is not only stunned silence before a mystery, it is sheer astonishment at the eruption of an excess that beggars our concepts. And yet language will speak, since speak it must, and so it says, what it can only say tautologically: *das Sein 'west,'* Being 'be's.' But what 'be-ing'! Philosophy's 'answer' cannot be an answer in any ordinary sense, it can only be an 'answer' that is itself 'excessive,' that 'answers *to*' the *thaumadzein* that elicits it by speaking, if it speaks at all, in hyperbole. The wonder of Being! An over-flowing abundance! A miracle! A mystery indeed!

That said, nevertheless, how is philosophy to *think* such excess, such an answer that is not-an-answer but an answering-to? A clue may be found in the notion of Being's over-flowing abundance as a *bestowal* that let beings be. As Witherall suggested, perhaps it is to think Being as a *gift*, a gift that gives (empties) itself in giving beings being.

Being as Gift

Before we turn to that 'elsewhere,' however, it is important to follow Heidegger's thinking of Being further. Despite the remnants of cosmology, it has radical implications that have not yet been tapped. For a question remains. How is philosophy to *think* the excess of Being, how best to think an 'answer-as-excess' that is 'not-an-answer' but an 'answering-to'? A clue may be found in Heidegger's notion of Being as a *bestowal [Schenkung]* that 'lets beings be.' He appears to be suggesting that the 'excess' of Being is Being's *letting*, and that this 'letting' is best understood, metaphorically, as the *gift* of Being. As Witherall suggested, drawing on Heidegger, thinking Being as *gift [Geschenk]* means thinking it as an over-flowing abundance that endlessly gives (empties) itself in letting beings be, thinking Being as a giving of the gift of be-ing to beings: *Es gibt Sein.* If so, by adopting this motif Heidegger is making yet another 'turn' in his thinking of Being. Thinking the 'excess' or 'letting' of Being as Gift would not supercede but would supplement thinking of Being as the Nothing (cf. Richardson 477). Is this reading into Heidegger something that is not there? What does Heidegger say?

That Being as gift is indeed for Heidegger of central importance may be seen in his letter to Richardson that serves as the Forward to the latter's book: "One who has no sense for perceiving the granting [*Gebens*] of such a gift [*Gabe*] to man will no more comprehend what is said about the sending [*Schicken*] of Being than the man born blind can ever experience what light and color are" (Heidegger in Richardson, xxii-xiii;

translation slightly altered). We have already seen that he understands Being as the 'excess' called *thaumadzein* by the Greeks, the 'strange wonder' which launched the 'excessive answers' of philosophy itself as 'thinking of Being.' As he commented in the lecture *On Time and Being* and repeated in the *Four Seminars:* "It is a matter here of understanding that the deepest meaning of being is letting. The text 'Time and Being' attempted to think his 'letting' still more originarily as 'giving.' The giving meant here speaks in the expression *Es gibt. Es gibt,* letting as such, the gift of a 'giving which gives only its gift, but in the giving holds itself back and withdraws.' Letting is then the pure *giving*, which itself refers to the it [*das Es*] that gives" (Heidegger, 2012, 59-60; 1972, 8/8). Richardson, echoing these remarks in commenting on similar passages, says that for Heidegger Being is "pure gift. [It is] the emergence of Being itself which bestow[s] itself spontaneously in pure bounty as gift (*Schenkung*)" (Richardson 411, 413; cf. Heidegger, 1975d, 41-42, 62/32-34, 75). It is the 'gratuity' of Being.

If indeed, as thus appears, 'gift' has come to be the key metaphor for Heidegger in his thinking of Being, then the problem is to decipher what it means without, if possible, falsifying its ontological content or truth. Both Rubenstein and Witherall offered interpretations.

Rubenstein's thesis was that the double movement of wonder (*thaumadzein*) as 'shock and awe' (*SZ*: anxiety-cum-joy) not only revealed but *was* the gift of being. However, in her comments on Levinas' critique of Heidegger, she argued that "it is hardly clear that the *il y a* is distinct from primordial *donation*" (Rubenstein, 211, n. 53; my emphasis). But there *is* a difference, since, as she also noted, for Levinas the *il y a* generates "the distinction between being and nothingness ... it is said to 'overflow with plentitude' from *beyond* being" (Rubenstein, 215, n. 135; Rubenstein's emphasis). This is an intriguing comment, not because it seems to reprise Heidegger's notion of the 'ontological difference,' but because it gives a tantalizing hint of something else in the 'Es' of Heidegger's 'Es gibt Sein,'that something more that needs to be said about Being itself from a 'place' that is 'elsewhere,' a 'no-place' or 'nowhere' from which both Being and the Nothing emerge. We have already alluded to that possibility in the previous section. Obviously it is one to which we will have to return.

Witherall provided a more detailed analysis of gift as both metaphor and metaphysics. While we rejected his attempt to give the metaphor a metaphysical gloss, we suggested that his interpretation contained clues that help to understand why, for Heidegger, the metaphor of gift moved to the center of his thinking of Being.

For Witherall the answer to the Why question is that Being is that which gives itself to beings "somehow at the same time." His basic thought, he said, was that "that the existence of something instead of nothing is a gift ... and it must be evaluated as such when we try to understand it... Being is given gratuitously ...It is both free and unnecessary" (Witherall, 122-123). These metaphorical propositions, for that is what they are, like Heidegger's, beg for further clarification. We know what it means, in ordinary contexts, for a gift to be given *freely, gratuitously*, for no particular reason, unconditionally, with no strings attached, no expectation of a response. We also know what it means for a gift to be *unnecessary*. The relationship was not dependent upon the gift given, though of course a gift often functions to give expression to a new relationship or further cement already-existing bonds. Absent these features it might be difficult to interpret it as a 'gift.' There is another feature present, though more rarely, in such an act of 'bestowal,' namely, an element of *self-sacrifice* on the part of the giver. The gift may have cost more than the giver could readily afford, in fact in an extreme case, it may have 'emptied out' the giver's pockets.

Now what could it mean to say that these features can be applied, if only metaphorically, to the 'Being of beings', the fact that beings exist? That latter phrase expresses in plain prose the content and truth of the metaphorical statements 'Being lets beings be' and 'Being gives itself to beings': they are a "restatement," Witherall says, "of the fact of existence itself" (Witherall, 123). The metaphor of the gift of Being is not an invitation to metaphysics. It does not stand in need of metaphysical rescue, nor need scientific explanations apply. Simple experience with a dollop of 'ontological wonder' does the trick. But then how do these moving metaphors apply to what seems a simple, everyday 'fact'? What makes them *appropriate* responses to the fact of Being-cum-beings? Because the 'simple, everyday fact' of there being something rather than nothing is, ultimately, a mystery – a mystery that can only be expressed in metaphors, not metaphysics. How do these metaphors express that existence is a mystery? To say that being(s) exist 'freely, gratuitously' is to say, analogously, that being exists 'for no reason,' 'cannot be explained,' is 'without why' – in other words, is a mystery. To say that the existence of beings(s) is 'unnecessary' is again to say that no necessary reason or explanation can be given – that it is a mystery. Thus, the metaphorical proposition, 'Being gives itself to beings' claims both that "the source of the gift is ineffable and that the gift is without justification" (Witherall, 154).

There are, however, two aspects of Heidegger's understanding of the 'gift of Being' metaphor that resist easy 'translation.' The first is the notion of the 'self-sacrifice' of Being in 'giving itself' to beings. We have cited a limited analogy in the ordinary case of making a sacrifice in giving a gift. But for Heidegger, Witherall says, "Being gives itself so completely that it is exhausted, and has thereby emptied itself into beings [It exists over] the abyss of Nothingness" (Witherall, 138). This notion of a gift as self-sacrifice cannot easily be accommodated within our usual experience of giving a gift, though it has its obvious counterparts in the sacrificial 'death' of God in Christ and the Buddha's sacrifice of himself in a previous lifetime to feed a hungry beast. Perhaps this religious origin is what is reflected in Heidegger's notion of the self-emptying of Being. But can it make sense in a non-religious context? Heidegger's resort to a quasi-religious metaphor is a reminder of the problematic relation between metaphysics, expressed in the concepts of philosophy, and metaphor, expressed in the symbols of religion. One solution might be the logic of the infinite in mysticism. Mystical theology asserts that God remains infinite even while emptying Himself out in the finite (cf. Witherall, 131). Heidegger is certainly familiar with mystical thinking, particularly Eckhart. The problem is that mysticism too is still a religious logic.

The second aspect of the gift of Being that is even harder to fit with ordinary gift-giving, one that reinforces the 'religious' character of Heidegger's notion, is that despite its self-emptying, the abundant, overflowing self-surpassing 'giving' of Being is *continual.* Despite being exhausted it is inexhaustible, despite being an emptiness it is a fullness, despite having given itself completely it gives itself infinitely, without end. Nothing in the human world of gift-giving can be said to be continually refreshing itself, re-filling itself from a 'fullness' that is never depleted. We are left with the question whether there is not a non-religious way of making sense of the metaphor of continuous self-sacrificial giving which Heidegger ascribes to the Being of beings.

One might ask, for example, 'Why does Being give itself to beings?' The simplest, most straightforward answer would be: because that is what 'Being' means. The 'because' simply makes explicit in the predicate what is already contained in the subject. This may seem like a tautology, and in fact *is* a tautology, but as Heidegger would say, it is not a 'mere' tautology. It is rather *t'autos-logos*, 'same-saying,' language at the edges of literal speech saying in a tautological metaphor that 'whereof one cannot speak' (Wittgenstein). Assuming, therefore, that the Being question can even be intelligibly asked, an assumption challenged in the first part of this study, it is not clear that any answer would simply be a *restating* of it in the language of metaphor and tautology. The metaphor of gift, like the metaphor of Being itself (for that in the last analysis is what 'Being' is), is thus but a linguistic pointer to a mystery that, as Arendt said, invites pondering, not 'answering.' The 'answer' takes the form of a non-answer or an anti-answer – an 'answer' in name only. The 'gift of Being' is a metaphor twice over that evades all interrogation. As Witherall said, "such an answer will not make the fact of existence less awesome, but it can succeed in bringing human beings closer to the centrality of this fact." The metaphor does something metaphysics cannot do: it "answers a mystery with a mystery" (Witherall, 155). Job is confronted by a riddle wrapped in a mystery inside an enigma, but, we read, strangely "he is comforted." By what? By the gift of Being itself.

Bringing humans 'closer to the centrality of this fact,' making it possible for humans to find 'comfort' in the face of an ultimate mystery, the 'strange wonder' that repels all philosophical questions and expels all metaphysical answer – that is the task Heidegger set himself in *thinking* the gift of Being. But to *think* Being as 'the gift that never stops giving,' to *think* the 'excess' or 'letting' of be-ing as the unique 'gift,' paradoxically opens the way to an *answer* to the Why question. That 'answer' takes the form of an 'answering to,' a *response to* the gift of Being. Thus Heidegger sees *thinking* the question of Being as *piety* before the mystery of Being itself, and *thinking* (*Denken*) the gift of Being as a *thanking* (*Danken*).

Heidegger II: Thinking (of Being)

'Thinking' in Heidegger's use of the word has a number of features, many of which are listed in the 'Nachwort" to *Was ist Metaphysics*, where Heidegger characterizes thinking as acquiescence, attunement, consent, self-surrender, echo, docility, and 'sacrifice' (Heidegger, 1998g, 46-50/233-237). However, insofar as thinking of Being proceeds from the experience of Being as *wonder* (Rubenstein) and *gift* (Witherall), three aspects stand out: thinking as questioning (including the 'piety' of thinking), thinking as tautologous, and thinking as thanking. Heidegger's life-long preoccupation as a thinker has been with the question of Being. His entire oeuvre has been an effort to ponder the question – variously formulated – 'What is the meaning (truth) of being?' 'Why are there beings instead of nothing?' So the task of thinking for Heidegger is to think being, to ask the question of being, and, if possible, to answer the question of being. In other words, the attempt to think *Being* becomes the question, what does it mean to *think*? (cf. Richardson, 16). What does it mean to 'think being'? And what does it mean to 'answer' that question? These simple questions, as Heidegger found, conceal enigma upon enigma.

First of all, what Heidegger means by 'thinking' in the phrase 'thinking (of) being' is not what is usually meant by thinking either in ordinary or philosophical, especially metaphysical use. To think being is to question *Being*. But what does it mean to *question* Being? What can one ask? What can one answer? What can one *say*? Clearly it must be questioning of a different kind, questioning in some other sense, not a questioning that challenges Being, an attempt to force Being to reveal its secrets, but a questioning that is a response to Being, response that not only lets beings be but that also 'lets Being be.' Heidegger says, "Thought accomplishes this letting [-be]" (Heidegger, 1998a, 54, 111/240, 270-271; cf. Richardson 541). But what kind of 'questioning' is that? In a gnomic remark, Heidegger even calls the so-called questioning (of) Being the 'piety' of thinking. A strange kind of 'questioning,' a strange kind of 'thinking'!

So how does one think Being? How does one question mystery? The questioning is strange, the answering is strange, the thinking is strange. But it become even more so when, as we shall see, we are told that thinking Being is thinking by tautology, thinking that 'says nothing'! It seems, in short, that what Heidegger means by thinking is not thinking in any sense that would be normally recognized, that what he calls questioning is not questioning in any of the familiar senses, and that the answer to such questioning is not an answer that would count in the halls of academe. Rather, what Heidegger seems to mean by 'thinking the question of Being' is a linguistic shorthand for an endless, bottomless, open-ness to the primordial wonder of Being, a thinking that raises a Why question for which there is no answer, thinking as a pointer to the mystery of Being without Why.

But there is a further problem. There is an ambiguity, in fact a manifold one, signaled by the 'of' in the phrase, the 'thinking (of) being.' There is, first, the question whether thinking of Being refers to the traditional metaphysical approach to Being or the 'other thinking' of Heidegger's *Seinsdenken*. As Heidegger said, the phrase, the 'thinking of Being,' must be "shorn of that ambiguity which allows it to cover on the one hand metaphysical thought (the thinking of the Being of *beings*) and on the other the Being-question, i.e., the thinking of *Being* as such (the revealed-ness of Being)" (letter to Richardson, xiv-xv; my italics). Then there is the ambiguity between the subjective and objective genitive contained in that little preposition, in fact two of them. There is the double reference to the thinking 'of' Being as thinking that is 'called' by Being, on the one hand, and thinking as that which 'answers to' Being, on the other (Heidegger, 1998a, 54/240; 1968, 132/218-219; 1998g, 10, 13/279-280, 282; cf. Richardson, 249, 542). Finally, there is another ambiguity in that 'of,' this one between two different aspects of that response to Being. On the one hand there is what we might called the 'objective' or 'cognitive' or 'propositional' aspect of thinking 'of' Being in the sense of thinking 'about' or talking 'about' Being, and on the other the 'subjective' aspect of responding *existentially* to the 'call' of Being, for example, in gratitude for the gift of Being. As Witherall observed, Being is 'given to us,' and as "the 'to us' indicates, it ineluctably calls for a response" (Witherall, 123). Thus, in talking about the 'thinking (of) Being' it is important to keep these three different significations of that relational preposition in mind. For Heidegger, therefore, thinking 'of' Being is a questioning, but one that, like the Being it thinks, calls not for an answer but an 'answering to,' a response to the mystery, the wonder, the gift of Being.

In summary, for Heidegger what does it mean to 'think Being'? How is one to think about and respond to Being? Heidegger focuses on three ways: by *thinking as questioning* Being; answering (to) the mystery, the wonder, of Being propositionally by *thinking as tautology*, thinking that 'says nothing,' or rather thinking as *t'autos logos*, thinking that 'says the Same'; and by answering (to) the gift of Being existentially by *thinking as thanking*.

Thinking as Questioning

For Heidegger thinking [*Denken*] is a co-equal partner with Being [*Sein*] in the thinking (of) Being [*Seinsdenken*] that marks the path-of-thought [*Denkweg*] on which he was always 'on the way' [*unterwegs*]. And that thinking is understood above all as an endless thinking-by-questioning [*Denken als Fragen*]. Why? Why is Being the most thought-worthy [*Denk-wurdigsten*]? Why is it the 'most question-worthy' [*Frag-wurdigsten*]?

Being as Question-Worthy

Heidegger says, "What gives itself [as thought-worthy] is the gift of the most question-worthy" (Heidegger, 1968, 149, cf. 108, 111-115/243-244, cf. 175, 182-191; cf. Richardson 439). The meaning of Being, the subject of his thought-path from at least *SZ*, is that *topos* which above all is worthy of thought and therefore of endless interrogation (Heidegger, 1968, 113/184-186; cf. Richardson, 616-617). Why is the thinking of Being primarily interrogative? Why does it require the thinker to 'think-by-question'? Because it is 'called for' by Being itself. It is Being which 'demands' that the thinker pose "the only question worth posing, the Being-question itself, which demands that the thinker think Being in its question-worthiness" [*Frag-wurdigkeit*] (Heidegger, 1998e, 15-16, 24- 25/144-145, 150-151; 1975d, 50, 58/ 62, 71; Richardson 253, 416). Thus, for Heidegger 'thinking' is not questioning in general, that is, it refuses to limit itself to limitations of ordinary or metaphysical thinking (cf. Richardson, 251). Rather, it is a questioning (of) Being in the sense of that double genitive – a questioning *by* and *about* Being itself. Such thinking, Heidegger says, is "a way of thinking that, instead of offering presentations [*Vorstellungen*] and concepts [*Begriffe*], experiences and proves itself as a *transformation* in the relation to Being*" (Heidegger, 1998d, 27/154; cf. 1998g, 44/232; cf. Richardson 481; my emphasis). As Heidegger adds, expanding on that 'transformation' and anticipating a section to follow: "Such thinking would be a *thanks-giving* to the thought-worthy...which would guard the thought-worthy inviolable in its question-worthiness" (Heidegger, 1968, 159; cf. 115, 128, 162-163/146; cf 160-161, 187-188, 212; Richardson, 615; my emphasis).

Why does Heidegger think of questioning (of) Being in that way? Because "it is by a question that we best express the primal wonderment that most characterizes authentic thought. This wonderment is familiar to us as the astonishment before the 'wonder of wonders,' [Being, that is] that beings are" (Heidegger, 1998g, 46-47/233-234; Richardson, 487-488). As Richardson comments, "What is wonder-ful here is the fact that the process by which they [beings] are comports negativity as well as positivity, i.e., the mystery as such of Being. Is the wonderment here consciously a translation of the Aristotelian *thaumadzein*?" (Heidegger, 1975a, 259/104; 1998g, 34, 41, 46/ 90, 95-96, 233-234; 1963, 142; Richardson, 487-488). Here another reason why thinking (of) Being takes the form of a primordial questioning is introduced. It is because Being 'hides' its 'positivity' in the darkness of a 'negativity,' it is because Being enshrouds itself in and as aboriginal mystery. It is because Being 'conceals' itself that it 'presences' itself as worthy of thought, of questioning. Only by a primal questioning of Being as a Nothing can thinking protect the mystery of Being (cf. Richardson 21, 439).

What kind of thinking-as-questioning is able to guard the mystery of Being? A thinking, a questioning that, says Heidegger, paradoxically "is at once both gentle and rigorous. Its gentleness consists in a tranquil release, in submissiveness (*die Gelassenheit*) to the overpowering mystery; its rigor consists in the re-solve that does not destroy the mystery but compels it into the open space of its own truth, i.e., that lets it come-to-presence as mystery" (Heidegger, 1998c, 26/152; cf. Richardson 253; Heidegger's emphasis). At the close of his essay on the reign of technology, thinking-as-calculation, Heidegger introduces a term that nicely if provocatively captures this combination of *milden Strenge* and *strengen Milde* that characterizes the thinking-as-questioning (of) Being: *piety* (*Frommigkeit*). The more we think Being in its negativity, that is, as aboriginal mystery, he says, the more question-worthy it becomes, "for interrogation is the piety of thinking." (Heidegger, 1977c, 44/335; cf. Richardson, 617). Under the resonant umbrella-term of piety Heidegger shelters thinking-as-questioning Being in its negativity and mystery.

We will return to this intriguing notion in an excursus in a moment, but first it should be noted what the piety of thinking is not. It is not an *answer* to the question (or questioning) of Being. Piety is not an answer but an 'attitude' or response, an *'answering to'* the 'call' of Being. As we have seen, the thinking (of) Being "never can be answered. It is and remains essentially a question." For Heidegger, the importance of thinking is measured rather "not by the question as answered but by the question as asked." Thus, if there is in any sense an 'answer' to the question of Being, it is only to the extent it helps understand Being better as 'the question-worthy as such,' in other words, only if such an 'answer' leads to ever more questioning. For Heidegger, "What is desirable is not to absolve the questioning by an answer but simply to achieve by it a deeper fidelity to Being-as-question-worthy." What is important is *piety* in response to Being as that which is supremely and uniquely worthy of *thinking* (Heidegger, 1968, 141, 145, 161/159-160, 233, 238; 1975b, 161/160; cf. Richardson, 15, 29, 615-616).

Excursus: "Questioning is the Piety of Thinking" ("Das Fragen ist die Frömmigkeit des Denkens").

Before passing on from thinking-as-questioning to thinking-as-tautology, it may be useful to conclude the discussion of questioning with a few comments on Heidegger's thought-provoking remark that questioning is the piety of thinking. For Heidegger 'piety' does not refer to a relapse into theology. On the surface, at least, it is a word with heavy religious overtones. It reminds one of Schleiermacher's 'feeling' (*Gefuhl*), or the pietism behind Kant, or the spiritual sensibility of German mystics like Eckhart. Yet, Heidegger insists, "The unconditioned character of faith and the question-worthiness of thought are two different domains a chasm apart" (Heidegger, 1968, 110/177-178; cf. 2000, 5-6/7-9). On the other hand, there is a difference between the questioning of the 'science' of metaphysics (Aristotle), its attempt to provide an explanatory framework for the knowledge of being, or the 'calculative thinking' of technology, and the questioning with which Heidegger, in perhaps an echo of Plato's discussion in the *Euthyphro*, equates true piety. (We might, after Plato and Aristotle, equate piety with *thaumadzein*, wonder). Rather, for Heidegger questioning-as-piety protects the mystery of Being. That which is most *fragwurdig* (question-worthy), not *fraglich* (questionable), is precisely that which, paradoxically, cannot be questioned, submitted to interrogation, that to which there is no answer, no explanation. It is a *koan*. It calls for the piety of thinking. What is thinking? It is keeping open to the mystery of Being. How does thinking 'keep open'? By questioning. Questioning is keeping open to the mystery of Being. It is the piety of thinking. Piety – wonder at and reverence for Being – is what guards the mystery of Being.

Robert Gall, in *Beyond Theism and Atheism: Heidegger's Significance for Religious Thinking*, expands upon the further implications of Heidegger's evocative remark. "Heidegger is trying to be provocative but at the same time quite 'traditionally' philosophical. The essay is a challenge to the idea that 'technology' gives us all the answers, that it is our 'salvation.' There will be no more questions (eventually); technology will solve all our problems. But look at the ambiguity of the title of the essay, particularly of the word *nach*: the Question About- After-From [*Nach*] Technology. There is a question about the faith and optimism that people have in technology (think of all those people who proclaim the liberating power of the Internet and online college). There are still questions *after* [*nach*] technology gives us its answers. If we think about it, technology gives us questions to ask even as it supposedly 'solves all our problems'. Technology is a danger, but where danger is, [Heidegger says], the 'saving power' grows. The 'saving power' is the power of questions and questioning. Thinking is about asking questions, not accumulating answers. The thinker submits to questioning, is devoted to questioning; that is how we become who we are (to paraphrase Nietzsche). It is that 'devotion' and 'submission' that are the meaning of 'piety' here. What is traditional about such a call is that it recalls Socrates, who did not claim to have all the answers but thought that wisdom lay in owning up to and opening oneself up to one's ignorance. If one does that, one asks questions rather than presuming one has the answers Socrates defended himself in the *Apology* by invoking 'the god' as having given him the command to question his fellow Athenians. Against the charge of impiety, Socrates suggests that he is actually pious, devoted to 'the god', insofar as he asks questions. The *Euthyphro* highlights the ambiguity of 'piety,' the two kinds of piety that we find in the Western tradition: that of Socrates and that of Euthyphro. Euthyphro thinks he is pious because he is doing what the gods require. The gods have the answers; there is no need to think about what one should do. Socrates tries to show Euthyphro that Euthyphro's 'faith', his confidence that he is right and doing what is required, raises questions, and that Euthyphro really needs to think about what he is doing rather than blindly proceeding to prosecute his father. Questioning, even questioning the gods, makes one pious. In so doing, we submit to who we are and what we are given: to think" (Gall, 2014).

To review and preview: For Heidegger the function of thinking-as-questioning is to *be open* to Being, to the strange, wondrous fact that there are beings rather than nothing, and to *keep open* to Being and beings, not to *close off* that wonder by metaphysical, scientific or technological 'explanations.' Questioning is the way thinking stays open to that originary wonder (*thaumadzein*), guarding and protecting the mystery of Being, not by proposing 'answers' but by receiving and accepting the *wonder* of Being and responding with thanks to the *gift* of Being.

Thinking as Tautology

How is thinking-as-questioning related to thinking-as-tautology? Is tautology supposed to be some sort of answer to the question of Being? On the face of it, that does not seem possible, for tautology is traditionally regarded as an 'empty' mode of discourse that 'says nothing.' That does not seem a promising route to take in search of an answer to the *Seinsfrage*. The move from questioning to tautology seems especially problematic given Heidegger's own words on the subject. Early in his career as a thinker he had spoken negatively about '*nichtsagenden Tautologie*' (Heidegger, 1998d, 22/111), and even later he spoke in non-committal fashion about that particular linguistic expression, saying, for example, "If someone continually says the same, for example, the plant is a plant, he is speaking in a tautology" (Heidegger, 1960a, 14/13-14; cf. Schoeffer, 203). So it comes as something of a surprise, even a shock, when in a late work he speaks positively of tautology in connection with the saying of Parmenides, '*esti gar einai*,' 'Being namely is.' Heidegger says: "I have long considered this saying; for a long time I have even been *ensnared* in it. [T]his is clearly a tautology. Indeed! This is a *genuine* tautology: it *names the Same* only once, and indeed as itself." Even more surprisingly, he extends his observation beyond what might seem merely hermeneutical puzzlement over an enigmatic Greek epigram. He makes the astonishing claim that tautology is that mode of discourse distinctive of thinking itself. "I name the thinking here in question tautology. It is the *primordial* sense of *phenomenology*. In this regard we must thoroughly recognize that tautology is the only possibility for thinking what *dialectic* can only veil" (Heidegger, 2012, 79; 80-81; my italics). Clearly something extraordinary has happened here, something that would appear to have overturned the entire approach to the Being-question that Heidegger had been following til then. Talk about a *Kehre*! Not: thinking as the *questioning* (of) Being, but: thinking as the tautological *saying* or *naming* of Being.

Needless to say, these two comments of the late Heidegger raise a number of questions. The most obvious is, what can he possibly mean by saying that thinking is tautologous, given that it seems a universal opinion in philosophical and literary circles that tautologies are, in Heidegger's own words earlier, *'nichtsagend'*? Is that why he felt for a long time 'ensnared' in Parmenides' tautological saying? What does Heidegger mean by saying that Parmenides' saying is a 'genuine' tautology? Are there different kinds of tautologies, real ones versus pseudo-ones? Even so, how does a particular tautology being 'genuine' serve as any kind of answer to the claim that it is 'nichtsagend' or that, put differently, it does no more than 'say/name the same'? Further, why is tautology said to be 'phenomenology' in a 'primordial' sense? And finally, why is tautology said to be the only way for thinking something that dialectic only covers over?

In order to unpack this unexpected 'turn' in his late thought and at the risk of becoming 'ensnared' ourselves in explicating these puzzling, even bizarre and in any case undeveloped comments, two studies will be helpful, one on the *logic of tautology* in philosophical, especially mystical thinking (as has been well-documented, Heidegger was steeped in the works of German mystical thinkers, especially Eckhart), and one on the distinctive role of *Heidegger's tautologies* among his many other linguistic innovations – paradox ("the essence of truth is un-truth"), *coincidentia oppositorum* ("Being : Nothing : Same"), the 'hermeneutical circle' as 'virtuous' not 'vicious' circle, and the unusual use of the colon ("the essence of language : the language of essence"). The first of these works is by Benavides, *Tautology and Contradiction in the Language of Mysticism* (1982), the second is Schoeffer's *Die Sprache Heideggers* (1962). With this assist it may be possible to understand why, at a late stage in his work as a thinker, Heidegger came to think that the 'answer' to the question of Being could best be expressed by turning to tautological 'saying/naming' of Being of the sort that had long 'ensnared' him when he pondered that ancient 'word' of Parmenides.

The Logic of Tautology

Benavides' study of the logic of tautology and contradiction focuses on the use of these rhetorical formulae by mystic thinkers in the Western Neoplatonic and Asian Buddhist traditions. Heidegger, of course, was well-read in the former, especially Eckhart and quite familiar with the linguistic innovations and strategies they employed in their efforts to express the 'ineffability' of the mystical experience. He was also attracted to the alternative linguistic, conceptual and anti-ontological strands of the 'East,' especially Taoism. But while he drew on these resources he differed in the use to which he put them. Thus, while there is a striking resemblance at the formal-structural level between the language of the mystics and Heidegger's language of Being, there is a fundamental difference at the material-content level. Heidegger's concept of Being is consciously directed against what he calls the 'onto-theo-logic' of mystical thought, its concept of a transcendent of God or Gottheit as the highest being and ground of all being. And while Heidegger's *Seinsdenken* bears similarities to the 'deflationary' metaphysics of Buddhist thought with its notion of 'emptiness' (*sunyata*) as the interdependent co-arising of all beings 'empty' of 'own-being' (*svabhava*), Heidegger's own 'deflationary' notion of 'the Nothing' refers not to the lack of 'own-being' by beings but to the fact that there are beings at all, 'empty' or not. Accordingly, though Benavides shows how the logic of tautology and contradiction (paradox and *coincidentia oppositorum*) is exemplified in the language of Neoplatonic and Buddhist, especially Madhyamika thinkers, this same analysis can be applied at the formal-structural level to Heidegger's language about Being.

A question that needs to be addressed at the outset is: If tautological and paradoxical statements are to be taken seriously for the purposes of thinking, whether such utterances are "irrational, empty, or whether they are, in fact, attempts to deal with the most elementary – and unavoidable – aspect of what is the case: the fact *that* it is" (Benavides, 58, my italics). The 'intentionality' of such linguistic formulae calls attention to that strange and wondrous fact of existence. By seeing the world *sub specie paradoxae* or *sub specie tautologiae*, we are brought to see the world as it truly is (Benavides, 3-4). Such statements are attempts to express "the 'ground' – in a logical and not metaphysical sense – of reality" (Benavides, 72), what Heidegger would refer to as the 'groundless ground' of world's being. As 'anti-structures' that negate the normal structures of our discourse, paradox and tautology express the 'structural negativity' of that intentionality (Benavides 4-5, 12-14). Put differently, they constitute at the extremities of either end of discourse an 'anti-system' that indicates the limits of the logical possibilities of discourse and thought (Benavides, 72). To assist in this function they embed 'anti-concepts' like the negative verbal constructions of the German mystics and the nirvana and sunyata of the Madhyamika (Benavides, 40, 139). To this can be added Heidegger's neologism, the Nothing.

Paradox. As we have seen, Heidegger employs paradox to this end, the most extreme rhetorical configuration being the uniquely formulated *coincidentia oppositorum* conveyed by a pendular colon with the addition of a colon of identity hinting at a tautology concealed beneath the contradictory linguistic surface: "Being : Nothing : Same." The coincidence of opposites, in which the world is seen *sub specie paradoxae* (Benavides, 30) is only the most extreme case of metaphor, the rhetorical trope that unifies separate opposing realities in an effort to capture the 'oscillation' between being and nonbeing as 'mutually annulled' while simultaneously 'mutually implicated' (Benavides, 30-32, 35). Such linguistic innovations and the transformation of thought they bring about are not 'irrational' nor are they arbitrary. Thus, in the case of mystical experience, for example, "the negative 'mystical' content is inseparable from the negative form; so via mystica, as via negativa, is via linguistica" (Benavides, 40). For Heidegger, as we have seen, they are 'called for' by the experience of the mystery of Being itself. Benavides here inserts an important cautionary note: one should not be taken in by 'metalanguage under the guise of metaphor' – nor, one might add, vice versa (Benavides, 66). Already the Neoplatonic thinker Plotinus observed that even the verb 'to be' itself was being used in a metaphorical way. Tillich's description of 'Being' as a symbol when employed in theological contexts was a contemporary reformulation of the same point. And in the Buddhist tradition, it was the radical Madhyamika thinker, Nagarjuna, who averred that *sunyata*, 'emptiness,' was but a metaphorical way of making the point that things are without 'own-being' *(svabhava)* and therefore, empty *(sunya)* (Benavides, 76, 154). Thus the resort to paradox, to talk about the 'coincidence of opposites,' is the result of an inevitable struggle with "the tension between words and silence." In the case of Eckhart or Nagarjuna, theirs was "a mysticism with the need to speak"

(Benavides, 49). The same can be said of Heidegger's paradoxical equation of Being and Nothing. Out of the silence of the mystery of Being the thinker feels compelled to say the 'word' (of) Being.

From Paradox to Tautology. Heidgger employs both paradox and tautology in his response to the 'call' of Being. What is the relation between these two extremes at either end of philosophical discourse? In the *Tractatus Logico-Philosophicus*, Wittgenstein says that the tension between contradiction (paradox) and tautology is "a necessary one" (Wittgenstein, *Tract.*, 4.46 to 4.661; cf. Benavides, 71, 74). Heidegger's addition of the colon of identity, 'Same,' to 'Being : Nothing' likewise suggests a necessity in the relation but also the direction of an answer. While both tautology and contradiction (paradox) are, as noted, 'limit cases' of the possibility of discourse, nevertheless in the final analysis it is tautology that is "the ground of the process of signification" (Benavides, 74). As Benavides observes, in the case of Cusanus the *coincidentia oppositorum* prove to be "less a contraction than a tautology, a contradiction without contradiction." For Cusanus "in the 'absolute same' being and non-being are the same itself" (Benavides, 101-102, 107). Shades of Heidegger! Similarly, just as Cusanus turns the *coincidentia oppositorum* into a tautological *non-aliud* ('not-other), so with Nagarjuna, "the *mahayana* notion of emptiness (*sunyata*) turns the contradiction against itself and transforms it into a tautology" (Benavides, 129). In fact, says Benadvides, Cusanus' whole philosophy is "an attempt – in circles, as it were – to express in the simplest possible way the ground – the 'that' – of reality. [Cusanus] is attempting to reach the most elementary ground of reality: the simplest possible way of accounting for all that is the case, including the process of accounting itself, the concept that explains everything and also itself, whose existence and non-existence determines the existence and non-existence of everything," (Benavides, 106, 108-109). So too, Heidegger's 'groundless ground' – Being : Nothing : Same – is not simply a *coincidentia oppositorum* but a 'genuine' tautology.

Tautology. Wittgenstein, who never ceases to astonish with his lapidary insights into language, observed that "tautology says nothing because it says everything," thus putting that traditional linguistic canard against tautology firmly to rest (Wittgenstein, *Tract.* 4.462-4.463; Benavides, 60). In other words, tautology constitutes "the simplest possible way of accounting for all that is the case, including the process of accounting itself.... the concept that explains everything and also itself." Tautology, as Wittgenstein says, does not *add* anything to the world, it does not in that sense 'say' anything *about* the world. Rather, as Benavides aptly puts the Wittgensteinian point, it is a *'monologue of'* the world. Tautology functions as the "unsubstantial point at the center of all propositions. It leaves to reality the whole – the infinite whole – of logical space. It vanishes inside all propositions." (Wittgenstein, *Tract.*, 4.463, Benavides, 65-66, 93, cf. 96). Thus, tautologically, Cusanus' *'non-aliud'* and Nagarjuna's *sunyata* 'say nothing'; rather, "they erase themselves, leaving the world as it is (*yathabuta*)" (Benavides, 162). Tautology, says Wittgenstein, is "the common factor of all propositions that have nothing in common with one another" (Wittgenstein, *Tract.*, 4.4661; Benavides, 70-71, 92). In the view of the world *sub specie tautologiae*, if the world is 'all that is the case,' then "the *that* and not the *how* of the world is what is mystical" (Wittgenstein, *Tract.*, 1; Benavides, 66). "The 'that' is the world seen *sub specie tautologiae*, a 'that' which makes a 'what' and a 'how' not only impossible, but also unnecessary." Inasmuch as Being is neither the 'what' or the 'how' of the world, it is "the neutral – or 'empty' ground of reality, the tautological 'that' of the world, of everything 'that is the case'" (Wittgenstein, *Tract.*, 1, 6.44; Benavides, 93). Cusanus and Nagarjuna attempted, by way of the *via tautologiae*, to 'say' what is the absolute presupposition of all language and thinking about the world: the fact that the world is. To do this it was necessary that their propositions be 'anti-propositions,' their concepts 'anti-concepts,' tautologies that disappear inside everything that is the case. To 'say everything' it was necessary that they appear to 'say nothing' – that they speak and think in tautologies. As Heidegger came to discover, for speaking and thinking (of) Being it was necessary that he too think-in-tautology.

Heidegger's Tautologies.

We have already seen examples of Heidegger's thinking in the form of questioning and negations. We now turn to the distinctive role of tautology among his many other linguistic innovations – paradox ("the essence of truth is un-truth"), *coincidentia oppositorum* ("Being : Nothing : Same"), the 'hermeneutical circle' as 'virtuous' not 'vicious' circle, and the unusual use of the colon ("the essence of language : the language of essence"). His tautologies are examples of *figura etymologica*, a rhetorical construction that features the unity of the subject (the 'object') and the verb (the 'activity'), highlighting the unity of *Sprache* and *Sache*, language and object of thought or reality itself. According to Schoeffer, "The essential linguistic achievement of the figura etymologica in Heidegger's formulation is actually a tautology in which the 'object' and 'activity' are expressed as identical. The subject of the sentence is absorbed into the predicate and vice versa. True, in the sentence the unity of the 'one' formally is with itself, a 'split,' but it is not visible or thinkable in terms of its content as a statement [*Aussagesatz*]. The coming about [*Vollzug*] of the object [*Sache*] and the coming about [*Vollzug*] of the language occur together" (Schoeffer, 209-210, 212, 217). Thus Heidegger turned to thinking-as-tautology in order to ensure that the content of the linguistic form be the *same* as the subject-matter of thought (Schoeffer, 217) while at the same time avoiding the 'is' structure of the *identity* of subject and predicate.

We will return to the problematic aspect of this unity in a moment. But first, Heidegger's understanding of tautology as *figura etymologica* provides an answer to some of the questions above, in particular that of the difference between what Heidegger calls a 'genuine' tautology, a tautology in the strong sense, and tautologies that are such in only a 'peripheral' or weak sense. To illustrate this distinction between two types of tautology, the first group are tautologies in Heidegger's 'genuine' or strong sense, the second are tautologies in a weak or 'peripheral' sense (Schoeffer, 203-204).

'Genuine' Tautologies

- *Das Wesen west* ("Essencing essences.") (*WW* and other writings)
- *Das Nichts selbst Nichtet* ("The Nothing itself nothings.") (*WM* 34)
- *Welt ist nie sondern weltet.* ("World is not, it worlds.") (*WG* 44)
- *Welt west indem sie weltet.* ("World is in that it worlds.") (*VA* 178)
- *Wie aber west das Ding? Das Ding dingt.* ("But how does the thing exist? The thing things.") (*VA* 172)
- *Die Zeitlichkeit ist nicht sondern zeitigt sich. Zeitlichkeit zeitigt.* ("Temporality is not, rather temporalizes itself. Temporality temporalizes.") (*SZ* 328; cf. *KM* 170, *WG* 46)

'Peripheral' Tautologies

- *Das Fragen dieser Frage ist...bestimmt von...* ("The questioning of this question is determined by...") (*SZ* 7)
- *Wovor die Angst sich angstet ... wovor die Furcht sich furchtet.* ("Before which anxiety is anxious... before which fear is fearful") (*SZ* 186)
- *Diese Einheit einigt.* ("The unity unites.") (*KM* 59; cf. *WG* 16 etc)
- *Diese 'Moglichkeit,' die das 'moglicherweise' allererst ermoglicht.* ("This 'possible-ness' that first makes possible the 'possibly.'") (*KM* 109; similar in *SZ*)
- *Die Weise, gemass der diese Vorstellung vorstellen.* ("The way in which this representation represents.") (*KM* 130)
- *Dergleichen wie eine regelnde Regel.* ("The same as a ruling rule.") (*KM* 141)

In the first group there is an inseparable unity between subject and verb, object and activity carrying an internal, reflexive sense – they are *sich selbst vollziehend* [in themselves self-actuating], rhetorical examples of an 'accusative of internal adjective' that results in an intensity and compactness of the thought-structure. As Schoeffer says, "In general, expressing an activity, they do in the verb exactly that which they themselves already are, they actuate themselves. The object is in the most originary way active, between it and the doing nothing can be inserted, no difference exists" (Schoeffer, 208). In other words, a 'genuine' tautology involves the strong claim that the meaning conveyed by the formula cannot be expressed, explained or grounded in any other way. As Heidegger says – and, says Schoeffer, the similarity to Spinoza's *per se concipitur* ('conceived through itself') is striking: "*Welt west, indem sie weltet. Dies sagt: das Welten von Welt ist weder durch anderes erklarbar noch aus anderem ergrundbar*" ("The world is in that it worlds. This says: the worlding of the world can neither be explained by means of something else, nor can it be grounded in something else" (Heidegger, 1975c, 178/179-180; Schoeffer, 208). Or again: "Also concerning temporality and the Nothing, fundamentally no other propositions can be made about them other than those brought to pass in a self-actualizing way [*entelechierartig*] in their own essenc-ing, which is their own activity" (Schoeffer, 209). In the second group, the 'peripheral' tautology, on the other hand, the activity represented by the verb can be expressed in another, non-tautological way without sacrifice of meaning (Schoeffer, 207-208). Thus, for example, with tautological-appearing expressions like "*die Frage fragt, die Moglichkeit (er)moglicht, die Regel regelt*" ("the question questions, the possibility makes possible, the rule rules"), Schoeffer notes,"one can replace the verb in them with others evidently without any loss in understanding the statement: thus "*die Frage sucht zu ergrunden, die Moglichkeit erlaubt, die Regel ordnet*" ("the question seeks to establish, the possibility permits, the rule orders" (Schoeffer, 208).

The reference to the unity of *Sprache* and *Sache* in a tautological 'proposition' in contra-distinction to the 'is' structure of subject-predicate proposition (Satz) in which the two are 'split' (*Zerlegung*), and in particular the difference between a tautology and the identity statement 'A is A,' points to a broader problem, one which Benavides also highlighted and one that applies to Heidegger as well. The question is this: Does language dictate limits to thinking, and if so to what extent? The matter concerns "How far, namely, the subject-predicate structure, the propositional structure of the Indo-European sentence, determines the nature of Western thinking, in general how narrow or wide are the limits of thinking stuck in the nature of linguistic predication." The issue traces to the difference between subject and predicate caused by the 'is' which lies at the basis of every proposition, a"clear, thoroughgoing distinction in West European languages" (Schoeffer, 210, cf. 212-213). The problematic of the 'is' structure of the subject-predicate sentence is one Heidegger tries to address by way of various linguistic strategems: "Heidegger's refusal to define, his use of images to express that which is essential, his resort to 'sayings,' to the essential 'names' [of Being], his use of variations of verbs in the group '*wesen, walten, wahren*' [to be, to prevail, to preserve] his thinking by way of questioning and negations – all are ways to avoid the implications of normal predication and nevertheless: to 'say'" (Schoeffer, 212). In other words, the question which his turn to the figura etymologica addresses is, says Heidegger, "whether the nature [*Wesen*] of Western languages in itself is stamped only by metaphysics and thus finally by 'onto-theo-logic,' or whether these languages preserve other possibilities of saying and that means at the same time a 'saying' that is 'not saying' [*sagenden Nichtsagens*]" (Heidegger, 1960b, 72/66; Schoeffer, 212-213).

It is here that an intriguing new possibility enters the pictures, for among Heidegger's attempts to avoid the implications of the subject-predicate 'is' structure of the Western propositional form is his tentative exploration of the possibilities for thinking found in Asian language structures and intellectual traditions. That 'clear, thorough-going distinction' between subject and predicate in the 'is' structure of Western languages contrasts with "its hiddenness, no, its non-existence in Chinese" (Schoeffer, 210-211). As Schoeffer notes, "In the form of his own thinking [*Form seines eigenen Denken*] the philosopher detects the inexorable effect of the fixed and yet not fixed imperative of the form of language [*Sprachform*]. Not surprising, therefore, is Heidegger's ever clearer growing 'interest' in the thinking of the East carried out in a totally different form of language" (Schoeffer, 213). Heidegger's 'interest' in the thinking of the 'East,' motivated by his attempt to avoid the limits imposed upon thinking (of) Being by the 'is' structure of propositions, thus not only resonates with Spinoza's pantheism and German mystical thought (Eckhart, Cusanus) with its Neoplatonic background, but also with Chinese Taoism and Indian Buddhist traditions that draw on Nagarjuna and Madhyamika thought.

Heidegger's Meta-Statements on Tautology. In the light of these studies by Benavides and Schoeffer on the nature and function of tautology Heidegger's meta-statements on tautology in the Zähringen Seminar of 1973 become intelligible:

- why for a long time he was 'ensnared' by the tautological saying of being by Parmenides
- what he meant by a 'genuine' tautology
- in what sense tautology "names the Same only once, and indeed as itself."
- why he came to think tautology was distinctive of 'thinking'
- why tautology could 'think' what 'dialectic' could not
- why tautology was thus the 'primordial' sense of 'phenomenology'

Why did Heidegger arrive at the view that tautology, not questioning, was what thinking (of) Being called for? Clearly he came to think that the fundamental 'attitude' of thinking was not one of *interrogating* but rather of *responding* to the 'call' of Being. As Richardson surmised, in Heidegger's later work he seemed to have rejected the formula of thinking-as-questioning in favor of thinking-as-attending to the 'appeal' of Being. Interrogating was subordinated to attending-responding as one of but not the most basic of thinking's functions, for even in thinking-as-questioning, the 'call' of Being held primacy for Heidegger (Richardson, 617). Thus it was thinking-as-tautology as the 'saying (of) Being' that came to assume the central place of prominence. It was in the 'same-saying' of tautology, as both Benavides and Schoeffer showed, that the task of thought – to bring the primordial relation of Being and language to phenomenological fulfillment [*Vollzug*] – was accomplished in the most extreme and compressed way possible, something which the statements of metaphysics, determined by the 'is' structure of traditional philosophical discourse, even that of Hegelian dialectic, were ill-equipped to do.

Thus for Heidegger the tautology of tautologies proved to be a restatement of the 'saying' of one of the earliest Greek, pre-Socratic thinkers, Parmenides: *'esti gar einai,'* 'Being namely is.' From Heidegger's tautologies of 'world,' *"Welt ist nie sondern weltet."* ("World is not, it worlds."), and *"Welt west indem sie weltet."* ("World is in that it worlds.") one can extrapolate the tautologies that 'answer' his earliest and enduring preoccupation as a thinker, the question of the meaning of Being. They alone express what is 'the only possibility for thinking'– the thinking and saying (of) Being: *"Das Sein ist nicht sondern west."* ("Being is not but be's.)" "Historically, only one saying (*Sage*) belongs to the matter of thinking. It lets Being ... be" (Heidegger, 1998a, 111/236). Thinking-as-tautology *is* thinking (of) Being.

Thinking as Thanking

If thinking-as-tautology is a response to the 'call' of Being on the level of linguistic structure, another 'answer to' takes place on an existential level – thinking as a form of thanking (*Denken als Danken*) – thinking as gratitude for the 'gift' of Being, for *'es gibt Sein,'* the primordial fact that there are beings rather than nothing. Thanking is the form thinking takes when thinking Being as gift. If tautology is thinking reduced to near speechlessness in wonder at the mystery of Being, 'saying nothing' in an attempt to 'say everything,' thinking as thanking is humility, *Gelassenheit*, not a mastering but a letting-be of Being as the 'giving' that lets beings be. Thanking is the fundamental 'attitude' of thinking as submission to Being, letting Being be itself as the Being of beings (cf. Richardson, 21, 480, 601-2, 604).

But what exactly does it mean to say thanking is a kind of *thinking*? Thinking is an intellectual activity, e.g. questioning, an epistemological effort to learn the truth of something. Thanking on the other hand, is an expressive or performative act, a *doing* what the word *says*: to *say* thank you *is* to thank, to *express* gratitude. Thinking is also a doing, but saying the word 'think' is not thereby to think. Does Heidegger mean something different by 'thanking' than what is ordinarily meant, something that makes it into a species of 'thinking'?

What Heidegger means by 'thinking.'

Thinking. says Heidegger, is usually conceived of as a metaphysical search for grounds or an instrumental rationality, a teleological or utilitarian relation of means and ends. But if thinking is not that sort of cognitive activity, what is it? It is, says Heidegger, a 'thoughtful' encounter with the mystery of Being. It is thinking 'called' to think that which 'be's' without grounds – without why. As he says: "Insofar as Being is, it itself has no ground. Yet this is not so because it is self-grounded, but rather because every form of grounding, even and precisely that which occurs through itself, remains inappropriate to Being as ground." Thinking is thus a thinking that lets Being be. It is a response to the 'call' of Being: *"Es ist, insofern Sein west"* ("It is insofar as Being be's") (Heidegger, 1975e, 325/40; Richardson, 602). Thinking exists only because of, and in response to, the mystery that there are beings rather than nothing.

Further, thinking is central to Dasein's being. As we recall, the question of Being puts Dasein's own being in question. In other words, this kind of thinking goes to the heart of Dasein's own existence: "[T]he essence of man rests in thinking the truth of Being" (Heidegger, 1975e, 343/58). As inherent in the essence of Dasein (Heidegger's existentialist version of Descartes' "I am a thing which thinks"), thinking (of) Being is the '*structural*' side of the 'double aspect of thought': it corresponds to the structure of Dasein as 'ek-sistenz,' as a standing-out in the 'truth' (*a-letheia*) or 'openness' ('unhiddenness,' *Unverborgenheit*) of Being (cf. Richardson, 525, 600, 602). Thinking lies at the center, the 'heart' of Dasein as an 'ec-static' relation to Being. In fact, what Heidegger means by thinking is more akin to feeling or mood than to what usually passes for thinking as metaphysical, teleological or instrumental rationality. Feeling or mood is more 'reasonable,' more intelligently perceptive, because more open to Being than reason in a reduced sense of rationality (Heidegger, 1977b, 150-151; cf. Robbins, 20003; one thinks here of Quentin Smiths' distinction of a 'metaphysics of feeling' from a metaphysics of 'rational meaning' or 'rational meaninglessness.')

Why Being 'calls' for thinking

Being, says Heidegger, 'needs, wants' [*braucht*] us, whereas Dasein, for its part, 'needs, wants' that which 'needs, wants' it in order for both Being to 'be' and Dasein to 'ek-sist.' Being and thinking exist in a structure of 'mutual wanting,' a relation with feeling connotations. "We have the power only for that which we want. But in turn we truly want only that which for its own part wants [*braucht*] us ... insofar as it addresses itself to our essence as that which sustains this essence." Thus, Being comes to Dasein as a 'call' that 'calls for' thinking, a thought-ful response. The 'appeal' of Being, the mystery that there are beings rather than nothing, 'calls forth' thinking, 'e-vokes' [*heisst*] thinking, "sets thought on its way, summoning, commissioning, enjoining, soliciting, at-tracting, laying-claim-upon it" (Heidegger, 1968, 1, 82-83, 97/3-4, 117-119, 150-151; Richardson, 598, 601). How does Being 'call' for, give rise to, thinking? Here Heidegger introduces his central metaphor contained in the expression, '*es gibt Sein*': "What [Being as thought-worthy] grants, the gift it bestows on us, is nothing less than itself" (Heidegger, 1968, 3, 85/4, 120-121; cf. 1998a, 80/285, where Heidegger stresses the basic accord of *es braucht* with *es gibt*). "Being 'grants' to thinking its to-be-thought." In other words, Heidegger now interprets Being's 'wanting' of thinking as a "a giving of Being itself as eminently thought-worthy. In hailing the thinker into Being, Being imparts itself to him as a gift, and this gift is what constitutes the essence of the thinker" – the 'heart' of man (Heidegger, 1968, 1, 86, 92, 97/3-4, 126-127, 139-140, 151; Richardson, 598-599).

In what sense thinking is thanking

Heidegger says, "Thought thinks when it responds to [Being as] the eminently thought-worthy" (Heidegger, 1968, 10/28; cf. Richardson 602). The question is: What makes this responding a *thanking*? Heidegger also says, "*Pure* thanks lies rather in this, that we simply think that which solely and properly is to-be-thought." (Heidegger, 1968, 94/145; cf. 1966, 66-67; 1963, 81, 142; 1998g, 49/236; my emphasis). But does this get us any further? The question remains: *why* is thinking (of) Being a *thanking*? And why does he call thinking (of) Being '*pure*' thanks? We could turn to etymology for help, though etymology can only get us so far, in fact can mislead rather than shed light on the matter. The word 'thinking' (*Denken*) in German derives from *Gedanc*, which suggest both *Denken* and *Danken* (thanking) (cf. Richardson, 599). But does this answer our question as to the use of these terms by Heidegger? We repeat: in what sense can thinking (of) Being be construed as a thanking vis-a-vis Being?

Thinking is a response to Being. What kind of response? A response which lets Being be. But this 'letting be' is a submission to, an acquiescence to, the mystery of Being. As Richardson puts it, "Thinking as thanking consents to ek-sistence through complete acquiescence to Being. Effectively, Dasein, once Being has released it to itself, must reciprocate by releasing itself to Being" (Richardson, 602). This 'release' (*Gelassenheit*, 'letting-be-ness') corresponds to Dasein's *authentic* being, what Heidegger in *SZ* called 're-solve.' Here we encounter the second or 'functional' element in the 'double aspect of thinking': thinking as thanking corresponds to Dasein as re-solve, as 'achieved authenticity' (Heidegger, 1975e, 321/35-36; cf. Richardson, 525, 602, 604).

This equation of thinking as acquiescence with thinking as thanking, thanking in a 'pure' form, needs a bit more explication, however. As Richardson elaborates: "Being's supreme gift to the thinker is the very Being by which he is a thinker: ek-sistence. Does it not warrant acknowledgment on man's part? Such an acknowledgment in its purity, however, is not in the first place a requiting of this gift with another gift. On the contrary, the purest form of acknowledgment is simply the accepting of the gift, i.e., assuming it, acquiescing in it, yielding to its demands. Acceptance, then, is the most original form of thanks." Dasein "accepts the gift of thought as such. For Dasein to accept thought as thought is to do what lies within its power to accomplish thought. This is by that very fact the fulfillment of thinking. Thinking thus conceived in the moment of fulfillment is clearly thanks-giving" (Richardson, 601, commenting on Heidegger's notion of thinking as thanking in *Was Heisst Denken?*). In other words, Richardson concludes, "This liberated, liberating self-surrender of Dasein to Being as it comes-to-pass in the event of truth is more than simply a response to Being's appeal, it is a profound and total gesture of gratitude – the only fitting one – for the marvelous bounty. Thought thus understood becomes the wellspring of all gratitude in man. To think in foundational [*wesentlich*, 'originary'] fashion, then, is to thank: in both cases, Dasein accepts; Dasein reciprocates" (Richardson, 480; cf. Heidegger, 1998g, 49-51/236-237; cf. 1963, 81, 142).

Thus thinking (of) Being as a 'thanking' of Being takes the form of gratitude for the fact that there are beings rather than nothing, while its 'purity' lies in its *Gelassenheit*, its letting Being and beings be – its rejection of attempts to master the mystery, instead the 'simplicity' of its acceptance of the gift of Being. The mystery and gift of Being are preserved and protected in the purity of this grateful re-solve. As Heidegger says, "Man can [preserve the truth of Being] only through the re-solve of Dasein" (Heidegger, 1975e, 321/ 36; cf. Richardson 598-599).

Thanking as an Aesthetic Response to the Gift of Being

In *Was Heisst Denken?*, a book in which Heidegger introduced the notion of thinking-as-thanking (*Denken als Danken*) that he considered central to his thinking (of) Being, he writes: "Joyful things, too, and beautiful and mysterious and gracious things, give us food for thought... if only we do not reject the gift by regarding everything that is joyful, beautiful and gracious as the kind of thing which should be left to feeling and experience, and kept out of the winds of thought" (Heidegger, 1968, 31, cited in Robbins, 2003). The feeling or mood most attuned to things that are 'beautiful, mysterious, and gracious' is joy, the joyful affirmation of what Heidegger calls the 'play' or 'dance' of Being. One is reminded of Nietzsche for whom the world is seen as a manifestation of beauty, the playful, artistic, joyous gift of the overflowing creativity Being itself. The 'attunement' or mood of thinking (of) Being is an originary joy. Thus thinking as thanking is joyful thinking in response to the gift of Being. True, in *SZ* as Rubenstein showed, Heidegger depicts fundamental thinking is *zunachst und zumeist* (first and usually) anxiety, an awe-ful dread (*Scheu, Furcht*) in the face of the "abyss" of Being. But the other 'side' of anxiety is joy. In joy, Being is received in its plenitude as gift – the *es gibt Sein* that 'gives' when, in its fearful face as the Nothing, it 'withdraws' in the 'giving' of beings. Where anxiety recoils in shock and terror at the abyss of Being, joy is a gracious acceptance and thanking (*Danken*) for the favor (*Huld*) and grace (*Gunst*) that Being has 'bestowed' upon Dasein by 'giving' itself as the fundamental *Sache* (matter) for thinking. In joy, thinking becomes a gracious thanking that requires no explanations arising from a need to fill a lack, from a desire for answers as to the 'ground' of Being. In the gracious thanking of joyful thinking Being *west* ('be's') as its own ground, without why.

Thinking-as-thanking submits itself to the gratuitousness of the gift of Being, given without why, unearned and without recompense, costing nothing, unwarranted, without cause or purpose. Gratified by the gratuitous grace of Being, thinking-thanking perceives the 'beauty' of the gift of Being. In acknowledging the beautiful gracefulness of Being, thinking-as-thanking also recognizes its 'goodness.' Not only the source of joy (derived from the Latin *gaudium*, source also of grace and gratitude), Being is also the ultimately 'bountiful' (derived from the Latin *bonus*, 'good,' from which is also derived 'beatific'). In the midst of the 'play' and 'dance' of Being, thinking-as-thanking is 'beatified,' made supremely happy, in receiving the 'goodness' of Being's 'bounty' 'given' freely and liberally by the 'generosity' of the *'es gibt Sein.'* In the beatific abundance and goodness of the grace of Being, in the midst of the play and dance of the truth of Being, thinking-as-thanking is joyfully fulfilled. And yet Being withdraws from being fully understood – it remains mysterious. When thinking-as-thanking seeks an explanation for the disclosure of Being, the *'es gibt Sein'* withdraws once again, and wonder gives over once again to mere curiosity. Thinking-as-thanking in the aesthetic mode of pure joy at the gift of Being is again covered over, and what is called thinking 'falls back' into the 'inauthentic' thinking of metaphysics and, ultimately, technology.

Thanking as a Moral Response to the Gift of Being

There is another 'felt' mode of thinking-as-thanking, namely, thinking as an ethical response to the gift of Being. Witherall described the theistic interpretation of this moral response as an ethics of gratitude for the love of God. In reprising his remarks, we will try to recast them, so far as possible, in terms that fit Heidegger's decidedly non-theistic understanding of Being. How can thinking-as-thanking elicit a moral response to the 'gift' of Being? How can it be interpreted as an ethic of gratitude, even of love?

Thinking (of) Being as Originary Ethics. Before turning to Witherall's analysis for concrete suggestions, let us first look for clues in Heidegger's remarks on 'originary ethics' in his *Humanismusbrief.* Though he does not directly address the content of that 'ethics,' Heidegger does provide some hints as to its nature and 'origin.' His concern is to locate that 'ethics,' if not identify it as, a way of 'dwelling' vis-a-vis the mystery of Being. The Greek word *ethos* is usually translated as "the character of a culture, era, community, institution, or individual revealed in its attitudes, aspirations, customs, values and belief" (OED). But Heidegger re-interprets *ethos* as the 'abode' where such attitudes are 'housed': "*Ethos* means abode, dwelling place." What in *SZ* Heidegger spoke of as Dasein's *In-sein*, 'being-in' the world, he here calls the *ethos* or 'dwelling' that characterizes the 'essence' of man's be-ing (*SZ/BT* 53ff/79ff): "The word names the open region in which man dwells. The open region of his abode allows what pertains to man's essence, and what in thus arriving resides in nearness to him, to appear. The abode of man contains and preserves the advent of what belongs to man in his essence" (Heidegger, 1998a, 106/269). What is that 'open region' that 'approaches' and 'belongs' to Da-sein's 'essence'? What is the 'essence' of man as Da-Sein? The '*Da*' of *Sein*, the 'open region,' the disclosure, the un-hiddenness, the presence, the thinking (of) Being. But this thinking (of) Being is *ethics* itself: "If the name 'ethics', in keeping with the basic meaning of the word *ethos*, should now say that 'ethics' ponders the abode [*Aufenhalt, dwelling*] of man, then that thinking which thinks the truth of Being as the primordial element [*essence*] of man, as one who eksists, is in itself the original ethics" [*ursprungliche*, 'originary' ethics] (Heidegger, 1998a, 109/ 271).

For Heidegger it is a 'saying' of another pre-Socratic thinker that "preserves the ethos more primordially than Aristotle's lectures on 'ethics.'

A saying of Heraclitus which consists on only three words says something so simply that from it the essence of the *ethos* immediately comes to light... *ethos anthropoi daimon*." Heidegger provides three translations. First, the 'usual' translation: "A man's *character* is his daimon." Then a second, half-literal, half-Heideggerian one: "Man *dwells*, insofar as he is man, in the *nearness* of god." Then a third, fully Heideggerian translation/interpretation: "The (familiar) *abode* is for man the *open region* of the *presencing* of god (the unfamiliar one)" (Heidegger, 1998a, 109/271; italics mine, to call attention to the shift from the usual reading to the Heideggerian re-reading). To emphasize the contrast between the 'familiar' ('usual,' *zunachst und zumeist;*) and the 'unfamiliar' (revelatory) dimension of the disclosure of Being to mortal man, Heidegger refers to Aristotle's report of another 'saying' of Heraclitus, one that upends our understanding of the usual, quotidian practices of life and casts them in an entirely different, unexpected light. Some foreign visitors come to see Heraclitus in his humble, sparse abode. They expect to see the famous thinker deep in profound thoughts, hoping to engage him in entertaining conversation, perhaps to extract from him some words of wisdom. Instead they find the shivering thinker in the poverty of his life warming himself at his stove, 'a common and insignificant place.' Disappointed, they are about to leave. Sensing their 'frustrated curiosity,' "the failure of an expected sensation to materialize," Heraclitus invites them in, saying:"*Einai gar kai entautha theous*, 'Here too the gods are present'" (Heidegger, 1998a, 108/270). Heidegger comments: "This phrase places the abode (*ethos*) of the thinker and his deed in another light. Whether the visitors understand this phrase at once–or at all–and then saw everything differently in this other light the story does not say." The *ethos*, "the atmosphere surrounding the thinker." casts everything familiar, everything everyday and taken for granted, into another, unfamiliar and thought-provoking light – the light of *theous*, 'the gods' – or in Heidegger's metaphorical interpretation, the 'open region' of the 'presencing' of Being itself.

For Heidegger, therefore, 'originary ethics' is understood as the 'originary' *transformation* of what it means to be human, to be the '*Da*' of 'Sein,' the 'place' where the 'event' (*Ereignis*), the 'advent' of Being, occurs, the *topos* where the thinking (of) the revelation (of) Being *ereignet*, comes to pass. But what more can we say about this *ethos*, this thinking-as-the-'ethics' (of) Being? To answer this question Heidegger resorts not just to poetic metaphor but to language that is 'religious' in its associations. The world of 'the gods,' the world of wonder, *thaumadzein*, vis-a-vis Being, wears a duplicitous face. Thinking the mystery of Being invokes at once and ineluctably both terror [*Erschrecken*] and awe [*Scheu*]. The thinking (of) Being as 'originary ethics' confronts Dasein with both healing [*Heil*] and evil [*Unheil*]: "Being itself is what is contested. To healing [*Heil*] Being first grants ascent into grace [*Huld*]; to raging [*Grimm*] its compulsion to malignancy [*Unheil*]" (Heidegger, 1998a, 114/273). The 'grant', the 'gift' of Being is a double-edged sword: beyond mere moral 'good and bad,' it reveals the 'originary' *ethos* of 'good and evil' – of being and nihilation.

Thinking-as-thanking, as gratitude for the gift of Being, is an ultimate affirmation in the face of Being as the source of both healing and malignancy, being and non-being. It embraces Being in both its truth (unhiddenness) and its untruth (hiddenness). "Every affirmation [*Bejahung*] consists in acknowledgment [*Anerkennen*]. It lets that toward which it goes come toward it." Only in that way can thinking move from 'originary ethics' to the ethics of *nomos*, the morality of law and reciprocal obligation (Heidegger, 1998a, 112, 114-115/272, 274). Heidegger thus answers Socrates' challenge to Euthyphro: "Do the gods love piety because it is pious, or is piety pious because the gods love it?" Is ethics grounded in religion, or is religion just ethics writ large? Clearly for Heidegger it is 'the gods,' that is, Being, 'originary ethics,' which takes precedence and ethics in the traditional sense which follows. But how are we to understand and to express this 'originary ethics' if we cannot consult our moral intuitions, the guidelines of long-established ethics? Heidegger imagines his questioner asking: "Whence does thinking take its measure? What law governs its deed?" His answer: It is the law that governs Being itself, the 'law' of thought-full 'dwelling' in the 'house' of Being "through the humbleness of its inconsequential accomplishment. In all this it as if nothing at all happens through thoughtful saying." The 'law' that 'governs' Being is the 'law' of thinking that lets Being be. What 'law' is that? The 'law' of tautology, of 'saying the same': Being be's.

Originary Ethics as Gratitude for the Gift of Being. Originary ethics is thinking (of) Being. But thinking (of) Being is also a thanking: *Denken als Danken.* Then originary ethics must also be a thanking, gratitude for the gift of Being. Originary ethics is not ordinary ethics, it is prior to that, 'primordial,' 'older,' more 'origin-al' than that, that which 'origin-ates,' gives rise to, ethics in the ordinary sense and provides it with its 'measure,' its 'law.' It is that which characterizes the 'essence' of Dasein's 'dwelling,' its 'being-in' the world, its 'comportment' [*Verhaltung. Einstellung*] toward the world, its fundamental (*ursprunglich*, 'originary') orientation or attitude toward Being. What is the nature of that orientation or attitude, that gratitude for the beings that 'be'? What is the specific content of that 'originary thanking'? To return to the question posed above: How can thinking-as-thanking evoke a *moral* response to Being? Heidegger never fully develops an answer to this question, though remarks in *SZ* provide a hint, perhaps enough to expand upon with the help of Witherall's remarks on the ethics of gratitude as a response to the gift of Being.

Heidegger on Sorge (care). In *SZ*, as noted earlier, Heidegger describes the structure of Dasein's being-in-the-world as that of 'care' (*Sorge*), a word on which he rings a series of changes, describing the various forms which care can take, in particular *Besorgnis* (concern) and *Fursorge* (solicitude), of which the latter, along with the root-word itself, are the most important. It is tempting to take these in an 'ontically' concrete and positive sense, *Sorge* as 'caring' for in the sense of feeling affection for, rather than in the more 'negative' connotation of the dictionary sense of anxious worry about or taking care of. Likewise one would like to take *Fursorge* in the emotionally more positive sense of being concerned for someone, rather than in the more 'negative' dictionary sense of looking out for someone's 'welfare' in a social-welfare sense. But Heidegger wants to redeploy these terms in an emotionally neutral sense to denote the phenomenological 'structure' of Dasein's being-in the world. True, he draws on the *Umgangsprache* meanings of the words to give them 'existential' resonance in keeping with his analysis of *Angst* as the basic orientation or attitude of Dasein's *being-in* the world. But despite the provenance of these phenomena in the Christian anthropology of Augustine, Luther and Kierkegaard, which he refers to in a footnote (*SZ* 190/*BT* 492 n.4), he clearly means to put them to a rather different use in the context of an 'ontological' analysis of Dasein's relation to Being. If we are to understand how Dasein's 'dwelling' in the world can be understood as an 'originary ethics,' as gratitude for the gift of Being, in a manner consistent with Heidegger's non-theistic understanding of Being, it is necessary to look elsewhere.

Witherall on Gratitude for the Gift. Thinking (of) Being in tautologous terms does not entirely answer the question of the meaning of being. Nor does the metaphor of 'gift' necessarily answer the question. One may fail to hear the 'call' of Being that "awakes to the wonder" evoked by the question of the meaning of Being. Or one may be disoriented by the ambivalent nature of the 'strange wonder' of Being. And yet the gift of Being is 'an offer one cannot refuse,' one, as Hick said, we cannot refuse existentially. Yet we can do so epistemologically – or, for importantly for the current discussion, morally. It is an invitation and a choice to respond to existence in a certain way, a way expressed as gratitude for a gift.

But even if one does choose the 'pattern of meaning' to be dwelling in gratitude, one cannot escape the weight of that choice or the anxiety that goes with it. It may be true we do not choose to exist, but we are free to choose to respond to Being as a gift. That acceptance involves a leap into the Nothing, the shadow side of Being; affirmation of the gift of Being is an act of abyssal freedom. The gift of Being asks not for a security blanket in the form of a metaphysical explanation, it asks, like all moral dilemmas, for a response, an affirmation, a 'Yes' – the choice to let Being 'be' and "to appreciate it as such" (Witherall, 133). Witherall: "In moments of despair, when we call out 'Why is there a world?' the answer is forthcoming: this world is our gift. We can use it or neglect it, but it remains true that it is given to us. If we are stunned by the realization that the world is spectacularly gratuitous, then we have at least come to a final point. If all that we can see are 'mere things,' things which we take for granted, we should reflect that existence is given to, and responds to this as a gift.... the final significance of the gift lies in the way that we appreciate it" (Witherall, 155-156).

But how is one to assess the 'significance, the 'truth' of such a response? Perhaps the primary criterion is the way of life to which that choice, that comportment or attitude leads. As Witherall observed, the 'metaphorical /metaphysical' structure of the gift of Being "is reflected in fundamental attitudes more than fundamental doctrines." And basic among these attitudes is gratitude, thankfulness, for the gift of Being. "The metaphor becomes a pattern of meaning into which we may fit ourselves" (Witherall, 146,153) – a 'pattern of meaning,' that is, *a way of being,* what Heidegger calls *dwelling.* The logic is circular, but it is a hermeneutical one, a 'virtuous' circle. Heidegger is never specific about the moral particulars of a dwelling that "lets Being be," but it needs to be asked, what is the way of 'seeing' and 'being' that issues from gratitude for the gift of Being? It must be, as Witherall says, "an interpretation of the gift of Being that expresses our fundamental attitude toward being-in-the-world. A truly satisfactory response to the question is a response which comes from the whole of life" (Witherall, 146). In other words, it must unite the intellectual and emotional, the thinking and thanking aspects of our life. The 'measure' of the 'truth' of such a choice will be its relationship to both the question of the meaning of Being and the question of the meaning of our own existence. If we choose to live a life of gratitude for the gift of Being, the truth of our life will be measured by our faithfulness to that choice, by the embodiment in our way of dwelling of the values that flow from that attitude, that perspective.

There an interesting double-entendre in the hackneyed phrase 'taking things for granted.' What does it mean to take 'things' for 'granted'? Heidegger says *es gibt Sein*, Being gives itself to beings, Being lets beings be. In other words, Being *grants* them their being. Then to take things for 'granted' is precisely *not* to see them in the 'usual,' 'normal,' 'everyday' way (*zunachst und zumeist*) but rather to see them in a new light, in the 'light' of Being as the miraculous 'things' they are, as embodiments of the ever-fresh, ever-new mystery of Being itself. As Witherall says, "The idea that there are 'mere things' is an illusion. Each immanent thing is a gift, it is something miraculous, if only for its existence. The idea is that we should respond to the world of beings with respect, with love and gratitude, and with a sense of the hidden meanings that lurk in the obscurity of the everyday" (Witherall, 155). Gratitude is what gives value to a moral way of being-in and being-toward beings, toward the 'things' of this world, a way of dwelling that is lived in accord with that respect and love. What gives beings their meaning? The gift of Being. Why does Being give itself to beings? Being 'gives itself' to beings because that is what 'Being' means. Being 'lets' beings be. Being is 'why' there are beings rather than nothing. It is a tautology, a *figura etymologica*. It is the way Being 'speaks' to us. Thanking, gratitude, love for beings is the way we 'answer' the gift of Being.

Concluding Remarks

Before we turn to Asian thinking on Being and Nothing, let us recap Heidegger's 'answer' to the question of the meaning of Being, his thinking (of) Being as encapsulated in the thought-provoking formulae: 'Es gibt Sein' and 'Being:Nothing:The Same.'

Es gibt Sein

To begin with, Heidegger was not asking Leibniz's question, "Why is there something rather than nothing?" he was asking "Why are there beings rather than nothing?" Being is always the Being *of beings*, not the Being of *something* rather than nothing. Why does he reject Leibniz's formulation? Because of its *theological* implications, as if the 'nothing' referred to by Leibniz was an *absolute* nothing to which the *absolute* being of God could be counter-posed. And yet, as a comparison with Asian thinking will make clear, Heidegger's language, his thinking, must nevertheless, at first glance, be seen against the background of that theological doctrine, was itself not possible apart from its contestation with a onto-theo-logical thinking not only indebted to Greek metaphysics but also steeped in the symbolic resonances of theistic traditions of the West (cf. *SZ*, n. iv, 190, n. vii, 199/BT, 492 n.4, n. 7). Thinking of Being as that which 'lets beings be' against the background of 'the Nothing' could be seen as a *re-thinking* of the motif of 'Creation *ex nihilo*' (the 'gift of Being'). Certainly theologians have been quick to think it so. By counter-posing the notion of 'nothing' to 'beings' rather than 'something,' however, Heidegger signals that, unlike the theological doctrine, this 'Nothing' is *relative*, that is, it is not an absolute counter-concept to, say, God's Being, but is no other than Being itself: Being:Nothing:The Same.

The question he was faced with, therefore, was "What is the *be-ing* of beings and how can we speak of it in 'relation' to (the) nothing?" In other words, he was not asking about the 'being' (the nature, essence, the 'what') of beings, as metaphysics and science do, to set beings up for manipulation by technology. Rather he was asking about the *be-ing* of beings, the *be-ing* of beings as that which *west, ereignet,* 'happens.' For Heidegger Being was not simply the (static) 'fact' that 'there are' beings or 'there is' (*es gibt*) Being. Rather he heard in the '*gibt*' an active, verbal sense of a 'giving', an ongoing temporal bestow-ing of the *be-ing* of beings. His thinking of Being is therefore neither 'ontology' in the Greek metaphysical sense, nor 'ontology' in a religiously-inflected sense. It is not a new species of 'onto-theo-logical' thinking. It is rather, in an entirely novel sense, a radical 'cosmology' of Being, featuring radical ideas of the 'world' as that which '*weltet*' and 'eternity' as the 'temporality' that '*sich zeitigt*,' a "primordial temporality which is 'infinite'" (*SZ*, 427 n. xiii/ *BT*, 499 n. 13).

His thinking of Being thus goes 'beyond theism and atheism,' that is, beyond not only the concept of Being in metaphysics but also the concept of Being in religious or mystical thought. It might seem similar to the concept of Being in Tillich. Tillich said that it was as 'atheistic' to say that God 'exists' as it was to deny God's existence. He talked instead of the God 'beyond the God of theism.' And yet Heidegger's thinking of Being is more radical still insofar as for Tillich, unlike for Heidegger, Being is still conceived as the ontological ultimate that 'overcomes' Non-being, that takes Non-being into itself, thus reprising the metaphysical and religio-mystical traditions of thinking of Being that characterize the 'onto-the-logical' thinking of Being in the West. In other words, for Heidegger the Nothing is not the counter-concept of *Being* (as we will see in Asian philosophy). Rather the Nothing, as the 'veil' of Being is the counter-concept to *beings*. Both Being and Nothing are 'the Same' in relation to *beings*.

Being:Nothing:The Same

What about that tautological formula, 'Being:Nothing:The Same'? What does Heidegger mean when he says Being and the Nothing are 'the Same'? How is it related to his other 'originary' pairs: Dasein and Being, Being and beings, or Thinking and Being? Heidegger elaborates upon his tautological formula, by way of commenting on Parmenides, fragment 5: *to gar auto noein estin te kai einai* (Heidegger, 1968, 146-149/ 241-244). The usual translation, he says, runs: "for it is the same thing to think and to be." What about *to auto*, 'the same'? 'Same,' says Heidegger, however, does not mean, as we might first think, 'exactly alike,' 'indistinguisable,' in short: 'identical.' In Greek 'identical' is *homoion,* not *auto.* Being and thinking are 'the same' but not 'identical'; they are different. But, Heidegger then enigmatically says, "it is just in their difference that they do belong together" (Heidegger, 1968, 147/241). Then is the 'relation' of Being and Nothing, of thinking and being, 'dialectical,' one of 'synthesis', or is it some third thing, something more primary, more originary? In fragment 8 Parmenides says: "for not separately, apart from being, can you find thinking" *(ou gar aneu tou eontos henrseis to noein).* In other words, they 'belong together.' Says Heidegger: "They belong together in this way, that the essential nature of *noein*, named first, consists in its remaining focused on the presence of that is present. *Eon*, the presence of what is present, accordingly keeps and guards *noein* within itself as what belongs to it. Let us note well – *eon emmenai*, the presence of what is present, and not what is present as such and not Being as such, nor both added together in a synthesis, but: their duality, emerging from their unity kept hidden." (Heidegger, 1968, 148/241- 242). He then adds significantly, what will prove to be of telling importance when we turn to Asian thinking: "And another thing, however, is clear: the saying *to gar auto noein estin te kai einai* becomes the basic theme of all of Western-European thinking – the *eon emmenai*, the presence of what is present, the duality of what the *one* word, the participle of participles, the word *eon* designates: what is present in presence" *(*Heidegger, 1968, 148/242- 243). Thus, "Thinking," in Heidegger's specific use of the term, "is thinking only when it recalls in thought the *eon*, That which the word indicates properly and truly, that is, unspoken tacitly. And that is the duality of being and Beings" – what we have referred to earlier, in a nod to Asian thinking, can now be seen to constitute the *non-dual duality* of thinking and being. Non-dual duality is the nature of 'the Same', non-dual duality points to the *Way* (*Weg*) in which Being and the Nothing 'belong together.' The 'Same' of Being and Nothing, of Parmenides' being and thinking, "is what properly gives food for thought. And what is so given, is the gift of what is most worthy of question" (Heidegger, 1968, 149/244).

Looking ahead to the relation of Heidegger's thinking of Being, as captured in the formula 'Being:Nothing:The Same' – its similarity and/ or difference to Asian thinking of Being and Nothing – several things are clear: for Heidegger Being is always the Being of beings: without beings there is no Being and vice versa, without Being, no beings; and, without thinking, Being cannot 'be.' Being needs (*braucht*) Dasein and vice versa. The essence of thinking is the revealing/concealing of Being. Being 'is' only as disclosed to Dasein, only as brought to language in the thinking (of) Being. Not only is there no Being without beings, there is not ontological difference between the two apart from thinking, apart from the Da of Sein. Further, though Being and Nothing are 'the Same,' though they 'belong together,' the ontological difference between Being and beings, as disclosed by the Nothing, remains. Finally, contra Levinas, there is no indeterminate 'something' beyond being and nothing, beyond being and thinking.

Thinking of Being

Turning from Being to Heidegger's *thinking* of Being, for Heidegger, answering the *question* of Being means thinking the *mystery* of Being. The 'answer' to the question, 'Why are there beings rather than nothing?' takes the form of a tautology, a same-saying: 'because' Being *be*'s. Thinking the mystery of Being in turns leads to, or rather *is, thanking* for the *gift* of Being. For Heidegger thinking – whether the thinking of the philosopher, the theologian, the poet, the artist, the historian, even the scientist – is (or should be) an act of thanking. If it is not a form of thanking, then it is not a form of thinking. It is an undermining, a demeaning, a perversion of thinking. Heidegger has been criticized for not having developed 'an ethic.' This is true. His defense is that every great thinker only thinks one thing. That may or may not be true. In his case, at least, that 'one thing' was the question of Being. This single-mindedness does not mean, however, as we have seen with Witherall, that one cannot develop a moral attitude, a way of being in the world, from out of that thinking (of) Being. As has been argued, Heidegger's answer to the question of the meaning of Being – the truth of the tautology that Being 'be's – can be joined with the beauty of joy in the beings that Being 'lets' be and an ethics of gratitude for the beings that Being 'gives' to be. Such thinking is thus not only an act of *piety* that 'guards' and 'shelters' Being but also an *ethos* ('originary ethics') of being-in-the-world as care (*Sorge*), love and compassion. *Denken als Danken* is the ultimate affirmation (*Bejahung*) of Being, the ultimate *Yes – Yes,* "the most positive word in the English language" (Joyce). *And Molly Bloom said: "yes I said yes I will Yes."*

Arthur Danto's Preface to his study of Nietzsche can with equal justification describe Heidegger's 'strange' thinking of Being as well: "His purpose was to crack the habitual grip on thought in which language holds us, to make us aware of how much our minds are dominated by concepts from which we can hardly escape, given the rules our language follows. Then, realizing the conventional nature of our language, we might try to create fresh concepts and so whole new philosophies... His language would have been less colorful...but then he would not have been the original thinker he was, working through a set of problems which had hardly even been charted before. Small wonder his maps are illustrated, so to speak, with all sorts of monsters and fearful indications and boastful cartographic embellishments." Strange answer. Strange thinking. Wondrous strange.

Critical Remarks

Throughout this study we have been following the thread of a guiding theme: the Why question and the various ways thinkers have tried to answer it. Heidegger in particular brought together the different dimensions – cosmological and ontological, cognitive and existential – put forward by others who wrestled with the question. Heidegger's thinking of Being, however, is not without problems of its own. Critical reflection on his thinking of Being is necessary, therefore, to indicate why, in the next part of our study, we turn to East Asian thinking, in particular the Kyoto School, for help in thinking about the central focus of this study.

Already at the outset we confront two new problems. The first is that Heidegger himself seems to have turned in his later work to East Asian sources, especially Taoist and Zen Buddhist, for help in reformulating his thinking of Being. The point, however, is not to enter into scholarly debates about questions of influence upon Heidegger by East Asian sources or upon East Asian philosophers by Heidegger. It is whether East Asian traditions can provide resources for thinking further about our guiding question: "why is there something rather than nothing?" A second and potentially more serious obstacle is that the focus of East Asian thought traditionally and still today has not been on Being but on something that has been anathema to thinkers in the West from Plato on – the experience and concept of Nothingness. How that phenomenon can be of any help to a Why question formulated in terms of the centrality of Being may prove to be one problem too many.

Whatever the case, we need first to examine the critical issues that remain in Heidegger's thinking of Being. This might suggest alternative ways of interpreting the Why question that might possibly exist in East Asian traditions. Of course the reverse could also be true. The reason why certain positive features of Heidegger's thinking might seem problematic to East Asian thinkers could highlight limitations in their own ways of thinking. If so, it may be that the search for an answer to the Why question will have to be pursued further.

Turning first, therefore, to Heidegger there are several areas in his thinking of Being that seem problematic as a solution to the Why question. These include the formulation of the Why question itself; the concepts of Being, the Nothing, and the ontological difference; the relation of human being/Dasein to Being; and, encapsulating these, what I term his 'existential cosmology.'

The Formulation of the Why Question

We have argued throughout this study that the Why question asks, "Why is there *something* rather than nothing?" Previously we distinguished this formulation from the one preferred by Smith, "Why does the *world-as-a-whole* exist rather than nothing?" We have also contended that the Why question is not the same as Heidegger's formulation, "Why are there *beings* rather than nothing?" Heidegger's posing of the question presupposes the existence of both beings and the world. For Heidegger the question of Being cannot be discussed apart from the Being of *beings*, not the Being of *something tout court. But if so, this means that his thinking of Being does not address the Why question after all.* Should this matter? Perhaps for Heidegger as for Smith this is a distinction without a difference? Or could it be that, in turning to alternative interpretations of the question of Being, both are operating in a reactive mode, namely, against what they perceive as the onto-theological thrust of the Why question in its original formulation by Leibniz? If so, that leaves open whether there is yet another way of understanding the Why question, one that does not bring clouds of theistic glory in its wake, one that poses the question from an standpoint of thinking that does not presuppose a transcendent theistic grounding, pace Leibniz, but that does not resort to a 'deflationary' thinking oriented to beings-as-a-whole or the world-as-a-whole.

We noted one such possibility, Levinas' radical 'anti-ontology' of the *il y a*, a primordial 'nonplace' prior to the difference of being and nothing. The *il y a* generates "the distinction between being and nothingness." And yet, in a manner reminiscent of Plato's Idea of the Good, that primordial 'something' is said to be "'overflow with plentitude' from *beyond* being." This mysterious source of being and nonbeing appears uncannily akin to Heidegger's *Ereignis*, the 'Es' which 'gives' birth to both Being and the

Nothing, a "unity kept hidden" (Heidegger, 1968, 148/242; cf. 1972, 5/6), a 'non-duality' that issues in a duality. *Ereignis* came to displace Being as the central 'guiding word' in Heidegger's evolving thought. As a result the Why question was reformulated once again. It now concerned not the Being of beings but rather "what brings about Being as the givenness or availability of entities? Heidegger's answer to this question was *Ereignis*" (Sheehan, cited in Ma, 2008, 33). In Heidegger's novel usage '*Ereignis*' is not used in its ordinary German meaning as 'event.' Rather, it refers to the *Er-eignis*, the (hidden) 'identity' that "appropriates Being and man to each other, and thereby lets every thing come into its own. What happens [*ereignet*] is Appropriation [*Ereignis*], the primordial relation, the belonging-together of man and Being. This relation, thought by Heidegger under both aspects of identity and difference, is more fundamental than the 'elements' in it. The elements, man and Being, don't constitute the relation; the relation constitutes the elements" (Poggeler, 1987, 67; Stambaugh, 82).

The non-dual nature of Ereignis is That whereby Being and the Nothing 'belong together,' whereby they are 'The Same.' It would seem, in short, that for Heidegger, and *ceteris paribus* for Levinas too, *Ereignis*, the 'nonplace' prior to being and nothing that gives rise to beings, functions like the transcendent Absolute of traditional metaphysics, namely, as the Ground, Source or Origin of beings *beyond* the distinction of being and nonbeing, a 'plenitude' that is itself ungrounded, without a source or origin, without a Why. But if so, then neither Levinas' *il y a* nor Heidegger's *Ereignis* answer the question: *What is the nature of that 'hidden unity,' that primordial 'place' that is a 'non-place'?* What more, if anything, can be said about it? Can such a thinking be made sense of in the Western tradition, even in the mysticism of an Eckhart or Cusanus? If not, perhaps it can be understood only if transposed into another conceptual register altogether, one that is fundamental to the traditions of East Asian thinking. Perhaps the Why question needs to be reinterpreted in terms of an 'anti-'or 'an-ontological' thinking that looks for an answer not in terms of 'being' or something 'beyond being,' but in terms of nothingness or emptiness.

The Presupposition of Being

As just noted, for Heidegger, as for the entire Western metaphysical tradition, one thing is indubitable: the presupposition that Being, however conceived, is the foundation of all philosophical thought. According to Heidegger, a saying of Parmenides established this assumption at the beginning of Western thought: "*to gar auto noein estin te kai einai* becomes the basic theme of all of Western-European thinking.... the *eon emmenai*, the presence of what is present, the duality of what the *one* word, the participle of participles, the word *eon* designates: what is present in presence" (Heidegger, 1968, 148-149/242- 243). Given this assumption, given the priority of the Being question for Heidegger, his thinking of Being appears to have taken Western metaphysics and ontology as far as it can go. If so, this raises the question whether there is an alternative based on a different grammar which either does *not* take Being as its starting point or that at least does not presuppose the priority of being over against nothingness – in other words, the possibility of a radically different, inverted reading of Heidegger's mantra, Being:Nothing:Same.

For Heidegger, however, that question could not arise; his thinking remained framed within the Western assumption of the priority of Being. As Schoeffer pointed out, when Heidegger contemplated the question of the extent to which the subject-object language structures of Western thinking, based on the verb 'is,' set limits to the possibilities of philosophical reflection, he confined himself to asking whether *Western* languages might still harbor "other possibilities of saying and that means at the same time a 'saying' that is 'not saying' [*sagenden Nichtsagens*]" (Heidegger, 1960b, 72/66; Schoeffer, 212-213). In other words, he did not feel the need to ask whether philosophy could look *outside* those languages for other possibilities for the thinking of Being. It would have made for him no sense. It is true, as Schoeffer and others have richly documented, that Heidegger made tentative forays into "the possibilities for thinking found in Asian language structures and intellectual traditions. Heidegger's ever clearer growing 'interest' in the thinking of the East carried out in a totally different form of language" was to that extent "not surprising" (Schoeffer, *ibid.*). The problem, however, is that despite the apparent resonances of Heidegger's later thought with East Asian traditions, despite even the possibility of "hidden influences" (May) of East Asian ideas and thought-structures imported into the framework of his own thinking, the fact remains that though Heidegger may have taken the thinking of Being as far as it could go, he could not take it as far as East Asian thinking about Nothingness or Emptiness without abandoning it altogether as a thinking of *Being*. To that extent he could not shake himself free of that Western presupposition. But further, he did not see the need to do that which for him would have been by definition an impossibility. For Heidegger philosophy meant *Western* philosophy, and Western philosophy meant the thinking of *Being*

If, however, Heidegger's thinking of Being does *not* answer the Why question after all; if, further, his 'answer' of *Ereignis* does not explicate the nature of that 'hidden unity' of Being and Nothing, does not explain why Being is always and ever the Being of beings, does not illuminate that primordial 'place' that is a 'non-place,' then must we feel bound to his in any case highly questionable, even parochial confinement of thinking, of philosophy itself, to the concepts and 'grammar' of the Western language-traditions? Must we accept the presupposition that 'being' is the master-word of all and only that thinking that can address these issues? If not then that raises the question, what *is* the 'relation' of Being and Nothing? If it is not dialectical, not one of synthesis, what is the nature of their alleged 'sameness,' their alleged 'belonging together'?

Perhaps there is some third possibility, something more primary, something more originary, something not yet dreamed of in Heidegger's thinking of Being:Nothing:Same. There is another *philosophical* tradition, one that employs a similar sounding yet radically different mantra: Being *sive/soku hi* (or/is-and is-not) Nothing, Nothing *sive/soku hi* (or/is-and-is-not) Being. In that tradition there is an emphasis, as the mantra suggests, on attachment-that-is- non-attachment, non-attachment that is attachment. Non-attachment to Being or Nothing as metaphysical concepts for that which is real. Non-attachment to wonder and awe, love and joy as existential responses to that which is taken as real. But is it possible to speak of 'attachments,' conceptual or existential, that are 'non-attachments' and vice versa, ways of thinking that 'de-tach' us from our usual, ordinary ways of seeing and 'attach' us to, open us up to, 'extra-ordinary' ways of seeing and being, ways of seeing and relating to that which is miraculous *in/as* the ordinary, ways of seeing the ordinary *as* a miracle? Ways of seeing and being in which that which is 'ordinary' is detached from the 'ordinary' and attached to the 'extra-ordinary,' the miraculous?

If so, what happens to Heidegger's innovative construction, 'the ontological difference? What happens to the distinction between Being and beings? Stambaugh argues that with the concept of *Gelassenheit*, the letting-be of beings in their mystery, "Heidegger has left behind one of the most fundamental distinctions, not only in *Being and Time*, but throughout all his writings, the distinction ontic/ontological, beings/ Being, the ontological difference" (Stambaugh, 87). A wonderful insight! This is but another way of saying that the ontological difference *collapses* into the be-ing of beings, beings' be-ing. Be-ing:beings:same. After all, what was the *origin* of the so-called ontological difference? As the 'other-though-same' of the Nothing, the be-ing of beings was said to be the mystery of Being itself. But cannot the proposition be reversed? Is not the mystery of Being/be-ing (none other than) the mystery of *beings*? If so, if Being is a mystery, it is because beings themselves, as such, are in the first place the wonder-filled, miraculous mystery.

The Centrality of Human Being

Another assumption, central to Heidegger's thinking of Being, as his work from *Being and Time* to his later concept of *Ereignis* seems consistently to testify, is his insistence that the phenomenon of human being (*Dasein*) is co-primordial with that of Being itself. This is made clear by his rewriting of *Dasein* as *Da-Sein*, the 'there' or 'place' where Being is disclosed. As noted earlier, Dasein as the Da-of-Sein is said to be 'needed' (*braucht*) by Being in order for Being to be able to 'let beings be,' in order for the 'ontological difference' to 'take place' (*ereignen*). Being only 'is' (*west*) insofar as Dasein 'ek-sists.' As Heidegger said already early on, and never wavered in saying, "Only so long as Dasein *is* ...'is there' Being" (*SZ*, 212/*BT*, 255). The problem, however, is if the ontological difference, the difference between Being and beings, does indeed collapse in Heidegger's later work, if Being is as it were 'reduced' to the be-ing of beings, if the proper locus of the mystery of 'Being' is in fact the mystery of the be-ing of beings themselves, as such, what does this do to the alleged 'need' of Being for the Da of Sein to 'let beings be'? And if the centrality of human being to the disclosure of Being is called into question, how does that bear in turn on the 'need' for Dasein to be 'held out into the Nothing' in order for the Being of beings to be disclosed? And, finally, what does that do to the 'relation,' the 'belonging together,' the 'hidden unity,' the 'Same' of Being and Nothing?

Existential Cosmology

We come now to an issue that has not really been addressed so far but that is perhaps the hidden secret of Heidegger's thinking of Being – not the alleged 'hidden influence' of East Asian thought, though exposing it may have the result of pointing us in that direction. It is rather a problematic that could prove equally central precisely because it is an 'existential' (human-centered) one. The question is this: Is Heidegger's formulation of the Why question still partly dependent on a cosmological-metaphysical understanding of beings and the world? Or rephrased: Is Heidegger's thinking of Being not in the final analysis a 'deflationary' one that equates ('reduces'?) the mystery of 'Being' to the mystery of the *world's* be-ing? At first glance it would seem not insofar as Dasein's relation to the world, i.e. beings-as-a-whole, appears to be filtered through something else instead, its primordial relation to the Nothing, understood as the veil of Being. The being of the world is understood, existentially, from the standpoint of Being. Nevertheless, Heidegger's thinking of Being is, in an entirely novel sense, a *cosmology* of Being featuring a co-primordial idea of the 'world' of which it can ultimately be said only that it '*weltet*' and a co-primordial idea of 'time' as a 'temporality' of which it can ultimately be said only that it '*sich zeitigt*' – an 'eternal' be-ing understood as a "primordial temporality which is 'infinite'" (*SZ*, n. xiii, 427/ *BT*, 499 n. xiii). In that sense Heidegger's thinking of Being is not a 'pure ontology' but an *existential cosmology*. Though it is grounded in existential-ontological analysis, it is 'cosmological' insofar as its reference is to the 'world' of 'beings.' That is why for Heidegger the Why question is not understood ontologically as asking 'Why does something exist rather than nothing?' Rather it is understood cosmologically as asking, 'Why do beings, that is the world, exist rather than nothing?'

If so, this means that the Why question has further, more radical implications that have not yet been tapped in Heidegger's thinking of Being. It leaves us with the question whether there is another way of understanding experiences like wonder, mystery, miracle, joy, love, and reverence that is not 'cosmological' in a feeling- metaphysical sense as

THOMAS DEAN

in Smith, nor 'cosmological' in an existential-ontological sense as in Heidegger. Is there another way of thinking of Being that avoids the pitfalls of nihilism or relativism, on the one hand, without relapsing into the dead-end of metaphysics, on the other. Is there a way of thinking of Being that points to the 'absolute nothingness' of being itself?

Relative versus Absolute Nothing

The above reflections on Heidegger's questionable (*frag-wurdig*) reformulation of the Why question, the problematic presupposition of Being, the alleged centrality of human being, and the deflationary nature of his existential cosmology all lead to the central issue in any search for an alternative way of thinking in East Asian thought - the nature and role of 'the Nothing' in Heidegger's thinking of Being. Heidegger's dramatic saying: "Being:Nothing:Same" misleads one into thinking that in their 'belonging-together' Being and the Nothing stand on the same ontological niveau. But in fact the mantra conceals the relativity of Nothingness vis-a-vis Being. As Heidegger's revealing metaphor makes clear, the Nothing is not the counter-concept of *Being*, it is the 'veil' of Being, it is a *relative* Nothing. Rather the Nothing is the counter-concept to *beings*. Thus it is doubly relative. Both Being and Nothing are 'the Same' in *relation* to *beings*. The Nothing is relative to Being, the shadow side of Being as it were, but it is also relative to beings, for its essential (*wesentlich*) ontological function on 'behalf' of Being is to 'disclose' their be-ing as it simultaneously 'conceals' that of Being itself. For Heidegger, therefore, the Nothing is not *absolute* but *relative* in 'relation' to both Being and beings. By counter-posing the notion of 'nothing' to 'Being' and 'beings' rather than to 'something,' Heidegger signals that, unlike the theological doctrine, this 'Nothing' is *relative*. It is is not an *absolute* counter-concept to, say, God's Being; it is not the absolute *nihil* of Creation. Thus, *pace* his analytically-minded detractors, Heidegger would agree, following in the footsteps of Parmenides and Plato, that talk of *absolutely* nothing in fact makes no sense – *me on*, 'nothing' *relative* to 'something,' yes, but *ouk on*, nothing in an *absolute* sense, no. That would be a misuse of words, an error traceable to a philosophical misconstrual of the grammatical function of the little word 'not.'

A residual sense, a longing perhaps, for an alternative view of 'nothing,' or at least a search for resources to think of it in another way, may explain why from time to time Heidegger displayed interest in 'anti-ontological' elements in East Asian thinking. But as already noted, while similarities can be found between Heidegger's thinking of the Nothing in relation to beings and the 'deflationary' metaphysics of the Buddhist concept of the *'emptiness'* (*sunyata*) of all beings, that is, their *lack* of 'own-being' (*svabhava*), Heidegger's 'deflationary' notion by contrast refers to a Nothing that discloses the *be-ing* of beings. Thus while, following Heidegger, we too will turn to East Asia to see if we can find there conceptual resources for a more adequate way of thinking the Why question, it will be important to keep in mind a cautionary note. We may find that the East Asian concept of Absolute Nothing, does not, any more than Heidegger's concept of relative Nothing, constitute a fully satisfactory answer to the question that has guided this inquiry: 'Why is there something rather than nothing at all?' If so, to repeat what was said above, it may be that the search for an answer to the Why question will have to be pursued further.

Bibliography (Volume One)

WESTERN SOURCES AND COMMENTARIES

Allen, Chad, review, 1996, "Smith's *The Felt Meanings of the World* and the Pure Appreciation of Being Simpliciter," *Journal of Philosophical Research* 21, 69-80.

Aristotle, 1941a, "Categories," *The Basic Works of Aristotle*, ed. Richard McKeon, New York: Random House.

Aristotle, 1941b, "De Sophisticis Elenchis (On Sophistical Refutations)," *The Basic Works of Aristotle*, ed. Richard McKeon, New York: Random House.

Aristotle, 1941c, "Metaphysics," *The Basic Works of Aristotle*, ed. Richard McKeon, New York: Random House.

Augustine, 1972, *The City of God*, trans. Henry Bettenson, London: Penguin.

Austin, J.L., 1962, *Sense and Sensibilia*, ed. J. Warnock, Oxford: Oxford University Press.

Ayer, A. J., ed., 1959, *Logical Positivism*, Chicago: Free Press.

Badiou, Alain, 2011, *Wittgenstein's Antiphilosophy*, transl. by Bruno Bosteels, New York: Verso.

Benavides, Gustavo. 1982, *Tautology and Contradiction in the Language of Mysticism*, Ph.D. diss., Department of Religion, Temple University, Philadelphia PA.

Bergo, Bettina, 2011, "Emanuel Levinas," *Stanford Encyclopedia of Philosophy* (online).

Bergson, Henri, 1998, *Creative Evolution*, tr. Arthur Mitchell, New York: Dover.

Carnap, Rudolf, 1959, "The Elimination of Metaphysics Through Logical Analysis of Language," rept. in A.J. Ayer, ed, *Logical Positivism*, Chicago: Free Press.

Cohen, S. Marc, 2008, "Aristotle's Metaphysics," *Stanford Encyclopedia of Philosophy* (online).

Capobianco, Richard, 2010, "The *Ereignis* Interview," 6.29.2010.

Crease, Robert P. & Mann, Charles C., *1987, The Second Creation: Makers of the Revolution in Twentieth-Century Physics,* New York: Macmillan.

Danto, Arthur, 1965, *Nietzsche as Philosopher,* New York: Macmillan.

Davidson, Matthew, 2013, "God and Other Necessary Beings," *Stanford Encyclopedia of Philosophy* (online).

De Sousa, Ronald, 2013, "Emotion," *Stanford Encyclopedia of Philosophy* (online).

Edwards, Paul, 1972, "Why," *The Encyclopedia of Philosophy*, vol. 8, 296-302.

Edwards, Rem B., 1972, *Reason and Religion: An Introduction to the Philosophy of Religion*, New York: Harcourt Brace Jovanovich.

Findlay, J. N., 1970, "The Logic of Mysticism," *Ascent to the Absolute*: *Metaphysical Papers and Lectures,* London: Allen & Unwin.

Flew, Anthony, 1966, *God and Philosophy*, London: Hutchison.

Gall, Robert, 2014, personal communication, email, May 13.

Gardiner, Patrick, 1967, "Schopenhauer," *The Encyclopedia of Philosophy*, Paul Edwards, ed., New York, Macmillan, vol. 7, 325–332.

Hamlyn, D.W., 1967, "Contingent and Necessary Statements," *The Encyclopedia of Philosophy*, Paul Edwards, ed., New York, Macmillan, vol. 2, 198-205.

Hargby, Ingvar, 1959, "Double Awareness in Heidegger and Wittgenstein," *Inquiry*, vol. 2, no. 4, Winter, Oslo: Scandanavian University Press, ed. Arne Naess, 235-264.

Harmon, Gilbert, 1985, "Is There a Single True Morality?", in David Copp and David. Zimmerman, eds., *Morality, Reason and Truth*, Totowa NJ: Rowman and Allanheld.

Hawking, Stephen, 1988, *A Brief History of Time*, New York: Bantam.

Heidegger, Martin, 1975a, "Aletheia (Heraklit, Fragment 16), *Vortrage und Aufsatze*, Pfullingen: Gunther Neske, 1954, 257-282 /"Aletheia (Heraclitus, Fragment B 16), *Early Greek Thinking,* trans. David Ferrell Krell and Frank A. Capuzzi, New York: Harper & Row, 102-123.

_____, 1977a, *Basic Writings,* ed. David Ferrell Krell, Harper & Row.

_____, 1975b, "Bauen Wohnen Denken," *Vortrage und Aufsatze*, Pfullingen: Gunther Neske, 1954, 145-162/ "Building, Dwelling, Thinking," *Poetry, Language, Thought*, trans. Albert Hofstadter, New York: Harper & Row, 1975, 143-161.

_____, 1998a, "Brief uber den 'Humanismus,'" *Platons Lehre von der Wahrheit, Mit einem Brief uber den 'Humanismus'*, Bern: Francke Verlag, 1954 [1947],53-113/ "Letter on 'Humanism,'" *Pathmarks*, ed. William McNeill, Cambridge: Cambridge University Press, 239-276.

_____, 1975c, "Das Ding," *Vortrage und Aufsatze*, Pfullingen: Gunther Neske, 1954, 163-185/ "The Thing," *Poetry, Language, Thought*, trans. Albert Hofstadter, New York: Harper & Row, 163-186.

_____, 1953, *Der Feldweg*, Frankfurt am Main: Vittorio Klostermann.

_____, 1960a, "Der Satz der Identitat," *Identitat und Differenz*, Pfullingen: Gunther Neske, 1957, 11-34/ "The Principle of Identity," *Essays in Metaphysics: Identity and Difference*, trans. Kurt F. Leidecker, New York: Philosophical Library, 11-32.

_____, 1996, *Der Satz vom Grund*, Pfullingen: Gunther Neske, 1957/ *The Principle of Reason*, trans. Reginald Lilly, Bloomington: Indiana University Press.

_____, 1975d, "Der Ursprung des Kunstwerkes," *Holzwege*, Frankfurt am Main: Vittorio Klostermann, 1963, 7-68/ "The Origin of the Work of Art," *Poetry, Language, Thought*, trans. Albert Hofstadter, New York: Harper & Row, 15-87.

_____, 1977b, "The Origin of the Work of Art," *Basic Writings*, ed. David Ferrell Krell, Harper & Row, 143-187.

_____, 1975e, "Der Spruch des Anaximander," *Holzwege*, Frankfurt am Main: Vittorio Klostermann, 1963, 296-343/ "The Anaximander Fragment," *Early Greek Thinking*, trans. David Ferrell Krell and Frank A. Capuzzi, New York: Harper & Row, 13-58.

_____, 1977c, "Die Frage nach der Technik," *Vortrage und Aufsatze*, Pfullingen: Gunther Neske. 1954, 13-44/"The Question Concerning Technology," *The Question Concerning Technology and Other Essays*, trans. William Lovitt, New York: Harper & Row, 3-35.

_____, 1995, *Die Grundbegriffe der Metaphysik*, Frankfurt am Main: Vittorio Klostermann, 1983/*The Fundamental Concepts of Metaphysics*, trans. William McNeill and Nicholas Walker, Bloomington: Indiana University Press.

_____, 1960b, "Die Onto-Theo-Logische Verfassung der Metaphysik," *Identitat und Differenz*, Pfullingen: Gunther Neske, 1957, 35-73/ "The Onto-theo-logical nature of Metaphysics," *Essays* in *Metaphysics: Identity and Difference,* trans. Kurt F. Leidecker, New York: Philosophical Library, 33-67.

_____, 2000, *Einfuhrung in die Metaphysik,* Tubingen: Max Niemeyer, 1957/*Introduction to Metaphysics,* trans. Gregory Fried and Richard Polt, New Haven: Yale University Press.

_____, 1998b, "Einleitung zu 'Was Ist Metaphysik,'" *Wegmarken,* Frankfurt am Main: Vittorio Klostermann, 1967, 195-211/"Introduction" to *What is Metaphysics, Pathmarks,* ed. William McNeill, Cambridge: Cambridge University Press, 277-290

_____, 1963, *Erlauterungen zu Holderlins Dichtung,* Frankfurt am Main: Vittorio Klostermann/*Elucidations of Holderlin's Poetry,* Amherst NY: Humanity Books, 2000.

_____. 1966, *Gelassenheit,* Pfullingen: Gunther Neske, 1959/*Discourse on Thinking,,* trans. John M. Anderson & E. Hans Freund, intro. John M.Anderson, Harper & Row, New York: Harper & Row.

_____. 1994, *Grundfragen der Philosophie,* Frankfurt am Main: Vittorio Klostermann, 1984/*Basic Questions of Philosophy,* trans. Richard Rojcewicz and Andre Schuwer, Bloomington: Indiana University Press.

_____, 1950, *Holzwege,* Frankfurt am Main: Vittorio Klostermann.

_____. 1962, *Kant und das Problem der Metaphysik,* Frankfurt am Main: Vittorio Klostermann, 1951/*Kant and the Problem of Metaphysics,* trans. James S. Churchill, Bloomington: Indiana University Press.

_____, 1975f, "Logos (Heraklit, Fragment 50," *Vortrage und Aufsatze,* Pfullingen: Gunther Neske, 1954, 207-229/"Logos (Heraclitus, Fragment B 50," *Early Greek Thinking,* trans. David Ferrell Krell and Frank A. Capuzzi, New York: Harper & Row, 59-78.

_____, 1977d, "Nietzsches Word 'Gott ist tot'"*Holzwege,* Frankfurt am Main: Vittorio Klostermann, 1963, 193-247/ "The Word of Nietzsche: 'God is Dead,'" *The Question Concerning Technology and Other Essays,* trans. William Lovitt, New York: Harper & Row, 53-112.

_____, 1998c, *Platons Lehre von der Wahrheit, Mit einem Brief uber den 'Humanismus',* Bern: Francke Verlag, 1954, 5-52/"Plato's Doctrine of Truth," *Pathmarks,* ed. William McNeill, Cambridge: Cambridge University Press, 155-182.

_____, 1963, *Sein und Zeit*, Tubingen: Max Niemeyer/*Being and Time*, trans. John Macquarrie & Edward Robinson, New York: Harper & Row, 1962.

_____, 1972, "Time and Being," *Zur Sache des Denkens*, Tubingen: Max Niemeyer, 1969/*On Time and Being*, trans. Joan Stambaugh, New York: Harper & Row.

_____, 1982, *Unterwegs zur Sprache*, Pfullingen: Gunther Neske, 1960/*On the Way to Language,* trans. Peter D. Hertz, San Francisco: Harper & Row, 1982.

_____, 1975g, *Unterwegs zur Sprache, "Die Sprache,"* Pfullingen: Gunther Neske, 1960, 9-33/*Poetry, Language, Thought*, "Language," trans. Albert Hofstadter, New York: Harper & Row, 189-210.

_____, 2012, *Vier Seminare,* Frankfurt am Main: Vittorio Klostermann, 1973/*Four Seminars*, trans. Andrew Mitchell and Francois Raffoul, Bloomington: Indiana University Press.

_____, 1998d, *Vom Wesen des Grundes,* Frankfurt am Main: Vittorio Klostermann, 1955 /*On the Essence of Ground, Pathmarks*, ed. William McNeill, Cambridge: Cambridge University Press, 97-135.

_____. 1998e, *Vom Wesen der Wahrheit,* Frankfurt am Main: Vittorio Klostermann, 1943 [1930]/*On the Essence of Truth, Pathmarks*, ed. William McNeill, Cambridge: Cambridge University Press, 136-154,

_____, 1998f, "*Vom Wesen und Begriff der* phusis. Aristotles' Physik B, 1," *Wegmarken*, Frankfurt am Main: Vittorio Klostermann,1967, 309-371/ "On the Essence and Concept of *phusis* in Aristotle's Physics B, 1", *Pathmarks*, ed. William McNeill, Cambridge: Cambridge University Press, 183-230.

_____, 1968, *Was Heisst Denken?*, Tubingen: Max Niemeyer, 1954/ *What is Called Thinking?,* trans. Fred D. Wieck and J. Glenn Gray, Harper & Row.

_____, 1998g. *Was ist Metaphysik?*, Frankfurt am Main: Vittorio Klostermann, 1960/*What is Metaphysics?, Pathmarks*, ed. William McNeill, Cambridge University Press, 277-290, 82-96, 231-238.

_____, 1975h, "The Way Back Into the Ground of Metaphysics," Kaufmann, Walter, ed., *Existentialism from Dostoevsky to Sartre*, New York: New American Library, 265-279.

_____. 1998h, *Wegmarken*, Frankfurt am Main: Vittorio Klostermann, 1967/*Pathmarks*, ed. William McNeill, Cambridge University Press.

_____, 1949, "What is Metaphysics?," trans. R.F.C. Hull and Alan Crick, *Existence and Being*, ed. Brock, Werner, Chicago: Henry Regnery, 325-361.

_____, 1977e, "Wissenschaft und Besinnung," *Vortrage und Aufsatze*, Pfullingen: Gunther Neske, 1954, 45-70/"Science and Reflection," *The Question Concerning Technology and Other Essays*, trans. William Lovitt, New York: Harper & Row, 155-182.

_____, 1958, *Zur Seinsfrage*, Frankfurt am Main: Vittorio Klostermann,1956/*The Question of Being*, trans. William Kluback and Jean T. Wilde, New York: Twain.

Heschel, Abraham Joshua, 1959, *God in Search of Man, A Philosophy of Judaism*, New York: Meridian.

Hick, John, 1990, *Philosophy of Religion*, New Jersey: Prentice-Hall.

Hick, John, 2004, *An Interpretation of Religion: Human Responses to the Transcendent*, 2nd ed, New Haven: Yale University Press.

Horwich, Paul, 1995, "truth," *The Cambridge Dictionary of Philos*ophy, ed. Robert Audi, Cambridge: Cambridge University Press, 812-813.

Hume, David, 1960, *A Treatise of Human Nature*, ed. L. A. Selby-Bigge, Oxford: Clarendon.

Irigaray, Luce, 1993, *Ethique de la difference sexuelle*, Paris: Les Editions de Minuit, 1984/*An Ethics of Sexual Difference*, trans. Gillian C. Gill, Ithaca NY: Cornell University Press.

Irigaray, Luce, 1999, *L'oubli de l'air chez Martin Heidegger*, 1983/ *The Forgetting of Air in Martin Heidegger*, trans. Mary Beth Mader, Austin TX: University of Texas Press.

James, William, 1950, *Principles of Psychology*, New York: Dover.

_____, 1968a, "The Sentiment of Rationality," *The Writings of William James*, ed. John J. McDermott, New York: Random House, 317-345.

_____, 1968b, "The Will to Believe," *The Writings of William James*, ed. John J. McDermott, New York: Random House, 771-735.

Kant, Immanuel, 1958, *Critique of Pure Reason*, trans. Norman Kemp Smith, London: Macmillan.

Kierkegaard, Soren, 1985, *Philosophical Fragments*, trans, Howard V. and Edna H. Hong, Princeton: Princeton University Press.

Lamberth, David C., 1999, *William James and the Metaphysics of Experience*, Cambridge: Cambridge University Press.

Lalonde, Gerald, 2009, personal communication, email, July 4.

Leslie, John and Robert Lawrence Kuhn, ed., 2013, *The Mystery of Existence, Why Is There Anything At All*, Hoboken, NJ: Wiley-Blackwell.

Levinas, Emmanuel, 1969, *Totalite et infini*, Leiden: Martinus Nijhoff, 1961, /*Totality and Infinity*, trans. Alphonso Lingis, Pittsburgh, Duquesne.

_____, 2001, *De l'existence à l'existant*, Paris: Librarie Philosophique, 1993/ *Existence and Existents*, trans. Alphonso Lingis, Pittsburgh, Duquesne.

Marcel, Gabriel, 1960, *The Mystery of Being*, Chicago: Henry Regnery, 1960.

_____, 1961, *The Philosophy of Existentialism*, New York: Citadel, 1961.

Miller, Barry, 2002, "Existence," *Stanford Encyclopedia of Philosophy* (online)

Monk, Ray, 1990, *Ludwig Wittgenstein: The Duty of Genius*, New York: Penguin.

Munitz, Milton, "1967, "Cosmology," *The Encyclopedia of Philosophy*, ed. Paul Edwards, New York, Macmillan, vol. 2, 237-244.

_____, 1965, *The Mystery of Existence*, Delta.

Murdoch, Iris, 1993, *Metaphysics as a Guide to Morals*, New York: Penguin.

Nagel, Thomas, 2004, "Review of Bede Rundle, *Why there is Something rather than Nothing*," *The London Times Literary Supplement*, 12 December.

Nancy, Jean-Luc, 2000, *Être singulier pluriel*, Paris: Galilée, 1996/*Being Singular Plural*, Stanford: Stanford University Press.

_____, 1997, *L'oubli de la philosophie*, Paris: Galilée, 1986/"The Forgetting of Philosophy," *The Gravity of Thought*, Amherst NY: Humanity, 7-74.

Otto, Rudolf, 1958, *The Idea of the Holy*, Oxford: Oxford University Press.

Parfit, Derek, 1998, "Why anything? Why this?," *London Review of Books*, 20:2, 22 January, 24-27; 20:3, 5 February, 22-25.

Plato, 1963a, "Euthyphro," *The Collected Dialogues*, ed. Edith Hamilton and Huntington Cairns, New York: Pantheon, 169-185.

_____, 1963b, "Republic," *The Collected Dialogues*, ed. Edith Hamilton and Huntington Cairns, New York: Pantheon, 575-844.

_____, 1963c, "Sophist," *The Collected Dialogues*, ed. Edith Hamilton and Huntington Cairns, New York: Pantheon, 957-1017.

_____, 1963d, "Theatetus," *The Collected Dialogues*, ed. Edith Hamilton and Huntington Cairns, New York: Pantheon, 845-919.

Poggeler, Otto, 1963, *Der Denkweg Heideggers*, Pfullingen: Gunther Neske.

_____, 1987, "West-East Dialogue: Heidegger and Lao-tzu," Graham Parkes, ed., *Heidegger and Asian Thought*, Honolulu: University of Hawaii Press, 47-78.

Polt, Richard, 2001, "The Question of Nothing," *A Companion to Heidegger's Introduction to Metaphysics*, ed. Richard Plot & Gregory Fried, Yale University Press, 57-82.

Post, John, 1987, *The Faces of Existence, An Essay in Nonreductive Metaphysics*, Ithaca: Cornell University Press.

Prior, A. N., 1967, "Existence," *The Encyclopedia of Philosophy*, ed. Paul Edwards, New York, Macmillan, vol. 3, 141-147.

Quine, W.V.O., 1969, "On What There Is," *Ontological Relativity and Other Essays*, New York: Columbia University Press.

_____, 1960, *Word and Object*, Cambridge, Mass: MIT Press.

Richardson, William J., 1963, *Heidegger: Through Phenomenology to Thought*, The Hague: Martinus Nijhoff.

Ricoeur, Paul, 1985, *The Symbolism of Evil*, Boston: Beacon Press.

Robbins, Brent Dean, 2003, *Joy and the politics of emotion: Toward a cultural therapeutics via phenomenology and critical theory*, Ph.D. diss., Duquesne University, Pittsburgh, PA.

Rubenstein, Mary-Jane, 2008, *Strange Wonder, The Closure of Metaphysics and the Opening of Awe*, New York: Columbia University Press.

_____, 2014, *Worlds Without End: The Many Lives of the Multiverse*, New York: Columbia University Press.

Rundle, Bede, 2004, *Why there is Something rather than Nothing*, Oxford: Oxford University Press.

Sartre, Jean-Paul, 1956, *Being and Nothingness, An Essay on Phenomonological Ontology*, trans. Hazel E. Barnes, New York: Philosophical Library.

_____, 1969, *Nausea*, trans. Lloyd Alexander, New York: New Directions.

Schlick, Moritz, 1962, "Meaning and Verification," "Unanswerable Questions," *Philosophy in the Twentieth Century*, eds. William Barrett and Henry D. Aiken, New York: Random House, vol. II, 23-51.

Schoeffer, Erasmus, 1962, *Die Sprache Heideggers*, Pfullingen: Gunther Neske.

Schopenhauer, Arthur, 1966, *World as Will and Representation*, vol. II, ch. XLVI, trans. E.F.J. Payne, New York: Dover.

Smart, Ninian, *Reasons and Faiths*, 1958, London: Routledge and Kegan Paul.

Smith, Quentin, 1998, *Ethics and Religious Thought in Analytical Philosophy of Language*, New Haven: Yale University Press.

_____, 1986, *The Felt Meanings of the World: A Metaphysics of Feeling*, West Lafayette, IN: Purdue University Press.

_____, 1981, "On Heidegger's Theory of Moods," *The Modern Schoolman*, 58:4, May 211-235.

Stambaugh, Joan, 1987, "Heidegger, Taoism, and the Question of Metaphysics," Graham Parkes, ed. *Heidegger and Asian Thought*, Honolulu: University of Hawaii Press, 79-91.

Steup, Matthias, 1995, "problem of the criterion," *The Cambridge Dictionary of Philosophy*, ed. Robert Audi, Cambridge: Cambridge University Press, 653.

Tillich, Paul, 1955, *Biblical Religion and the Search for Ultimate Reality*, Chicago: Chicago University Press.

_____, 1958, *Dynamics of Faith*, New York: Harper & Brothers.

_____, 1973, *Systematic Theology*, vol. I, Chicago: Chicago University Press.

_____, 1959, "The Two Types of Philosophy of Religion," *Theology of Culture*, New York: Oxford University Press, 10-29.

Troxell, Mary, n.d., "Arthur Schopenhauer," *Internet Encyclopedia of Philosophy* (online)

Van Buren, John, 1994, *The Young Heidegger: Rumor of the Hidden King*, Bloomington: Indiana University Press.

Van Inwagen, Peter, 2014, "Metaphysics," *Stanford Encyclopedia of Philosophy* (online).

Watts, Alan, 1972, *Behold the Spirit: A Study in the Necessity of Mystical Religion*, New York: Vintage.

Wicks, Robert, 2017, "Schopenhauer," *Stanford Encyclopedia of Philosophy* (online).

Wittgenstein, Ludwig, 1984, *Culture and Values*, trans. Peter Winch, Chicago: Chicago University Press.

_____, 1965, "Lecture on Ethics," *The Philosophical Review*, LXXIV, 3-17.

_____, 1966, *Lectures and Conversations on Aesthetics, Psychology & Religious Belief, 1938-1946*, ed. Cyril Barrett, Oxford: Blackwell.

_____, 1961, *Notebooks 1914-1916*, ed. G. H. Von Wright and G.E M.Anscombe, Oxford: Blackwell.

_____, 1953, *Philosophical Investigations*, trans. G.E.M. Anscombe, New York: Macmillan.

_____, 1922, *Tractatus Logico-Philosophicus*, London: Kegan Paul.

Witherall, Arthur, 2002, *The Problem of Existence*, London: Ashgate.

Printed in the United States
By Bookmasters